THEODORE
DREISER

OTHER BOOKS BY RICHARD LINGEMAN

Don't You Know There's a War On?

Small Town America

THEODORE
DREISER

AN AMERICAN JOURNEY

Richard Lingeman

An abridgment of:
Theodore Dreiser: At the Gates of the City, 1871–1907
Theodore Dreiser: An American Journey, 1908–1945

JOHN WILEY & SONS, INC.

NEW YORK • CHICHESTER • BRISBANE • TORONTO • SINGAPORE

Copyright ©1993 by Richard Lingeman
First published in 1993 by John Wiley & Sons, Inc.

This work is an abridgement of:

Theodore Dreiser: At the Gates of the City, 1871–1907
©1986 by Richard Lingeman
Theodore Dreiser: An American Journey, 1908–1945
©1990 by Richard Lingeman

Abridged edition published by arrangement with G. P. Putnam's Sons.

Library of Congress Cataloging-in-Publication Data:
Lingeman, Richard R.
    Theodore Dreiser : an American journey / Richard Lingeman. —
Abridged ed.
        p. cm.
    "This work is an abridgement of: 'Theodore Dreiser : at the gates
of the city, 1871–1907', and 'Theodore Dreiser : an American journey,
1908–1945" —Publisher's info.
    Includes bibliographical references and index.
    ISBN 0-471-57426-0
    1. Dreiser, Theodore, 1871–1945—Biography. 2. Novelists,
American—20th century—Biography.   I. Title.
PS3507.R55Z6652   1993
813'.52—dc20   92-40559

Printed in the United States of America

10 9 8 7 6 5 4 3 2 1

To Anthea

and

To the Memory of

My Father,

Dr. Byron N. Lingeman

Listen: I will be honest with you; I do not offer the old, smooth prizes, but offer rough new prizes.

— WALT WHITMAN

No facts are to me sacred, none are profane; I simply experiment, an endless seeker, with no Past at my back.

— RALPH WALDO EMERSON

Contents

Book II: An American Journey, 1908–1945

Prologue

The career of Theodore Dreiser was one of the most obstacle-ridden in American letters. As a transitional figure between the genteel era dominated by William Dean Howells, Mark Twain, and Henry James, and the rebels of the twenties, he was a messenger picking his way through a minefield of censorship, prejudice, and snobbery, clearing a path for the generation that went over the top after him and took the literary high ground.

At first his mission was a lonely one, his only allies a handful of mentors in his youth, a few friends, two or three sympathetic editors, and a worshiping wife; he was driven by naive, undisciplined genius and a passion for truth that was like a natural force. Although he had learned his craft in the raucous Tenderloin of late-nineteenth-century journalism and ten-cent mass magazines, his innate honesty remained intact, uncorruptible. In his first novel, *Sister Carrie,* he sought to provide a true picture of social conditions, of the way the world works, "of the game as it is played."

He was no self-conscious rebel, though, no literary anarchist setting off bombs in a literary Haymarket Square. In many ways he was a conventional young man with a vague idealism about art and literature that cut him off from the commercial hustle of the Gilded Age, though he was not immune to the success virus by any means. Born in 1871 to a poor family headed by a fanatically religious German immigrant father and a "pagan," indulgent mother, he was, like most second-generation children, full of American dreams of power, sex, affluence, and status. He had cut his teeth on Horatio Alger as a boy, and like many in his generation he envisioned himself becoming another Andrew Carnegie or John D. Rockefeller. But he regarded money as the key to a finer sphere, naively envisioned in terms of beauty, luxury, fame, and the love of women. Lacking the discipline for the traditional slow Algerine climb up the clerical ladder, throwing away the chance for a university education, and sensing from his childhood immersion in poverty that the race was unequal, he drifted into journalism, and there his seedling literary ambitions took root.

In adolescence and young manhood, he was introspective, awkward, prudish. Sex mesmerized him, a hot flame he feared getting too close to. Burning, he married. She was a gentle, small-town girl from Missouri, Sara Osborne White; it was a prolonged courtship fueled by romantic agonies of thwarted desire. He placed literary fame on the same pedestal on which he had put his fiancée, abandoning a lucrative carrer grinding out "specials" for popular magazines. He had a simple faith that if he wrote something good, true, and artistic, he would win the favors of the dream goddess, just as he had won his wife, and continue his days as a literary gentleman, neither a high-paid confectioner of popular society romances nor a hack pandering to "low" tastes.

But there was a rebellious streak in his makeup; he had a voluptuous, sensual temperament, a love for dreamy idleness, that lured him even as he was straining on the success treadmill; he also had an iron stubbornness with a cynical, perverse (some would say evil) twist. Something in him—resentment, distrust—instinctively rebelled against the reigning genteel tradition. In the light of his background, it seemed false, irrelevant to everything he had experienced, beginning as a boy in Terre Haute, Indiana. While he paid obeisance to the establishment figures such as novelist William Dean Howells and poet Edmund Clarence Stedman, and sought their patronage, they sensed something not "right" about the tall, voluble, awkward Hoosier with a cast in one eye and edged away.

That was perhaps for the best, for he was a natural who had to go his own way. Until his first novel was published, he sought to placate the dominant morality with compromises, but he had gone much too far along the road to the new literature—a democratic novel, its pages open to characters previously considered vulgar, which spoke unself-consciously in the flat tones of Middle Western speech and focused on life as it is rather than as it ought to be.

Dreiser's early life, the subject of Book I, is a remarkable story of failure and victory. He saw the most brilliant truth-telling young writers of his generation struck down by illness, drink, or despair, and for a time, in the early 1900s, it was a near thing whether he himself would live or die, or if he did live, whether he would ever write again. His battle to survive was the crucial period of his life, and the story has never been fully told.

Looked at in retrospect, his life towers like a lonely mesa, striated with layers of American time, beginning in nineteenth-century Indiana and encompassing those epical social temblors that altered the landscape—the mass migration to the cities, the widening fissure between rich and poor, the rise of industry, the centralization of economic (and political) power in the corporations and trusts. It offers many glimpses of journalism in the pre-Yellow and Yellow eras, of New York City in the Mauve Decade, of America in the age of enterprise and the age of progressivism; of the optimism and budding imperialism of the early 1900s, as reflected in the popular magazines of the day; and of the literary tides and cross-currents that boiled up in the twentieth century.

•　•　•

Dreiser's story begins with a newspaper item from a compilation in the Sullivan, Indiana, public library which I happened on almost by chance, given the haphazard organization of the material by its compiler, a local historian named Dr. Maple. The event described in the Sullivan *Democrat* of May 3, 1866, occurred five years before Theodore Dreiser was born, yet the family legend that grew out of it would throw a long shadow over his childhood: "We learn that man named Paul Dresser [sic], engaged at Jewett Brothers' Woolen Factory, near the depot, was seriously injured last Saturday. In erecting a scaffold for finishing the cornice of the building, a piece of timber fell, striking Mr. Dresser on the head and knocking him senseless. His injuries are not fatal."

In family legend John Paul Dreiser's failure in America, which dragged his large brood down into poverty, had its germ in the incident described in the clipping. As a result of the injuries he suffered from the blow to the head, his son Theodore later wrote, repeating what he had heard, he became "queer" and obsessed with religion. Disabled by the accident, he lost the managership of a prosperous woolen mill and was cheated by his partners. Because of an obsessive belief that he must either pay off his debts or face an eternity in purgatory, and the mentally warping effects of his fanatical Catholicism, he was never able to recoup.

So went the story—at least as Theodore heard and believed it. As a result of the accident, John Paul Dreiser lost his chance for financial success and became a "morose and dour figure, forlorn and despondent, tramping about the house, his hands behind his back and occasionally talking to himself." His spirits traced a pendulum course between the torments of hell and the faint hope of heaven.

Like many legends, this one contains a core of truth, but it was colored and distorted by the tellers, and Dreiser added his own embroidery when, in his fifties, he set it down in his autobiography, *Dawn*. One of the most truthful autobiographies ever written, it is still the work of a novelist, who shaped and rearranged the facts available to him.

Book One

. . .

AT THE GATES
OF THE CITY,
1871 – 1907

Part One

. . .

BOYHOOD

1 / *The Immigrant*

> I will not say this is a true record. What I have written is probably no more than accumulated and assorted hearsay, collated and arranged after the facts.
>
> —Dreiser, *Dawn* (1931)

Johann Paul Dreiser debarked at New York City in 1844, one of thousands of young Germans escaping the Prussian military draft, whose tentacles had stretched to his birthplace, Mayen, an ancient provincial town of some four thousand people near Koblenz in Alsace-Lorraine that had grown up around a feudal castle. A prominent landmark was St. Clemens Catholic Church, which had an odd, twisted spire, the result of a structural flaw when it was built in the fourteenth century. The populace was overwhelmingly Catholic (4291 out of 4395 people in 1843). Dreisers had lived in the Mayen area for centuries; the name means of "of Dreis," a neighboring village where the family originated in the Middle Ages. Theodore Dreiser always believed that his German ancestors were "of no great standing." Actually, they were solid burghers; the family home was a large stone structure in the center of town near the church. Six Dreisers had served as mayor, and a street bore the family name. Paul Dreiser's father, also Johann, was a farmer and a strict, almost saintly man, according to another son, Henry: "I have never met a man so honorable and straightforward. . . . I do not know why he did go to confessional as . . . even in his thoughts [he] committed no sin; he was charitable, he was good, although he was a Disciplinarian and very severe with his children. I had many beatings from him, which I have not forgotten to this day."

Since Johann had twenty-two children to chastise, his arm must have been oaken. He had married three times, and Paul, who was born in 1821, was raised by two stepmothers. Such a home situation was not calculated to hold an ambitious young man either emotionally or economically. Since only the oldest son would inherit his father's land, Paul took up a trade, becoming a weaver and dyer of wool.

Upon his arrival in the United States, Paul Dreiser seemed eager to get ahead and did not settle in one of the German enclaves in the cities. He made his way to Somerville, Massachusetts, where he found work in the woolen mills. Around 1849, accompanied by a *Landsmann* named George Heinemann, he struck out for the West. Peddling housewares to farmers' wives to pay their expenses, the two men made it to Middletown, Ohio, where Dreiser obtained a job in George Ellis's woolen mills, located near the lock of the Miami Canal just south of Dayton. Ellis, a seasoned wool man from Leeds, England, had moved to the state fifteen years earlier after learning the American end of the trade in Philadelphia.

Paul's skill and industriousness won him a patron in Ellis. When the latter moved to Terre Haute in 1853 to found the Ellis Woolen Factory, he sent for Paul, who came accompanied by a wife, the former Sarah Mary Schänäb. A strong, pretty farm girl with a radiant smile, Sarah was of German-Moravian ancestry. She was born in a log cabin on May 8, 1833 six miles west of Dayton. Nine years later, the family moved on to Kosciusko County, Indiana, where they became prosperous farmers. Around 1850 Paul Dreiser worked in a woolen mill in Fort Wayne and somehow met Sarah, with whom he fell "madly in love."

Sarah's parents were Mennonites—"plain people"—who were deeply opposed to the Church of Rome in particular and to intermarriage in general. Not surprisingly, when Sarah fell in love with the wiry, devoutly Catholic immigrant twelve years her senior, her father was adamantly opposed. But Paul Dreiser was a determined man who hungered for a wife and home after seven years spent bouncing about his new country, and Sarah was a rebellious and headstrong girl. The couple eloped to Piqua, Ohio, where they were married on New Year's Day 1851. Her father promptly disowned her, but she kept in touch with her brothers and sisters after they left the family homestead. Two years or so later, they moved to Terre Haute. They had three children, but two died in 1854 and the third in the following year.

In 1857 Sarah conceived again, and this baby—John Paul, Jr.—lived. They were residing on First Street near Walnut, less than a block from the Ellis mill. Paul was working as a spinner, but his employer had better things in mind for him. The following year Ellis made a down payment of three hundred dollars on a lot for the couple, at Second and Poplar streets, and Sarah sewed for the garment makers on Wabash Avenue to help pay for the house. By 1863 Paul was foreman at the Ellis mill, which was enjoying flush times as a result of the Civil War and the government's demand for soldiers' clothing.

That same year, Ellis purchased and completely refitted the Sullivan Wool Manufactory in Sullivan, Indiana, a hamlet of about eight hundred souls located twenty-five miles south of Terre Haute. In March, however, he sold the mill to the brothers D. M. and E. D. Jewett, of Terre Haute, and they hired Paul to manage it. That July Dreiser sold his Terre Haute house for $375 and moved to Sullivan.

The Jewetts' venture was ill-starred, however. In June of the following year the factory burned to the ground. It was during the construction of the new mill that Dreiser suffered the accident that would reverberate through Theodore's early years.

The family version of the accident compresses its aftermath considerably. Paul's decline was not nearly so precipitous as the legend had it. How long he was disabled is not known, but the belief of Theodore's oldest sister, Mary Frances, that the Jewett brothers "ruined the business during Father's illness," and Theodore's repeated hearsay that they made off with some deeds while his father was incapacitated, is inaccurate. For, in March 1867, apparently fully recovered, Paul entered into a partnership with the Jewett brothers. That same year he purchased two lots in town—adding a third in 1869—and erected a house that was larger than the small cottage near the depot and the old mill the family had previously occupied.

Sarah, who had a soft heart, was active in charitable work among the parishioners. Years later, local merchants recalled her as a kindly and intelligent woman. One family that never forgot her benefactions was the Bulgers, a large, impoverished Irish clan that would reappear in Sarah's life.

All in all, then, the Sullivan years were good ones for the Dreisers despite the accident. Clearly, Paul was becoming a man of substance in the community. A local resident remembered "the large family seated in church as so many peas in a pod . . . they were an impressive spectacle . . . a devout Catholic family." Their house, on North Broad Street, was in "one of the best residential sections in town," a former neighbor said.

By 1869, however, legend and reality begin to converge. The brothers announced that the partnership with Paul Dreiser had been dissolved, the latter "withdrawing from the firm." Mary Francis, known by the rest of the family as Mame, believed her father had been a victim of "Yankee treachery." Paul was, after all, an immigrant. It appears that the partners had a falling out, and perhaps Paul was angered by some kind of sharp practices on the Jewetts' part. In May 1870 Chauncey Rose purchased the mill for more than $10,000 and installed Paul as his manager. In the 1870 census roll, dated August 30, John Paul Dreiser is identified as a "wool manufacturer," the owner of real estate valued at $1750, and a personal estate worth $500. Although he was scarcely a wealthy man, he was modestly prosperous.

Still, sometime that fall or winter, Paul lost his position. The immediate cause was a storm that blew away the mill's top story. In February 1871 Rose sold the mill to Peter Hill and Eli and Anthony Milner for $7000. The $3000 markdown was probably owing to the damage wrought by the storm.

Paul Dreiser's downward spiral had begun. In March 1871 he sold his home for $1400, and on April 17 he conveyed a tract known as the "millowner's lot" to Hill and the Milners for $125.

By September the family was back in Terre Haute. Paul and Sarah Dreiser purchased a large house on the southwest corner of Twelfth and Walnut streets for $1200, paying $200 down and assuming a mortgage of $1000. The 1872 Terre Haute directory, however, listed the occupation of Paul Dreiser as "laborer."

Within the space of two years he had sunk from manager of a mill to laborer. The cause of Paul's sudden drop remains obscure, but nothing on the record suggests that he was either cheated out of his rightful share or that the blow on the head had made him mentally unstable. In truth, the Sullivan mill, built in the immediate afterglow of Civil War prosperity, had in a few years become a loser; damage from the storm was the coup de grace. The stories of his being mentally unbalanced or cheated are the rationalizations of a son with ambivalent feelings toward his father, and a loving daughter. Theodore said it was all Paul's fault; Mame, not his fault at all. Theodore attributed much of his father's failure to qualities in him that he disliked, primarily his religiosity, which allegedly drove him to pay off sizable debts and made him unfit for the world of business.

The central truth is that Paul Dreiser's failure in Sullivan was the family's fall from grace, their expulsion from the Eden of middle-class respectability. Never again would their status in the community be so assured, and at times it would be precarious indeed. The memory of belonging to that elevated sphere caused Theodore and the other children, with Sarah as chief propagandist, always to consider themselves better than their fallen state, but it left him in a state of chronic foreboding echoing the primal disaster. It also made him identify with the heroes in so many melodramas and dime novels of the nineteenth century: the young man or woman of good birth who is plunged into poverty as a child but who rises by hard work or virtue and whose true nobility is revealed in the dénouement. The Horatio Alger dreams of recovering his rightful place mingled with the fear that failure—disaster—would be his lot.

John Paul Dreiser faced a bleak prospect in the new home in Terre Haute. The outlook was not helped by the arrival of his ninth child on August 27, 1871, a boy who was christened Herman Theodore Dreiser at St. Benedict's Catholic Church on September 10—the day before the final papers were signed for the family's new home.

2 / *Dawn*

All this industry we see about us is man's response to man's increasing desires. The utter savage has no more wants than the
brute — the *partially* perfected man wants not only the earth
but the infinite, and the one man dreams, another thinks, and
all work, and the whirligig of time, and the rush and whir
of the busy struggling generations go hand in hand through
the centuries and the eons.

— H. W. Bechwith, *History of Vigo
and Parke Countys* [sic] (1880)

Even in the relatively pastoral pre–Civil War era the distant rumble of industry
could be sensed in Terre Haute. Abundant coal and some iron ore were to be
found nearby, and dreams began to swell like iridescent bubbles: Terre Haute
would be the Pittsburgh of the Middle West. Then came the postwar boom.
The population mushroomed from twenty thousand to seventy thousand in the
three decades following the Civil War as immigrants, largely from Germany
and Ireland, streamed in to perform the heavy labor.

In the 1870s and 1880s, the town completed its shuddering metamor-
phosis into a city. Those who had grown up during Terre Haute's prewar years
remembered the vanished era with a keen nostalgia, strengthened by the contrast between it and the smoky, bustling city. Theodore's eldest brother, Paul,
Jr., would cling to a pastoral image of the city as would the labor leader and socialist Eugene Victor Debs, who knew Paul when both were boys. Debs would
later extol his hometown as "that sacred little spot," that "beloved little community . . . where all were neighbors and all friends," that "enchanting little
village."

•   •   •

Two years after Theodore arrived, Sarah gave birth to her tenth child, completing the Dreiser family. She was forty. Sarah Dreiser had produced a vigorous

9

brood, most of whom lived long lives. In order of appearance, the German names they were christened with were:

Johann Paul, born 1858 (Paul)
Markus Romanus, 1860 (Rome)
Maria Franziska, 1861 (Mary Frances, Mame)
Emma Wilhelmina, 1863 (Em)
Mary Theresa, 1865 (Theresa, Terese, Tres)
Cacilia, 1866 (Sylvia, Syl)
Alphons Joachim, 1867 (Al)
Clara Clothilde, 1869 (Claire, Tillie)
Herman Theodore, 1871 (Theo, Thee, Dorsch, Teddy)
Eduard Minerod, 1873 (Edward Meinrad, Ed)

Sarah's strong maternal presence dominated the children's lives, particularly Theodore's, who perhaps because he had been, in Mame's words, "puny beyond belief, all ribs and hollow eyes and ailing and whimpering," at birth received special solicitude. He remembered being rocked in Sarah's arms and confessed, "I was always a mother child, hanging to her skirts as much as I was permitted until I was seven or eight years old." And for the rest of his life he clung to her idealized memory—her "velvety hand" whose touch was like balm, her "sweetness and grace of mind," her "genial smile," her "natural understanding . . . tolerance . . . charity for all," her "glamour—the pearly radiance of romance and tenderness" she cast "over everything she did, said, thought," the "comfort of the mere presence of her." He was not alone in his worship of his mother. Paul, Jr., as the songwriter Paul Dresser, had no rivals as the chief exponent of the "mother song" in the 1890s; Mame simply wrote, "My Mother beyond doubt was one of the greatest women of all times."

To Theodore "her body, sheltering knees," were "home, shelter, blessed-ness, perfection, peace, delight," a refuge in a world whose terrors the imagi-native child magnified. Once, to keep him from venturing into the cellar, Sarah told him a "cat man" lurked in the darkness to pounce on small boys and eat them. The figure became omnipresent in his mind, and when Theodore heard the monotonous rasp of the locusts, he thought they were cat men perched in the trees. When the youngest were mischievous, Sarah would announce she was going to leave them forever, pack a bag, don her black shawl and Mennonite bonnet, and stride out the door. Once Theodore was so wrought up that he fainted.

This tactic left its mark: fears of abandonment haunted Theodore the rest of his life. It was as though his mother conditioned him to feel that her absence was the worst possible disaster ("Oh years later, when she was really gone, I knew why I cried!" he exclaims in *Dawn*). As he wrote in the 1920s: "Long after I had passed my thirtieth year and when she had already been dead for years, I still used to dream of her as being alive but away, threatening to go off and leave me and awoke to find myself in fear. Even to this day dreams of her inevitably evoke a great sadness and longing in me. . . . "

Sarah Dreiser conveyed to her children in a hundred subtle and not so subtle ways her sacrifices for them; she manipulated their emotions in myriad ways. For all the miraculous healing power of her tenderness, her emotional claims could be exorbitant, for what greater power is there than sweet, sacrificial abnegation—the velvety hand that conceals "hooks of steel"?

The upshot in Theodore's case was a fixation on his mother and a deep ambivalence toward his father. In his attitude toward his father, Theodore was reflecting Sarah's own resentment of her marriage, which she communicated to him. Ed, who managed to extricate himself from Sarah's dominance, always remembered his father warmly and never felt the bitterness toward him that Theodore did.

A vivid childhood memory of Dreiser shows Sarah making Theodore an accomplice against his father. She is sitting in the parlor in a white dressing gown, a faint light filtering through the curtains. Theodore crawls to her and begins stroking her toes, protruding through a hole in her shabby shoes. "See poor mother's shoes?" she croons. "Aren't you sorry she has to wear such torn shoes? See the hole there?" Her voice, which "could make me cry at any time," upset him.

"Are you going to grow up to be a big man and work and bring me nice shoes?"

"Work, work, yes, I work," the little boy stammers.

Finally, "a sudden swelling sense of pity that ended in tears. I smothered her shoes and cried." In the dimly lit room, a sobbing child, a mother bent over him, wed in shared sorrow.

•   •   •

He attended St. Benedict's parochial school on Ninth and Walnut, although the Fourth Ward School, a brand-new square structure with a cupola, was only a block away from their home. Paul, of course, insisted on religious indoctrination for his offspring despite the extra expense. The school was established for children of St. Joseph's German congregation. German was spoken, and lessons, including grammar, were rudimentary. The boys were required to doff their caps and say "Praise be Jesus Christ!" to the grim-faced priests patrolling the halls, who barked "Amen!"

The rote learning of parochial school did not nip Dreiser's budding curiosity. "When friends called at the Dreiser home," a friend of the family recalled, "the little wise-looking child drew up a chair and listened to everything with a knowing air." Freud might have called him a scopophiliac child—always looking, absorbing, grasping. When a watchman who had given the boy candy every day on his way to work died, Theodore was taken to the funeral and lifted up to peer in the coffin. He tried to snatch the gleaming coins that covered the corpse's eyes. Death was a mystery: what had departed that once vibrant body that was now like the shell of a locust?

Sunday Mass was another mystery. When someone—his father perhaps— explained to him that God was present in the communion wine and wafers, the child cried, "Give me God! Give me God!"

3 / "The Damndest Family"

> At the same time, this city of my birth was identified with so much struggle on the part of my parents, so many dramas and tragedies in connection with relatives and friends, that by now it seemed quite wonderful as the scene of almost an epic. . . . I will only say that from the time the mill burned until, after various futile attempts to right ourselves . . . we finally left this part of the country for good, it was one unbroken stretch of privation and misery.
>
> —Dreiser, *A Hoosier Holiday* (1916)

A lowering cloud hung over John Paul Dreiser's economic prospects during the years the family lived at Twelfth and Walnut. The directory lists him variously as "laborer," "spinner," and "sorter"—and once as a "blacksmith." Stunned by the national recession of 1873, Terre Haute was hit hard in 1875 by "a great business depression as a result of flood and high water," according to a local historian. And the wool business was undergoing structural changes that would make small concerns like the Ellis mill and skilled craftsmen like Paul Dreiser obsolete.

Given John Paul's skills and experience, Theodore could not understand why his father drudged along in temporary positions rather than managing another mill. In *Dawn* he writes, "He could still have borrowed money and secured control of a mill if he had had the courage." Supposedly (family legend again), Terre Haute's richest man and a silent partner of the Jewetts, Chauncey Rose, offered to advance him the necessary capital, but Paul's unreasoning fear of going into debt caused him to decline, and Theodore theorizes that "by now he was so depressed by various ills that he could not bestir himself in the proper way."

Possibly the Sullivan failure had shaken his self-esteem. But, even if he retained the driving ambition of his earlier years in America, the economic cards were stacked against him. Borrowing money and opening a mill of his own was not a realistic option, given the decline of the wool trade in Terre Haute.

The family clawed for a handhold on middle-class respectability but skid-ded inexorably down the slippery slope to hunger and want. Dreiser remem-bered "long, dreary, gray, cold days: meager meals, only fried potatoes or fried mush at times." Sarah, who had grown up on a prosperous farm with a well-stocked larder, was hard pressed to put food on the table and began to question her husband's authority for the first time.

He was being challenged from another quarter as well — his children. The oldest ones were now in the full heat of adolescent blood. The first to rebel was Paul, Jr. Fourteen years old when the family moved back to Terre Haute, he had grown into a big, husky boy with a knockabout sense of humor and an appetite for pranks. Such antics angered his austere father, who decided, in Mame's words, "to devote his eldest son to the service of God." In 1872 the young Paul was shipped off to the St. Meinrad Seminary in southern Indiana, which offered a preparatory course leading to the study of the priesthood.

Paul, Jr., lasted about two years. He left St. Meinrad in 1874, voluntarily or otherwise, and hung out with a group of would-be thespians. The group graduated from impromptu song and dance performances in the streets; then Paul joined a minstrel show known as the Lemon Brothers that toured the surrounding small towns. But business was poor, and their money ran out. Stranded, Paul headed for a friend's farm, hoping for work as a hired hand. He remained there awhile and then lit out for Cambridge City in search of Father Alerding, the visiting priest at Sullivan who had stayed with the Dreisers.

Eventually Father Alerding persuaded the boy to go home and face the music. Soon he was in trouble with the law. The Sullivan *Democrat* picked up the story: "A young man named Paul Dresser was arrested at Terre Haute last Monday (2-21-76) and fully convicted by the mayor on the charge of burglary. His father formerly resided here." According to the Terre Haute *Express*, the target of the attempted burglary was Miller's Saloon. Paul, Sr., had to borrow money to post the three-hundred-dollar bond, adding to the family woes.

The next-oldest boy, Rome, was also heading down the primrose path. He had a regular job with the *Journal* as a press feeder, but at night he donned loud clothes and joined the sports in front of the Terre Haute House, known as the "Terrible Hot House," a toothpick dangling from his mouth to give the impression he had just eaten in the dining room. Rome seemed indifferent to the family's precarious position in the community, living entirely for himself with "vainglory, indifference, colossal selfishness."

When Mame became involved with a wealthy citizen whom Dreiser calls Colonel Silsby, who gave her money, Rome tried to persuade her to direct some of the largesse his way, but she refused. However, he did inveigle her into beg-ging fifty dollars from the president of a local lumber company, coaching her to tell him that the family needed it to pay the rent. Rome gave fifteen dollars to Sarah and blew the rest on lottery tickets. His next scheme was an attempt to blackmail the vice president of the same concern, but the man smelled a con. When Mame arrived at his door for the prearranged meeting accompanied by her husky brother, he threw them out. When Silsby heard of Rome's latest caper, he told Sarah, "You have the damndest family on record." The Dreisers were becoming a scandal and a byword in the town.

Paul, Sr., was trying desperately to provide for them, but the Ellis mill closed down. He worked for a time as a sort of handyman for fifteen dollars a week, a good wage, but his insistence on sending the children to parochial school and his continuing tithes to the Church kept the family poor. Theodore formed a lifelong resentment of his father's self-absorbed piety. He remembered him in "wornout clothes, a derby or soft hat pulled low over his eyes, his shoes oiled (not shined) in order to make them wear longer . . . trudging off at seven or eight every morning, rain or shine, to hear his beloved mass."

To the boy he seemed to escape into illusions — religious opium dreams — while his family suffered.

Meanwhile, Paul's wife was undermining his authority. She plotted to protect the girls in their amorous liaisons and once hid Paul, Jr., in a shed so his father would not beat him after another scrape with the law. She forgave the errant Rome and spoiled Claire, Theodore, and Ed. Paul watched all this with growing anger: his wife was a moral backslider as far as he was concerned. He envisioned the family in the European way, as an economic unit, with the boys learning a trade and the girls working as maids until they married someone of their own "station." Understandably, he could see nothing good coming of wealthy men's attentions to his daughters. But the father's tirades simply made the girls more rebellious. Emma later told Theodore she did not care about marriage or work (she held various jobs, including a stint in the mill), only clothes and men. "I don't know whether it was because we were poor or because Father was so insistent on the Catholic faith, but I was wild for anything that represented the opposite of what I had. Father was always talking about honorable marriage, but I didn't want to get married."

With his poor command of English, their father was unable to communicate with them. His thoughts got jumbled in the translation, and his words came out contorted with terrifying threats of hellfire and damnation. The children, in turn, saw and heard an old man ranting in a thick accent. He seemed to condemn anything that was pleasant — candy, parties, clothes, dancing, all the things they wanted to do. The Church he spoke for, with its strict nuns and German ways, also was foreign to them. And so they turned against him and embraced the American customs he found so immoral.

Sarah instinctively sided with them. Although Dreiser called her a "pagan," she was, in her way, as concerned about respectability as Paul was. But she had been disowned by her parents for following her passion, and it would have been hypocritical of her to censure her daughters for going out with men.

She was not class-conscious in the Old World manner like her husband; she thought her children good enough to do anything they wanted. When they got into trouble she could only pity them, pick them up, bandage their wounds. Siding with them, she could control and possess them.

•   •   •

The precociously observant Theodore sensed a primal battle being waged. Ultimately, though, Paul's authority depended not on tradition or righteousness but on his ability as a provider. As Dreiser put it:

> They fought over how the children should be regulated, who should correct them, what should be said or done. . . . She could not stand to see the children beaten or abused and to his charge that they were plunging straight to hell under her too yielding supervision, her reply was that he could not make a decent living for them, that he was too narrow and hard and she did not propose to see them governed by his theories. Let him first provide a good living and then talk.

One can imagine Sarah's social terrors as their poverty deepened and she sensed the neighbor's gossip about her children's various delinquencies. When Paul, Sr., was sick and there was no money, she had to send the oldest ones to the railroad tracks to gather lumps of coal that had spilled out of the tenders. "It was during this time," Dreiser recalled in later years, "that the severe phases of poverty which so impressed me occurred."

In May 1878 Paul, Sr., sold the house on Twelfth and Walnut and moved to a much smaller place, near a lumberyard and the railroad tracks.

Now Sarah put into effect a curious plan: she and the three youngest children—Claire, Theodore, and Ed—would move to Sullivan. There they would live cheaply in a little house with a garden where they would grow vegetables. To earn money they would take in boarders, perhaps. Paul and the older girls would set up a household in Terre Haute, with Paul, Jr., and Rome coming and going. Al would be packed off to live on her brother's farm near Manchester, Indiana.

The plan was justified as an economy measure, but there was probably more involved. The rift with her husband over the children's discipline and education (she favored public schools for them) had hardened. By now the oldest children—Paul, Jr., Rome, and Mame—were beyond help, so far as she was concerned, but at least she might save the youngest three. At some deeper level, though, Sarah was taking flight—from the strains of her marriage, from her husband's sexual demands (and having more children), from the disgrace of their poverty. Her life had been fearfully hard the past five years, and the thought of returning to Sullivan, where she had been happy and the family had been respected, must have been seductive.

The night before they left, Paul assembled them in the parlor and sang a German folk song:

> Now we are about to travel out of the gate of the city, I sit down to say good-bye, good-bye, good-bye, good-bye, farewell!

Theodore blotted the song out of his memory until his brother Ed sang it for him half a century later. The parting was more painful then he knew. Nor could he appreciate that the song, a relic of medieval times, expressed regret for leaving the security of the city. To go outside the gate meant that one was either a traveler, with all the attendant perils, or an outcast.

4 / Her Wandering Boy

'Twas not thro' word of anger, 'twas not thro' love of gold,
'Twas not through pangs of hunger, he wandered from the fold,
But just a restless nature that none could understand . . .
Next eve there came a knocking, upon the homestead door,
"Your last words, mother, saved me, I won't leave you any more."
— Paul Dresser, "You're Going Far Away, Lad;
or I'm Still Your Mother, Dear" (1897)

Sarah's scheme almost collapsed at the outset. She wrote to the Bulgers, the Irish family she had patronized in better days, and was told that economic conditions were not favorable to her boardinghouse venture. Determined to leave anyhow, she and the children moved in with a woman named Sue Bellette, an orphan she had befriended in Terre Haute who had married a fireman in Vincennes, thirty miles to the south. It turned out that the firehouse, a large building with several floors and numerous beds, served as the town brothel as well.

As soon as Sarah determined that conditions were a bit more favorable in Sullivan, she packed their things and they boarded the train. The place of their former glory was still a placid county seat with a population of about twenty-two hundred. It had little industry, though there were a few coal mines in the vicinity.

Sarah found a small house at the edge of town, on the wrong side of the Evansville and Terre Haute Railroad tracks. Green fields of corn and wheat stretched to the east, and to the west was a common covered with a rank growth of weeds and with a slaughterhouse in one corner. The rent was only seven dollars a month, and they moved in with no furniture other than a couple of straw mattresses and a chair borrowed from friends. Full of enthusiasm, she scrubbed down the house and made it into a bare but comfortable abode. To earn immediate money she took in washing — the traditional small-town occupation for impoverished widows and abandoned wives.

Like her pioneer forebears, Sarah believed in the great good place just over the next hill, but she must have had some misgivings about her social position; only a decade before she had been the mill manager's wife. As was her way, she communicated her doubts to the children. Theodore, at least, sensed them, for he remembered being deeply ashamed of having to deliver the baskets of clothes and making his rounds via back-street routes. He also remembered going to school barefoot and being told to get some shoes when the weather got cold. Since there was no money to buy them, he and Ed dropped out for a time, then went back. Ed later said Theodore exaggerated; they had gone barefoot in summertime as was the small-town custom and had shoes when winter came. But Theodore was acutely self-conscious and imagined that everyone in town looked down on them. His solution was to hold himself aloof, clinging to an imagined superiority. Sarah had managed to instill in them a sense of the family's vanished glory; their present lowly state was merely temporary, and better days were ahead.

But she had to lavish affection on him constantly; he cried easily and had bad dreams about the slaughterhouse next door. Twice a week, Spilky, the owner, would herd the hapless animals from an adjacent field into the shed that served as his charnel house, and the boy could hear their frightened bleats and squeals. Afterward, Spilky would emerge and toss bloody chunks of meat into a wagon. In his nightmares Theodore saw ghostly pigs and steers with lolling tongues and wide, panicky eyes racing frenziedly about.

He could escape from his fears in rambles about the countryside. He also remembered sitting on the porch on summer nights, his mother rocking, inhaling the fragrance of the roses she had planted, and telling them stories or gazing up at the stars.

Paul, Sr., sent them money and visited occasionally. In time the girls returned one by one, drawn by Sarah's psychic chains. The first to turn up was Sylvia, who was soon followed by Emma. The two of them spent most of their time dressing up in their best clothes and then promenading around the courthouse square, ogled by the local dudes. After some near disastrous flirtations — Sylvia almost ran off with a traveling salesman — they became bored and decided to go to Chicago, which a friend of Emma had been extolling as a place of glamour and excitement. At the last minute Sylvia had to back out — the ticket agent she cajoled into giving her a free fare changed his mind — so Emma went alone, dreaming of the fine clothes she would someday buy and the handsome, wealthy men she would meet.

Next Mame arrived bearing more troubles than all the others combined: She was pregnant, perhaps by the old but still vigorous Colonel Silsby. The man, whoever he was, had directed her to a country doctor who was reputed to perform abortions, but when she arrived she discovered that he was dead. So she slunk back to Sarah and confessed the worst — she was not even married.

Her mother took charge, comforting Mame ("Perhaps you will be a better girl for it"), keeping her out of sight until the baby came. Sarah delivered it herself, and when it turned out to be stillborn, she buried the tiny corpse in the yard under cover of darkness.

Eventually these extra boarders moved on, and after about a year Sarah replaced them with the paying kind. In addition to a taciturn man who was, it turned out when detectives came to arrest him, an escaped convict, there were a few miners and railroad workers. The most distinguished guest was Professor Solax, a dapper book agent. He was peddling *Hill's Manual of Social and Business Forms*, an eclectic compendium of useful information on etiquette, letter writing, composition, U.S. history, literature, and poetry.

During their second winter, Sarah must have felt that the poorhouse had become a real possibility. The boardinghouse languished and she took in washing again. Paul, Sr., was laid off, so his contributions stopped. As wintry gusts rattled the windows, Sarah felt the icy breath of failure. The children were sent to the mines to gather loose chunks of coal to keep the fire going in the stove. There were days when there was nothing to eat but cornmeal, and Dreiser remembered walking to the gristmill in order to save a few pennies. For years after, the onset of winter or the sight of a poor neighborhood filled him "with an indefinable and highly oppressive dread . . . thoughts and emotions which had a close kinship to actual and severe physical pain."

What deepened the trauma of this time was Sarah's discouragement. She sank into a "dumb despair," plodding listlessly about her tasks or sitting in her chair rocking. With no idea what to do, she could only hope something would turn up. The effect of her attitude must have been psychologically devastating to Theodore, who was so dependent upon her. The haunting dread that some disaster was about to strike took on exaggerated proportions amid this latest crisis.

One day in February 1882, a loud rapping was heard at the door of the Sullivan cottage. When Sarah opened it, young Paul burst in and swept her into his arms. To the children, who barely knew him, he seemed an emissary from some higher, finer sphere, dressed in a thick fur coat and silk hat and carrying a walking stick. His presence lit up the room, "like the sun, or a warm cheering fire."

He passed out presents and pressed soft green bills in his mother's hand. They sat mesmerized as he recounted his adventures over the past three years. For a time, he traveled with the Lightning Liniment troupe, appearing frequently in Terre Haute and Evansville. He performed in blackface, sang, danced, told jokes, and played the elaborate pipe organ on the wagon (his mother somehow had started him out with piano lessons). When he and his fellow performers had put the crowd in a good mood, the pitchman would appear to extol the virtues of Lightning Liniment for aching muscles and a host of other ills.

Next he joined the bill at the Evansville Apollo Theater, an open-air beer garden where the city's large German population spent summer evenings and Sunday afternoons soaking up Würzburger and *Gemütlichkeit*. Paul's comic blackface routines were well received, and he moved up to a star turn at the Opera House. On the side, he wrote a column of quips and doggerel for a weekly paper called the *Argus*. He was also composing songs, and he passed out copies of *The Paul Dresser Songster*.

A big man, around six feet tall and weighing two hundred pounds, Paul was nonetheless light on his feet. His routine consisted of broad, shamelessly corny pratfalls, jokes, and comic songs, which went over well with the entertainment-starved rural audiences to whom the arrival of the medicine show was a major event.

In Evansville he was popular for his "big smile . . . and his great big happy ways," one old-timer recalled. "I do not believe he had an enemy in the world. He . . . was never at a loss for an answer so that it became a common expression, 'You can't get ahead of Paul.' " A man who worked with him on the *Argus* remembered him as "big and good natured, with a disposition that was always sunny." He was well remembered for his generosity. Once he gave his last dollar to a beggar, telling a crony: "It looks as if that old man has no friend in the whole world but now with my dollar he has a friend . . . and even if I get cold and hungry I am happy that temporarily I made it better for him."

At one point he decided to have a try at New York. Green as a sassafras shoot but brimming with self-confidence, he attempted to get an interview with Augustin Daly, author of the hit melodrama of the 1860s, *Under the Gaslight*, and now the owner of a palatial theater on Broadway with a resident stock company that featured John Drew, Mrs. Scott-Siddons, Ada Rehan, and other leading thespians. After haunting the stage door for days, he managed to speak to a supercilious functionary who told him, "No mah deah boy; we have all the talent we desiah." Undaunted, Paul had some cards printed up reading: MR PAUL DRESSER/DALY'S THEATER/STAGE ENTRANCE—NO FURTHER. After being deluged with those cards, Daly sent for him and gave him a place in one of his road companies.

Paul found other work during his New York sojourn. In September 1891 a theatrical paper ran the announcement that "Paul Dresser, eccentric comedian and vocalist" would open at Miner's New Theater in the Bowery. The following month he is listed second on the bill of the National Theater, his "Mirthful Morsels, Songs and Parodies" preceding such headliners as Parker and His Dogs, the Lanier Sisters, and Emerson & Clark. Earlier that year he was featured at the Buckingham Theater in Louisville, Kentucky, where a local press agent dubbed him "the sensational comique." He also put in a stint with the Thatcher, Primrose and West Minstrel Show.

Undoubtedly, Paul left out some of his racier adventures on the road, for he was already acquiring a taste for women and whiskey, and he exploited the itinerant actor's power to arouse the buried passions of small-town girls. Nor, probably, did he tell them much about his new Evansville friend, Sallie Walker, other than to say she would call on them. Sallie was the main reason for his mooring in Evansville.

When she did arrive a few days later, Sallie turned out to be a beautiful, dark-haired woman, well-dressed, refined, and several years older than Paul. She stayed for the space of one train (as they said in that era of ten or twelve trains a day), discussing Paul's and her intention to move the family to Evansville. Soon after she left, boxes of groceries and fruit arrived. For Sarah and Claire there were also some secondhand dresses of a rather flamboyant style.

What Paul probably did not tell his mother was that Sallie Walker (real name: Annie Brace) was a madame, the proprietor of Evansville's most elegant brothel. Sarah must have guessed that Sallie was no Sunday school teacher, but she was not one to inquire too deeply into the background of her children's friends. The important thing was that the family was saved; the good life had returned.

5 / City Lights

In 1889 Chicago had the peculiar qualifications of growth which made such adventuresome pilgrimages, even on the part of young girls, plausible.

—Dreiser, *Sister Carrie* (1900)

In late spring 1882 Paul, Jr., came and put Sarah, Claire, Theodore, and Ed aboard a train for Evansville. Late that night, when they emerged in the street, Theodore gazed with sleepy eyes at the crowds of people and the rumbling wagons, lit up by rows of gas lamps. After the somnolence of Sullivan, they had been plunged in the hurly-burly of a small city of about twenty-five thousand people. It seemed like a "fairy land" to Theodore.

Paul piled their luggage into a jitney and they clopped out Main Street to 1415 East Franklin, located in a new addition at the edge of town. The house was spanking new—a half-story brick cottage set in a large yard and surrounded by a picket fence. When Theodore, the next morning, ran out to explore, he discovered a barn, a garden, a chicken run in the back, and open country beyond. To Sarah it was a palace—new furniture, carpets on the floors, and a well-appointed kitchen. The sight of such luxury brought tears to her eyes, causing Paul to cry too. The wandering boy and the mother who kept the light burning in the window—it was the stuff of a sentimental ballad, and Paul would use the theme often in the coming years.

Evansville is located on high ground at a point where the viscid brown Ohio River makes a sharp bend to the south. Main Street ran down to a stone levee, where white steamboats docked, their tall chimneys belching black smoke, their paddle wheels churning up a boiling wake. Cotton bales, boxes, and barrels were piled about in front of great warehouses, and black roustabouts lounged or labored. Along Water Street, as the levee was known, was also located the vice district.

On weekends Paul would journey out to the house on East Franklin with gifts for Sarah and the children. He spent hours chatting with his mother in the kitchen, playing comic songs on the piano, or hitting flies to Theodore and Ed, whom he had equipped with gloves and bats to go with the Evansville team uniforms their mother had sewed for them.

His younger brothers had become such inseparable companions that Paul dubbed them "Frassus" and "Fitus." With the other boys in the neighborhood, they sometimes put on plays inspired by performances they had seen at the Opera House on passes donated by Paul. Al, who had rejoined the family, was always the villain. He was a husky youth now, toughened by hard work. He and Ed, who excelled in sports, were a contrast to Theodore, who had little aptitude for such things, though he joined in. Theodore preferred to take long walks or read. Sometimes Ed accompanied him on those rambles, and he later recalled:

> [Theodore] would do most of the talking, but he was always interested in my questions and answers. . . . Theo would suggest we pick a subject, any subject under the sun, and talk about it. We talked and talked for hours. It was amazing the way everything and everyone in the world interested him. He wasn't aggressive or anxious in the same way [most] children are. His manner was earnest and gentle; and in place of a random curiosity quickly satisfied, he was interested strongly in people, what they were doing and thinking . . . everything.

Once, when they were playing with some other boys on the riverfront, jumping from barge to barge, Theodore slipped and fell in. Just as he was about to be swept away, Ed and another boy pulled him out. This narrow escape confirmed a fear of water Theodore had begun to develop when he and Rome were in a boat on the Wabash River. A small steamboat passed by, rocking them with its waves. When Theodore began to scream, Rome rocked harder, laughing his guttural, sinister laugh.

The oppressive fears associated with Catholicism became more deeply rooted during the years Theodore lived in Evansville. Though Sarah would have preferred that the children go to public school, Paul, Sr., came down from Terre Haute to make sure they were enrolled in the Holy Trinity parochial school near Third and Vine. Theodore resented the rote learning, which consisted of a little grammar, arithmetic, and spelling and mainly indoctrination in Church history. The object was to prepare the students for first communion at age twelve; after that it was assumed they would be put out to work in a factory.

Most of his education Theodore picked up on his own, wandering about the city, observing people at work—a potter shaping a formless mound of glistening white clay at his wheel, or men in a foundry feeding scrap into the furnace's fiery maw. He also read avidly the books he found in their new house—Gray's "Elegy," Oliver Goldsmith's "The Deserted Village," Ouida's *Wanda* and Bulwer-Lytton's *Ernest Maltravers*. More interesting, though, were the illustrated weeklies and dime novels he purchased with nickels from Paul (the price of most "dime" novels was five cents).

Many of these stories had urban settings, and they served to instruct America's predominantly rural and small-town populace in the wonders and pitfalls of the city. Dangers, moral and otherwise, there were aplenty, but success and happiness crowned the efforts of the virtuous shopgirl or clerk who adhered to a simple moral code learned at mother's knee. A favorite genre was the working girl who was kidnapped or lured by villainous thugs for unmentionable purposes. Trapped, she would buckle on the armor of righteousness, as does the heroine of *Night Scenes in New York: In Darkness and by Gaslight:* "Hear me, Lyman Treadwell; I am but a poor shopgirl; my present life is a struggle for a scanty existence; my future a life of toil; but over my present life of suffering there extends a rainbow of hope . . . the grave is but the entrance to eternity. And you, villain, ask me to change my present peace for a life of horror with you. No, monster, rather may I die at once!"

The premier urban hero appeared in the Horatio Alger stories—always poor but honest (and often well-born) lads. Theodore sampled the volumes in Alger's proliferating library—*Luck and Pluck, Wait and Win*, and several others, learning that industry, frugality, and saving the boss's daughter from a runaway horse were the routes to modest prosperity.

With Paul's financial support, and with Sylvia, Emma, Al, and Paul, Sr., adding their mites, the Evansville branch of the family was fairly prosperous. The trouble was, the whole arrangement rested on Paul's relationship with Sallie. Apparently, she put up most of the money for the household, probably regarding it as a way of ensuring her young lover's affections. Later, Paul explained to Theodore that Sallie had purchased the house and that he contributed money for expenses, but deed records show it belonged to Edward F. Goecke and was rented to Paul, who made the payments. Since Paul had a taste for high life and could not have been earning a large salary at the Opera House, the money probably ultimately came from Sallie.

In *Dawn*, Dreiser writes that Paul was an "unregenerate sex enthusiast," and in a passage he cut from the final book he writes that after one escapade his brother contracted syphilis, which he cured with the standard mercury treatments. However, a lesion erupted on his nose, leaving a pitted scar which Paul always covered with a small piece of flesh-colored tape. Once he ran off with one of Sallie's girls but returned and begged Sallie's forgiveness. She took him back and fired the girl, but when he launched an affair with a respectable woman from a wealthy local family, she kicked him out for good. Respectability was something Sallie couldn't fight; also, as a professional, she must have felt contempt for a man who would put pleasure before business.

Deprived of Sallie's financial assistance, Paul joined a minstrel company and later moved on to New York City, where he established himself as a blackface comedian at Tony Pastor's nightclub on Fourteenth Street and then played at the London Varieties.

As for Sarah, she pulled herself together and planned the next move. This time she set her sights on Chicago, about which she had been hearing a lot from Rome, Mame, and Theresa. All the children save Al, who had a girlfriend and a steady job in a furniture factory, were gravitating there. Its rapid growth was the wonder of the Middle West, and there were said to be jobs for the asking. Paul, Sr., was working again at the Ellis mill and did not want to join them; at sixty-two, he was too old to give up a position in hand.

So they packed once again, and once again boarded the train. Theodore had acquired some of his mother's blind faith in the good place over the next hill, and he had heard the enthusiastic tales about the magic of city lights from his older brothers and sisters. But these constant uprootings and the dizzying rise and fall of their fortunes instilled in him a deep anxiety. Later in life he could never leave a place (or a person he was close to) without a sickening sense of doom and disaster.

The first signs of Chicago hove into view through the train window: the flat prairie broken by a line of telegraph poles marching to the horizon; houses set on raw earth in a gridwork of unpaved streets, signs already in place—new developments. Then the houses grew more numerous and gave way to blocks of flats, factories, grain elevators. Looming against the sky were two ten-story buildings—Burnham and Root's Montauk Block and William Le Baron Jenney's just-completed Home Insurance Building, the first iron-and-steel-framed structure and precursor of the "skyscraper." Finally, the family clambered off in Dearborn Street Station, with its tall clock tower, and plunged into a maelstrom of novel sights, sounds, and smells.

To Theodore Chicago was the wonder of his life. By the time they reached their new home, a six-room, third-floor rear flat on the corner of West Madison and Throop, he was drunk on it. He hung out the apartment window, gaping at the crush of people and horses and wagons on the street below. In the beer garden atop the Waverly Theater across the street, he could hear a band playing and see pennants flapping in the breeze. Peddlers with pushcarts sold vegetables or purchased rags, iron, and bones. As night fell, the clamor subsided and new sounds wafted through the window—music and laughter from the beer garden, the hum of voices from the throngs of pleasure seekers. Gaslights dripped pools of radiance, and in the windows of the flats across the way figures swam in and out of view in the yellow glow of oil lamps. Theodore watched the spectacle until he fell asleep, exhausted, at the window.

In 1884 Chicago was swollen with new arrivals. It had risen from the ashes of the 1871 fire more vital and energetic than ever. In the two decades from 1870 to 1890, its population increased fivefold, from 368,000 to 1.3 million, and its area from 35 to 185 square miles. Great grain elevators towered over the tangled ganglia of tracks, and factory chimneys belched black smoke. By 1890 there would be ten thousand manufacturing establishments turning out

$64.5 million worth of goods—foundries making steel, stockyards with sprawling mazes of open pens where herds of cattle waited to be butchered. On the dirty, noisome Chicago River, intestine of the city's wastes, a fleet of barges and scows hauled coal and produce. The vibrant hum of commerce, the promise of fortunes to be made, hung in the air. "It is the only great city in the world to which all its citizens have come with the one common, avowed object of making money," remarks a character in Henry B. Fuller's novel *With the Procession*.

The appetite for unskilled labor was voracious. Young women were needed as shopgirls in department stores such as Mandel Brothers; Field; Schlesinger and Mayer; Carson, Pirie, Scott; and The Fair, or as machine tenders in the shoe factories and garment-making concerns at four to ten dollars a week. Untrained young men fresh from the farm or the boat performed heavy labor in the factories, stockyards, foundries, mills, train yards, grain elevators, and warehouses, and in thousands of smaller tributary concerns.

Lured by the promise of work, the newcomers poured in, and in such numbers—fifty thousand a year—that wages were chronically depressed. The American-born farmers among them had been driven off the land by plummeting commodity prices, forced in part by the overproduction made possible by new machines such as Cyrus McCormick's reapers. Further impetus was provided by inflated freight rates rigged by Chicago railway magnates, which ate away farmers' profits, and by deflated currency and high interest rates, set by the city's bankers, which made it impossible for them to pay off their mortgages. To the greenhorn and the rustic, the city was a shimmering mirage of hope, promising not only economic opportunity but excitement, sociability, glamour, comfort, and ease.

The neighborhood the Dreisers lived in, on the borderline of a bastion of respectability known as Union Park, presented a vivid social canvas. A cataract of shouts, laughter, and quarrels spilled down the dumbwaiter shaft in their building. The apartment above was occupied by a woman with a drunken husband, and once Paul, Sr., was forced to call a policeman after he had beaten her into insensibility. Eventually he abandoned her, and Sarah temporarily adopted their child until the wife could get back on her feet.

They had not been in Chicago long before Theodore began to overhear scraps of conversation that had a familiar ring. The gist of them was that the family economy was again shaky. Paul, Sr., was unemployed, and Rome, now twenty-four, was incommunicado. Paul, Jr., twenty-six, had recently stopped sending money because of romantic problems. Theodore and Ed sold newspapers—daringly boarding trolley cars and working the packed crowd of homebound commuters until the conductor kicked them off—but sank their profits into licorice whips and cream caramels.

Mame, now a tall, striking young woman of twenty-three with a full figure and a warm smile, had become involved with a genial casketware salesman named Austin Brennan, who was nearly twenty years older than she. Although Brennan had a good income and hailed from a socially prominent Irish family in Rochester, New York, he was a playboy and bon vivant.

The twenty-year-old Theresa was keeping company with an aging, wealthy widower to whom Brennan had introduced her and whom the ever-hopeful Sarah treated as a bona fide suitor. Emma, twenty-one, also had an affair perking with an older man, a cultivated, prominent architect. He had set her up in a hotel on South Halstead Street. Theodore had visited her there once, and she showed off her silver toilet articles and a closet full off dresses.

His sisters' apparent success impressed him but was also confusing. He felt vaguely ashamed because, as his father complained, they "were selling themselves too cheaply, that men were using them as mere playthings." Yet they seemed happy and prosperous and independent. Where, exactly, was the immorality?

None of their illicit prosperity made its way to Sarah, however. As the family fell behind on rent and furniture payments, she decided it was time to move to Warsaw, Indiana, which had the virtue of being near a plot of land that she had inherited. More important, she had brothers and sisters living in the area. Warsaw was the seat of Kosciusko County and was considered a pleasant town with good schools. By now Sarah was determined that Theodore, Ed, and Claire would have a public education.

The Dreisers were a family that clung to the margin of the middle class, but had come to be identified with the poor, outside the pale of bourgeois respectability.

6 / Awakenings

> From contemplating most of the small towns with which I have come in contact . . . I have to come to dread the conventional point of view. The small mind of the townsmen is anti-polar to that of the larger, more sophisticated wisdom of the city. . . . I never was in such a place for any period of time without feeling cabined, cribbed, confined intellectually if not emotionally.
>
> —Dreiser, *A Hoosier Holiday* (1916)

Warsaw was a pretty town in 1884. In summer it seemed to be washed by brilliant Alpine light. The flat green terrain was the opposite of Alpine, but it was dotted with lakes; two were near the town, and one, Center Lake, was right at its edge. The relaxed gaiety of arriving vacationers (for the town was something of a resort), the bright-colored sailboats and canoes on the gleaming blue lake, and the bathers on the shore gave it a festive air.

The population then was around thirty-three hundred, and while there was no large industry or wealthy few, a thin upper crust of sorts existed. Its manners and morals were set by the wives of the town's successful grocers, landlords of office blocks, owners of the biggest hardware store and meat market, chiefs of the flour and planing mills, and assorted lawyers, doctors, and politicians.

Into these social waters, placid on the surface but full of concealed snags, plunged Sarah and her three youngest children. Sarah settled the family in a large old brick house known as the Grant Place. With living cheaper, and both Pauls resuming their financial contributions, the family's situation was stabilized. Theodore, for the first time, felt a sense of belonging.

The public school was next door, and the children were enrolled soon after their arrival (there were tirades from Paul, Sr., later, but Sarah held firm). After the authoritarian Catholic schools, the place seemed like heaven to Theodore. His seventh-grade teacher was a kindly woman named May Calvert, who had warm blue eyes and long blond hair and was only twenty. He fell in love with her, and she, sensing he was a "mother boy," gave him special attention, coaching him in grammar, which was his weakest subject. Despite her efforts he failed it, but she promoted him anyway, saying he was too bright to be held back. He bloomed under her attention and for the first time found school interesting.

Also interesting were the girls in his class. Among the beauties were Augusta Phillipson; Myrtle Weimar; Carrie (Cad) Tuttle, who had thick tawny hair; her sister, Maud, who was plump and blond; and Berta Moon, with jet-black hair and a slim figure. He was too shy to speak to them at first, for he had formed the idea that he was unattractive and unlikable.

At Miss Calvert's urging Theodore obtained a card at the town's small public library and rifled its shelves. There he discovered Hawthorne's *The House of the Seven Gables* and *The Scarlet Letter*, fellow Hoosier Lew Wallace's *Ben-Hur*, Charles Kingsley's *The Water Babies* (a kind of Darwinian fable for children that strangely fascinated him), the novels of James Fenimore Cooper, and the poetry of Longfellow, Bryant, Whittier, and Poe (whom he liked the best of all). He also read the romantic effusions of popular writes such as Laura Jean Libbey, who supplied "some phase of impossible sentimentalism which my nature seemed to crave."

After about a year the family moved to the old Thralls mansion, a rambling, twelve-room brick structure built fifty years before by a prominent judge but now in a state of decrepitude. There was a pond in back, where logs for the planing mill were massed, and Theodore, Ed, and their friends jumped about on them, lumberjack style. The place also had an orchard, several chestnut trees, a large garden, and a grove of ash trees from which they took firewood.

Theodore made a few friends, including the Shoup brothers, whose father was co-owner of the flour mill and whose mother was Sarah's niece, but it didn't escape his notice that he and Ed were never invited to their homes. He sensed an invisible line which his family could not cross.

The boys spent hours loafing and talking in the woods, with sex, a subject about which the thirteen-year-old Theodore was becoming curious, the chief topic. A boy named Gavin McNutt gossiped knowingly about Warsaw's sexual underground; he knew which young woman was in trouble and which young rake would have to leave town. Theodore's closest friend, Harry Croxton, served as scientific consultant by dint of his having attended a "sex hygiene" lecture by an itinerant savant, who solved the mystery with the aid of a pointer and male and female anatomy charts. Croxton passed on the professor's lurid warnings about the horrors of venereal disease and the awful consequences of masturbation: pimples, sterility, madness, death.

Such talk inflamed Theodore. He reread the lustier passages of Shakespeare and Fielding; a picture of an actress in tights turned him into a quivering jelly of adolescent lust. He began fantasizing about the girls in his class, though when he confronted them he was painfully shy and averted his eyes, lest they divine his desires. He formed a kind of idealized passion for the mousy, ethereal

Myrtle Weimar—she reminded him of pictures of Quaker maids he had seen in books—while the sensuous-looking Carrie Tuttle stirred him in a physical way. Myrtle had no connection with the seething inside him. All he hoped for was a chaste kiss.

His only sexual experience came with the baker's daughter, who was about his age and already known as a town "pump." As he walked by the shop one day, she cried, "Bet you can't catch me!" and ran to the back. He followed her into a shed. After a brief mock struggle, they sank to the floor, and in a chaotic blur of sensations, his pent-up desires found a sudden, blinding release. Afterward, however, he could only think of Croxton's warning about a horrible pox known as the clap, and he never went back to her.

He knew that he had no chance with the "nice" girls, and never even dared a kiss, convinced that because he was homely and lacked "money, daring, this and that, [they] would never permit . . . such familiarities as the baker's daughter. . . ."

Before long Theodore found the inevitable outlet—the "ridiculous and unsatisfactory practice of masturbation." Already ashamed of his secret desires, he acquired a habit that was condemned in every pulpit and pseudoscientific pamphlet in the land.

In a passage Dreiser expurgated from the published version of *Dawn* as too risqué, he tells of sitting on his bed and fantasizing about Carrie Tuttle and the other girls in his class; an erection ensued, and he manipulated it. The ejaculation was intensely pleasurable but also terrifying. He jumped up, thinking he had injured himself. A few days later, the fantasies recurred, and he repeated the process. He resolved to stop, but the urge would seize him and he would hurry to his room or the bathroom and "in a kind of fury and excess of passion and delight give himself over to this form of self ab-use [sic]."

After some months of this he began to notice alarming physical symptoms. One night, at the dinner table, he felt a whirring sensation in his head and a ringing in his ears, followed moments later by a wave of vertigo so severe that he would have fallen had he not been sitting down. He had to excuse himself and go to his room and lie down.

Theodore decided he was having a nervous breakdown, which was nature's way of restoring his system to "parity." He had been overtaxing his body, or, as he put it nearly fifty years later, "paying out of one treasury by drawing too swiftly and too heavily on others." He retained the Victorian belief that emissions of semen represent a sort of overdraft on one's "energy bank." This was the prevailing opinion.

In the ensuing months Theodore worried that he was wasting away. Desperate for advice but too shy to ask, he copied a prescription from a home medical guide and a friendly pharmacist filled it. When his mother received the bill, she asked him about it. He stammered incoherently, but she did not press him, suggesting, in a voice "as soft and pleasing as that of a sweetheart," that he see Dr. Wooley, the family physician. He never did, but he also never forgot what he sensed (however she intended it) as the seductive undercurrent in her voice, implicating her in his sexual awakening.

•　　•　　•

Like a bad omen, Rome reeled into town. Emma and Sylvia followed, both of them voluptuous and spoiling for romance. They promenaded around the square in flashy city clothes, Emma in patent leather shoes with white tips, and Sylvia in rings and furs. Paul, Sr., who was temporarily in residence, called them "shameless creatures." After trolling their allures, they landed two sports from the upper crust: the son of the bank president and that of the leading butcher. One night, when they came home after 2:00 A.M., Paul was waiting up for them. He announced he was throwing them out: the door was closed to them forever. Sylvia wailed, Emma screamed, and Sarah shouted, "You are too rough! You always were! What will the neighbors think!"

The next day at school a boy who lived in the neighborhood asked Theodore if someone had been sick the previous night. A few days later another boy slyly referred to Emma and Sylvia as the "Ticket sisters," using the last name of one of their swains. The innuendo was clear: only fast girls went out with Harry Ticket. Theodore was reminded of the time in Evansville when some locals teased him about Paul's relationship with Sallie Walker. He had a premonition that "scandal hung over our household—a household . . . darkened by doubts as to its own validity and decency."

The family's social fortunes went downhill after that. Emma was banished to Chicago, but Sylvia remained, bored and sulky. Later that winter the trouble that Emma was courting fell on her like a load of hay. She was smitten by a forty-year-old clerk named L. A. Hopkins, a slight, dapper man with a mustache who was nicknamed "Grove" because of his resemblance to Grover Cleveland and his amorous proclivities. He worked for Chapin and Gore, a chain of saloons that catered to a working-class clientele, and had a wife and an eighteen-year-old daughter living on the West Side.

Mrs. Hopkins got wind of her husband's adultery and hired a private detective to trail him to the apartment on the South Side that Emma shared with Theresa. Determined to catch Hopkins in flagrante delicto, she, the detective, and some friends went to the love nest at one o'clock in the morning. According to the Chicago Mail, Mrs. Hopkins climbed in the front window and spied the guilty pair asleep.

What made the story a three-day wonder in Chicago journalism was the fact that Hopkins absconded with $3500 in cash and $200 worth of jewelry from his employer's safe. After taking the money, he and Emma boarded a train to

Montreal (Canada had no extradition treaty with the United States at that time). Once there, Hopkins got cold feet or had a change of heart and returned all but $800 of the money to Chapin and Gore, who declined to press charges. He and Emma then went on to New York City for a new life. A reporter covering the incident concluded that the theft was planned in advance. Hopkins was responsible for closing the warehouse every other Sunday night, the day he fled. Two days before the theft, neighbors said, a letter had arrived for Emma. Shortly after receiving it, she summoned an American Express truck to pick up her trunk and take it to Hopkins' office. The smitten clerk was not acting on a drunken impulse.

Two detectives came to Warsaw to question Sarah about her daughter (Mrs. Hopkins had told police about the Dreiser sisters' involvement). At least their real names never appeared in the stories in the Chicago papers with their lurid headlines (A WOMAN IN THE CASE, A DASHING BLONDE, and EMBEZZLER HOPKINS HAD A FAIR COMPANION WHEN HE SKIPPED FOR CANADA). However, Sarah was shaken, and she never dared tell her husband about the affair.

But another scandal occurred that could not be covered up. Bored and lonely, Sylvia threw herself at Don Ashley (as Dreiser calls him), a well-off young man-about-town with a reputation as a gambler and a womanizer. Sarah had the naive idea that her daughter was moving up in the world and permitted Syl to entertain Ashley in their home before meeting him (her complaisance when her daughter's marriage prospects were involved was seemingly boundless). That fall, however, Theodore noticed his sister acting strangely. He sometimes compulsively went into the girls' rooms when they were out, drawn to the hothouse of female scents—hair, perfume, powder—and stole some small token. He wanted to penetrate this intimate, musky sphere; the tendrils of desire he would have normally sent out to girls his own age turned back on him, becoming ingrown, incestuous. But on that occasion, Sylvia was there. He noticed a bottle marked "poison" on her bureau and queried her about it. She mumbled that it was medicine. Then she shut herself in her room weeping, refusing to eat. Sarah coaxed her secret from her: she was pregnant, and Ashley was the father.

Sarah thought of bringing a paternity suit against Sylvia's seducer, but the lawyer she hired was beholden to the Ashley family and stalled her. Finally, Sylvia was sent to Emma's in New York City to have the baby. Sarah had heard that Emma was prospering but probably did not know the source of their money: she and Hopkins were running a bedhouse, to which streetwalkers brought their clients. Hopkins had ingratiated himself with Tammany Hall and had an arrangement with the local precinct. As a result, Emma was living high—lavish clothes, carriage rides in Central Park and sumptuous dinners at Delmonico's. She was glad to take in her sister.

After Sylvia gave birth, she refused to keep the baby, and once again Sarah was stuck. She took the little boy, who was named Carl, and his presence in their house sealed their doom in Warsaw society. The child was passed off as a relative, but Warsaw's moral guardians were not fooled. For Theodore it was a dismal period, a gloom from which he never completely emerged. "I was more or less in a state of doldrums concerning us," he recalled. "We were just naturally bad perhaps and could not be made much better." He, Ed, and Claire were now outside the pale. They could only yearn for the other world in Warsaw — that of the superior social set one read about in the society pages of the *Daily Times*, the young people who sailed in bright-painted boats on Central Lake and went to garden parties lit by strings of Chinese lanterns, like soft pastel moons. He envied them: "They were constantly going off somewhere on weekend excursions. . . . They were better clothed and carried themselves with an air of ease and sufficiency to which I did not feel I was entitled."

The sense of being an outcast oppressed him terribly. Torn between his father's religious morality, which he rejected even though he feared it, and his mother's gentleness and compassion, which he preferred but which seemed linked to one family disaster after another, he was in a quandary. He resented having to bear the obloquy of Sylvia's transgression, yet "seeing what my own sex feelings were I could not be very hard on her." Unlike Claire (who was closer to Paul, Sr., than any of them and already something of a prig), he could not condemn Sylvia. But he was in no position to flout convention. Like any child his age, Theodore wanted to be liked and accepted. He had been thrust into a state of nonconformity he had not chosen and scarcely understood.

He became increasingly solitary — reading, taking long walks, lying in a hammock watching the birds wheeling against the sky. School provided his only happy times. His latest teacher, Miss Fielding, had taken a shine to him and encouraged him to cultivate his mind as a way of achieving success. The superintendent of schools had also become interested in Theodore after reading a composition he had written about discovering a dead Jewish peddler in the woods. May Calvert had already put him on to Samuel Smiles's success primer, *Self-Help*, and the superintendent urged him to study the rise of the German empire and read Shakespeare.

The Dreiser family left few traces of their sojourn in Warsaw. There is on record the adult recollection of Theodore by a contemporary which gives a brief, painful glimpse of his youth: "We knew Dreiser . . . in his high school days in Indiana. He was a gawk then; kept to himself, had no dealings with the other boys; went along the street with his head down as if afraid to look anyone in the eye. We boys thought he was 'queer,' and in the main were as ready to avoid him as he was to keep away from all companionship."

In the summer of 1887, not long before his sixteenth birthday, Theodore read an account in a Chicago Sunday supplement describing the raucous, vibrant, pushcart life on Halstead Street, which brought back vividly the sights of the metropolis. "If only we could return to the city," he thought. "There our neighbors would not care what we were." He went to Sarah and announced, "Ma, I'm going to Chicago."

She protested that she wanted him to finish school and make something of himself, but Theodore argued he would get an education somehow. "I don't want to sit around this place any longer," he said. "We can't get anywhere here. People only talk about us." Sarah could make no argument to that. Her hopes of winning respectability in Warsaw lay in ruins.

She gave him three dollars and packed a shoebox with a cold chicken, half a pie, and some apples. Theodore left that same day on the Nickel Plate line, without even saying goodbye to Ed and Claire.

7 / A Start in Life

Ah the horror of the commonplace, of disgrace, of shame, of
being shut out, ignored, forgotten, left to wander friendless
and by myself. How often have my hands beaten in spirit at
least at those doors and windows on the other side of which I
fancied joy or a hope of beauty to be. How often have I stood
outside and looked in wishing and longing with a too full
heart.

—Dreiser, *Dawn* (1931)

As the now familiar environs of Chicago rushed past the train window, Theodore
felt an infusion of hope. He had sworn he wouldn't look up his sisters when he
arrived; he intended to prove himself—this bashful, skinny boy whose most
recent job had been picking vegetables on a farm near Warsaw (he lasted one
day) and who had no visible talents other than reading and daydreaming.

In a pleasant neighborhood that reminded him of the small town he had just
left, he found a boardinghouse, run by a motherly old lady called Mrs. Pilcher.
Immediately guessing that he was trying to "make a start in the world," she
offered him a small front bedroom for only $1.50 a week. She understood how
it was with young men; she had a son starting out in Kansas City.

The next morning he was up early and out tramping the streets. He made
the rounds of shops in the neighborhood, but it was always the same: "No
Help Wanted." He purchased a copy of the *Daily News* and scanned the "Boy
Wanted" columns, but when he went to the addresses, he found that he was
not what was needed—too puny or lacking the required skill.

Soon he was down to his last two dollars. He rationed the contents of the
shoebox his mother packed, but when it was gone he had to lay out eighty-five
cents for food. Then an encouraging letter arrived from Sarah with two dollars
enclosed. She wrote that if Theodore could find work, and if Al, Theresa, and
Mame could be induced to contribute their shares, she would join them and set
up a new household. That galvanized him into renewing his search. Spotting
a DISHWASHER WANTED sign in the window of a Greek restaurant, he went in,

and the proprietor, John Paradiso, hired him on the spot; he was used to rapid turnover on this job.

Eventually Theodore looked up Theresa but, too embarrassed to say where he was working, he told her he was clerking in a Halstead Street haberdashery at the respectable sum of seven dollars a week. The two of them immediately discussed how to put Sarah's plan into action. Theresa, "a shadowy, self-effacing girl" blessed with the common sense her sisters lacked and closest of all to her mother, began looking that same afternoon and found a suitable flat on Ogden Avenue. The rent was thirty-five dollars a month, but with Al, Mame, Theodore, Theresa (who was working as a dentist's assistant), and Paul contributing, in addition to what Ed and Claire would bring in once they got jobs, survival seemed possible.

Sarah was summoned immediately, and Theodore and Theresa met her at the station, a commanding figure leading a safari of fellow travelers carrying her boxes and trunks. Al joined them a day or so later. Then followed Mame, who bustled about suggesting various improvements that would make the flat appropriate to her newly elevated social level.

While in Warsaw Al had tried a stage career in amateur minstrel productions and displayed a talent for writing comic songs. But now he was anxious to find a trade. When Al said he wouldn't mind a cushy position in a gent's emporium too, Theodore was forced to confess where he was actually working. Al asked him to quit so they could make the rounds together.

Telling his mother he had been laid off by the haberdashery, Theodore plunged once more into the economic storm. At a hardware company he was put to work cleaning stoves, but a sadistic co-worker kicked him after he balked at lifting a heavy stove. Brandishing a stove leg, Theodore was angry enough, for once, to fight. Next he worked as assistant to Theresa's boyfriend, Davis, a painter of stage sets and backgrounds for photographers.

Then Rome blew in from parts unknown and, between drinking bouts, took Theodore in hand. He had a railroad buddy with the Chicago, Burlington and Quincy who would fix up his brother with a job as a freight-car tracer. Rome's friend said the job paid forty-five dollars a month—eleven dollars a week! But Theodore would have to commute to the Hegewisch Yard, ten miles outside of the city, on the 6:40 A.M. train.

Rome convoyed him the first day. He had had a few eye-openers, and during the ride he launched into a diatribe against rich men like Armour and Pullman, who were amassing great fortunes while most poor slobs toiled for pittances to support the magnates' "sissy sons and daughters." As Theodore watched in horror, Rome repeatedly stabbed the velvet plush on the seats with a penknife, saying, "Oh, the company's rich. It can afford it."

The job of tracer consisted of locating freight cars scheduled for shipment. Theodore scampered about the huge railyard looking for tags that corresponded to the cabalistic notations on a sheaf of slips given him by the foreman. A kindly brakeman volunteered some advice, but Theodore finished his stint in a state of total confusion. Still, he found beauty in that industrial setting: "The shadows, the red, white, blue, green and yellow switch lights winking and glowing like flowers, the suggestion of distant cities . . . "

On the train home, he observed his fellow laborers, most of them foreigners, silent, toil-worn men, clutching their lunch buckets with cracked, grimy hands: "inured to a lean and meager life which horrified me and yet made me sad." He wondered if they were a foreshadowing of his own future. Would he be a workingman like them—like his father? The thought filled him with "a morbidity that was almost devastating."

Running around in the freezing December drizzle, he had caught cold, and the next morning he was too sick to go to work. The pity in his mother's eyes as he described the job made him feel sorry for himself, and when he was better he did not go back. Soon he was tramping the streets again. The family was living on such a tight margin that Theodore's six or seven dollars a week spelled the difference between solvency and eviction. Their combined monthly earnings during this period never came to much more than seventy dollars. After rent, furniture payments, and food, there was nothing left. Sarah, the family rock, was, as usual, planted on shifting sands.

After days of fruitless search, Theodore found a place as a box rustler and stockpiler at Hibbard, Spencer, Bartlett & Company, a huge wholesale hardware concern.

As the days went by, Theodore noticed two well-dressed young men from the East, sons of friends of the owners who were learning the business. By their condescending airs they made it clear to the others that their sojourn here was a mere interlude before they assumed their rightful positions. Their arrogance made him conscious of the unfairness of a society in which well-born boys had a head start in the battle for place.

But the co-worker who made the deepest impression on him was a Dane named Christian Aaberg, a "shambling man with a wrinkled, emaciated, obviously emotion-scarred face." Looking well over forty, Aaberg bore the stigmata of alcoholic martyrdom. On Monday mornings, shaky and puffy-eyed from a hangover, he would moan "My gott, how drunk I was yesterday! Oh these women! These devils of women!" He had a *manqué* air about him, hinting of an aristocratic upbringing, which he subsequently confirmed. Now, however, he was poor, making ten dollars a week and drinking up most of it. His talk was sprinkled with allusions to heretic philosophers and writers he had read— Ibsen, Nietzsche, Schopenhauer, Strindberg—and they would discuss intellectual matters as they sorted bolts or stacked pots and pans. His message echoed Miss Fielding's in Warsaw: "Mind and mind alone, makes the essential difference between the masses and the classes."

When not sitting at Aaberg's feet, Theodore spent a good deal of time gazing out the window at the crowds below or daydreaming. Chicago hummed with the frenetic trading at the wheat pit, the talk of a World's Fair in 1893, John D. Rockefeller's plans for the University of Chicago. Theodore's head was filled with "buzzing dreams of leaving Chicago and becoming a great man."

Though he needed the job, it was harming his health. The dust he breathed daily was playing havoc with his lungs. He also had a nervous stomach and suffered from constipation. He was tortured by the fear that his sexual excesses had rendered him impotent. With all this turmoil in mind and body, he became languid, rising with difficulty each morning, dragging through the day, and returning home exhausted.

But then Miss Fielding turned up at Hibbard, Spencer. She had left her job in Warsaw to become principal of a school in a Chicago suburb. Having saved some money, she wanted to use it to give Theodore a year at Indiana University. This was to be an experiment; perhaps he had an aptitude for something better, which college training would help him discover; perhaps not. At any rate, she wanted him to try. Theodore snatched at the lifeline. Miss Fielding knew the president of Indiana University and arranged for Theodore to be admitted as a special student. She would pay his two-hundred-dollar tuition and provide him with a monthly allowance of fifty dollars for room, board, and expenses.

He had no idea of what he would study, only a vague notion that in an industrializing, commercial society a young man who wanted to get ahead should acquire "technique" —a professional skill.

8 / *The Freshman*

> I attended the state university at Bloomington for several
> years, acquiring nothing save a disrespect for cut and dried
> methods of imparting information. This is not wholly true,
> however, for the beauty—natural and architectural—which
> invested the scene carried me to mental heights not previ-
> ously attained.
>
> —Dreiser to Richard Duffy (1901)

Bloomington in 1889 was a country village of a few hundred souls—a "charming place," Dreiser called it in a letter to a friend a few years later, probably
gilding memory. When he got off the train he carried a single suitcase and wore
one of Paul's cast-off suits cut down for him. He had three hundred dollars in
his pocket, two hundred of which was earmarked for tuition.

After years of dreary jobs, Bloomington seemed a peaceful haven. The campus had groves of trees and a creek winding through. Several modest stone and
brick buildings housed classrooms and the library, and the six hundred students
either lived in fraternity or sorority houses or boarded at private homes near
campus. The university was a "social" school, attracting the sons and daughters of some of Indiana's most prosperous citizens: substantial bankers and hardware merchants, lawyers, manufacturers, and well-to-do farmers. A continuous
whirl of parties and dances centered around the secret societies to which the
elite youth belonged—the young men who would go into their fathers' businesses or pursue careers in law and politics, and the young women who would
become their wives and doyennes of small-town society.

Theodore chose the required freshman subjects, suggesting that he was
aiming for a degree. He did not get off to a blazing start. As he later recalled:
"I never learned, all the time I was there, quite what it was all about. I heard
much talk of -ologies and -tries without grasping quite the fundamental fact
that they were really dealing with plain, ordinary, everyday life—the forces
about us. Somehow I had the vague uncertain notion that they did not concern
ordinary life at all."

But Theodore's university year gave him the leisure to think and dream and enabled him to associate with a kind of youth he never would have met otherwise. Some were as poor as he was, but wealthier boys also befriended him with the innate democracy of their small towns. He was an outsider, but not to the extent he later described. He joined Philomathean, for example, the leading literary society, and was elected secretary.

Theodore boarded with a widow and made friends with Will Yakey, who came from a well-off family and was an athlete and ladies' man. Why he was drawn to the gawky, painfully shy freshman is hard to fathom. Perhaps it was only proximity (they slept in the same bed); also, Yakey seems to have felt sorry for Dreiser and became his protector, finding him girls and urging him to do exercises to strengthen himself. But Theodore rebelled when the other overstepped the invisible line between friendliness and condescension.

He found another patron, a wealthy sophomore named Day Allen Willy, who also made an effort to fix him up with girls. The efforts proved fruitless because of Theodore's shyness and belief that he was homely. Whenever Willy found him a putatively willing coed, Theodore's fears of impotence prevented him from seducing her.

"Never in my life have I been more heart hungry—or sex-hungry if you will—than I was then," he remembered, "and never . . . was I so completely out of almost everything." This was an exaggeration; but everywhere, it seemed, youth and love were in ferment, while he stood in a corner and watched. Theodore sensed he didn't belong in the social whirl, and he was neglecting his studies. He moved out of the room he shared with Yakey, found another boardinghouse inhabited by young men who were as déclassé as he was, and buried himself in his studies.

At the new place he made friends of a different sort. One was a cheerful boy named Howard Hall, who was puny like Theodore. The two of them pursued fitness in hikes, exploring the caves in the hills outside Bloomington. Another was Russell Ratliff, who was working his way through school by running a student laundry service. They were drawn to each other by a mutual interest in philosophy. Together they read and discussed the writings of the contemporary thinkers who were revising philosophy in light of Charles Darwin's theory of evolution—Herbert Spencer, Thomas Huxley, Alfred Russell Wallace. Ratliff agonized over the Darwinist interpretation of society. What relevance had it to the growing disparities between rich and poor, the running warfare between capital and labor, the prevalence of vice and crime? Ratliff introduced Theodore to Tolstoy's *What to Do?*, which called for men to return to simple physical labor, each working only to provide for his own needs, eliminating exploitation of the poor by the rich. But Darwinism seemed to deny the possibility of altruism. Weren't most men selfish, grasping, driven blindly by instincts? The two were unable to reconcile their views (unlike Tolstoy, who simply rejected Darwinism and sociological positivism).

Dreiser visited his family during Christmas holiday, a stay enlivened when Willy blew in and took him for a tour of the city's red-light district. Theodore refused to let his friend buy him a prostitute, however; he was too fearful of the reality of the sex he dreamed of. Taking stock of himself during the Christmas break, he decided that college had brought him no closer to acquiring the *technique* one needed to rise; his scientific inclination was thwarted by his poor record in geometry, a prerequisite to further study. He had no interest in business or law. Somehow he would rise, but college seemed too dry, too bookish. It was all very well for youths like Yakey and Willy, who would return to their small towns, where their way would be smoothed by family connections. For him, however, the future was opaque.

In later years Dreiser emphasized his failure at the university. Actually, he had had a respectable freshman year. True, his grades were not stellar, but he probably could have improved them in his sophomore year. Socially, he found a niche, even if it wasn't the one his outlandish dreams called for; he belonged, as mentioned, to the literary society, which was where his interests lay, and a contemporary group photograph shows that he also joined a spelunkers club. Certainly Theodore liked the prestige of being able to call himself a "college man" and on occasion claimed to have spent "several years" at the university.

•   •   •

Upon his arrival home in June 1890, Theodore found his family still precariously together. Economic pressures had eased temporarily, but the clashes of these sharply individualistic temperaments raged on. It was a remarkable brood. Though most of them, for want of a good education, had not developed their talents to the fullest, their temperaments had bloomed riotously. They were driven this way and that by strong emotions, but Sarah remained their center of gravity.

As the summer drew on, they all noticed changes in her. She had grown unusually stout, and the added pounds slowed her down. Theodore would always remember his mother padding heavily about her daily rounds: up at 4:00 or 5:00 in the morning to prepare breakfast, washing dishes, cleaning, sweeping, sewing, resting awhile and telling stories to whoever gathered around. Now her bottomless well of strength was going dry, and the spectacle of her deterioration threw terror into their hearts. One day she could drag herself around no longer; a heavy lassitude seemed to have settled on her, reminding Theodore of that winter in Sullivan.

He had taken a job with a real estate promoter named Asa Conklin, a Civil War pensioner who had inherited five hundred dollars and intended to parlay it into a fortune in the city's rampant land boom. Theodore's job was to call on prospects, and he was given the use of a horse and buggy, which he used to take his mother for rides. But the excursions did little good.

Sarah's health continued to deteriorate. One day in October, when Theodore took her for a drive to view the autumnal foliage, she told him, "You know, I feel so strange these days, I hate to see the leaves turning. I'm afraid I won't see them again."

"Oh, ma, how you talk!" he said. "You're just feeling blue now because you're sick."

"You think so? Well, maybe. But I have such strange dreams. Last night I dreamed my father and mother were near me and motioning to me."

Remembering the great store she put in such portents, Theodore's heart sank. He begged his sisters to call another doctor, who told them nothing more could be done for Sarah. She slipped in and out of a coma.

One day Theodore came home at lunchtime to check on her. Theresa told him she was feeling better and seemed cheerful. When he entered the bedroom, Sarah asked him to help her sit up. Theresa insisted she lie back and rest, but Sarah refused. She began to struggle, kicking off the covers. Theodore rushed to the bed and with great difficulty hoisted her into a sitting position. He went out for a moment, and when he came back, she was on the side of the bed. Then she strained forward as though trying to walk, shuddered, and collapsed. Theodore rushed to her side and supported her soft bulk as she sank to the floor. Her deeply weary eyes stared blankly for a moment, then glowed with a preternatural light. But the light clicked out; a veil closed over.

"Mamma! Mamma!" Theodore cried. Theresa was at his side in an instant, clasping Sarah, chafing her hands, breaking into a spasm of uncontrollable sobs. Rushing in, Paul, Sr., saw his wife lying on the floor and knelt beside her. "I'm old. I should have gone first!" he moaned.

Soon the others came in, one by one—all save Sylvia and Em, who were in New York; Rome, who was wandering; and young Paul, who at that moment was giving a matinee performance in Chicago. Ed had to fetch Al and met him on his way home. "She's dead! She's dead!" Ed called the moment he saw his brother.

Al looked at him strangely for a moment and then said, "Well, that's the end of our home."

9 / *An End and a Beginning*

> Well might I write above the gravestone of my youth: "He yearned."
>
> —Dreiser, *Dawn* (1931)

They were a family rocked by a catastrophe. Old Paul sagged in a chair, mumbling to himself. Each in his or her own way grasped the truth. It was the end of the family. The woman who had woven an emotional web of tenderness that enmeshed them all was gone, leaving an emptiness at the center.

To Theodore his mother's death was a seismic shock. "The earth seemed truly black and rent," he said later. "The ground shook under me. I dreamed sad, racking dreams for years." In those dreams Sarah was alive but about to abandon him forever, as she had threatened to do when he was a child. Sometimes she was in a boat, drifting slowly away through a woolly fog.

The family went about the preparations for her burial like automatons. Old Paul had summoned a priest as soon as his grief gave way to fear for her immortal soul. But when the little Bavarian cleric arrived, he was appalled to learn that Sarah had not been to church in many months and demanded to know why he had not been summoned earlier. Old Paul wrung his hands, while the children looked on with growing anger. Sarah had drifted away from the Church, and her husband had let the matter of her salvation slide.

The officious priest was insensitive to the heartbeat of this family. All he knew was that the rules had been broken, and for this the punishment prescribed was burial in unconsecrated ground. Old Paul was devastated—the everlasting shame of it! While he pleaded, the others, led by a spirited Theresa, screamed at the pastor. Finally, a compromise was hammered out whereby the family pledged to pay for Masses and burn candles in Sarah's name, and the priest said he would allow her to be buried in a Catholic cemetery.

Old Paul tried to assume the leadership of the family, but it was no use. The soul of this household was gone, leaving only rivalries and centrifugal ambitions. Theodore was hard pressed for cash. Asa Conklin, his employer

44

at the real estate office, was an ineffectual businessman, and so little money was coming in to the firm that Theodore's wages were in arrears.

He saw himself as a failure; after nineteen years of life he had no skills, no place, no prospects. In the grim light of his situation he regretted not returning to Indiana University; when the student newspaper queried him about his plans, he supplied them with the following item for the January 1891 issue: "Theodore Dreiser, through Freshman last year, is working in Chicago at present, where his home is. He expects to return to I.U. next year." The expectation was no more than a wistful hope; Dreiser was too proud to admit that he was unemployed and near penniless.

His ambition to succeed still burned. In his dreams the upper class was the "one to which I properly belonged." Poverty was a black hole, the lives of common working people brutish, grinding with drudgery (though they enjoyed greater sexual freedom than the middle class). His mother had always aspired to a niche in the middle class for her brood, but after their Warsaw experience, Theodore was repelled by the bourgeois proprieties. It seemed to him that the moneyed aristocracy lived the truly glamorous life in America, and the press gave them idolatrous coverage, as though they were American royalty—which, in a way, they were.

Now Theodore was shaken by the glandular storms of adolescence and harried by the necessity of earning a living—most likely doing work he hated. So the dreaming part of his brain worked overtime in compensation, blowing bubbles of sexual fulfillment with beautiful women, of riches and ease, of himself as the head of a "thrashing great business," or a famous writer or philosopher, or as the consort of a rich woman—or even as an ordinary Union Park businessman coming home to a cozy flat, the aroma of dinner cooking on the stove, a wife and child greeting him lovingly.

Sustained by his dreams, he tramped the streets and finally found a place as a driver for a large laundry. It was hard work—twelve hours a day, including Saturdays, when he did not get home until midnight. But the job kept him out in the open air, and his health improved. It was an adventure to drive his wagon through raucous, clogged streets, and making deliveries and pickups gave him entrée into a cross section of homes, from mansions to tenements.

The female workers at the laundry inflamed him. Most of them were immigrants—German, Irish, Polish. With their plump arms bared, their skirts tucked in to expose smooth white calves, and their faces pink from the steam, they exuded a coarse sensuality. Upstairs, other, more genteel women handled the skilled labor—ironing shirt collars or doing delicate piecework. These were prim old maids or young girls, dainty in shirtwaists and long skirts.

He became friendly with a dark-haired cashier named Nellie Anderson. Born to Scottish immigrant parents, she was two years older than he. Their flirtation soon evolved to furtive kisses at the end of the day. Although Nellie was shy and genteel, she was no prude and gradually permitted more serious kisses and hugs, though she never allowed his avidly groping hands to stroke her breasts and body. He liked her parents, but when he sensed that they were eyeing him as a likely son-in-law, he got cold feet. He feared entrapment in marriage, and Nellie was too conventional for him.

His career at the laundry flourished. When a rival firm dangled a two-dollar raise before him, Theodore snapped at it. His new employers were three Jewish brothers, who thought Theodore might bring his old customers with him. They assigned him to a new route, however, which took him into the business heart, where the congestion was fierce. The brothers were never satisfied with his performance, accusing him of laziness; he found them vulgar womanizers. The culmination of his dislike for them came when he collided with another wagon, damaging the new vehicle beyond repair. The accident had been the other driver's fault, but the brothers blamed him and he was summarily fired. Afterward their uncle suggested to him that all would be forgiven if he would testify in a lawsuit against the other driver's company. Theodore refused.

Now he was tramping the streets again, wondering if he "would always be getting poor places and losing them." But one of his women customers, who had been impressed by his energy and efficiency, recommended him to her husband, Frank Nesbit, whose business was selling clocks, rugs, lampshades, and other bric-a-brac of garish taste and shoddy workmanship on the installment plan. In need of a collector, Nesbit hired him on the spot. His duties were to pick up weekly payments from the purchaser's of Nesbit's gimcracks.

The job took him to slums, where he knocked at the doors of mean shanties with rubble-strewn yards. Fat black women leered invitingly at him; blowsy widows told him how lonely they were; strumpets rose naked from their beds and slouched, yawning, to get the money to pay him—or offered him their services instead. He walked down streets paved with cedar blocks that had splintered and rotted, emblems of the city's heedless growth. In middle-class neighborhoods housewives sometimes signaled him to go around to the back door so their neighbors wouldn't see they were buying on time. Pictures registered in his brain: "The palls of heavy manufacturing smoke that hung low over the city like impending hurricanes; the storms of wintry snow or sleety rain; the glow of yellow lights in little shops at evening; mile after mile, where people were stirring and bustling over potatoes, flour, cabbages. . . ."

He began to paint word portraits in his mind of what he saw. Sometimes he would chant these "word-dreams" as he walked, fancying himself an orator like the Reverend Frank W. Gunsaulus, a prominent evangelist spellbinder of the day. He began writing them down, and when he had a respectable number of them, he sent them to Eugene Field, whose "Sharps & Flats" column in the Chicago *Daily News* printed verse and short items by outside contributors. Field never replied, but Theodore hardly expected him to: the act of sending them led to a vague idea that he might write for newspapers.

Although his college days seemed a dream, the intellectual interests kindled there were still vibrant. He was searching for a religious faith that was relevant to the modern world, an alternative to his father's Catholic dogmatism. The social gospel—a movement to engage Christianity in the solution of contemporary problems—appealed to his idealistic side. The city spawned a notable group of dissident preachers—men like Gunsaulus and H. W. Thomas, a fiery old man who had been expelled from the Methodist ministry for his radical views. They demonstrated to Theodore the possibility of a nondoctrinal, rational religion. He listened to Thomas's sermons at McVickar's Theater and attended meetings of the Ethical Culture Society.

Accompanying him to these affairs was a new love, a friend of Claire at The Fair named Lois Zahn. Claire had brought her home at Christmastime, and although Lois was seeing another man regularly, a thirty-five-year-old clerk with a steady job who wanted to marry her, she was attracted to Theodore and flirted with him. She admired his height, now a gangling six feet, and his soft, light brown hair, which he combed in a pompadour.

During that Christmas of 1891, Theodore felt a growing pressure to make some decision about his future, to choose some profession in which he was at least interested, rather than continue working at jobs he loathed. What precipitated these thoughts was the loss of his position with the Nesbit company. His growing prosperity had made him desire more of the little luxuries. He had varied the routine of fifteen-cent meals of ham and beans at little restaurants frequented by other clerks with one-dollar-fifty-cent feasts at fancy places like Delmonico's. He also longed for better clothes, a necessity for impressing the girls he would someday meet, and settled his aspirations on a new overcoat. When one of Nesbit's customers paid off her bill in full, to save the trouble of making weekly payments, he was struck by an idea. Other customers had paid him in full. Why not keep the money the next time it happened and give Nesbit the thirty-five-cent installment? He would eventually pay off the entire debt, so he was not really cheating the boss.

The scheme seemed foolproof; soon he had accumulated twenty-five dollars, with which he bought a handsome woolen overcoat that would protect him from the frigid gales off Lake Michigan. But he had overestimated the docility of his clients. A woman complained that her clock was not working. When told that collector Dreiser's records showed she still owed money, she insisted she had paid him in full. Nesbit, who had probably seen this trick before, summoned Theodore immediately and demanded to know where the money was. Unable to brazen it out, he confessed. Nesbit had taken a liking to him and shook his head sadly. "Theodore," he said, "if you're going to begin anything like this, you know, you're on the straight road to hell, and I can't keep you." Deeply ashamed, Theodore went home and wrote a letter of apology, promising to pay back the money. He never did, but he never again stole from an employer.

While he was between jobs at Christmastime, he took a temporary post doling out toys for the Chicago *Herald*'s help-the-neediest campaign. Although he was disillusioned to learn that the toys were shoddy and secondhand, he stuck it out because the ad had promised "promotion possible," meaning, he hoped, a reporter's job. This turned out to be a false hope, but the boy's ambition was set ablaze. The *Herald*'s offices, with their marble floors and bronze decorations at the entrance, proclaimed important matters were taking place within. What reporters actually did, he could only imagine. They were sent out to write up a story about a traffic accident or a murder, he supposed, and that seemed easy and exciting. Whenever he saw a minor collision on his daily rounds, Theodore would compose an account in his mind.

He also imagined that newspapermen consorted on a daily basis with the great, the wealthy, and the famous. Their press cards were tickets to the grand world, and he envisioned himself exchanging sage observations with some magnate and then writing them up in his mahogany-paneled office.

It was a time of endings and beginnings. The beginnings were barely begun, but the ending had a sonorous finality to it. He and Claire, in rare agreement, decided to move, and Ed agreed to come along. When the three youngest announced their intention to leave, old Paul became distraught, pleading with them to stay, but Theodore was implacable. He delivered an ultimatum: they would stay only if Mame's airs were curbed. But their father's authority had been eroded by a thousand little rebellions among his fractious children over the years.

Paul said goodbye at the doorway, looking old and frail. "I'm sorry, Dorsch," he told Theodore. "I done the best I could. The girls they won't ever agree, it seems. I try, but I don't seem to do any good. I have prayed these last few days. . . . I hope you don't ever feel sorry."

Part Two

• • •

APPRENTICESHIP

10 / *The Cub*

We are dealing now not with an ethically correct and moral
youth who answers to all the important moral, social and religious conceptions of the day but with a sentimental boy of
considerable range of feeling.
                                    —Dreiser, *Newspaper Days* (1922)

Goaded by the knowledge that only sixty-five dollars in savings stood between
him and the streets, Theodore began to lay siege to the offices of Chicago's papers. He selected the *Globe*, the smallest and least prosperous of the city's dailies
and the black sheep of Chicago journalism. Its owner was a man named Mike
McDonald, who had made his money as Chicago's gambling czar. While serving his fellowman in this fashion, Mike drew the notice of the reform element
in town and became its favorite target. The great organs of Victor F. Lawson
(the *Morning News*, later the *Record*) and Joseph Medill (the *Tribune*) thundered
against him. The criticism got under McDonald's skin, and he decided to buy
a paper and hit back at the reformers and police brass. (Harsh treatment from
the press had also moved Charles Yerkes, Chicago's "traction king," to found
his own newspaper, the *Inter-Ocean*.) It was an era of personal journalism, and
every owner freely injected his biases into his news and editorials. Medill, a
foe of horse racing, once led a successful crusade to close Washington Park,
a favorite turf venue for Chicago society to see and be seen. When his sports
page reported the general unhappiness among the haut monde, Medill fired
the entire staff. McDonald's favorite exposés were of police corruption and the
failures of reform administrations to curb vice.

Theodore began his siege by sitting near a door opening into an alley. From
his post he could watch the reporters at their desks. At one end of the room, behind a railing, like Quakers on the facing bench, were the desks of the editors,
including the city editor, who ritually told him, "Nothing today. There's not a
thing in sight." His tone was not unkind, though, and Theodore did not lose
hope. Theodore became a familiar face to the six or seven reporters who made

up the *Globe's* staff, and some of them tossed him scraps of advice on the job situation at their paper and tips on potential jobs at other places.

After he had kept a faithful vigil for two weeks, John Maxwell, the copy editor, a corpulent man with cynical eyes, asked him what he was doing there. When Theodore told him he wanted a job, Maxwell said, "Why did you pick the *Globe?* Don't you know it's the poorest paper in Chicago?"

Theodore explained that was why he had chosen it, on the theory it would have a faster turnover. Maxwell nodded approvingly and advised him to hang around. In June the Democratic National Convention would convene in the city to choose its presidential candidate, and the *Globe* was sure to hire some part-timers as it expanded its coverage.

After a month or so, his chance came. Gissel, the *Globe's* single editorial writer, a house mastiff who mauled McDonald's enemies, had written a novel — a nostalgic tale of boyhood in the popular *Tom Sawyer* vein — and had the idea that his former high school classmates would buy copies because of their fond memories of him. He proposed that Theodore call on every one of them, and if he did a good job, he could have a tryout on the paper. Since he was an experienced door-to-door man of sorts already, Theodore jumped at the offer and managed to sell more than a hundred.

Having done his job and relayed to Gissel exaggerated reports of his ex-classmates' enduring love for him (most hardly remembered him) he confidently awaited his elevation to the staff. Nothing happened, until Maxwell insisted he be hired as one of the extra reporters the paper was taking on for the convention. Theodore got the job at fifteen dollars a week, with the guarantee of at least two weeks' work.

And so, decked out in new clothes — light check trousers, a bright blue coat and vest, a brown fedora, and squeaky yellow shoes — the new cub began his assignment. Theodore's knowledge of politics was vague; he read the newspapers and had ingested a smattering a John Stuart Mill, Tolstoy, and other social philosophers, but he had not the slightest grasp of the intricacies of Tammany Hall, free silver, and patronage.

The reporter heading the *Globe's* election team told him to hang around the lobbies of the hotels where the delegates were staying. With his nickel-plated press star pinned on his lapel, Theodore importuned whoever was warming a chair, feeling a rush of self-importance when he said the magic words, "I'm a reporter from the *Globe*." On his first day he collared Senator "Pitchfork Ben" Tillman, who said he didn't want to be bothered. Clutching this inscrutable fragment, and his firsthand impression of the Richelieu Hotel lobby during a political convention, Theodore hurried back to the office and filled nine pages of foolscap on both sides with vague speculations on the Democratic Party and the future of the Republic. His violation of the most elementary rule of journalism—don't write on both sides of the paper—was only the first of the sins he had committed. The city editor turned him over to John Maxwell for salvage. Maxwell asked Theodore to tell him exactly what he had seen, and listened for a time to the torrent of incoherent impression before saying, "No, no! . . . It's not news." He proceeded to explain what news was, adding that the *Globe* had a political reporter who would sketch the big picture. He suggested that Theodore concentrate on discovering the name of the party's likely nominee, since there was no obvious front-runner.

He returned to the hotel and buttonholed Tammany Hall boss Richard Croker, who brushed him off. Then, gossiping in the bar with some fellow journalists, he bruited the name of a southern dark horse. Senator McEntee, who happened to be standing nearby, tipped him off to an important meeting of the party leaders in progress. Rewritten by Maxwell, the story made the front page:

CLEVELAND AND GRAY THE TICKET

Cleveland and Gray will be the ticket. This was decided upon last night at a meeting of the leaders of the party held at the Richelieu hotel in the apartments of ex-Secretary [of the Navy William Collins] Whitney.

This momentous result was achieved almost solely by the efforts of Mr. Whitney, who has been moving heaven and earth to destroy the last vestige of opposition to Mr. Cleveland.

It is a concession to the Tammany men, who dictated the nomination of ex-Gov. [of Indiana Isaac Pusey] Gray for second place. Gray was [New York Governor David Bennett] Hill's choice for the tail end of the ticket should the latter have been nominated, but as the Tammany men learned that this was impossible, they took what they could get—the second place.

Save for the fact that Adlai E. Stevenson ultimately was the convention's choice for the second slot on the ticket, it was a solid scoop.

Grateful for Maxwell's help on the story, Theodore placed his hand on his shoulder. The other stiffened. "Cut the gentle con work," he snapped. "Life is a Goddamned stinking, treacherous game, and nine hundred and ninety-nine men out of every thousand are bastards. . . . Don't think I'm not one, or that I'm a genial ass that can be worked by every Tom, Dick and Harry."

Despite his misanthropy, Maxwell liked Theodore and was a valuable ally, persuading the *Globe*'s management to hire him as a full-time reporter when the convention was over. He covered small fires, arrests, and assorted mayhem, dreaming of one day joining his idol, Eugene Field, on the journalistic heights. Field had become a national celebrity (and considerably richer) through the popular children's verse he wrote—including "Little Boy Blue" and "Wynken, Blynken, and Nod." (Less well known was the bawdy doggerel he recited at stag parties.)

At the *Globe* Theodore was squarely situated on the far side of the journalistic tracks; the paper drew from the sludge of Chicago's pool of reporters. The most prominent name on the staff was typical of these castoffs. He was John T. McEnnis, who took over as city editor after Theodore had been on the job several months. McEnnis was a brilliant writer, but he had a headline-sized thirst. After losing a succession of jobs because of drinking, he had sunk to the *Globe*. Raucous and uncouth-looking, clad in a long frock coat and a pair of shiny black trousers that were perpetually caked with tobacco, food, and liquor, he had a bulbous red nose like J. P. Morgan's.

As it turned out, McEnnis took a fatherly interest in Theodore, giving him encouragement and useful advice, and then borrowing a dollar for whiskey. Part of the attraction, perhaps, was that he liked Theodore's writing and saw in him a reflection of his own youthful promise. McEnnis assigned him to do a feature article for the Sunday edition about a vile slum near the river known as Cheyenne. Such neighborhoods weren't new to him, but now he had the duty of getting them down on paper. Coming upon Cheyenne on a hot summer night, he noted the denizens, most of them immigrants, sleeping on the sidewalks, in doorways, and on the roofs. The area was unutterably filthy:

> From surrounding basements issue the sickening heat of laundries, or equally as bad, the fumes of whisky and the odors from the underground restaurant. The alleys reek with decaying garbage and human filth, the vile odors carrying disease and death to those already weakened and enervated by such environment. No really healthy face greets the eye. No ray of intelligence beams from the faces of the wandering, jaded inhabitants.

Maxwell applauded his effort and told him, "Maybe you're cut out to be a writer after all, not just an ordinary newspaper man." Soon Theodore was touring the morgue, pondering the fate of the unidentified dead:

> A cheap coffin, six feet of earth, a headstone bearing a number only and the potter's field has gained an addition.
>
> The morgue-keeper was asked for some stories of unidentified bodies. He replied:
>
> "An unknown has no story."

Maxwell and McEnnis preferred straight news stories, but personal journalism was popular at the time, and Theodore showed a knack for it, though he also did a notable exposé of fake auction shops that caused a considerable stir. But he liked doing Sunday supplement features, full of color and lurid details. Charles Dickens was the model, and the idea was to give readers a roller-coaster ride from the lower depths to the haut monde, employing the free-roaming gaze of the novelist and ending on a moral note, lest it be thought that the newspaper was sanctioning the vice portrayed in such loving detail. This kind of writing could be called sensationalism, but it unleashed the imaginations—and pens—of tyro novelists. Many writers of the nineties and early 1900s—Stephen Crane, David Graham Phillips, Richard Harding Davis, Brand Whitlock, Harold Frederic—served literary internships in the city rooms.

Theodore also published his first piece of fiction in the *Globe,* a fable headed "The Return of Genius." The author used the pseudonym "Carl Dreiser" at Maxwell's behest. (Maxwell had nicknamed him Carl, but Theodore told his family he wanted to credit his nephew, Sylvia's unwanted child, who was still living with them.) The story tells of a young writer "whose younger years were spent in poverty and sorrow" and who longs for fame, riches, and pleasure. The God of Genius appears and offers him "glory and an undying fame" on one condition: that he never know of them on earth. The Genius agrees and is whisked to a fabulous palace where he enjoys every luxury. But at last he begins to miss the admiration and praise of men. The god appears once more and sends him back to the world, where he is stripped of his immortality. "In thine own hand is the power—the strength," a voice whispers to him. "Achieve thine own glory. It is for thee alone to do this. In effort, will thy genius be sharpened. Aid from the gods would but destroy thee."

His own life among men—and women—was in better shape. He had taken a pleasant room in Ogden Place, overlooking Union Park, with its green lawns surrounding a small lagoon. His affair with Lois was progressing favorably. He was half in love with her and she more than that with him, though she continued to see her faithful Harry as insurance. But he continued to court her, driven by his sexual yearnings. One night Dreiser persuaded her to accompany him to a cheap room on Halstead Street. It was his first experience with taking a woman to bed; his old fears of impotence welled up, and he had a premature ejaculation. The excitement and her gentle remonstrances—"I don't mean to cry. I can't help it"—were probably the causes, but Theodore regarded it as another defeat. They met again, but he could not bring himself to take her virginity, though she was willing. Frustrated, she told him, "Dorse, I think you're the most bashful man I ever knew."

It was a measure of how tightly the old bugaboos about masturbation gripped him that years later Dreiser thought of his precipitousness as "impotence." In a passage later expurgated from *Newspaper Days,* he writes, "though I ejaculated copiously, I still imagined I was impotent due to youthful errors and bordering on senility." Inexperience and an inordinate fear of making Lois pregnant—not only because a child would tie him down to her but because of his memories of his sisters' experiences—probably go far in explaining his unsatisfactory performance. He considered "potency" equivalent to ejaculating inside a woman, which created the risk of impregnation. Dreiser's anxiety served as a psychic coitus interruptus. It induced a compulsion to withhold that was overridden by his strong desire, with the result that he "spent" uncontrollably.

Had the affair progressed, he would have felt obligated to "do right" by Lois even if they didn't have a child, and he didn't want to marry her. In his heart of hearts he felt superior to her: his boundless ambitions included some vague, ineffably beautiful and wealthy feminine figure who would embody all his dreams of success. Against such a fantasy Lois seemed commonplace.

Theodore's "buzzing dreams of living in Chicago and becoming a great man" left little room for Lois, and his eyes constantly roved to others. One day, as they were about to go to an Ethical Culture Society lecture, she told him, "You don't care any more. I'm going back to Harry." Theodore halfheartedly protested his affection, but he knew she was right; he didn't care enough to give Lois what she really wanted—marriage, or at least living together.

Meanwhile, events in his life were moving at such a pace that Lois was already receding into the past. Impressed by the job he had done on the auction-shop series, McEnnis urged him to seek a position on a larger paper, where he could get the training he needed. The editor suggested as a likely possibility the St. Louis *Globe-Democrat,* which, under the editorship of the great Joseph McCullagh, was one of the best papers in the West. The *Globe-Democrat's* traveling correspondent, who was a friend of McEnnis, was in Chicago to cover the preparations for the 1893 World's Fair and dropped by to see his old colleague. McEnnis suggested that Theodore work for him on a free-lance basis as a legman, conducting man-in-the-street interviews. This served as a tryout, and when Theodore completed the work successfully, McEnnis told the *Globe-Democrat* man to ask McCullagh to take him on. In a few weeks a wire came offering a reporter's job at twenty dollars per week, and on October 29, 1892, Theodore drew his last pay envelope from the Chicago *Globe.*

Theodore thought of telling Lois about the job, but procrastinated until the night before he was to leave. After a farewell dinner with McEnnis, he went to her house but found she was out with Harry. Angered, he decided to punish her by not saying goodbye. The next morning, as the train passed by her house, Theodore felt a keen pang of sadness. Parting, change, pained him, always.

11 / St. Louis Days

> I went into newspaper work . . . and from that time dates my
> real contact with life—murders, arson, rape, sodomy, bribery,
> corruption, trickery and false witness in every conceivable
> form. The cards were put down so fast before me for a while
> that I was rather stunned. Finally, I got used to the game and
> rather liked it.
>
> —Dreiser to H. L. Mencken (1916)

St. Louis's largely German and southern population of four hundred fifty thousand was hard-working and prosperous. The city had a lively press, with four major dailies of regional, if not national, stature: William Hyde's *Republic,* small and struggling; W. E. Scripps's *Chronicle;* the *Globe-Democrat,* edited by McCullagh, "Little Mac" in Eugene Field's poem; and the *Post-Dispatch,* which had exploded into prominence in the 1880s under the brilliant, neurasthenic Joseph Pulitzer, who boosted circulation with his crusades against municipal corruption. By the time Theodore arrived, Pulitzer had moved on to New York, purchased the ailing *World,* and used his patented editorial mix of sensation and crusading journalism to drive its readership to the top of the city's papers.

Theodore was unaware of the intensely competitive journalistic world he was entering, but he was consumed by a desire to rise—"ambitious, until my very heart aches . . . ," he wrote his childhood friend Emma Rector. One day he thought of becoming a business magnate, the next a newspaper publisher. His first meeting with Little Mac turned his fancies in still another direction: He would become a great editor.

McCullagh was a short, solid man who inhabited a tiny office piled to the ceiling with newspapers. Painfully shy and introverted, he kept the only three chairs covered so visitors would not be encouraged to linger. Under his editorship the *Globe-Democrat* had prospered. It concentrated on presenting world, national, and regional news in a sober, almost stodgy style, but its editorials were crisp and sometimes whimsical. When the "old man" wrote one, his mordant wit crackled through every paragraph. McCullagh had won his spurs as a correspondent in the Civil War, and now he was a venerated figure in the city, especially among the farmers and small-town people of the region, who made pilgrimages to the *Globe-Democrat* and stood outside his office in attitudes of hushed reverence. But reporters considered him a remote and chilling figure. When another paper scooped him, he would wait at the water cooler and fire the first reporter who appeared (and rehire him a few days later).

Those first weeks in St. Louis were lonely ones. When Theodore went home to his small hall bedroom, the walls seemed bare and cold. He missed an enveloping feminine presence—his mother, his sisters. He had an "intensely uxorious nature" and needed "feminine ministrations," so he gravitated to boardinghouses run by widows, who maintained the homelike atmosphere he craved. After a time, he was drawn to the landladies themselves. His first boardinghouse was run by a fat and fortyish woman who wasted little time in confiding that her husband was consumptive and neglected her. When she became bolder and touched him suggestively he "flushed like a girl." But her overripe coyness sickened him, and one night he sneaked out.

He found another room in a neighborhood near Broadway and the theatrical and restaurant district. His new landlady was Mrs. Zernouse, a stocky, attractive, Slavic widow with two young children. She provided a clean, spacious room with high windows, which Theodore decorated in what he conceived as a bohemian style—tapestry-cloth curtains, a bookshelf for his few volumes, and a plaster statue of Venus on the mantel. The nude fascinated Mrs. Zernouse, who took it as a sign that he was a devilish fellow. Unlike his previous landlady, she was attractive in a coarse, peasant way. She teased him constantly about the statuette, which embarrassed him.

While covering a church revival meeting, Theodore picked up a girl his own age. Emboldened when she let him hold her hand, he invited her to his rooms. He began kissing her and then undressed her, negotiating over each article of clothing, until she balked finally at one last flimsy, token undergarment. But by then he had won, and they spent a delicious night together. It was his first full sexual experience, and she seemed to enjoy their lovemaking. She left at dawn without giving him her address, and he never saw her again.

When Mrs. Zernouse came in to clean, she spotted a hairpin on the sheets. Rather than being shocked, she made bawdy remarks, and soon they tumbled into the still unmade bed. She was passionate in her transports, uttering abandoned cries and achieving a climax quickly. Theodore, in his inexperience, took her ardor as a sign of abnormality. This liaison continued until he tired of her, feeling she was beneath him socially and intellectually. Too cowardly to make a clean break, he rented another room, gradually moved his things, and tiptoed out late one night for good.

Again his landlady was a widow who was drawn to Theodore's stripling charm. Petite and prettier than the others, she was also more socially acceptable and owned a large brick house on Chestnut Street with windows trimmed in white stone. The affair proceeded like the previous one. When Theodore returned after midnight, she would come up and slip into his bed; or he would go to her bedroom. She was demonstrative, giving him little love bites, coiling her legs tightly about him, and uttering muffled cries. "Do you like that? Do you like to do it to me?" Her behavior shocked Theodore; he thought "the mere act of silent, secretive friction was enough." Although his doubts about his ability to perform had been vanquished, in the aftermath he was filled with black remorse, scoring himself as a "wastrel," a criminal fornicator.

Dreiser's sexual nature was split: one part of him was drawn to women of experience who were openly sensual and took the lead in the affair ("made their way" with him). But another part sought an ideal, which meant fresh, young girls with petal-smooth faces and innocent eyes, like the nymph in the painting "September Morn." In contrast to the sexually demanding older women, these visions were sweet, shy, and demure. As he wrote Emma Rector, "I adore the womanly traits, when confined and not roughened by the world." But only the women of a certain age were available, while the dream girls eluded him.

He found a few male friends of his own age—two mainly, artists at the *Globe-Democrat* named Peter B. McCord and Dick Wood, who affected a bohemian lifestyle and liked to talk long into the night about art and life over growlers of beer. Wood dressed like a *fin-de-siècle* dandy—flowing black tie, loose-linen shirt, soft felt hat, cape, and boutonniere of violets, like the character Des Esseintes in Huysmans's novel *A Rebours*.

Like Wood, McCord was a small-town boy from the Middle West. He wore practical work clothes and an unkempt black beard; his wide-ranging curiosity led him to works of natural philosophy. He loved to perpetrate elaborate hoaxes, often assuming a false identity. Though brought up a Catholic, McCord seemed to Theodore a true pagan, a free spirit who had sloughed off the constricting skin of convention and come to an acceptance of life in all its grim and pleasurable facets.

Tiring of amorous landladies, Theodore had moved to bachelor's quarters in a large building at 12 South Broadway, inhabited by other reporters. Like most newsrooms, the *Globe-Democrat*'s held a number of reporters with literary ambitions, whose example made Theodore think seriously of becoming a writer of some kind. Several former newsmen from St. Louis had achieved commercial success in New York, notably the playwright Augustus Thomas, who had put in a short stint as a reporter for the *Post-Dispatch*.

Two of the oddest fish in American journalism were spawned in the Queen City's newsrooms. One was William Cowper Brann, who went on to found a monthly Texas newspaper called *The Iconoclast,* which preached atheism and antipuritanism. Unfortunately, Brann also followed Pulitzer's lead in exposing political corruption and was fatally shot by the object of one of his crusades.

The other notable figure, who had acquired only a local reputation in Theodore's day—and that a bad one—was William Marion Reedy. In the 1880s Reedy had been a star feature writer on the *Republic* and the *Globe-Democrat,* but drink, the curse of the working press, almost felled him. After McCullagh rusticated him, he was reduced to toiling for a gossip sheet called *Star Sayings.* In 1890 he joined forces with two other St. Louisans (one of them, a tough investigative reporter named Red Galvin, became something of a nemesis to Theodore, beating him out of several scoops by superior cunning) to found a weekly called the *Sunday Mirror.* Reedy, a paunchy Irishman with a cherubic face and bulging eyes, was an insider par excellence and knew St. Louis politics intimately. But he continued to scandalize propriety with his alcoholic escapades and, later, his marriages to a prostitute and a madam.

Reedy would become the leading champion of realism in literature in Theodore's generation. The realism in the air in St. Louis at this time was distinctly foreign in origin; called "naturalism," it was signed by names like Emile Zola and Guy de Maupassant. There was an acolyte of the Parisian school at the *Globe-Democrat,* a jovial young reporter named Bob Hazard, who had been dining out for years on an unpublished novel he had written with a fellow journalist named Grubb, who was later murdered in an opium den. Hazard's story, reputed to be too daring to be published in the United States, was a pastiche of Zola and Balzac and was set in Paris. The plot involved an actress-heroine named Theo, whose lover, a newspaperman, is wrongly accused of murder and goes to the guillotine despite her efforts to save him. This tragic tale was spiced with midnight suppers and other sinful Parisian diversions. In one daring scene Theo has a fight with a rival and spanks her with a hairbrush.

That Hazard and Grubb's novel was unpublishable in the United States made Dreiser aware of the gulf between what American contemporary novels portrayed as life and what he had seen as a reporter. One night, dressed in evening clothes, he might cover the Veiled Prophets Ball, assiduously reporting the feminine fashions on display, and then rush to a shabby slum dwelling where a father had just murdered his children. The pitiful story was good for a stick to titillate readers at breakfasttime. However, when he obtained information on a compromising relationship between a visiting medium and a local society woman, which the man's landlady had viewed through the keyhole, he was told it was unprintable.

A similar schism existed in Theodore's own nature. His attitude toward women was that of a young romantic, yet he knew from experience that women too had desires. He watched the whores who worked near his office, lolling on the front steps or sashaying languidly down the street—and sometimes he hired their services or just talked to them. (Office rumor had it that he procured girls for Mitchell, the city editor, though Dreiser does not mention this in his autobiography.)

Following Hazard's advice, he wrote a comic opera about an Indiana farmer who is transported back in time to the Aztec empire and is acclaimed as a god. (The plot owed something to Mark Twain's novel *A Connecticut Yankee in King Arthur's Court*.) The Hoosier hero is corrupted by his absolute power and becomes a tyrant, but a beautiful Aztec maiden teaches him mercy and compassion, and he transforms his domain into a republic. Theodore timidly read the libretto to Wood and McCord, who, to his relief, pronounced it promising.

A surviving fragment of *Jeremiah I* suggests that his friends' enthusiasm was excessive. Although the comic premise—a farmer plopped down in an ancient, exotic culture—was promising, the script is talky and full of labored, rustic jokes, as the following extract shows. Farmer Peaskin has just materialized in the throne room of the Royal Aztec Palace. A beautiful maiden rushes in:

> IAVE. (Falling towards Peaskin who beats a hasty retreat up the throne steps.) Great Spirit—save me, otherwise I must die.
> PEASKIN. Huh? What's that there?
> IAVE. Great Sovereign of my people, since you have come, deign to command that my life be spared.
> PEASKIN. (Viewing her doubtfully.) Deign that your life be spared? Course I'll deign it. Well I'll be plum cursed.
> IAVE. (Sobbing.) Most masterful Spirit!
> PEASKIN. Who? Me? (Descends steps.) Say, look up here. What's ailin' you? Be you sick? Git up.

With his energy, inquisitiveness, and powers of observation, Theodore was a natural reporter. In the noise and confusion of the newsroom, under the pressure of the daily deadline, he acquired the habits of speed and concentration. Description and narrative force, not style, were his strong points. When getting the facts bored him, he let his imagination do his legwork.

One of his copy editors, Captain Webb, remembered him as "a splendid writer," but "better as a writer than in getting news."

> Though you sent him for a "story" and he might not get it, he always, as I recall, brought back some story. He had an inventive fictional mind. But you must watch his copy. On a good "story" he might get carried away from the facts by his own emotion. Or again, he might come in with a yarn you just knew didn't happen.

Perhaps in tribute to his inventive powers, Theodore was assigned to write a column of hotel news called "Heard in the Corridors." Hazard, who had previously written the column, told Theodore that when there were no visiting firemen, he could invent talks with imaginary people. Dreiser reported, for example, a story related to him by "Olney Wade of Elizabeth, New Jersey."

It is a highly fictionalized account of the life of Christian Aaberg, the cynical Dane at Hibbard, Spencer, and Bartlett. As "Wade" tells it, Aaberg, the son of a nobleman, squandered his annuity on drink and was reduced to running an elevator. Then he inherited seventy thousand dollars and bought a country place, where he devoted himself to full-time debauchery. He died young, surrounded by "books and fine wines."

"Heard in the Corridors" was something Dreiser did with his left hand while continuing to handle general assignments. In the city's rough-and-tumble journalistic life, he learned that to lie and cheat was all right; the only sin was to be scooped. His dreams had undergone a severe overhauling during his spell in St. Louis, he later wrote Emma Rector. "Worldly experience" had "shattered the ideals" of youth, and he looked back on "the years of labor I have endured . . . with a feeling akin to sorrow and almost disgust." Corresponding with Emma filled him with halcyon memories of the Sullivan days, when they had played together on the Rector farm, eight miles from the town.

He provided a romanticized but probably accurate portrait of himself at age twenty-two:

> When you look at [my picture], you will see egotism written in every lineament; a strong presentiment of self love in every expression. I have a semi-Roman nose, a high forehead and an Austrian lip, with the edges of my teeth always showing. I wear my hair long, and part it in the middle, only to brush it roughly back from the temples. Then I'm six feet tall, but never look it, and very frail of physique. I always feel ill, and people say I look cold and distant. I dislike companionship, as far as numbers go, and care only for a few friends, who like what I like. I prefer writing to reading and would rather see for myself, than hear or read all the knowledge of the world. You will not like me, I'm sure.

The cynicism he half-boasted of was the protective coating over a sensitive nature that was lacerated by the horrors he had seen as a reporter—for example, a train wreck he covered.

One Sunday afternoon he was idling at the *Globe-Democrat* office when a man burst in and told him excitedly that a passenger train had run through an open switch and crashed into some tanker cars filled with oil on a spur track three miles from Alton, Illinois. None of the editors were in at the time, so Theodore hurried to the scene on his own initiative, planning to telegraph his copy from the station. Shortly after he arrived there was a tremendous explosion. Flames burning around the tanks had caused two unruptured tanks to heat up, turning them into huge bombs which hurled shrapnel—jagged chunks of white-hot metal and scalding gobbets of oil—onto the crowd of bystanders. "Many forms were instantly transformed to blazing, screaming, running, rolling bodies, crying loudly for mercy and aid. These tortured souls threw themselves to the ground and rolled about on the earth. They threw their burning hands to tortured, flame-lit faces. . . . They clawed and bit the earth, and then, with an agonizing gasp, sunk, faint and dying, into a deathly stillness."

He tore off his coat and tried to beat out the flames on one shrieking human torch, to no avail.

All the while his mind was recording the carnage, thinking how to describe it. When a train bringing doctors and nurses arrived from Alton, he hurried to the depot where the dead and dying were taken. He watched physicians bend briefly over the charred figures on the litters. Most of them were beyond help. A throng of relatives wandered about vainly seeking a recognizable face among the seared masks. A group of parents, whose children had gone to the site of the wreck, milled in the hall asking for information. Theodore went from stretcher to stretcher, asking the occupant his or her name and address, telling those who protested, "Someone will want to know about you."

Theodore returned to the explosion site to interview eyewitnesses, who told of narrow escapes or of futilely trying to assist agonized victims. A man aiding one human torch cut away the man's clothes; in pulling off the sleeve of his coat, the skin of the victim's hand stuck to it and came off like a glove: "I tried . . . to console him in his awful plight. . . . He recognized my voice, and, with his burned and sightless eyes turned toward me, he managed to inform me that he was my old friend, James Murray."

Finally, the city desk ordered Theodore to return and write up his story. When he arrived at the newsroom, reporters who had already read his brief telegraphed dispatches were talking excitedly. He went straight to his desk; as he finished each page, a boy would snatch it away and run it to the copy desk. A knot of reporters gathered around him. At last it was done, and the next morning's front-page headlines proclaimed:

BURNED TO DEATH
One of the Most Disastrous Railroad Casualties Ever Recorded
Six People Killed Outright and a Score of Others Will Die
The Fearful Holocaust Brought About by an Open Switch
—Total Destruction of the Big Four's Southwestern
Limited Express—Heartrending Scenes

Theodore went out again to compile further grisly details and to cover the coroner's investigation that was in progress. The two accounts add up to a remarkable job of reporting—long, vivid, gruesome (in the style of the times), yet ballasted with facts. Such was Theodore's lack of confidence in himself, however, that in the aftermath he was seized by a fear that he had been wrong to chase after the story without getting permission. Mitchell, the city editor, disliked him and might think he had a swelled head; perhaps he would be fired. He was so late returning from his second trip that he missed his daily assignment, so when Mitchell told him that McCullagh wanted to see him right away, his heart sank.

"You called for me, Mr. McCullagh?" Theodore said timidly.

"Mmm, yuss, yuss!" the editor replied, not looking at him. "I wanted to say that I liked that story you wrote, very much indeed. A fine piece of work, a fine piece of work!" He reached into his pocket, extracted a thick roll, and peeled off a twenty-dollar bill. "I like to recognize a good piece of work when I see it. I have raised your salary five dollars, and I would like to give you this."

12 / *Love in the White City*

I went to Jackson Park and saw what is left of the dear old
World's Fair where I learned to love you.
—Dreiser to Sara Osborne White (1898)

Dreiser took advantage of McCullagh's patronage to request a job he coveted—
that of theater critic. It was a part-time post, but at least it would give him
some respite from stories of death and poverty. As he ruefully recalled, the
theater was "a world of unreality which unfortunately fell in with the wildest
of my youthful imaginings." Although part of him recognized the falsity of
the stage illusions—the glamorous drawing rooms, plush and gilt, fairy tales
of mythical kingdoms inhabited by fat comedians and pretty soubrettes in sexy
knee-length dresses or tights—he succumbed to them nevertheless.

His reviews consisted mainly of a recitation of the plot and the names of the
players, garnished with a few complimentary phrases. He favored the romantic
action and realistic settings of plays like *Paul Kauvar:* "Those who are interested
in the exciting times of the great French revolution, with its streams of blood
and mountains of dead bodies, can get an inkling of the dramatic realism of
it all. . . . " Plays with compelling love scenes also elicited rhapsodies from the
Globe-Democrat's critic. Theodore's predilection for gushing tributes got him
into trouble, however, when in a review of a performance by Mme. Sissieretta
Jones, known as "the black Patti," he wrote that her voice "brings back visions
of the still glassy water and soft-swaying branches of some drowsy nook in the
summertime." The applause was "wild and long." He didn't know that to praise
a black person in language traditionally used for whites was an unforgivable
trespass of the color barrier in St. Louis.

A rival Democratic paper (despite its name, the *Globe-Democrat* was Republican) pounced on the review in a snide editorial that attributed the sentiments
to McCullagh and twitted him for his admiration of "the colored lady, name
of Jones," his "fervid tribute to this chocolate-hued diva." It was another example of Mac's "black Republicanism." Another paper, without referring to

Theodore's notice, set him straight on the facts: "The African temperament is essentially and hopelessly inartistic."

But Theodore's worst gaffe as theater critic was yet to come. The city editor had resented Theodore's appealing over his head to Little Mac for the critic's job and was doing everything he could to pay him back. One night, when Theodore looked forward to covering the openings of three plays, stopping briefly at each and sampling the performance before writing his notices, Mitchell ordered him to cover a streetcar holdup. Theodore hastily wrote his reviews from the press releases (a common practice among reviewers) and hurried off to his assignment. Unfortunately, heavy rains across the river in Illinois had washed out sections of the track, and the actors in two of the shows did not arrive. McCullagh was again the butt of jokes among the wiseacres who gathered at such journalists' watering places as the La Clede and Phil Hackett's bar, and again the Democratic editorialists went after him in full cry. General descriptions of the shows would have been bad enough, but Theodore had ventured some criticism of the acting. For example, on the prizefighter Peter Jackson, who was starring in *Uncle Tom's Cabin,* he commented that while he could be judged only by the standard of James J. Corbett, John L. Sullivan, and other pugilists who were then the rage as theatrical-circuit performers, "he is even better than the standard, and manages to lay aside that very suggestive, not to say sluggestive, air of trouble-picking which accompanies constantly his guild brothers." Theodore was probably remembering Sullivan's performance a few months previously, before which the ex-champ had "dallied with the 'black bottle' as only John L. can dally with it." When a man in the balcony laughed at his drunken antics, Sullivan challenged him to a fight and then shambled through the performance, handling his leading lady "so carelessly that the paint on her left cheek was rubbed off, giving the woman much pain and embarrassment."

The other papers were not impressed by the critic's sage observations on fighters as actors. After alluding to Mac's alleged praise for "the colored Patti," the *Chronicle* quoted the words about Jackson and those about Lewis, an actor in the other missing show. It concluded: "McCullagh is becoming a faddist in the phenomena of the occult. Was it a manifestation springing from an unknown, unseen beyond that inspired his criticism on Peter Jackson and Jeffrey Lewis?"

When this disaster blew up in his face, Theodore realized he was in for a severe reprimand or worse from Little Mac, whom he revered. To save his editor the trouble, he left a letter of resignation and slunk away without a word to any of his colleagues. For several days he remained in his room, afraid he might meet someone he knew on the street. When his money ran low, he obtained a job at the *Republic,* the smallest and shakiest of the city's dailies, for only eighteen dollars a week. The city editor, H. B. Wandell, was a small, birdlike man with piercing eyes who drove his reporters hard, demanding sensational stories that would enable the *Republic* to beat the *Globe-Democrat*. He demanded novelistic touches of color and atmosphere. "Remember Zola and Balzac, my boy, remember Zola and Balzac," he exhorted.

Theodore was assigned to writing Sunday specials and acted as a traveling correspondent. On one of these assignments he covered a story that haunted him for years. It was a typical border-state occurrence: the lynching of a Negro for raping a white woman. This particular assault was a brutal one; an ex-convict named John Buckner had ravaged two women, one white and one black, near the village of Valley Park, fifteen miles from St. Louis. A posse was quickly formed, and he was arrested at his family's home and taken to the jail in Manchester.

Theodore's first dispatch from the scene told of Buckner's (referred to as the "brute" and the "demon") "fiendish brutality"; in keeping with the contemporary mores the word "rape" was never mentioned, though the description of his assaults left no doubts as to his intentions. The first story closes with a mention of the possibility of a lynching, and as if egging the townsfolk on, the editors at the *Republic* headlined it:

THIS CALLS FOR HEMP
St. Louis County the Scene of a Shocking Outrage

A NEGRO'S DOUBLE CRIME
Two Women Criminally Assaulted . . . One Being Colored and the
Other White—Desperate Struggle of the Latter for Her Honor—The
Brute Captured and in a Fair Way to Be Summarily Dealt With

That night a mob formed and headed for the jail, where they brushed by complaisant guards and abducted the prisoner. In a lengthy follow-up story the next day, Theodore described the scene. The moon had gone down, but in the light of the yellow flames of lanterns the Negro's face could be seen, "distorted with all the fear of a hunted beast . . . waiting more like an animal than a human being." He was taken to a bridge in a cart, and a rope tied round his neck. Then, "with a swish and a plunge his great hulking body strained at the cord." Later, Theodore, who may or may not have been present at the lynching, visited the dead man's home, and described the scene: "Through the broken panes of a miserable log window the pale, cloudbroken moonlight cast its sheen and shadow on the gaunt form of the dead, while near it, in a dark corner, wept the mother of the erring boy alone."

Here a glint of compassion breaks through in a story that otherwise reflects the racist point of view of the lynchers. A hastily called coroner's jury found that Buckner "came to his death at the hands of a person or persons unknown" and the *Republic* headlined Theodore's second account approvingly.

TEN-FOOT DROP

The Brute Who Assaulted Mrs. Al Mungo and Miss Alice Harrison Is Taken From His Home by a Band of Quiet, Determined Men and Sent Into Eternity Before the Dawn of the Day Following His Fiendish Outrages

That story was not the one that won him his spurs at the *Republic,* however. What caught Wandell's—and, more important, the publisher's—fancy was a humorous account Theodore wrote about the preparations for an annual charity baseball game between the Owls and the Elk lodges, sponsored by the paper. Here Theodore tapped a hitherto unrevealed talent for low comedy. He invented a do-or-die rivalry between the principals, as this excerpt shows: "Mr. Joy said he had not kicked in anybody's rib for some time and Mr. Melchin said that the taste of the last ear he chewed off had completely faded away, so that both are pining for the enemy and the enemy is equally pining for them. The contest is to be for nine innings only and no gouging. Any kind of bat from a rail to a board fence is permissible, and no one will be permitted to hit the ball twice at the same time."

He found he could dash off each article in an hour, leaving him time to dally with his current landlady. What is more, the series brought him more local celebrity than anything he had previously written. Local gentry would clap him on the back in the bar at the La Clede or in hotel lobbies. But Dreiser had a sneaking suspicion of this talent; it was all too easy, too superficial—the writing as well as the fame—and later he decided that tragedy rather than comedy was his forte: "Mere humor, such as I could achieve when I chose, seemed always to require for its foundation the most trivial of incidents, whereas huge and massive conditions underlay tragedy and all the more forceful aspects of life."

•   •   •

The popularity of his series on the charity baseball game led to another choice assignment: escorting a group of prize-winning schoolteachers to the World's Columbian Exposition in Chicago, which had just opened. The contest was sponsored by the *Republic,* and Theodore was supposed to record the young women's reactions to the fair's wonders.

He was at this time a presentable enough young man, with a taste in clothing that ran to the outré. "Jock" Belairs, a police reporter for the *Republic,* later recalled Dreiser as "the best dressed newspaperman I ever knew . . . a classy dresser," who liked to don evening wear when the assignment called for it. Theodore affected soft collars and flowing ties like Dick Wood wore. Another colleague, however, thought he had "a genius for overdressing. Just the wrong touch in his effort to be altogether correct . . . he was so ambitious, so anxious to appear as one 'to the manner born.' " Dreiser's description of himself as a youth was more succinct: "a parvenu."

After the initial awkwardness, Theodore introduced himself to the school-marms on the train and found himself a caliph in a harem of Middle Western beauties who vied for his attention. Only one of the girls held back, and for this reason she interested him. She was tiny and sweet-faced, with eyes like a startled doe's and long auburn hair, which she wore in braids pulled together in a bun. He sensed in her "an intense something . . . that was concealed by an air of supreme innocence and maidenly reserve." She somehow seemed older, more mature, than the others. Perhaps her reserve conveyed that, or perhaps it was her eyes, alternately pensive and vulnerable. Her hair was the color of his mother's, and her first name, he learned, was the same, though she had dropped the "h"—Sara White. She was from Danville, Missouri, but taught at a grade school in Pattonville, a village near St. Louis. Called Sallie by her friends, her family nickname was "Jug," a sobriquet given her by a beau named Bob Rogers because she wore brown so often that she resembled the little brown jug of the song.

The Chicago World's Fair was the wonder of the 1890s, a great festival of technology, science, and commerce presented to audiences of some twenty-seven million visitors who came from every corner of the nation. Built at a cost of upward of ten million dollars, it was Chicago's celebration of its preeminence among Middle Western cities. Visitors were dazzled by the Court of Honor, the central complex of exhibition pavilions arrayed around Grand Basin, at one end of which towered a statue of the Republic—all constructed of a plaster-fiber mixture called staff, which was painted white to simulate marble. In one of his daily dispatches to the *Republic,* Theodore declared it the incarnation of Athens: "One can understand . . . why the Grecians were proud and how it came that men could meditate the sublime philosophy that characterized the mythic age." Most Americans regarded the creation as the apotheosis of the "white city," a utopian vision of urbanism cleansed of all its present flaws, embodying the highest ideals of the age.

Two cultures jostled at the fair—the reigning high culture and the upstart popular culture of the multitudes who streamed to Chicago for an experience they would remember the rest of their lives. They rode to Jackson Park in transit magnate Charles T. Yerkes's streetcars and ate their box lunches around the fountain he had endowed with its replicas of the Niña, the Pinta, and the Santa María; or rode the Ferris Wheel, America's first, with its large gondolas holding twenty-five people (one of them carried members of John Philip Sousa's band, playing repeatedly "After the Ball," the hit of the fair); or toured the art exhibits and were shocked by the nudes; or heard a black man named Scott Joplin play ragtime piano music; or glimpsed the future at the Electricity Building with its stoves, fans, and dishwashers; or thronged the Midway Plaisance to watch Little Egypt and her troupe gyrating in what was politely called *la danse du ventre.*

Theodore saw the fair through the people's eyes. In a description of a night scene he wired to the *Republic,* he restored humanity to the dreamscape—"a massive crowd, a surging throng," which came "in droves—armies, thousands" to see a display of the illuminated fountains:

> They made one black and motionless mass. From such a ground-work of human-
> ity, up sprang the waters. High they leaped, rolled, rushed and then curved and
> gracefully descended to the surface below. . . . It was only when the whistle wailed
> out its reminder of the lateness of the hour that the fountain ceased. . . . Then the
> great enthusiastic mass tramped its way out and rejoiced that it had been fortunate
> enough of all the world's children to have seen such a display.

Idealism and realism clashed in many venues. At the Congress on Lit-erature a young writer from the West named Hamlin Garland, whose collec-tion of short stories, *Main-Traveled Roads,* had recently been praised by William Dean Howells, called for a new kind of literature, which Garland alternatively termed "veritism" and "local color"—a literature that was authentically Amer-ican rather than imitative of Europe and that used homespun American speech. In his column Eugene Field kidded Garland for preferring fictional heroes "who sweat and do not wear socks."

●   ●   ●

Oblivious to the debate, Theodore inhaled the sights, often escorting Miss White and her pretty younger sister, Rose. He found in Rose a liveliness that the older girl lacked and was attracted to her, but Sallie White held him with a stronger magnetism. She was quiet and genteel, complementing Theodore's egoism and gaucheness. Her earnestness and intelligence drew him out, yet made him temper a little his usual stammering volubility. In keeping with her gentleness of manner, Sallie had a delicate constitution and spent the hot part of the days in the hotel parlor. When Theodore tried to kiss her, she begged him not to be "sentimental," so he courted less inhibited girls in the party. But Sallie White intrigued him, and he resolved to write her when he returned to St. Louis.

During Theodore's Chicago excursion, he visited his father, whom he found living alone and querulously complaining that the other children neglected him. Theodore took him to the fair several times. The gloomy, ranting figure who had loomed over his childhood was now, he saw, a forlorn old man.

Back in St. Louis, Theodore called on some of the schoolteachers he had met at the fair, but the memory of Sallie White's almond eyes and auburn hair persisted. Finally he wrote her, and she replied after a decent interval, telling him that she was planning to visit relatives in the city and that he might call on her. He bought a new suit for the occasion, "a heavy military coat of the most disturbing length, a wide-brimmed stetson hat, Southern style, gloves, a cane, soft pleated shirt." He also wangled press passes to the latest shows, determined to sweep Sallie off her feet by exposing her to a whirl of urban sights. He took her to the best restaurants and for afternoon strolls in the park, attired in his finery, which he changed before returning to the newsroom.

Sallie entertained him in the parlor of the home where she was staying, playing the piano while he eyed her petite, perfectly formed figure. Afterward, they would hold hands and he would beg her to let down her luxuriant hair. Sometimes she agreed, but she resisted his pleas to sit on his lap. Her coolness had the effect of inflaming Theodore all the more. He wrote her long letters, which, she later said, made her love him. The courtship grew serious, and Sallie agreed to an informal engagement.

Theodore was growing restless. If he continued on his present course, he might at best eventually become an editor on one of the city's papers, or at least a prominent local reporter, settling down to a home and family with Jug. But the thought of such a conventional future seemed stifling (he could not admit to himself that perhaps the idea of marriage itself was oppressing him).

In December 1893 Dreiser wrote to Emma Rector: "New York's the place for special writers and literary effusions are my strong 'fast ball' . . . so that I must go. Not now however. I'm a newspaper man at present with all the untoward instincts of one and not until I have achieved a certain status of perfection will I be able to throw off the shell as they say and spring out into that other much desired sphere."

Then a reporter friend from Chicago named Hutchinson, who had moved to St. Louis, told him of his plan to buy a country newspaper near his home in Ohio and asked Theodore to be his partner. To Theodore the pretext was as good as any. He fancied becoming an influential small-town editor, commenting on local politics. But this dream meant throwing up a good job in the depths of the financial panic of 1893. When Dreiser gave notice to his employers, they offered him a raise, but he was too proud to accept. His motives were a contradictory mix of wanderlust and yearning for the stability of small-town homelife. Also, the journalistic grind was wearing him down; he felt constantly tired and couldn't sleep. In early March 1894 he said goodbye to his comrades at the *Republic* and took the train. Ostensibly it was bound for Ohio; actually, it was the first leg of a journey to New York, the ultimate city.

13 / *Wanderjahre*

> I was more interested in moving on and in seeing everything
> than in staying anywhere. I was constantly speculating as to
> my permanent abode. When, if ever, was I to have a home of
> my own.
>
> —Dreiser, *Newspaper Days* (1931)

His immediate destination, however, was a tiny village called Grand Rapids, which consisted of a main street, some slatternly shops, and a few houses. The stationmaster pointed the way to the Hutchinson farm.

The next day Hutchinson took him to the nearby town of Weston, where the office of the *Wood County Herald,* the paper he wanted to buy, was located. Their capital consisted of the hundred dollars Theodore had saved and the little that Hutchinson could borrow. The paper, Hutchinson told him, could be had for two hundred, which seemed a lot after they saw the office. The press was in bad shape, and the type was worn. The names of about five hundred subscribers were listed in a dusty old ledger.

The thought of investing in such a rickety enterprise and trying to please an audience of narrow-minded merchants and farmers was appalling, and Theodore dissolved the partnership on the spot.

In his loneliness he wrote Jug long letters—some of them running to fifty or sixty pages—in which he poured out his feelings. This was the first truly expressive writing he had ever done; he disgorged "all the surging and seething emotions and ideas which had hitherto been locked up in me," for which reporting offered no outlet. From the start, his creative drive was powered by erotic energy.

After a few days of relaxation, he decided it was time to move on, and he chose nearby Toledo as his next way station. There he tramped the streets, gazing longingly at the comfortable homes in which people lived happy lives. Finally, screwing up his courage, he entered the office of the *Blade* to inquire if they needed a reporter. They didn't—at least not on a full-time basis—but he hit it off with the city editor, a plump, apple-cheeked young man named Arthur Henry, who had worked for the Chicago *Herald* while Theodore was on the *Globe*. As it happened, a streetcar strike was in progress, and the company was running a car manned by scabs. Violence was expected and Henry needed a reporter to ride in the car. Theodore was soon on his way to the car barn to find out what was happening. That evening he returned with his story—there had been no violence—and Henry thought it so good he personally shepherded it through the typesetters and proofreaders, making certain no one would tell the publisher, who was antilabor.

Theodore's sympathies were with the workers. To show that the company's intention was to break the union, he posed as a union man from St. Louis looking for a job and was told that no union men were wanted. Actually, Henry's wife, Maude, a strong feminist who had badgered the paper until it hired her, wrote the main story, and Theodore wrote sidebars.

Dreiser handed in a couple of other trivial pieces. In one he described the countryside in poetic terms, and Henry, recognizing a kindred literary spirit, took him to lunch. They talked for three hours. Henry had ambitions of being a novelist and a poet, and dreamed of going to New York. He had written a book of fairy tales for children, and he and Maude performed plays with other members of Toledo's bohemian set at their old mansion on the Maumee River. That night, when Theodore and Arthur reconvened for dinner, they were bonded as soulmates. As Dreiser later wrote, "If he had been a girl, I would have married him."

Theodore hung around a few more days, but his new friend had nothing to offer him save an occasional free-lance assignment, so Dreiser decided to move on. After a spell in Cleveland, Dreiser traveled to Buffalo, where he hung on *sans* job until he noticed a ticket broker's sign advertising cut-rate fares to Pittsburgh. By 10:00 that same morning he was on the train speeding south, and by 7:00 he was in Pittsburgh.

14 / The Young Man from the Provinces

Just about then, in Pittsburgh, where I was working as a newspaper man, I came across Balzac and then I saw what life was—a rich, gorgeous, showy spectacle. It was beautiful, dramatic, sad, delightful, and epic—all those things combined.

—Dreiser, interview (1911)

As Dreiser crossed the steel-arch bridge over the Monongahela leading from the station to the business district, he looked up and saw a row of perhaps fifty great smokestacks extruding bright orange tongues of flame into the sky.

The next day he studied the local papers to get a line on what sort of journalism was practiced in Pittsburgh. He noted that the news columns were filled with brief reports of industrial accidents, a litany of maimings and deaths. He was also struck by the obsequious way the press chronicled the doings of the local industrial aristocracy. Junkets to New York for theatergoing and shopping, jaunts to shooting lodges in Virginia for the duck season, sailings to Europe, dinner parties, balls and fetes were slavishly reported. Juxtaposed with the stories of industrial carnage, these society notes made the world of the rich seem an empire built on pain.

Later, he explored those disparate worlds, taking a trolley to Homestead, site of the great strike of 1892, during which the workers occupied Andrew Carnegie's steel plant and fought off boatloads of imported Pinkerton detectives. After four months the people of Homestead were starving, and the state militia was patrolling the Carnegie works. Many workers were blacklisted; the rest returned to their jobs. Carnegie had won. As Secretary of the Treasury Charles Foster observed about the Homestead strikers, "They were talking about . . . Carnegie being too rich, while they were poor." Revolutionary talk—a fissure had opened between capital and labor.

Now, in Homestead, Theodore explored a defeated city. The young veritist Hamlin Garland also visited Homestead in the spring of 1894, on an assignment for *McClure's Magazine,* and he recorded these impressions:

> Higher up the tenement houses stood in dingy rows, alternating with vacant lots. The streets of the town were horrible. The buildings were poor; the sidewalks were sunken, swaying and full of holes. . . . Everywhere the yellow mud of the street lay kneaded into a sticky mass, through which groups of pale lean men slouched in faded garments, grimy with soot and grease of the mills.

At the *Dispatch,* an editor told him to come back in ten days; there might be something. Upon his return to his boardinghouse, Theodore found a telegram from Henry offering him a position with the *Blade* at eighteen dollars a week. Taking a pen, Theodore changed the eighteen dollars to twenty-five and then showed it to the editor at the *Dispatch,* who was impressed and hired him at the higher figure.

When Theodore reported for work the next morning, the city editor briefed him on the ground rules: no stories on labor relations (the labor reporter handled those considered printable), nothing derogatory about religion, nothing critical of society, no scandals in high places. "I'd rather have some simple little feature any time," he told Theodore, "a story about some old fellow with eccentric habits, than any of those scandals or tragedies."

One of his first assignments was an interview with Speaker of the House Thomas B. Reed. Theodore was curious to know what the congressman thought of Jacob Coxey's "Industrial Army," the raggle-taggle band of unemployed men that was marching on Washington to present a petition of grievances. Reed opined that the movement showed "the general unrest of the people," adding that unfortunately the administration in Washington did not seem to appreciate its significance. (In his autobiography *Newspaper Days,* Dreiser unfairly portrays Reed as a mossback who branded the men "revolutionaries.")

The labor reporter, a stocky, soft-spoken young man named Martyn, explained to Theodore how the owners imported cheap foreign labor to displace the union men, and how, after the Homestead strike, wages had gone down 25 percent while the workday was increased from eight to twelve hours. He took Dreiser on a tour of the "courts," where as many as twelve people were packed into each of the two-room flats, and one outdoor wooden latrine served the entire building. Of course Martyn never wrote about those things; he had a wife and a child, and needed his job. The gap between what the reporter knew and what he wrote seemed, if anything, wider here in Pittsburgh than in St. Louis.

For a time, Theodore was assigned to the police beat in the city of Allegheny, just across the river. Every morning he checked in at the courthouse to see if anything of interest was brewing. Usually he was free to spend the rest of the day gossiping with the other reporters and the municipal functionaries, or reading at the library, another monument to Carnegie's philanthropy. The steel magnate had donated a similar building to Homestead, but, as a worker there told a visiting journalist, "After working twelve hours, how can a man go to the library?"

Theodore had plenty of time, though; the library became his university. It was there that he discovered Balzac, one of the writers Wandell had urged him to emulate. Taking down a volume entitled *The Wild Ass's Skin* one day, he lost himself in the story of Raphael, the idealistic young man from the provinces who comes to Paris. The shock of recognition was profound: they dreamed the same dreams of conquering the city and suffered the same rebuffs.

Another novel, *The Great Man from the Provinces,* spoke even more directly to his own life, with its tale of Lucien de Rubempré, the naive young poet who is sucked into the mephitic swamp of Parisian journalism, where cynical reporters sell their principles to the highest bidder. Theodore was filled with awe at Balzac's teeming mural of Parisian life. All those grasping, greedy people were dispassionately scrutinized: no attempt was made to idealize them. Their fates were determined by the dice of chance; some rose, others fell, but all hungered for the same glittering prizes—wealth, fame, position. This view of life hit Theodore with the force of a revelation. Now all the world looked Balzacian to him. Pittsburgh's bridges became *ponts* of the Seine. Why couldn't a young novelist anatomize an American city as Balzac did Paris?

When the city editor suggested he do humorous feature stories about eccentric old men and the like, Theodore took as his inspiration Lucien's column of observations on Parisian life, "The Man in the Street." His first effort was well received, and he was turned loose to roam around the city and write about whatever struck his fancy. Sometimes he reported what he saw; sometimes he engaged in pure fancy; and sometimes—rather, most of the time—there was a bit of both. The talent for humor Dreiser had unleashed on the Owls-Elks baseball game in St. Louis was revived. But now there was a faint undertone of morbidity. An amusing bit of whimsy about a housefly describes the insect as "a suicide by inheritance. Unnatural and untimely death is his delight." One such specimen, deciding every man's hand is against him, what with flypaper and people constantly shooing him off tasty morsels, chooses to end it all in the vinegar jar; another prefers the gravy bowl. In a more serious piece, "Hospital Violet Day," Theodore displays considerable charm in describing the death of an old man named Fritz in a hospital ward amid the jokes of the other patients and the perfume of spring flowers. Another article is a sustained flight on the many ramifications of blue Monday, from the cranky magistrate who hands out a stiff sentence, to the housewife facing piles of washing. But wait—there is a "little heap" awaiting one good woman, the childish wearer of the clothes gone forever. The little garments are to be washed and then "stowed away with heartaches and teardrops, the real symbols of life's greatest pain." A recurrent motif is a lonely grave in which one of the city's anonymous throng is laid, epitomizing the urban dweller's fear of dying alone and unmourned. "An unknown has no story."

Balzac had broadened Dreiser's sympathies perceptibly. Another author who galvanized his imagination was George du Maurier, whose *Trilby,* a tale of artists in the Latin Quarter, was appearing as a serial in *Harper's* and causing a sensation.

But *Trilby* had a more urgent personal message. The story of Little Billee's love for Trilby and his devastating loss when she is lured away by the evil mesmerizing Svengali set Dreiser imagining that he would lose Jug. Not that he was entirely faithful. Emma Rector was probably not the only girl with whom he carried on a flirtation; his desires tormented him. And there were prostitutes, many of them immigrants' daughters from the courts of Homestead. One woman delighted him with the "words and expressions she used when rutting . . . or positions she was willing to take."

More memorable, though, was the hard-bitten whore whose bare arm was covered with needle scars. When Theodore lectured her on the evils of morphine, she exclaimed in a flat, tired voice: "Oh great God! What do you know about life?"

15 / *A Moth to the Lamp*

> New York . . . had the feeling of gross and blissful and parad-
> ing self-indulgence. . . . Here . . . were huge dreams and lusts
> and vanities being gratified hourly. I wanted to know the
> worst and the best.
>
> —Dreiser, *Newspaper Days* (1931)

Theodore's anxiety about Jug's fidelity was fueled by a recurrence of his panicky fear that life was sliding through his fingers. Surely she had already tired of waiting for him and found someone else. Desperate to see her, he took a vacation in the summer of 1894 and journeyed to Missouri.

Jug was living at her father's home near Danville, a village really, which clung to the title of county seat but felt the strong pull of nearby Montgomery City, a place of some fifteen hundred people that had become the terminus for the Wabash Railroad. In the battle for survival among towns, being bypassed by the railroad meant sure decline.

Whites had been living in the country since 1824, when Morgan B. White, Sr., arrived from Kentucky to take up a large plot of land and become, according to the county history, "a man of some consideration." The family traced its origins to Virginia, and people in the county used another word to sum them up: "aristocrats."

Jug's father, Archibald Herndon White, son of Morgan B., Sr., was a prominent farmer and politician. Now in his sixties, he and his wife, Ann Drace White, had reared an extremely close-knit family of three sons and seven daughters, all of whom Theodore was sure would amount to something. Like their mother before them, the girls had gone to Danville Academy, "a very successful and good school attended by daughters of prominent families from all parts of Missouri as well as other states."

This attractive homestead was a jarring contrast to the courts of Homestead — not to mention Theodore's own anarchic kin. He could not help but compare the White family's rocklike stability, its honored place in the community, its superior "breeding" (though not wealth) with his own impoverished, itinerant childhood. He was beguiled by the picturesque rural setting, and Jug seemed more desirable than ever.

The summer heat, the humid air, the drone of the bees in the honeysuckle vines, stirred potent desires in both of them. When they met in the hall or an empty room, they would urgently kiss; now she was as ardent as he was. One humid night, when the heat lightning flickered on the horizon and the distant thunder rumbled, their lovemaking spilled over the old bounds. As fat raindrops began spattering the leaves, they hurried inside. The rest of the family was asleep, and they met in the sitting room after Jug had changed into a flimsy nightdress through which Theodore could feel the soft contours of her body. As the rain drummed against the French windows, they sank into a stupor of passion, she half-fainting. He carried her to her room, and only Jug's pleas for him to protect her because she could not help herself prevented him from taking her.

After a week, Theodore tore himself away. A stopover in St. Louis to visit McCord and Wood depressed him, and he left as soon as he could. He had some vacation time remaining, and in a recent letter Paul had again urged him to come to New York. After a winter on the road, his brother was boarding with Emma and Hopkins and looking forward to an idle, pleasant summer. He promised to show Theodore the city and to introduce him to journalist cronies who could help him get a job on a great paper like the *Sun* or the *World*.

Theodore stopped over in Pittsburgh only long enough to pick up a change of clothes at his rooming house and to telegraph Paul that he was coming, and then caught the New York express. When he got off the train in Jersey City the next morning, Paul was there to meet him in the huge, glass-roofed train shed, from which they took the Hudson River ferry to Manhattan. They landed at Cortlandt Street in Lower Manhattan, and Paul hailed a carriage. Theodore's first view of the city was of the narrow alleys and drab tenements along the East River. Paul told him not to judge prematurely. Wait until he had seen *his* New York.

They went directly to Emma's place at 215 West 15th Street, near Seventh Avenue. Theodore found his sister much changed. The plump, delectable beauty of her youth had faded; she was now stout and worn-looking. Still, she was the same uncomplicated, affectionate Em, who would always be his favorite sister. She made a huge breakfast for them—steak, biscuits, and gravy. Paul, after alleging he was on a diet, tucked in with gusto—in honor of Thee's arrival, of course.

Emma, Theodore would learn, was now enduring the drab aftermath of her love story with Hopkins, who had been ousted from his Tammany Hall sinecure as a result of the Lexow Committee's investigations of political corruption, and was unemployed. Emma had taken in roomers for a time—that is, bona fide roomers, Hopkins having also lost his police protection—but now Paul was subsidizing the household.

Not only had Hopkins failed as a provider, he had turned to other women. Emma had resigned herself to this behavior and stuck by him. Subdued after her early flings, she was a proper homebody, slavishly devoted to her two children, Gertrude and George.

The next day Paul took Theodore for a walk up Broadway. They began at Fourteenth Street and Union Square, once the heart of the theater district. Paul pointed out some of the landmarks from his earliest days in the city. Broadway above Fourteenth Street was a fashionable thoroughfare, a glittering channel cut across the grid pattern of streets, lined with theaters, fancy emporiums, and luxury hotels. Paul thought it too hot to walk and hailed a hansom cab, and they were borne slowly uptown on the sluggish current of traffic. Buildings of ten or even twelve stories, with ornate façades and jutting cornices, loomed on either side. Like a tour guide, Paul called out the names of their famous occupants— Tiffany's at Fifteenth Street, Park and Tilford's fancy grocery, and the studio of Sarony, photographer of actresses and society women. Theodore gaped at the crowds surging along the sidewalk—the Broadway "parade." The men were all nattily dressed in silk hats, frock coats, and spats. Women in voluminous skirts and mutton-chop sleeves formed small, chattering flocks that were ogled by the sports standing in little knots on each street corner.

At Twentieth Street, Paul pointed out the offices of Howley, Haviland, the song publishing firm in which he was a silent partner. The area had become the center of the infant sheet-music business, anchored by the old, established firm of Oliver Ditson Company, which had its offices on Eighteenth and Broadway.

At Twenty-third Street they came upon Madison Square Park, on which fronted palatial hotels such as the Bartholdi and the Fifth Avenue, where presidents stayed and where influential politicians gathered in the bar at the Amen Corner. Dominating the north side of the square was the Garden, its soaring tower capped by the gold statue of Diana and her bow. Continuing up the street, they passed luxury hotels including the Albermarle and Gilsey House, home to "Diamond Jim" Brady and theater folk, including, at times, Paul. To the west, on Sixth Avenue, his brother told him, was the Tenderloin, a district of dance halls and brothels, now nailed shut by the Reverend Charles Parkhurst's antivice crusade, which had put a reform administration in City Hall. They stopped for a drink in the barroom of the Hoffmann House Café, with its huge painting, "Nymphs and Satyrs," by Bourguereau.

After finishing their drinks, they walked the rest of the way, past more luxury hotels—the Broadway Central, the Marlborough, the Grand, the Imperial—and theaters such as the Metropolitan Opera House and the Empire. At Forty-second Street they reached the northernmost outpost of Paul's world, the Hotel Metropole.

Inside was a huge lounge with a long, darkly gleaming mahogany bar and brass rail and leather banquettes around the wall. Paul led him to a table, scattering greetings like papal blessings. A stream of cronies came up to his table to pay their respects, and Paul had a joke or an anecdote for each, smiling, gladhanding, calling them "sport" and "old fellow," introducing his brother as "a writer from out West." Theodore later learned that Paul's bonhomie was in part motivated by business concerns. In addition to writing songs, he was "outside man" for Howley, Haviland, his job to charm composers into joining the firm and to cajole tenors and soubrettes into plugging its songs. It was "good old Paul" and glasses of whiskey and booming laughter.

The remainder of Theodore's week was a blur of impressions. Almost daily Paul would make a ceremonial progress up Broadway, retailing along the way the latest funny story, giving it a full performance at each stopping place, with appropriate gestures and accent. This was Paul's element, Theodore realized; the laughter and backslapping were as much nourishment to him as his heavy breakfasts at Emma's.

Sex was another appetite, and Paul satisfied it as greedily as he ate. One day when they were standing with a group of sports on a Broadway corner, Paul suggested they nip over to a special brothel he knew, a "French" place. When Theodore mumbled some excuse, Paul explained, "Don't you know what people mean when they say 'French,' sport? It's not just that they're French girls. It's the different way of doing it. They go down on you—blow the pipe—play the flute. Aren't you on?" Under Paul's prodding, he agreed, and the group headed en masse for the Tenderloin, with Theodore feeling he was "undertaking a dreadful, perilous and shameful adventure."

When Paul was preoccupied with business matters, Theodore made forays on his own. He journeyed to upper Fifth Avenue, where brownstone mansions squatted in haughty splendor, two or three to a block, now boarded up for the summer while their occupants cavorted in Newport or Saratoga. He toured Wall Street and slum areas; the contrasts between rich and poor in New York seemed even more glaring than in Pittsburgh. Here the poor appeared more hopeless and the rich more arrogant. He was struck by the words Paul had spoken to him that first day on Broadway: "Sometime you ought to write about these things, Thee. . . . The people out West don't know yet what is going on, but the rich are getting control. They'll own the country pretty soon. A writer like you could make 'em see that."

His final Sunday in the city, he accompanied Paul on an excursion to Manhattan Beach, a fashionable resort for the urban upper middle class and the group just below that looked up to them as a model. Businessmen, politicians, clerks, and their wives and girls, were headed for this pleasure dome; the trains and ferries were packed with smiling people, the women in lace-trimmed summer frocks and the men in white flannels and striped blazers.

When dusk fell, they sat on the broad veranda of the Manhattan and watched the fireworks display over the water. As the dull booms intoned, the sky was lit by silver starbursts that rained liquid fire on the dark ocean. Theodore envied Paul, so sleek and confident and superbly equipped for success in such a world, which Theodore could observe only from the fringe. He sensed the vulgarity of all this prosperity around him, founded on speculation and political corruption, yet he admired it. Out of the moil of cupidity, lust, and vanity that made up the city's seething energies had come this fabulous spectacle— Manhattan Beach. He exulted: "I have never lived until now."

The next morning, with the scenes of the previous night still incandescent in his mind, Theodore boarded the Limited for Pittsburgh, determined to return as soon as he could save enough money to stake him to a gamble on this city.

16 / *First Principles*
in Pittsburgh

> To understand how science and religion express opposite sides
> of the same fact—the one its near or visible side, and the
> other its remote or invisible side—this it is which we must
> attempt. . . . We see good reason to conclude that the most
> abstract truth contained in religion and the most abstract
> truth contained in science must be the one in which the two
> coalesce.
>
> —Herbert Spencer, *First Principles* (1862)

For the next three months he scrimped, spending a nickel for a breakfast of
coffee and a doughnut and fifteen cents for dinner, his only substantial meal, at
a greasy spoon. Still thin and gangling, his 140 pounds distributed sparingly
over his six-foot-one-inch frame, he almost succeeded in ruining his health by
the time he had accumulated two hundred and forty dollars.

The decision to try New York City marked the end of Theodore's Wanderjahre. His peregrinations had shown him America "in the furnace stage of its
existence." He had begun to understand that the trusts were gaining control of
the country. Having seen the demoralized state into which labor in Pittsburgh
had sunk, he had felt pity toward the weak on whom the strong fed. But at
the same time, he admired the titans of business who were building factories,
mines, and railroads.

The most enduring impression his wanderings leave is of a young man
seeking a niche in life, yet uncertain of how to achieve it and lacking in education and skills—face pressed against the window, gazing with desirous eyes at
the mansions of the wealthy. As he later told Jug, he was "an ambitious young
man without a competence . . . working for a place and a name."

Flowing from Dreiser's inability to find his place in society was his per-
plexity about his—and all humankind's—role in the cosmic scheme. A single

book that he read in Pittsburgh did more to shape his political and philosophical ideas than any other. That was Herbert Spencer's *First Principles.* As he wrote later, it "quite blew me, intellectually, to bits." Spencer had been a revelation to an entire generation of British and American intellectuals, and though his vogue in America was beginning to wane, its reverberations would continue in American literature until well into the twentieth century. And, of course, Spencer's ideas on the "survival of the fittest," a phrase he coined, found favor among industrialists to whom it was a license for ruthless acquisitiveness.

Spencer packaged moral philosophy as science. He synthesized Darwin's theory of evolution, Malthus's demography with its iron law of population, Ricardo's economics with its iron law of wages, and Lamarck's biology with its doctrine of the inheritability of acquired characteristics, into a great, over-arching theory.

Spencer was a brilliant spinner of theories, proceeding magisterially in such books as *Social Statics, The Principles of Sociology,* and *Synthetic Philosophy* to construct a vast edifice that comprehended all human knowledge. The trouble was that he preferred theorizing to evidence. In this he was the polar opposite of Charles Darwin, the patient grubber of facts. (Darwin once wrote of Spencer, "his conclusions never convinced, and over and over again I have said to myself, after reading one of his discussions, 'Here would be a fine subject for half-a-dozen years' work.' ")

Though Spencer's prose style was ponderous, it was lucid, and the grand sweep of his generalizations and the laws he propounded carried an aura of authority that won him converts among writers, intellectuals, autodidacts, and village atheists in nineteenth-century America.

Some of his readers experienced a revelation akin to a religious conversion. Andrew Carnegie, Spencer's most famous American disciple, said, "I remember that light came as in a flood and all was clear. Not only had I got rid of theology and the supernatural but I had found the truth of evolution."

Paradoxically, the man who inspired these conversions was a radical materialist. Trained as an engineer, he envisioned the universe as a great machine driven by divine hydraulic power. Force was the basis of motion and matter. Force was the propellant of Evolution. Spencer believed that evolution—in animals, human beings, and human society—moves from the homogenous to the heterogeneous, from cell to organism, from nebula to universe. Out of the inchoate flux and "undulations" of matter and motion, of action and reaction, came specialization and complexity. Humanity evolved from the primitive to the civilized, becoming ever more virtuous, altruistic, and happy. Evolution was God's plan, a divine momentum propelling humankind ever upward and on.

Spencer taught that all should be free to pursue happiness, but he never asked if all were equal at the start. He implied not that we get what we deserve, but that we deserve what we get. Traits of character were inherited; character determined fate, and a bad fate meant a bad character. The fittest survived; the unfit were culled for the sake of the betterment of the race.

Theodore was chastened by the precept that his failures in life were determined, that he was a mere atom in the great void. Now he understood the things he had seen as a journalist—the venalities, the suicides, the murders, the inhumanities. All were explained, Spencer taught, by the fact that desires—"nascent excitations"—were the spark plugs of the human engine; they ignited consciousness into action, propelling men and women along the lines of least resistance to seek pleasure. There was no free will; virtue was avoidance of pain, "the correspondence of certain inner physico-chemical actions with certain outer physico-chemical actions."

Life rewarded the strong: "Personal ends must be pursued with little regard to the evils entailed on unsuccessful competitors." This message confirmed Theodore's observations in Pittsburgh of the strong battening on the weak. And he also took comfort from Spencer that the desires that tormented him had been bred into him; they were a fact of nature. What the individual tried to do mattered little and his morality or lack of it mattered not at all.

In furnace-stage America, in the crucibles of its premier steelmaking city, the novelist was formed. Balzac made Dreiser see "for the first time how a book should be written. . . . I did not expect to write like Balzac but to use his method of giving a complete picture of life from beginning to end." Reporting had opened a window on the real world, and the view had convinced him that the lives of the great mass of men and women were hard and brutish, mirroring the ceaseless struggle in nature. Life was far from what it was represented to be by the priests and ministers; by the good, solid people like the Whites who lived in their dream world, the great American rural homestead; by the novels of sentiment and idealism. All those people were spinners of illusions.

But reporting had also shown him that nature had endowed him with a talent, writing, with which he could express his chaotic feelings. Reading Balzac, he had sensed that a novelist could write about what he saw, about life as it was lived. The rise and fall of individuals was a paradigm of the undulations of the Spencerian universe. In literature one could reenact the defeats of one's own dreams—and attain wealth, fame, and immortality in the process. Miss Fielding had told Theodore that *mind* was the touchstone of success, and now he had heroes who exemplified her advice: Spencer and Balzac. Philosophy and art were the royal roads to power. Two years later, he would call Spencer an intellectual Napoleon ("At the approach of his victorious mentality all living things bowed in vassalage, and he exacted the tribute of their reason and meaning from all") and Balzac "the Alexander of literature," whose conquering imagination penetrated into every corner of society and every guarded niche of the human heart.

●　　●　　●

One night in late November 1894, he stopped at the Press Club and fell into a conversation with the *Dispatch*'s political editor, who asked Theodore why he stayed in Pittsburgh. He was young and unencumbered—why didn't he go up to New York? Theodore blurted out that he hoped to.

The next day Theodore gave his notice to the city editor, who did not seem surprised. The following Saturday he drew his final paycheck, and at four o'clock that afternoon, with a bag and the two hundred and forty dollars he had saved, he boarded the express for New York. His life, he might have thought, had been a series of train journeys—Terre Haute to Sullivan, Sullivan to Evansville, to Chicago, to Warsaw, to Chicago again, to St. Louis, Toledo, Cleveland, Buffalo, Pittsburgh . . . journeys without arrival.

17 / *Fear of the City*

> Some transition is needed between the two states of being a
> somebody at home and of being a nobody in Paris; and those
> who pass too abruptly from one to the other experience a feel-
> ing of annihilation.
>
> —Balzac, *Lost Illusions* (1837)

New York in November 1894 was not the summertime city he had last seen.
Paul was on the road, and Theodore missed his brother's bolstering presence.
Emma's household was in a gloomy state. Hopkins was still unemployed, and
he seemed to have given up trying to find a job. Emma greeted Theodore
joyfully—relieved, he later learned, because she counted on his taking up the
financial slack left by Paul's departure.

New York had sunk into an economic slump that cast a pall over his own
prospects. Paul's newspaper connections might have helped him, but he was
too proud (or naive) to exploit them. The papers reported that unemployment
was severe. There were one hundred thousand men out of work in the city,
and as Theodore passed the Sisters of Mercy Convent on Fifteenth Street, he
could see lines of shabbily dressed men stamping their feet to keep warm as
they waited for admission to the soup kitchen the sisters ran.

One damp, chilly day he boarded the Sixth Avenue elevated and traveled
downtown to Park Row, where the offices of all the city's major newspapers
were located. He planned to start job hunting at the *World*—Joseph Pulitzer's
paper, where a former St. Louis reporter might receive extra consideration, since
Pulitzer had begun his rise to power in St. Louis.

As he walked through City Hall Park, Dreiser could see the *World* building
at 32 Park Row, towering sixteen stories above him, capped by a golden dome.
It was by far the tallest of the newspaper offices on the block (indeed, the second
tallest building in the city, next to the twenty-story American Surety building),
dwarfing the *Tribune's* nine-story redstone structure with its slender clock tower.
It seemed calculated to make him feel insignificant. Nerving himself, Theodore

entered the large doors and took the elevator to the city room on the eleventh floor. Immediately he was set upon by a pack of hostile office boys who refused to take his card identifying him as a correspondent for the St. Louis *Republic*.

Repulsed by the phalanx of sentinels, Theodore tried the other papers along the Row. At each he was greeted with indifference or contempt. It soon became clear that no paper in the city was hiring: he was only one of hundreds of out-of-work newspapermen. The confidence in his ability, the pride in the standing he had earned, whooshed out of him.

He sat awhile in the park, gazing up at the imposing row of newspaper offices, their windows staring back blankly. The park was full of bums and tramps, known as "benchers." He felt a kinship with them, which changed to cold fear. In what way was he superior? He too was a face in the crowd. While he was sitting with the bums of City Hall Park, "the idea of *Hurstwood* was born," Dreiser wrote in *Newspaper Days*. He did not mean the fully developed George Hurstwood of *Sister Carrie*. Rather, it was a vision of a shabby bum — the *fate* of Hurstwood — that suddenly flashed before his eyes.

In the ensuing days and weeks, Theodore toured the newspaper offices, meeting stony indifference. Finally, angered by the arrogance of the office boys at the *World,* he bulled past them into the city room. As the pack closed in, he stared in awe at the huge room, full of reporters scribbling stories and copy editors working at desks on a platform in the center. Cries of "Coppee!" rent the air.

As the watchdogs tried to drag him off, a tall, slender young man noticed the commotion. Handsome, his brow lined with premature wrinkles, Arthur Brisbane would, in 1895, become Sunday editor of the *World,* leading Pulitzer's army in the yellow journalism war against William Randolph Hearst's *Journal*. Brisbane calmly asked the now beleaguered hopeful who he was and what he wanted. When Theodore told him, Brisbane escorted him to the city editor's desk. "This young man wants a job," he said. "I wish you would give him one." With a quick nod, he was off.

After Brisbane left, the city editor eyed Theodore fishily and told him he would be taken on as a space-rate reporter. He would be paid $7.50 per column (twenty-one inches of newsprint) or a proportion thereof, depending on how long his article ran, plus expenses and fifty cents an hour while out on the assignment. His first published story — an account of a meeting on "How to Improve Tenement Life" — was boiled down to a few inches, and he received $1.86 for his efforts.

That sum should have signaled him that space-rate reporting was a losing game, for him at least. In his best week he made only $12.50 — a bit more than what a skilled steelworker got but well below the rate for beginning reporters, which was $15 to $20 a week. Actually, Dreiser seems not to have realized that most reporters at the *World* worked on space, and top performers, such as David

Graham Phillips and Albert Payson Terhune at the *World,* Stephen Crane at the *Herald,* and Lincoln Steffens at the *Evening Post,* earned up to $75 a week at it.

Most space-raters, however, were part of the labor pool the publishers maintained to keep wages down. The field of journalism was overcrowded and intensely competitive because so many newsmen were drawn to the city.

The *World* had beaten out Charles A. Dana's *Sun* in circulation after Pulitzer's arrival in the 1880s. The *Sun,* somewhat more staid, was a writer's paper, and went in for long, elegantly crafted features. Dana was obsessed with good writing, and was known to fire a reporter at the drop of a solecism. His staff people were encouraged to take their time with their stories, and turn out a finished essay. Pulitzer's motto, posted prominently in the city room, was "Terseness—Accuracy—Terseness." When Hearst took over at the *Journal,* his byword was speed, speed, speed; and when he challenged Pulitzer to a circulation war, the final stage of devolution was reached: "Sensation, sensation, sensation."

It was into this milieu that Theodore dipped a tentative toe—a world of ruthless newspaper barons, thoroughbred reporters, and whiskey-drinking hacks, glamorous figures like Richard Harding Davis and David Graham Phillips, and sleazy types like Frank Butler, a flabby man in food-stained clothes who looked like "a dropsical eagle that had spent the night in a coal bin."

Theodore nursed a resentment toward Davis and Phillips and their kind—those well-groomed young college men in fine clothes who seemed the favored ones and who spoke familiarly of high governmental and society figures. He resented their glib talk of "reform," sensing in it the condescending charity of the rich. His experience with reform was that it had cost Hopkins his job, leaving his sister Emma hard up. Always, it seemed, the Dreisers were the victims of the forces of respectability.

Lacking Davis's and Phillips's inbred self-assurance (or Stephen Crane's precocious genius), Theodore was condemned to sit on the bench with the other space-raters, treated like a cub, a nobody—he who had been a star in St. Louis. Now he could not seem to hit upon a story that would catch the city editor's glazed eye.

During the endless hours he spent in the reporters' room, he met other hangers-on from the West. One of them, a reporter from Pittsburgh, was trying to support a family on "space" and finding it impossible. Another told him about a mutual friend, a city editor they had known in St. Louis, who had committed suicide in a West Street hotel.

"What was the trouble?" Theodore asked.

"Tired of the game, I guess," was the reply. "He didn't get along down here as well as he had out there. I guess he felt that he was going downhill."

The vision of the derelict that came to Theodore in City Hall Park lurked in the back of his mind. How was he any better than the other hopefuls drawn to New York?

Meanwhile, life at Emma's had grown more uncomfortable. Hopkins spent most of his days lounging dispiritedly around the house, "waiting for something to turn up," and Theodore watched him (seeing him through Em's eyes) progressively going to seed, not shaving, wearing old clothes, refusing to take the odd jobs his political cronies offered him out of charity. "He had turned fifty and he came to feel life was over for him," Dreiser later wrote. With Christmas approaching, Emma was desperate. There was no money for presents, and her husband was proposing that they rent rooms to transient lovers again.

The idea of Em operating a bedhouse outraged Theodore. When it came to his blood sister, his attitude was protective like Paul's. Theodore could not stand the idea of any of his sisters being used. Branded in his memory was the humiliation of the Warsaw and Chicago days when Em and Theresa were playthings for rich men.

He had developed a strong antipathy to Hopkins. There was something vulpine about the man, something predatory in his eyes that reminded Theodore of Rome's feral selfishness. But there was also something there that mirrored what Theodore was also feeling: fear. They were "suffering from the same terror of life or New York." This fear, causally linked with failure, was in the eyes of the derelicts in City Hall Park. It was like a contagious disease—the disease of poverty.

Theodore had by now concluded that Em's marriage was intolerable; she and the children must leave Hopkins. When he broached the idea to her, however, she broke into tears. She told him how much she had loved Hopkins in Chicago—had been insane about him, really. And she had been partially to blame for the affair, she confessed. She had been so wild then—a flirtatious girl, sympathizing with Hopkins when he told her now miserable his life was with his first wife. Now that her youth was gone, it was no wonder he was indifferent. It would be hard for her to survive on her own; keeping house was all she knew.

Gradually, Theodore wore down her resistance. They devised an elaborate ruse. Telling Hopkins he was going back to Pittsburgh, Theodore took a room near the Bowery. Next, he wrote a letter and had a friend on the *Dispatch* mail it from Pittsburgh. Emma showed the letter to Hopkins and told him that she was going to join her brother and that he would have to look out for himself. Hopkins was sufficiently roused by this ultimatum to find a job as a hotel clerk in Brooklyn. After he had gone, Em had the furniture moved to a new apartment on West Seventeenth Street. The two never saw each other again. Hopkins died a year or so later. Theodore had seen him once in Brooklyn, a ruin of a man. (By another account, Hopkins returned to his wife in Chicago.)

Theodore continued to warm the bench in the reporters' room at the *World*. Now he was just a legman, obtaining facts for others to write. He covered a streetcar strike in Brooklyn. Often he went to the city morgue to check out a report of a suicide. If there was some colorful angle, or (even better) if the victim was a pretty young girl, a suicide story was worth a few inches. Finally, the day came when he could take no more of the indifference with which he was treated at the *World*. When he brought in a story about one of the waxen maidens of the morgue, the city editor told him perfunctorily to give it to a rewrite man. Theodore protested: "I don't see why I should have to do this. I'm not a beginner in this game. I wrote stories and big ones before I ever came to this paper."

"Maybe you did," the editor replied, "but we have the feeling that you haven't proved to be of much use to us."

Sensing his imminent firing, Dreiser quit. After drawing his last meager check and walking out the city room door, past the watchdogs, who had been right — he belonged on the streets with the rest of the "hams" — Theodore swore he would starve rather than work for a newspaper again. His chances were reasonably good of doing just that.

18 / *Street Scenes*

DID HE BLOW OUT THE GAS?
A shabbily dressed man who was without an overcoat registered as John Smith on Thursday night at the Bryant Park
Hotel, No. 660 Sixth Avenue, and was assigned to a bedroom. The hotel porter, John Meyer, detected gas escaping
from the room yesterday and burst open the door. Smith was
lying dead on the bed. . . . The body was taken to the Morgue.
The hotel people think it was an accident.
                              —New York *World*, February 16, 1895

Not much is known about Theodore's movements during the next months. He
still had some of his savings left, and could afford to free-lance for a while. He
was becoming accustomed to living frugally.

Having failed at journalism, he decided to heed Brisbane's suggestion and
become a magazinist. He first tried penning short stories for distinguished publications like *Harper's Monthly, The Atlantic Monthly,* the *Century,* and *Scribner's
Magazine.* But after studying them assiduously, he concluded they had only the
remotest connection to life as he knew it. The female characters exemplified the
highest ideals of chastity. The men were either drooling satyrs to be vanquished
by a stern look of blue-eyed rectitude or else misguided boys to be redeemed
by the superior power of feminine virtue.

Wandering the streets, he stored up impressions in the honeycombs of his
subconscious. The exotic corners of the city and their teeming humanity were
what he really wanted to write about, but the kind of word pictures in his head
did not translate readily into newspaper copy. When Dreiser suggested doing
stories about the great contrasts between wealth and poverty, editors would say,
"Old stuff! Old stuff! Think up something that everybody doesn't know about."
Once he encountered Mark Twain strolling along Doyers Street in Chinatown,
elegantly clad in a fur-collared overcoat and a top hat, tapping the sidewalk
with a gold-headed cane. Having read that Twain was scheduled to meet with
his lawyers to untangle the bankruptcy of a publishing company in which the

humorist had an interest, and knowing that the papers were interested in "old authors who were about to fail," Theodore tried to get an interview. Twain, however, shooed him away, saying, "I'm not to be interviewed in this way. I don't mind you newspapermen interviewing me—and saying that you saw me. But no more than that. Otherwise I'll have to deny it." Cowed, Theodore muttered that he understood, and then cursed himself for missing his big chance.

No other story so salable came his way; perhaps he didn't look very hard. Rather, he explored the side streets and stared at the strolling girls, "of the painted cohorts of the city," in Stephen Crane's phrase. Their pimps, dressed in high Bowery fashion—tight pants, silk hat, black scarf, polished boots— hovered in the background, waiting for them to lure marks into a back room, where they could roll them. At night the "jays" would descend on the area looking for excitement in notorious saloons such as Ahearn's or the Atlantic Gardens.

Bums were everywhere, drawn to the saloons, where for the price of a schooner of beer—a nickel—they could nurse a bowl of hot, greasy soup at the free-lunch counter. According to Jacob Riis, the Danish-born police reporter who had, four years previously, written a book on New York's poor, *How the Other Half Lives,* ten thousand homeless men descended upon the Bowery every night, seeking a place to sleep in the cheap lodging houses. For a quarter they could purchase the luxury of a partitioned room, fifteen cents got them a dormitory bed, and for a nickel they could sleep on the floor crammed between other unwashed bodies. Riis reported that sanitary police inspecting one such inn of the homeless found twelve adults in a room measuring thirteen by thirteen feet—three of them in bunks and the rest on the floor; three others were sprawled in the hallway. It was in such a flophouse that Stephen Crane stayed when he wrote his sketch "An Experiment in Misery," which appeared in the New York *Press* in April 1894. When he entered, Crane "felt his liver turn white . . . there came to his nostrils strange and unspeakable odors that assailed him like malignant diseases with wings. They seemed to be from human bodies closely packed in dens; the exhalations from a hundred pairs of reeking lips; the fumes from a thousand bygone debauches; the expression of a thousand present miseries."

After Riis published his book, young journalists regarded the Bowery as a testing ground. Lincoln Steffens, a Californian of respectable upbringing just arrived in the city, wrote excitedly to his parents that he was going to "the vilest part of the horrible East Side amid poverty, sin and depravity. Will it degrade me? Will it make a man of me? Here is my field, my chance."

A similar sense of quest may have stimulated Theodore. He watched bums gathered in Chatham Square, waiting for the flops to open; the breadline (here the term was coined) of hungry men that formed every night at Fleischmann's Vienna Model Bakery on Tenth and Broadway, waiting for employees to distribute the day's leftovers; the foundling home where unwed mothers stole up to leave their babies in an anonymous crib; the crowd of men jamming the door of a mission soup kitchen.

When he wandered over to the Italian neighborhood around Mulberry Street, site of the famous "Bend" that Riis pinpointed as the nadir of the other half's misery before its noisome tenements were torn down, Theodore was more enthralled by the teeming, vivid life spilling out on the streets than by the statistics of poverty. He saw clots of gossiping old women in black dresses, mothers breast-feeding their infants on the stoops, girls leaning out the windows to flirt with pushcart men selling cut-rate bruised vegetables and decaying chickens. Riis had eavesdropped on the hidden dramas inside those sagging brick structures—the "sweater [sweat] shops" on Hester and Bayard streets, where pale Jewish girls toiled; tiny, fetid rooms in which large families lived in squalor; courts like those at Homestead, with stinking privies hard by the single hydrants from which the residents took their drinking and washing water; narrow alleys that led to stale-beer dives where the dregs of the poor could buy a tomato can of the rancid stuff for a penny.

The ragged bums were the chief face of misery on the streets that winter of 1894–1895. During Crane's two-day experiment in misery, he had joined the benchers in City Hall Park. Like Theodore, he gazed up at the lofty newspaper offices of Park Row and the *World's* shining gold tower like the minaret in an old Persian painting. Crane had been shaken by a sudden vision of the great gulf between him and those buildings. They were "emblematic of a nation forcing its regal head into the clouds throwing no downward glances; in the sublimity of its aspirations ignoring the wretches who may flounder at its feet."

Theodore too was seeing the city from the bottom up, with the eyes of one of the city's itinerant poor. Dorothy Dudley writes, "In adversity his father was growing into him, superseding, undermining the 'pagan' mother, so much adored." He came to understand better Paul's nights in those lonely rooms while he was away from his family, and the blow to his pride and manhood of being out of work. Spencer's Unknowable had superseded his father's harsh God. "Life was desolate, inexplicable, unbelievably accidental—luck or disaster," he told Dudley.

As the winter wore on, Theodore realized he was sinking into the undifferentiated mass of nameless, tattered men, scarecrow arms flapping against the cold. After submerging so far, you reached a depth from which there was no return. You acquired a permanent air of defeat; your eyes were hunted, feral, your gait shuffling and weary.

At one point, reduced to sleeping in flophouses, Theodore found his own experience in misery more than he could bear. Now he was one of those anonymous men, hearing them groan in their sleep, smelling their reeking bodies. One bitter cold night, he later said—perhaps apocryphally—he walked down to the wharves by the East River, intending to hurl himself into the frigid waters. As he picked his way along the pier, he half-tripped over a bulky object, hard yet yielding. It was a sack of potatoes. He was hungry; he hadn't eaten all day. Collecting some small sticks and boards lying about, he made a fire and cooked them. The fire warmed him until they were done. The food restored him; the find was an omen that his luck would turn, that his destiny held.

• • •

If the idea for the character of Hurstwood, the tragic saloon manager of *Sister Carrie,* came to him that day in City Hall Park, it acquired stronger outlines during his sojourn on the Bowery. A number of influences converged on him — the spectacle of the bums in Chatham Square, the smells of the flophouses, the thoughts of suicide, the cold and the hunger, the recrudescent fears of poverty and his father's failure — the lean days in Terre Haute. Even in the chance encounter with Mark Twain, dapper in his fur coat and top hat but stalked by the specter of bankruptcy, Dreiser saw an old writer who had been cast aside. What if a man tumbled from the golden coach into these mean streets?

Out of such thoughts as these and the sights around him came a number of urban sketches that he would write, describing the sweatshops, the life in the tenements, the men in the breadline, lining up at the flophouse, the benchers — the tragic last act of *Carrie.*

19 / *The One-Man Band*

It becomes not only a pleasure but a duty occasionally to pierce some of the more iridescent soap bubble illusions of the many concerning some phases of life as we read and speculate about it.

—Dreiser, "Reflections" (1896)

In May Theodore went to the Howley, Haviland office to see if Paul had returned (he hadn't), and while there he overheard Pat Howley and Fred Haviland talking about starting a song magazine. Oliver Ditson's, the song publishing house where Haviland once worked, had profitably published the *Musical Record* since 1878, and there were others. They contained the words to numerous songs and were aimed at the trade—music shops, teachers, students, and performers. Howley, Haviland had something of this sort of publication in mind, but one that would advertise their songs to a nonprofessional audience.

The song that had launched the firm was "The Sidewalks of New York," an infectious waltz about street life written by an actor named Charles B. Lawlor and a hat salesman named Jim Blake. It was a perfect number for the ubiquitous Italian organ grinders, who soon were playing it on every corner, just as the verse had said: "While the 'ginnie' played the organ on the sidewalks of New York." That success was followed by another, "I Can't Tell Why I Love You But I Do," written by a teenage prodigy named Gus Edwards, who would become one of the top songwriters of the early 1900s. With profits starting to roll in, Howley quit his job, and Haviland joined him after his then employer got wind of his moonlighting and fired him.

The sheet music business was undergoing a rapid transformation from cottage industry to mass-production operation, and Howley, Haviland was in the vanguard of the young Turk publishers who were operating out of their hats but determined to cut a slice of the huge profits that could be made. In addition to cheaper printing made possible by the rotary press and photoengraving, a nationwide distribution network for sheet music was in place. No longer were songs peddled at intermissions of minstrel shows and in a few specialty shops. Now they were sold in department stores and music shops in every city and large town. Thousands of copies, retailing for fifty cents each, could be shipped by rail and reach these outlets in a matter of days, should the demand arise. Techniques for stimulating that demand had also improved, and *Ev'ry Month* was designed to be a cog in the promotional machinery.

Hearing Howley and Haviland's talk about issuing a song magazine, Theodore immediately nominated himself as its editor and proposed that they publish a real magazine as a wrapper for their songs. It would attract readers who would buy the sheet music. Any profits from sales of the magazine would be gravy. Pat and Fred liked his idea and hired Theodore at ten dollars a week until the first issue was out, and fifteen dollars a week thereafter. Pat and Fred envisioned the magazine as a shoestring operation, serving primarily as a vehicle for the firm's songs. The editor had bigger ideas.

Theodore had all summer to plan his premier number, scheduled to make its debut in September, after people returned from their summer vacations. He took as his model the ten-cent magazines like *Munsey's,* which he read avidly and which appealed to the aspiring young urban middle class (of whom he was one, after all). Frank Munsey had pioneered some money-saving innovations that made his low cover price possible. He used photographs lavishly because the development of the halftone engraving process made them cheaper than woodcuts. He also created departments on topics that appealed directly to readers (theater, society, fashion, and the like). They were written by anonymous free-lancers, enabling Munsey to avoid competing for high-priced authors, who in the case of a Rudyard Kipling or a Robert Louis Stevenson commanded as much as thirty-five thousand dollars for a book-length serial. Theodore borrowed those ideas, and the dime cover price as well.

The chief buyers of sheet music—and popular magazines, for that matter— were young women. The upright piano was becoming a standard fixture in the parlors of middle-class homes supplanting the bulkier and more expensive organ, with its paneled mirrors and elaborate carvings. Thousands of young women dutifully added piano playing to their attainments and performed the latest tunes for family and beaux (Jug had impressed Theodore in this fashion during their courtship days in St. Louis).

The average *Ev'ry Month* reader probably bought the magazine for the two or three songs contained in each issue, which cost her only ten cents, compared to fifty cents for a copy of sheet music. So one of them informed the editor-arranger at any rate:

> Thee I wish you would send me and Ed every
> month regular as Ed plays the violen [sic] and
> I would like it for the music there is in it.
> Sister Emma

To give the illusion of numerous contributors, Theodore adopted several noms de plume. In the Christmas issue, he was "The Prophet," who signed the "Reflections" column, an editorial grab-bag of notes and philosophical observations that led off the magazine. He was also "The Cynic," the author of an essay called "The Gloom Chasers" (a reworking of a humorous article he had written for the Pittsburgh *Dispatch*); "Edward Al" (a combining of two of his brothers' first names), who conducted "The Literary Shower"; "S. J. White" (a wave to Jug), who wrote the article "We Others"; "Th.D.," the play reviewer, and probably the anonymous author of the column on flowers in the back of the book. In the August 1896 issue his first published short story (aside from the youthful "Return of Genius") appeared. Entitled "Forgotten," it was an amalgam of Paul's song "The Letter That Never Came," telling in prose the sad story of the quiet man lying in a hospital bed asking each day if there is a letter for him, and "Hospital Violet Day," the *Dispatch* piece about flowers and dying in a hospital. Theodore also clipped short poems from other magazines as fillers. He wrote Jug that they had been selected as love poems just for her.

Eventually Theodore's friends responded to his calls for help. From St. Louis Peter McCord contributed fiction, verse, and humorous pieces under his own name and such pseudonyms as "James McCord," "J. Rhey McCord," and "The Enthusiast" (a counterbalance to "The Cynic"?). Dick Wood sent some romantic fiction and Decadent verse. Later, William Marion Reedy was represented with an obituary of Joseph McCullagh. (The taciturn editor had committed suicide by jumping from the window of an upper story of his house. Aloof to the end, he left no note.) And Arthur Henry, who had quit his job with the Toledo *Blade* to become a free-lance writer and publicist, offered some poems and philosophical effusions. There were also occasional articles on political issues. John P. Altgeld, the progressive governor of Illinois, for example, was represented by an attack on the misuse of the injunction in labor disputes.

In time, as the magazine began to generate some revenue, Theodore was able to buy fiction and commission articles by New York City writers, paying them a penny a word. George C. Jenks, an out-of-work Pittsburgh newsman who had moved to the city, took over "The Literary Shower." The title was a steal from *Town Topics*'s "The Literary Show," conducted by avant garde critic Percival Pollard. Virginia Hyde wrote a series on well-known contemporary women calculated to appeal to *Ev'ry Month*'s feminine readership. Others were recruited to write on fashions, society, and the theater. Glenn Willets, a scion of an old New York family, specialized in stories and articles about society; bearded Morgan Robertson contributed sea tales. Theodore also purchased syndicated stories by better-known writers, such as Stephen Crane's "A Mystery of Heroism" and Bret Harte's "A Night in the Divide." But his staple was romantic fiction designed for his feminine readers.

But if *Ev'ry Month* had become a women's magazine, Theodore edited it with one woman in mind: Sara Osborne White. He wrote her out in Missouri that she was the magazine's "mascot," and promised that her name would be smuggled into every issue.

"All of the literary people I meet here tell me I'm the most easygoing editor in town," he confessed, "and I think I must be. Here in my office I do more thinking about you than I do about my various duties and frequently I abandon all details and announce myself 'out' to all comers just so I may have an hour's peace in which to write you." Still, "Like Dinah's meals in Uncle Tom's Cabin, 'Ev'ry Month' comes out of chaos all o.k."

After only a year, circulation rose to sixty-five thousand and the magazine grew to forty-four pages, with advertising up from three pages to nine. A full-time advertising representative was hired, and Theodore had his own "editorial stationery" printed up on blue paper.

Despite circulation gains, however, his future as an editor was increasingly shaky. *Ev'ry Month* was not a moneymaker, at least in the eyes of Pat Howley and Fred Haviland. (Haviland claimed in later years that the firm dropped a total of fifty thousand dollars on it, a considerable loss.) It lacked the mass impact of a journal like *Munsey's* because it was still basically a song magazine, and Pat and Fred did not wish to make the necessary editorial investment to give it wider appeal. And so it remained something of an anomaly and very much a one-man journal. The "Reflections" column had become Theodore's personal sounding board, a podium from which he propounded his moody observations and pessimistic philosophical musings, laced with Bryanish Populism and at times radicalism—all of which could not have pleased Pat and Fred.

Looking over the shoulder of "The Prophet" were his mentors, Herbert Spencer and Charles Darwin. Dreiser had taken up the latter in earnest, and in November 1896 wrote Jug that he had just finished reading a chapter in which the Master explained why the male courts the female. Acknowledging his fiancée's opposition to the doctrine of evolution on religious principles, Theodore boasted that *he* was "firmly grounded in the belief" and gained "as much satisfaction from observing the truth of it, as some would in observing the nearness of a novelist's fiction to actual life," betraying his literary as well as his scientific values.

But evolution provoked darker thoughts. "We are born, struggle and die . . . the lever that moves the Universe is pain," he wrote in *Ev'ry Month*. "This is the law, cold, hard, immutable . . . the law of self-preservation and upon it all must take their stand and press forward or die." He was thinking of his own desperate ambition and the struggle to survive in the city. He had written to Jug about thoughts of suicide.

Perhaps because he took the doctrine of the survival of the fittest so personally, "The Prophet" was ambivalent about it. He was, like Spencer, opposed to direct government action to help the victims of the powerful ("the man is wrong who cries for the State to do something for the unfortunate. . . . The State cannot legislate brains into people and therefore it cannot relieve their lack of shrewdness nor make them successful. It can only offer a free field and encourage enterprise"). New York's poor suffer and die in their dark tenements; it is the immutable law. And yet, unlike Spencer, Dreiser refuses to say that their misery is due to improvidence, alcoholism, or bad character. The true cause of their plight is environment, lack of education and equal opportunity.

Nor did he share completely Spencer's views that wealth was the reward for natural superiority. In one column he scorns the "money-desire" and the "evil of American rapacity," as evidenced by a recent financial panic in the West. The "money changers (and they are not Jews nowadays)" were behind it, and they "may soon learn that it is evil to crave immense prosperity." In another he equates conditions in the factories with slavery, writing: "[Do] you think slavery is abolished? Read New York State's factory inspector's report on conditions in the 'sweaters.' "

He also finds the success ethos inimical to community: "Our age is largely successful from a commercial view, and it is largely friendless." "For all else a man is still a man however often he may fail."

●   ●   ●

Fred and Pat's economy lectures made little impression on Dreiser, for he asked for a raise and a share of the profits, which he apparently believed were cascading in. He was thin-skinned and oversensitive, aloof and solitary. The location of his office was symbolic of his place in the firm: he occupied a tiny aerie above the main room, which was reached by a narrow flight of stairs.

As he complained to Jug, "I am practically alone, month after month." He admits this might be his fault: "I know I am terribly selfish, have a high opinion of my own importance and often place it disagreeably in evidence." Because of his unconventional views, he told her, "They say here that I am a perverted cynic." Although his bosses were "plutocrats and cantankerous goldites," he assured her that "I stand quite alone, but unterrified." But he was pushing his luck by resorting to Populist rhetoric. Paul, a Democrat, might have sided with him politically, but Theodore's relations with Paul were not the best, and he proceeded to further alienate his brother by publishing an article by Arthur Henry which mocked Paul's style of slapstick comedy.

In early 1897 Henry arrived in the city, he later wrote, with "nothing but my ticket, a night-dress, eight dollars, a pipe and a poem. . . . " He headed for East Twentieth Street in hopes of selling two philosophical works. Theodore accepted them, wrote him a voucher for fifteen dollars, and took him to lunch.

As they passed through the bustling office, Henry asked Theodore the meaning of all the hubbub. Those people were "succeeding," Dreiser explained with lofty disdain. "And you?" Henry asked.

"I am drawing a good salary. The things I am able to get the boss to publish that I believe in are very few," Theodore replied. "The rest must tickle the vanity or cater to the foibles and prejudices of readers. From my standpoint I am not succeeding."

Over lunch, Henry told him he should be writing novels, poetry, plays. Under the spell of his friend's charm (he once described Henry as "a lover of impossible romances which fascinated me by their very impossibility"), Theodore began to envision greener pastures. Not long after their lunch, in the summer of 1897, Dreiser was fired, as he probably wanted to be.

He left in August, after preparing the September issue, which featured Henry's "Philosophy of Hope." Despite its stormy ending, his *Ev'ry Month* experience had been a valuable one. It had given Dreiser absolute freedom, for a time, to speak his mind, and he had "got it through {his} skull what a magazine was." He left the table while still ahead of the game.

20 / Broadway Paul

> While cynics might refer to the little simple melodies [I write] as trash and the words as maudlin sentiment, to me with apologies to none the grandest word in the English or any other language [is] Mother.
>
> —Paul Dresser (1897)

Paul undoubtedly took Pat and Fred's part in the dispute with Theodore. Push Paul too far, as Theodore had done, and his customary geniality faded. The imbroglio over the conduct of *Ev'ry Month* led to a coolness between the brothers that was mainly on Theodore's part. For Paul, family ties transcended everything. "But she's your sister" or "he's your brother" was his ultimate verdict on all the sibling squabbles he adjudicated.

After Theodore's departure, Paul became more directly involved in the affairs of *Ev'ry Month*. In the fall of 1897 he told a St. Louis newsman that he had come to town to solicit advertising and would "hereafter devote his time to writing songs and in building up his new magazine Ev'ry Month."

Thanks to Paul's songs, the money was rolling in. His two biggest hits appeared in 1895 and 1897: "Just Tell Them That You Saw Me," based on an encounter Paul had with someone he knew from Terre Haute who, when asked if he has any message for the home folks, speaks the words of the title; and "On the Banks of the Wabash." Each song sold more than five hundred thousand copies, meaning a total of eighty thousand dollars for Paul and an equal amount in profits for the firm—huge sums in that era.

If Theodore had stuck around a bit longer, he might have shared in the new prosperity. It seems doubtful, though, that more money would have made him happy. He later ruefully described his attitude toward Pat and Fred as one of snobbish superiority. He felt the same way about Paul, but he probably liked his songs more than he let on. Certainly he had a fondness for a lot of popular music. In a letter to Jug, he describes a pleasant scene at the Howley, Haviland offices on a warm summer evening, listening to his friend Theo Morse, a young composer, playing his latest songs, "Baby" and "I Want You My Honey." The music lulled him into reveries of her. His interest in songwriting extended to rewriting lyrics for Howley, Haviland.

Theodore's most successful job of lyric writing was for Paul, though it came about in such a casual way as to seem almost inadvertent. As Dreiser recounts it in his story "My Brother Paul," he, Ed, Paul, and a few others were lounging about at the office. Paul was noodling on the piano, trying out various melodic fragments that popped into his head. Unable to come up with anything, he asked his brother to give him an idea, and Theodore suggested that he compose something about a river, as Stephen Foster had done with the Suwannee. Paul liked the idea; he greatly admired Foster. But which river? Why not the Wabash? Theodore asked. After all, Paul had played along its banks as a boy in Terre Haute. Dubious, Paul proposed that Theodore write the verse, a story on which to hang a chorus.

Theodore took a pencil and paper and retired to a corner, grumbling that he knew little and cared less about writing a song. After about a half hour he returned with a rough draft of what would be the verse of "On the Banks of the Wabash":

> *Round my Indiana home there waves a cornfield,*
> *In the distance loom the woodlands clear and cool.*
> *Often times my thoughts revert to scenes of childhood,*
> *Where I first received my lessons, nature's school.*
> *But one thing there is missing from the picture,*
> *Without her face it seems so incomplete.*
> *I long to see my mother in the doorway,*
> *As she stood there years ago, her boy to greet.*

He also planted the germ of a chorus, basing it on the title of his unwritten play, *Along the Wabash*. His effort didn't give Paul a lot to go on. For one thing there was really no story or situation. Still, Theodore's idea appealed to him; it tapped his nostalgia for the old home place, where Mother was standing in the doorway waiting for her boy to return.

As Theodore tells it, Paul sat down at the piano, plinked out a suitable melody, rewrote the chorus to fit, and was finished in a matter of hours. According to an article Theodore wrote in 1898, "the words of 'On the Banks of the Wabash' were written in less than an hour of an April Sunday afternoon, and . . . the music did not require a much longer period." Although he did not mention his own role in the song's composition, he noted, "I know whereof I speak."

That account appeared in *Metropolitan Magazine*. In a letter to Jug earlier that year, Theodore boasted, "Yes, dearie, I wrote the words as I said, of 'On the Banks of the Wabash.' " And years later Ed Dreiser told his daughter, Vera, that it had happened much as Theodore had said it did. Paul, however, never publicly acknowledged his brother's contribution in the various versions he gave the press of how "The Wabash" came to be written.

The most accurate journalistic account was the one that had Paul writing the song in Chicago in May 1897. Max Hoffman, an arranger with the Witmark Music Publishing Company, who worked with Paul when the latter was visiting Howley, Haviland's branch office in Chicago, remembered being summoned to Paul's hotel room in June 1897 and finding him laboring over a melody on his portable organ. Paul told Hoffman he wanted him to make a piano arrangement for a new song. He had the tune, but was still working with a dummy lyric. First, Paul had Hoffman play the melody over and over while he tinkered with the words. By the time he had finished, the dummy lyric was completely changed. Hoffman was struck by the beauty of one of Paul's new lines, "Thro' the sycamores the candle lights are gleaming," and thinking it must have been inspired by the lights reflected on the dark waters of Lake Michigan.

This account does not necessarily conflict with Theodore's. The dummy lyric was probably his, and Paul's main concern was coming up with a chorus that would fit his basic melody, which entailed considerable expansion on his brother's idea. What he produced was superb:

> Oh, the moonlight's fair tonight along the Wabash,
> From the fields there comes a breath of new mown hay.
> Thro' the sycamores the candle lights are gleaming,
> On the banks of the Wabash, far away.

"On the Banks of the Wabash" had its tryout in a vaudeville show playing at the Alhambra Theater in Chicago. Charles K. Harris, author of "After the Ball" and a friend of Paul, recalled that it received an ovation, and Paul wired Howley, Haviland to rush the song out. After a few months it began to build, and in September Paul reported to the song's dedicatee, a Terre Haute girl named Mary South: "The 'Wabash' is going fine. I have sold over five thousand up to date. Had an order for 300 from Lyons Healy Chicago in this morning's mail." A year later he wrote: "The 'Wabash' is still the great hit of the day. Our sales this week up to date have reached nearly 10,000 copies."

"The Wabash" went on to sell well over a half-million copies. Not only did it bring Paul bags of money, it won him fame in his hometown, something that meant a lot to him (in 1913 it was chosen as the Indiana state song).

Part of the reason he was so successful was that he sincerely believed in what he wrote. "When he sat down to write a song his heart and soul were in it," said Charles K. Harris. "Money meant nothing to him."

Tears would roll down Paul Dresser's plump cheeks when he was composing one of his poignant ballads. "I write for the masses, not the classes," he often said. "On the Banks of the Wabash," his biggest seller, was one of the greatest home, heart, and mother songs ever written—authentic in its emotion, with a simple, wistful melody that carries an ineffable yearning. "The Wabash" flows through the heartland of the American psyche.

Why did Paul fail to acknowledge Theodore's role in "On the Banks of the Wabash"? The answer is that by the time he had finished it, the break with Theodore had occurred. Out of a mixture of pique, ego, and protectiveness toward his reputation, Paul appropriated the song.

In addition to whatever rancor Theodore felt over Paul's appropriation of "The Wabash," there were temperamental differences between them. He disapproved of his brother's free-spending ways and his numerous affairs, most of them with tarts or actresses. Paul's frank carnality offended the Puritan in Theodore. When he and Ed shared a hotel suite with their older brother, Paul would parade around nude every morning with a towel draped over his matutinal erection. This practice so disgusted Theodore that he moved out. Smugly engaged to Jug, he wrote to her that Paul "loves all women too well generally to love anyone in particular for long. He is fickle, fat and forty and worse than ever."

But envy tinged those sniffy words. Mai Skelly, at the time one of Paul's protégées, remembered Theodore eyeing her at the *Ev'ry Month* offices in a hungry way that she found unpleasant. Theodore would see his brother sweeping her off (Mai's mother in tow as chaperone) to Sherry's or Delmonico's and be reminded again of Paul's superior attainments as a lady's man. Ironically, the more handsome Ed, who had moved to the city in 1897 and whom Paul was helping become an actor, stole Mai from his oldest brother. They fell in love at a party given by the playwright Clyde Fitch, at which Mai sang "On the Banks of the Wabash." Ed won a role in Richard Harding Davis's play *Soldiers of Fortune,* and, with Paul's blessing and financial help, Ed and Mai were married in June 1899 at St. Patrick's Cathedral.

21 / A Season of "Success"

I had made the amazing discovery that I could write a rather hack type of magazine article, [and] I ran into Orison Swett Marden, in the editorial offices of the *Christian Herald*, the most successful all-around Christian paper of its day.

—Dreiser (1932)

Once again Theodore was on his own hook, but he was better prepared to survive than when he first arrived in the city. He decided to try the life of the free-lance writer again. After editing other writers for two years, he felt able to turn out a salable article and had gained confidence in his ideas. He had also made useful acquaintances among editors, writers, and artists. Lastly, he had material in hand—an article he had written for a series on women artists running in *Ev'ry Month*. It appeared in the November *Puritan* under the title "Our Women Violinists." He also had pieces in the November *Truth* and in the *Metropolitan,* the latter signed "Theodore Dresser."

For his November harvest of stories, Theodore received two to three hundred dollars, and his career as "specials" writer was launched. For the next two years he sailed ahead, with awesome energy and prolificacy. "I have an easy pen," he boasted to Jug. There was a plethora of new publications hungry for material, but to make a good living, the "magazinist" had to produce in volume. Here Theodore's newspaper experience, which had taught him to write rapidly under pressure, was an advantage. He was used to letting the copy editors clean up his stories, however, and magazines put much of the burden on the free-lancer, so the prose in his early efforts was cliché-ridden and crude.

The free-lancer's best course was to gain entrée at a few journals and build up a reputation as a reliable contributor. Eventually, he or she might become a columnist or contributing editor, drawing a regular stipend. For a time Theodore had a working relationship with *The Cosmopolitan*; in 1899 he became contributing editor to *Ainslee's,* where a friend, Richard Duffy, was an editor. In exchange for articles and ideas, he was guaranteed seventy-five dollars every other week.

A chance encounter in the fall of 1897 gained Dreiser his most steady outlet and eased him over the bumpy transition from *Ev'ry Month* to the free-lance life. He was contributing unsigned squibs to the *Christian Herald,* and at its office in Bible House on Eighth Street he met opportunity in the person of Orison Swett Marden. Marden was a friend of Louis Klopsch, publisher of the *Herald,* who had taken over the failing paper a few years before and turned it into a moneymaker, and himself into a millionaire. Klopsch, a German Jewish immigrant, raised millions of dollars for famine relief in India, China, and other countries through his paper.

Sensing that the formula of stories about eminent achievers whose lives exemplified his credo—"Unceasing struggle in adversity brings triumph"—would be equally lucrative in a magazine format, Marden decided to found a weekly called *Success.* Klopsch agreed to back the new publication and assigned *Christian Herald* managing editor George A. Sandison to help get it started. Sandison suggested Theodore as a potential contributor and introduced him to Marden.

Dreiser quickly established himself as a reliable *Success* peddler, and over the next three years contributed about thirty articles and a poem to the magazine. A man who got value on the dollar, Marden published every word Theodore wrote, using leftover scraps as fillers. And when he found that Theodore's copy needed editing, Marden informed him in the spirit of the sweatshop operator who deducts for ruined materials, "By the way, we shall have to charge you about ten dollars on each article for editing the manuscript." Marden's literary ethics were not the highest. He took sixteen of Theodore's pieces and used them, without permission or credit, in a series of *Success* anthologies, including *How They Succeeded, Little Visits with Great Americans,* and *Choosing a Career.*

The articles themselves are stilted, reverential; each pompous maxim is recorded stenographically. Carnegie on thrift: "It is the first dollar saved that tells." Carnegie on starting at the bottom: "If by chance the professional sweeper is absent any morning do not hesitate to try your hand at the broom." One suspects that some of the interviews were conducted by letter, or even cobbled together from various public pronouncements. At times the hyperbole is numbing. "No more significant story," Dreiser began an article on department store owner Marshall Field, "none more full of stimulus, of encouragement, of brain-inspiring and pulse-thrilling potency has been told in these columns." In the office of the meat-packing magnate Philip D. Armour "a snow storm of white letters [fell] . . . thickly upon a mass of dark desks." There was something awesome in this "mobilization of energy to promote the private affairs of one man."

Dreiser dutifully elicited the data Marden wanted: the hero's boyhood poverty, his early struggles, the virtues that helped him climb the ladder, his tips for the young man who wanted to emulate him, his views on the importance of money (most success cases deprecated money—perhaps because they had so much of it), and his sermons on the virtues of hard work, thrift, honesty, and so on.

But one senses an underlying ambivalence, and in the interview with the wealthy corporation lawyer Joseph H. Choate, his questions seem to reflect a private agenda. Dreiser opens their conversation by asking, "I wish to discover whether you believe special advantages at the beginning of a youth's career are necessary to success."

After gruffly demanding to know his interrogator's definition of advantages ("money, opportunity, friends, good advice, and personal popularity," was the reply), Choate denies that a head start in the race is crucial—certainly it was not in his case. Later he says flatly, "I never met a great man who was born rich." At this point the reporter blandly interpolates, "This remark seemed rather striking in a way because of the fact that Mr. Choate's parents were not poor in the accepted sense. The family is rather distinguished in New England annals." Choate, he notes, graduated from Harvard, and "Influence procured him a position in a Boston law office."

Theodore pressed on: "If equally valuable opportunities do not come to all hasn't an individual a right to complain and justify his failures?" Choate agreed that some men were less fortunate than others, but if such inferior individuals should demand the privileges of their betters, they must prove that they are worthy of them. The interlocutor then wonders if some youths might not overestimate their abilities. He was probing another hole in the success credo: if it instills in young people the illusion that they might succeed, what happens when that illusion is shattered by reality? Doesn't such an overreaching contain the seeds of tragedy? Theodore's fear that he might not achieve his own ambitions was a painful one. The previous year he had written Jug that he was haunted by the thought that "nature had made me a mind fitted above my station."

In the panegyric to Carnegie, the alert reader might have caught an allusion to a development that had further shrunk the field of opportunity—the rise of the large corporation. Carnegie hailed the opportunities for advancement in such enterprises, but his implication was that it was no longer possible to build a business empire from scratch as he had done. In a talk with the Chicago preacher Reverend Frank Gunsaulus, this point emerged more clearly. "The modern young man is more or less discouraged by the growing belief that all things are falling into the hands of great corporations and trusts, and that the individual no longer has much chance," Gunsaulus said.

The businessmen Dreiser really admired were the emerging successors to the robber barons, men with a social conscience such as John H. Patterson, president of the National Cash Register Company, who provided his workers with schools, hobby shops, gymnasiums, and sermons. And he much preferred interviewing artists or writers such as William Dean Howells or the naturalist John Burroughs, whose life in a mountain hut he had built with his own hands exemplified the lesson that "all success is not material," that mere dollars are nothing, and that "the influential man is the successful man, whether he be rich or poor."

A glimpse into his true state of mind was provided by Myrta Lockett Avary, who was working for Klopsch when Dreiser was contributing to *Success*. One day Theodore stopped at her desk to talk about a picture layout, and they fell to chatting. Avary was a widow from the South who had come to New York to make her way, and she felt a sympathetic current flowing from Dreiser: "the ugliest man I ever saw, but also the most interesting." The talk came around to the work she was doing, and he told her: "You should make your name here." He paused significantly, then added, "If they'll let you."

22 / *The "Specials" Writer*

Man's ingenuity finds many contradictory channels for its expression. The labor to perfect those sciences which tend to save human life goes on side by side with the labor to create new and more potent methods for its destruction.

—Dreiser, "Scenes in a Cartridge Factory" (1898)

The connection with *Success* was an augury; Dreiser's magazine career was soon flourishing. By February 1898 he bragged to Jug that with his present "standing and ability," he should be able to average $5000 a year. He moaned about overwork, but it was all to make enough money so they could marry. They were officially engaged now; he had sent her a ring in June 1896.

As it turned out, 1898 was a boom year for the firm of Th. Dreiser & Co. He sold nearly fifty articles and poems, and easily cleared $5000, as he had predicted. He was doing solid hackwork, learning the ropes fast, attempting to make as much money as he could. With the twentieth century fast approaching, futuristic pieces on the brave new world of technology were in demand. Interurban trolleys, for example, were still enough of a novelty for Dreiser to recount his experiences on a journey from New York to Boston.

Another part of him was drawn to nature and scenic areas like the Brandywine River, which he proposed to Jug as a honeymoon destination; historic places, such as Germantown (where his mother's ancestors had first settled) and Tarrytown; or literary sites, such as Nathaniel Hawthorne's Salem and William Cullen Bryant's home. Theodore found romance in old places and called for their preservation. The progress that would tear them down in favor of commercial structures was "reprehensible" and "shameless." In "The Harlem River Speedway" he advocated planting grass and trees along a new urban roadway, and in "The Haunts of Nathaniel Hawthorne" he criticized the trolleys and electric lights in Salem that "glared upon and outraged its ancient ways."

Dreiser showed himself sensitive to the artistic potential of photography in an article on Alfred Stieglitz, the first ever done on him. At that time Stieglitz was experimenting with a mass-produced Kodak Detective on the theory that if he rid himself of clumsy paraphernalia—the heavy box camera, the tripod, the hood, the glass plates—he might better record city scenes. In the developing process, Stieglitz discovered, one could crop a picture and highlight the central point of interest. Theodore marveled that "by purely photographic methods" Stieglitz had succeeded in conveying "the impression produced by the original scene . . . the clear crowning reality of the thing." He decided that Stieglitz's "Winter on Fifth Avenue," a dramatic portrait of a cabdriver in a snowstorm that caused a sensation when it was first exhibited, "had the tone of reality. . . . The driving sleet and the uncomfortable atmosphere issued out of the picture with uncomfortable persuasion."

On occasion, a glimmer of description shines through in Theodore's own photographic prose, as though he had suddenly seen things with his own eyes rather than with those of the conventional-minded readers for whom he usually wrote. Such glints were rare; usually he stuck to ladling out a thick gruel of facts. He was writing too fast to speak in his own voice and had adopted a sort of droning vivacity. One imagines him lucubrating at the Salmagundi Club on West Twelfth Street, where as a nonresident member he had the use of the study, or at the Bible House, where Marden gave him desk space, filling half sheets of yellow foolscap with his crabbed reporter's script. Dreiser was a writing machine; his speed and ability to sustain it for hours at a time accounted in part for his fecundity. But he also learned to use his material thriftily, plagiarizing from himself, expanding or rewriting previously published pieces and reselling them, reheating leftover research.

Yet recycled material makes up only about one-fifth of his production during 1898 and 1899. Apparently no editor ever found one article identical to another. Duffy did send him a panicky note saying that a profile of the sculptor Henry Shrady, which was going to press, had turned up in identical form in the Sunday supplement of the *World*. It seems unlikely that Theodore would have resold the article under Duffy's nose; perhaps it was all a misunderstanding. At any rate, he continued to write for *Ainslee's*.

One of his worst sins was overshooting space limitations. J. C. Brill at *Munsey's* wrote him that a five-thousand-word article he submitted must be cut to three thousand, and an editor of *The Cosmopolitan* told him, "We would also like permission to materially change or rewrite and condense the manuscript." Some of his freshest pieces appeared in *Ainslee's*, where his friend Duffy seems to have given him his head. Duffy was one of the first of his contemporaries to recognize that Theodore was destined for something better than special writing.

There were some damaging complaints about factual errors from sharp-eyed readers. One claimed that the route Theodore had followed on his trolley trip from New York to Boston was geographically impossible. Another said an article on the Winchester Arms Company for *The Cosmopolitan* contained "matter copied bodily without credit from the catalogue" of the firm.

The pressure Dreiser was working under partially explained the lapses. In the case of the Winchester article, he had visited the factory. It could even be said that he was meeting wartime demand—the Spanish-American War had begun in April 1898. A blast of frenetic patriotism, fanned by William Randolph Hearst's *Journal*, swept the land. Joining the rush to the colors were reporters and artists like David Graham Phillips, Frank Norris, Richard Harding Davis, Stephen Crane, and Frederic Remington, who signed up as correspondents or combat illustrators and shipped out for Tampa, Florida, the staging area for the upcoming invasion of Cuba. Theodore did not join them, for reasons unknown. Perhaps he believed his health was not sufficiently robust; nor did he share the urge to prove himself and the valor of the Anglo-Saxon "race." Yet he did share the patriotic sentiment, and regarded the invasion of Cuba as aiding an "oppressed" people. He joined the chorus with a war poem that appeared in several newspapers and was later collected in an anthology of patriotic verse. Called "Exordium," it begins:

> *Right with naked hands hath beaten*
> *At the haughty gates of crime;*
> *She hath for their freedom battled*
> *With all nations, through all time;*
> *She has marched through snows of Winter*
> *With her blood-stained feet—sublime.*

In contrast to the dozen or so war songs Paul wrote, including one with the memorable title, "Your God Comes First, Your Country Next, and Then Your Mother Dear," Theodore's contribution to the home front morale consisted of "Exordium" and four articles he wrote in the span of a month on wartime subjects—carrier pigeons, a shipyard where battleships were built, a cartridge factory in Bridgeport, and the Winchester Arms Company. His attitude toward the fray in these pieces was more philosophical than patriotic. For example, in the article on the Winchester company, he reports that he left the plant thinking that the deadly weapons made inside were the enemy of war, because they make it "so swift and decisive, that after a while there may be no longer need of war."

The issue of expansionism came to a head in the Senate debate on the peace treaty with Spain, signed at the end of 1898, annexing the Philippines. His hero, Bryan, while favoring ratification, thought the United States should free the conquered territories. In 1900 the Great Commoner ran for president as an anti-imperialist, appealing to a small but growing peace movement in the country that enlisted such writers and intellectuals as Howells, Mark Twain, and William James. Theodore apparently didn't share those sentiments.

When he interviewed former House Speaker Thomas B. Reed at his home in Maine, in September 1898, Dreiser managed an off-the-record gibe that did not appear in his article but which he reported to Jug. Reed, whom he thought resembled Paul physically and in his clownishness, had grown disillusioned with the imperialist sentiments of the Republican party and resigned as speaker. When they talked about the war, Reed said, "Think of all the hundreds of men who lost their lives in the recent war." Theodore replied, "Oh, but think of the thousands and thousands who have lost their opinions," a reference to Reed's desertion of his party because of its support of the war. Theodore explained to Jug, "This was a direct shot at his conservatism." Imperialism was a young man's game—espoused by political comers like Roosevelt and Senators Henry Cabot Lodge and Albert J. Beveridge, and Theodore cast Reed as an old fogey.

One young man who had lost his life was the artist Louis Sonntag, Jr., who had done covers for *Ev'ry Month*. While in Cuba drawing pictures of ships for Hearst, Sonntag had contracted malaria, as did so many of the Boys of '98, and died. The tragedy reminded Theodore of the fragility of youthful dreams. In memory of his friend, who had introduced him to New York's artistic scene, he composed a poem that was published by several newspapers. Called "Of One Who Dreamed," it was crude in language but heartfelt:

> *Lord! one whose dreams were numerous has gone,*
> *Who living loved and toiled and blessed each dawn.*
>
> . . . .
>
> *Lord in thy law some good must balance pain*
> *Else were this all too much—a struggle vain.*

23 / *I'll Have You*
No Matter What

> I lived in my love for you and my letters. . . . I was cursed, I
> thought because my imaginings could not be made real. . . .
> I dwell in my imagination and you who came into my life
> were admitted to it.
>
> —Dreiser to Sara O. White (1896)

Dreiser sometimes feared he was engaged in a vain struggle. All his work now, article after article, was consecrated to becoming a success so he and Jug could marry—yet that goal seemed to recede before him.

Their formal engagement had stretched into two years, and they had had an "understanding" since he lived in St. Louis, four years ago. Yet since he had quit the *Republic* they had met only twice. In the intervening months he made love by post to a fantasy Jug, building "silvery castles" about her, he wrote. His objective was "a little quarter of our own with you and pretty furniture in it to make it lovely. I want money to buy you rich dresses and soft luxurious lingerie and best of all I want you with me in a warm voluptuous embrace for nights and nights unending." He longed for the time when

> *Your little shoes and my big boots*
> *Are under the bed together.*

His ardent sentiments disconcerted the small-town Methodist in Jug. She complained frequently that he was being indiscreet, at one point warning him that someone at the post office was steaming open their letters. Theodore refused to bowdlerize, complaining, "I hate to be careful. It's like being made to mind."

Years later, Jug had her way retroactively. To Dreiser's discomfiture, she had kept his courtship letters, written from 1896 through 1898. She—or someone else—blacked out sentences and destroyed entire pages. There is little question that the main purpose was to remove erotic passages. He might have replied that if his sexual feelings had exceeded the bounds of decorum, he couldn't help himself. As he wrote in one of those letters, "Nature . . . has given me a cross of passion."

• • •

After Theodore visited her in spring of 1896, their first meeting in twenty-one months, parting was such a painful wrench that it left him in a state of "almost fainting misery." During that visit she had reciprocated his physical passion up to a point. "What a lover you are. You are Sapphic in your fire," Dreiser exulted. In June he sent her a ring. Perhaps at their last meeting Jug had let him go "too far" on the strength of his promises and felt compromised, though he reminds her that it wasn't entirely his fault: "You abetted me with love and sentiment."

But Theodore had not let their lovemaking get out of hand. As he told her later, there were times when she had been "helpless" and would have "succumbed" if he had persisted in his "tender urging." But sex without marriage would have been empty. "I want you—and not your physical virtue . . . the other without you could only have brought me misery." Unspoken was his realistic but almost neurotic fear that she would become pregnant—or even feign pregnancy.

After that visit, Jug pressed him to set a date. Theodore, preoccupied with making *Ev'ry Month* a success, put her off. This led to a crisis in their relationship in the summer of 1896. Jug played a desperate game, flaunting her independence, hinting that others found her attractive, and finally, not writing him.

By mid-August she had reduced the flow of her letters to a trickle. He suspected that she had found someone else. When Jug went to Colorado to visit her brother he warned her, "Everything in such soft and languorous climate appeals to you. . . . In such a time there might come another, and then where would be I." Worrying about her inconstancy had made him "nervous and disquieted," he complained. "You have too much of my heart." He was experiencing for the first time the torment of being the lover but not the loved. It was agony.

Jug seems to have sensed his vulnerability and twisted the knife, hinting of flirtations, that she had been "reckless." He begged her to tell him if she had changed, but clung to the last shreds of self-respect: "I do not want you if you have been, as you say, reckless." Alluding to the necessity of earning enough money to support her, he moaned, "It is one of the misfortunes that overtake ambitious young men who have not inherited a competence. I left you that I might eventually draw you inseparably to me and it would be but another fine irony of my fate if my venture should prove my loss of you."

Soon afterward Jug relented, and in Dreiser's letter of September 11 he mentions rereading her last letter "so many times that I almost know it by heart." He praised her "siren hair" and asserted, "When your hair is down about your forehead and ears you always look so much just like one of Rossetti's maidens," though she is not meek and sorrowful like them. He couldn't live with a girl like that and is "awful glad to have a sweetheart who is gay and aggressive." Recovering his self-respect, Theodore can write of the possibility of her meeting other men. She was free to do so, so long as she did not "accept introductions where a love match is hoped for."

At Christmas he begged Jug to send him a glove and one of her slippers instead of a present. While passing the *Century* Magazine building (a citadel he yearned to penetrate) in Union Square, he had a fantasy of Jug standing nude on a marble pedestal, and he mentally arranged her in various "classic attitudes." She is both angel and repentant Magdalen, saint and sinner. Her face had a "sacred modesty," a "saintlike beauty," but she was also his "divinely formed madonna," his "little red-halo-ed Venus." Those reveries were tinctured by his earliest erotic stirrings in Warsaw, when he was drawn to sensuous blond earthy girls like Cad Tuttle and to ethereal, saintly maidens like Myrtle Weimar. In the idea of Jug, the sensual and the saintly had coalesced.

It was an unstable compound. At times Dreiser had an urge to desecrate her purity. He spoke of wanting "to despoil your saintlike beauty. Like a bouquet of thornless roses you tempt me to crush you to withering in my arms. . . . Can you have such as me?"

He all but confessed that his fantasies led to autoerotic activity. He described himself lying in bed late one morning with only his pillow to embrace, thinking of her. And then "the imagination becomes all powerful and I grasp with a tremor of passion at nothing and bury my face in my pillow with despair." He sought to implicate her in his fantasies. From the rear window of his hall bedroom at 232 West Fifteenth Street, he watched women in the apartment across the courtyard undressing. They reminded him of the risqué dances on the Midway at the Chicago World's Fair. If Jug were with him, he would draw the curtains and "my own girl would engage me with her beauty as no one else can—ever has before."

The real Jug behind the veils of erotic illusion continued to press him on the question of when his big boots and her little shoes would end up under the bed. Theodore was held back by his procrastinating nature and his absorption in becoming a success.

He was also gun-shy. Whenever Jug tried to get him to talk about the actual ceremony, Dreiser became a quivering wreck. Marriage "seems like wandering into a state absolutely blind"; he wished there were "houses already furnished for lovers and a book to buy which would tell husband and wife just what to do." The thought of standing up before dozens of Arch White's friends and neighbors in a Methodist church in Montgomery City struck terror in his heart. Public displays of affection were repugnant to him; people who did it were "like animals." As a way out of his anticipated misery, he lobbied for an elopement, offering to pay her way to New York if she would agree. He also proposed a kind of trial marriage.

In June he visited her, and when they parted, his agony at the prospect of another separation was greater than it had been two years before. He had gone to the station, he told her, in a catatonic state. As the train bore him away from her, he wrote a poem to her. Then: "As the hurrying engine sped onward marking each new village with a long cry of steam and each farther main road with four lonely shrieks, I sped ever backward through the far night to my Jug. . . . "

In April he had promised they would be married in September. In August he swore he would come for her within "the next forty days." Neither pledge was honored. In Dreiser's autobiographical novel, *The "Genius,"* Angela Blue, the heroine, is subjected to similar delays and becomes ill. Her sister—the fictional counterpart of Rose White—finally scolds him for worrying about amassing sufficient money to provide Angela with luxuries.

He also wrote in *The "Genius,"* and said as much to his biographer Dorothy Dudley, that he had had affairs with other women during the long engagement. If Theodore did dally, he remained true to the ideal Jug. "You have my every passionate physical thought," he swore, "and more I cannot give. If I shared the latter with others in this state of extreme love for you, you would be wronged, but I do not. . . . When I take you in my arms as my own you can know for certain that since my lips first touched yours they have never touched another in either affection [remainder of sentence expurgated]."

Those words were written in 1897, and throughout 1898 his protestations of love grew. He longed for their wedding night, "when nothing shall be withheld from me. . . . We will unite, close, final, perfect—mingle our very beings—sigh exhausted and repaid."

On a riverboat to Buffalo, where he was going to gather material for an article, Dreiser watched a couple enter their cabin and then eavesdropped on their "sighs and light laughter," wishing that Jug were there and that they could go to their own cabin. In August he assured her, "I'll have you no matter what."

October came, and still they weren't married. The letters Jug preserved break off in September. But up to that point he is a young man eagerly anticipating the physical bliss they had so long denied themselves, acutely conscious of time slipping by: "It seems as if something dinned into my aching ears all the time the cry 'Losing time, losing time.' . . . "

• • •

Perhaps because she too was panicked by the rush of time (she was nearly thirty; he was twenty-seven), she agreed to an elopement. They were married on neutral ground, in Washington, D.C., on December 28, 1898. Rose, and perhaps her brother Richard Drace White, were the only others present; it was probably an informal wedding in a Methodist minister's study. For Jug it was the culmination of four years of waiting, living at home like a spinster (she had given up teaching). For Theodore, it was the actualization of a dream that had sustained him during those years on the road, in lonely hall bedrooms and boardinghouses in Cleveland and Pittsburgh and New York.

By the description in The "Genius," marriage tapped reserves of thwarted sexual passion in Jug. They were both ardent but inexperienced. When he was in his sixties, Dreiser confessed to his niece Vera, "It is true that my first marriage was not as happy as it should have been. I was not the most successful sexually of young men when I married Jug." And what woman could live up to his dream Jug? Reality tarnishes, and perhaps the discoloration began to set in during the honeymoon. There is a hint of that in Theodore's assertion to Dorothy Dudley that the only novel by William Dean Howells he ever liked was Their Wedding Journey, an odd choice even at a time when Dreiser had sternly repressed his earlier admiration of the man. The book was, after all, Howells's first novel, a charming but slight account of a young couple's honeymoon trip. Dreiser, however, extolled it: "not a sentimental passage in it, quarrels from beginning to end, just the way it would be" (an inaccurate description, incidentally; perhaps Dreiser was confusing it with Howells's A Modern Instance, which is about a divorce).

But Dreiser's best-known verdict on his marriage was his claim at the end of Newspaper Days that he had wed Jug when "the first flare of love had thinned down to the pale flame of duty." In view of his love letters to her, to say he married her out of duty is stretching matters. True, he had doubts; true, too, he had private reservations about the vows he took, particularly the one that went "forsaking all others." But his later protestation that if convention had not stopped them and they had had sexual relations before marriage, he would not have been trapped, was history soured by disillusionment. The truth was that Theodore's own desires trapped him, and his need for Sara was strong and more than just physical. The words he wrote in Sister Carrie, in a passage about Hurstwood's love letters that was cut from the published book, were a more apt description of Dreiser's state of mind at the time: "Under the influence of a contagion as subtle, expansive and pervasive as love, the mind is above the normal in its power of imagination. . . . Things said or written under such circumstances should have no more significance attached to them than is attached to a ripple of laughter or a burst of song. . . . "

24 / Summer on the Maumee

> Married! Married! The words were as the notes of a tolled bell.
> —Dreiser, "Rella" (1929)

They took an apartment at 6 West 102nd Street, in a new five-story building. The Upper West Side was a predominantly middle-class area, just emerging from the pioneer stage. New brick and brownstone row houses and new apartments, like the Dakota (an elegant castle in the urban Badlands when it was built in 1884), along Central Park West (which was fashionable), were mingled with vacant lots, shanties, and even a few farmhouses. The neighborhood was an enclave of upward strivers and "respectable" workingmen and their families. Six-room flats could be rented for $35 a month. A new place like the one Theodore and Jug moved into had the latest conveniences: a dumbwaiter in which garbage was lowered to the basement, a speaking tube connected with the front door, a call bell for the janitor, steam heat, and hot and cold running water.

Save for Sylvia, who was keeping company with a Japanese photographer named Hidi Kishima, there were no other sisters or brothers around to welcome Jug into the family. The Dreiser clan had entered another of its centrifugal phases. A Christmas reunion in 1896, at which Paul and Theodore passed out the gifts and Brennan passed out from overeating, had been the last major family gathering. But scattered as they were (and as fractious as ever), they were still bound by Sarah's invisible hooks of steel. Paul, the eldest, who most resembled her physically, had assumed Sarah's role to a degree. He had several needy cases to take charge of. The ethereal Theresa had married her sweetheart, the scenery painter Ed Davis. It was a real love match, but Davis's mother resented her new daughter-in-law and made life hell for her. Theresa told Theodore she dreamed that her mother-in-law was dead—a portent she took seriously, being a Dreiser. The premonition was a double-edged sword. Mrs. Davis did die. But in October 1897, while wheeling her bicycle across the tracks of the Lake Shore and Michigan Southern Railroad in Chicago, Tres was struck by a train.

Death was instantaneous, Paul wrote his friend Mary South. He had come to the city on business and ended up burying his sister—or rather, temporarily placing her body in a mausoleum until he could take it to Rochester, New York, where, having no say in the matter, Tres was laid to rest beside her mother-in-law. "Poor Theresa," Sylvia wrote in what could be an epitaph. "Her life was not a sunshiny one."

Another sister who had lived through heavy weather was Emma, but in her case the clouds had temporarily lifted. Three years after leaving Hopkins, she married John Nelson, whose occupation is unknown but who had trouble finding employment in it, whatever it was. They lived in Bayonne for a time, and Emma was obliged to take in boarders. In a letter to Theodore, she portrayed herself as having been wronged by Mame and cut off from Paul's largesse. Mame "talked about us all, even you," and Paul said he "had no use for me as I only rooked him for money but that he would do anything for Mame. I don't care but I will never write him or see him again."

Mame and Brennan were looking after Father Dreiser and little Carl, who was no longer little and who had been shunted around from one sister to another, a leftover stray from Sarah's time. In 1898, on a visit to Chicago, Paul reported to Theodore that he found Carl "in rags" and had to provide money so the boy could go to school. Carl was apparently a troubled boy. He must have suspected that his position in the family was an anomalous one; probably he knew by now that Sylvia, his real mother, had abandoned him. (A few years later, barely out of his teens, he committed suicide.)

On the same trip in which he found Carl in a state of neglect, Paul also discovered a seriously ill Claire. Not long after taking a tuberculosis cure, she had hemorrhaged, and Paul gave her the money she needed to return to the sanatorium. The "same tale of woe—wow—" he told his brother. Claire dreaded a "slow, miserable" death from consumption, she wrote Theodore from Arizona. She was not afraid of dying, but prayed that the end would come quickly.

• • •

Such was the family Jug had married into. Although in 1899 she may not have met any of her new brothers and sisters, she must have gained enough of a general idea from Theodore to sense the glaring contrast with the White clan. Jug's brothers and sisters were now grown and off pursuing their lives, but theirs was the normal moving-on of small-town young people who have been sheltered in the pod until ready. Theodore's family, by contrast, had been blown apart. John Paul Dreiser, battered by the industrial storms, was now a beached hulk, while Arch White, though not wealthy, was a solid citizen.

Like most women of her time, Jug had oriented her entire life around the goal of being a good wife. She was an excellent cook (her biscuits became famous among Theodore's friends), sewed her own clothes, and looked after her husband's wardrobe assiduously, darning his socks and laying out his underwear. Theodore soon became happily uxorious. She helped him with his writing, correcting his grammar and spelling and making fair copies of manuscripts. Sometimes, in the middle of an article, he would tire, but rather than stop, he would dictate passages to her and take up the pencil again when he was rested.

And so they passed the winter, Jug making the apartment into a home and Theodore writing articles. It may well be that his failure to tell others about the marriage resulted in some awkward moments when his city friends called and were surprised to find a wife installed. Did Theodore's reticence betray a lack of pride in Sara, as he later wrote in *The "Genius"*?

By June 1899 he had saved enough money to take up Arthur Henry's long-standing invitation to visit him and Maude at their House of Four Pillars, an old, rambling affair. Located in the village of Maumee, it had fourteen airy rooms that provided cool refuges from the baking Ohio sun. The Greek revival pillars and veranda looked out on an apron of grassy lawn sloping down to the unpretentious, meandering river, beside which ran an abandoned barge canal with overgrown towpaths, moss-laden rocks, and rusting gears. Henry had fixed up a study in the basement, which had wood-paneled walls, a fireplace, a bearskin rug, and a rocking chair for Theodore with wide arms that could serve as a writing desk. His plan was that they would work side by side.

Theodore had reached a pleasant upland meadow in his career, where he could pause and take satisfaction at how far he had climbed. In only two years he had become a successful specials writer, as he had predicted to Emma Rector he would. Concrete recognition had recently come in the form of membership in the Indiana Club and a listing in the first edition of *Who's Who in America*: "Dreiser, Theodore, journalist-author . . . connected with daily papers, Chicago, St. Louis, Pittsburgh, 1891–5; editor Every Month [sic], musical magazine, 1895–7; then in sp'l work for Cosmopolitan magazine, contributes prose and verse to various periodicals. Author, Studies of Contemporary Celebrities, Poems. Residence, 6 W. 102nd St. New York."

The entry was accurate save for the "author" credits: neither of the books listed had been published. *Studies of Contemporary Celebrities* was to have been a collection of interviews from *Success* and other magazines. A Cincinnati house had offered him an advance of $500, but the firm went bankrupt.

Although he had accumulated enough poems to make a slim volume, no publisher had taken them. Nevertheless, he had told an interviewer from McClure's Syndicate that William Dean Howells had "expressed a hearty liking" for them and that the Dodd, Mead Company "had the book in hand." There is no evidence that Howells ever praised Theodore's verse publicly or privately. Whatever Howells's verdict, Theodore was in need of a sponsor for his verse.

The obvious person was Edmund Clarence Stedman, who was a patron to young poets as William Dean Howells was to fledgling novelists. One might well suspect that Theodore first sought to smooth his path to the great man with a little flattery, for in the March 1899 issue of *Munsey's* appeared an idolatrous article entitled "Edmund Clarence Stedman at Home" by Theodore Dreiser. It contains a purported description of the poet's Lawrence Park abode—a suburban artists' enclave about which Dreiser had written one of his first magazine pieces—as well as quotations of his verse and a bit of biographical data. But there is no interview with Stedman, though by a verbal *trompe l'oeil* the reader almost believes that one took place.

What is interesting about the piece is that a substantial section of it is plagiarized—doubly plagiarized, one could say. At first remove it draws on an article Theodore wrote for *The New York Times Illustrated Magazine* the year before; that article—and, to a greater degree, the one in *Munsey's*—borrowed almost verbatim from one by Ann Bowman Dodd in *The Critic* in 1885. True, Theodore does say that the writer who comes on Stedman "at this late day . . . must be content . . . to leave the account of the poet's long active life as it has been written down by other pens." But no credit is given to Dodd. What is more, the Stedman house Dodd described was in New York City, not in Lawrence Park.

Apparently, though, Theodore was eager to put his praises of the Wall Street versifier on the record, and the reason for his eagerness may well have been that he hoped Stedman would give his collection of poems a boost with a publisher. In April he wrote the bard of Lawrence Park to ask permission to submit some poems; the reply was favorable. Months passed, however, before the verdict came down. On June 9 Ella Boult, a secretary, wrote Theodore that while Stedman found his "characteristic and best mood the contemplative, exemplified in such pieces as 'Compensation,'" he did not think the poems sufficiently "above the average," and "it is impossible for verse to succeed in book form unless it is distinctly above the average." Also, Theodore's work was too "lacking in dramatic or lyric quality" to appeal to the present generation.

To this polite dismissal, Theodore replied arrogantly that he did not need to be told his poetry was unlikely to sell. "A critically admired volume stands more as an exponent of a man's mental calibre than as a source of revenue or general fame." His bravado showed he was developing a prickly literary ego.

Philosophy and emotion wrestled in Dreiser's poetry. In some the influence of Spencerian doctrine was apparent. When in "Bondage" he wrote of the "ceaseless drag of all desire," he meant desire as Spencer did, as the prime mover within each individual:

> And this thing hunger—ceaseless, yearning pain—
> Its slave you are. Denying is so vain.

Some one hath touched you saying: "Feel desire."
His will you do—you run, you run, aspire!

Much of his poetry reflected the sensibility of a romantically gloomy young man. The language was often halting and clumsy, though heavy with sincerity. Death and the passage of time were his favorite subjects. In "Resignation," for example, Dreiser wrote of kissing the "cool, damp soil/The door, I hope, to peace, to God." We have a "few bright days, a few brief years . . . and lo, the end appears." Then nature takes us, "As tho' it never yet had been."

Although Stedman's letter did not shake Theodore's belief in his poetic talent, the rebuff came at a timely moment, turning him to other forms of expression. It was Arthur Henry who gave him the needed push that summer at the House of Four Pillars. His temperament was the catalyst, and his chipper optimism and quixotic bohemianism counteracted Theodore's gloominess and inclination to drift.

Henry wanted to write a novel but was reluctant to undertake it unless his friend was working on one too, at his side. Theodore also had an idea for a novel but lacked confidence in it. So Henry nagged him to try some short stories as finger exercises. Sitting in his wide-armed rocking chair in the basement of the big house, Theodore made his first attempt: "It was a hot day in August. The parching rays of a summer sun had faded the once sappy green leaves of the trees to a dull and dusty hue."

After each paragraph, he considered giving it up, he later told H. L. Mencken; he thought it "asinine." But Henry praised his efforts and kept him at it until he finished.

As the story—called "McEwen of the Shining Slave Makers"—opens, McEwen is sitting on a park bench in the heart of a large city, a green island of calm in the tossing urban sea. Suddenly, he is transformed into an ant, forced to survive in the Darwinian world of nature. He becomes embroiled in a great battle between his tribe, the *Sanguineae* (a species of black ant; the naturalistic details of the story were drawn from John Lubbock's *Ants, Bees and Wasps*), and a marauding party of red ants. Mortally wounded, McEwen is on the verge of death when he is suddenly restored to human form. He gazes at the ant battle on the ground, a ferocious, no-quarter contest, and has a vision of life as "strange passions, moods, and necessities . . . worlds within worlds, all apparently full of necessity, contention, binding emotions and unities."

In other words, the "God-damned stinking, treacherous game" that Maxwell had said it was in the newsroom of the *Globe* in Chicago; that it was in New York City in 1894. Like McEwen, Theodore had been thrown in it to live or die. But he did not see it entirely in Darwinian terms. The vision of a bloody struggle was tempered by a Tolstoyan recognition of humane values— "binding emotions and unities." McEwen experiences cruelty, but he also acts altruistically, risking his life for his comrade, Erni, and experiences kindness from members of his own tribe. And the story has a vision of nature within the city: two separate yet indivisible spheres, "worlds within worlds," each a metaphor of the other.

Theodore wrote four more stories that summer. In the second he shifted from allegory to realism, drawing upon his own family experiences. Entitled "Old Rogaum and His Theresa," it tells of the daughter of a German butcher in Greenwich Village who seeks to escape from her stern Old World father, a carbon copy of John Paul Dreiser. Like Theodore in Chicago, Theresa Rogaum is drawn to the street, "with its stars, the street lamps, the cars, the tinkle and laughter of eternal life." She walks out with a young man from the neighborhood, a reputed "masher," as Sylvia and Emma had done in Warsaw. Old Rogaum beats and berates her and finally locks her out—as old Paul threatened to do to Sylvia and Emma.

Later, the butcher discovers the body of a young girl on his doorstep, and for a heart-stopping moment thinks it is his Theresa. But she turns out to be a young prostitute who has committed suicide. Rogaum has had a glimpse of what Theresa might become if he continued to lock her out (a policeman tells him that the dead girl's father had done the same). And so when his daughter returns—she had been with her boyfriend—he forgives her. The conflict between youthful desire and paternal authority is dramatized, and Rogaum's tyranny is considered monstrous while his daughter's innocent longing for love is natural. Yet Rogaum loves his daughter, as Theodore was coming to see that old Paul had loved Emma and Sylvia.

The next story, "Nigger Jeff," drew on the lynching of the young black man who raped two women that Dreiser reported for the St. Louis *Republic*. The details follow the newspaper account closely, although to make the rapist more sympathetic, he is not a psychotic, as his real-life counterpart evidently was, but a victim too, in a way. A reporter who believes life's rewards and punishments are justly meted out watches as the mob besieges the jail where the suspect is being held, outwits the law-abiding sheriff, and carries off the trembling, pleading prisoner. The reporter passively records the lynching, but the ground opens up beneath him: his Sunday school morality has crumbled. He visits the cabin where the corpse is laid out (noting that the "bar of cool moonlight lay just across the face and the breast," as he had done in his article); the mother is weeping in the corner, just as the real-life mother had been. He comprehends that life is a muddle of beauty and pain. As he leaves, the sound of the mother's weeping in his ears, the reporter sorts out the elements of the scene, its color and pathos, "with the cruel instinct of the budding artist that he already was." He suddenly understands that "it was not so much the business of the writer to indict as to interpret." It was not his function to condemn the rape or the lynching but to *show* what happened, to convey his own emotional interpretation of the events, his sympathy with the victims of justice, rather than the journalistic facts.

The story transcends social considerations to focus on the tragic *mise-en-scène*—the dead boy, his face lit momentarily by the cold bar of moonlight, and the Pietà-esque figure of the mother. They stand for pity and mercy, qualities absent from justice, legal or otherwise. As he leaves, the reporter silently vows, "I'll get it all in! I'll get it all in!"

Another story Dreiser wrote that summer, called "The World and the Bubble," a fantasy, has been lost, but a hint of the idea that may have animated it can be found in "The Bubble of Success," an unpublished essay. In it he declares that "deluded selfishness" is the source of all progress. Youths are impelled by illusions of a more glamorous life, but when they achieve their goal, they are disillusioned. Success seen from the outside is a pretty bubble, but once one is inside, it is not what it seemed or what the world said it was. Human progress is a great bubble chase: "The planner of this curious existence has set before men's eyes a rainbow and at its end a misty pot of gold beyond the distant hillside in order that all humanity may run on and on, achieving, accomplishing but never enjoying." (About the same time, Dreiser described his sole antidote to disenchantment: "I think sometimes that nature is the only thing in life that has not changed for me, the one thing that did not begin as an illusion and conclude as a fraud.")

The fifth story was a fantasy called "When the Old Century Was New," an attempt to write something appropriate for the approaching debut of the twentieth century. It was a parody of the popular historical romances of the time, with their detailed allusions to quaint dress and manners. His conceit was to show New Year's Day in New York in 1800. Walton, the central figure, goes about his daily rounds, happily discussing marriage with his fiancée and encountering historical figures such as John Adams and Thomas Jefferson. But Dreiser injects in the story a sense of foreboding, of dark clouds gathering on the horizon. Walton is oblivious to foreshadowings of problems that will flare up at the century's end—primarily industrialism and the widening gap between rich and poor. Walton uncomprehendingly notes "the aristocracy, gentry and common rabble forming in separate groups." A ground base of social realism grows increasingly insistent under the dominant romantic theme, and the story closes with a reference to Walton's blindness. He cannot see "The crush and stress and wretchedness fast treading this path of loveliness."

• • •

That summer on the Maumee was an immensely important breakthrough for Dreiser: half-formed moods and thoughts coalesced in fictional form—his vision of the city as urban nature, for example; his sense of the artist's duty to

see life whole and record it unjudgmentally; the discovery of his family, particularly his sisters and father, as a subject for fiction; the rejection of romanticism
for realism. And he also revealed prophetic intuition of the dark underside of
progress: *pace* Spencer, society was not necessarily turning out for the best. Life
was the unending pursuit of illusion, a rainbow chase. When he returned to
New York, he would no longer be content just to write articles and lugubrious
poems.

While he was in Ohio, Theodore had received a letter from *Demorest's* requesting "something particularly striking and significant for a leading article
for November." The article he wrote would be different from anything he had
previously done and take him another step in his pursuit of the bubble of literary fame.

25 / Curious Shifts
of the Free-lance

> Genius struggles up. Talent often lingers and wears itself out
> in journalism unheard of.
> —Dreiser, "The Literary Shower" (1896)

Dreiser returned to New York that September poorer but with five short stories
in his trunk. Henry, who had more confidence in their salability than he did,
urged him to send "McEwen of the Shining Slave Makers" to the august *Century*.

The *Century* submission was a long shot, and Theodore needed to restore
his savings after a summer of idleness. So it was back to the life of magazine
journalism for him, and for Arthur Henry too. They formed a literary partnership, collaborating on articles and sharing the fees fifty-fifty. Their objective
was to make enough money to enable them to work on their novels. During
their extended stay that summer, the Dreisers had literally eaten the Henrys
out of house and home. Theodore had lent Arthur two hundred dollars; Henry
signed over to his friend a half interest in the second-mortgaged house, meaning
that Theodore took over the mortgage payments. The three of them returned
to New York, leaving Maude to hold the bag, as she later put it bitterly.

Henry moved in with Theodore and Sara at the flat on West 102nd Street,
and, working together and separately, they lined up assignments from various
editors and divided them. Each had certain areas of expertise: Henry, for example, specialized in municipal government, and Theodore fancied himself an
authority on education and natural sciences. But they worked on any ideas they
could sell, and collaborated interchangeably on the research and writing. Arthur
was the better editor of the two, and he polished Theodore's copy; the latter
was a far more prolific writer. Henry might do all the research and Theodore the
writing, or vice versa. Dreiser made periodic trips to the Library of Congress
in Washington, where he copied reports by trade associations. Sometimes they

cut several articles out of a bolt of research. If one got stuck midway, the other would tackle the conclusion.

Each would also act as the other's agent. This practice occasionally caused mixups. Once Theodore sold Woodward at *Pearson's* an article on peach growing that had been rejected by *Munsey's*. Then, a week or so later, Henry strolled into *Pearson's* editorial chambers. When Woodward told him he was ravenous for material, Henry hurried home and dug out the peach article. Woodward recognized it as Theodore's idea, and Henry explained (he wrote his partner, who was summering in Missouri) "that some time ago you and I had investigated the subject of American Food products and finding that it was a very important and prolific field had divided it up between us."

Sharing out of a common pot was a good idea, since their money dribbled in so irregularly that one — usually Henry — might be insolvent while the other was flush. But it also kept their joint finances in a constant muddle, and neither was businessman enough to straighten them out. An idea of their casual book-keeping emerges in a letter Henry wrote to his partner: "You owe me $26.19 out of the fruit article. Had you got the check for the song article, you would have owed me one half of that, plus the $29.20. Sorry you didn't get the song article check. If you can spare it send me $70.19 out of the fruit article and keep all the money for the song article when it comes."

The *ménage* on West 102nd Street was, platonically, *à trois*. As Henry characterized their relationship, "up to a certain point" they "had share and share alike" in Jug. He admired Jug's beauty — her "girlish figure and glorious mass of red hair," as he wrote once — and regarded her as "a complex combination of child and woman, a being of affectionate impulses and stubborn fidelity, devoted to the comfort of her husband and managing in some mysterious fashion to reconcile her traditional beliefs with his unorthodox thoughts and ways." Once, when Theodore and Jug were sojourning in Danville, he wrote, "I too wish with all my heart that we could be constantly together, walking, talking and writing of what seems great and worthy to us. I am not able to get either inspiration or comfort from others I meet. . . . The fact is that you are the only inhabitant of the same world with me." And in his letters Theodore spoke with equal affection. It was Henry, and Henry alone, who encouraged him in the idea that he could write something "great and worthy."

Theodore continued to procrastinate, but his feet were on the path leading to *Sister Carrie*. Some of his articles reveal a subconscious drift, and hint at themes that he later developed in full measure. One of those was the "particularly striking and significant" lead article for the November 1899 issue of *Demorest's*. A significant departure from Theodore's hackwork, it was called "Curious Shifts of the Poor" and represented his first venture into New York local-color realism, in which descriptions of life in the Bowery were de rigueur. In it he depicts a line of ragged, shambling men at a soup kitchen run by the

Sisters of Mercy Convent near Emma's old place on West Fifteenth Street. He describes the way the snow piled up, unheeded, on "the old hats and peaked shoulders" of the men, how they watch the closed door "as dumb brutes look, as dogs paw and whine and study the knob."

Other haunts of the homeless are described in "Curious Shifts": Madison Square when theatergoers are heading home and the fire signs blaze and a man known as the Captain collects money for derelicts; the breadline at Fleischmann's Vienna Model Bakery at Tenth Street and Broadway. The story showed that Theodore was compelled to write something at once more personal and more objectively truthful than his usual magazine articles. With it he announced himself a follower of the realists—Stephen Crane, Hamlin Garland, and William Dean Howells. Indeed, Crane had described similar scenes in a sketch called "The Men in the Storm." Howells had also visited the breadline at Fleischmann's Bakery and written a self-conscious little essay about it. He was so entangled in the irony of himself observing the hungry bums, a plump, benevolent-looking man with a white mustache, bundled up in a warm fur coat, that he did not even claim to have been present, saying he had been given the account by a friend, who had been urged to go to the Bowery by "young newspaper men trying to make literature out of life and smuggle it into print under the guard of unwary editors, and young authors eager to get life into their literature."

In "Curious Shifts of the Poor," Theodore mentions the appearance of a carriage that could have been Howells's. One of the men in line at a flophouse sees it and jeers, "Look at the bloke ridin'," and another sneers, "He ain't so cold." " 'Eh! Eh! Eh!' yelled another, the carriage having long since passed out of hearing." While Crane and Dreiser joined the men in the storm, William Dean Howells watched from inside his carriage.

Part Three

. . .

SISTER CARRIE

26 / She Went to the City

She went to the city, 'twas all they would say,
She went to the city, far, far away . . .
She grew kind o' restless and wanted to go,
Said she'd be back in a few weeks or so,
She went to the city with a tear in her eye, but she never
returned.

—Paul Dresser (1904)

In late September 1899 (if not at Maumee) Theodore had sat down at the dining-room table and written in pencil on a half sheet of copy paper the title of a novel—"Sister Carrie." He told Dorothy Dudley that his mind "was blank except for the name. I had no idea who or what she was to be. I have often thought there was something mystic about it, as if I were being used, like a medium."

To his friend H. L. Mencken, Dreiser later described the genesis of *Sister Carrie* somewhat differently. Arthur Henry, who had begun a novel called *A Princess of Arcady,* wanted company, and began to "ding-dong" his friend about writing one too. Finally, "I took a piece of yellow paper and to please him wrote down a title at random—*Sister Carrie*—and began." And so, it appears from the manuscript, he did. At the top of the first page are the words of the title, and the first paragraph provides the essential information like a good newspaper lead:

When Caroline Meeber boarded the afternoon train for Chicago her total outfit consisted of a small trunk, which was checked in the baggage car, a cheap imitation alligator skin satchel holding some minor details of the toilet, a small lunch in a paper bag and a yellow leather snap purse, containing her ticket, a scrap of paper with her sister's address in Van Buren Street, and four dollars in money. It was in August, 1889. She was eighteen years of age, bright, timid and full of the illusions of ignorance and youth.

Aside from minor editing, page one of the manuscript appears to be just as it flowed out in Theodore's tiny, penciled script, but it seems unlikely that the story popped into his head. Actually, he had been brooding over elements of it—the character of Hurstwood, for example—for some time. Richard Duffy recalled that before Dreiser started writing, he had prepared a "story backbone, showing his characters moving to an inevitable fate." The theme reminded Duffy of Thomas Hardy, "the master Dreiser recognized and venerated."

The two-word title was a mnemonic key that unlocked a private storehouse of memories. Theodore apparently forgot the "sister" part once he was under way, and it was Jug, serving as copy editor, who later inserted a phrase explaining that "Sister Carrie" was a "half-affectionate" nickname. The true origin of the title lay in family history. Theodore had a sister Carrie, who alone of his sisters always closed her letters to him:

I remain your
Sister Emma

The two words at the top of the half sheet of pale yellow copy paper were a private incantation, summoning up the story he intended to tell, the story of Emma absconding from Chicago with her lover, L. A. Hopkins. Knowing few details of Emma's 1883 flight from Sullivan, he was forced to invent, making Carrie a more universal figure, the country girl "venturing to reconnoitre the mysterious city. . . ."

The first chapter of *Sister Carrie* echoes the moralizing tone of popular, cautionary books with a pious passage about the fate of girls in the city: "Either she falls into saving hands and becomes better, or she rapidly assumes the cosmopolitan standard of virtue and becomes worse." But Theodore identifies the city itself, not an unscrupulous man, as the seducer, and in doing so he breaks the bonds of conventional morality. Metropolis has its "cunning wiles," and "The gleam of a thousand lights is often as effective, to all moral intents and purposes, as the persuasive light in a wooing and fascinating eye."

Carrie differs from the popular-novel heroines in other ways. On the first page, she is revealed to be suspiciously lacking in strong ties to Columbia City, Wisconsin, and sheds only a brief tear as "the threads which bound her so lightly to girlhood and home were irretrievably broken." Later, when the possibility of returning to her hometown arises, she cringes at the thought of the "dull round" of rural life, which seems infinitely inferior to the city.

The popular novelists' heroines clung to the past, the old democratic, religious, morally upright village. Theodore remembered no such place: in the four Indiana towns he had bounced among, the Dreisers had been poor or social outcasts.

In another departure from the sentimental conventions, the author shows Carrie allowing herself to be befriended by Charlie Drouet, the genial traveling salesman, "masher," and eventual despoiler of her virginity. Though she is on her guard, she does not send him packing as her more virtuous dime-novel sisters would have done. By the time the train pulls into Chicago, she has given him her address.

Carrie is the prototypical young woman of her times, alive to the promise of love and excitement. She was a girl Theodore encountered on a train in 1898 while traveling on a magazine assignment. As he described the scene to Jug, he had noticed her staring at him and "took advantage of her uncomfortable position to help her arrange her seat, and so began a talk, which lasted from 12:30 midnight to 5 A.M. . . . " The girl in the parlor car was "wholly untrained and quite of the shop girl order."

The chance meeting provided the inspiration for the scene on the Chicago-bound train in his novel. He put a bit of his younger, sartorially resplendent St. Louis self into the character of Drouet (rhymes with *roué*). Both he and the salesman were "mashers"—fops who hope to attract women by their finery. Then Theodore did a curious thing: he spliced in a passage, slightly paraphrased, from a story by George Ade, "The Fable of the Two Mandolin Players and the Willing Performer." The excerpt described the masher's parlor-car technique and was the first of several instances in which Dreiser interpolated documentary material—want ads, news stories, dialogue from plays, and the like—into his manuscript to give verisimilitude. He also used the real names of places, buildings, theaters, restaurants, and theatrical figures. In this case, however, Dreiser chose Ade's fiction for "documentation": he plagiarized. Could it be he feared that Jug, who was reading the script as he went along, would be jealous?

The name "Carrie," which he wrote automatically at the head of his manuscript, tapped his earliest sexual memories. One of the girls in Warsaw who had figured in his fantasies was named Carrie Tuttle—"Cad" for short. "Cad" is Drouet's pet name for Caroline Meeber. This tawny-maned grade-school temptress was one of the first objects of Theodore's awakening sexual desires.

Carrie Meeber also embodied the other side of his pubescent erotic fantasies: the ethereal, unattainable Myrtle Weimar. The kinship to Myrtle is visible in Carrie's most characteristic facial expression—a kind of sadness communicating unfulfilled desire. Her "mouth had the expression at times, in talking and in repose, of one who might be upon the verge of tears," and her eyes have shadows about them, which make her seem even more pathetic. Not that she was inwardly sad; it was simply an accident of nature. He had once described Jug as a "repentant Magdalen," whose eyes were "meek" and "sorrowful."

Carrie's first impressions of Chicago were drawn from Theodore's memories of his arrival there in 1884. In his first draft he had set the story in August of that year, but he had second thoughts and changed the year to 1889. This was necessary so that later scenes of Hurstwood's downfall could take place during the depression winter of 1893–1894. But at the beginning of the story, Carrie's "illusions of youth and ignorance" were his own in 1884.

Carrie's first job is at a shoe factory, operating a machine. Led to her work station by a surly foreman, she sees "a line of girls . . . sitting on a line of stools in front of a line of clacking machines," a scene Theodore drew from a visit to a factory in New Jersey that spring. (The repetitive image recalls Herman Melville's description of female workers in a New England paper mill: "rows of blank-looking girls . . . all blankly folding blank paper . . . " standing "like so many mares haltered to the rack.") The work is too hard; the shop is dirty; the workers are exploited; she is not strong enough. The other girls are friendly but common; all they talk about is their boyfriends. The male employees are louts who flirt with her. As she leaves, one of them calls out, "Say, Maggie, if you'll wait I'll walk with you." The allusion to Stephen Crane's Maggie (who works in a factory before becoming a prostitute) consigns Carrie to the same fate.

After losing her job when she becomes ill, Carrie halfheartedly begins the demoralizing process of hunting for another one and by chance meets the tempter, Drouet, who takes her to a restaurant. Forlorn and cold, Carrie basks before the cheery blaze of his hospitality. His is the remembered warmth of Paul, arriving at the door of the Sullivan cottage in the dead of winter. As they are about to part, he presses into her hand two soft, green, ten-dollar bills.

• • •

Drouet "would need to delight himself with Carrie as surely as he would need to eat his heavy breakfast." He flirted with women "not because he was a cold-blooded, dark, scheming villain" but because he was driven by "inborn desire." As for Carrie, though she has qualms, she is drawn tropistically, like a sentient plant, to the drummer's sunny generosity. Like him, she is a sinner only insofar as her conscience rules her, and she has, after all, "only an average little conscience, a thing which represented the world, her past environment, habit, convention, in a confused, reflected way." She is unformed, a creature of emotion, "a harp in the wind."

And so Carrie is seduced by Drouet, and afterward she offhandedly wonders, "What have I lost?" Looking in the mirror, she sees a blooming young woman. On the street she saw one of the girls from the shoe factory, and "a tide rolled between them." Going back would be impossible; she had no choice. "She was alone; she was desireful; she was fearful of the whistling wind. The voice of want made answer for her." With that passage, the structure of Victorian morality shudders.

27 / *Under the Gaslight*

> The forces which regulate two individuals of the character
> of Carrie and Hurstwood are as strange and as subtle as de-
> scribed. We have been writing our novels and our philoso-
> phies without sufficiently emphasizing them—we have been
> neglecting to set forth what all men must know and feel about
> these things before a true and natural life may be led.
>
> —Dreiser, *Sister Carrie* (1900)

Just before the point at which Hurstwood meets Carrie, Theodore found himself
blocked. After writing nine chapters rapidly, his momentum ran out. Stumped
by the problem of describing how the manager seduces Carrie, he told Dorothy
Dudley, "It seemed to me the thing was a failure, a total frost."

Rather than stew about it, he put the manuscript aside and went off to
write some articles. His novel very much on his mind, he worked on an article about workers in the textile mills in Fall River, Massachusetts (though
Henry apparently helped with the research for it). *The Cosmopolitan* found it "a
picturesque account of the lives of factory girls" but rejected it, as did Henry
Mills Alden at *Harper's Monthly* and John Phillips at *McClure's*, though they
recognized its power. A study of an industrial town, the article is more than
merely picturesque, and one suspects it was too strong for editors of the day
(it was never published). The workers' drab, joyless lives in "the great stone
prisons of work" are contrasted with the few seaside resorts, condemned by the
Baptist minister yet offering "the one touch of beauty, the one breath of fresh
air" in this town of "gray streets and grayer mills."

Theodore had money problems and demanded $100 from *The Cosmopolitan*
for an article on boys' clubs and $75 for one on the need for good roads. The
editor, John Brisben Walker, had no recollection of offering those sums and
told Theodore through a subordinate to take $75 and $50 or leave it.

Dreiser also quarreled with the *Century* over its rejection of "McEwen of
the Shining Slave Makers." An accompanying note said a reader had found
the story scientifically inaccurate. Theodore protested to associate editor Robert

Underwood Johnson that the story was based on authoritative scientific information. Also, he objected to "being left to the mercy of a scientific reader, who, to me, must stand as the Editor of *The Century*." Johnson replied starchily that the story had been read by a regular member of the editorial staff, that it had been rejected because the magazine disliked allegory, and that an apology was in order. Theodore replied that he stood corrected insofar as his accusation that the editors of the magazine hadn't read the story, but he had no apologies for his defense of the story's accuracy.

Theodore fought for his work in lesser forums too. He chastised Ellery Sedgwick, who had taken over the editorship of *Frank Leslie's Popular Monthly*, for rejecting "A True Patriarch," a sketch about his father-in-law, Arch White. Sedgwick explained that Theodore's contribution lacked a plot: "the 'average reader' whom you so much dislike would wonder in reading it where the 'story' was going to begin." But Dreiser was experimenting with a fictionlike treatment of factual material; he had moved beyond the formulaic plot of mass-magazine stories.

●   ●   ●

After a six-week lapse, Dreiser resumed the writing of *Sister Carrie*. Hurstwood's attraction to Carrie ignites over a game of euchre at the Ogden Place flat. The manager determines that by the Lord, he will have this woman—even if it means euchring his friend Charlie. Hurstwood is nearly forty; in 1900 he would be considered a middle-aged man. His marriage "ran along by force of habit, by force of conventional opinion. With the lapse of time it must necessarily become dryer and dryer—must eventually be tinder, easily lighted and destroyed. . . . The whole thing might move on in a conventional manner to old age and dissolution. Also it might not."

Borne along by an erotic subcurrent of desire for his heroine, Theodore identified with Hurstwood's attraction for a girl twenty years younger than himself. The character of the manager was becoming solider than the wraith who had appeared in the back of Dreiser's mind that day while he was in City Hall Park. The question, of course, was who had that derelict been? His answer is George Hurstwood, who is placed just below the topmost rung of urban success. He is a combined greeter, maître d', and manager of what Drouet, an admirer, calls a "way-up swell saloon." When presiding at Hannah & Hogg's saloon, Hurstwood is a bit like Paul working the crowd at the Metropole. Even Hurstwood's business relationship with Hannah & Hogg resembles Paul's with Pat Howley and Fred Haviland (since the saloon was a real one in Chicago, it is perhaps only coincidence that the two sets of partners have the same first initials). Hurstwood is a front man who "lacked financial functions," as was Paul.

Of course, there are many differences between the two men; Hurstwood is a powerfully original characterization. Paul was more jovial, an impression his enormous girth and ready smile helped convey. Hurstwood exudes an aura of dignity, probity, and inner strength. Hurstwood has a social-climbing wife and two equally ambitious children, owns a fine brick house on the North Side, a horse and a trap, and is worth forty thousand dollars (though most of his property is in his wife's name). He is "altogether a very acceptable individual of our great American upper class — the first grade below the luxuriously rich." Hurstwood pays the bills, with only an occasional grumble, and lives in a high style. But he is not the generous soul that Paul was. When a beggar approaches him as he is emerging from the theater accompanied by Carrie and Drouet, he ignores him. Hurstwood's dress and suave manners confirm his standing. When Carrie invidiously compares Hurstwood's soft calf-leather boots, polished to a dull sheen, to the salesman's shiny patent leathers, she has grasped the class language of clothes. In the city, clothes and manners are signs of wealth, power, and status.

Hurstwood is a master social artificer; in his "black eyes" dwells "a cold make believe" and he feigns bonhomie toward his clientele. He lives a dual life in which "circumspectness" is the byword and getting caught is a cardinal sin ("He lost sympathy for the man that made a mistake and was found out"). He is a secret patron of "those more unmentionable resorts of vice." When he invites Drouet to return later in the evening, the salesman half-jokingly asks, "Is she a blonde?" Hurstwood ignores the question — not because he takes affront, but because he is discreet.

Hurstwood is at the height of his reflected splendor in the yellow glow of gaslight, when streams of pleasure-seekers flow toward the restaurants and the theaters — in the evening, "that mystic period between the glare and the gloom of the world when life is changing from one sphere or condition to another. Ah, the promise of the night. What does it not hold for the weary. What old illusion of hope is not here forever repeated!"

Into Hurstwood's world of pretense slips Carrie, like a fairy-tale heroine, lured by mirages of "wealth, fashion, ease," seeking "that shadow of *manner* which she thought must hang about her and make clear to all who and what she was."

Under the sun of Drouet's generosity Carrie blooms. She becomes more sensuous: "Her form had filled out until it was admirably plump and well-rounded. . . . Her dresses draped her becomingly for she wore excellent corsets and laced herself with care."

As she grows more fluent in the city's language, its signs of status, wealth, and power, she is drawn to Hurstwood as someone who holds the key to a richer life; in contrast, the good-hearted drummer seems vulgar. Then Drouet cajoles Carrie into appearing in an amateur production sponsored by his Elks lodge.

Acting opens up a potent world of illusion, which can conjure up the life Carrie dreams of; it is a "secret passage" to that finer world. The play she acts in is Augustin Daly's melodrama *Under the Gaslight,* a "society play." Carrie plays the heroine, Laura, whom blackmailers expose as a foundling, adopted by a wealthy woman. But when she is unmasked, her blue-blooded friends turn against her as an "impostor." As her former fiancé explains: " . . . there is something wolfish in society. Laura has mocked it with a pretence, and society, which is made up of pretences, will bitterly resent the mockery."

When Carrie hears the actor speak her cue, she is filled with an emotional kinship with the character she is playing. For she too is a pretender. Hurstwood calls her "Mrs. Drouet" (though he suspects that she and the drummer aren't married), and Drouet has given her the stage name "Carrie Madenda" because he doesn't want to introduce her as his wife. Carrie is beginning to see that she lives in a mirror house of deception: Drouet pretends he will marry her; Hurstwood will pretend he is not married. Brimming with emotion, she conveys the pathos of the heart of the melodrama, and the formerly restless audience falls silent.

When Carrie speaks Daly's pathetic lines ("Remember, love is all a woman has to give, but it is the only earthly thing which God permits us to carry beyond the grave"), her two lovers in the audience are almost sick with sexual desire. Hurstwood, with his somewhat finer sensibility, feels she is speaking just to him and "could hardly restrain the tears," while Drouet resolves that "He would marry her, by George. She was worth it."

Shrouded in Laura's chaste white gown, Carrie seduces Hurstwood and Drouet from the stage. The world of gaslight, all shadows, gilt and plush, pink flesh and secret sexuality, becomes a theater of desire.

28 / *Atoms Amid Forces*

> Nature is so grim. The city, which represents it so effectively,
> is also so grim. It does not care at all. It is not conscious. The
> passing of so small an organism as that of a man or a woman
> is nothing to it.
>
> —Dreiser, "The Man on the Sidewalk" (1909)

In the next half-dozen chapters, Hurstwood's passion for Carrie is exposed,
setting off a chain reaction of confrontations. The scenes shuttle from one major
player to another. Hurstwood stews about how to respond to the threatening
letter from his wife's lawyers, then throws up his hands and escapes to the gilded
gaiety of his saloon. Drouet returns to the flat, intending to persuade Carrie to
have another go at living together, but she is out and he leaves, saying in those
laconic Middle Western cadences which Dreiser renders with perfect pitch: "You
didn't do me right, Cad." (Only George Ade at this time had recorded the speech
of ordinary Americans so truly.) If Carrie had been home, things might have
turned out differently, for her job hunting was fruitless. So it goes — chance,
missed connections, drift, procrastination.

These people make up the most realistic gallery of urbanites yet to appear
in an American novel, save in Howells's *A Hazard of New Fortunes* or Fuller's *With
the Procession*. But Howells had assembled a cast of people from familiar social
soil — the South, Boston, Ohio — in the city; and Fuller's affectionate, satirical
portrait of a vanishing world was focused on the old New England merchant
class. The people in *Sister Carrie* are all arrivistes: they are from no discernible
origins, and their status is based on money. Hurstwood's social-climbing wife
and children crave admission to the Lake Shore Drive set as hungrily as Carrie
does, though they are far more sophisticated about it.

Carrie is a passive striver, a materialist but not a gold digger. Hurstwood
considers her a higher type of woman than those he usually dallies with. It is her
wholesome rural innocence that arouses him, and Carrie is instinctively aware
of her power. But when she allows herself to be seduced, instead of condemning
her, Dreiser launches into a solemn discourse on the lack of an adequate scientific basis of morality (despite the "liberal analysis of Spencer and our modern

141

naturalistic philosophers"). The implication is that outmoded contemporary standards will be superseded by more scientific ones founded on truth rather than convention and hypocrisy.

Struggling against the economic undertow that is pulling her into prostitution, Carrie intuits that her body, like her labor, is a commodity, and she had better barter it to the kindest bidder, who at the time is Hurstwood. She is learning, unlike Emma and Sylvia in Warsaw, not to give herself too cheaply, not to become a "plaything" of a man, as she tells Drouet. Carrie remains an old-fashioned heroine in that she "falls," and a modern woman in that she rises in spite of her lapses.

•   •   •

In the climactic Chicago chapters, the shallow, ephemeral nature of human contacts in the city colors the action. Dreiser's vision of city life grew out of his youthful impressions of Chicago, with his adult experiences in New York grafted on. The former are more benign. The Middle Western metropolis is seen as a place of enchantment and wonders, but also as a young giant, growing and flexing its muscles; an adolescent city, in a state of becoming. "Its population was not so much thriving upon established commerce as upon the industries that prepared for the arrival of others."

Like Chicago, Carrie has youth and hope; the young city is her natural habitat—as it was Dreiser's. Chicago was a place where your neighbors did not care who you had been. As soon as Carrie steps off the train, she is immersed in a new element, "a lone figure in a tossing, thoughtless sea." Dreiser frequently uses storm or sea imagery to represent urban social forces, and he portrays the city as a Darwinian jungle where only the strong, the fit, the lucky, can survive.

But in Dreiser's vision, nature is also creative, fertile. Carrie symbolizes the forces of the sun, youth, generation and growth; Hurstwood represents night, pleasure, ease, age and death. Hurstwood regards Carrie as a lily "which had sucked its waxen beauty and perfume from below a depth of waters which he had never penetrated, and out of ooze and mold which he could not understand." Herbert Spencer wrote that nature traced a recurrent cycle: out of mold and decay, new life rises up. In Carrie's beauty Hurstwood seeks his own renewal, not understanding that he is caught in the descending cycle of death.

> If it were not for the artificial fires of merriment, the rush of profit-seeking trade and pleasure-selling amusements . . . we would quickly discover how firmly the chill hand of winter lays upon the heart;—how dispiriting are the days during which the sun withholds a portion of our allowance of light and warmth.

The axis of the book was about to shift—from Carrie to Hurstwood, from Chicago to New York City, from summer to winter.

29 / Strange, Bitter, Sad Facts

At times, sitting at my little dining table in the flat I then
occupied at 102nd Street near Central Park West, New York,
I felt very much like Martin Luther must have felt when he
stood before the Diet of Worms. "Here I stand. Otherwise I
cannot do. God help me."

— Dreiser, "Autobiographical Attack
on Grant Richards" (1911)

The writing of the last part of the Chicago section of *Sister Carrie* consumed
December and most of January. At the point in the story where Hurstwood, like
Emma's L. A. Hopkins, steals the money from his employers' safe, Dreiser was
again unable to continue. He told H. L. Mencken the sticking point: "I couldn't
think how to have him do it." To his biographer Robert Elias, years later, he
recalled he had wanted to present the crime in such a way that Hurstwood's
guilt or innocence was ambiguous.

He was also uncertain about Hurstwood's psychology—specifically, the
mental laws of dissolution that bring him down. This may have been his motive
for interviewing the inventor Elmer Gates, "our foremost American investigator" of the workings of the mind. With the profits of his inventions Gates had
founded a facility for pure research called the Elmer Gates Laboratory of Psychology and Psychurgy, in Chevy Chase, Maryland, and was conducting experi-
ments into learning, perception, and the physiological effects of the emotions.

Not long after Theodore's visit, Gates wrote him a friendly note, mentioning Theodore's interest in "taking up experimental psychology" and suggesting
further reading. He later contributed two articles on free will to *Success*. The
wizard of Chevy Chase drew a distinction between will and volition. He regarded will in the traditional sense of moral or rational choice; volition, however, "is not intellection; it is not emotion, it is not organized feeling, and,
finally, it is not the power to choose." A chain of neuromuscular responses
constituted a purposive act, an act of volition. Such a theory could explain
Hurstwood's theft scientifically: he acted out of volition, not free will.

Of more interest to Theodore were Gates's ideas on the chemical changes in the body produced by emotions. Gates propounded the theory that positive emotions and truthful thoughts engender "anastates," which make the brain healthy and help the organism adapt to its environment. False ideas or evil emotions produce poisons called "katastates," which "slowly destroy the structure in which its memory is enregistered." A katastate "prevents normal and sane judgments and consequently prevents successful adaptation to environment and therefore tends to destroy or limit the life of the organism in which it is embodied." Good and evil, virtue and vice, health and sickness—all could be ultimately analyzed in a test tube. The ideas also provided Theodore with much-needed intellectual—*moral*—support at a crucial time.

•   •   •

Arthur Henry was no longer in residence on West 102nd Street. He was off on a dalliance. While delivering some manuscripts to a typing service that Theodore patronized, Henry had met the owner, a woman named Anna Mallon. He was lonely, and Maude was in Ohio. She was tall, intelligent, literarily inclined, and six years older than he. And she ran a successful business. In Anna's office on lower Broadway, twenty or so young women at rows of desks clattered away, with Anna seated at the front of the room like a teacher. This arrangement reminded Henry of a classroom, so he dubbed the typewriter girls "the Infants," or "Infantas," a play on the "Infant Class." He nicknamed their boss "Sister Anna" because she had attended a convent school; also, there was a nun in his novel. And then there was "Sister" Carrie.

Preoccupied with Anna, Henry withdrew from the literary partnership. This added to Theodore's financial insecurity. But he missed Henry's emotional support even more. They were so close that Theodore resented his friend's abandonment of him and morally disapproved of his abandonment of Maude for Anna. This jealousy would fester until a later time.

Upon his return, Henry read what Theodore had written, assured him it was wonderful, and chided him for ever doubting himself. Moreover, he could point to a dividend of his friendship with Anna: they would receive cut-rate typing services, which would come in handy since *Sister Carrie* and *A Princess of Arcady* would have to be typed for submission to a publisher.

His confidence restored, and bolstered by Gates's theories, Dreiser tackled the crucial scene in which Hurstwood steals the money. When he told Mencken that the problem had been "how to have him do it," he really meant that he was reluctant to show Hurstwood committing a criminal act as Hopkins had done.

The simplest solution was to portray Hurstwood's folly as a temporary aberration, the result of great strain. Moreover, Hurstwood takes more whiskey than is his wont, so by the time he goes to his office to total the day's receipts, he is a bit tipsy. (Emma had told Dreiser that Hopkins was drunk when he took the money, though, as we have seen, contemporary newspaper accounts strongly suggested that the crime was premeditated.) Still, it would not do to have Hurstwood drunk; that would denude the act of any moral significance. And so he is presented in a heightened state, in which his normal inhibitions are weakened but still present. He "trembles in the balance between duty and desire"; the "ghostly clock of the mind" alternately ticks "thou shalt" and "thou shalt not." Here Dreiser recalled his own youthful lapse when he pocketed the money he had collected for the novelty company in Chicago and bought a new overcoat with it. The power of temptation over "the individual whose mind is less strongly constituted," he writes, addressing the moralists directly, may not be apparent to "those who have never wavered in conscience," but it is very real—as he proceeds to demonstrate with Hurstwood. At this point, Elmer Gates's ideas on the separation of will and volition may have been in the back of Dreiser's mind. He was seeking a way to have the manager *do it* and yet *not do it*.

Hurstwood continues to procrastinate. He puts the money back, realizes it is in the wrong place, takes it out. Finally, his mind lurches to a decision of sorts: "There was something fascinating about the soft green stack. . . . He felt sure now that he could not leave that. No, no. He would do it." But doubts again paralyze him, and at that moment the lock accidentally clicks shut. He has procrastinated so long that chance has taken the decision out of his hands. Now there is nothing for it but to take the money and flee. "*Did he do it?*" Society would say yes, but those privy to the manager's mental debate cannot be so sure. Later, after he has tricked Carrie into fleeing to Montreal with him, when he has time to think about what he has done, Hurstwood realizes the magnitude of his blunder—that it has shut him out from Chicago, his old life, and condemned him to a future that is "dark, friendless, exiled." He is outside the gates. But he also thinks, after seeing the stories of his defalcation in the papers, that society's view is not right either. For it sees "but a single point in a long, cumulative tragedy. All the newspapers noted but one thing, his taking the money. . . . All the complications which led up to it were unknown. He was accused without being understood." *Understanding*—the final plea of the criminal, the exile, and the only absolution society can give. He cannot plead innocence; he can only beg forgiveness and ask that the verdict be set aside because of the circumstances.

• • •

In the second, New York section of *Sister Carrie*, winter seems to have set in permanently. Events are lit by the cold, washed-out rays of a winter sun or the crimson glow of a Broadway fire sign. New York is different in other ways. It is an imperial city; Chicago is a country town. (Carrie is impressed by the absence of green lawns and houses in New York; she does not like it much.) In this sea full of whales "Hurstwood was nothing."

The atmosphere is charged with the energy of great schemes; it is an opiate enslaving the newcomer to "dreams unfilled—gnawing, luring, idle phantoms which beckon and lead, beckon and lead, until death and dissolution dissolve their power and restore us blind to nature's heart." New York's dreams are more destructive because they are more remote and unattainable than Chicago's. A young man is vulnerable to them, but he has "the strength of hope" to sustain him through the inevitable setbacks. A man Hurstwood's age is less prone to illusion but, lacking hope, more susceptible to disappointment because he sees more keenly the contrast between his present and his desired state. Regret and "nostalgy" for the old days begin gnawing at his morale, and aging works its wasting ravages. Here, in diagnosing Hurstwood's state, Dreiser resorts to Gatesian psychurgy invoking "certain poisons in the blood, called katastates," generated by remorse, which "eventually produce marked physical deterioration." Hurstwood's sickness was "a deep and cancerous sense of mistake which ate into his energy and force."

Once, Hurstwood had been inside the bubble of success; now he is outside. He understands that there is a city within the City: "Men were posted at the gates. You could not get in. Those inside did not care to come out to see who you were. They were so merry inside there that all those outside were forgotten, and he was on the outside."

As for Carrie, she adapts to her new circumstances, living quietly as a young matron known as "Mrs. Wheeler" (Hurstwood's pseudonym), passing idle hours with trashy novels, supervising her maid at the housework, or cooking dinner for her husband.

Then she meets a neighbor, a smart urbanite named Mrs. Vance, who awakens her old melancholy, her old desires. They go to the theater and afterward join the Broadway fashion parade. Carrie feels dissatisfaction with her clothes as she is raked by the supercilious eyes of splendidly dressed men and women.

Awakened, Carrie looks at Hurstwood with a more critical eye. She has long since lost her awe of him. She is loyal and affectionate enough but there is little love between them. And when Mrs. Vance takes her to Delmonico's, she meets a man who opens her eyes to a higher sphere, just as Hurstwood did when she was living with Drouet. He is Bob Ames, an inventor from Indianapolis. Ames is the closest thing to a spokesman for Dreiser's ideas in the novel. It is Ames who comments on the high prices at the restaurants, evincing disapproval of the conspicuous consumption of the Gilded Age. He is an intellectual; he urges her to read Hardy and Balzac and deprecates Bertha Clay's *Dora Thorne,* which Carrie had found only "fair" herself (it is the story of a poor girl who marries a rich young man and is rejected for living above her station). Alone, rocking in her flat, Carrie dreams of finer things and remembers her moment of glory on the stage. Ames had told her it was a fine thing to be an actress. . . .

•   •   •

And so Carrie and Hurstwood bemoan their separate states, but each is set on a different trajectory—Carrie's upward, Hurstwood's downward. When he and his partner lose their lease on a saloon, Hurstwood is reduced to seeking an ordinary job, but his applications are rejected because he is either too old or looks too important for the position. When winter sets in, he holes up in the flat, huddling by the radiator's warmth, rocking and reading his papers. He takes charge of the household after Carrie, with his acquiescence, lands a job in the chorus line in a comic opera. Now his manhood is slipping away.

Once, after her caustic remarks become too much for him, he bestirs himself to get a job as a scab motorman in Brooklyn. When, despite police protection, the strikers seize him and throw him to the ground, the last raiments of the old, resplendent George Hurstwood are stripped away. He hurries back to his warm room where he can read about the strike in the *World*.

Carrie, meanwhile, continues her adventitious rise. This "apt student of fortune's ways" advances to a small speaking part after the comedian happens to make a remark to her and she responds with a pert ad-lib that brings down the house. She moves on to a bigger role in another show. The director dresses her as a Quakeress and orders her to frown throughout the comedian's routine. Again, she somehow piques the audience's fancy and is a hit. As the critic of the *Evening Sun* writes: " . . . the vagaries of fortune are indeed curious."

After Carrie walks out on him, Hurstwood sells the furniture—his final stake—and heads for the Bowery, where in a shabby hotel room he reads the paragraph in the *Sun* recording Carrie's latest success and thinks: "Ah, she was in the walled city now. Its splendid gates had opened, admitting her from a cold, dreary outside. She seems a creature from afar off—like every other celebrity he had known.

" 'Well, let her have it,' he said. 'I won't bother her.'

"It was the grim resolution of a bent, bedraggled but unbroken pride."

•   •   •

Throughout the month of March Theodore wrote in one long sustained burst. His self-doubt had dissipated, the tragedy was marching inexorably to its foreordained end, and his writing grew leaner, more telling.

Richard Duffy received periodic progress reports from the author. "Every few days," Duffy recalled, "he would make the breezy announcement that since he last came on view he had written as many as 20,000 words." This had been Theodore's way throughout the writing of the book—tremendous bursts followed by fallow periods when he grew discouraged.

At nights he would pace the floor, and Jug would get out of bed and sleepily match his steps. Like Carrie, he found solace in rocking and folding and refolding his handkerchief. As Duffy remembers him at this time:

> He always sat in a rocking chair, if he could find one, and he sat in it to rock, his long frame crouched at the shoulders, while he folded a handkerchief into the dimensions of a postal stamp with the slow patience of a Japanese drawing a maple leaf. If he was not talking he would be humming the refrain of "On the Banks of the Wabash" or of some other popular song. He had hundreds in his head.

Dreiser was straining under a compulsion to render life truthfully. He remembered working into the night at the dining-room table: "I would come to strange, hard, bitter sad facts in my story . . . and I would say shall I put that down and something within the very centre of my being would say, 'You must! You must! You dare not do otherwise!' "

•   •   •

A Broadway fire sign apotheosizes Carrie's celebrity. Hurstwood, shambling through the dirty snow, a muttering, ragged, subhuman figure, hesitates before a poster of her and moves on. He stops at the window of a luxury restaurant and gazes at the gleaming napery, the steaming dishes, framed in the glass that barred him from this world (his old world) like a poster advertising the grand life. "Eat," he mutters. "Eat. That's right eat. Nobody else wants any."

While Carrie and her friend Lola sit in Carrie's new suite in the Waldorf, a warm and brightly lit bubble, Hurstwood shambles to his destiny. A heavy snow is falling, and Lola wonders if they can go sleighing. Carrie, who is reading Balzac's *Père Goriot* and is sorry for the old man's suffering, worries about the people out in the cold. Lola sees a man fall in the snow and laughs merrily. "How sheepish men look when they fall, don't they?"

At the door of the Bowery flophouse, Hurstwood moves in a crush of shabby men. He pays his fifteen cents and goes to his allotted cubicle. Leisurely, like a man with all of the time in the world, he stuffs his overcoat in the crack beneath the door and carefully lays down his cracked old hat. He stands under the gaslight a moment, then turns on the jet without igniting it. He stands there a moment as the fumes, the sweetish aroma of dead lilies, insinuate themselves into his nostrils. Then, "hidden wholly in that kindness which is night" ("Ah, the promise of the night. What does it not hold for the weary. . . . It is the lifting of the burden of toil"), he lies down, saying, with finality, "What's the use." In the stately dignity of that scene, one of the most moving in our literature, Hurstwood, brought low, becomes great—a man who played the game and lost, dying with a bent but unbroken pride. Four years earlier Theodore had foreshadowed the theme of his book when he wrote in *Ev'ry Month,* "A man is still a man however often he may fail."

Seated at his dining-room table, a pile of yellow half sheets before him, Dreiser wrote:

"The End. Thursday, March 29—2:53 P.M."

Part Four

• • •

THE NOVELIST
STILLBORN

30 / At the Outworks of the City

> After it was done considerable cutting was suggested by
> Henry and this was done. I think all of 40,000 words came
> out.
>
> —Dreiser to H. L. Mencken (1916)

Even as Dreiser was writing the final chapters, Anna Mallon's typists were work-ing on the earlier ones. Eventually, they outran the author. When they finished Chapter 49, in which Ames and Carrie converse at a dinner party and a current of attraction flows between them, the young women had become so caught up in Carrie's story that they sent Dreiser an impatient note:

> Dear Mr. Author:
> We have finished the last iniquitous chapter of
> Sister Carrie, and are now ready for something hot and
> sizzling. So please send her down.
>
> Impatiently,
> THE INFANT CLASS

Anna Mallon was also enthralled and wrote to Dreiser to compliment him on the scene, saying she would "impatiently await the closing chapter." The fact that the young "typewriters" found Carrie's tale "iniquitous"—meaning risqué—should have sounded a warning bell to the trio at West 102nd Street. These were the young women whom the "obscenity" laws were designed to protect by quarantining them from the virus of immorality. That they enjoyed the story was a testament to how outmoded those laws had become.

Not to Jug, however. She served as technical adviser on matters of feminine dress, but this role merged with that of censor when she deleted the intimate references to Carrie's keeping her body sweet and wearing "excellent corsets." She also prettified Carrie's speech to make her more ladylike. Thus, rather than charging that Drouet had "lied" to her, the little pilgrim says he "deceived" her. Such locutions subtly changed Carrie's personality, making her more genteel than the raw country girl from Columbia City Dreiser had in mind.

Dreiser was willing enough to delegate to her minor matters of propriety. Rather than write "bitch," he has Hurstwood call his wife a "confounded _____." Jug filled in the blank with "wretch," and he accepted the substitution. When he wrote "bastard," she let it stand.

Dreiser conveyed the subject matter honestly. His journalistic style was attuned to the facts of the contemporary world, and it was more compatible with common speech than the genteel style. It was well adapted to conveying a sense of the contemporary urban scene—society, environment, above all, ordinary speech—and the manners and customs of turn-of-the-century Americans. In contrast, the genteel style was designed to evade vulgarity—to muffle, idealize, or euphemize it. When Dreiser fell into genteelisms himself—when he had Carrie walk "trippingly," for example—his mind was in never-never land; his true voice was speaking when, describing the fresh-from-the-country Carrie, he writes, "her feet, though small, were set flatly."

If his prose was also set flatly, rather than running trippingly, he generally avoided the trap many later realists fell into of telling a humdrum story tediously, resulting in novels that ran on as drearily as a small-town Sunday afternoon. The humdrum details were there, to be sure, most tellingly in the delineation of the breakup of Hurstwood and Carrie's marriage, when they quarrel over the price of steak and his small economies grow into an obsession. The manager's dwindling bankroll, meticulously audited, becomes an account book of his life slipping away.

Structurally, the shifting urban scenes, from Broadway to the Bowery, from flophouse to Waldorf Hotel, are like the shuttles of the loom of destiny. Dreiser's mind worked in dialectic fashion; he showed reality by contrasts: Carrie contrasts the Hansons' flat with her meal with Drouet in a luxurious restaurant; Hurstwood contrasts his sterile marriage with the renewed youthfulness of his love for Carrie—and on and on. Through this interweaving of antitheses, life is presented in the round. Ultimately Carrie will ascend to her suite at the Waldorf while Hurstwood will be borne to an unmarked grave in potter's field. The author's brooding eye records both fates without moralizing. Accorded equal stature and dignity, the three commonplace protagonists become larger than life.

After the hectic events of the Chicago scenes and the hollow dazzle of Carrie's rise on the New York stage, the pace of the novel becomes like the rhythmic tread of a ceremonial procession. The earlier action is slowed by the philosophical digressions characteristic of the Victorian novel—though in Dreiser's case the models were Balzac and Hardy, the best ones. Also, many of these passages are integrated into the bone and tissue of the book. And they are juxtaposed with scenes of great force and economy, told almost entirely in dialogue and gesture (for example, the scene in the restaurant that climaxes with Carrie's acceptance of money from Drouet), anticipating the techniques of later novelists such as Ernest Hemingway and F. Scott Fitzgerald. Like Carrie, the book is a mixture of the old and the new, a bridge between the nineteenth-century novel and the twentieth. For that matter, the pervasive pessimism underlying the story, its assumption that desire and selfishness are the motive forces of most human behavior, that chance and inscrutable forces rather than ethics or Providence control human destiny, would also become dominant themes in twentieth-century literature.

The chief flaw in *Sister Carrie* is Dreiser's penchant for abstractions, his godlike pose of applying fundamental laws. He becomes like the Spencerian Unknowable—an almost inhuman intelligence. There is a corresponding love-lessness in his characters that is true to their natures but that the author does not entirely comprehend. At the same time, Dreiser's great strength is his empathy with his characters, which reaches its peak in the final scenes about Hurstwood. In the supreme effort to make believable the climactic downfall of this, the most strongly imagined figure in the book, Dreiser *became* Hurstwood, producing his every thought, his every emotion, from inside himself.

The published version of *Sister Carrie* closes with a kind of epilogue, or rather a coda reprising the themes of the book, added after Dreiser had written "The End." His only explanation of the new ending came in an interview, seven years later, with a reporter from the New York *Herald:* "When I finished it I felt that it was not done. The problem was . . . to lead a story to a point, an elevation where it could be left and yet continue into the future. . . . I wanted in the final picture to suggest the continuation of Carrie's fate along the lines of established truths." Nothing occurred to him immediately, so he hiked to his favorite spot on the Palisades, the sheer cliffs across the Hudson from Manhattan, and lay down beneath a shelf of overhanging rock. "Two hours passed in delicious mental revery. Then suddenly came the inspiration of its own accord." He reached for his pencil and scribbled the new ending in his notebook. Finis.

Casting a bit of cold water on this romantic account is the existence of thirteen pages of notes with the original manuscript. Except for the beginning, which was written by Dreiser, the notes are in Jug's hand. Apparently he started to jot down some ideas, became tired, and dictated the rest to her. The notes are a rough outline for the coda that ultimately appeared in the published book.

The notes show that Dreiser was, as he suggested to the interviewer, attempting to bring his book full circle, back to Carrie. Rather than state what happens to her, though, as Balzac did in his epilogues, he summarizes her character to foreshadow her future. She is driven by feeling, rather than reason; "beauty," rather than desire for fine things or even sex, as one might have thought, lures her on. Dreams call her; she will always be dissatisfied with present reality. Ames has instilled in her a new ambition—acting in a comedy drama; she has become "the old mournful Carrie—with the unsatisfied longing." Ultimately, she can only be happy sitting in her rocker and dreaming: "Dream boats and swan songs—such joys as never were."

As Chapter 49 was originally written, the reader would expect that Ames and Carrie fall in love, perhaps marry, but a strong theme in Dreiser's dictated soliloquy was the need to dash that expectation. "Ames is not a matrimonial possibility," he says flatly. "That is not his significance." And so he rewrote the Ames-Carrie tête-à-tête to eliminate all hints of warmth between them. In the new draft the inventor tells her bluntly that she should use her gift for conveying emotion and pathos in serious drama; if Carrie continues to live solely for herself, she will lose this gift. She must live for others through her art—use her talent to express their feelings. Ames's final words to her are brusque and commanding: "If I were you, I'd change."

In the original scene between Ames and Carrie, Ames forgets his reservations about "the moral status of certain types of actresses," and when he bids Carrie farewell, he is "wide awake to her beauty." The "blind strivings" passage that follows suggests that even if Carrie does enter into a relationship with Ames, "the light is but now in these his eyes," and tomorrow it will be someone or something else. Perhaps Dreiser did not intend it so, but a censorious reader might interpret the phrase to mean there would be other men for her. Dreiser had written himself into a moral trap. The only way to get out was to alter the passage beginning "O blind strivings of the heart," which closes the scene between him and Carrie, so that it carries a note of disapproval for Carrie's past conduct, and transpose it to the end of the novel.

Carrie is left in a kind of stasis that is out of keeping with the realism of the rest of the novel. In her rocking chair, she moves yet goes nowhere. Is it some Spencerian state of equilibrium beyond desire, when all motion stops? But deprived of the Ames possibility, the author throws up his hands, leaving his heroine cloistered from further contamination by the world.

The apologia for Carrie is complete. When she came to the city, she was "poor, unsophisticated, emotional." The "drag to follow beauty" was so strong that she abandoned "the admired way, taking rather the despised path leading to her dreams quickly." But who shall cast the first stone? "Not evil, but goodness more often allures the feeling mind unused to reason."

•   •   •

The new ending was dispatched to the Infants, and by early April 1900 the typescript of *Sister Carrie* was done. Again the editorial team sharpened its pencils and fell to. Now Henry began to take charge in a more visible way.

At first his contributions were stylistic. He worked hard at making Dreiser's sometimes tortured sentences rest easier on the page. But as Jug had done in a different way, he occasionally ignored the awkward power of Dreiser's style and substituted something slicker and blander. Theodore let himself be edited, but he was not sitting by idly. Contrary to his later reputation as a careless writer, Dreiser tinkered with many clumsy sentences. He seemed determined to make his prose correct.

After this final polishing, Carrie was ready to go out into the world. Dreiser decided to aim high: he chose Harper & Brothers, still a leading house despite its recent reorganization in bankruptcy by J. P. Morgan, and still the publisher of Mark Twain and William Dean Howells. Might the Dean of Critics intercede on behalf of another young novelist from the West as Dreiser speculated in an article about him in the March *Ainslee's*? Another consideration was that Henry Mills Alden, the editor of *Harper's Monthly*, had been sympathetic to his nonfiction work.

Alden gave the manuscript a quick reading and told Dreiser that, although he liked it, he thought it unlikely that Harper's would publish it. But at the author's behest he forwarded the script to the parent firm with some favorable words appended. On May 2 the novel came back. The accompanying reader's report called *Sister Carrie* a "superior piece of reportorial realism" with excellent touches of local color, particularly the rendering of "below-the-surface life in the Chicago of twenty years ago." But, it continued, the author's touch was "neither firm enough nor sufficiently delicate to depict without offense to the reader the continued illicit relations of the heroine. . . . I cannot conceive of the book arousing the interest or inviting the attention . . . of the feminine readers who control the destinies of so many novels." Those words may have produced consternation at West 102nd Street. Dreiser may have prepared a heated mental rebuttal to the criticisms, but he desperately wanted his novel out.

With Dreiser lacking sufficient detachment to make the necessary adjustments, Arthur Henry took command. He went through the entire typescript, lightly penciling brackets around suggested cuts. Dreiser followed him with a soft-leaded pencil, drawing heavy black lines through sentences and paragraphs, where he agreed.

The majority of the trims homed in on phrases that could be construed as "immoral"—passages that cast doubt on the sanctity of marriage, for example, or that alluded to sexuality even in an indirect way. Thus, the section about Carrie being ogled by prospective employers was dropped. Carrie's answering warmth to Hurstwood's amorous pleas was extirpated. References to Drouet's and Hurstwood's philandering also had to go. Although the book was strong enough to stand the cuts, something was lost—the social comment on the plight of the working girl in the job-hunting section, for example. The removal of references to Carrie's feelings about Drouet and Hurstwood made her seem

THE NOVELIST STILLBORN

frigid; but her pangs of conscience after Drouet seduces her were also dropped, making her even more of a cipher. Hurstwood becomes a man who has remained faithful to his wife all those years, despite his coolness toward her. Some of the subversive cynicism had gone out of Dreiser's book.

Now, it would seem, *Sister Carrie* had been scrubbed of all blemishes. Surely she was ready to make her debut in polite society. Her next destination, it was decided, would be the firm of Doubleday, Page, a new house formed only the previous year by Frank Nelson Doubleday and Walter Hines Page.

31 / A Novel Amid Forces: The Spendings of Fancy

> I had the definite and yet entirely illusory notion that because
> [*Sister Carrie*] was considered excellent by a number of per-
> sonal and critical friends it must sell and sell well. All one
> had to do was to take it to a reputable publisher and get it
> published. Presto—fame and fortune.
> —Dreiser to Fremont Older (1923)

Frank Norris's presence as a reader of Doubleday, Page may well have influenced Dreiser's decision to send *Sister Carrie* there next. As it happened, Rose White arrived for a visit in April while Theodore was revising *Sister Carrie*. She had come across Norris's *McTeague* and was praising it to the skies. On her recommendation, Dreiser read it and found it a revelation—"the first real American book I had ever read," he told H. L. Mencken years later.

Norris sat up all night reading the manuscript of *Sister Carrie*. A few days later, he announced to a visiting writer, Morgan Robertson, "I have found a masterpiece. The man's name is Theodore Dreiser." Robertson said he had known Dreiser as the editor of a small-time song sheet called *Ev'ry Month*. Well, whatever he had been, Norris said, he had written a great book which Doubleday, Page *must* publish, and he intended to convey his personal feelings to the author immediately. Norris did so on May 28:

> My Dear Mr. Dreiser:
> My report of *Sister Carrie* has gone astray and I cannot
> now put my hands on it.
> But I remember that I said, and it gives me pleasure
> to repeat it, that it was the best novel I have read in
> M.S. since I had been reading for the firm, and that it
> pleased me as well as any novel I have read in any form,
> published or otherwise. . . .

On June 8 Norris invited Dreiser to come to his rooms at the Angelsea Hotel at 60 Washington Square South, an establishment popular with artists and bohemians of the paying sort, and told him the book was officially accepted. What else they talked about can only be conjectured, but they probably hit it off. Dreiser must have felt a kinship with the tall, slender Californian with prematurely graying hair. Both had fallen under the sway of Darwin, and both regarded the city as the great subject for modern novelists. Their great difference was that of class: Norris, of "good stock," believed in the superiority of the Anglo-Saxon "race" and, like Zola, believed that heredity determined character, whereas Dreiser, the immigrant's son, pitied the downtrodden and could not accept fixed distinctions based on class or race.

The day after their meeting, Page had written to offer his congratulations on "so good a piece of work." However, Norris's enthusiasm for *Sister Carrie* outstripped that of another editor, Henry Lanier, who was opposed to the presentation of such low types in a novel. "People are not of equal significance," he explained to Dorothy Dudley. But he agreed with Norris's estimation of the book's power and integrity. Page also had reservations about the characters. Still, he called it "a natural" and agreed it must be published. When he met with Dreiser to discuss terms, Page voiced his reservations and urged him to fictionalize all the names and places. An oral agreement was made on the spot. Publication was scheduled for the fall.

With his novel accepted, Dreiser could feel that he had, in the words of Richard Duffy, "scaled the outworks of the walls of the City." He was rapidly spinning illusions of literary fame, if not fortune, and planned to make his living as a novelist—"to join the one a year group." A couple of subjects were fermenting in his brain, and he scraped together some money, planning to head for Montgomery City, where he could live off his in-laws' hospitality.

In Missouri he set to work on a novel he would call *The Rake*. He had delegated to Arthur Henry the task of handling any problems that might arise in his absence, and Theodore's friend hovered over the book as though it were his own. On July 14 Henry wrote that he had had a discussion with Lanier about the use of real names. When Lanier insisted that all of them be changed, they had a "warm argument," Lanier contending that Dreiser was "straining after realism." He implied that unless the changes were made, the book would not be published. Henry agreed that the name Hannah & Hogg ought to be altered because the theft took place there, but insisted that all the others were necessary. Lanier also wanted a new title—something more "pretentious." Henry urged Teddie not to back down, but said he should make a decision on all these matters quickly.

When Henry's letter arrived, Dreiser took it as confirmation of a premonition he had had two days earlier "that there was something in the wind that boded ill to me." He even asked one of the blacks who worked for Arch White where the local "Old Mammy" — the fortune teller — lived, but for some reason could not bring himself to consult her. Then he fell into "a deep gloom" and that night suffered a "physical derangement of the nervous system" and was unable to sleep. "There is a tenth sense stirring in the minds of men. . . . " he wrote Henry in explanation of his premonition. Four days later another letter from Henry arrived:

> Dear Teddie:
> It has dazed me. I am amazed and enraged.
> Doubleday has turned down your story. . . .

Doubleday had returned from Europe. After hearing Norris's enthusiastic endorsement, he took the manuscript to his home in Oyster Bay, Long Island, to read over the weekend. Monday morning, we may fairly presume, he stormed into the office and summoned Page. A stunned Frank Norris described his reaction to Henry, who relayed it to Dreiser: " 'Doubleday,' [Norris] said, 'thinks the story immoral and badly written.' He don't make any of the objections to it that might be made [i.e., those raised by Page and Lanier] — he simply don't think the story *ought* to be published by anybody first of all because it is immoral."

Norris's initial reaction was to advise Dreiser to seek another publisher. He offered to try to place it with Macmillan, and told Henry if they acted at once, there would still be time to get *Sister Carrie* out in the fall. In a note to Henry before their talk, Norris makes no mention of Doubleday's opposition other than to assure Henry that "Page — and all of us — Mr. Doubleday too — are immensely interested in Dreiser and have every faith that he will go far."

• • •

The following morning Henry returned to the publisher's offices at 34 Union Square and raised the question of whether the firm had a legal obligation to publish the book because of Page's oral agreement with Dreiser. Norris agreed that it probably did, and suggested Henry see Doubleday. When Henry described Page's representations, Doubleday admitted that he could be forced to publish, but said that it would be a great mistake for Dreiser to insist, since "[Doubleday] would make no effort to sell it as the more it sold the worse he would feel about it."

After Henry left, Doubleday apparently conferred with Page, and they decided to try to talk Dreiser into withdrawing the book. In a letter dated July 19, which he sent to Dreiser c/o 6 West 102nd Street, Page asked "to be released from my agreement with you." What had happened, he explained, was that the more everyone at the firm thought it over, the more strongly they believed that "the choice of your characters has been unfortunate. I think I told you that, personally, this kind of people did not interest me, and we find it hard to believe they will interest the great majority of readers."

Curiously, none of the principals would cast Doubleday as the main villain. Dreiser's initial attitude toward him was that "he must have ample reasons" for his objections. Henry reserved his fire for the other editors; he called Doubleday "sincere" but "mistaken." As for Norris, he seems to have snatched at a scrap of rumor that would let Doubleday off the hook. Sometime after Dreiser returned from Missouri, Norris told him that Mrs. Doubleday had actually raised the fuss. Where he got that information is unknown, but it lent support to Norris's theory that Doubleday would come 'round once the critics hailed the book as a work of genius. Thus began the legend that Neltje Doubleday had torpedoed *Sister Carrie,* a story that Dreiser in later years retailed to Mencken and others and to his biographer Dorothy Dudley.

Dudley could find no confirmation for this tale, however. Henry Lanier told her flatly, "It was Frank who made the trouble. He hated it enough without other influence, called it 'indecent,' and begged us at once to break the contract." Neltje Doubleday was a much admired woman, and her main interest was in writing books about birds and gardening, which her husband published and which sold well. Her favorite charity was the Red Cross, not "purity leagues" or rescuing fallen women, as Dudley implies.

Neither Dreiser's nor Arthur Henry's letters at the time mention the lady. Dreiser's are dominated by concern about the personal embarrassment he would suffer if the book did not come out. In a letter dated July 23, he equivocates, telling Henry that if he and Norris think it best to submit the book to Macmillan — well and good. However, if the manuscript is returned to him by Doubleday, Page, he will refuse to accept it, and he thinks it should remain with the house until the "matter has been adjudicated."

Despite the setback, Theodore felt his career was secure — "Not that, after all, it is essential that I should have a career," but his views "are needed by society and will work for its improvement — the greater happiness of man." He planned not to tell Jug about the contretemps, and asked Henry not to either. And he forwarded a handwritten reply to Page, asking Henry to have it typed before sending it. Dreiser wrote that if the book were not published, the setback to his literary career "will work me material injury." The words *material injury* would alert any lawyer to a possible suit; furthermore, honor required that the agreement be carried out. Let readers be the final judge of the book's quality: "The public feeds upon nothing which is not helpful to it."

When Henry received the draft of Dreiser's July 23 letter to Page, he wrote, "We arrived at exactly the same conclusion. . . . I will not take the MSS from them even as a loan for fear they would think we might weaken. And then too it would give them the chance for an argument that they do not have now with the book still in their possession." But in his accompanying letter Dreiser had proposed that the Macmillan route be explored if possible.

Page sent a second, slippery, avuncular letter on August 2, in which he noted that James Lane Allen had finished a novel a year ago that was postponed in favor of another book. If a popular writer like Allen could delay a book, why couldn't Dreiser? Page dangled the possibility of doing some articles for *World's Work*, which would be launched shortly.

In his reply, Dreiser conceded nothing. Regarding Page's contention that he could postpone without harm to his career, he observed: "I do not have much faith in the orderly progression of publication as regards novels. A great book will destroy conditions, unfavorable or indifferent, whether these be due to previous failures or hostile prejudice aroused by previous error. Even if this book should fail, I can either write another important enough in its nature to make its own conditions and be approved of for itself alone, or I can write something unimportant and fail, as the author of a triviality deserves to fail."

Back in New York, Dreiser confronted Page and Lanier, who remembered him as "crushed and tragically pathetic" during their fifteen-minute talk. Lanier tried to persuade him that it would be unfair to his book to let the firm issue it when the head of the house was so staunchly opposed. Dreiser did not waver. He gave the two editors an ultimatum: if they did not publish, he would take legal action.

The junior members met with Doubleday, who called in the firm's lawyer, Thomas H. McKee. McKee, who thought Dreiser had a good case, advised Doubleday that he was legally bound to publish *Carrie,* and that the minimal criteria for publication included printing copies and filling orders from bookstores, if any. Frank Doubleday was a man of his word; he would honor a promise made by his partner as though it were his own. But he would also make good his threat to discourage the book's sale.

Years later, Dreiser would regret his obduracy. His first inclination had been "to take the book under my arm and walk out," but Norris and Henry had persuaded him to stand on his contract—"of all silly things."

32 / A Novel Amid Forces: Fortune's Way

> You would never dream of recommending [it] to another person to read. Yet . . . as a work of literature and the philosophy of human life it comes within sight of greatness.
> —Seattle *Post Intelligencer* (1901)

On August 20, 1900, Doubleday, Page signed a contract with Dreiser for the publication of a book called *The Flesh and the Spirit;* however, Dreiser penciled "Sister Carrie" underneath the typed line. Had Doubleday insisted on a "pretentious title" per Lanier's suggestions? If so, Dreiser resisted. Nor is it clear if the publisher proposed the chapter titles that Dreiser and Henry concocted at the last; probably it was their idea—an attempt to make the book more literary. The dedication was to "Arthur Henry whose steadfast ideals and serene devotion to truth and beauty have served to lighten the purpose and strengthen the method of this volume."

Buoyed by the triumph of his hopes, Dreiser had plunged into his second novel, *The Rake*, writing ten chapters or so in an initial burst. *The Rake* was about the adventures of a young newspaperman named Eugene. So autobiographical was it that Dreiser later spliced one of the scenes into the manuscript of *Newspaper Days*, merely changing the hero from third to first person.

He continued to fight even as the book was readied for the printers, and it is quite possible that his manner further irritated the autocratic Doubleday. In September the publisher (who seems to have taken over the editing of the book) wrote him under the frosty salutation "Dear Sir," curtly agreeing to the title *Sister Carrie* and demanding that real names be changed, that all the "profanity" be removed, and that certain passages be altered. Dreiser began his reply on a conciliatory note, saying he had changed several of the names per request and had struck out sentences that were considered "suggestive." But some of

Doubleday's demands he could not agree to. A reference to Delmonico's had been questioned; Dreiser thought the restaurant was sufficiently well known to remain. After all, Richard Harding Davis frequently referred to Delmonico's; why couldn't he? As for alleged profanity, "Since when has the expression 'Lord Lord' become profane. Wherein is 'Damn,' 'By the Lord,' and 'By God.' "

The ways of the censor were indeed capricious and arbitrary. Names such as the Waldorf, the Broadway Central, and Charles Frohman, the producer, which Dreiser said he had changed, appeared in the final book, while others were altered. As a general rule, only the names of businesses mentioned negatively were fictionalized. Some "by Jesus"es and "by the Lord"s were excised; others were not.

Still, a pair of sharp eyes belonging to someone at the publishing house continued to vet *Sister Carrie* for risqué bits until the book was on the presses, and emendations were made even after Dreiser had returned the corrected author's proofs (which he had had Richard Duffy read as a check). For example, the timing of the pro forma marriage of Carrie and Hurstwood in Montreal was changed so that it occurred before they consummated their "complete matrimonial union"; instead of counting his money in a "dingy lavatory" Hurstwood counted it in a "dingy hall"; Hurstwood's patronage of "those more unmentionable resorts of vice" and Drouet's query "Is she a blonde?" were jettisoned. Now the much-laundered Carrie was spotless.

For her debut she was outfitted in the drabbest possible garb, lest anyone be allured by her. The cheap-looking, dull brick-red binding and plain-black title lettering would have been more appropriate on a plumbing manual. As Dorothy Dudley wrote, it was "an assassin's binding." Nor did the size of the first printing bespeak much enthusiasm on the publisher's part — 1000 copies, of which 450 remained unbound, pending orders. To discourage the latter, the title was not listed in the Doubleday, Page catalogue, though Zola's *Fruitfulness* was (in a bowdlerized translation and described as an exposure of "an evil . . . which is sapping the vitality of France" but full of "clear, sound healthy feelings"), as were *Bob Son of Battle* and *Spencer and Spencerism*. Henry's *A Princess of Arcady* is praised as a "charming idyll," "a delicate romance," and a "striking contrast to the strenuous and often unpleasant fiction which is so common today." The firm's salesmen probably made no effort to cry up *Sister Carrie*. No advertising was taken. The price was $1.50, the standard charge for a novel at the time.

At least one story Dreiser told in later years, crediting it to Frank Norris and Thomas H. McKee, was not true — that all copies were stored in the basement at the Doubleday, Page offices. Orders from wholesalers were filled, and copies did appear in the stores. Painfully few of them, though: only 456 volumes were sold between November 1900 and February 1902, netting Dreiser $68.40 in royalties.

The only bright spot in the picture was Frank Norris. True to his word, he sent out copies to reviewers—more than one hundred of them—accompanied by personal letters. Isaac Marcosson, a young book columnist for the Louisville *Times* and an admirer of Norris, recalled receiving one, and his review—highly favorable—was the first to appear after the official publication day, November 6. Other reviewers followed suit, in a somewhat desultory fashion, and *Sister Carrie* was fairly widely reviewed, for which Norris deserves the major credit.

What is more, the reception was generally favorable; even the most hard-shell moralists could not find any specific obscenities to complain about. Of course there was some clucking over Carrie's fall and rise. For example, *Life,* at the time a humor magazine, found nothing funny about her career and warned: "Such girls, however, as imagine that they can follow in her footsteps will probably end their days on [Blackwells] Island or in the gutter." The reviewer for the Newark *Sunday News* (recruited by Dreiser's friend Peter McCord, who was working on the paper) correctly noted that "after having yielded up that which woman holds most precious . . . this strange heroine feels but the lightest pangs of remorse or shame" and faulted the author for his "failure to appreciate the power and depth of certain feminine instincts." But that was one of the few sour notes in a review that went on to hail Dreiser's "great talent—possibly genius."

Another seeming censure when taken out of context were the observations of the Chicago *Tribune* that *Sister Carrie* was "a presentation of the godless side of American life" and "Not once does the name of the Deity appear in the book, except as it is implied in the suggestion of profanity." But the point being made was that a novel dealing with this segment of society "has been waited for through many years." People like Drouet and Hurstwood existed, so they should be shown.

What was mainly complained of was the unrelenting unpleasantness of the realism, the absence of edification or idealism, the plethora of slang and the lack of a "literary" style. For a few reviewers the book was too somber, but many others praised this quality, though remarking that it would doom it to unpopularity. Such statements became, in effect, self-fulfilling prophecies. And so many reviewers felt duty-bound to discuss the book's morality that it acquired a sort of guilt by association.

Marcosson was among the few reviewers who celebrated *Sister Carrie* as an exploration of new fictional territory. "Out in the highways and hedges of life you find a phase of realism that has not found its way into many books," he began. "It reeks of life's sordid endeavor; of the lowly home and the hopelessly restricted existence. Its loves, its joys, its sorrows, are narrow. There is little sunshine. It is plain realism." At last, here was a book about the "other side of the social scale."

Also perceptive was the anonymous reviewer for the *Commercial Advertiser,* a lively New York paper sympathetic to new movements in the arts. The *Advertiser's* critic took the eighteenth-century French economist Turgot's maxim that "Civilization is at bottom an economic fact" as his text and traced its working-out in the story of Hurstwood. We have all known such men, he wrote, suave, well-fed, and successful. But the case of Hurstwood illustrates Turgot's rule: if the economic pilings on which their lives are built are swept away, they will sink into destitution, loss of self-respect, moral squalor. It was astute recognition of Dreiser's sense of the economic tragedy at the heart of American life.

And out in St. Louis William Marion Reedy found in *Sister Carrie* a major step forward: "its veritism out-Howells Mr. Howells and out-Garlands Mr. Hamlin Garland." Despite its photographic truth, the novel had "an art about it that lifts it often above mere reporting" and "there lurks behind the mere story an intense fierce resentment of the conditions glimpsed." Yet it was a moral tale despite its directness, which, Reedy correctly noted, "seems to be the frankness of a vast unsophistication. . . . The story, as a whole, has a grip that is not exercised upon any unwholesome taste." *Sister Carrie* was about the "commonest kind of common people, yet the spell is there. . . . You find your-self trying . . . to analyze the charm away. But you cannot."

The review was the beginning of a long comradeship on the literary battle-ground. Dreiser had found an eloquent champion, and they began corresponding. He gained other converts, though pitifully few of them: Marcosson; Edna Kenton of the Chicago *Daily News,* a young woman who had migrated to the city like Carrie; Alfred Stieglitz, who gave copies to friends; George Horton of the Chicago *Times Herald;* H. L. Mencken, a fledgling Baltimore reporter; and a few score anonymous reviewers in places such as Hartford, Detroit, Albany, Indianapolis, and Seattle. Most of the book's discoverers were young and on the fringes of the literary world, newspaper men and women many of them, who had passed through the same tank towns and Middle American cities that Theodore had on their flight from conventional small-town upbringings, and who hungered for writers who were as true to American life as Tolstoy was to Russian and Hardy to English. And there were a few others, anonymous souls, scattered across the arid cultural plains of the nation, who read his book in small-town frame houses and city hall bedrooms in the watches of the night and thought, *I am not alone.*

●　●　●

In all, about thirty reviews straggled out over the course of a year. Some, like the one by McCord's friend at the Newark *Sunday News,* were not published until well into 1901. Fewer than five could be characterized as downright negative, and about ten were mixed. Although the positive reviews probably did not win over the consumers of light popular fare, who made up the great majority of the book-buying public, surely there were more than 456 readers for *Sister Carrie* in the United States. After all, Norris's *McTeague* had sold in excess of four thousand copies in hardcover. Why didn't Dreiser's novel reach a similar number?

Reedy had a hunch as to the explanation, which he noted at the beginning of his review: *Sister Carrie* "has been neither extensively advertised by its publishers, Doubleday, Page & Co. nor enthusiastically reviewed, if, indeed, it has been reviewed at all, in any of the journals of criticism." A few other reviewers also noted that the book had slunk out like a freed convict, and Horton wondered why the publisher of *Sister Carrie* would spend a good deal of money pushing a trivial work like *An Englishwoman's Love Letters* when it had the real thing.

The lack of advertising influenced the booksellers. The almost universal opinion in the trade was, "It is a 'dead one' from the shopkeeper's point of view" because the publisher did not back it up. That, of course, is a common fate for first novels; still, a less hostile publisher might have, on the strength of the reviews, taken out some advertising. A rather pretty garland of quotes could have been woven, though again one cannot say for a certainty that such an ad would have made a dent in the wall of indifference *Sister Carrie* met.

The dominance of romantic and historical fiction was now a cultural fact. *When Knighthood Was in Flower* and *Richard Carvel* were best sellers. Borne into the twentieth century on a rising tide of economic prosperity, their armies and navies victorious in Cuba and the Philippines, Americans were indeed turning to historical romances, which William Dean Howells had deplored in his first "Easy Chair" column for *Harper's Monthly* in 1900. The Era of Good Feeling under McKinley and Mark Hanna would give way to the middle-class progressivism and big-stick diplomacy of Theodore Roosevelt, who called upon Americans to feel "the mighty lift that thrills 'stern men with empire in their brains.' " The prevailing orgy of Anglo-Saxon race pride represented a backlash among the old American stock against the waves of immigrants imported by the money barons to work in their Pittsburgh mills and Lower East Side sweatshops. In such a climate, who would notice a novel about a chorus girl, a drummer, and a saloonkeeper written by the son of a German immigrant?

•   •   •

Not long after his novel came out, Dreiser ran into Howells at the Harper offices. "You know," the older man said, "I didn't like *Sister Carrie*," and hurried off. At that moment the generational fault line cracked open. To endorse a woman like Carrie Meeber would have run counter to Howells's deepest instincts; let the next generation admit her into literature—he had gone as far as he could in boosting the new realism. The seeds of free expression Dreiser had planted must lie dormant for another decade.

In 1900 Stephen Crane died in Germany, where he had retreated to fight a last battle with tuberculosis. His constitution had been weakened by the malaria he contracted covering the Spanish-American war in Cuba, and his will to live had been vitiated by financial worries. Deeply and foolishly in debt, Crane had turned to writing romances for quick money. Asked by a friend why he had abandoned realism, he replied, "I get a little tired of saying, 'Is it true?'"

Part Five

. . .

DOWN HILL AND UP

33 / Losing the Thread

> Similarly, any form of social distress—a wretched, down-at-
> heels neighborhood, a poor farm, an asylum, a jail, or an in-
> dividual or group of individuals anywhere that seemed to be
> lacking in the means of subsistence or to be devoid of the nor-
> mal comforts of life—was sufficient to set up in me thoughts
> and emotions which had a close kinship to actual and severe
> physical pain.
>
> —Dreiser, *Dawn* (1931)

By mid-December 1900 it must have become clear to Dreiser that his brave
hopes of critical and public vindication had been wildly optimistic. The many
good reviews seem not to have assuaged the pain of failure. By his testimony
ten years later, they might have been about someone else's book. Asking himself
if he had believed the reviewers who hailed him for writing a work of genius,
he answers, "I'm quite sure I didn't. I was the most surprised man—or boy,
for I was a boy in mind, all the same, that you ever saw." Frank Doubleday's
verdict of "immoral" was the judgment that mattered most deeply; it worked
under his skin like a splinter and festered.

Possibly the first manifestation of this self-doubt was his abandonment of
the novel he was working on, *The Rake.* The title alone suggests that Theodore
was sailing into perilous moral waters again, perhaps writing about his youthful
amours. After the Doubleday shock, he may have grown doubtful that he would
find a publisher for such material.

In January 1901 he began a new book. The inspiration for its heroine,
whom Dreiser called Jennie Gerhardt, was another of his sisters. Something
had impelled him to sift the ashes of his earliest memories in Terre Haute.
That something could only have been the death of John Paul Dreiser on
Christmas Day 1900, at the age of seventy-nine. Theodore received the news
in Montgomery City, where he and Jug were spending the holiday. Paul was
living with Mame and Brennan in Rochester when he died. He spent his
last days peacefully, tending the Brennans' garden, going to early Mass daily.

Sylvia's abandoned Carl was living with them too, though Carl would now have been sixteen or seventeen and probably was about to strike out on his own. Evidently, the idea of his father living with Mame—the daughter who had disgraced him in Terre Haute with her affair with Colonel Silsby—struck Theodore as the seed of a novel. A stern, Old World father who had disowned his daughter in her youth spends his final days in her care; presumably he has forgiven her, as she has forgiven him (perhaps Mame had even told him as much).

Theodore began writing the story of Jennie on January 6, 1901, less than two weeks after his father's death. But his haste did not mean he was indifferent to his father's passing. In a letter he wrote to Richard Duffy only a day or so after his father died, some of Theodore's grief must have shown through. In his reply, dated December 30, Duffy expresses concern about his mental state: "I am very sorry to hear of the bereavement you have suffered in the death of your father. . . . I hope you will force yourself to bear this trial with fortitude, the more so, since it has seemed to me that you are lately inclined to ponder sadly. Ponder and weigh life's bundle of waste, I know you must. It is the heritage of your philosophic Teutonic ancestors." Duffy must have noticed depressive tendencies in Dreiser in New York and feared that the latest blow might intensify them.

Disregarding his friend's advice that his next book contain "a truly humorous character," Dreiser plunged into the Jennie Gerhardt story, which begins with scenes of cold and hunger in Terre Haute, memories of gathering lumps of coal along the railroad tracks. He wrote with considerable speed, finishing five chapters in six days and ten by February 3. The first ten chapters were the ones most directly grounded in his childhood.

Back in New York City after the holidays, Theodore was confronted once again with the problem of making a living. It must have been clear by then that he could expect little in the way of royalties from *Sister Carrie*. As a belt-tightening measure, he and Jug moved to a cheaper apartment at 1599 East End Avenue, along the East River. From his window Dreiser could see Black-wells Island, where were located the city's prison, insane asylum, and charity hospital, and "the sight had a most depressing effect on me," he said.

The first winter Arthur Henry joined them to re-create briefly the old *ménage à trois*. Henry had envisioned a "cozy winter" in which both of them would work on their novels (he was also starting another one). First, of course, they would churn out some articles and lay up sufficient money to finance their next literary ventures.

Dreiser pushed ahead on his novel, completing nearly forty chapters. He had thirty of them typed by the Infant class, with the idea of showing them to a publisher and obtaining an advance to live on while he completed the book.

He decided to query George P. Brett, head of Macmillan, who had written him that he liked *Sister Carrie*. But in his letter, Theodore confessed that "an error in character analysis makes me wish to throw away everything from my fifteenth chapter on and rewrite it with a view to making it more truthful and appealing." Doubts had begun to set in. Brett showed interest but said the firm never advanced money on an uncompleted book.

The reception at other houses was even less hospitable. At the Century Company the manuscript was returned to him by a secretary without even a form rejection; A. S. Barnes declined (later, when the house was considering reissuing *Sister Carrie,* a reader was so shocked that he threw it into his fireplace); and John Phillips, of McClure, Phillips, told him that if that was his idea of literature, he should go into another line of work.

Dreiser was also circulating copies of *Sister Carrie* in the hope that someone might give his aborted child a miraculous second life. His idea was that he would offer a publisher the rights to both his novels. He made a preliminary inquiry to Doubleday, Page about buying the plates and unsold stock not long after he returned to the city. A statement prepared by the publisher in February puts the value of what is on hand at about seven hundred fifty dollars. It concludes with the following cryptic statement: "New royalty arrangement might be made more favorable to ~~author~~ [sic] publisher—author is sick. Sell for cost less 15%." Apparently, the idea was that Dreiser would buy the plates out of his royalties. What his sickness was is not known. It could have been a particulary debilitating case of the flu or bronchitis.

Then came an upswing in *Carrie's* fortunes. In May the London publisher William Heinemann asked for permission to bring out a British edition of *Sister Carrie* (Frank Norris had sent him a copy) in his Dollar Library series, which was devoted to publishing young American writers. There was one problem: the price of books in the series was fixed at four shillings (the equivalent of a dollar), and Dreiser's novel was too long to sell at that price. Could he condense the first two hundred pages to about eighty? Already a bit punch-drunk from cuts and changes, Dreiser was queasy about wielding the shears once more. Fortunately, Arthur Henry volunteered to undertake the job. He accomplished it with dispatch, compressing Carrie's story and making a new, tighter book in the process, one that probably should have been called "The Death of Hurstwood," since the manager becomes the focus. Heinemann was pleased and bent all efforts to have his edition out in late July.

If this news cheered Dreiser, the effect was only temporary. For his other literary affairs were not prospering. He was not selling articles at his old pace. In 1898 he had published almost fifty articles, poems, and stories; in the year and a half after he finished *Sister Carrie,* he sold only thirteen. And several of them had been researched before or during those miraculous six months in which he completed his novel. He began to think that a conspiracy of rejection had formed against him, not only among book publishers but among magazine editors.

The truth of the matter was that Dreiser was no longer able to grind out "specials"; he had lost touch with the market—possibly by choice. His antipathy to magazine writing could be traced back to the summer on the Maumee, only two years before. That discovery of untapped powers had permanently disqualified him for hackdom. Now all he was capable of writing were impressionistic sketches (e.g., one called "Hell's Kitchen"). A few of the short stories he had begun in the summer and fall of 1899 he sold, but it was a slow business. It had taken him two years of continuous effort to get "McEwen" and "Nigger Jeff" published, and it was Duffy who finally took them for *Ainslee's*. Reedy ran "Butcher Rogaum" in the *Mirror*, and "A True Patriarch" was taken by John Phillips for *McClure's*, after some haggling over the price (Dreiser, obviously out of need, had demanded more than the hundred dollars Phillips offered).

• • •

By June Dreiser still had no publisher to back his second novel and faced the task of recasting almost two-thirds of what he had written. He had sold nothing in months, and his money was dwindling. Then Arthur Henry breezed in from a sojourn with Anna and invited him and Jug to spend the summer at Dumpling Island, a few hundred feet off the coast of Connecticut. Though the cast of characters had changed (Anna in place of Maude), it must have seemed an opportunity to renew the fellowship and productivity of that summer on the Maumee. Dreiser accepted, with Jug planning to join them in July, after a stay with her family. It would be like old times, helping each other on their new novels, the best of comrades.

34 / Nancy, Ruth, Tom, and I

> In all the world, there is no lovelier retreat than this island, where Nancy, Ruth, Tom and I were together for a month. And yet, we became more and more unhappy as the days passed.
>
> —Arthur Henry, *An Island Cabin* (1904)

Henry never wrote his novel; instead, he turned to autobiographical back-to-nature books, which were then in vogue—perhaps as a reaction against too-rapid urbanization. The idea for the first of these came that summer in 1901; he would call it *An Island Cabin*. It would tell about two couples—Ruth and Tom, Nancy and himself—who escape to the perfect retreat and spoil it because they have brought their city troubles along.

When Theodore debarked from the small sailboat used to haul water and supplies, he saw a large, unpainted saltbox house surrounded by sand, rocks, and tangled scrub growth. Henry, who had thought his friend would love the rugged natural beauty of the setting, was shocked to hear him complaining. The place was filthy; the dishes were greasy and the knives rusty; the floor needed scrubbing; the bedding was damp; the food was atrocious. Henry had vowed to live on two dollars a week and was subsisting entirely on a diet of fish, potatoes, and onions. Dreiser was in no mood for Thoreauvian simplicity and thought the back-to-nature regimen a pose. Since the island was only a few hundred feet offshore, however, they were hardly roughing it.

Waiting for Jug and Anna to arrive, they spent most of the time loafing, talking, or reading. They held long philosophical colloquies under the stars, Dreiser in a rocker that was providentially among the sparse furnishings, and Henry stretched out on a blanket and pillow. One night they argued about the nature of the universe. Henry thought it "wise, generous and tender," tending toward "harmony, beauty and order." "Men rob and murder and deceive," he said, "and yet the sum total of their conduct from the beginning until now is progress toward a loving fellowship."

Dreiser scoffed. Rocking in the darkness, he opined that the universe might be an individual, like President McKinley or Chancellor Bismarck, or J. P. Morgan or John D. Rockefeller—but he doubted it had the strength of purpose of such great men. Or "it might be a crab or a leaf or an atom of the air, and man but a minor subdivision in its make-up." It didn't matter, really. "Any conception of life is good if held in reverence," he said. "Reverence is man's salvation." But modern man lacked an object of reverence. He had outgrown traditional religious beliefs; science had toppled the old gods and left nothing in their place.

Those unguarded words were signs of a spiritual crisis. Many turn-of-the-century Americans faced a similar one. The naturalist John Burroughs, whom Dreiser interviewed for *Success,* was one of the many intellectuals who bemoaned the contemporary loss of faith.

> How the revelations of science do break in upon the sort of private and domestic view of the universe which mankind have so long held! To many minds it is like being fairly turned out into the cold, and made to face without shield or shelter the eternities and infinities of geologic time and sidereal space. . . . The race of man becomes the mere ephemera of an hour, like the insects of a summer day. . . . We feel the cosmic chill.

Dreiser knew this ephemeral feeling. "We are insects produced by heat and wither and pass without it," he had written in *Sister Carrie* in another context. The chill of gray days plunged him into gloom; the chill of the cosmic winds affected his inner weather. Stripped of self-esteem by the collapse of his inflated ambitions, he was as vulnerable as Hurstwood after his fall from Chicago celebrity. And he felt himself sinking into that state of apathy and drift he feared and that had given rise to the dark, fictional alter ego.

●　　●　　●

At last Jug came. They were late meeting the train and found her sitting on her luggage, pouting—at which, Henry reports, Dreiser "pulled her from the trunk and beat her publicly that all men might know he was the master of his house," a description Henry probably intended jestingly but which accurately reflected his own psychological treatment of Maude and, later, Anna.

Her presence was like the return of the sun. She loved the island and found the living conditions ever so jolly. Immediately establishing herself in the kitchen, she cooked mouth-watering dishes with the materials at hand. Dreiser proudly made over the kitchen to suit her. When Anna Mallon arrived, he told her, "I found a lot of your trash around here and threw it into the sea. When [Jug] is in a place two minutes, it begins to look like home."

Anna's reaction is not recorded, but this was the first of many such flare-ups between Dreiser and her. He was full of "half-playful, half-cynical jibes and railleries," Henry recalled, and Theodore's sharpest thrusts were aimed at Anna. The odd emotion of jealousy Anna aroused in Theodore must have been troubling. He had, in his way, loved Henry more than any other human being save Jug and his mother; now he was wondering if he had made a fool of himself, or worse. Even if there were no homoerotic overtones to his attraction, he had fallen totally for an illusion. As Maude wrote many years later, "It was inevitable that Dreiser should come under the benign influence of the calm, clear gray eyes, the idealism, the reasoning mind of Arthur Henry . . . always ready for adventure, for gay laughter, for hard work when necessary, but ingrained with the . . . fairy-taled happenings of early youth." Now the enchantment was broken, leaving Theodore hurt and angry, betrayed and abandoned.

At the end of July he and Jug returned to the city.

35 / Fortune's Wheel

> It is quite true that to the victor belongs the spoils, and to the strong the race, but at the same time it is sad to think that to the weak and vanquished belong nothing.
> —Dreiser, "Reflections" (1896)

Back in New York, his money running low, Dreiser returned to magazine writing, but not to salable articles about lady harp players and trolley trips. He was still writing out of a personal vision.

Dreiser sold three articles on the down-and-out to, of all places, *Success*. One of them was a spin-off from "Curious Shifts of the Poor," focusing on the character of the Captain, who conducted his nightly auction in the theater district to raise money for the city's legions of Hurstwoods. Another was an inspirational tale about a cripple, and the third described how the lives of tenement dwellers had become twisted under the never-ending pressure of economic survival. Although such stories were somewhat downbeat, Orison Swett Marden published them, billing the one about the Captain as a "distinct commentary on the social conditions of our day." The old success peddler was sensing the winds of change. The national mood was increasingly progressive; a popular backlash against big business was building, and in a year's time S. S. McClure would launch the muckraking era in popular journalism.

The only article Dreiser wrote in this vein was "A Mayor and His People," a profile of a socialist mayor, an honest and enlightened public servant who is cast out by powerful economic interests he has offended. He sent it to *McClure's*. Lincoln Steffens, who was acting as managing editor, wrote a detailed critique of the piece and recommended that the author "make it over into what we want." That touched off an exchange of letters, with Steffens insisting that Dreiser must make his story "either a definite account of the facts or a fiction story. . . . As it stands it is neither one nor the other." Dreiser did a bit of fiddling with the piece but stubbornly ignored Steffens's instructions. The latter returned it, saying, "it is plain that . . . anything of yours is to be taken as left not changed."

Meanwhile, out of the blue, Ripley Hitchcock, an editor at Appleton, wrote him to praise *Carrie* and suggest that if Dreiser could write another novel that was "less drastic," he would be interested in publishing it; then his firm would reissue *Carrie*. (Hitchcock had a precedent for this approach. He had turned down Stephen Crane's *Maggie: A Girl of the Streets* in manuscript but published a trade edition after the success of *The Red Badge of Courage,* which he also handled.) For some reason Hitchcock could not follow through on the offer, but his interest made Dreiser think once again about the possibility of a reincarnation for *Carrie*. Doubleday was not cooperative. The company asked $500 for plates and unbound books. As J. W. Thompson of the firm informed Dreiser in a letter dated September 23, 1901, even that price represented a loss to the company of between $150 and $200.

Dreiser, who had nothing like $500 in the bank, talked about taking out a note for the amount, which was agreeable to Thompson if Theodore could find a financially reputable individual to cosign it. Then fortune's wheel took another spin. Rutger B. Jewett, trade book editor at the J. F. Taylor Company, a young house, was interested in publishing Dreiser's second book and also reissuing *Sister Carrie*. "I believe in you and in your work," Jewett wrote him, "and intend to make it possible for you to finish that second book by advancing enough for you to live on while you do it." Dreiser leaped at the chance. Under the contract signed September 30, J. F. Taylor agreed to buy the plates and unsold stock of *Sister Carrie* from Doubleday for $500. It also undertook to reissue the book "either for the coming winter or spring trade, whichever seems the more advisable, under the same name or some suitable title." In return Dreiser gave the company an option on his next novel—the story of Jennie Gerhardt, of which he had supplied a synopsis. In a separate letter of agreement, dated November 6, Taylor promised to pay Dreiser $100 a month on account for a year.

Taylor had founded his firm in 1898, primarily to reprint European and American classics, but he had recently formed a small trade department, headed by Jewett. Though Jewett was most interested in *Carrie,* Taylor, a cautious businessman, was worried that Doubleday had "killed" the book. As Jewett explained, Doubleday, Page had sprinkled enough copies in the stores so that booksellers would say, "Well, we gave it a trial, and still have the books we ordered." And so Taylor suggested a title change to make the book seem to be a new one.

•   •   •

In the wake of the agreement with Taylor, Dreiser received some heartening news from abroad. The reviews of the Heinemann edition surpassed his wildest imaginings. What is more, they came out together, an authoritative, nearly unanimous chorus of yeas. Nearly all of the major literary organs were represented. The *Spectator* praised the "really powerful" study of Hurstwood and called *Sister Carrie* "an engrossing and depressing book." The *Academy* found it "thoroughly good, alike in accurate and synthetic observation, in human sympathy, in lyric appeal and in dramatic power." The London *Daily Mail* commented: "At last a really strong novel has come from America; a novel almost great because of its relentless purpose, its power to compel emotion, its marvelous simplicity."

The British reviews, as Dreiser later wrote, have "done me proud." But they were far too late to resurrect *Sister Carrie* in America. And although the Heinemann edition got off to a fast start in the stalls, it ended up selling only about one thousand copies and earning the author some eighty dollars in royalties.

Heartened by his critical reception in England, Dreiser decided to flee winter's spirit-deadening chill for the Blue Ridge Mountains and dig in for a siege of writing. After receiving his first monthly check from Taylor in early November, he closed his apartment, packed Jug off to her family, and headed for Bedford City, Virginia, near Roanoke.

36 / The Crannies of the World

The deep blue blacks of the dome, picked out with millions
and millions of stars. How they do glisten. Underneath is this
little town, its cottages hugging the ground and the soft glow
of the windows seeming to struggle in a feeble way against
the immensity of the blind universe without. —Oh the little
lamps, the wee little humans! How they struggle between the
crannies of the world.
—Dreiser to Mary Annabel Fanton Roberts (1901)

Once he was out of New York, Dreiser's spirits soared. Bedford City was "home
like, southern and high and dry," he wrote J. F. Taylor. He found a good boardinghouse, and his room had a view of the mountains, a great improvement over
Blackwells Island. Mrs. Clayton, his landlady, set a bountiful table, and his appetite was sharp. On November 14 he wrote to Mary Annabel Fanton Roberts,
who was editing the manuscript of the Jennie Gerhardt story, that a mild winter
was promised, and he rhapsodized over the mountains—"great towering lonely
figures with a blue haze always hanging over them." In such a setting, he felt
certain that his "malarial feeling" would be replaced by a "desire to work."

The reference to malarial feeling is Dreiser's first to the general sense of
debility that would dog him for the next year. There is no evidence that he
actually had malaria; perhaps it was the aftermath of a serious case of flu. He
was trying to give a medical label to a cluster of complaints—apathy, aches and
pains, and increasingly frequent bouts of insomnia, that old nemesis.

But in Bedford City, the illness, whatever it was, went into remission. The
spectacular scenery of the Blue Ridge Mountains and the pristine air intoxicated
him. Jauntily he told Mrs. Roberts to send him the manuscript she was working
on "heavily edited. . . . Pull it together close—everything can go except the
grip. That I must have in it." Part of his reason for egging Mrs. Roberts on
was that he was already getting some gentle prodding from his new publishers.

Dreiser must have felt like he was reliving a bad dream when he read this
sentence in Jewett's letter: "To the majority of readers some moral coloring

seems essential. One of the criticisms for instance which some of the women readers have brought against your story of Carrie is that it points no moral. . . . As you sketched your second story to me, the moral was on every page but the reading public needs a certain amount of explanation."

Taylor's suggestion could have planted in Dreiser's mind the worry that his supposedly liberal new publishers were Frank Doubledays under the skin. Such fears could not have been helpful at this stage, when he needed to regain his original enthusiasm, pick up the dropped thread of the story, and follow it wherever it led.

Taylor's views on *Sister Carrie* could only have increased Dreiser's anxiety. Taylor felt, Jewett reported, that the relationship between Carrie and Ames should be developed into a love story in order to "win a much warmer audience" for the book. In a "thoroughly womanly way," Jewett explained, Carrie would confess to Ames that she loved him and suggest marriage. But Ames would turn her down because of her past. Cruel, perhaps, but "it is exactly the position that 99 men out of every 100 would take." Not that Jewett approved of such a view, but it was the way of the world—"simply the damnable result of a dual code of ethics, one for woman, another for man." The change would be a "little" one, which would not affect the main outline of the book, and the outcome would be the same: "Carrie would not marry the man just as you do not allow her to, only more would be made of the situation . . . and vital color given to the picture."

Dreiser replied noncommittally. "No one could be more open to thoughtful suggestions than I am," he assured his publisher. "I try to steer my course by the light that I can get from all sources."

Jewett must have scented evasion, for he returned to the proposal in a subsequent letter. This time, however, he envisioned Carrie nobly refusing to marry Ames "because of the mistakes of her past life. That her experiences, shame, suffering, and empty triumphs could have made her big enough for this sacrifice is not only possible but probable. In fact, I know it to be the case with just such a woman on the New York stage to-day." While the revision seemed only a minor change to Jewett, Dreiser could not have seen it that way.

Then, on December 4, Taylor suggested postponing publication of *Sister Carrie*. Jewett had led Dreiser to believe that the new edition would be out the following spring. Now Taylor was telling him that "our experience has taught us that it is almost impossible to bring out a book that has once been on the market, unless something has occurred in the interim which would insure the success of the reissue. Applying this principle to *Sister Carrie*, he thought they should hold off until after the new novel had "made a success," creating a demand for Dreiser's earlier work.

Taylor had in effect introduced a new condition into their agreement—that Dreiser's second novel be a success. Though Theodore's reply has been lost, it must have shown flashes of his old truculent self, for Jewett felt compelled to write soothingly, "I do not wonder after your experience with Doubleday that you feel suspicious of possible unfair treatment in the case of this book. We want however to do what is perfectly square and honorable with you." The firm stood ready "to issue the book again in its present form for you this spring if you wish," but in view of reports from the company's salesmen, it would be best not to republish *Sister Carrie* without the requested changes, including a new title.

Shaken by the rumblings from New York, he made little progress on his novel in Bedford City. His initial optimism rapidly dissipated; he also missed Jug. He was so lonely that he became friendly with a black tailor and dry cleaner named J. E. Bowler. Actually, Bowler was a remarkable man, so if loneliness drew Dreiser to him, it was soon replaced by liking and respect. Intelligent and ambitious, Bowler was a strong supporter of civil rights in the Booker T. Washington sense of self-improvement — without overstepping the color line.

Their acquaintance flowered into a sporadic correspondence that continued over the next decade. (In one of those letters, Bowler notes that it was the first time he had ever written to a white man on matters having nothing to do with business.) Bowler found Dreiser to be a man of "large sympathy." They talked of philosophy (what else with Dreiser?) and of Bowler's fierce ambition to better himself.

After a month of futile effort in Bedford City, Dreiser fled to Missouri to spend the holidays with the White family. Arch White had little use for fame or riches, but he must have felt paternal concern about his daughter's welfare. Dreiser's financial prospects could not have looked too secure at this point. He no longer even had a permanent address, and Jug was forced to live at home. Such things a father could understand, while glowing British reviews and contracts for future books were a distant urban fantasy. Dreiser's increased moodiness must also have given the patriarch cause for concern.

Still, in the warmth of the White family circle at Christmastime, Dreiser cheered up and sent Duffy a description of the festivities as well as thanks for a copy of Walt Whitman's *Leaves of Grass* and a testament of friendship. He also passed around to his in-laws the Christmas issue of William Reedy's *Mirror*, which contained his story "Butcher Rogaum's Door."

• • •

In February Dreiser and Jug struck out on a restless odyssey through the South. From Red Sulphur Springs, West Virginia, he reported to Duffy that the water "is supposed to be good for insomnia. Hence my presence." They had been traveling so much that he received two of Duffy's letters at once. Dreiser wrote that he was "interested" in Henry's "Island Cabin" story, which was being serialized in the New York *Post,* and wondered if McClure would bring it out as a book. "Hen has rather gone out of my life recently and so a bit of news now and then would be welcome." The novel was "proceeding slowly but proceeding."

Duffy had cheered him with a sheaf of Thomas Hardy's poems, which Dreiser found "rousingly beautiful." Hardy was "the greatest figure in all English literature." He also praised Whitman: "Time will put him above all other American poets up to now."

After a few weeks the Dreisers landed in Hinton, West Virginia, a town near another hot springs. Perhaps Theodore's mysterious malaise could be cured by some magic waters. He persisted in believing his troubles were physical. But what if they were not?

37 / The Wild Ass's Skin

> I wandered here & there in Virginia & West Virginia, unable
> to write. My mood made worse by the fact that the money
> that was being sent me was being used up & I was getting no
> where.
>
> —Dreiser, "Down Hill and Up" (1920)

Now gloom pervaded Dreiser's reports to Jewett, and the editor wrote him on
March 17, "The last time I saw you I told you that if you did not learn how to
laugh some times just for the sake of relief you would go crazy, or die of grief."

Jug's life was getting no cheerier, as her husband grew more restless and
moody. He soon tired of the charms of Hinton and moved on to Lynchburg, Virginia, leaving her behind. Not liking it there, he continued to Charlottesville.
Thinking he was still in Lynchburg, Jug sent him a postcard there saying she
would arrive on the No. 4 train and that he should meet her at the station.
She must have had some anxious moments at the Lynchburg station. It may be
that Dreiser was subconsciously abandoning her. Jug was a solace to him but a
financial burden. She returned to Missouri not long after this, leaving Dreiser
to fight it out alone in Charlottesville for two more months.

Thrown back on himself, Dreiser's distrust of his publisher flared up anew
when he read the March issue of the trade publication *The Bookman*. It reports
that *Sister Carrie* would be republished in the spring by J. F. Taylor & Co. "in
more attractive form, and, let us hope, under a new and more significant title."
Furthermore, the author intends to make some changes in it; specifically, he
will expand the role of the third man in the book with whom Carrie is involved,
"whose path crosses her own at the close of the book, but in an abortive manner,
which leaves an impression of artistic imcompleteness and faulty observation."

Replying to Dreiser's query, Jewett confirmed that he had indeed talked
to *The Bookman*'s stringer, "Cooper of the Commercial Advertiser," whom he
described as an admirer of *Sister Carrie* "very keen to strike a blow for the book
wherever and whenever opportunity opens." Jewett fed Cooper a story about
the changes, making it appear that they were the author's idea. Since Dreiser

hadn't agreed to make the changes, he must have found the promise of them disturbing.

Dreiser told Jewett in early April that he could expect the novel's opening chapters shortly. Jewett prodded Dreiser to come up with a title, but when Dreiser suggested *Jennie Gerhardt,* Jewett requested something more "abstract" and accused his author of having a fatal fascination for heroines with diminutive first names. If he did use her in the title, he should use her formal first name, Jane. Thus, he might call the book "Jane Gebhardt."

The misspelling detonated another minor explosion in Charlottesville, and Jewett was obliged to reassure his thin-skinned author that it was an innocent typo. Again he begged Dreiser to erase the Doubleday past: "You have a mind . . . that needs filtering to remove the taint of old suspicion." Dreiser cooled off and suggested that the novel be called *The Transgressor,* which Jewett liked, perhaps because it had a strong moral ring to it.

The obligation to finish his new book in time for fall publication was becoming more onerous with each passing day. To keep Jewett temporarily happy, Dreiser set in motion a small deception. He gave his editor the impression that the opening chapters were new, or at least a complete reworking of an earlier draft. Actually, the ten chapters he forwarded at the end of April were those Anna Mallon's employees had typed the previous spring.

•   •   •

The plot of *The Transgressor* concerns a poor girl from Columbus, Ohio — Jennie — who meets the distinguished Senator Brander, a somewhat Bryanesque figure, while she and her mother are working as cleaning women at the principal hotel in Columbus.

Brander, a man of fifty, is attracted to the eighteen-year-old Jennie's wholesome beauty and takes pity on her family, which is suffering severe poverty because the father, William, a German immigrant glassblower, is out of work. Brander begins taking her out, and, despite the great difference in their ages, he proposes marriage. The neighbors, however, are critical. They "saw only a family, in the Gerhardts, given to making mistakes" — like the Dreisers in Warsaw. Gerhardt, a strict Lutheran under the thumb of puritanical Pastor Wundt, is ashamed. He berates his wife for her moral laxity in bringing up the children ("Such a wife! Such a home! Such a family! . . . She would make streetwalkers of them all!") and forbids Brander to see Jennie again.

But Sebastian — "Bass" — the oldest son, who is working as an installment-payment collector à la Theodore, and in his off hours playing the dude à la Rome at the Columbus counterpart of the Terre Haute House, loses sixty dollars of his employer's money in a poker game. Fearing he will be fired, he begs Jennie to go to Brander that night and borrow the money. To save her brother, she does, and Brander seduces her. The senator promises to marry Jennie but dies of a heart attack before he can do so.

Jennie is pregnant. When Gerhardt learns of this, he expels her from the house. Bass, Jennie, and her mother hatch a plan whereby Bass will go to Cleveland and get a job, and the family will follow. Gerhardt, meanwhile, sells the mortgage-encumbered house, pays off his debts, and moves to Youngstown, Ohio, where there is an opening in his craft. The mother and the other children join Bass in Cleveland. Jennie, who in the meantime has given birth, goes to work in a factory, but the combined family income, even with old Gerhardt contributing most of his paycheck, is barely enough for them to survive. After the father is badly burned in an accident, he is unable to work and needs constant medical attention.

With overdue bills piling up and the family facing eviction, Jennie is accosted on the street by Lester Kane, the handsome, rakish son of a wealthy Cincinnati carriage manufacturer. Overcome by his charm, she shyly describes her family's troubles and accepts ten dollars. Kane persuades her to sup with him at a fancy hotel that provides private dining rooms to patrons interested in seduction. After much soul-searching, Jennie decides she will keep the assignation: "The lesson Brander's action had taught her was coming back. . . . The world would buy beauty. It could be induced to pay something for her soul." At the hotel, though, she loses her nerve and breaks into tears (as Emma had done in Evansville under similar circumstances). Kane takes pity on her and sends her home with forty dollars. As far as he is concerned, he is merely postponing his pleasure.

Kane is a charming bachelor in his mid-thirties, much in demand socially, who travels around representing the family business interests (something like the role assigned to the jovial, pleasure-loving Austin Brennan). Marriage is a fine institution, Kane thinks, but not for him. The next time he is in Cleveland he asks Jennie to meet him, and they go to lunch. In a scene strongly reminiscent of Drouet's seduction of Carrie (this was not the only time Dreiser reflexively harked back to his first novel), he urges her to go to New York City with him. He will provide for her family—even buy them a new house. Jennie hesitates, but she feels a "drag of affinity." Lester sweeps away her last shreds of compunction by taking her to a fancy dry-goods store and buying her an expensive wardrobe, as Drouet had done with Carrie.

Screwing up her courage, she explains to Mrs. Gerhardt that a Mr. Kane wants to help them and has invited her to accompany him to New York. Her mother promptly asks, "Will he marry you?" Yes, Jennie replies, "the lie falling like a leaden weight from her lips to her heart."

In New York she is stirred, Carrie-like, by the fashion parade on Broadway. As for Lester, his attraction to Jennie is that of the strong for the weak, which Dreiser regards as a law of life. He is a man who takes what he wants: "The

Macheavellean [sic] manner in which Lester thus complicated Jennie's sense of consideration for her mother with the need of yielding to him while at the same time destroying any illusions as to the nature of his feeling for her, was calculated to upset and undo that little wanderer—to make her feel the helplessness of her portion."

The story continues with Lester moving to Chicago and setting up Jennie in an apartment, where his sister discovers by accident his illicit relationship.

There the original manuscript ends. It should be apparent why, two years earlier, Dreiser had misgivings about its publishability and the "appeal" of his characters.

Lester is an unattractive figure—a rake, a rich Drouet, without the latter's saving goodheartedness. Jennie doesn't love him, so what can she possibly see in him but his money? She nobly sacrifices her virtue for her family, but Dreiser can bring no emotional poignancy to that theme. Her decision to sell herself is presented so tentatively, as though he had grave misgivings, that it lacks conviction. Then he shows her reveling in her new luxuries, making her seem materialistic, and seems to half-approve of the masterful way Lester overcomes her resistance.

Unable to attain the necessary detachment from his material, still stuck in his first book, Dreiser desperately tried to rewrite and rearrange, but when he patched here the story became unraveled there. The facts of Mame's life stubbornly refused to yield to imaginative flights; they remained inert, sordid.

He slogged on, and in early June sent his typist, Miss Gordinnier, the first batch of manuscript. Unable to stay in Charlottesville any longer, he set out on a tramp northward. He hoped that the exercise would calm his frayed nerves, but there was an element of panicky flight in his trek—almost a fugue state. He later told an interviewer, Isaac Goldberg, that he was seized by "an aching desire to be forever on the move." As each month passed, his debt to his publisher mounted another hundred dollars. Dreiser had wished for freedom from financial pressures so he could write, and magically Jewett had appeared and offered it to him. But in his present depressed state, the boon was coming to resemble the magical wild ass's skin in Balzac's novel. The more Theodore used it, the more it shrank and the more he suffered.

A gauge of his state of mind is a letter he wrote to Howells not long before leaving Charlottesville. In a review of a biography of Longfellow in the April *Harper's,* Howells had written that the beauty of the poet's work was more apparent to a man in his later years, "when impartial chance decimates the rank in which he stands, and leaves him safe only till the next round at best. Those who fall become the closer friends to those who remain untouched."

After quoting this passage, Dreiser writes, "There is something so mellow, kindly and withal so lonely about it that I venture to offer, if I may, a word of fellow feeling and appreciation ere the 'next round' take you and it be too

late." In the "fitful dream" that is life, he is heartened by the "mental attitude"
of the three writers he most admires—Hardy, Tolstoy, and Howells. And he
closes with an unconsciously morbid flourish:

> If the common ground is to be credited with the flowering out of such minds as
> yours I shall not be disturbed to return to the dust. There is enough in the thought
> to explain the wonder of the night, the sparkle of the waters—the thrill of tender
> feeling that runs abroad in the odours and murmurs and sighs. Buried Howells
> and Hardys and Tolstoys shall explain it to me. I shall rejoice to believe that it is
> they who laugh in the waters—that it is because of such that the hills clap their
> hands.

What Howells thought of this funereal communication is not known, since
he never replied.

• • •

By early June Dreiser had walked as far as Rehoboth Beach, Delaware, where
he settled temporarily. As soon as Jewett learned his address, he fired off an
urgent query: "What and where is the delay?" The firm had made up a dummy
of *The Transgressor* for its salesmen and was anxious to have the book. His back
to the wall, Dreiser confessed the truth: he could not possibly finish in time.
On June 20 Jewett bowed to the inevitable: "If the book cannot mature in
time for September publication it will be better to postpone the issue until the
following February. . . . Do not get discouraged."

Actually, Miss Gordinnier was just finishing up another batch of manuscript—about twenty thousand words in all—and she forwarded it to Delaware
when she learned of Dreiser's whereabouts. She had enjoyed Jennie's story, she
reported: "Am sorry I did not have the first chapters . . . the story having great
interest for me, it being so truly everyday and human. It is a surprise to me that
a man can so comprehend the minute details of household life as you have." As
the Infants had done with *Carrie,* she identified with Jennie, and like them she
provided an ingenuous warning: "Unless Jennie reaps the proverbial whirlwind
in the closing chapters I fear me that the issue of your book . . . will break up
the typewriting profession, not to mention other employments." Why be a
working girl if you could be a kept woman like Jennie?

38 / *The Ache of Modernism*

> I was hard up, and everything seemed futile. . . . Life seemed
> an endless chain without meaning.
> —Dreiser to Dorothy Dudley (1932)

When Miss Gordinnier's letter reached him in early July, Dreiser's wandering
had landed him in Philadelphia, where he had taken a room at 3225 Ridge
Avenue, toward the outskirts of the city. Why Philadelphia? Perhaps he did
not feel ready for New York. Also, his friend Peter McCord had been living in
Philadelphia and had worked for the *North American* (the town's "yellow sheet,"
he told Dreiser). McCord pulled strings to enable Dreiser to do some unsigned
pieces for the paper.

J. F. Taylor's check in June was the last because of Dreiser's failure to meet
the deadline. He now owed the publisher seven hundred dollars unless he could
somehow finish *The Transgressor*. But first he must bail out his sinking financial
ship, and the free-lance seas seemed hostile at this point. Henry Mills Alden
returned a story with a curt-sounding note: "It is not the kind of material we
want in whatever shape it may be put."

The *Harper's Monthly* editor was probably not banishing Dreiser from his
pages. His colleague at *Harper's Weekly*, John Kendrick Bangs, asked Dreiser to
write a piece on "Christmas in the Tenements" for the appropriate December
issue. Managing editor R. C. Penfield cautioned, "We do not want too much
'misery' in the story, but I don't know that you know too much of it, for publication at least . . . a Christmas number should be bright and cheerful and you
can find much in this line among the tenements, I am sure, to write about."
Dreiser must have had a bitter laugh.

The usually hospitable Duffy rejected "The Mayor and His People," explaining that *Munsey's* was now mainly in the market for light, amusing material. Convinced there was a conspiracy of rejection against him, Dreiser sent a
story to *The Atlantic Monthly* under McCord's name. Years later he told Dorothy
Dudley that the magazine had informed him he was "morally bankrupt" and
wanted nothing more to do with him.

To cap it all, Jewett was somewhat less than enthusiastic about the last batch of chapters of *The Transgressor*. "You elaborate certain parts of the narrative to excess," he wrote, mentioning the section dealing with the Gerhardts' problems of economic survival in Cleveland; "the reader becomes confused and weary." Nothing incurable, but obviously Dreiser was floundering—and in need of an Arthur Henry to advise him. But by this time Henry's *An Island Cabin* had appeared, with its unflattering portrait of the querulous and eccentric Tom. The average reader would not know who Tom was, of course, but his real-life counterpart could picture New York editorial insiders laughing at Theodore Dreiser.

• • •

"Christmas in the Tenements" would be the last full-length magazine article Dreiser wrote for many months. It was also one of the best of his urban sketches in the vein of "Curious Shifts of the Poor." Amid dogday heat he conjured up holiday scenes of ragged children at shop windows gazing longingly at the cheap baubles with "an earnest, child-heart longing which may never again be gratified if not now." He had a personal understanding of a child's cravings. If they are left unfulfilled—or, worse, denied by a hard, puritanical father—he believed, the child's life is permanently warped. He also tried to show that at Christmastime "sympathy, love, affection and passion" were just as prevalent in the slums as they were on Fifth Avenue—that the child's desires were the "indissoluble link which binds these weakest and most wretched elements of society to the best and most successful." It was a Howellsian-Tolstoyan message with a Dreiser twist: desire, not love, as the solvent of class barriers.

Jug joined him in September and became a helpless onlooker to his increasingly futile struggles. All Dreiser's efforts at self-cure having failed, he decided to seek professional help. On October 22 he called at the offices of Dr. Louis Adolphus Duhring, a leading dermatologist, two blocks from the University of Pennsylvania Hospital. Among Dreiser's medley of symptoms were various skin disorders, ranging from a burning sensation on his fingertips to eczemalike rashes and itching feet. In addition, he complained of chest pains and headaches, that he was losing his hair, had an abnormally large appetite, and couldn't sleep. He said at times he felt exhausted and down in the depths.

When Dreiser had finished, Duhring told him he was suffering from "nervous exhaustion"—neurasthenia, a condition to which the doctor himself had succumbed. Although problems arising in the nervous system were difficult to deal with, Duhring had a theory that certain drugs could alleviate them. To be sure, this was a controversial regimen, and most specialists in nervous diseases would not agree with him. If Dreiser wished to undergo the still-experimental therapy, Duhring would administer a course of several different nostrums that the patient must take in sequence. He must also avoid being alone too much, seek "amusing and companionable society," and go to the theater. The doctor's first prescription was a mixture of antipyrine (an analgesic) and sodium bromide (a sedative), for which he collected eight dollars.

Duhring also recommended that his patient keep a diary of his symptoms, and this Dreiser did religiously, noting everything from bowel movements to his mental state. Based on what he wrote, a modern diagnosis would be a moderate to severe case of depression. Dreiser exhibited nearly all the textbook symptoms: apathy, chronic fatigue, insomnia, procrastination, abnormally large appetite, guilt, remorse, anxiety, a fear of depleting his resources (in his case sexual), and various physical complaints (headaches, dyspepsia, constipation).

He thought his problem might be "confusing physical opposition to labor with illness," or else, "I am in a much depressed mental state." But he concludes that he is probably suffering from "purely mental exhaustion from past excesses both of sexual passion and mental labor." Regarding the former, he notes that "my tendency to overindulge in thoughts concerning the sexual relation, as well as in the relation itself" caused a "nervous ache in the region of the genito-urinary organs." He tried total abstinence but was not always successful: "*Wednesday, Nov. 19th* Rose at seven after having foolishly taxed myself by copulating with Mrs. D. but I could not control my desire."

Curiously, the words "but I could not control my" were written in Jug's hand. Either Dreiser had used a crude phrase which she later cleaned up or she had been the one who could not control her desire. As mentioned, she was ardent, and it could be that she chafed under Dreiser's self-imposed regimen. But proper young women did not admit such behavior, and she probably assumed that Duhring would read the diary.

In blaming his troubles on carnal overindulgence, Dreiser repressed his loss of sexual desire for Jug, which became associated with the shame and guilt learned from the antimasturbation propaganda he read as a boy. Like many Victorian males, he had put his love object on a pedestal; his respect for Jug's social superiority roused the sleeping incest taboo. As Freud noted, "whoever is to be really free and happy in love must have overcome his deference for women and come to terms with the idea of incest with mother and sister." Jug's aggressiveness in the sexual relation would only have repelled Theodore more, reinforcing his feelings of inadequacy.

Of course, the lifelong bachelor Dr. Duhring could not have had much understanding of sexual problems. His treatment was, as he said, unconventional; most experts on neurasthenia advised against using drugs. The standard cure called for months of absolute bed rest accompanied by frequent meals. The malady was said to be largely prevalent among urbanites, leading to the hypothesis that the novel pressures of city life and rapid technological and social change were also to blame. In short, neurasthenia was a manifestation of what Thomas Hardy called "the ache of modernism."

●   ●   ●

On November 10 Dreiser makes his last mention of his inability to work on the book. He complains of "mental wildness" and "brain ache"—and of being haunted by a "disturbing sense of error." Five days earlier, Jewett, sensing something was wrong, made what turned out to be a final plea: "Open the door and sweep out the rubbish of distrust. . . . I know that when the book is finished it will be good." He also returned "the papers and chapters which you desire." The reason Dreiser wanted the manuscript became clear in his next letter. He notified Jewett that he was sick, unable to finish *The Transgressor,* and that he had burned the manuscript. He would try to pay back the money he owed them someday. Jewett sent him a kindly reply: "Brace up, stop worrying, and rest your head as well as your body. You exaggerate greatly the obligation under which you think you are staggering. I gambled on a manuscript and when the manuscript is finished I believe that the result will justify my plunge."

It would be more than seven years until Dreiser seriously took up the story of Jennie Gerhardt again, ten before it was published. Much later he explained that he had lost interest, that it had become no longer "vital" to him. There was some truth in that; Jewett and Taylor were not entirely to blame, for Dreiser was himself dissatisfied with the novel, and because of his deepening depression, he could not rekindle his enthusiasm for it. But his distrust of Taylor and Jewett, coupled with the fear that the book would be denounced as immoral, also sapped his energy and self-confidence.

On November 14, four days after his final attempt to work on *The Transgressor,* Dreiser undertook a magazine assignment that enabled him to express his true feelings about morality and immorality in fiction. It was a four-hundred-word editorial for a new publication called *Booklovers Magazine.* The editor, Seymour Eaton, had advertised for "short, pungent, vigorous" editorials for his magazine, "anything which hits the nail on the head." He promised to "pay cash and good prices," which probably brought Dreiser to his door in hopes of making a few quick dollars.

Entitled "True Art Speaks Plainly," it was a despairing protest against censorship. The only guide to morality in art, Dreiser wrote, could be expressed in three words: "Tell the truth." The artist must express what he or she sees, "honestly and without subterfuge: this is morality as well as art." Censors were not really worried about "the discussion of mere sexual lewdness, for no work on that basis could possibly succeed." What they feared were books that challenged the status quo. Censorship sought to suppress the subversive truth: "Immoral! Immoral! Under this cloak hide the vices of wealth as well as the vast unspoken blackness of poverty and ignorance; and between them must walk the little novelist, choosing neither truth nor beauty, but some half-conceived phase of life that bears no honest relationship to either the whole of nature or to man."

The cry of immoral literature "has become a house of refuge to which every form of social injustice hurries for protection . . . the objection to the discussion of the sex question is so great as to almost prevent the handling of the theme entirely." He could have been speaking of his own inability to handle it in *The Transgressor.*

A single sentence in his diary was almost as eloquent: "Ah me—Ah me, who is it that tells the truth and is happy."

•   •   •

His insomnia continued to torment him, and it assumed the classic pattern of depression: fitful sleep early in the evening, followed by wakefulness from about 3:00 A.M. until morning. Duhring had prescribed bromides in low doses, and when they failed to promote sleep he gave his patient scopolamine, a drug of the belladonna family, and chloral hydrate, a pre-barbiturate sedative and the traditional ingredient in Mickey Finns. He was also prescribing a cocktail of small amounts of arsenic, strychnine, and quinine, which was supposed to stimulate the blood.

Over a period of two months, Dreiser swallowed a medicine chest full of drugs, some of them capable of producing bizarre mental reactions when taken in sufficient amounts. Scopolamine, for example, can induce "twilight sleep," hallucinations, and a psychoticlike state. Arsenic and strychnine in nonfatal doses produce similar effects. And bromides, which tend to accumulate in the system, cam produce the condition known as "bromism," with symptoms that include skin rash, headaches, and constipation, all of which Dreiser mentioned in his diary. Also, in cases of depression the adverse side effects might be worse. (A contemporary pharmacology textbook states: "Bromide has no rational place in the management of patients with depression.")

These drugs could have accounted for some of the odd physical and mental symptoms he recorded in the diary, and his obliviousness to their origin made them all the more disturbing. He was a little like the "jay" who has been slipped a Mickey Finn and wonders why the world is spinning out of control.

39 / *Hurstwood's Way*

> [Hurstwood] buried himself in his papers and read. Oh, the
> rest of it—the relief from walking and thinking. . . . So he
> read, read, read, rocking in the warm room, near the radiator
> and waiting for the dinner to be served.
>
> —Dreiser, *Sister Carrie* (1900)

Duhring's advice that he seek "amusing and companionable society" was ignored, though not by choice. Theodore and Jug knew almost no one in Philadelphia and had little social life. They lived quietly at a boardinghouse at 210
Spruce Street.

A few friends from New York came to call. Duffy arrived in November,
and the anticipation of his visit was enough to put Dreiser in a "nervous condition." Duffy viewed his friend's mood swings as the artist's *Sturm und Drang*.
("I understand now better than ever before how much you suffer and enjoy. One
complements the other.") They tramped about Manayunk, an industrial suburb near the Dreisers' boardinghouse, engaging in a philosophical debate. The
verbal joust put Dreiser in an overwrought state, and he noted in his diary that
day: "Find that I suffer from a peculiar illusion as to the necessity of varying the
progress of an idea—changing the direction of my thoughts—which is purely
a result of mental overwork."

Another caller was Charles D. Gray, a friend who had picnicked with Jug
and Dreiser in happier times. Gray spent Christmas Day with them, talking
over old times and overindulging in seasonal fare, for which Dreiser was later
punished by indigestion. Gray was welcome in another sense: he paid back part
of the thirty-five dollars he owed Dreiser.

But those visits were about the extent of their social life, and Jug must
have had a good deal of time on her hands. She devoted herself to nursing her
husband, bathing his forehead when the "brain aches" came on, rubbing his
chest with Chicago Oil when he had a cold, reading to him, and correcting
his manuscripts. There was precious little copy editing for her to do, however,

even after Dreiser abandoned his stalled novel and tried to write some shorter pieces.

•   •   •

On January 26 Jug returned to Montgomery City. He could no longer afford her keep. He did not even have enough money to pay for her ticket and asked Joseph Coates, editor of the progressive *Era* magazine, for an advance on the fees for two articles he had sold him: "The Problem of the Soil" and "A Mayor and His People." After seeing Jug off, Theodore returned to his room and brooded over his loss. Now he was alone, and he had no hope of her returning until he could make some money. But he wrote little. Instead, using Coates's library card, he borrowed books and sat in his room reading.

He chastised himself for sinking into a Hurstwood-like torpor and felt "doomed to rot." But the next day found him in a euphoric mood, and he wrote, "I might as well use my time to improve my knowledge of current novels since I shall want to be writing another one myself some day." He had set himself a program of reading all the contemporary realists, beginning with Howells's *The Rise of Silas Lapham* and John Hay's *The Bread-Winners,* and proceeding through books by Garland, Harold Frederic, Robert Grant, Brand Whitlock, and Henry B. Fuller.

The next afternoon his psychic barometer dropped sickeningly: "All the horror of being alone and without work, without money and sick swept over me and I thought I should die." He was so homesick for Jug he almost wept. He even thought of asking Coates to send him the balance due on the two articles so he could go to Missouri. "I must get something to do something for a change or I will utterly go mad," he wrote.

The awareness that his funds would cover his board and room for just one more week strangely elated him: a decision was being made for him. Intimations of impending changes infused him with fresh hope. With the fifteen dollars Gray still owed him and thirty-five to forty more from Coates, he could go to New York. When he could actually obtain the money was uncertain; he was reluctant to dun Coates, and Gray's check might arrive too late for him to pay his next week's board. If it did, Dreiser resolved to throw himself on the mercy of the streets. That would be better than prolonging his stay in Philadelphia. Like Hurstwood, he was drifting with the current.

He thought of applying for manual labor but decided against it because he believed he was destined to do "literary and socialistic work and that very shortly I would be able to do it." He decided to try a charitable society that provided free meals in exchange for chopping wood. But the place was in a "very poverty-stricken neighborhood" and the "idea of an appeal was too painful." On another day, he went to the streetcar barns to ask about a conductor's job, as Hurstwood had done, but was relieved to find the employment office closed.

He had half convinced himself that his health was improving and that he would soon be on his feet again, "writing articles and finishing my story." His mind was teeming with ideas that he was sure he could convert into magazine specials. He promptly entered a Horn & Hardart restaurant and ordered a fifteen-cent bowl of mock turtle soup, leaving him only thirty-seven cents.

A few days later the weather turned fine, and he walked, singing to himself for joy, feeling that life was so beautiful that he could not remain poor always. He would grow strong and be able to write. And, "Love was to come back and play its part in my life again." He wrote that shortly after being plunged into grief by Jug's departure. He was hopelessly torn: he wanted her, he wanted a new love.

All he could do now was wait for his dreams to materialize, but the thought was hard to bear: "Not now. Not now. Somehow now is almost always commonplace. We see when we return that we have to wait. To be alone, to live alone, to wait, wait, wait, that is the lot accorded us and only the dreams are real. The substance of them is never with us—never attainable." He had come full circle to the coda of *Sister Carrie*. In his rocking chair, reading, he could only dream of a better life, waiting wearily for this storm to pass.

But Dreiser was groping his way out of the cave; his desire to write was the guiding thread that would lead him to daylight. After Jug's departure his diary changes, as though a burden had lifted. The hypochondriac's querulous litany gives way to shards of narrative. His ordeal was being transmuted into a tale in which he was the protagonist: "... thinking how I would write all this. What a peculiar story my life would make if all were told."

Another sign that his mind was groping toward health were the poems he wrote—chinks in his writer's block. As far back as November, he had been dashing them off. After taking a walk, Dreiser "felt lonely and wrote a little poem." It survives. Scrawled on the back of an envelope, it is about an old man "tottering in ugliness . . . muttering in despair." His springtime is over, and "it is now winter." But out of the earth come the flowers: "Life of the world springs up from dead life/Have faith and go in peace if you would be born again." He was searching for comfort in Spencer's philosophy—the idea that decay produces life. Yet there was also a religious undertone. Shattered by fears, his mind clutched for wholeness in the symbolism of religion, if not its dogma, at the Catholic service in Manayunk and at other churches he attended while in Philadelphia. He expressed this emotion in another poem (never published):

> *To thrill with the touch of cool water*
> *To walk the good earth singing, singing*
> *To breathe deeply, think tenderly*
> *In no way to treasure bitterness*
> *But to feel that life is good and so proclaim it*
> *This shall be for a prayer unto your maker*

It shall be for a testament that
he hath made you whole.

On February 10 he overcame his reluctance to ask Coates for the rest of the money *Era* owed him. Coates agreed to give it to him in a few days, and they talked for a while about *The Transgressor,* which Coates had just read. He found the writing overwrought in places, but when Dreiser told him the story in his own words, just as he had it, fully formed, in his mind, the editor was enthusiastic. "We will hear more of you yet," he said.

On Tuesday, February 17, Coates's check arrived, but it was election day and the banks were closed. After recording this latest reversal, Dreiser writes:

Though one has neither houses nor lands, nor affection nor companionship he can still live. It isn't pleasant I'll admit but it can be done. How I am trying to tell you.

Then, with the words "I wish those who are doubtful about the" the diary breaks off.

40 / *Touching Bottom*

A world or given order was passing. . . . For days and weeks and months and years I seemed absolutely alone with a vast sea that urged and persuaded without explaining. I was to change, but I could not see why. The wonder of it, the indifference of it, the inexplicableness of it, seized me as with an icy hand. I was afraid. I did not want to die.

—Dreiser, *An Amateur Laborer* (1904)

"In the chill glow of a dying February day," with thirty-two dollars in his pocket, Dreiser arrived in New York City. He took the ferry across the East River to Brooklyn. The tidal flood was like a moat separating him from the gleaming skyline of Manhattan. But in Brooklyn he could live more cheaply. He intended to tour the editorial offices and collect some assignments, sound out employment possibilities, then return to his hideout and write. When he had made enough money he would send for Jug and take an apartment in Manhattan.

Although Paul, Sylvia, Ed, Mame and Brennan, and Emma lived in and around the city, he did not call on them. Too proud to ask for their help, he was also too ashamed of his present state—he, the novelist, reduced to this. Besides, when had he ever helped them?

After debarking from the ferry, he wandered the streets of the Williamsburg section, looking for lodgings. He kept to the waterfront streets as though magnetically drawn to the urban Styx. Eventually he came upon a neighborhood of shabby tenements, factories, livery stables, and a few large brownstones that had seen better days.

He found a small, four-story brick tenement at 113 Ross Street, a downhill thoroughfare near the Brooklyn Navy Yard and the Wallabout Channel. The landlady, a Mrs. Curry, tall and angular with piercing eyes that matched her black dress, led him up creaking stairs to the top floor, where there was a single room furnished with a rocking chair, a black walnut bookcase filled with religious tracts, and a highboard bed. It was clean and only $2.50 a week. Dreiser took it. If he rationed his money carefully, eating at a boardinghouse nearby, walking rather than taking trolleys and ferries (though it was a long way from his dwelling to the Brooklyn Bridge), he could hold out for several weeks.

Shortly after his arrival, a letter from Ripley Hitchcock caught up with him. Having recently resigned from Appleton, Hitchcock planned to join another house, A. S. Barnes, and was writing to "bespeak an opportunity of seeing your next novel." Dreiser replied that "a long illness—quite a year and a half of nervous prostration—has completely destroyed all my original plans." He said his novel was about three-quarters done, adding more accurately that he had "no immediate prospects of finishing it this spring, as I hoped." He was still "down in the dumps in regard to 'Sister Carrie,' " despite the excellent notices it received in England. He concluded on an optimistic note: "I seem to be just emerging from a long siege of bad weather and am only now looking to my sails again."

He set up a meeting with Hitchcock and scaled down his claims as to *The Transgressor,* saying he could show him only a fragment of the story, the same material Hitchcock had perused more than a year ago. He was making "radical changes" in the manuscript. Moreover, there were "certain things relating to this story which make it impossible for me to offer any hope that we can come to any arrangement concerning it." (He was probably referring to his contract with J. T. Taylor.)

Nothing much came of their discussion. The possibility of Barnes reissuing *Sister Carrie* came up, but Hitchcock had not changed his view that a second "less drastic" novel should pave the way for *Carrie*'s rehabilitation. Since *The Transgressor* still belonged to Taylor, that course was an impossibility, and Hitchcock was in no position to commit his company to buy out Dreiser's contract.

The friendly interest from Hitchcock was the last Dreiser received from a publisher. He collected a few magazine assignments but no job offers. He also tried Park Row but found nothing. Lowering his sights, he called on some local papers in Brooklyn. One editor told him flatly he was overqualified for the staff opening; another promised him a job as the paper's Long Island correspondent for fifteen dollars a week but later reneged.

Gradually, Dreiser withdrew into his little room on Ross Street. He tried to write at the little leaf-table in his tiny room, but it was useless. He spent most of the time staring at an evil brown stain on the peeling wallpaper where the rain had leaked in. His nights were riven by insomnia. "Day after day," he remembered, "I rose to a futile effort to produce some literary article which I might sell and night after night I lay down to a sleepless couch, the ravages of worry and brooding keeping me wide awake."

Most days he would walk the streets. Guilt and self-recrimination, the depressive's companions, matched his strides. Always inclined to fatalism, he was drowning in it. Dreiser believed his troubles had been "foreordained—

worked up by invisible and adverse powers." He conceived the theory that "all life—animal and vegetable—was bound up, so far as their individual conditions were concerned, in a great overruling Providence—fate, power or star, under which they were born, by which they were protected, with which they were compelled to suffer or prosper accordingly as this particular force, Providence or star was successful in the larger universe of which it was a part." Now his star was having a bad time, and he must wait until the plot in the vast sidereal drama took a more favorable turn.

The god Science had forsaken him. He feared omens of death, which his mother had believed in, such as a howling black dog he saw in Philadelphia; he half believed that the 13 in his house number was the cause of his ill luck. And Dreiser's theory that his troubles were due to an unlucky star was a kind of eccentric astrology, in which he had more than a casual interest.

But whatever solace he found in astrology, superstition, and religion was only temporary. Dreiser was cursed with a pessimistic vision too profound for any of the traditional spiritual nostrums to work. As he wrote later, "It seems as if my mind had been laid bare, as if by a scalpel, to mysteries of the universe, and that I was compelled to suffer blood-raw, the agonies of its weight."

Hurstwood-like, he nursed his dwindling funds. His only expenses were his weekly rent of $2.50 and another $4.50 for board. Premonitions of impending disaster would periodically jerk him out of his apathy, and he would mutter, "I must do something!" But only manual labor was available. He would slink by the factories, offices, and warehouses in the area, eyeing them furtively. On the few occasions when he was able to nerve himself to enter, he would be struck by a "cold fear of inability" and hurriedly retrace his steps. Once, when he started to join a group of men in an employment line, rough, healthy laborers all, he sensed their curious stares forming a wall against him and scuttled off. He imagined they were asking, What is this frail intellectual doing here?

When his money was almost gone, Theodore decided to try a private charity. The charity head explained that all he could do was to give Theodore letters of introduction to places that provided temporary jobs. Once he was outside, Dreiser tore up the letters and threw them in the gutter. The letterhead of the charitable society would stigmatize him as a beggar wherever he presented it, and his pride could not bear that.

Then he received a ten-dollar check for a poem he had dug out of his trunk and sent to a magazine, and when that sum was almost gone, he remembered an old debt and collected it. He moved into a smaller room that had just become available in his lodging house. It cost only $1.25 per week, and he gave up eating at the boardinghouse, taking his meals at cheap restaurants in the area. By this resort, and by eating little, he cut his food expenses to two dollars a week.

•   •   •

His money played out like a lifeline through his hands. He cut his meals down to a bottle of milk and half a loaf of bread a day, supplemented by an occasional apple or potato he picked up in the gutter at the Wallabout market. He was emaciated-looking; his weight had dropped to 130 pounds. (Hurstwood's, after his bout with pneumonia, had fallen to 135.) He began to have hallucinations. At night, he felt a sensation that Something was coming; he could hear its footsteps in the hallway and then feel it beside his bed. The hairs on the back of his neck would stand up as a hand groped toward his head on the pillow — then he would jump up and light the lamp and confront his empty room.

He was also subject to queer distortions of perception. He imagined that lines and angles were slightly off plumb, and twisted his chair in a full circle, attempting to realign himself with the universe. Out of doors he noticed a similar phenomenon — streets, trees, curbs, all looked out of kilter. And when he read a newspaper, the columns slanted maddeningly. He shifted the paper around, vainly trying to straighten them.

Those perceptual distortions probably had a medical explanation. Dreiser's weaker eye had now lost its adjustment to the stronger one. Normally, images seen by his stronger eye dominated, but because of the mental stress he was undergoing, he began seeing through the weaker, astigmatic one (which he had seen a doctor in Philadelphia about, without receiving treatment), precipitating perceptual distortions. His symptoms resembled those of the condition called cyclophoria: floors seem slanted, right angles become obtuse, houses appear to be leaning over. Experiencing these bizarre visions is very disorienting to the sufferer and can exacerbate the original mental distress.

He saw himself as another person — or rather two persons. One was "a tall, thin, greedy individual who had struggled and thought always for himself and how he should prosper." And the other was a silent, philosophical creature who was watching him with aloof detachment, "taking an indifferent interest in his failures." The other self — he called it his "oversoul," in the Emersonian sense of a higher, universal consciousness — was the philosophic Dreiser, the creator of Carrie and Drouet and Hurstwood, the detached, self-conscious artist who must "get it all in." It was indifferent, cold, and remote, but not malign. "He was very wise and sane and I had great faith in him. . . . In all probability he would bring me through. Something would happen."

41 / *Just Tell Them That You Saw Me*

"I long to see them all again, but not just yet, she said,
'Tis pride alone that's keeping me away.
Just tell them not to worry, for I'm all right don't you know,
Tell mother I am coming home some day."
—Paul Dresser, "Just Tell Them That You Saw Me" (1895)

The dual sense of himself recurred as he dragged about the Brooklyn streets in his stuporous state, but it continued oddly to hearten him. Not that he had much cause for optimism. He was down to his last few dollars; he felt dragged out and looked terrible—as his sister Mame told him when he appeared on her doorstep one day.

He had somehow summoned up the resolve to have still another try at finding an editorial job in Manhattan, and after a day of fruitless rounds, he found himself on Fourteenth Street near Union Square, only ten blocks from the Brennans' apartment on Washington Square. He was pricked by a desire to see his sister, despite their strained relationship in recent years. Perhaps writing *The Transgressor* had reminded Theodore of her hard life, which made him more sympathetic toward her.

When Mame opened the door, she was shocked and insisted he stay for lunch, which turned out to be a five-course spread, since Brennan was a dedicated trencherman. Dreiser wolfed down his portion, his first decent meal since he gave up eating at the boardinghouse. In response to his sister's anxious questions, he said he had been going through a session of neurasthenia but was feeling better. When she invited him to join them on a country outing, he declined, too proud to tell her that he could not afford the rail fare.

The Brennans' apartment was by no means luxurious, but with its drapes, pictures, and heavy carpets it seemed a palace. To live like this, to have plenty to eat, to sleep in a soft bed! A longing for material comforts filled him with a rush. Shelter and food—a mind unmoored in them was adrift in a storm. When he parted from Mame and Brennan, he gave her a false address. He knew she was in touch with Paul. If Paul learned where his younger brother was, he would seek out his shabby lodgings.

On his way to the Twenty-third Street ferry, he stopped at Fourth Avenue to inspect the excavations for the new subway. The wind suddenly picked up and whipped his hat away, whirling it down somewhere in the inky depths. The loss upset him. He was now down to exactly three dollars and thirty-one cents, and a new one would cost him at least two dollars. Not only did it keep his head warm in the cold wind, the hat stood for respectability, dignity, status. He had resisted pawning an engraved gold watch that he had bought in St. Louis. That and his frock suit, his overcoat, and a silk topper, which were stored in his trunk at Ross Street, were the last vestiges of his former status.

But if he did buy a new hat, he would not have enough for food, for his room rent was due tomorrow. He stood in the dark, lashed by the cold winds, at the brink of the shadow-pooled pit. Never, he later wrote, had he felt so keenly "the vastness, the indifference, the desolation of the world" as he did that night. He could only resign himself to the workings of fate. It would either save him or finish him off; he was powerless to affect the outcome. He walked along Fourteenth Street until he found a hat store, where he bought a cheap brown woolen cap for fifty cents—a workman's cap, but at least it would keep his head warm.

The next day he paid Mrs. Curry the $1.25 he owed for rent, leaving him one dollar and fifty-six cents. He figured if he cut out lunches and lived on milk and bread, he would finish the week with a bit over a dollar. That he would use to go to Manhattan, where he would put his trunk in storage and wander the streets until he found some kind of charitable institution that provided free beds.

That week a letter came from Paul, who had written to the fictitious address Dreiser had given to Mame. The number was in the same postal district, and an efficient clerk redirected it to the correct location. Paul demanded that Theo come to see him, or else he would go to Brooklyn. Dreiser did not reply.

As his final day at Ross Street drew near, he felt a slight lift of spirits. Surely nothing worse could happen to him now. Saturday morning he ate half of the loaf he had bought the night before, packed his truck and his grip, stuffed some letters from publishers in his pocket to use as references, walked out of his room and the house at 113 Ross Street, and took the ferry across the East River.

He stood at the rail watching a cloud of sea gulls swooping down to snatch bits of garbage floating on the choppy green waters. Fighting, eating, going hungry—emblems of nature's blind profligacy. And on the far side, amid the shining buildings of the city, the teeming crowds in the streets, all of them scrabbling for subsistence like the gulls. He decided that the questions of who succeeded and who failed had little to do with the Darwinian concept of fitness. Some were born with money; others beauty. He had been born with a gift to write; it was not something he had acquired or studied for. It would have been better to be born with money or beauty, but he must accept his lot.

Leaving the ferry, Theodore walked along Twenty-third Street. Now he must deal with the urgent question of where he would sleep that night and the nights to come until he found a job. Then he remembered a journalist friend who had worked for the New Haven Railroad as a conductor following a nervous breakdown. He had heard that George Henry Daniels, the general passenger agent of the New York Central, had literary inclinations. The New York Central employed thousands of people; surely it would have a menial or clerical job for him. And, after all, he had published an interview with the company's president, Chauncey Depew, in *Success.*

Impelled by this desperate hope, he walked up Fourth Avenue to the Grand Central Depot, a red-brick edifice with three tall clock towers on Forty-second Street; inside were the administrative offices of the railroad. Resuming his identity as a literary man had a tonic effect. The airs he unconsciously assumed got Theodore through the outworks to the office of the passenger agent's secretary. After he had described his plight, showed his letters from publishers, and made some allusions to his last meeting with Depew, the secretary was impressed. Daniels was out, but could Dreiser come back in an hour? He could and did and found awaiting him a letter signed by Daniels himself asking the chief engineer of the railroad to extend all courtesies to the bearer.

Elated, Dreiser allowed himself to be bucked down the chain of command until he ended up with the engineer of maintenance of way, A. T. Hardin, who had charge of thirteen thousand employees who performed roadwork on the Central's far-flung empire. Hardin listened patiently as Dreiser, encouraged by a sympathetic listener of his own kind, poured out his story. After all, neurasthenia was a respectable complaint—the American Disease, afflictor of overworked dynamos in business as well as the arts. Hardin said he used a Whitely Exerciser when the pressures of overcivilization became too much for him, or retreated to his country place. He admired Dreiser's determination to take the physical-labor cure, but thought the job of track worker too strenuous. He would ponder the matter over the weekend.

Dreiser now had hope. There was one small problem, though. He had no money for food, and he had left his half loaf of bread on a windowsill outside the chief passenger agent's office. When he went back for it, it was gone. Then he remembered his watch. He had once written about the Provident Loan Association, which had been set up by some enlightened citizens to extend loans to poor people who brought in trinkets that conventional pawnbrokers would not accept. He went there, and to his surprise, the clerk offered him twenty-five dollars.

He could live for weeks on that! It would enable him to survive until his first railroad paycheck came through. He treated himself to a full-course meal and decided to spend the night at the Mills Hotel, another enlightened institution for the poor, which rented clean rooms for twenty cents a day. But first he felt an urge to luxuriate in the spring sunshine and decided to take the Hudson ferry to Fort Lee and hike along the Palisades. He joined the afternoon fashion parade up Broadway, intending to buy a decent hat at a shop he knew on Forty-second Street.

As he was approaching the Imperial Hotel on Thirty-second Street, Dreiser noticed a tall, fat man elegantly turned out in a Prince Albert coat, gray pants, and white spats. Ducking his head, he tried to hurry past, but a familiar voice pulled him back.

"Hello, Paul," he said. The old resentment welled up, and he replied sullenly to Paul's barrage of anxious questions.

But Paul would not be brushed off. He was appalled by his younger brother's appearance. "Look, old man," he said. "I'm going away tonight. I've got to go to Buffalo, but I want you to let me loan you something until I come back."

And he reached into his pocket and extracted a fat roll of bills. "I know you're in hard luck. We've all been that way from time to time." Paul tried to press the money into Theodore's hand, but the other brushed it away. It became a ridiculous scene, Theodore insisting angrily that he didn't want the money, Paul pleading with him to take it.

Dreiser looked into those blue eyes that were so like his mother's. He was on the verge of tears and would have thrown his arms around Paul if there hadn't been so many people around. He stuffed the roll in his pocket, muttering that he would not spend a penny of it.

Paul made him promise to come to the hotel the following Monday. Then he was gone. Theodore strode along Broadway, thinking that a world with Paul in it could not be such a hard place. He took the elevated down to Bleecker Street, where the Mills Hotel was located. It was an imposing nine-story structure of cream-colored brick set in a neighborhood of run-down tenements, a monument to the philanthropy of Darius O. Mills, who had built it as a refuge from Bowery flophouses.

Once inside, Theodore found himself among the same cast of bums, down-and-outers, and lost souls that one saw along the Bowery. For many this was a way station on the familiar road that led to Blackwells Island and the boat on the East River. He noted that the walls of each cubicle were raised on jacks above the floor. It would be impossible to commit suicide in this room. There was not even a gas jet.

He spent a restless night amid the constant hubbub created by the men in neighboring cubicles who cried out in their sleep or talked to themselves while their neighbors cursed them and shouted, "Chop it off!" Monday came, and he walked toward Paul's hotel, emerging from a chrysalis. He must get back his health and then earn a living. He must have some money—"Enough to be clean and decent and mentally at rest." He must never again be poor. As he entered the ornate portals of the Imperial (one likes to imagine), the shadowy figure following him, a man in a shabby overcoat and a battered hat, hesitated, turned away, and shambled off. Soon, Hurstwood was swallowed up by the crowd.

Part Six

. . .

THE LOST DECADE

42 / The Way Back

After a long battle I am once more the possessor of health. That necessary poise in which the mind and body reflect the pulsations of the infinite is mine. I am not overconscious. I trust I am not under so. All that is, now passes before me a rich, varied and beautiful procession. I have fought a battle for the right to live and for the present, musing with stilled nerves and a serene gaze, I seem the victor.

—Dreiser, *An Amateur Laborer* (1904)

At the nadir of his life, his older brother pulled him away from the abyss. Paul's first move was to bundle Theodore off to a sanatorium he regularly visited. Its official name was the Olympia Hygienic Institute, but most of its habitués called it simply Muldoon's, after the former wrestling champion William Muldoon, who owned it. Nestled in the gently rolling Long Island hills, it drew a wealthy clientele who were run down from overwork or debilitated by the excesses of the flesh. Muldoon badgered and hectored them back to health.

Under Muldoon's regimen, Dreiser's health steadily improved, and he began to know what a normal night's sleep was like. After only a month's stay, he had resumed negotiations with Hitchcock on a new edition of *Sister Carrie* and had written an article about the sanatorium, "Scared Back to Nature," which appeared in the May 16 *Harper's Weekly*. Perhaps because he was still under Muldoon's lash, Dreiser speaks of the "marked strain of autocracy" of the host and "a certain helpless servility" among the guests. Yet he must have felt Muldoon's authoritarian methods were good, for he quotes him approvingly as saying they were designed for "wresting a man's mental control from him in order to increase his mental energy. If his will has nothing to do with the arrangement of his day, his mind is much more likely to contemplate nature and to rest." Dreiser later credited the hazing and strenuous exercise with taking his mind off himself and checking his morbidly introspective tendencies.

• • •

After two months at the sanatorium, he was sufficiently recovered to go to work for the New York Central, remaining there from early June until Christmas Day 1903. Theodore was an unlikely railroad hand, not strong enough to do heavy labor, eagerly engaging his perplexed co-workers in philosophical discussions, insisting on his superior status as a recovering neurasthenic.

He retained a foothold in the middle-class world by boarding in Kingsbridge with a cultivated widow named Mrs. Hardenbrooks, who had been impressed by his literary credentials, and her family, which included a widowed daughter. Dreiser told Dorothy Dudley that he had an affair with an unnamed woman around this time, and in his autobiographical novel, The "Genius," written in 1911, the hero, Eugene, does take up with the landlady's daughter, a well-off, unconventional beauty named Carlotta, who is married to an absentee gambler. But the real daughter was rather plain, and Dreiser mentions no affair in An Amateur Laborer, an unpublished nonfiction account of his railroad experiences written in 1904.

The life of an amateur laborer soon palled. "I saw that I was as unfitted to be a hewer of wood as I was to be president of the railroad," Dreiser recalled. In addition to providing timely financial aid, Paul sent his brother a stream of encouraging letters. Occasionally he would enclose a "V" for spending money or invite him to have dinner in town.

There were others cheering him on as well: Duffy, of course, and Coates, whom Theodore had known only while he was in Philadelphia, but who was obviously impressed with him. Jewett had sent him buck-up letters at Muldoon's, and when he learned Dreiser was working on the railroad, he applauded: "Good for you. Health is bound to come to you through some strenuous channel. Keep a stiff upper lip, and you will come out all right." Despite Dreiser's outstanding debt, he also forwarded a royalty check from Heinemann for British sales of Sister Carrie.

His railroad experience did provide Dreiser with a firsthand view of the "labor question," just as his stay at Muldoon's had yielded an unglamorous view of the ruling class. In the space of seven months he explored both sides of the Great Divide in American society. After seeing both classes close up, he found little to admire in either. The Muldoon's crowd was grasping, money-obsessed, and self-indulgent, while the workers were beaten down, conniving, with a "sour, pugnacious view of life." Yet he envied the physical strength and dexterity of the workers and came to see that they deserved more help from society. Their lot was a grim one, an unending round of toil enforced by the lash of economic necessity. In "The Toil of the Laborer," a long essay he wrote not long after leaving the railroad, Dreiser seemed to call for economic security for all: "That none should suffer, that none should want! This after all seemed the worthiest thought that sprang at the sight of the toil-weary man."

•   •   •

A more immediate consequence was that he gave up the free-lance life and became an editor again. Paul was instrumental in his return to the magazine world. He was writing a farce called *Boomerang* with Robert H. Davis, managing editor of the New York *Daily News,* which was starting a Sunday supplement, and Paul asked his collaborator to take his brother on staff. One suspects Paul would have supported Theodore had he wanted to resume working on his novel. He could certainly afford to. Now a full partner in the renamed Howley, Haviland and Dresser, Paul was still turning out hits, though none of them was as big as "On the Banks of the Wabash."

In October 1903 Paul wrote an impatient Theodore that Davis "will do something for you after January 1." On the strength of that offer Theodore left the railroad just before Christmas. He and Jug took their furniture out of storage and moved to a modest apartment at 399 Mott Avenue in the Bronx—with the help of a fifty-dollar check from Paul. Jug's brother Pete White also aided them with a loan, telling them not to worry about paying it back.

In January 1904 Theodore began the job on the *Daily News,* turning out feature stories on lurid or sentimental topics such as "The Love Affairs of Little Italy" and "The Cradle of Tears" (a New York foundling home). It was while he was at the *News* that he began "The Toil of the Laborer." After finishing it, he took up *An Amateur Laborer,* working on it at the office in his spare time. He had increasing amounts of that. In June the Sunday supplement was canceled, and he was unemployed.

•　　•　　•

As so often happened in Dreiser's writing career, after the initial burst he ran out of steam on *An Amateur Laborer.* He could never decide whether to make it autobiographical, which was how he initially wrote it (with the subtitle "The Case of the Author"), or to recast it as a novel.

What he wrote in 1904, when the events were still fresh in his mind, remains the truest account of his breakdown; in later years Dreiser expurgated or embroidered the record he set down. For example, in "Down Hill and Up," an essay written in the 1920s, and in a letter to H. L. Mencken, he told of seriously contemplating ending it all in the "icy cold and splashing waters" of the East River, only to be diverted by an interloper—an Erie Canal boatman in one version and a jovial drunken Scotsman in another. Although Dreiser undoubtedly had suicidal thoughts during this period, there is no mention of an attempt in *An Amateur Laborer.* And when he drew upon his railroad experiences in his autobiographical novel, *The "Genius,"* he toned down the hardship aspects considerably.

Although the passing of time mellowed Dreiser's recollections of his bout with neurasthenia, it was a watershed in his life. The helplessness and humiliation of his poverty lacerated his soul. He was worried for months afterward that the damage was permanent: "To be maimed as an insect. To get a hurt that would not heal." Henceforth, he would strive to live with the paradox that nature was cruel and profligate and blind, yet to be alive was good.

He had felt the lash of social prejudice that falls on the helpless sufferer of mental torments. The mentally ill person, he wrote in *An Amateur Laborer*, is "debarred . . . from broad and pleasant social contact. He is injured. Therefore he is not morally whole. Let him go forth and wander by himself. He does not any longer belong to the sane and healthy order of society."

He also learned that the truth teller is often cast outside the walls of the city. Censorship was used by the dominant class to banish truth by branding it an obscenity. "Immoral" meant politically and socially suspect. Art had political consequences.

Theodore did not relish being an outsider—neither the ultimate isolation of madness nor that uniquely urban loneliness he had experienced in Brooklyn. While living at Mott Avenue in the Bronx, he wrote a short sketch entitled "The Loneliness of the City" that articulated a longing for human fellowship. It described the anonymous lives of his fellow tenants in the building, who chase after wealth, fame, and pleasure. Only in times of calamity do they recall "the importance of the individual relationship . . . friendship, affection, tenderness." The sketch closes with this admonition: "After all is said and done, we must truly love one another or we must die—alone, neglected despised and forgotten, as too many of us die."

•   •   •

He exercised regularly, followed Muldoon's regimen of calisthenics, taking a bath and drinking several glasses of hot water upon rising—"work and cleanliness," the old wrestler had stressed. And he toughened his mind by reading philosophy—Schopenhauer, Kant, and others.

He must change, Dreiser told himself in Brooklyn. It would not happen in a day, or a week, or a year, but he set his life on a new course. As he had written at the time of the *Sister Carrie* debacle, "Fortune need not forever feel that she must use the whip on me."

43 / The Best of Brothers

Where are the friends of other days,
Friends that I loved so well;
Friends that I never turned away,
Is there no one to tell?
— Paul Dresser, "Where Are the Friends
of Other Days?" (1903)

Between 1900 and 1911 Theodore Dreiser published no novels, and he almost disappears from the pages of American literary history. Yet his "silent decade" was not a time of withdrawal or prostration. Those years were marked by ambition and a strong attraction to power and money. Being Dreiser, he never pursued those two goals with the single-minded zeal of a *Success* subject, but there was a good deal of the bourgeois in him, and during these years that side of his nature was in the ascendant. The writer, the bohemian, the nonconformist, were accordingly eclipsed — though, as his various employers (some of the most neurotic dynamos in the American success-worship pantheon) soon learned, he remained prickly and independent. Exposed to the rough game of commerce, Dreiser found he liked it; the vulnerable, failed novelist of the post–*Sister Carrie* days developed a tough hide.

But he still clung to his dream of being a novelist, and to his obsession with reissuing *Sister Carrie*. His bitterness toward Frank Doubleday (and wife), exaggerated as it was, was like adrenaline to an athlete, energizing him in a single-minded fight to win justice for his book.

That book, it should be said, lived on in a kind of limbo, the flame of its reputation kept flickering by a handful of critical champions such as William Marion Reedy and a few score intelligent readers who passed their dog-eared copies among friends. One of the younger generation who remembered was Edna Kenton, now a Chicago book critic. In 1905 she wrote Dreiser out of the blue to express her continuing admiration of him for having written "the strongest, best biggest novel of American life that so far has been printed," and to ask if there were any plans to reissue it. Dreiser told her *Carrie* was still in the doldrums, but he was looking for a publisher with courage enough to bring it out. "Maybe—the gods providing—when I take up my pen again, the world will be a bit more kindly disposed," he concluded. "I am older now, a little bit wiser and not so radical I was going to say, but it wouldn't be true—simply sorrowful and uncertain." Kenton replied, "Surely a courageous publisher is not entirely nonexistent, though Americans indeed are not yet at that stage in their art life where they relish the Slavonic [sic] touch in the native novel. But I . . . cannot lose faith in that book and its ultimate great success."

But the country was changing. A rebellious minority of the younger generation was about to put its stamp on American culture. They were the ones to whom the legend of *Sister Carrie*'s suppression would become a manifesto in the battle for freer expression in literature and in morals and manners. A transitional group between Dreiser's and the cynical rebels of the 1920s, they were imbued with Victorian idealism and moral seriousness. But they were also alive to the whisper of desire: the "sex question" would become prominent on their social and literary agendas.

This was a generation that, as the critic Randolph Bourne said, rebelled at the monotonous daily fare of "classics" served up in the literature classes at freshwater universities and Ivy League institutions alike, and raided the library shelves for sustenance—Hardy, Tolstoy, Flaubert, Turgenev, Meredith, Moore, and the other modern writers who were not taught in their courses. The realism wars of Howells's day were as remote from them as the Peloponnesian Wars; they took as axiomatic the proposition that literature should represent the truth about life. The "daring" French writers like Zola and de Maupassant, while not widely available, were no longer exotic cultural contraband. In theory at least, the young people saw no reason why American writers could not tackle the same subject matter. Indeed, Zolaesque novels such as Norris's *The Pit* and Upton Sinclair's *The Jungle*, as stomach-turning as *l'Assommoir*, were best sellers in the early 1900s, riding the wave of reform of the progressive era. The muckrakers, who were enjoying a tremendous vogue, made the daring social and political subject matter of the "economic novels" of the nineties—political corruption, big-business chicanery, exploitation of workers—familiar reading matter for a mass audience.

The young intellectuals also repudiated the saccharine romantic view of life purveyed in the popular fiction of their day. Dorothy Dudley recalled, "Young people were tired of vicarious romance. They must have experience themselves . . . and have it quickly." They wanted novels that held the mirror up to life. They poured into the cities, questing, eager, not yet sexually "emancipated" like the bohemians of the twenties (the young women among them still believed in chaperoned introductions leading to engagement and marriage), but in rebellion against American "puritanism" that stifled freedom and experimentation in the arts.

The young people would turn on establishment authors such as Longfellow, Whittier, Holmes, Lowell, and, through guilt by association, Howells. Pick and dynamite in hand, they set out to clear away the "crumbling idols" as Garland had done in his day (and Howells in his and Longfellow in his). In 1905 most of the revered ancients were either dead, living off the annuity of their reputations, or unread. Many of the tottering survivors had been translated into living monuments as members of the recently founded American Academy of Arts and Letters, of which Howells was the inevitable first president and Garland a member and eager booster.

Similarly entrenched were the guardians of purity in literature, led by the indefatigable smut-smiter Anthony Comstock. In 1906 Comstock and his vigilantes at the New York Society for the Suppression of Vice raided numerous publishers and vendors of allegedly obscene books and attempted to close the Art Students League in New York because nude models were used. The annual report of the society for that year claimed that one thousand pounds of obscene books and stock had been impounded and destroyed.

Still, there was a growing resistance to Comstockery. Attacks on Shaw's play about a former prostitute, *Mrs. Warren's Profession,* had the predictable effect of creating long lines at the box office. Art lovers, who saw nothing wrong with nudes, rallied to the support of the Art Students League. And censorship was not monolithic; there were quirky cracks in the façade. For example, the critic James Huneker noted that the Metropolitan Museum of Art did not use fig leaves on its statuary, though the Louvre and other great museums in Europe followed that "needlessly offensive custom."

As for Dreiser, he continued the hunt for a "courageous" publisher. He made his first breakthrough while working at Street and Smith, the dime novel and mass magazine empire ruled by the brilliant, cultivated Ormond C. (Million Dollar) Smith, who is supposed to have said, "The worse the swill, the more the public will buy." Dreiser's first job was editing *Diamond Dick* and the Jack Harkaway stories, a popular series of boys' adventure yarns written in the 1870s, which Street and Smith was reissuing. His task on the latter, he recalled, involved "cutting them in two and tacking an end to the first half and a beginning to the second, thereby doubling the output for the firm."

An admiring co-worker on the Street and Smith assembly line was Charles Agnew MacLean, who had read and liked *Carrie.* Both men had ambitions beyond rewriting dime novels, and they hatched the idea of forming a publishing company, buying the plates and stock of *Sister Carrie* from the J. F. Taylor Company, and issuing it as the first title on their list. Dreiser was making only fifteen dollars a week and was in debt, so MacLean had to come up with the necessary five hundred dollars. The deal was consummated in January 1905, and Jewett wrote to congratulate MacLean: "You are purchasing one of the best American books ever written."

Dreiser had a financial motive for reviving *Sister Carrie*. He still owed J. F. Taylor seven hundred fifty dollars, representing the advance on *The Transgressor*. Not that Taylor was dunning him, but he did invite Theodore in for a discussion of their contract. The upshot of this meeting was an amicable agreement that Dreiser would attempt to sell the rights to *Carrie* and his second novel to another publisher and reimburse Taylor out of the proceeds. A year later Taylor was still inquiring about Dreiser's plans to repay him; eventually he did, but it took Dreiser another year to find a publisher.

The nebulous partnership between Dreiser and MacLean was dissolved after they quarreled. Dreiser later told Dorothy Dudley that MacLean had been jealous of his rise in the company and worked behind his back to undercut him. Actually, both men rose. Dreiser was soon made editor of a new "home" magazine called *Smith's*. His first issue appeared in April 1905, with a publisher's note promising not to "tamper with the higher education or attempt to alter the present formation of the universe" and to render the reader "some assistance in enduring the little sorrows and tragedies of life." *Smith's* was said to be aimed at "the every-day reader who seeks entertainment" and would not be a "class" magazine. Theodore's premier issue received a glowing review from brother Paul: "Great—fine, exstatic [sic]—imperishable genius art thou."

Although he sounded his usual cheery self, Paul was having business worries. He and Pat Howley had a falling out with Fred Haviland, for reasons that are unclear but probably arose out of squabbles over money. Haviland's wife, Mabel, later recalled that the three partners had "made lots of money but none of them held on to it."

Paul and Pat bought out Haviland for $8000 and tried to make a go of it with a company of their own, but went bankrupt in 1905 and had to sell their song catalogue at a distress price. (A year later Howley bought it back for peanuts.) Then Paul founded his own firm, using money lent to him by Ed Dreiser and by Mai and her mother. Ed served as president of the company, although he had little experience in song publishing. Paul was given a twenty-five-dollar weekly allowance and told to closet himself with his portable organ and write more hits.

But the hits didn't come. Tastes had changed; ragtime, which Paul deplored, was having a vogue. The day of the "mother" song had passed. Also, Paul now had loftier aims. In an interview with the New York *Sun* in mid-1905, while he was still technically Pat Howley's partner, Paul complained that although he had a trunkful of good songs—"genuine songs of feeling that ought to stir the heart"—the music-buying public wanted only junk. Now he was composing socially significant songs, he told the reporter from the *Sun*. He was appalled at how "the rich of this country are getting richer and richer, and the poor are getting poorer and poorer." Then, heaving his monstrous bulk to the piano (he weighed over three hundred pounds), Paul played and sang the chorus of a song he had written:

> *The People, the People are marching by*
> *The cry of the downtrodden, far and nigh*
> *Is heard in the homes where the weary sigh*
> *The People, the People are marching by.*

Paul's social conscience was emerging at a bad time. He needed to write the songs he did best, which, sentimental as they were, derived from his honest emotions. But the row with Haviland had embittered him, and he had grown disillusioned with the Broadway crowd that plucked him like a golden chicken. It was said that he had fifty thousand dollars in outstanding loans that he could not collect.

And so, while Dreiser's star was now on the rise, Paul's had entered a dangerous phase. The Paul Dresser Publishing Company quickly flopped, leaving Mai's parents and Ed out twenty-five hundred dollars. Paul's financial affairs were in a hopeless tangle; he had lost the songwriter's only asset, his catalogue. His only hope was to compose another "Wabash," and, surprisingly, despite all his troubles, he did succeed in writing the big one: "My Gal Sal." He persuaded his former protégé Louise Dresser, now a vaudeville headliner, to introduce it, and he put her picture on the cover. Her renditions were well received, but for a time "Sal" remained what was known in the trade as a "stage hit"—one that pleases audiences—rather than a "selling hit." Eventually it would earn a lot of money, but not in Paul's lifetime. The millions of people who played the song in parlors all over America and heard it in vaudeville theaters never knew that its inspiration was the madam of a high-class Evansville brothel.

By late 1905 Paul was broke, and he had to ask Emma, now living on West 106th Street, to take him in. Paul was given a small room, in which he set up his portable organ and tried to compose. To economize, he took his meals at the home of Mai Dresser's Aunt Kate. He was suffering from pernicious anemia, rheumatism, dropsy—accumulation of fluid in the tissues—and had a bad heart. Sensitive about his girth because sometimes women laughed at it, he went on crash diets, taking nothing but milk or orange juice and losing forty or fifty pounds in the course of a few weeks. The diets, followed by eating binges, surely overtaxed his heart. And his fall from Broadway celebrity depressed him. He "emanated a kind of fear," Dreiser recalled.

After work, Theodore would visit him. They would reminisce about the old days, and Paul would urge him to take notes and write a book about him.

On January 29, 1906, a wire from Ed announced the dreaded news: PAUL IS DYING. Dreiser hurried up to Emma's place and found his good brother laid out on the bed, "his soft hands folded over his chest, his face turned to one side on the pillow, that indescribable sweetness of expression about the eyes and mouth—the empty shell of a beetle." He was forty-eight.

Although Paul had told Emma there would be enough for everyone, he died penniless. The New York *Telegram,* a theatrical paper, commented in its obituary, "He made two or three fortunes solely from his compositions" but did not elaborate. The White Rats, an organization of vaudevillians, volunteered to pick up the funeral tab.

Le tout Broadway turned out for the funeral, at St. Francis Xavier church on West Sixteenth. Paul had been a parishioner there, and in his homily Father Van Rennselaer (who, when Paul skipped Mass, would hunt him down like the Hound of Heaven), said that Paul had been a good Catholic who, no matter how far he strayed, always returned home to the Church. Then the priest read the lyrics of "The Judgment Is at Hand," the last song Paul wrote:

> *And then came an angel, majestic pure and grand,*
> *Calling "Arise, Ye" Judgment is now at hand.*
> *"As ye have sown, so shall ye reap,"*
> *Just as the Master planned*
> *Arise ye all, seek not to hide*
> *The judgment is at hand.*

44 / The Gates of the City

> Ah, she was in the walled city now. Its splendid gates had
> opened, admitting her from a cold, dreary outside. She
> seemed a creature afar off—like every other celebrity he had
> known.
>
> —Dreiser, *Sister Carrie* (1900)

Paul's death closed a chapter in Dreiser's life. He was now at the age—thirty-five—when he could look back on the New York of the 1890s, Paul's New York, as a vanished era. His memories were tinted by its afterglow—his first walk up Broadway with his brother, the Sunday night at Manhattan Beach, the *Ev'ry Month* days, the stockboys bundling up copies of "Just Tell Them That You Saw Me," the organ grinders playing it on every corner. . . .

The legal ownership of Paul's songs was eventually untangled—but they could earn something only if a publisher brought them out in sheet music. Most of them were as dead as the era that spawned them, save "On the Banks of the Wabash," "My Gal Sal," and a few others. Ed was able to lease the selling rights of "Sal" to a publisher on a 5 percent royalty basis. The song started slowly but gradually caught on, and Ed earned a good sum out of it over the years, so perhaps Paul had paid back the borrowed money after all.

There were other severances with the past. Theodore's feud with Arthur Henry over the unflattering portrait in *An Island Cabin* erupted. The occasion was the reissue of that book by A. S. Barnes in 1904, along with Henry's new book, *The House in the Woods*. Not long after Dreiser left the New York Central and took the apartment on Mott Street, a letter from Henry arrived. The tone was friendly but a bit defiant. Henry said he could understand why Dreiser would nurse ill will toward him, but he could not resist challenging him to "prove you can face *all* the facts and that you are not simply nursing a grudge and come down here this evening. Hitchcock and I want to see you about your future work and mine."

Dreiser was infuriated and sent a scorching reply:

Here is the way to face all the facts. If your feelings have undergone no change and [sic] I accuse you of flagrant abuse of those unchanged feelings in 'An Island Cabin.' Let the book be brought out, not at a dinner or in the presence of those who do not know, but here in my own rooms, between us, and where those others [Jug] who do can be quickly gathered. If there is no evidence of this flagrant abuse how long do you suppose I will be delay [sic] in taking you to my ~~arms~~ [sic] heart again. And if there is, how long can you honestly refuse to acknowledge it and to make me the amends a wrong demands.

Henry persisted, requesting a meeting "to see if it is not possible to come to a friendly and affectionate understanding again." Apparently they did meet, but Dreiser was his usual obdurate self. When all efforts had failed, Henry wrote a preface to the new edition, in which he denied, rather unconvincingly, that the character of Tom had anything to do with Dreiser: "Tom as I have depicted him could not be the author of *Sister Carrie*. . . . He is a shadow of no value, except to enforce the moral I used him for."

After Dreiser vetoed the conciliatory preface, Henry wrote him: "It is very clear to me that this book is not responsible for the interruption of our friendship. That was doomed before the book was written." He accused Dreiser of listening to gossip about him and Anna and making accusations to her that "should have come directly, and at once, from you to me." In time the anger between them cooled, but only the ashes of their former friendship remained.

The old world was breaking up, and a new order was forming. Even Theodore's brother Al—who, Theodore always said, had more talent than any of them—was in trouble. While she was in Chicago seeing to Paul's reinterment, Mame found Al in a down-and-out condition and wrote Theodore, "Poor dear All [sic], he is having a hard time and oh how I wish we could help him—he had a great heart and so full of love—" Not long afterward, Al vanished, resurfacing twenty years later in California.

In different ways and degrees, Dreiser had been dependent on Paul, Al, and Arthur Henry, but now he no longer needed them. Under his editorship, *Smith's* was prospering. In the June issue the editor proclaimed that all periodicals must live by the law of the jungle: "*Success* is what counts in the world, and it is little matter how the success is won. It is a hard, cold fact with little comfort in it for the unsuccessful, but it is still a fact that we must recognize."

Fortunately, *Smith's* was one of the fit. Out of a stockpile of memories of the magazines that had fueled his dreams of New York and his experiences at *Ev'ry Month* and as a free-lancer, Dreiser had patched together a periodical with instant popular appeal, aimed at young married couples. The first issues tended to be lightweight, emphasizing slick fiction with alternating masculine and feminine appeal, and features like "Art Studies" (photographs of beautiful,

fashionably dressed actresses); "The Passing Hour," an illustrated chronicle of
the doings of Society and European royalty; and "The Out-of-Town Girl in New
York," a fashion column aimed at the Carrie Meebers among his readers.

With the magazine's future presumably assured, the editor proclaimed in
the June issue that henceforth *Smith's* would shoulder its social responsibilities.
In the July number he criticized his countrymen's pursuit of the "Almighty dollar" and announced "a change in the spirit of the American people." The wage
earners, the bone and sinew of the Republic, were demanding that "modern
conditions be at one with moral health and national honor." They were calling
for "the *right* use of national wealth, for integrity and civility in public office,
for honesty and fair-dealing in the business world, for sanity and liberality in
schools and colleges, and for kindness and humanity everywhere."

Thus did Dreiser align *Smith's* with the progressive sentiments abroad in
the land, which he shared despite his lingering Social Darwinism. In subsequent issues he presented an article by Cleveland's reform mayor Tom Johnson,
an old hero, on municipal socialism, and one by Kansas Governor E. W. Hoch
recounting his battle with Standard Oil's lobbyists in his state. He also published articles on "The Public and the Post Office," "Wanted: A Parcels Post,"
"How Our Railroads Regulate Us," and "The Coming Socialism."

But he lightened the editorial mix with dollops of "service" features, fashion
articles, and popular fiction to hold the allegiance of readers interested primarily
in entertainment. Thus, in August Dreiser announced with some typographical
fanfare that he had signed exclusive contracts with the "Three Most Popular
Authors in the World"—Mary J. Holmes, Mrs. Georgie Sheldon, and Charles
Garvice, whose books had aggregate sales of *"ten million copies."* In later issues,
the editor expounded his tastes (Dreiser was nothing if not confessional with his
readers). He vowed to publish only stories that "reflect American manners and
customs, thought and feeling," but also confessed to a predilection for tales that
depicted a character's rise from rags to riches. He never abandoned his boyhood
faith in ambition and self-improvement, and it cost him little enough to share
it with his readers, however much he might brood on the profounder currents
beneath life's raging seas.

Those darker preoccupations he vented in occasional short sketches such
as the *pensée* published in 1905 in *Tom Watson's Magazine* (to which Duffy had
migrated) called "A Lesson from the Aquarium." Observing how some fish
guard their eggs from predators, how the hermit crab will evict another of
its species from a shell it covets, and how suckerfish attach themselves to
sharks for protection, Dreiser points to analogues in the human world. Capitalists who control a franchise would love to emulate the fishes' skill in driving
away predators; real estate sharpers would envy the crab's success in acquiring
the property it covets, and, "What weakling, seeing the world was against

him, and that he was not fitted to cope with it, would not attach himself, sucker-wise, to any magnate, trust, political or social (we will not call them sharks) . . . ?"

In January 1906 he cut out an editorial in the New York *Tribune* entitled "The Materials of a Great Novel." Commenting on the recent death of Charles T. Yerkes, the "traction king," the editorialist noted the fight over Yerkes's estate, estimated to be worth more than twelve million dollars and now carrion for the legal jackals. Yerkes's story would indeed make a great novel, the editorialist continued, though not one suitable for a William Dean Howells or a Henry James: "The tale is too intricate and various and melodramatic for any kind of living novelist . . . by divine right it is the property of Balzac." Balzac was, of course, dead, but his American acolyte, Theodore Dreiser, filed away the clipping for future reference.

The antibusiness climate must have seemed hospitable to a muckraking book on a financier like Yerkes. Then too, it would be an opportunity to write about this corporate buccaneer and evoke the pillage of America in the furnace years of capitalism. Here was a man with sybaritic tastes, a connoisseur of art and beauty, an inveterate womanizer, whose mistress lived opulently in a mansion not far from his Fifth Avenue palazzo (linked by a tunnel, the gossip writers reported). With an imperious disdain for public opinion, Yerkes had indulged desires that burned in Dreiser's secret heart.

Dreiser's nerves were attuned to the moneymaking energies in the air; he was beginning to enjoy the success game, though he could stand off and contemplate it philosophically. In the dissolution of Yerkes's fortune, he saw the final dissipation of Motion that Spencer had said was the ultimate equilibrium. And, in a more personal way, he was applying the bitter lessons of Ross Street, associating his weakness with the feminine side of his nature, turning to an admiration of strength and physical or business prowess. No more did he write about Tolstoyan altruists. A novel about their antithesis, the egoistic Charles Tyson Yerkes, began to take form in his mind.

•   •   •

Meanwhile, as a rising magazine editor, he demanded and got an increase in salary to sixty dollars a week. His place in the Street and Smith factory seemed assured, but, as he had done at *Ev'ry Month,* Dreiser made enemies in the upper reaches of management, MacLean among them. Some sort of infighting was touched off. Perhaps Dreiser demanded a more royal budget; perhaps it was his innate stubbornness and rebelliousness. As he admitted to Dorothy Dudley, "I was always difficult to deal with."

The escape hatch was the editorship of *Broadway Magazine,* a "white-light" monthly, the term for publications that reported on lurid doings in the theatrical quarter. Under Roland Burke Hennesey, who founded it in 1898, it had achieved a flash success by featuring pictures of women in tights and racy gossip of the demimonde by a columnist called The Red Soubrette. Hennesey had sold out, however, and after his successor cleaned it up, the paper fell on hard times. Its circulation now stood at an anemic twelve thousand.

As chance would have it, the present publisher was Thomas McKee, the former Doubleday lawyer. Dreiser's work at *Smith's* caught his eye, and McKee remembered him as a brilliant, if stubborn, young man. So, in April 1906, even as his enemies at Street and Smith were whetting their dirks, Dreiser received a letter from Caleb L. Litchfield, who seems to have been acting editor, asking if he would like to discuss his ideas for improving the *Broadway*. What Litchfield and McKee had in mind was a moral face-lift. The *Broadway* was to shed its disreputable image as a white-light monthly and, while keeping its New York orientation, become respectable enough to be displayed on the center table in the average God-fearing American's parlor.

That evening Dreiser sketched his ideas for rehabilitating the faded soubrette. He proposed a department that would cover celebrities; regular articles about the "play of the month"; and coverage of the art world, including halftone reproductions of paintings of beautiful women ("a careful supervision to be exercised as to merit and purity"). There would be articles on subjects like "The City of Crowds" (the title of a piece he had already written for *Smith's*), "The Richest Ten-Acre Field in the World" (Manhattan real estate), "Our Underground Life" (subways), "Sorting Three Million Letters" (the post office), interviews with "any personality which makes a real stir in the city," and portraits of society hostesses like Mrs. Stuyvesant Fish. The magazine should also cover current fads like the bolero, "the new Italian peasant dance . . . being practiced by the wealthy." Such an article might appropriately be "illustrated in pretty poses by a good looking girl."

Those hastily cobbled ideas won him the job. His salary would be sixty-five dollars a week to start, rising to one hundred dollars if circulation reached one hundred thousand.

Not long after he was hired, the magazine was purchased by Benjamin Bowles Hampton, a young dynamo from Illinois who had made a fortune in the advertising business. Hampton retained McKee as publisher and Dreiser as editor. Years later, when Dreiser was a major literary figure, Hampton told Dorothy Dudley, "The minute I set eyes on him, I figured the man was a genius. I said to myself, 'Jesus, here's a wow.'" Hampton may have embellished his memories, but during the first months of Dreiser's tenure he was preoccupied with affairs at his ad agency and gave his editor a free hand.

Hampton was throwing fistfuls of money into the enterprise, so Dreiser could engage writers and artists at eighteen to twenty-five dollars a week. A cloud of out-of-work journalists gathered like flies on a cow pat, including

Charles Fort, who shared Dreiser's fascination with the cosmos and offered some bizarre metascientific speculations of his own. As assistant editor and manuscript reader he hired an intelligent young woman named Ethel M. Kelley, late of Bryn Mawr College. She thought her boss a commercial hack—until she read *Sister Carrie*.

Another of Dreiser's discoveries was a cynical young man from the West named Harris Merton Lyon, who casually agreed with Dreiser that a piece he had done for the previous editor stank. They talked, and Lyon revealed his ambition to be a serious writer. Dreiser admired his brashness, his disdain for sham, and his intoxication with the city. (Lyon once told him, "God, how I hate to go to bed in this town! I'm afraid something will happen while I'm asleep and I won't see it!") Seeing in Lyon the young arriviste in the city he had once been, Dreiser took a paternal interest in him, perhaps the closest to fatherhood he ever came. Lyon wrote polished vignettes on urban life that caught the sophisticated tone Dreiser was seeking in the magazine and contributed ironic short stories in the vein of his idol, de Maupassant.

Within a year Dreiser had earned his bonus: circulation had risen above the hundred-thousand mark. He had transformed *Broadway* into a mirror of the glamorous side of New York life, with occasional excursions into its more grim or exotic byways. In its way it was a city magazine, a prototype of *Vanity Fair* and *The New Yorker*. It served as a bridge from the scandalous white-light magazines that catered to the outlanders' view of New York as Sodom-on-the-Hudson, to those that viewed the Rialto and the city in which it was set through worldly, unmoralizing eyes. Dreiser's achievement was, in the words of the columnist for *The Standard & Vanity Fair*: "the prettiest piece of transformation work seen in New York for many a day. He turned in a river of good literature and snappy special articles, changing the magazine completely except in name. People began to sit up and take notice of the *Broadway*. Instead of sneaking around the corner to read it, they carried it in the sunlight and were proud of it."

As a result of his raise, he and Jug were able to move to a larger apartment in Morningside Heights and live in bourgeois comfort. Life might have continued in this more or less pleasant vein but for Ben Hampton, who began taking a more active role as publisher. With his restless energies and robust ego he could not be happy in the countinghouse; he hankered for some editorial glory. He had grand ideas of making the *Broadway* into a muckraking organ and increasing circulation in the bargain. He could not have helped but notice how Thomas Lawson's series "Frenzied Finance," a sensational exposé of Wall Street, had boosted the circulation of *Everybody's* to one million copies in 1904. Dreiser had done a good job, but Hampton regarded him as too literary. He later said Dreiser was miscast as editor of *Broadway Magazine*—"Christ in Hell," as Hampton put it with an adman's hyperbole.

By Dreiser's account, Hampton's final maneuver was to form an editorial advisory committee headed by himself and made up of his loyalists on the staff. Dreiser was effectively bypassed; no longer did the magazine reflect his tastes. It was time to move on again. He had by now acquired the reputation of being a magazine doctor, the man to call in when the patient was failing and heroic remedies were needed.

The Delineator, a ladies' magazine owned by the Butterick Company, which sold tissue-paper patterns of the latest fashions, was just such an invalid. The magazine's main function was to sell patterns, but the company's president, George W. Wilder, realized that to do that, the "Del" needed bright editorial matter to attract readers. His last editor, who had also served as art director, had committed suicide over an unhappy love affair with a society woman, and Wilder needed a replacement immediately.

And so, in June 1907, even as Ben Hampton was putting into effect his editorial plans, not the least of which was changing the magazine's name to *Hampton's,* Dreiser received a letter from Wilder (who, with lofty unconcern, misspelled his name "Dreyser") informing him, "If you would call at this office to see me tomorrow (Friday) morning at or about eleven o'clock you would be doing me a courtesy that I would very much appreciate." Actually, Wilder had learned from John O'Hara Cosgrave, editor of *Everybody's,* in which Wilder was a silent partner, that Dreiser wanted to jump Hampton's ship.

Dreiser boarded the Sixth Avenue elevated train to Spring and MacDougal streets, where the Butterick Building loomed up, its three-planed front commanding a magnificent view of the southern tip of Manhattan. He took the elevator to Wilder's office on the fifteenth floor, where, amid trappings of corporate splendor, he was offered the editorship of *The Delineator* and the two other members of the Butterick trio, *The Designer* and *New Idea Women's Magazine,* at a starting salary of seven thousand dollars a year, with bonuses keyed to increasing circulation. He accepted Wilder's offer. The gates had been opened; he had attained the inner city.

45 / A Pirate Selling Ribbons

> From now on it shall be the NEW DELINEATOR—new in
> humanitarian energy; new in serviceable tenderness; new in
> willingness and desire to aid and to see that idea of the fathers
> that has come down to us from the times of the Pilgrims shall
> not be brought to nothing.
>   —Dreiser, "Concerning Us All" (1908)

In an age of muckraking and progressivism, the thirty-five-year-old *Del* seemed
old-fashioned. It was the kind of magazine mothers would recommend to their
daughters as they did Butterick's conservative dress styles ("Safe fashions for
home people"). Arthur Sullivant Hoffman, who served as managing editor under Dreiser, described it as "a fashion sheet with an omelet of magazine material
poured loosely on and around it."

As it happened, Dreiser was as intimately acquainted as any man could be
with the dreams of the young women from the villages and farms who joined
the rush to the cities beginning in the 1880s. *Sister Carrie* was testimony to
that. He understood that, though their interests were mainly centered on home
and family, they had to live in a hard world; they were affected by social conditions impinging on the domestic sphere. The audience for the Butterick trio
consisted largely of rural and small-town women (including their displaced sisters in the city), and Dreiser had grown up in small towns in the Middle West.
Frances Perkins, then a writer and social reformer, who tried unsuccessfully to
sell him an article, thought Dreiser was the first to use the phrase "west of the
Mississippi River" to refer to a state of mind and level of sophistication as well
as to a geographical region. So, whatever impelled George Wilder to anoint
the author of the "immoral" *Sister Carrie* as the savior of the prim Butterick
magazines, he had made a shrewd choice.

• • •

After cleaning out his desk at the *Broadway*, Dreiser moved into a large office
on the twelfth floor of the Butterick Building. In this edifice two thousand em-

ployees toiled at putting out the magazines and paper patterns that were the company's stock in trade. The building resembled the prow of a great ocean liner, and one might imagine the basement, where great presses clanked and thundered (the world's largest printing plant), as the engine room, manned by grimy stokers. On the bridge, the fifteenth floor, Wilder and his corporate lieutenants held forth, while down on the eighth were the hard-eyed quartermasters of the business department.

What the captain's quarters were like can only be conjectured; Dreiser's (when the interior decorators had finished) were merely opulent. He had picked up the idea somewhere in his magazine travels that decor was power—the more lavish, the better for the executive image. William C. Lengel, who in 1910 came to be interviewed for the job of secretary to the great man, remembered thick drapes and massive pictures, chosen to harmonize with the color scheme of green and bronze, which conveyed solid, understated luxury. Dominating the room, rather like a potentate's throne, was a massive black desk on a raised platform, which Dreiser later confessed he had positioned to give him the psychological advantage of looking down on visitors. Behind it sat a hulking figure who continued writing for five minutes before deigning to notice Lengel.

He was a tall man—six feet one inch, to be precise—who wore a gold pince-nez attached to a black ribbon and was dressed in heavy professorial tweeds with a contrasting vest. A young reporter named Sinclair Lewis, who interviewed Dreiser around this time, observed his bulging waistline (Dreiser weighed a prosperous 180 pounds) and decided he looked like a "wholesale hardware merchant." He was not handsome; some called him ugly. The novelist Fannie Hurst—then a young writer just in from St. Louis with a batch of short stories under her arm—remarked on his "strange lantern of a face," which gave no sign of greeting. The features beneath the high, sloping forehead and unruly hair the color of wet straw were puffy as though molded from putty. His sensuous lips were parted over even, prominent teeth, and the cast in one eye made it difficult to tell if he was looking at you or not. Hurst had the impression that Dreiser was "regarding me without seeing me, focusing on somewhere in an area between, rather than into, my eyes." On first meeting, Dreiser seemed gruff and autocratic, but those who knew him best agreed that his manner was partly for show; that he was a shy, often kindly and emotional man, a bit uncouth and incapable of small talk.

Everyone who met him was intrigued by his nervous habit of pleating his handkerchief; few realized the habit was the only outward manifestation of a highly nervous temperament. Nina Carter Marbourg, a frequent contributor to the magazine, sensed this inner unease, calling him "the most nervous man I ever saw in an editorial chair." Frances Perkins also thought him "queer"—that is, neurotic.

Yet, his quirks and tics aside, Dreiser was clearly in charge. He presided over editorial meetings impassively, a kind of Buddha figure, speaking briefly, quick to praise, slow to censure. In a worshipful portrait, Charles Hanson Towne, who was his fiction editor, pictured Dreiser as a "dominating personality" and a decisive executive, a rock of strength in a tossing sea of ringing telephones and harried editors. Lengel, however, remembered subeditors coming out of his office swearing and women subeditors emerging with tears in their eyes. He was known to tear up an issue at press time in order to get in a compelling story. Writers complained of the magazine's sitting on articles for six or nine months, and Dreiser explained to one irate author that he and his staff had been unable to decide what to do with his piece. When Dreiser gave orders, Lengel said, he tried to be jovial, but his "curious eyes and that twisted mouth made his attempted lightness seem arrogant and dictatorial. What he intended as joviality was mistaken for sarcasm." He was called a slave driver who badgered his subordinates mercilessly, demanding ideas, ideas, ideas. On one of his nervous prowls he happened into the office of Sarah Field Splint, head of the children's department, and told her, "You can stay on as long as you have ideas. But once you stop you'll have to leave. I don't want any hard feelings." "There won't be any hard feelings," replied Splint, on the verge of tears. Nearly every morning Dreiser brought in a sheaf of notes for stories and features, which his secretary copied meticulously on special forms for presentation at weekly editorial meetings. "He was exceedingly tolerant at the criticism of his offerings, and, at these meetings at least, never showed any impatience or raised his voice," Lengel wrote.

The tyrant image was largely dissipated by familiarity. The younger members of the staff found that once they broke through his autocratic crust, Dreiser listened to their ideas or problems. They in turn admired his novel. A woman on the staff had disliked and feared Dreiser until she read *Carrie.* Then she felt a strong loyalty to him because he had written "the one big serious true American novel with blood in it—not ink." Even those who had not read the book came to respect his ability and his professionalism. Ray Long, who succeeded him at *The Broadway,* said he learned the editor's trade by reading copies of Dreiser's letters to contributors in which he outlined story ideas. The humorist Homer Croy, one of several Missourians Dreiser hired (Lengel was another), because his wife was from the state and he had been a newspaperman in St. Louis, wrote, "In Philadelphia there were two great names—George Horace Lorimer and Edward Bok. In New York—Dreiser." Perhaps the comparison to the legendary editors of *The Saturday Evening Post* and *Ladies' Home Journal* was a little strained, but it was not far off the mark.

Ensconced in his luxurious office with a view of the East River, he sometimes gazed out the window, lost in thought. Towne wondered if he was dreaming of a new book. Elia W. Peattie, one of his editors, thought him wildly miscast, later calling him "a pirate selling ribbons."

Out of a kind of *nostalgie de la boue,* he liked to walk in the Italian slums from which the Butterick Building jutted up like an alien monolith. He inhaled the color, the noise, the jostling humanity. Lengel remembered him each evening walking with a rolling gait along MacDougal Street to the elevated train, humming spirituals or popular tunes of the nineties.

When Lengel asked Dreiser why he wasted his time editing a women's magazine when he could write a novel like *Sister Carrie,* Dreiser shrugged and said, "One must live. Don't you know the story of that book?" Later, he told him. A sad story, but one that, ironically, had a happy ending.

46 / "The Game as It Is Played!"

—And what is your Mr. Dreiser doing these days?
—Dreiser?
—The author of *Sister Carrie!* . . . Americans do not know that England looks on *Sister Carrie* as the finest American novel sent over in the last twenty years and to Dreiser as the biggest American novelist who has sent us anything. . . .

—William J. Locke, British novelist in an interview
on arriving in New York City (1908)

Ben Hampton told Dorothy Dudley he had deeply admired *Sister Carrie* and always wished he had been the one who put up the money for its republication in 1907. Probably he had been too busy consolidating his control to notice that Dreiser had succeeded in finding a new publisher on his own. Knowing of her boss's desire for a new edition, Ethel Kelly gave it to a friend named Flora Mai Holly, who was starting out as a literary agent, to try to sell. Holly was herself a true believer and familiar with the book's history. At the time *Sister Carrie* came out, she had been working for *The Bookman* and had heard the trade gossip about *Carrie*'s abortive publication.

To avoid any lingering traces of old prejudices, Holly placed the book with a new firm, B. W. Dodge and Company. Dodge was a shrewd, unconventional publisher who was looking for a way to launch his company with a big splash and was willing to take a chance. He had been a salesman for Dodd, Mead and worked up to an editorial position before quitting to found his own house. His business affairs were disorderly, but Dodge was ebullient and full of schemes for making money ("stunts" he liked to call them). He also had a talent for charming wealthy people—"moneybags"—into backing his ventures. His only major weakness—a fatal one, as it turned out—was a considerable thirst for hard liquor. He was, in Dreiser's words, "a lovable alcoholic."

Holly set up a meeting between author and publisher in late January 1907, and by early March they had agreed on a contract in which the author agreed to buy fifty shares of stock in B. W. Dodge and Company at $100 a share. Dodge had talked Dreiser into underwriting his own book. He was to pay $1000 down, which would cover production costs and leave something over for advertising and promotion. The remaining $4000 would be deducted from royalties.

In return, Dreiser became a director of the new firm, entitled to a share of its profits, if any. As subsequent events showed, he intended his stock purchase as a serious investment and hoped to make money out of it. He took an active role in the company's affairs, both to protect the value of his shares and to have a say in the publication of his novel.

Dreiser and Dodge devised a two-pronged strategy for *Carrie*'s rehabilitation that called for advertising the novel's literary merits and publicizing the story of its "suppression" so that the public would think of it as virtually a new book. If people caught a whiff of the risqué, well, so be it; the first part of the strategy would preempt any charges of pandering to the public's appetite for sensation.

Proceeding on the first front, Dreiser wrote letters to *Carrie*'s prominent admirers informing them that *Carrie* was at long last being resurrected and asking permission to use a quote in the advertising brochure. On the other front, Dreiser wrote a long account of the Doubleday story, mentioning no names. This was not used in the brochure that Dodge eventually disseminated among booksellers. Instead, Dodge indulged in a tease: "This book was accepted by a leading American publisher, but strangely enough immediately withdrawn; meantime an English edition was published and had an instantaneous success. As its suppression in this country was our gain, we have no comments to make, but again ask you to read the comments of others who can fairly be supposed to be unprejudiced judges."

And so *Sister Carrie* made her second debut on May 18, 1907. Dodge and Dreiser had made certain that this time the little knight did not venture forth half-equipped. No assassin's binding for the new model: she was decked out in bright red cloth of good quality, and the title was stamped in gold letters. There was only one illustration, a full-color frontispiece in which Carrie, looking pert in her "little Quaker" costume, is shown curtsying before the curtain. The warm dedication to Arthur Henry had been removed, however, as had the borrowed passage from George Ade.

To supplement the promotional brochure, which was aimed at booksellers, Dodge took out advertisements in the newspapers. Here, his huckstering was more uninhibited. He trumpeted the book's uniqueness ("The Curtain Raised on a Generally Unwritten Phase of Life"), its power ("Startling in reality"), and, not least, its daring ("Sensational revelations"). The literati were cued ("The realism of a Zola without the faults. One of the most remarkable novels in literature . . . "), but the general public was not neglected ("and everybody is going to read it").

Not everybody did, by any means, but sales got off to a brisk start. In the first three months after publication, more than 4600 copies were sold, and eventually the total reached about 8500—small in comparison to the 200,000-copy sale that year of Robert W. Chambers's society novel *The Younger Set,* or the even higher sales of *The Lady of the Decoration* by Frances Little, in a Century Company dollar edition—but respectable. In 1908, after sales had cooled down, Grosset and Dunlap brought out a cheap edition of 10,000 copies, taking the excess stock off Dodge's hands. The book's critical reception finally established Dreiser's reputation as an important American novelist.

This time the reviews came out in a single authoritative wave, rather than intermittent ripples. He now won the approval of critics for the mainstream papers. The Washington *Evening Star*'s reviewer wrote that the novel was "one of the most important books of the year"; Agnes Repellier of the Philadelphia *Public Ledger* called it "literature of high class"; the Los Angeles *Times* described it as "somber, powerful, fearlessly and even fearfully frank"; and the New Orleans *Picayune* averred it was the "strongest piece of realism we have yet met with in American fiction."

There were dissents, of course, and the moralists fulminated. The *Ohio Journal,* for example, warned, "Such books are to be shunned . . . there is so much in the world that is fresh and clean, elevating little stories . . . that are worth telling." The Chicago *Advance* warned, "The book is not a good or wholesome one for women to read." In the heart of Watch and Ward Society country, the Boston *Transcript*'s reviewer found it "a matter for regret that [the author] should devote his creative energy to a woman and two men who never quicken our nobler impulses."

But the *Transcript*'s reviewer said that Dreiser had succeeded in investing his sordid characters "with the dignity of psychological insight and literary perception, and with an interest—often rebellious—which never flags." She made it clear that the book did not appeal to prurient tastes, and as a feminist she was not puzzled by the title. It stood for "the sisterhood of woman: her temptations and her opportunities, her wrongs and her rights, her obedience to the ordinary demands of the moment, her responsiveness to the appeal of sex, her power to develop out of and above it into independence of thought and action." Perhaps too polite to say it, she meant that this was no portrait of a lady. Carrie Meeber Wheeler Madenda was a modern woman.

It took a member of the younger generation—a literary radical—to recognize the transcendent cultural issue involved. Writing in the Houston *Post,* the reviewer saw in *Sister Carrie* "one more evidence of a broader American intellectual freedom." He continued:

> Possibly the day may come when George Moore's *Memoirs of My Dead Life,* will not have to be expurgated as if for children, when it is issued in the United States. No wonder England, no wonder France, no wonder Germany look patronizingly down

upon us—a nation of grown men and women for whom publishers must expurgate books before they are allowed to read them! "The land of the free," "freedom of the press"—the words are empty. . . . The time is coming some day—I care not whether it is within twenty-five years or within a century—when the United States will have to "stand for"—if it comes to the point of compulsion—an American Tolstoi, Turgenieff, Flaubert, Balzac, Nietzsche, Wilde, de Maupassant.

The reviewer was Harris Merton Lyon.

•   •   •

In an interview with the New York *Times* after *Sister Carrie*'s successful second debut, Dreiser said he was too busy editing *The Delineator* to write novels. He spoke of the dramas of ordinary life, and the twists and turns of fate. He told the reviewer, "The mere living of your daily life is a drastic drama. . . . The banquet of tonight may crumble to the crust of the morning."

Perhaps he was thinking that, only four years earlier, he had been a beggar; now he was an invited guest at the feast. From his office on the twelfth floor of the Butterick Building he could see all the way to the southern tip of Manhattan, where the two rivers converged—the East, river of the nameless dead, and the Hudson, river of power and dreams. Two streams in his life had also converged: his constant struggle for money and power and his idealistic battle for art, expression, and truth. Beyond their confluence lay the open sea, awaiting further voyages.

"I simply want to tell about life as it is," he told the interviewer. "Every human life is intensely interesting . . . the personal desire to survive, the fight to win, the stretching out of the fingers to grasp—these are the things I want to write about—life as it is, the facts as they exist, the game as it is played!"

Book Two

• • •

AN AMERICAN
JOURNEY,
1908 – 1945

Part Seven

. . .

THE EDITOR

47 / The Bohemian Within

"Are you writing anything else?"
"I have another book partly finished, but I don't know when I shall get it done. I have not the time to work on it, much as I want to."

—Dreiser, interview in *The New York Times*
Saturday Book Review (1907)

When Dreiser told the reporter from the New York *Times* that he had a book "partly finished" but had no time to work on it, he was referring, of course, to *The Transgressor*. That aborted novel continued to live a phantom existence. In 1905 Grant Richards, a British publisher who on one of his scouting trips to New York had heard about *Sister Carrie* from the novelist Frank Norris, asked if he might be the British publisher of Dreiser's next novel. He urged Dreiser to send him a copy of the manuscript as soon as it was finished: "I don't want to wait a day longer than I can help before I read it."

No manuscript was forthcoming, but Richards wrote Dreiser encouraging letters from time to time and visited him on his annual author-hunting trips to New York. At last, in March 1908, Dreiser sent the British publisher twenty chapters of the manuscript of the story of Jennie Gerhardt. Richards expressed his "keen pleasure that the promise of 'Sister Carrie' is being fulfilled. . . ." He closed with a lighthearted aside: "I believe the book will healthily depress every one of its intelligent readers."

Richards's jesting remark almost put Dreiser off the novel for good. He replied that maybe he had "better drop that yarn and take up something else. Perhaps my later mood will not be so sombre. . . ." Richards quickly soothed him: "All I can say is that if I did not convince you that I thought 'Jennie' was a very fine piece of work, indeed, a fit and worthy successor to 'Sister Carrie,' then I must have expressed myself very clumsily and inadequately. It is my 'absolute conviction that the thing is really worth while.' I should publish it with enthusiasm and pride." But a fear that the story was too grim and "immoral" gnawed at Dreiser.

Indeed, although he dreamed of returning to full-time writing, a fear of failure haunted him. Moreover, the power and prestige of his present job were addictive. He liked fashionable clothes, enjoyed travel, and demanded a well-endowed table. Sartorially, his tastes ran to heavy tweeds—"quality" stuffs, Johnson & Murphy shoes, and Knox hats. "The label gives you a certain standing," he explained to William C. Lengel, one of his secretaries. He probably had social ambitions. Ludwig Lewisohn, an aspiring novelist who had become one of his protegés, was surprised to hear that this literary radical was a regular in the Sunday fashion parade on Riverside Drive, resplendent in a top hat and Prince Albert coat.

Still, he was showing signs of restlessness. In July 1909 Dreiser purchased for $1000 a disreputable and bankrupt magazine called the *Bohemian.* In a letter to H. L. Mencken he explained that he hoped to "have some fun with the project." He seemed to regard it as an editorial pasture, a place to kick up his heels against the restraints at *The Delineator.* He assured Mencken, however, that he was not about to relinquish control of Butterick publications. Mencken, who had come to Dreiser's notice by ghostwriting for a Baltimore physician a series on baby care that ran in the Del, replied that he was "in with both feet." Dreiser dispatched a more detailed editorial prospectus. First of all, he wanted to make the *Bohemian* "the broadest, most genial little publication in the field." Although he wanted no "tainted fiction" or "sex struck articles," he aimed at "a big catholic point of view, a sense of humor grim or gay, and articles on any conceivable subject. . . . I want bright stuff. I want humor. And above all I want knowledge of life *as it is*. . . . "

Mencken's first contribution, "A Plea for Profanity," suited Dreiser to a T, and he begged for more. Their friendship flourished in the shared recognition that neither was doing the work he wanted to do. Although Mencken loved journalism, he was in a hurry to make his mark in a literary way. As he wrote Dreiser: "I am getting along toward thirty and it is time for me to be planning for the future. Specifically, I want to write a couple of books for you within the next few years. Specifically again, I want to write a play that now encumbers and tortures my system. You will understand what a stew I am in."

Dreiser understood. Discussing fees for the baby-care series, Dreiser had said, "I suppose the low ebb of the literary life in Baltimore has something to do with" his resorting to hackwork.

When they met face to face in the late spring of 1908, Dreiser's initial impression was of the playboy son of a prosperous brewer dressed in a loud suit and yellow shoes for a night on the town. Unawed by Dreiser's cavernous office or his large chair designed to intimidate visitors, the five-foot-eight-inch Mencken lolled back insouciantly—a cocky, snub-nosed, jug-eared young man, his hair parted in the middle—and beamed at the great editor "with the confidence of a smirking fox about to devour a chicken."

On Mencken's subsequent visits to New York City he and Dreiser argued boisterously about literature, science, God, religion, and myriad other topics. Dreiser did not share Mencken's near worship of Nietzsche, calling the German philosopher "Schopenhauer confused and warmed over." Mencken inscribed his third book, *The Philosophy of Friedrich Nietzsche,* to his friend, "In memory of furious disputations on sorcery & the art of letters."

Dreiser's most important intervention in Mencken's life was to help launch him as a book critic. In the spring of 1908 Dreiser learned that a former Butterick employee, Fred Splint, was seeking a reviewer for the *Smart Set,* of which he had recently become editor. Dreiser recommended Mencken, and he was hired "with the rank and pay of a sergeant of artillery" and handed a pile of books. By fall he was reviewing at a furious pace—twenty-five volumes a month—praising realistic American literature and damning publishers' timidity and the genteel best sellers of the day. The following year he was joined on the staff by a kindred spirit, George Jean Nathan, a drama critic.

• • •

The *Bohemian* lasted four issues and died unmourned, save by Mencken. Dreiser's fling with it was a symptom of his restlessness in his job. Another, more serious dalliance revealed his unhappiness in his marriage. It started when he joined a group of ballroom dancing devotees called the Fantastic Toe Club and met an eighteen-year-old beauty named Thelma Cudlipp.

Thelma was studying at the Artists League and was the daughter of Annie Ericsson Cudlipp, a formidable widow from Virginia who was in charge of the stenographic pool at the Butterick Company. Hired by Dreiser, who had a soft spot for widows with families to support, she had been befriended by Jug, who invited Thelma and her mother to dinner and sometimes invited the young woman to sleep over after a night's dancing. Jug seemed to encourage her husband's outings with the younger crowd as a way of taking his mind off his Butterick responsibilities. She would call Mrs. Cudlipp and say, "Theo wants a party. Can you manage it, dear Mrs. Cudlipp? Bring your gayest young people."

Thelma's first intimation of Dreiser's interest in her came during a ball at the Staten Island Yacht Club. They had walked out on the veranda. "Do you like to dance with me as much as those younger men?" Dreiser suddenly asked her. Stirred, Thelma replied, "You must know I do, Mr. Dreiser." He told her to call him Theo and assured her that Mrs. Dreiser approved of their friendship.

"Then he kissed me," Thelma wrote in "October's Child," her unpublished memoirs. Throughout their friendship that was the only time he kissed her. Thelma was so innocent that she could not imagine anything more, in a physical way, in their relationship. She was as much in awe as in love. There were other meetings, dances, rendezvous at Long Island house parties, long walks, even meetings at a Butterick employee's apartment. He called her "Honeypot," a twist on Jug's pet name for him, "Honeybugs." He talked baby talk to her, and together they composed silly jingles that he proposed to make into a children's book, which Thelma would illustrate.

Mrs. Cudlipp did nothing to discourage what seemed an innocent friendship, and when Jug fell ill with rheumatic fever in the spring of 1910, she counted on the Cudlipps more than ever to provide amusement and companionship for her neglected Theo. It was at that point that the relationship between Dreiser and Thelma entered a dangerous phase.

He was making a grab for the brass ring of youth. Acutely, even neurotically conscious of the passage of time, he felt the cold blasts of forty bearing down on him. Even before Jug's illness, his sexual desire for her had cooled. It was now a marriage of convenience—his from the standpoint of comfort and hers from that of convention and social position. Nearly two years older than her husband, she turned forty in 1909. To Dreiser, that seemed middle-aged.

But she provided the home and mothering he both craved and subconsciously resented. As his niece Vera Dreiser, a psychologist, wrote in her biography, *My Uncle Theodore,* he was still inseparably bound to his much-adored mother, who had died twenty years before but who had "dwarfed his capacity to love, leaving him forever in a state of arrested emotional development. Consequently, he transferred to his young wife . . . the latent hostilities that rightly belonged to his mother." Poor Jug had unwittingly assumed the role of maternal superego in his life.

Many Butterick colleagues wondered what he saw in her; she seemed nice but small-townish. Dreiser felt that she had not kept pace intellectually with his rapid rise in the magazine world. In an editorial in *The Delineator* he was surely describing her: "In case a man has married a woman in one state or plane of his life and finds at forty or fifty that he has risen above that state, supposing the woman that he married at twenty no longer represents the spirit or interests of his larger existence—that she is neither beautiful or intellectual—has not kept pace with him in his upward progress—what does that man owe that woman?"

Jug begged him to let her have a child, thinking that fatherhood would steady him. But he adamantly refused, as he had throughout their marriage. He liked children well enough and could sincerely pity the orphans featured in *The Delineator*'s Child Rescue Campaign—they too had been abandoned. But having a child of his own would mean the end of his monopoly of Jug's maternal instincts. He told her that giving birth would ruin her figure, the implication being that she would become unattractive to him. And, obviously, he disliked the idea of having a child because it would strengthen her hold over him.

• • •

One evening in the spring of 1910, after an excursion to the Palisades amusement park with a group of young Butterick employees, Thelma and Dreiser were sitting alone in the living room of the 123rd Street apartment. He told her that their love had reached a stage when his "man's desire" must be satisfied. Suddenly Thelma glimpsed a slender figure framed in the doorway, her copper hair in braids that seemed to reach to the floor, her eyes flashing, her body trembling with a profound emotion. Jug called Thelma a foolish girl and threatened to tell her mother about the entire affair. Later, there was a horrendous quarrel between Dreiser and Jug—or so he wrote in *The "Genius."* The real-life outcome was the same as the one in the book: he refused to stop seeing Thelma.

Despite her illness, Jug fought ferociously to save her marriage. She wrote Thelma reproachful letters, ordering her to forget Dreiser. Aghast at the prospect of her daugher's becoming involved with a married man twice her age, the distraught Annie Cudlipp began playing a double game, trying to buy time in hopes that Thelma would tire of the romance.

In late July 1910 Dreiser wrote Mencken, "Mrs. Dreiser was quite bad but is better and looks as though she will be all right in the course of 10 days or two weeks." Beneath those bland words flowed an undercurrent of guilt. The thought that Jug might die and free him to marry Thelma had surely crossed his mind. He later wrote a story called "Free," about an unhappily married man who waited too long. His wife's death liberates him, but he is too old to enjoy his freedom. Bitterly, he tells himself he is "free—free to die." Dreiser evoked the stifling sense of entrapment he felt in his own marriage. Thelma was the glittering prize that would make his success complete. As he wrote her, "I NEED you. You are the breath of life to me. All my life I have longed for this."

48 / Amid the Ruins

Here was all the solid foundation knocked from under him.
. . . His shimmering world of dreams was beginning to fade
like an evening sky. It might be that he had been chasing a
will-o'-the-wisp, after all.

—Dreiser, *The "Genius"* (1915)

What was already a bad melodrama took a farcical turn when Fritz Krog, a
young protégé who was himself infatuated with Thelma, heard of Dreiser's
involvement. The unstable Krog became wildly jealous, threatening to kill his
rival, but then decided he didn't want to after all.

Meanwhile, Annie Cudlipp revealed the full story to George Wilder, the
president of Butterick company, and issued an ultimatum: if Wilder did not
put a stop to the romance, she would take the story to the newspapers. Not
only would she tell them that the editor of *The Delineator* was carrying on with
an eighteen-year-old girl, she would also reveal that Erman J. Ridgway, publisher of *Everybody's* magazine, which had recently merged with the Butterick
publishing group, was doing the same with one of *his* assistants. Faced with
that double-barreled threat, Wilder was forced to act. In late September 1910
a delegation headed by Ridgway and Wilder marched into Dreiser's sanctum.
Wilder offered Dreiser a choice: Thelma or his job. Dreiser refused to give
her up.

•   •   •

In fact, the Thelma scandal was only the proximate cause of Dreiser's downfall. As Arthur Hoffman, managing editor at the time, recalled, "Though
the young lady afforded occasion and might have been sufficient warrant,
office politics was out for his scalp long before that came up. Butterick
. . . was notorious for its office politics and the difficulties of its many editors." The infighting had heated up in the fall of 1909 after Butterick

purchased *Everybody's* magazine, owned by the Ridgway Company, and Erman J. Ridgway became a director of Butterick publications. Inevitably, Dreiser locked horns with Ridgway over budgets and editorial content.

Success may have made Dreiser overconfident. His first misstep was a six-part series on spiritualism in 1908, "Are the Dead Alive?" It was considered blasphemous by Bible Belt readers, generating a wave of angry letters, to which Dreiser was forced to reply in the magazine. Admitting that the articles "have raised a storm around our editorial head," he assured readers that he had not intended to proselytize for spiritualism, "only to give an unbiased, impartial presentation."

In an interview with a Boston *Globe* reporter who had inquired about *The Delineator's* "prospectus" for the coming year, Wilder was jocular, as was his style, but there was an edge in his voice: "Our editor is a wonder, —he changes his mind so fast there ain't no Prospectus." One thing Wilder is sure of: the magazine is going to discontinue the "Are the Dead Alive?" series and "a few other circulation destroyers, but even then I won't guarantee the editor from attacking the church—any old church—but I am going to try to keep him good."

Thereafter Dreiser trod softly when religion was the subject. He announced in the Christmas issue an upcoming series of articles on "the spirit of the new Christianity," the first being "Why One Hundred Sunday-Schools Have Succeeded." In 1910 he asked H. G. Wells to tone down a novel submitted to the Del for serialization. Although Wells's theme "might delight the highly intellectual women," he said, "it would possibly offend the rank and file." He asked Wells "to modify or eliminate in the remainder of the book the keen thrusts against morality and society. . . . "

With the advent of Ridgway, who was friendly with the Butterick president, Dreiser became increasingly isolated and vulnerable. He had little talent for corporate infighting. He was a creative editor who preferred generating ideas and working with writers to empire building. His style was to delegate authority to talented people, and after he became obsessed with Thelma Cudlipp, he let the reins on his department heads go slack. He withdrew from the battle at the wrong moment: just as Ridgway was busily forging alliances and installing his own people. Dreiser's protégés could sense the power shift, and some of them defected to his rival's camp to protect their jobs.

• • •

And so, unwilling to give up Thelma, Dreiser renounced his throne. He agreed to a face-saving resignation as of October 15, 1910. His departure came as a surprise to most of the staff. Few knew the real reason for his going, and even Lengel was in the dark for a long time. Fremont Rider, who been intimately involved in Dreiser's extracurricular business interests, was also unaware of his amorous affairs and sent a letter expressing his regrets. In his reply, Dreiser implied that he had resigned on a matter of principle: "I do not consider my resignation in the light of a loss. The big work was done there. . . . I had been fighting interference for sometime & finally stood the whole thing out."

He let slip his true feelings to Mencken in a hasty, unsigned memo: "I have just discovered that this is a very sad world." Later he explained, "Nothing's up save a big row. It's all over now though & I am considering several good things. My conscience hurts me a little though for first-off I should finish my book. And I may."

Temporarily separated from Jug, who was being nursed by her sister, he moved to a Park Avenue hotel to pine for Thelma in lonely splendor. His room overlooked the courtyard restaurant, and in the evening when the sounds of an orchestra wafted up and the little red lamps on the tables glowed like fire-flies, he felt unutterably sad. One day Lengel dropped in and found his former boss sitting disconsolately on his bed, endlessly folding his handkerchief, the picture of a broken man. Yet Dreiser insisted that he was all right and spoke optimistically of his prospects. He might buy into a publishing house or man-age a literary syndicate or edit a newspaper. He dickered for an interest in the Wildman Magazine and News Service, but negotiations broke down when he insisted on an equal partnership and refused to invest his own money.

He was, as he told Mencken, inclining toward finishing *The Transgressor* and so was hanging on to his savings. He wrote Thelma, who had been spirited by her mother to North Carolina to stay with relatives, that he was "not at all anxious" about his future and that Jug was "taking it all much better than I thought she would and I fancy things are going to come out nicely." As for the loss of his job—"You are worth it all—my worry, my position, the danger of publicity—everything—I gladly pay the price & would pay it again."

Meanwhile Annie Cudlipp was playing her last hand—double or nothing. She told Dreiser he could marry her daughter on two conditions: that he obtain a divorce and that he not see Thelma for one year. He agreed, but the prospect of a long separation plunged him deeper into gloom.

Actually, Annie's offer was a bluff—another attempt to buy time in hopes her daugher's interest would cool. Even the self-hypnotized Dreiser now sus-pected that Annie was leading him on.

In a letter to Thelma he begged her, "Oh, Honeypot be kind—be kind to me. You said once you would be mother & sister and sweetheart to me. I am a little pleading boy now in need of your love, your mother love." If Thelma had once loved him, a love that was part hero-worship and part schoolgirl crush, she was now having doubts; she had blundered into a terrifying grown-ups' world with lurking monsters of convention and sexuality. The man who had once been her idol was now begging her to be a mother to him.

To make sure that Thelma did not elope with Dreiser on her own, as Thelma recounts it in her unpublished memoir, her mother had a friend tell her all about sex and "man's desire." It was evidently a graphic lesson, laced with Victorian horrors, for it left Thelma disgusted and angry at Dreiser for wanting to subject her to such a nasty business. She agreed to go to London, where she would live with her uncle and study art at the Royal Academy.

• • •

Inwardly Dreiser was shattered, but unlike Hurstwood, he was not without resources. He had saved money; he had friends, editorial contacts, a literary reputation—and an unfinished novel on his desk. Richards, Mencken, and his literary agent, Flora Mai Holly, among others, urged him to return to writing. The influential critic James Gibbons Huneker had written him only recently: "I'm sorry for the Delineator's sake that you are leaving it and I hope you have something better. *But*—if you, Theodore Dreiser, could or would return to your old field, the gain for our literature would be something worthwhile. We have but one *Sister Carrie,* despite the army of imitators."

But how much easier it was to be a well-paid purveyor of Human Betterment to housewives than to subject himself to what he had called "the lonely tortures of writing." In what he saw as a country without culture, where the businessman called the tune, the serious artist was ignored or condescended to. As he would write in *The "Genius,"* "Why follow a profession or craft in which . . . all your days you were tolerated for your genius with a kindly smile, used as an ornament at receptions but never taken seriously as a factor in the commercial affairs of the world?"

But there was a price for the power and affluence he had enjoyed. Much later he candidly assessed the *Delineator* years:

> It was pathetic, as I look at it now, the things we were trying to do and the conditions under which we were trying to do them—the raw commercial force and theory which underlay the whole thing, the necessity of explaining and fighting for so much that one should not, as I saw it then, have to argue over at all. . . . My own experience with *Sister Carrie,* as well as the fierce opposition or chilling indifference which, as I saw, overtook all those who attempted anything even partially serious in America, was enough to make me believe that the world took anything even slightly approximating the truth as one of the rankest and most criminal offenses possible. One dared not talk out loud, one dared not report life as it was, as one lived it.

49 / A Woman's Story

> I have just finished one book—Jennie Gerhardt—and am half
> through with another. I expect to try out this book game for
> about four or five books after which unless I am enjoying a
> good income from them I will quit.
>
> —Dreiser to Mencken (1914)

Worried about whether Dreiser would continue to provide for her, Jug consulted
Thomas H. McKee, the lawyer who had tried to untangle Paul Dresser's song
copyrights in 1906.

When McKee called on her in the fall of 1910, he found her ill but anxious
to confide in someone. As the lawyer recalled to Dreiser biographer Robert H.
Elias, "Little by little she unfolded a tale of marital distress, giving details
which were strange even to my accustomed ears and of which I cannot speak."
When he asked her if she was willing to take legal action to force Dreiser to
support her, she demurred. Theo must not even know that she had spoken
with McKee; the publicity of a court proceeding would hurt his "standing,"
and she did not want that. His hands tied, McKee advised her to work out a
reconciliation and left.

Dreiser continued to send her money and paid a conciliatory visit, for he felt
sorry for her and did not intend to abandon her. But their separation continued;
Jug went off to Missouri to recuperate, and Dreiser moved from his hotel to a
rented room in the large apartment of Elias Rosenthal at 608 Riverside Drive.
The cultivated Rosenthal, an attorney, and his wife, Emma, a writer, frequently
entertained people from the aristic and business worlds. They also provided a
cover of respectability, for Dreiser was still worried about appearances.

Like other defectors from middle-class conventions, he sometimes fled to
Greenwich Village, a burgeoning Bohemian quarter. But he had little time for
play. None of his halfhearted efforts to launch a new career had panned out,
so he turned to the job of finishing the story of Jennie Gerhardt. He had no
publisher as yet, but he had received nibbles from several editors, including
Ripley Hitchcock at Harper & Brothers. As soon as Hitchcock heard that Dreiser

had departed from Butterick, he wrote to congratulate him on being "fortunate enough to be released from the strain of office work" and asked if he had a novel on the hob. Dreiser replied that he expected to finish one by December 1 and had engaged Flora Mai Holly, who had handled the republication of *Sister Carrie*, as his agent. Send along the manuscript, Hitchcock cried—in time to make the spring list.

• • •

Dreiser's prediction that he would finish by December was unrealistic. Nevertheless, he worked furiously and actually completed a version by early January, picking up where he left off as long ago as 1904, at the point in the story when the sister of Lester Kane, Jennie's wealthy lover, barges in on the apartment where the two are living together. Once he reached the place where Lester faces the disapproval of his family, he had been beset by doubts about how to handle the outcome of the story. Should the couple continue to live in sin, or should they marry? And if the latter, wouldn't the moralists protest that he was "rewarding" her?

He solved the problem with the Victorian device of a will. Lester's father dies, leaving a testament stipulating that if Lester abandons Jenny he will receive his full inheritance worth an estimated $1.5 million; if he marries her, he will receive $10,000 a year for life, but he will lose his share of the family fortune. Dreiser thus writes the moralists' choices into Archibald Kane's will, enforcing them with a pecuniary sanction. If Lester does the "right thing"— observes the convention—he will collect his full monetary reward and return to the good graces of his family. But he will also grievously hurt Jennie, a devoted woman, and destroy the only loving relationship in his aimless life. Conventional morality is ironically reduced to a financial calculation, opposed to human feelings.

Lester has three years to decide. Loath to hurt Jennie, he procrastinates and almost weds Lettie Gerald, a beautiful, wealthy widow and an old admirer. Marriage to Lettie would be a most attractive solution to Lester's dilemma, but in the end he realizes that Jennie's love is the only happiness he will ever know in a life that he finds increasingly meaningless, and so he returns to her for good.

Dreiser had toned down the rakish side of Lester's character. He also made Jennie more sexually magnetic and womanly, a more mystical temperament. These are improvements: Lester is no longer a Machiavellian seducer but a complex man who sees through social sham; Jennie is a life force rather than merely a seduced and abandoned waif.

In Dreiser's revised plot, marriage "rewarded" Jennie, but at least it gave her respectability. Perhaps that compromise would satisfy the prudes. Still, he was uneasy and circulated copies of the manuscript among friends for advice and criticism.

Among the first readers was Lillian Rosenthal, the twenty-year-old daughter of Elias and Emma, a plump and pretty young woman with a musical bent. Her literary background consisted mainly of reading some of the more "advanced" European authors, but that was enough to tell her that the optimistic ending rang false. Too shy to tell this to Dreiser face to face, she sent him her critique in a letter. The novel "establishes a standard for American fiction," she said, but "if Lester had married Lettie, the tragedy of Jennie would have been greater. Poignancy is a neccessity in this story, and it can only be maintained by persistent want on the part of Jennie. The loss of Lester would insure this." She timidly added that maybe such a change was unnecessary, for the novel was so strong that it "compels one to recognize the truth about life."

Dreiser teased her about claiming to know so much about life at her age, but inwardly he agreed with Lillian. As he had previously written Fremont Rider, who had also read the manuscript, "I am convinced that one of the reasons of lack of poignancy is the fact that Lester marries Jennie. In the revision I don't intend to let him do it. And I may use your version for the rest. . . . "

He told Rider the changes involved "very little work," though in fact they took him another month. In his revision, Lester marries Lettie. Dreiser added further poignancy by having Jennie's illegitimate daughter, Vesta, die of typhoid fever. Lettie elbows her way into New York's "400" and keeps a mansion staffed by liveried servants while her husband devotes himself to the pleasures of the table. Eventually his gourmandizing ruins his health, and he is struck by a fatal illness. Realizing he is dying, he sends for Jennie (Lettie is abroad) and tells her that she is the only woman he ever loved. Jennie stays by him until he dies, attends his funeral heavily veiled, and watches at the railroad station as his coffin is loaded on a train, thinking of the empty, lonely life ahead—"Days and days in endless reiteration, and then—?"

The book should have ended on that dangling question, but Dreiser tacked on a meditative coda, as he had done with *Sister Carrie*, summarizing the meaning of his heroine's life and, not incidentally, justifying her. The moving evocation of death amid life in that final scene of Jennie at the station was epilogue enough—the holiday travelers bustling about their journeys, the train announcer's litany of distant cities, the baggage handler bawling, "Hey, Jack! Give us a hand here. There's a stiff outside!"—and Jennie a still figure in the center of it all, her eyes fixed on "the great box that was so soon to disappear" bearing all the happiness she ever had or ever would know. The moral was that there was no moral. Human lives are subject to inscrutable purposes. As Lester tells Jennie, "All of us are more or less pawns. We're moved about like chessmen by circumstances over which we have no control."

•   •   •

Holly sent the revised manuscript first to Edward G. Marsh, a Macmillan editor, who rendered a quick negative verdict. He predicted commercial success but added, "There are some things about it . . . which I do not like." He did not elaborate, but Dreiser later learned that he felt it was too "broad," that is, explicit. The following day Dreiser wrote Mencken, "I sometimes think my desire is for expression that is entirely too frank for this time—hence that I must pay the price of being unpalatable. The next book will tell." And he told Grant Richards, "I had better be careful. My turn comes later."

That next book, which, he told Mencken with excessive optimism, was "half-finished," was called *The Genius*. It is the story of a young artist named Eugene Witla, who is harried by sexual desires, mesmerized by feminine beauty, and torn between art and commerce. Some of the surface details of the hero's career were drawn from that of Everett Shinn, one of the "Eight," a group of young painters who shocked the New York art world with a show in 1907 that featured city scapes painted in a gritty realistic style. Shinn was also a successful commercial artist, specializing in glib drawings of handsome tuxedoed young men and soignée young women, and Dreiser had used his work in the *Broadway Magazine* in 1906. Most fascinating to Dreiser was the gossip about his amorous escapades. Shinn, who would go through a string of wives, had a boyish quality that made women want to mother him, it was said. He epitomized the Bohemian sexual freedom that Dreiser, trapped in an unhappy marriage, had envied.

But Dreiser was not only telling Shinn's story; he was attempting to trace his own rough path to success and to come to terms with his fall from Butterick, his dead marriage, and his unrequited love for Thelma. Some of the grief he felt had added somber music to passages in *Jennie Gerhardt*.

• • •

Meanwhile, Dreiser's agent, Flora Mai Holly, had sent that manuscript to Hitchcock at Harper & Brothers. The response was favorable, which was fortunate, since next on Holly's list was Frederick A. Stokes, a conservative house. Sinclair Lewis, an editor at Stokes, had urged his boss, William Morrow, to sign up Dreiser. But Morrow demurred, on the grounds that Dreiser was a troublesome author and his books were immoral. He was by no means the only editor of that opinion along Publishers Row.

Hitchcock, however, thought he could tame the barbarian. After all, in the 1890s he had bowdlerized Stephen Crane's *The Red Badge of Courage* for Appleton, and it had become a best seller. Founded in 1817, Harper & Brothers had fallen on hard times by the turn of the century and been rescued from bankruptcy by J. P. Morgan.

The contract gave the publisher an option on Dreiser's next book, which was now shaping up to be *The Genius*. On April 17 he reported to Mencken

that "the 3d book draws to a close. It's grim, I'm sorry to state but life-like."
Too grim for Harper's, he thought, confiding to Grant Richards: "They may
not take number three."

He could take heart from Mencken's advance judgment on *Jennie*. Toward
the end of April, his Baltimore correspondent tossed his hat in the air:

> I have just finished reading the ms. —every word of it, from first to last—and I
> put it down with a clear notion that it could remain as it stands. The story comes
> upon me with great force; it touches my own experience of life in a hundred places;
> it preaches (or perhaps I had better say exhibits) a philosophy of life that seems to
> me to be sound; altogether I get a powerful effect of reality, stark and unashamed.
> It is drab and gloomy, but so is the struggle for existence. It is without humor,
> but so are the jests of that great comedian who shoots at our heels and makes us
> do our grotesque dancing.

Dreiser replied that his praise sounded "too good to be true" but it was a
great comfort. He added that Charles De Camp, an editor, and Huneker, "as
grim critically as any I know," had agreed with Mencken's opinion. Huneker,
who had done more than any single writer to introduce modernist European art
and literature to American intellectuals and whose colorful, racy prose Mencken
had taken as a model, wrote Dreiser that he had read *Jennie* through without
stopping from 11:30 in the morning until 10:00 at night. Though he had
qualms about the style, he thought *Jennie* "the best fiction I have read since
Frank Norris."

•   •   •

Distracted by *The Genius*, Dreiser had turned the initial cutting of *Jennie* over
to Jug. He had gone back to her, as she no doubt hoped, and she was probably
eager to be of use, seeking to revive those troubled yet hopeful days when she
helped edit *Sister Carrie*. She took the script with her to a Virginia spa, where
she could work on it while recuperating from her recent siege. In late April
she sent an edited version to Dreiser in New York. When he went through
it, he must have exploded. On *Sister Carrie* she had confined herself largely to
stylistic changes, though she managed to insert some genteelisms. Much of her
work on *Jennie* echoed the job she did on *Carrie*, but many of her changes were
obviously intended to tone down physiological or sexual references.

For example, Dreiser wrote a rather daring scene in which Jennie and Lester
discuss her becoming his mistress, in exchange for which he will provide for
her family. In Dreiser's version she timidly raises the question of pregnancy, and
Lester assures her she needn't worry about having a child because "I understand
a number of things that you don't yet. It can be arranged." That veiled reference
to contraceptives was too much for Jug, and she cut it.

Dreiser's claim in later years that Jug had wanted "to cut what she called the 'bad parts' " stemmed from that spring in Virginia, though he retroactively applied the charge to *Sister Carrie* as well. Nevertheless, he apparently accepted some of her changes, including the removal of references to contraceptives, for in the published version Jennie says, simply, "I couldn't have a baby," and Lester replies, "You don't need to have a child unless you want to, and I don't want you to." Dreiser sent the script to Hitchcock as a guide for his cutting. Hitchcock, whose own editing was "fairly well advanced" by that time, had told Dreiser that the manuscript would have to be heavily edited and retyped, at a charge of $600 to the author.

Actually, most of the cuts to the manuscript were by Hitchcock and other Harper editors. Probably about sixteen thousand words were excised. Hitchcock had also made some additions, Dreiser told the novelist W. B. Trites, who after reading the novel said he could detect Hitchcock's hand in it.

Dreiser had inserted a clause in the contract that allowed him to withdraw the novel if he was dissatisfied with the editing. In his resistance he was backed up by Mencken, who wrote him: "If anyone urges you to cut down the book bid that one be damned. And if anyone argues that it is over-gloomy call the police."

At one point Dreiser complained that Harper's had not let him see the edited script. To which Hitchcock replied jauntily, "Why you should abuse me I do not quite know, but I take it the harsh terms you use are really an expression of affection." In June, when galleys were being run, Dreiser asked to see the original manuscript to compare with the proofs. Hitchcock told him to wait until he had it retyped, probably hoping that on a clean copy his cuts and changes would not be noticeable. Dreiser did notice, however, for in July Hitchcock writes that he had "put back pages and pages of MS. in accordance with your request."

In fact, Hitchcock (and his literary assistants) did more than eliminate verbosity and untangle syntax; they rewrote sentences and slashed controversial matter. For example, when Dreiser describes the wife's conversion from the Mennonite faith to Lutheranism, he injects a mild touch of impiety. Hitchcock, a religious man who was active in church affairs, cut this, as he did a paragraph that describes Pastor Wundt's fulminations against lax parents, "whose daughters walked the streets after seven at night" and whose sons spent their time "loafing about the street corners." Dreiser's mild allusions to the rebelliousness of modern youth were perhaps regarded as too daring.

Later, Dreiser asked Mencken to read through the bound book to ascertain if it had been hurt or helped by the editing. Mencken replied that at first the cuts "irritated me a good deal," but on further thought, he had decided that they had not damaged the novel. That was not the whole truth; while Dreiser was sweating out the reviews, Mencken was reluctant to say anything that might discourage him. He expressed his real opinion to his friend Harry Leon Wilson, former editor of *Puck*: " . . . the Harpers cut about 25,000 words out of the ms. . . . Such ruthless slashing is alarming. The chief virtue of Dreiser is his skill at piling up detail. The story he tells, reduced to a mere story is nothing."

Apparently, Dreiser was in the end satisfied with (or resigned to) the editing, for Hitchcock wrote Holly in September: "We can congratulate ourselves that Mr. Dreiser's book is now in print and it has gone through with practically no demur on his part. He seems to have accepted my final work on the manuscript without any changes of consequence."

• • •

By July Dreiser had finished a draft of *The Genius* and, while it was being typed, relentlessly moved on to the fourth book on his literary schedule. This was a novel called *The Financier*, which was based on the life of traction magnate Charles T. Yerkes, robber baron and connoisseur of fine art and beautiful women. He spent all of July on research, reporting to Mencken on August 8 that the data for *The Financier* were "practically gathered."

That same day a literary column in the Chicago *Evening Post* carried a detailed story on *Jennie Gerhardt*, which quoted Mencken's letter praising the novel and rehashed the familiar legend of the "suppression" of *Carrie*. Dreiser's efforts to orchestrate prepublication publicity earned him a cautionary letter from Frederick A. Duneka, Harper's general manager, who warned that other journals might be offended by the *Evening Post*'s scoop. Dreiser was sorry it happened, he told Mencken, who was panting for advance galleys so that he could write his encomium in time to make the November *Smart Set*. Just be sure, Dreiser sent his Baltimore correspondent the typescript that Jug had worked on, "marked for cutting but it was not cut in that fashion."

Working from the unedited, uncensored version, Mencken delivered a lengthy review in which he hailed *Jennie Gerhardt* as "the best American novel I have ever read, with the lonesome but Himalayan exception of 'Huckleberry Finn.' " He called the book "assertively American in its scene and its human material, and yet so European in its method, its point of view, its almost reverential seriousness that one can scarcely imagine an American writing it."

His anxiety at a high pitch now that the book was in the stores, Dreiser asked the critic Edna Kenton to find out what Floyd Dell, editor of *The Chicago Evening Post Literary Review*, intended to do with the book. Kenton, a devotee of *Carrie* in its first incarnation, informed him that Dell intended to blazon *Jennie* to the world. He promptly forwarded Mencken's notice to Dell's wife, Margery Curry, cautioning, disingenuously, "but don't let Mr. Dell read it for I don't want his opinion crossed by the least thought for or against. . . ."

Dell not only read the *Smart Set* notice, he cited it approvingly in his review. But he sincerely conveyed his own reactions and tried to divine the source of the book's power. A great part of the effect, he decided, "must be due to the long-sustained simplicity of the narrative, rather than to the quality of any certain passage. Quiet sympathy, it seems, can be prolonged until it reaches the breaking point of poignancy. . . . " Like Mencken, he was attuned to the book's somber music, the contrapuntal themes of life and death, that coalesce in the final scene of Jennie at the station.

Those two reviews (Dell's appeared about two weeks after Mencken's) set the terms of the critical debate. Resolved, the two young critics had said, *Jennie Gerhardt* is a great novel. Most of the subsequent reviewers sided with the affirmative, greeting Dreiser as a major writer. *Contra* were the moralists such as the poet Edwin Markham, author of "The Man with a Hoe," a stark picture of the American peasantry, who was naturally sympathetic to the parts of the book that etch "with power the dark side of poverty with all its cares and despairs." But he condemned Jennie's decision to become Kane's mistress in part because he promises to help her impoverished family: "Is a woman ever justified in smirching her womanhood, in staining her virtue, in order to help her relatives—even to save them from starvation? This must be answered with an iron 'No' by all who take a deep look into life. The wise are aware that there are some misfortunes that are worse than starvation."

Even more damning was the reviewer for the Lexington, Kentucky, *Herald*, who wrote that the novel "is a long, full and unreserved statement of the lower motives and base instincts of the worst order of human animals. . . . There is . . . not one chapter that is not unutterably base; every line is upon such a low plane it is hard to believe that this is all."

Fearing such a reaction, Duneka had sent an advance copy to the influential critic Hamilton Wright Mabie of the Christian *Outlook* as a kind of test. The Harper's executive devoted most of his cover letter to apologizing for the novel's "rather unpleasant" theme and noting, "it is a fair question whether any really good end is subserved." He added that Dreiser's novel had "provoked more discussion before we decided to publish it than any book since *Jude the Obscure*." There were more disclaimers and apologies in that vein, ending with the lukewarm certification that in spite of its having been "written in almost violent sincerity, and in spite of its heroine being outside the pale, it is about as suggestive as a Patent Office Report or Kent's Commentary."

The conservative Mabie replied that he had liked *Jennie* more than he expected. The general tone was "reverential" and the portrait of Jennie "very winning." Indeed, "One had no sense of moral dirt except with regard to the men." He thought Dreiser showed considerable promise—if he could be "kept from getting obsessed by the general sex theme which has made so many writers insane."

Dreiser was furious when he learned that Duneka had sought out Mabie's views, and he urged the Harper's executive to read Mencken's notice in the *Smart Set* as an antidote.

•   •   •

As a reviewer for the New York *Tribune* later wrote, Theodore Dreiser *imposed* himself on American literature. That incursion began with *Jennie Gerhardt*. *Sister Carrie* was a greater book, but its publication in 1900 had been the tree falling in the empty forest. Even its successful reissue in 1907 had left Dreiser, as Sinclair Lewis had noted, a great American realist who had written only one book. Now, with *Jennie* out, *The Genius* seemingly completed, and *The Financier* in the works, the invasion was fully launched. And leading it was Mencken, who for the next five years would remain in the van.

Dreiser was quite aware that his friend occupied an exposed salient, writing him in November, "It looks to me from the drift of things as though your stand on Jennie would either make or break you. . . . They are tying you up pretty close to it." But Mencken saw his *Smart Set* review as the beginning of a grand fight and an opening to glory. He believed in what Dreiser was doing; his praise had been given with a full heart. But he was also ambitious and eager to push his own notions of a "European" literature in America. As he later said, "Dreiser simply gave me a good chance to unload my own ideas, which were identical with his." And so a literary alliance was forged, but it was still to be tested in battle.

Part Eight

• • •

ANNI
MIRABILES

50 / *Grand Tour*

Sunday Nov. 5th G. R. [Grant Richards] calls. . . . His chief characteristic, I should say, which I have long noticed is not an uncommon trait in Englishmen, is a strong sense of individual and racial superiority. . . . I am a very peculiar person. I like being managed at times—only at times. Sometimes it is a great convenience . . . to have someone step forward and take from your weary shoulders the burden of responsibility. . . . G. R. admires my work greatly. *At this time* he fancies I am a great writer. He likes my personality. Time will tell what becomes of all this. . . . I do not know. I hope it lasts.

—Dreiser (1911)

The favorable reviews by Mencken, Dell, and others were welcome, but Dreiser had been out of a regular job for a year now, and no money was coming in. He also had a wife to support in her accustomed style. Despite his differences with Jug over her editing of the manuscript (which he had resolved, at least in his own mind, by a determination henceforth to keep his literary and marital affairs separate), in June 1911 he had taken a smaller apartment at the Riverview Court, 3609 Broadway. It was a middle-class building, with a middle-class rent of fifty dollars a month.

Suppressing his money worries, he let Jug fix up the apartment as she liked. What Dreiser's long-term intentions were is unclear, but he felt guilty and so let her assemble the stage settings of a normal home life. But now they had a tacit arrangement that allowed him to go his way.

His relationship with Lillian Rosenthal had progressed to greater intimacy, and Jug tolerated his infidelities with gritted teeth. One evening in September while Mencken was visiting the apartment, Dreiser suddenly excused himself, pleading unspecified business, and was away for more than an hour. As soon as he left, Jug said bitterly, "He's gone around to that Jewish girl."

Mencken was a staunch advocate of the bourgeois proprieties (he classified adultery as "hitting below the belt") and treated Jug courteously. Yet privately he suspected she was jealous of her husband's literary fame. Also, he had seen Christian Science magazines in the house, and he wrote her off as a deluded believer. To him, Mary Baker Eddyism was the worst kind of pious snake oil.

Dreiser apparently hadn't told Mencken of his own interest in Christian Science, or else passed it off as mere scientific curiosity, knowing the other's violent dislike of any sort of "spiritualism." Not that Dreiser could be a convert; he once wrote, "I think I know as much about metaphysics as Mrs. Eddy & can read my God direct." Still, he had been much taken by Eddy's ideas of mind as the only reality. He believed: "So-called life is an illusion. There is a larger life which is the only reality." Eugene Witla, his alter ego in *The Genius*, submits to the ministrations of a Christian Science healer during a spiritual crisis, and Dreiser and Jug had consulted with practitioners in the manner of contemporary couples visiting a marriage counselor.

Haunted by a fear of death, Dreiser had investigated spiritualism in the "Are the Dead Alive?" series. Describing Jennie's grief after the death of her daughter, Vesta, he interjects, "If only some counselor of eternal wisdom could have whispered to her that obvious and convincing truth — there are no dead." Jug trotted along behind him on this and other notions, but it was sometimes a strain for her to keep up. She once wrote of his "great power to make people believe almost what they do not believe."

•   •   •

A promising five thousand copies of the novel were sold in the first month after publication, thanks to the wave of favorable reviews, and throughout October Dreiser bombarded Harper's with letters suggesting stunts to promote the book (selling it in hotels, for one) and complaining about the dearth of advertising. Bypassing Hitchcock, Dreiser took his complaints directly to Major Leigh, treasurer of the firm, a big, genial man who patiently explained to the nervous author that Harper's wanted *Jennie* to be a commercial success almost as badly as he did.

As more reviews assailing the novel on moral grounds appeared, religious groups were alerted and there were isolated instances of censorship — a book dealer refusing to stock it, a condemnation of the novel as unsuitable on moral grounds by the National Library Association. Leigh wrote Dreiser that the experience of *Sister Carrie* "was not helpful to the sale of *Jennie Gerhardt*. I am not arguing about whether it is right or not, — I am simply stating you a fact." He insisted that Harper's didn't consider *Jennie* immoral; if it did, the firm wouldn't have published it. Dreiser no doubt feared another Doubleday-style "suppression," but Harper's spent more than $1500 on advertising in the book's first month, a fair sum.

There was more praise from Great Britain, and Grant Richards arrived in New York in early November with some good news. As Dreiser relayed it to Mencken, "I have a good chance of getting the next Nobel prize for literature following Maeterlinck, if it's worked right." Richards was willing "to organize the sentiment in England where he says I am a strong favorite, through Frank Harris & others. . . . He thought some American critic of prominence ought to make the suggestion somewhere in which he could call attention & I spoke of you." Harris had ranked *Carrie* among the twenty greatest novels of all time.

Although the Nobel Prize boomlet went nowhere, Richards's visit to the States was a turning point in Dreiser's life. Dreiser invited the Englishman over for breakfast, and there he summed up his troubles in one word: "Money." He was well along with *The Financier,* he said (actually, about one-third done), but the real-life inspiration for his hero, Charles T. Yerkes, had spent the last years of his life in Europe engineering a takeover of the London Underground and dallying romantically in Paris and on the Riviera. To see the things that Yerkes had seen would take money, and he saw no way of obtaining it. He had $400 in the bank and bills coming due. He was, in effect, broke.

Richards, a tall, charming man who was about Dreiser's age, eyed the American sternly through his monocle and, as was his wont, took charge. Ridiculous, he said. Why couldn't Harper's advance him the money? Dreiser explained they might be reluctant to go beyond the original advance in order to finance a Yerkes-style grand tour. Richards told Dreiser he had overestimated the cost of touring Europe. Richards could show him how to do it economically and would put him up at his home while he was in England. As for funds, he would arrange that too. Tomorrow he was calling on executives of the Century Company, with whom he was on good terms, and he would talk them into parting with an advance for some articles on Europe for the *Century* magazine and possibly on Dreiser's next book after *The Financier.* In return, Dreiser would give him the English rights to his books. Dreiser was skeptical. Under the *Jennie Gerhardt* contract Harper's had an option on his next novel. Moreover, he doubted that the *Century,* a last bastion of the genteel tradition under its editor, Robert Underwood Johnson, would want him as an author.

When Richards met the next day with Frank H. Scott, president of the Century Company, he encountered some resistance. Dreiser was considered "risky" and a "difficult fellow," Scott told him. Richards argued that with proper handling Dreiser could be a valuable asset to Century, which needed new blood; he was probably aware that the genteel *Century* was losing its loyal readers through natural attrition while newer, livelier journals attracted younger people. Scott agreed to read *Jennie*, and copies were supplied to five other principal editors.

Events moved rapidly after that. On November 10, at a luncheon at the Century offices in Union Square, Dreiser found himself reminiscing pleasantly with Johnson about their disagreement over a story he had submitted in 1900. With everyone in a genial mood, a preliminary agreement was drawn up providing a $1500 advance for three travel articles for the *Century* and a payment of $1500 for a future novel should Dreiser eventually decide to defect from Harper's.

Then Richards put into motion the next phase of his plan. According to Dreiser, on Richards's advice he sent Harper's an ultimatum: advance him $2500 on *The Financier* immediately and $2500 more on completion. A yes-or-no answer must arrive by Friday, November 17, and the money by the following Monday, or else Dreiser would consider "other propositions before him," as he put it in a letter to Hitchcock. Those were stiff demands, and Dreiser characterizes them as a "bluff" devised by Richards to provoke Harper's into dropping him. The day after the Century lunch, he wrote Mencken, "Strictly between you & myself [the Century Company] would like me to move with my books to Union Square, but there's nothing definite about that. . . . "

Three days later Harper's called Richards's bluff, if that's what it was, agreeing to pay Dreiser $2500 — $2000 of that for *The Financier* and the remainder as an advance against royalties from *Jennie*. Major Leigh chided Dreiser for apparently forgetting "the fact that you have already agreed to deliver us a manuscript on terms set forth in your contract of April 29, 1911." Nevertheless, he said, Harper's recognized his need for European research on *The Financier* and would be happy to provide him some money. The check arrived the next day. The conditions were that Dreiser show Harper's the thirty-nine chapters of *The Financier* he had completed; if the publisher didn't like them, the money must be returned.

In fact, Dreiser preferred Harper & Brothers, despite his complaints about their niggardly advertising. Leigh had been kind to him, and he sensed the house was as good a publisher as he could get. Richards's claim—long after the fact—that he had no desire to come between Dreiser and Harper's was not entirely candid. He knew that Harper's had an active London office and expected to sell the British editions of Dreiser's books. That was written into the contract. Therefore, the only way Richards could get Dreiser's books was to decouple him from Harper's. The Englishman was a gambler—literally, for he was a regular patron of the casinos at Monte Carlo. He had the virtue of loving literature and the sin of being a poor businessman and a high liver, going bankrupt several times over the course of his career. But he published George Bernard Shaw (who chided him for being too literary), A. E. Housman, John Masefield, and James Joyce, among others.

•   •   •

They booked passage on the *Mauretania*, sailing November 22, and Dreiser scurried about putting his affairs in order. On his last day ashore, he was interviewed by a reporter for the New York *Sun*. Dreiser deplored the paucity of novels in the American grain, particularly set in his own Middle West—"that stretch of country which is universally called to mind by the term 'American,' in which a real and throbbing life exists, has been allowed no literary expression." He said that newspapers and magazines were "so far ahead of all the novels that have been published that there is no comparison. For they are vital, dramatic true presentations of the life that is being lived today." The novels of William Dean Howells, whose critical endorsement he had once courted, were a prime example of the prevailing reticence. They reminded him of a family he had visited. "I mentioned a certain episode. 'We don't talk of that,' I was told." So it was in Howells's novels, and those of others like him; the authors did not talk about certain phases of life. Later in his stateroom he wrote of his hopes that America would someday "love its realists . . . as it now loves its patriots— Nathan Hale and Ulyssess [sic] S. Grant, and Abraham Lincoln, and it will have the same noble basis for doing so."

In another interview, with critic Baldwin Macy, he explained his reasons for going to Europe. First, to research Yerkes's career. He predicted that in *The Financier* he would interpret "the American man of affairs and millionaire as he has never yet been interpreted. . . . It's a big theme, too big for a little handling, too big to look at from any one angle. . . . All I'm after is the source of his inevitability—why he is what he is." But he also wanted to see how his country measured up in the world. "I've got an idea about America," he said, "that over here we've got a monopoly on the biggest ideals, and the largest amount of raw material energy by which to execute them than any people on earth. . . . I'm going over to find out . . . how we rank really in our chances for the future among the rest of the nations."

Richards assumed the roles of host and guide. For Dreiser's hotel in London he chose the Capitol, a Victorian pile with a somewhat louche reputation but now supposedly respectable. But sounds of laughter and flirtation in the halls prompted Dreiser to observe in his diary, perhaps wishfully, that hotels had become modern-day sites of sexual license comparable to "Greek Arcadian days." He was less impressed by the elegant Carlton, where Richards took him to lunch in the Grill. Dreiser thought it a bit dowdy and inferior to the Waldorf-Astoria.

But Richards did not content himself with playing preceptor to his guest; he also pressed him to sign over the English rights to his books. On December 6, when Dreiser called at Richards's Dickensian offices in Henrietta Street near Covent Garden, the publisher had drawn up a preliminary agreement giving him the English rights to *The Financier*, the travel book, and *Sister Carrie*. In his diary Dreiser says he refused to sign, but Richards wrote him: "We made last night . . . an arrangement by which this house is to have the publication of 'The Financier.' . . . " He asserted that this letter would be a "sufficient agreement" between them; a "more formal contract" would be drawn up later.

That was not Dreiser's intention, and he probably felt under obligation to Harper's. But he seems not to have given Richards a definite no, in order to keep his options open for a better offer from Century. Thus far Richards had produced nothing from that particular hat, but he still dangled the hope of a long-term arrangement that would end Dreiser's financial worries.

That evening in Piccadilly Circus Dreiser picked up a prostitute named Lilly Edwards, accompanied her to her room, and questioned her about her life. She undressed and he examined her body with clinical detachment (she told him she was six months pregnant). He approved of Europe's tacit acceptance of the "social evil." As he later wrote Mencken: "The prostitute is as necessary as a lawyer & more so. She is the world's sex safety valve," a preventive of rape and other sex crimes.

But he yearned for the lost Thelma, who was no longer in London. Forewarned of Dreiser's visit by his letters, she had fled to America. He saw her face everywhere—a woman on the street reminded him of her, then a dancer onstage. When he found a horseshoe on a walk through the East End, his first thought was of "luck with Thelma . . . I dream of what I would do if she was to come to me."

Mingled with his longing for her was a panicky sense of growing old. In August he had turned forty, and everywhere, it seemed, he encountered reminders that he had crossed that great divide into middle age.

•   •   •

Outfitting himself in Saville Row suits and haberdashery, he made his debut in London society. But his Anglophilia suffered a blow when the *International* published a long, sneering review of *Jennie* sarcastically titled "The Lyrical Mr. Dreiser." The notice hurt. He had expected a triumphant reception from the British intelligentsia, but now every review seemed to be a slam. When he met John Masefield, not until they parted did the seaman poet mention Dreiser's books: he said he had liked *Carrie.*

Back in his hotel room that evening, he experienced spells of homesickness, loneliness, and depression. One seizure was so painful that he wrote in his diary, "If I were of a suicidal turn these things would end me. Try to reason myself out of it by counting all my blessings. Not possible. My principle [sic] difficulty is a longing for loving companionship. I have had so little of loving understanding on the part of a big woman."

•   •   •

Fortunately, Paris was next on his itinerary. After settling in at the Normandy Hotel, he and Richards cut a swath through Montmartre, ending up at the wicked Abbaye de Thélème bar, where Richards caught this word picture (printed in his novel *Caviare*) of Dreiser hurling small white pasteboard balls, lightly weighted with shot, at his fellow patrons: "With one foot on the ground, and another on his chair, he flung his missiles with a vigour that meant execution when they struck; his coat half off his back, his hair tousled, his face red, his eyes asparkle. He . . . had forgotten the United States!"

During the day they had met the painters Anne Rice and J. D. Ferguson, whom Dreiser was intrigued to learn were not only man and mistress but maintained separate studios—an ideal living arrangement, he thought. He was trying something along those lines with Jug but could not afford separate domiciles. He filed his impressions away for future use in describing Eugene Witla's Paris sojourn in *The "Genius."*

Aware of his affectional/research needs, Richards introduced him to a sometime actress, a Mme de Villiers, who, it turned out, supported herself by talents other than acting. She later invited Dreiser to her flat, and, after practicing on him the "French" technique, graphically described her heterodox sexual experiences, which included lesbianism. Dreiser found Paris a haven of sexual freedom and approved of the openly displayed pornographic books in the Rue St. Honoré.

His nocturnal rounds acquired the cachet of science with the arrival of Abraham Flexner, the playwright and social investigator who had done a study of prostitution in America for John D. Rockefeller, Jr.'s Bureau of Social Hygiene, and was now researching the subject in Europe. Also in the party was W. W. Ellsworth, vice president of the Century Company, who was in Europe on an author-hunting expedition and had recommended Richards to Flexner as a guide to the underside of Paris. The four of them spent an evening of research at Palmyre's, a notorious *boite* run by the woman in whose arms Toulouse-Lautrec was said to have died.

Then came news from Duneka about *Jennie*: 7720 copies sold through January 1, 1912, with total orders of 10,000. Also, the Harper's executive said, the firm would not let Richards have the English rights to *The Financier* without a sizable payment in return. Dreiser complained to Richards about the sales figures, concluding gloomily: "If I were you I wouldn't be so concerned about me. I am not going to be a best seller or even a half seller. My satisfaction is to be purely critical if even that. . . . I haven't the drag with the public—that's all." He'd never be a moneymaker, he said, probably seeking to put off Richards. But the latter was undeterred.

"Tush," he responded. "I think you're very easily discouraged." To him 10,000 orders seemed a capital showing. Though *Jennie* might not be a best seller, it "can be a big seller." He reminded Dreiser that ten weeks ago he was deeply depressed about his future; now he was touring Europe. He must not be "so damned mercurial."

• • •

At the end of January they left for the Riveria, accompanied by Richards's friend Sir Hugh Lane, a collector, dealer, and connoisseur of art. At Monte Carlo, Richards introduced Dreiser to the Municipal Casino. Filling out an admission form, Dreiser, still troubled about turning forty, gave his age as "39." Under profession he penned "*Rentier.*" In the company of the dapper, monocled Richards and the cultivated, elegantly bearded Lane, he transformed himself into a gentleman of means.

His evenings were devoted to a cocotte named Marcelle. At the luxurious Grand Hotel in Nice the expenses mounted up, and Dreiser accused Richards, to whom he had turned over a fair sum, of spending too freely. When Richards asked him for another "loan" (as Dreiser terms it in his diary) of £120—over $600—and proposed allotting him £100 for the rest of his trip, Dreiser demanded a full accounting, which insulted Richards.

On that sour note, Dreiser departed for Italy, leaving Richards and Lane fuming at his accusations. Modern-day Rome he dismissed as an "eighth-rate city," although "as a collection of ruins and art objects it cannot be surpassed." After four days, though, the antiquities had begun to seem "endless" and it would "take a lifetime to decipher them." He was also worried about expenses.

Yet he lingered, probably because he met Rella Abell Armstrong, an attractive American woman separated from her writer husband and living with her children in the Grand Continental. She proved a catalytic influence, recounting the lurid history of the Borgias, which so fascinated him that he made her write it all down.

He had found the key to Cowperwood and titans like Rockefeller, Jay Gould, E. H. Harriman, and others of that "race of giants" who used finance as "the one direct avenue to power and magnificence" as ruthlessly as the Borgias in their day had pursued the same ends. One must not judge them by Christian morality; they must be seen in the context of the "pagan" morality of ancient Rome, the grandeur of which whispered to him from these great ruins. Such a perspective, striking him at this peculiar time, was liberating.

•　　•　　•

Meanwhile there was news about his affairs in America. He expressed his continuing disappointment with the small sales of *Jennie* to Duneka and later remarked bitterly about the "munificent returns" of authorship. In a letter to Richards, he mentions hearing that Erman J. Ridgway might leave Butterick (his old rival was ousted because *Everybody's* was losing money) and adds casually, "I may go back there." This betrayal of his vocation threw Richards into a high dudgeon. He remonstrated that such an idea was "disloyal . . . to yourself and your qualities. The trouble with you is that you do really you know, get cold feet. You are in streaks." As for the fate of *Jennie*: "I've been seeing a lot of American publishers and I have been struck by the extent to which you have put it across there. . . . You have made a dent in the national conscience, all right." And in an earlier letter, he put his finger on one reason for Dreiser's lack of confidence: "Such things not having been done before from your country you have nothing to compare yourself with. . . . "

Dreiser did not tell Richards that Duneka's letter contained a positive note. After reading the first thirty-nine chapters of *The Financier*, Duneka said he was "trembling" for the rest—"Not that I doubt you but because of the greatness of it all." He urged Dreiser to turn in the manuscript by the latter part of July because Harper's was anxious to publish—*had* to publish the book by September 19. They were hemming him in further, cutting off his escape to Richards and the Century Company.

By now Richards had become sufficiently accustomed to his charge's moodiness to shrug off the assault on his financial integrity in Cannes; he never would grasp the depth of the poverty-haunted Dreiser's worries about money.

•   •   •

With time and money slipping away, Dreiser departed Rome on February 26 for Florence and Venice with stopovers in Spello, Assisi, and Perugia. And then it was on to Germany and the heart of his journey: the village of Mayen, his father's birthplace. The medieval walls still stood, as did the ancient castle and the twisted spire of St. Clements Catholic Church, where his father was baptized. Although it was late in the day, he went straightaway to the graveyard in search of the tombs of his ancestors. He was shocked to read the inscription on the first family marker he happened upon:

THEODOR DREISER
GEB'N 16 FEB 1820
GEST'N 28 FEB 1882

In his notebook he describes the "dear old graveyard all wet now with a spring rain & odourous of mold," and then writes: "I am the 13th grave in the 5th row beyond the first wall. . . . " He had gone back to his beginnings to discover his own end. The spectacle of his fate profoundly unnerved him, as though all his worries about time slipping away had culminated here.

After a chat with the innkeeper, who seems to have told him there were no living Dreisers around (if he had consulted parish records, he would have discovered that he had numerous cousins residing in the area), he paid a farewell visit to the old graveyard and caught a train to Frankfurt. There he made himself known to Julia Culp, a singer friend of Richards who was giving a concert. She had expressed admiration for *Jennie Gerhardt* and after her performance they shared a late supper. Dreiser accompanied her to her hotel, where, after insisting she must not be unfaithful to Richards, she allowed him to kiss her. She led him to believe there might be even more love play in Berlin, where he was to stay at her home and she was to join him when her concert tour was finished.

•   •   •

Ensconsced in Mme Culp's comfortable suburban villa, he tried to puzzle out the relationship between his absent hostess and her nominal husband, Herr Merton, a rather pompous gentleman who lectured Dreiser on German superiority. Walking about Berlin, Dreiser was moved to meditate on his various romantic liaisons back home. He decided that love was an explosive force, capable of wrecking lives—as his passion for Thelma had done his. Yet it was central to human existence: "the great fact is that love—complete chemical responsiveness to the universe—is the greatest thing in the world and as such is the most astounding, the most dignified & the most artistic . . . no individual sees what life really is emotionally and otherwise until he is in love. He is not complete. When he becomes so, the astonishing chemical reaction which takes place may result in anything."

On another excursion he happened upon a cemetery where a funeral was in progress. The mourners threw handfuls of dirt into the open grave, like a gaping wound in the earth, and a woman, who appeared to be the mother of the deceased, wept uncontrollably. Suddenly, he was crying too: "I fancy my tears are for the whole world—for grief such as this cannot be healed."

Mme Culp returned, but he soon discovered she was a tease, and when later she casually canceled a promised rendezvous in Amsterdam, he was infuriated. By then he was tired of cocottes and prima donnas and homesick for America. Back in London, Richards told him that his funds were low, reviving the suspicions he had on the Riviera. He decided that Richards either had pocketed some of the money entrusted to him or else squandered it so that Dreiser would be forced to "hypothecate" his future books with the Century Company. He was, of course, being unreasonable, but his fear of not having enough to carry him through the writing of *The Financier* was real. The upshot was that he cabled Harper's for an additional $500.

But then Richards suggested he invite Marcelle to England for a final fling. That he should propose this added expense astounded Dreiser—the man was "a true advocate of the devil." But Richards argued that it would cost him only ten pounds, and he acquiesced without further resistance. His *petite amie* arrived on the boat train at five in the morning, and they immediately repaired to his hotel room, where the porter had laid a fire.

Dreiser had originally wanted to sail on the *Titanic*, a modern, "smart" ship, which departed from Liverpool April 9, 1912, on its maiden voyage to New

York, but Richards persuaded him to spend a few more days in Paris. Thanks to the intervention of Richards's colleague Mitchell Kennerley, the British-born New York publisher, Dreiser was able to book a reasonably priced stateroom on the slower *Kroonland*, departing on April 13.

On his last night in London, Dreiser had a farewell dinner with Marcelle and Richards. Dreiser spent the evening wrapped in a sullen cloud of jealousy as Richards and Marcelle merrily conversed in French. When the party returned to the hotel, he ordered Richards to leave and spent a cool night with Marcelle, though in the morning, after his bath, he reports, "find myself passionate and the usual sex relation follows."

Later, Richards called, acting as though the previous evening's quarrel had not taken place, to report that the money from Harper's had arrived. They went to Cook's to draw the remainder of his letter of credit, finding only a few pounds left. Nonetheless, he presented Marcelle with a *pourboire* of 800 francs ($160) and a new hat, which Richards had chosen, and after saying an ambivalent goodbye to the publisher, he accompanied his *petite amie* to Dover, where he saw her off, and then boarded the *Kroonland*.

The return voyage was quiet. A purser confided the news of the *Titanic*'s sinking. He read an article about Dostoevsky and strongly approved of the Russian's "compassion for the tragedy of the obscure & the submerged."

As they drew near to New York, he stood on deck, watching the sea and thinking about the transience of life: "Youth is gone. With it is the possible fulfillment of the dreams of youth. . . . I think of Thelma—but that is all over. Nothing but work now—and it makes no difference anyhow."

He disembarked on April 22, 1912, and called on the Rosenthals that evening. Lillian played for him Irving Berlin's new hit song "Everybody's Doin' It."

Europe was the past, and America was the future, the new colossus of trade and industry, with its conquering capitalists and financiers (such as Yerkes). In Europe he had clearly realized that he was irrevocably an American writer. His subject was the energy and change of its cities, where achieving, not living, was the watchword, where life was attuned to a jagged ragtime beat.

He had clipped Edwin Markham's book review that day in the New York *American*, along with the story of the sinking of the *Titanic*, the technological marvel that seemed to carry with it to the bottom the Victorian hopes of Science and Progress. Declared the poet-critic: "America today is in a somber, self-questioning mood. We are in a period of clamor, of bewilderment, of an almost tremulous unrest."

51 / *The Financier*

> Like a wolf prowling under glittering, bitter stars in the
> night, he was looking down into the humble folds of simple
> men and seeing what their ignorance and their unsophistica-
> tion would cost them.
>
> —Dreiser, *The Financier*

His apartment having been sublet, Dreiser moved into temporary quarters at
the St. Paul Hotel. He obviously hadn't rushed to Jug, who was staying at the
Brevoort on lower Fifth Avenue, a raffish but not inexpensive establishment.
He had written her from Rome, apparently pleading financial hardship and
asking that she support herself or live with friends or relatives for a while;
perhaps he asked for a divorce. At any rate, she replied: "I cannot grant your
request, Theo—you know why." He had probably pleaded poverty, as a result
of his trip and the lackluster sales of *Jennie*, in hopes that she would relieve him
of his financial responsibility for her.

Though the marriage bond still publicly held, its frayed state was becoming apparent to Dreiser's sisters, and they began taking sides. Mame and Sylvia
gave Jug to understand that she was no longer welcome in their homes, while
his brother Ed's wife, Mai, and Claire Gormley, Theodore's youngest sister, both
devout Catholics, swung into Jug's camp. She moved back into the Broadway
flat in May, but Dreiser did not join her, instead taking a room at 605 West
111th Street, presumably explaining that he could work better living alone.

His publishers were pressing him for a complete manuscript by the end
of July, but in a concession to him had agreed to publish *The Financier* in three
volumes. That was a load off Dreiser's mind, for he calculated that at the rate he
was going a single volume would have run to more than five hundred thousand
words (he was being conservative as it turned out). But, as he explained to
Richards, the breaks between volumes occurred naturally, since Yerkes's career
had three phases, the first in Philadelphia, the second in Chicago, and the last
in London. He also told Richards that he had no quarrel with Harper's, who
"are civil & fairly decent as publishers." Four days later, on May 30, he wrote

that "by a private arrangement . . . which does not mean hypothecating either my future work or my time" he had reduced his debt to Harper's from $5000 to $2000. But he had kept the door ajar, telling Richards, "I have preferred to reduce the obligation in this way in order that in case I wish to leave there will be no great difficulties on this score." And he pointed out that the trilogy plan would enable him to take a break between volumes I and II to write the travel book for the Century Company.

Yet, two weeks after his return, he told the Englishman, "I am profoundly glad that I am on my home ground and out of your clutches." Richards was not amused; he was miffed at Dreiser's discourtesy in not writing him until two weeks after his arrival and, what is more, making no mention of what Richards conceived to be his pivotal role in saving him from going down with the *Titanic*. He protested: "One day you press me to your bosom and tell me you are not going to take any step in regard to your literary affairs without my approval and sanction . . . and the next you go allowing Harper to 'plan' your future." Four days later he refers to the "agreement" they had entered into on December 15 giving his firm the English rights to all Dreiser's books.

Under the circumstances, Dreiser needed Mencken, who had departed on his own to the Continent. Mencken returned in June, and Dreiser wrote, "For heaven [sic] sake keep in touch with me by mail for I'm rather lonely & I have to work like the devil." In addition to winding up the book, he was cutting and rewriting earlier parts. His first draft was overloaded with details of Cowperwood's financial manipulations. By extensive reading he had mastered the essentials of his subject, but he had trouble folding the raw facts into the narrative batter.

He had immersed himself in Yerkes's world, reading numerous financial histories, inventories of his art collection, and press accounts of the decor and furnishings of his New York mansion at Sixty-fourth Street and Fifth Avenue. Dreiser's chief source, however, was the files of the Philadelphia *Public Ledger*, which provided voluminous detail on Yerkes's financial manipulations and subsequent conviction for larceny and wrongful conversion of municipal funds.

Dreiser went about his research methodically, recording each important event of Yerkes's life on a separate sheet of yellow paper, either by handwritten note or in the form of a clipping pasted to the paper. He then arranged the sheets in chronological order to speed composition, and he followed the historical record in his narrative. In his obsession with getting the facts right, he corresponded with Joseph Hornor Coates, a Philadelphia editor he had met in 1902. Coates helped him gain access to the relevant newspaper files and served as technical adviser on Philadelphia history, customs, business practices, politics, and much else. In one letter Coates counsels Dreiser that "your young couple [Cowperwood and his first wife] would probably belong to the Merion Cricket Club and the Philadelphia Country Club." In another, he supplies a lengthy description of the stock exchange in Yerkes's time, pointing out that each broker had his own chair, which he sat in when he bid on stocks, like an auction. When Dreiser wrote back that this intelligence had ruined one of his scenes, Coates advised him to let the anachronism stand. Since he wasn't writing a biography or a history, he shouldn't "let an *unimportant* fact spoil a good fiction scene."

Dreiser heeded Coates's advice. And there were many places where the record was incomplete, especially relating to his hero's personal life—Yerkes's boyhood; his marriage to Susanna Gamble, a wealthy widow several years older than he; his adulterous affair with Mary Adelaide Moore, the daughter of a well-to-do pharmacist. Here Dreiser's imagination took over. He freely created scenes or altered or compressed events that were in the public record.

He also changed historical figures, sometimes in drastic ways. For example, Yerkes acted in league with other prominent Philadelphia financiers, but in the book, and to serve Dreiser's heroic conception of him, he is a lone wolf. Mary Adelaide Moore becomes the rebellious, passionate Aileen Butler, and her tame pharmacist father is transformed into Edward Malia Butler, a canny Irish political boss whose monopoly of city garbage collections, gained through bribes and favors, has made him a wealthy man. The character is closely modeled on a politico of that name and background whom Dreiser had interviewed and admired as a reporter in St. Louis. And he often manipulates the chronology of Yerkes's life, contracting his time in Philadelphia after his release from prison to speed up the narrative.

●　　●　　●

An article by Edwin Lefèvre on Yerkes entitled "What Availeth It?" in the June 1911 *Everybody's* was crucial in forming Dreiser's interpretation of him as a man who scorned conventional morality. As Lefèvre concluded, "He was not worse than so many other captains of industry. He merely was less hypocritical." That suggestion of defiance of the conventions appealed to Dreiser, as did one of Yerkes's maxims quoted in a newspaper interview: "Whatever I do, I do not from a sense of duty, but to satisfy myself." He did not need to overstrain his imagination to concoct Cowperwood's motto: "I satisfy myself."

●　　●　　●

In writing the chapters on Frank Cowperwood's boyhood, Dreiser drew on his own experiences, Yerkes's sparse autobiographical statements, and a biography of Jay Cooke, a near contemporary of Yerkes in Philadelphia. There are two pivotal events in the shaping of Frank's character. The first is a fight with a bully. Cowperwood cuts the other boy's face with a ring he is wearing (the reverse of what happened to Dreiser as a boy in Chicago in a similar fracas), learning that he must use craft and guile to become stronger than his enemies. The second occurs during a visit to an aquarium, where Frank watches a lobster and a squid cohabiting a tank. Eventually the lobster eats the squid, and the boy has a revelation: "How was life organized? Things lived on each other—that was it."

And so young Cowperwood comprehends that he must live off—use— others: "A real man—a financier—was never a tool. He used tools. He created. He led." Though not inherently dishonest, he regards laws and conventions as fetters, like the net of tiny ropes with which the Lilliputians subdued Gulliver. The great man takes care to observe the proprieties when it is in his interest to do so and to avoid getting caught at something illegal, but he must never let small men tether him, prevent him from pursuing his interests. (In a note scrawled alongside one of the clippings he pasted up, Dreiser wrote, "The strong man wants to be allow[ed] to do. The little man wants to stop him.") Cowperwood's cold eyes penetrate the veil of hypocrisy to the naked self-interest or desire underneath. Religion and morality are merely "toys of the clerics, by which they made money." The strong man manipulates the rules to his own advantage. (Watching a soccer game in Germany, Dreiser was inspired to write in his diary: "Morality and ethics are nothing but footballs wherewith people—strong people—play to win points.")

With such touches Dreiser transformed the historical Yerkes into Cowperwood, a projection of his own psyche. The cool, self-contained, supremely confident Cowperwood was the *beau ideal* of his anxiety-ridden, sometimes gauche creator. Yerkes was indeed a philanderer and an art collector, but his philosophy was "Wealth does not buy happiness; it buys luxuries." He was a man who had no illusions about what he was purchasing. Dreiser, however, sublimates his own strong yet guilt-hobbled sexual drive into the suave Cowperwood and transforms it into a quest for beauty, for the ideal. In a passage cut from the published version of *The Financier,* Dreiser writes that beautiful women "were like wondrous objects of art but to get the full value of their artistry [Cowperwood] had to be in close individual relationship with them and that could only be achieved through the affections"—sexual relations, a condition Dreiser set in his own love life.

Cowperwood also embodied a conflict within Dreiser. On the one hand he admired and envied the famous rogue builders of American capitalism, reflecting his own boyhood ambitions (it's no accident that Cowperwood's middle name is "Algernon"—after Horatio Alger) and his strong lust for power. On the other, his acute sense of social justice condemned them as exploiters of the common people.

The philosophy of Herbert Spencer, as adapted by Dreiser, suggested a resolution to this conflict between the great individual and the masses. Analogizing from the laws of physics to the laws of sociology, the British savant taught that every force produced a counterforce, every action a reaction, resulting in constant change until an ultimate balance — "suspended equation" — was reached. Dreiser borrowed this idea, gave it a personal meaning and eventually a name: the Equation Inevitable. He saw society as a Darwinian jungle; but he also saw it as ruled by Spencerian laws, which imposed a pattern on the endless struggle between the haves and have-nots, resulting in an eventual balance whenever one side became too powerful.

•　　•　　•

By July Dreiser was deep into revisions. Hoping to avoid arguments over cuts, Hitchcock had written him that "I want to have the book made with the fullest understanding between us." Nevertheless, Dreiser reacted so angrily to one of his critiques that Hitchcock had to telephone him and then write a letter the same day assuring him that the overall story was strong and that it was now a matter of pruning excessive financial detail.

Hitchcock had another worry. He suggested playing down the fact that this was only the first volume of a trilogy, citing the precedent of the American Winston Churchill's best-selling trio of historical novels, *Richard Carvel, The Crisis,* and *The Crossing.* The initial book must be presented to the public as complete of itself, and then, as with Churchill, "the rumor allowed to percolate" that the author would write another volume dealing with the characters introduced in the first. In furtherance of this plan, each volume of Dreiser's trilogy would have a separate title, rather than being titled *The Financier,* volumes I, II, and III, as Dreiser suggested.

Dreiser was willing to go along with Harper's scheme if it would increase sales, but the problem with it was that reviewers and readers might think *The Financier* incomplete. And, in fact, several oblivious reviewers did remark that the novel seemed to end abruptly.

•　　•　　•

Working furiously, Dreiser sent Hitchcock the concluding chapters of *The Financier* in mid-July. He had met his deadline, but it had been a brutal task, and he was not entirely happy with the results. Rightly or wrongly, he did not trust Hitchcock. Mencken was his only remaining sounding board. In late August he flashed a broad hint to Baltimore: "It looks to be a book of 700 pages or more unless I can cut it. Alas, alas." Could he send a set of galleys to his friend?

The sergeant of artillery snapped to. "Let me have those proofs by all means. . . . Don't let the damnable Harpers cut the story! A pox on all such butchery." But Dreiser too was worried about length, estimating that the manuscript contained 270,000 words—probably an understatement—and he was frantically revising. As a result, Mencken did not receive proofs until October 3—too late to write a review for the November *Smart Set*. Three days later he conveyed his personal reaction to Dreiser: "No better picture of a political-financial camorra has ever been done. It is wholly accurate and wholly American." Yes, it was too long; whole scenes of irrelevant description could go, but the massive documentation was one of the chief virtues.

Mencken had pulled his punches a little, for he wrote a more objective opinion to his friend Harry Leon Wilson, a writer and editor. Dreiser had "got drunk on his story" and piled on too many financial details. At the same time, he had said too little about Cowperwood's relationship with Aileen Butler, a point Mencken had made to Dreiser, suggesting that he should deal with "the girl's initiation and the constant menace . . . of pregnancy."

That suggestion must have seemed rather naive to Dreiser, given all the blows he had taken from moralistic editors and critics. Otherwise Dreiser took his resident critic's suggestions and made many cuts on page proofs, incurring a huge charge of $726.90 for author's alterations. He had excised seventy-seven pages in all. He told Mencken that he wished it had been two hundred, and asked him to suggest any chapters that could come out or be dropped in toto. "You always see a thing as a whole which is a Gods blessing."

•   •   •

Grant Richards's patience and forbearance finally ran out. A letter Dreiser wrote in July was the last straw. "Do you really think you ought to have it?" he teasingly asked, referring to *The Financier*. "Personally I get very dubious when I think that the one financial thing I really wanted you to do you did not do and rather wilfully and inconsiderately I think." By "the one financial thing" Dreiser was referring to Richards's alleged mismanagement of his money in Europe so that he had nothing left when it came time to return. Coming at this late date, the remark was a low blow, and Dreiser compounded the cruelty by adding in a subsequent letter that the reason he had not signed the agreement in Richards's office in April was that he "did not care to be rushed into any understanding I might regret." Now he was glad he hadn't.

Richards was deeply offended. On August 8 he wrote with chilling conde-scension: "My poor friend: When I read your letter I confess that I had a rather bad half hour." Now he understood what Dreiser had meant when he warned of his "suspiciousness," he said. "I should perhaps have known that there are men who can't believe that one is friendly, disinterested or enthusiastic from conviction. You searched for a motive for all the trouble I took . . . & you found one after your own kind. Well, I wish you joy of it."

Dreiser had indeed warned Richards: "There's something strange in my makeup. I quarrel with my friends." He had let that quality poison their friendship; moreover, wanting the trip to Europe and hoping for a better offer than Harper's had given him, he had let Richards develop expectations of a future association. And yet, Richards should have realized that Harper's would not give up Dreiser, with whom the firm had a perfectly valid contract. And he had offered Dreiser little but promises.

Much later Dreiser would say, "I would give anything not to have quarreled with him, and over money too! I owe him so much; that trip to Europe! It was like a tonic that lasted me for years; it was a new life to me."

•   •   •

What Dreiser did not know was that Richards now had an additional grievance: he had read in the first draft of *A Traveler at Forty,* as the travel book was called, Dreiser's indiscreet account of his relations with the cocottes to whom Richards had introduced him and with Mme Culp, not to mention blunt comments on some of Richards's friends. On December 12 Richards dispatched a scorching protest to Douglas Doty at the Century Company, who was editing the book. Dreiser had slanderously portrayed him as "a go between and a continual patron of . . . ladies of bad character. . . . Half of Dreiser's facts are wrong; and if right they are generally wrongly seen and lead to wrong deductions." He vowed to "come down on the Century Company with all the power of the law" if the offending matter was not removed. Doty could not be considered Dreiser's staunch ally, having told Richards in an earlier letter, "What you have to say confidentially about T.D. does not surprise me. He's a curious combination of real man and *mucker.*"

•   •   •

The Financier was published on October 24, 1912, to generally favorable reviews. Their effect was to ensure Dreiser's literary stature. As Mencken later wrote, "You are gaining a definite place . . . as the leading American novelist. . . . New serious novels are no longer compared to 'Silas Lapham' or to 'McTeague' but to 'Sister Carrie' & 'Jennie Gerhardt.' " Dreiser was regarded as an independent force, by far the most compelling writer on the American literary scene.

In addition to seeing his friend through the accouchement, Mencken tirelessly pounded out reviews, opening with a major article in *The New York Times Book Review.* He recited Dreiser's now familiar weaknesses as a novelist but, by subtle twists, turned each of them into a virtue. Possibly to Harper's consternation, he noted that *The Financier* was but a prologue to "the more important second volume [in which] the real drama of Frank Cowperwood's life will be played out." He also held forth in the Los Angeles *Times,* in the *Smart Set,* and in "The Free Lance" column in the Baltimore *Sun.*

"Dreiser is a real fellow and deserves all the help he can get," Mencken later wrote Willard Huntington Wright. "Some day, I believe, we will be glad to think that we gave him a hand. He is bound to win out." The good reception of *The Financier* seemed to indicate that a sea change in literary taste was taking place. Indeed, in 1912 — the year of the rise of ragtime, Woodrow Wilson's election to the presidency, and the defeat of William Howard Taft and Theodore Roosevelt, who represented the politics of the past — the old order seemed to be fading. A youthful minority was searching for new forms of expression, new values, new experiences — new freedoms. Historians would call this premature cultural spring the American Renaissance, and Dreiser was its chief harbinger in the novel. *The Financier* demonstrated that now a preponderance of the critics were sympathetically disposed to his efforts to critique, in Cowperwood's story, the rise of American finance capitalism in the post–Civil War area.

There had been novels aplenty about business in recent years, but until *The Financier* the business novel had been reformist or moralistic in impulse. Dreiser had approached the world of high finance in a radically new way. The antagonists in the story are not the representatives of religion's good and evil or of reform's decency and corruption; they are emissaries of natural forces, and they bring Cowperwood down not because his kind must be stopped, but out of countervailing selfishness, greed, jealousy. "We live in a stony universe whose hard, brilliant forces rage fiercely," Dreiser writes in the novel. "Life moves in an ordered hierarchy of forces of which the lesser is as nothing to the greater."

Dreiser's vision of man — "his feet are in the trap of circumstance, his eyes are on an illusion" — gives his book a deeper tragic resonance than its predecessors. And the historic scope of his theme, the monumental architecture of his story, and the exhaustiveness of his documentation make *The Financier* the greatest business novel written in America of its time — and probably of all time.

As Cowperwood was compulsively drawn to younger women, so Dreiser. Thus, he was eager to meet Anna Tatum, who had written him admiring, disputatious letters while he was in Europe and who had just arrived in New York from Pennsylvania. When they met in the dining room of the Brevoort, she blurted out, "I didn't know you were so homely." Dreiser stalked out the door. Anna was apparently not really dissatisfied with what she saw, for Dreiser later wrote in his diary that they lived together from May 1, 1912, to January 1, 1913; at least part of that time he was nominally living with Jug at 3609 Broadway.

When Anna met Dreiser she was no innocent, though she was a virgin. According to his diary, she had a lesbian affair with a doctor at the Woman's

Hospital in New York; but when she met Dreiser, she was spoiling for a liaison with a great writer and urged him to take her, which he did. She was slight, blond, and attractive, and also brilliant and well read. A graduate of Wellesley, she came from an old and wealthy Quaker family. During their affair, she related to Dreiser the story of her family, and he found it so compelling that he decided he would make a novel of it. What attracted him to it was the figure of the father, a stern, pious man like John Paul Dreiser. In Anna's version, her father's severity and domineering ways drove the children to rebellion. Anna was a case in point. She defiantly puffed cigarettes in public, began drinking after she met Dreiser, and read Verlaine, then little known in the United States.

Her family's story hit Dreiser hard. Hadn't his own father's fanaticism driven his sisters to leave home and rush into illicit affairs with older men? His brother Paul had run off to join a medicine show rather than face further beatings by his father, and two other brothers, Rome and Al, had also taken to the road at an early age. Out of those associations was born *The Bulwark,* a novel he would work on intermittently for the next thirty years.

52 / Chicago

Chicago is my love; I don't believe any one could be crazier
over a girl than I am over that city.

—Dreiser (1912)

After being released from prison, Yerkes went to Chicago. In December 1912, Dreiser followed him to research the second volume of the series, which he called *The Titan*. The city had changed since he was last there, in the 1890s; it had grown and acquired a veneer of culture, though the wind off Lake Michigan was just as raw in the winter, and the smell of the stockyards just as rank in the summer. As a young boy he had stood at the door of their flat on Madison and Throop dazzled by the sounds and bright lights. His memories of this city had been distilled into *Sister Carrie,* of which Floyd Dell had recently written in the *Evening Post,* "The poetry of Chicago has been adequately rendered, so far, by only one writer, and that in only one book."

Dreiser zestfully pursued his researches at the Newberry Library, within walking distance of his boardinghouse, filling hundreds of pages with abstracts from newspapers and municipal records on Yerkes. When he tired, he could stroll over to nearby Bughouse Square and listen to the open-air philosophers. He also called on Edgar Lee Masters, a lawyer who wrote poetry on the side and who had praised *The Financier.* He had practiced law during Yerkes's last years and gave Dreiser a letter of introduction to Carter H. Harrison, former mayor of Chicago and leader of the opposition to the traction magnate's attempt to bribe the state legislature and the city council into granting him a fifty-year monopoly of the city's street railways. Dreiser had letters to others who knew Yerkes, including one of the battery of attorneys he had kept on retainer solely to deal with heartbalm suits by discarded mistresses, who were paid off handsomely if they cooperated. Dreiser's relish for his story grew, as plum after juicy plum fell into his lap.

The two men hit it off. Lee Masters was also trapped in an empty marriage and hated the necessity of doing work he loathed to support his family. He had written several volumes of poetry, which he had published with his own money. He was a friend of William Reedy, the St. Louis editor of the *Mirror* and an

eloquent champion of new writing, including *Sister Carrie*. Reedy had published
articles by Masters on law and politics and tried to discourage his friend's poetic
ambitions, without much success. The conventional odes to autumn and Helen
of Troy kept coming, and out of friendship Reedy published a few of them under
a pseudonym.

In addition to his talks with Masters, his researches, and spells of writing
on *The Titan*, Dreiser seemed bent on researching firsthand Yerkes's amorous
career as well. He found a covey of lively, "advanced" young women at the Little
Theater, founded by Maurice Browne, a wandering Englishman who had landed
in Chicago. The Little Theater was a popular gathering place for the cultural set
where Bohemia and new money rubbed shoulders. Every weekday, subscribers
could take refreshments at the tearoom adjacent to the tiny auditorium, where
a samovar bubbled and cakes and sandwiches were dispensed. On Sundays an
open house was held in honor of some visiting celebrity, and Dreiser was guest
of honor at one of these levees and thereafter a frequent visitor.

Enter Elaine Hyman, at a Little Theater open house. She was with Floyd
Dell, a considerable figure in Chicago's Bohemia, with his small moustache, a
cigarette perpetually dangling from his lips, his soft hat and flowing tie, the
image of a dashing Latin Quarter poet. Elaine had been the star of Browne's
production of *The Trojan Women*. At her first meeting with Dreiser, she was
put off by the famous novelist's Hoosier twang, and she soon swept out of the
room, accompanied by Dell and an equally flamboyantly clad friend, the poet
Michael Carmichael Carr. But Dreiser was drawn to Elaine's unconventional
beauty. Tall, with an olive complexion and coal-black hair, she was Grecian-
looking. Her father was Jewish and her mother of New England stock, and the
two heritages warred within her. Her father doted on her and wanted her to
be a professor of literature. She was intelligent and well read; she sang, wrote
poetry, and painted. Her education had consisted mainly of tutoring by her
father and courses at the Art Institute.

It was perhaps inevitable that a girl so close to her father would choose the
older man. Dreiser, it should be said, had a way of broadcasting his helplessness
and need for mothering, and these qualities were attractive to Elaine, young as
she was. When Dell asked her why she chose Dreiser over him, she said, "He
needs me. You don't."

After a rapid, intense courtship, Elaine "gave herself" to him, Dreiser later
wrote in his diary. She was determined to join him in New York and become
an actress, and Dreiser had encouraged her.

•   •   •

He left Chicago on February 10, 1913, and stopped off in Baltimore for dinner with Mencken on the way to New York. They had much to talk over. Masters

and other Chicago freethinkers had awakened Dreiser to the bane of censorship. Mencken had been tilting with the Baltimore Society for the Suppression of Vice, and Dreiser asked Mencken to send him six sets of his "Free Lance" columns attacking the literary moralists, saying he was "going to place them where they will do real good."

Back in New York, Dreiser sent a financial-distress call to Major Leigh. He swore he had "led the simple life," but asked Leigh for $200 a month to see him through the writing of *The Titan*. Leigh was amenable, but Dreiser was required to turn over the manuscript of *The Genius* as a security; Harper's would have the right to publish it, if by October 1914 his other books hadn't earned back their advances. In effect, he was on a drawing account, pledging the royalties on past, present, and now, possibly, future works as security for the debt.

Dreiser was worried about not only the merits of *The Genius*, but also its moral acceptability. He might have been even more distressed to learn that Harper's was already uneasy about *The Titan*. In a confidential letter to Flora Mai Holly, written in the fall of 1911, Hitchcock told the agent that he must see the "last part" of *The Financier* (which at that point was still envisioned as a one-volume work) because of "certain delicate conditions involved. There may be something in the latter part which, from our point of view, would be wholly inadvisable . . . ." What Harper's was worried about was the reaction of J. Pierpont Morgan. In 1901 he and Yerkes had tangled over who would handle the financing of the consolidated London underground transit system, and Morgan had lost—something J. P. was highly unaccustomed to doing. The "last part" of Dreiser's novel would deal with Yerkes's London operations.

• • •

Meanwhile the manuscript of *The Genius* was encountering objections of another kind. Dell found it "badly written" and said no amount of cutting would improve it. Lengel told Dreiser that publication of it now "would do more to damage your career than to help it." He recognized many of the figures and incidents from the Butterick days and felt that Dreiser had "clung too closely to life . . . to give a calm portrayal." Nevertheless, at Dreiser's request he cut the script for possible serialization and showed it to Ray Long, editor of *Red Book*, which was based in Chicago. Long thought the writing was too diffuse. The story "could not possibly grip the reader."

Dreiser was not visibly disheartened by these reactions. He told Lengel that the book couldn't be published for two or three years, anyhow, and that he had been thinking of revising it. Still, he had "six or seven" other opinions that were favorable.

He was juggling too many other projects to devote much thought to *The Genius*. He was working furiously on *A Traveler at Forty*, and an early chapter, the one describing his meeting with the London prostitute called Lilly Edwards, appeared in the June *Smart Set*. In the latter part of May, Dreiser wrote Elaine Hyman that he had finished fifty-two chapters and was finding the work taxing. He wound up the travel book by mid-July (he had written some of it in England), turning in a five-hundred-thousand-word manuscript, by Doty's estimate. That seems incredible, and a surviving typescript is less than half that length. Despite Hitchcock's advice to make *The Titan* "relatively concise. . . . Pray let the reader infer something for himself," it was growing into another behemoth. For cutting Dreiser depended on Hitchcock and another editor, W. G. van Tassell Sutphen, who approached the task with some trepidation and later thanked Dreiser for "the forbearance with which you have accepted my literary surgery." As with *The Financier*, Dreiser was distressed about excessive length, even as he hated to see the book cut.

He was working too fast, and he knew it. Necessity, of course, was goading him, but he was also in a hurry to get down on paper the ideas and characters that were seething in his brain. As he later told a biographer, Dorothy Dudley, "The country is big; you can't write about it in a small peckish way; there's not time to polish. Later on I intend to rewrite my books, condense them. I have too much to do, too much to put forth. People need it. They need to know things."

He believed in the long novel, he told Anna Tatum, "because it is more life like. It gives both author and reader a better opportunity to grow into a deep sympathetic understanding with the characters." In keeping with this philosophy, the physical act of writing for him was akin to opening a valve, as one of his literary assistants once said. He had iron concentration, and the words flowed forth, steadily, the protuding wire on his stylographic pen whirling like a dervish as it stirred up the ink in the barrel. He could sit completely immobile. He kept a stack of typewriter paper on his desk, filling one sheet after another, placing the finished ones on another steadily growing pile or letting them drift to the floor to be put in order later.

●　　●　　●

All the while, Elaine was sending him frequent, yearning letters. In March the Little Theater made a tour of several cities on the Eastern Seaboard, and Dreiser took a room in a boardinghouse in Boston. Elaine slipped away from the others for clandestine meetings.

As immersed in work as he was, Dreiser urged her to come to New York. Her letters show she was eager to join her "lover husband," but her parents were a problem; they knew nothing about the affair, and she had to write him secretly. But she managed to cajole her father into subsidizing a try at a stage career on the condition that is she didn't find work after a reasonable time, she must come home. She adopted the stage name Kirah Markham.

At the end of May she took a room on East Fifty-ninth Street, where Dreiser undoubtedly was a frequent visitor; he may have even told Jug that he had taken a studio there. Kirah believed that he had broken with Jug; it was not that simple. The situation was confused, and the confusion was compounded when Dell arrived in the city in late summer. When he called at what he took to be "their" apartment, Dreiser greeted him genially and said he would leave so Floyd and Kirah could talk things over. "I suppose when I come back I'll see you disappearing around the corner," he joked, "Dell carrying the grand piano on his back." But the lady had chosen, and Dell, who had comforted her during her separation from Dreiser, moved on.

While he was still in the city, Dell's running quarrel with the pious publisher of the *Evening Post* came to a head, and he resigned in protest. After settling his affairs in Chicago, he joined the rebellion now fermenting in Greenwich Village.

• • •

With Dell now amicably out of Kirah's life, she, and Jug, and Theodore settled into a kind of stable triangle. Kirah made the rounds of the theaters without much success and helped her lover with his work. By October, Harper's was sending an edited manuscript of *The Titan* to East Fifty-ninth rather than 3609 Broadway. The affair could no longer be said to be secret. After she had moved to a new place at 23 West Fifty-eighth Street, Dreiser notified Willard Huntington Wright that "Miss Kirah Markham . . . maintains an interesting drawing room Sunday evenings."

Dreiser began expressing interest in a "liberal" publisher. He was unhappy with Harper's for business and literary reasons. The sales of *The Financier*, which had raced to a promising start in the latter part of 1912, tailed off in 1913 to only 1569 copies in the first six months and 1727 for the entire year. *Jennie* had sold 5000 copies in its second year, but now it had slowed to a trickle; the same held true for *Sister Carrie*. If *The Titan* didn't sell, he would slide deeper into debt, with only *The Genius* available to rescue him. But that manuscript bristled with potential moral problems.

His resentment against the censors was growing. When he received a rather innocuous letter from John O' Hara Cosgrave, a former colleague at Butterick, and now an editor with the New York *World*, asking him to join the Authors League and support its struggle to reform the copyright law, he shot off an angry reply. An authors' society that would fight "bureaucratic & reactionary interpretations of morals and individualistic thought in books, plays, sketches & the like" might interest him, but he could not see the worth of one dominated by "the pseudos, reactionaries and pink tea and chocolate bon bon brotherhood of literary effort" who were concerned primarily with "second serial and moving picture rights."

By fall he was asking Mencken to help him find another publisher. The latter advised him to talk to George H. Doran, who was reputed to be liberal-minded. Dreiser followed up the lead promptly and wrote Mencken that Doran "will give me full liberty this side [sic] criminal libel & will arrange for debts." Doran looked inviting because Dreiser had just passed through a terrible row with the Century Company over the *Traveler* manuscript.

53 / *The Woman Stuff*

After I am dead please take up my mss of The Financier, Titan
& Travel book & restore some of the woman stuff. . . .
—Dreiser to Mencken (1913)

The arrival of batches of the *Traveler* at the Century offices at Union Square
must have resembled a series of earth tremors. One can imagine the editors
reading the latest chapters with mounting alarm. Dreiser's encounters with
those gay Parisiennes, Marcelle and Mme de Villiers, are described, if not in
full. Two chapters are devoted to a Berlin prostitute named Hanscha Jower. A
charming dalliance in Venice (not mentioned in his travel diary) is given its
due, complete with a moral: "I think true passion is silent and lust is deadly."
Needless to say, as Dreiser wrote Mencken, the editors "objected . . . like hell"
to these vignettes.

The raciness of parts of Dreiser's manuscript seems to have precipitated a
battle within the Century Company between the new breed, represented by
Ellsworth, Doty, and others, and members of the *ancien régime*, led by Robert
Underwood Johnson, who wrote Hamlin Garland that Dreiser had included
descriptions of "illicit relations with five different women, with disgusting details." What is more, he had "made defense of his conduct from the moral
point of view—the most unblushing and immoral thing I have ever read." Already incensed by the efforts to rejuvenate the aging *Century,* Johnson regarded
Dreiser's articles as profaning the temple.

• • •

On the face of it, Dreiser appears to have lurched into another controversy
he should have avoided. Some of his copy he could hardly have expected to
be published. Probably he thought that all the furor about the "social evil"
made the subject of prostitution respectable. The topic was very much in
the air after a New York grand jury headed by John D. Rockefeller, Jr., began

probing the so-called white slave traffic in 1910, and the Chicago Vice Commission published its report on prostitution the following year. Magazines had been full of lurid articles about young women who were drugged by swarthy foreigners and spirited off to bagnios in Hong Kong or Rio de Janeiro. If Dreiser had not written about the subject with sociological objectivity, it was because he was a novelist, not a social scientist.

Describing his affair with Marcelle in Nice, he mentions that they kiss, then adds, "The rest need not be related. . . . " In his chapters on Hanscha Jower, however, Dreiser does say that he availed himself of the woman's services. His travel diary shows that he regarded their encounter as more than a casual sexual transaction: "Back to Alexander Platz where I get off & encounter Hanscha Jower. A most remarkable experience. All my life I have been seeking to encounter a woman of the streets who was safe, pleasant, innocent in a way. . . . Here she is, Hanscha Jower. Born in Tilsit, East Prussia. Lived in Stettin (pronounced Steteen). Large, soft, innocent, mild eye—like one of Ruben's [sic] women—like Jennie Gerhardt."

How many novelists are granted by life the opportunity to make love to a character in one of their books?

She took him to her little room and related the story of her life—how she had learned weaving but fell in love and became pregnant. The father of the child left her to join the army, and she worked for a time in the mills of Stettin, but the job made her ill. She tried clerking in a department store but had no head for figures. "Occasionally I went with a man. I had to." Dreiser gives his answer to Johnson: "It is so easy for those born in satisfactory circumstances to moralize."

In London, Richards slashed away with abandon at anything unflattering to himself or his friends. Worried that nothing would be left, Doty suggested Dreiser disguise identities wherever possible. At one point he tells him rather than kill the Paris and Riviera sections entirely, "it would be better to resort to fiction, —to eliminate your personality entirely and project a new character as a traveling companion."

Meanwhile, the rift within the Century Company widened. In July Ellsworth wrote Richards that the articles selected for the magazine were "much liked by the liberals, and rather frowned on by the elder statesmen—of whom, by the way, we have now very few left." Johnson had resigned the previous month after management rejected his proposal that the company start a new, popular magazine like *Ainslee's* while continuing to publish the *Century* in the old way.

With the domestic opposition vanquished, Doty and Ellsworth turned their fire on Richards. Ellsworth gently laid down the law:

> Mr. Dreiser thinks, and we all think, that you are asking him to take a great deal out of "A Traveler at Forty" which could be there just as well as not and hurt no one.

I read the galley proofs of the book last Sunday, and it seems to me wonderful, — one of the most remarkable travel books ever issued, and I believe it is going to become a classic. Why should you not be embodied, like a fly in amber, in this classic?

When the book was safely in galleys, Doty told Richards that he had restored some of the cuts, mainly descriptions of friends whose identities had by then been sufficiently disguised. Richards himself had been given the elegant pseudonym "Barfleur."

And so *A Traveler at Forty* went to press, Doty sighing with relief: "The damn book has surely worn me out!" Many cuts had been made, and some padding added, it appears. Mencken, after reading the advance galleys, sensed that something was missing. Although the section on Italy was "dragging in tempo," in the Paris chapters he noticed "an effect of reticence. You start up affairs which come to nothing." Dreiser replied, without elaboration, that he wished he had cut "the last half of the book more or left in a lot of woman stuff. . . ." He begged Mencken, "For heaven [sic] sake don't over emphasize the dullness of the Italian scene or you will have every critic in the U.S. yelping your remarks like a pack of curs." For he now believed that Mencken's reviews set the tone of his books' critical reception.

The published version of *A Traveler at Forty*, like the Venus de Milo in the Louvre, is only a torso, but there is enough of Dreiser left to make it identifiably his. In some places he exhibits a vivacity of style and humor, but his fatalistic philosophy runs through the book like a ground bass, reminding Mencken of Conrad: "He is an agnostic in exactly the same sense that you are—that is to say, he gives it up." Dreiser expresses, more openly than in any previous work, his skepticism of all laws and conventions: "For myself, I accept now no creeds. I do not know what truth is, what beauty is, what love is, what hope is. I do not believe any one absolutely and I do not doubt any one absolutely. I think people are both evil and well-intentioned."

His social comment is largely confined to England and consists of brief but telling descriptions of the London slums. As his diary shows, the gap between rich and poor, and the hopelessness and passivity of the latter, made a deep impression on him and permanently etched his opinion of England as a class-ridden country with a ruling elite that was indifferent to the fate of the poor. By contrast, America seemed a land of opportunity; at least young people of ambition and "genius" (like himself) had the hope of bettering themselves. A London shopgirl he talked to, unlike Carrie, could not conceive of marrying above her station.

Had the Hanscha Jower chapters and similar material been retained, the book might have shown a more darkly evocative picture of the underside of Europe, providing an ironic contrast to the guidebook Europe that remains. As published, *Traveler* is an editorially battered child. Only in the final chapters, culminating in Dreiser's account of how passengers aboard the *Kroonland* reacted to the sinking of the *Titanic,* does the book develop a cumulative emotional power. The ship, built by Britain in an effort to claim victory in the running competition between its and Germany's transatlantic passenger fleets, epitomized the bellicose commercial and nationalistic rivalry between the two nations. Its demise provided Dreiser with an unwitting epitaph to the prewar era.

•   •   •

Determined to recoup its sizable investment in Dreiser, after emasculating his book, the Century Company produced a handsome edition of *A Traveler at Forty,* with pencil sketches by William Glackens and a binding stamped in gold. The critical reception was respectful, for the most part, taking the book as a welcome detour from the heavy black line Dreiser was drawing on the literary map. Among the naysayers was, surprisingly — or perhaps not so surprisingly — Floyd Dell in *The Masses,* where he was now assistant editor.

His attack on Dreiser had as much to do with the generation gap as with bitterness over the loss of Kirah Markham. Dell spoke for the young radicals of the Village. He was irritated by Dreiser's pessimism about the possibility of political change and accused him of preaching the outworn Darwinism of the Victorian era. Dell, speaking for the Bohemian rebels around *The Masses,* sounded the radical tocsin: "We can have any kind of bloody world we bloody want." Later he continued this dispute with Dreiser in person, once shouting at him: "Look, this world is changing. . . . It's changing before your eyes — changing because of human effort."

Summing up, Dell complains that in *A Traveler at Forty* Dreiser takes "one last look at mid-nineteenth century Europe — a Europe of streetcorners and drawing-rooms, cafés and cathedrals, repartee and women, and over all a sense of lovely futility as of flowers and toys." But in hindsight, Dell's radical optimism is more dated than Dreiser's chronic pessimism. Bloody world indeed.

•   •   •

Dreiser may have seemed a political fossil to Dell and some of the Village radicals, but he was not entirely out of sympathy with them. He had acquaintances among the orthodox socialists (whom the *Masses* radicals thought stuffy), and the New York *Call,* a socialist organ, had reprinted the previous year his sketch about unemployment, "The Men in the Dark."

On cultural and social issues he was even more in step with the younger generation. Because of the troubles in his own marriage, he shared the ideas on the family, sexual morality, and contraception proclaimed by Emma Goldman, Margaret Sanger, and the Swedish feminist Ellen Key, who held that the marital union should not be enforced by law. *A Traveler at Forty* contains an attack on the Christian doctrine of the indissolubility of marital ties: "in marriage, as in no other trade, profession or contract, once a bargain is struck—a mistake made—society suggests that there is no solution save in death." (He had used the marriage vow—"forsaking all others," etc.—as an ironic epigraph for *The Genius*.) Dreiser also predicted that as new demands for greater "intellectual, social, spiritual freedom" bubbled up, the state "will guarantee the rights, privileges and immunities of the children to the entire satisfaction of the state, the parents and the children." Elsewhere, he expanded on that theme, saying that the state should raise children where the parents were unfit. But he continued to advocate the pro-feminist views he had encouraged, albeit cautiously, in the *Delineator,* telling one interviewer: "I am an intense individualist, and it seems to me that the beauty and interest of life will be increased in proportion to the growing number of great individuals among women as well as among men. I believe that the feminist movement, taken as a whole, has a distinct tendency to strengthen and enrich the individuality of woman."

He failed to link feminism with any specific program of laws or reforms; presumably, it must come naturally, as a product of the larger forces of change, led by great individuals—male and female.

• • •

Dreiser's convictions on artistic freedom would also have been acceptable to the Village radicals. There had been some developments on the censorship front, however, that suggested a counterrevolution was escalating. In September Anthony Comstock, head of the New York Society for Suppression of Vice, led a raid on the offices of Mitchell Kennerley, the British-born publisher who specialized in radical writers such as Vachel Lindsay, Joseph Hergesheimer, Max Eastman, and Walter Lippmann. What aroused Comstock's ire was a novel Kennerley had just published called *Hagar Revelly.* Written by an earnest social reformer, the novel sanctimoniously evoked the temptations and pitfalls faced by New York's underpaid shopgirls and included a couple of overwrought seduction scenes.

The threat that Comstock posed to publishers was dramatized by the raid: Kennerley was arrested and the plates and sheets of *Hagar Revelly* impounded. Previously, Comstock had concentrated his fire on fly-by-night pornography peddlers and publishers of sex manuals rather than mainstream publishers. Kennerley was personally erratic, his firm small and financially shaky, but he was a publisher of serious books.

Rather than withdraw the novel and pay his fine, Kennerley became the first publisher to fight the ban in court. He hired John Quinn, a literary lawyer and art collector, to defend him. Comstock, who was also an inspector for the

U.S. Postal Department, had charged Kennerley with sending obscene material in the mail in violation of the 1873 statute Comstock had helped write.

The trial judge urged the jury to deliver a guilty verdict, but the independent-minded panel declared Kennerley not guilty. His acquittal was hailed as a vindication of freedom of the press, and B. W. Huebsch, another publisher of modernist literature, pointed out that *Hagar Revelly* "went no further than a hundred novels of the past decade" and that it "possessed both literary merit and social significance."

But as Mencken noted in a letter to Dreiser, Kennerley had not been permitted to offer testimony of experts as to the book's artistic and sociological integrity. Furthermore, the jury was not allowed to consider the book as a whole, only Comstock's list of isolated allegedly obscene passages and words. Indeed, the decision was something of a fluke, probably contrary to law, by a runaway jury.

•   •   •

The reception for *A Traveler at Forty* was not encouraging: only 2745 copies sold in the last two months of 1913, followed by the usual falloff. In December Century advanced Dreiser $500 and in January $300, but that was it, Doty told him. There was no hope of any further money from Harper's, and he was casting about for another publisher who might take over all his books and sell them.

Mencken tried to buck him up, saying, "Certainly you'll reach the place where your novels will keep you. . . . 'The Titan,' with its melodrama, ought to make both a popular and an artistic success. And once you escape from Harpers, all of the books will pick up."

With *The Titan* now in press, after considerable last-minute sweat, Dreiser departed for Chicago—and Kirah.

54 / The Same Thing Over and Over

An eternal pox upon the Harpers.
—Mencken to Dreiser (1914)

Other than for a rest and an idyll with Kirah, Dreiser had no particular reason to go to Chicago. Probably he hoped to stir up publicity for the new novel. *The Financier* had sold well in the city and was for a time the number-one fiction title—Yerkes was well remembered. *The Titan* follows Yerkes's business career in Chicago closely, culminating in his grandiose plan to wrest a monopoly of the city transit system. Exiled by society despite his efforts to buy his way in with lavish soirées and civic gifts, he and his Mary Adelaide were left to take drives in solitary splendor. When he tired of his wife and sought comfort in the arms of others, Mary Adelaide turned to drink and raged up and down the empty, echoing corridors of their vast mansion on Michigan Avenue.

All of this Dreiser put in. He was accused of exaggerating Yerkes's amorous career, though much later he told biographer Robert Elias that he had learned from his researches that Yerkes had mistresses tucked away all over the country. But there was no real-life counterpart to the woman in the novel he calls Stephanie Platow, the art-smitten young actress—or rather none in Yerkes's day, for she is clearly based on Kirah Markham. It must have amused Dreiser to play fictionally with an affair he was having in real life, even creating a character based on Dell, a "young, smug, handsome drama critic," as one of Cowperwood's rivals for Stephanie's favors.

Cowperwood at last finds the ideal woman he has been seeking for years. She is Berenice Fleming, a schoolgirl when he first meets her but possessed of such promise of beauty and refinement that he plays Pygmalion, sculpting her with his money into a cultured young lady.

While Berenice is blooming in a hothouse finishing school, Cowperwood is pyramiding his street railways into a monopoly. Only one final step remains:

to create a holding company that controls the entire operation and to sell the watered stock at a huge profit. But to make the new company a success, he needs a long-term franchise; otherwise he will be at the mercy of the "sandbaggers," corrupt city council members who set up dummy companies ostensibly to compete with that of the franchise seeker and who demand that the latter buy them out before they will grant the privilege he seeks. To obtain a fifty-year monopoly, Cowperwood first bribes the state legislature, and then he approaches the governor. But the latter is incorruptible (the character is based on the reformer John P. Altgeld). Next Cowperwood focuses on the city council, as ripe a collection of boodlers as ever looted a city. But a downstate paper exposes his subornation of the legislature, and the Chicago press takes up the cry like a pack of hounds on the scent.

A typical headline of the time read: NEW GRAB BY YERKES; YERKES IS INSATIABLE. Dreiser's notes express amazement that the press could have treated the man who had become his hero so ferociously. ("Fighting Yerkes must have created circulation," he decides.) Cowperwood's enemies in the business community supported the vendetta, and Dreiser scores their hypocrisy in one of his notes: "Imagine them sitting solemnly on the fate of Yerkes!"

The novel reaches a climax with the defeat of Cowperwood's fifty-year franchise proposal at a turbulent meeting of the city council, which has been cowed by a mob of infuriated citizens, who threaten to lynch them if they vote their pocketbooks. Again, Dreiser dramatized a page from Chicago's history. But then he departed from reality. Cowperwood retires to his mansion to brood; enter Berenice, who declares her love and encourages him to resume the fight on another playing field. Actually, Yerkes was barely scratched by his defeat. He immediately went to the Sunset Club, a meeting place for the city's power brokers, and coolly defended his attempt to bribe the city council: "We do not want the eternal sandbagger after us all the time. When they say there is bribery in the City Council why not give us the fifty year franchise we ask for and thus stop the bribery." And then he sold his streetcar lines for a reputed $20 million and moved on to London, where the unfinished Underground offered a new challenge. But the Sunset Club scene might have detracted from Dreiser's romantic climax.

•   •   •

In late February Dreiser suffered a setback of his own. Harper's informed him that it would not publish *The Titan*. The reason, Dreiser laconically reported to Mencken, was that "the realism is too hard and uncompromising and their policy cannot stand it." (To Alfred A. Knopf he explained that Harper's found the book "hard, cold, immoral.")

"The Harpers be damned," Mencken fumed. "Jump to Doran, by all means," despite reports that he "is running to religious bosh." Ironically, Mencken had also been approached by a representative of Doubleday (probably Knopf, who started his long publishing career there), who asked if Dreiser would be interested in coming back. Only if Doubleday were the last publisher on earth, Mencken had retorted.

There were other reminders of *Carrie*. In the summer of 1900, Dreiser was out of New York and had to rely on his friend Arthur Henry to conduct negotiations for him. This time he depended on Anna Tatum and William Lengel, who had recently moved to the city to work for *Real Estate* magazine. Both sounded out publishers besides Doran, while Dreiser wrote to Charles Scribner, who was friendly but uninterested. Mencken's suspicion about Doran turned out to have been close to the mark. As Tatum reported, "He is a 'gentleman' and a conventionalist," and considered the book unsalable because Yerkes was an "abnormal American" and "the Grigsby woman" (Emilie Grigsby, Yerkes' great love and the prototype for Berenice Fleming) an adventuress.

Anna would be a rock in the ensuing days, although she was "literally penniless" and her father was dying. Kirah had supplanted her in Dreiser's affections, but now Anna found in him a cause commensurate with her idealism. As she told Dreiser, calling him by a pet name, "Oh, Dodo, how I love you. And how I love even more, the artistic ideal." Lengel too was eager to be of service to his old chief, even though he was immersed in getting out his first issue of *Real Estate*. Fortunately, he approached J. Jefferson Jones, manager of the American branch of the John Lane Company, whom Anna sized up as "a far more generous, idealistic type than Doran." Not only was he liberal-minded, he was also willing to take a chance on new and unconventional American writers. For a second opinion Jones passed on the galleys to Frederick Chapman, a literary adviser for Lane who was in New York City.

Other publishers were approached, and Alfred A. Knopf, who had left Doubleday to work for Kennerley, was interested. Knopf became known to Mencken and Dreiser as a champion of Joseph Conrad. Dreiser, however, did not think much of Kennerley, who had a reputation of not paying his authors.

Dreiser informed Knopf that he doubted Kennerley saw him as a "commercial possibility" but allowed him to read the manuscript and render "a frank honest opinion." But "the reading must be speedy as well as the decision," he added as an afterthought, which Knopf took as authorization to pass it on to his boss. Kennerley was outraged by the depiction of Grigsby, with whom he had been in love, and predicted she would sue. (She was now living in England and moved in the highest circles.)

While *The Titan* hung in limbo, Dreiser gave interviews to publicize it. One was with Ben Hecht, a young reporter on the Chicago *Journal*, who found

Dreiser's knowledge of the city's political and business history staggering. To a reporter from the *Evening Post* Dreiser held forth on censorship. He had identified so deeply with his hero that he seemed to conflate his troubles with censors and Yerkes's with civic reformers. Both of the latter were seeking to tear down the strong, the builders and creators. "A big city is not a teacup to be seasoned by old maids," he said. "It is a big city where men must fight and think for themselves, where the weak must go down and the strong remain." Let the fittest survive, so that "the future of Chicago will then be known by the genius of the great men it bred." He attacked Major Funkhouser, the city censor, who had banned the painting *September Morn,* calling him "Bunkhouser." Censorship, he warned, was " a terrible thing that is overtaking this whole country, appointing someone . . . to tell you and me what is right for us to think—mind you, think!"

•   •   •

Upon his return from an excursion downstate with Masters, Dreiser was visited by another trial—a painful attack of carbuncles. The condition required surgery, and he was given nitrous oxide. After the operation, and still under the effects of anesthesia, he began hysterically giggling, and Kirah, who was at his bedside, heard him exclaim, "I've got it . . . the secret of the universe, the same thing over and over . . . " Was that revelation inspired by the resemblance of his present troubles with Harper's to the *Sister Carrie* case—or was it a vision of the Spencerian universe, with its sempiternal rhythmic undulations, equilibrium after equilibrium until the final synthesis? Shortly after the operation he wrote Mencken that he was planning an article—"a new philosophic interpretation of earthly life."

Five days later, on March 21, he reported that his carbuncles had been vanquished. And there was even better news: Jones had sent him a telegram saying he would be "proud" to publish *The Titan.*

The mystery of the entire affair is why Harper's acted so precipitously. It had four thousand advance orders for the book and had printed sheets for ten thousand copies. Apparently, the abrupt cancellation order came from high up in the company, probably from George Harvey himself. The financial stewardship of the jaunty, enigmatic president of the House of Harper was under increasing criticism from his overseer, Thomas Lamont, of the Morgan bank, and changes had been demanded. Knopf told Lengel that Harper's feared a novel about financial chicanery might antagonize its leading creditor. "*Too much truth told* about the *high financier.* Do you *get it?*" Anna wrote Dreiser, presumably referring to Morgan. Volume III, dealing with Yerkes's battle in London against Morgan's agents, would, as Hitchcock had feared, pose a problem. George Harvey's position had become too shaky to risk offending his bankers. That portrait of the late Pierpont Morgan in his office glowered at him daily, and the old man's son was now in charge of the bank.

Although nervous about Dreiser's "immorality," Harper's seemed prepared to back him for the long haul. Now its objections were to *The Titan*, with its muckracking content, rather than to Dreiser himself. The firm insisted on keeping *Carrie* and *Jennie* on its list, and, as Dreiser wrote Mencken on March 31, "If you will believe it Harpers have asked me to permit them to publish . . . *The Genius*. This sounds wild but it is true and they backed it by an offer of aid. They feel they have made a mistake . . . the same people who think me unfit for publication. Am I mad or is this good red earth we are standing on."

●   ●   ●

Publicly, Dreiser took the Harper's affair with his characteristic fatalism, although inwardly he probably had some bad moments. He told Mencken that he was full of plans and projects, but he was still peering into the financial abyss. He now owed various publishers $3800, counting the money Century loaned him. He had complained to Knopf that no one wanted to back his career; publishers were interested only in immediate gains: "The book of the season is the thing and the opinion of small fry critics. My contempt for the situation is so great that I heartily desire to drop out at times."

He had Mencken's private prediction that *The Titan* would sell, as well as his enthusiastic endorsement of the novel as the best picture of an immoralist in all modern literature. Anna Tatum had rushed the typescript to the critic so he could write a *Smart Set* review before leaving for Europe April 11. Unfortunately, Mencken was too pressed with last-minute arrangements to do so and this time was not in the critical van. Confirming Dreiser's belief in his crucial influence, the reception for *The Titan* was on the whole tepid, notably in Chicago, where Dreiser had counted on brisk sales. A bellwether was Lucian Cary, who was sympathetic to Dreiser. While praising the accuracy of the Chicago backdrop, he thought the book too reportorial. "The story is always dangerously close to actual event," he wrote, "dangerously close because Mr. Dreiser has depended on this actuality to convey reality . . . outward facts are significant only when they are the sign of inward meaning. And Mr. Dreiser simply does not know the inward meaning. He has never for a moment stood in Frank Cowperwood's shoes and looked out upon the Chicago of twenty-five years ago with Frank Cowperwood's eyes." The schoolmarms, male and female, were out in force. Some complained that Dreiser was wrong to acclaim this rather commonplace financial freebooter as a superman. He was "a satyr not a titan" and "no more a

Superman than the barber around the corner." "The book tells a story, a sordid, disagreeable one," wrote the Chicago *Tribune*, "with many blemishes of split infinitives, unnecessarily coarse speech and rough colloquialisms." Adding to the growing collection of Dreiser's overworked words was "rich" (as in "rich" thrills or a person who takes "rich" strides); and such solecisms as "Quite like a character in a Japanese print might be" and "She was probably something like her own mother would have been."

Defenders praised Cowperwood as an accurate portrayal. To say, as some reviewers did, that presenting "abnormal" types like Cowperwood without any mitigating goodness was not realism was to confront Dreiser on his strongest suit—truth. The world of Chicago politics and finance in the latter part of the nineteenth century was not populated by exemplary characters, and Dreiser created a powerful portrait of a type of financier whose greed and amoral methods were representative of an age.

But Cowperwood is also motivated by an ideal higher than money and power, which becomes the means to this end: beauty in both its feminine and artistic incarnations. When he meets Berenice, he realizes he has finally found the meaning of his existence.

Dreiser's European diary attests to how deeply personal was this conviction. He was obsessed by the passage of time, the need for feminine warmth and beauty (an unconditional, maternal love). In Rome he had noted the need of even the most powerful and successful person for love—not any love, or ordinary love, or bland, steady uxorial love—but *new love,* love fired by romance, a restorative of lost youth, love like Venus-Aphrodite rising pink and new from the waves.

And what was art but a redirection (sublimation, if you will) of the erotic impulse? Love was madness; art was divine madness. Artistic beauty was a realization of the feminine ideal, only a picture's beauty never faded as a woman's did. Indeed, that was the reason for the eternal quest for Aphrodite—to find a fresh feminine beauty to replace the fading charms of the present love-object. And ultimately, only feminine solace—Eros, the eternal foe of Thanatos—could assuage the pain of encroaching mortality. He had written in his diary that even death he would not fear, if he could slip into it obliviously in the arms of a beautiful woman.

And so in this saga of Spencerian dissolution, Cowperwood seeks to stave off death—temporarily—by acquiring beauty through power and wealth. In *The Financier* Cowperwood recalls having read about a man who lived a shabby, lonely life in a little room for twelve years and finally committed suicide. He should have done it long before, Frank thinks, for he had long been dead. Most of us sink back into the undifferentiated herd, never having *lived.* Radical individualism—freedom—is man's boldest defiance of his inevitable fate.

Part Nine

. . .

THE VILLAGE

55 / Scènes de la Vie de Bohème

> Only youth and enthusiasm and love of freedom and color
> and variety together with all but unbelievable illusion and
> an incurable detestation of the humdrum and commonplace
> could have achieved it.
>
> —Dreiser, "Greenwich Village"

Back in New York, Dreiser rented a post office box and slipped away to the home of his sister Mame on Staten Island. Since Mame took his side in the battle with Jug, she provided a perfect hideaway. When William Lengel and his new bride, Nelle, called at 3609 Broadway, they found Jug alone. She said vaguely that Dreiser was "away," but she probably wistfully hoped that he might return; she always thought he needed her and would sooner or later realize it. She simply could not imagine that he was drunk on Cowperwood and needed others, not her.

Kirah Markham had joined a touring company, which opened in Philadelphia. He pursued her there and they had trysts in his rented room when she could sneak away. "Don't give this address to anyone," he wrote Mencken on April 5, 1914, from 4142 Parkside Avenue, adding that he was considering a permanent move to Philadelphia.

He wrote Mencken that he was about to tackle revisions of *The Genius*, which would "surely" be published next spring. At Mame's he had begun working on an autobiography, writing under her nose about things in her and the family's past she wanted forgotten. He called it *Dawn* and finished thirteen chapters by April 24. In an interview with the New York *Sun* more than a year before, he had announced that he would like to write "an absolutely accurate autobiography . . . a literal transcript of life as it is," to be called "The Sealed Book." Only Rousseau in the *Confessions* had made an honest self-revelation. Any halfway truthful account would demonstrate that "all lives are failures."

•　•　•

In May he was at Mame's, working and absorbing the reviews of *The Titan*. The novel's performance was turning out to be a disappointment: some six thousand copies sold in the first two months, but only two thousand or so more during the rest of the year. Not only was this a falloff from the not large total for *The Financier*, it meant that Dreiser would collect no royalties from either Harper's or Lane—all the more reason to revive *The Genius*. Possibly because of the controversy over volume II of the Cowperwood trilogy, Dreiser decided to shelve volume III (which would be called *The Stoic*). There was much more research to do on it, and Dreiser had continuing fears of libel (Berenice-Emilie was a central character).

In June he reported to Mencken that he was at last going to "try to edit" *The Genius* after having it retyped, adding with a broad hint, "I am such a poor editor." Mencken, of course, stood ready to oblige; he had designs on the novel. The letter to H. L. M. revealed Dreiser to be in good spirits: "I have many schemes or plans but only one pen hand—and meanwhile my allotted space ticks swiftly by. Greetings—and let's pray we keep good stomachs and avoid religion."

One of Dreiser's schemes involved the infant motion picture industry. Lengel's employer, Hoggson Bros., was planning to set up a movie company, Mirror Films, and Lengel suggested his old boss for the post of editor-in-chief, or some such title, responsible for choosing original scenarios or books and plays that could be converted into scripts, as well as writing some.

He was also testing the Broadway waters. The agent Gabrielle Welch was dickering on his behalf with a Boston producer who was interested in dramatizing *The Financier*. But that effort fell through when the producer refused to come up with an advance. Financial need was surely the main goad for his extra-literary forays, but that did not mean he was steering his own writing into more commercial channels. Far from it. He was working on some philosophical one-act plays.

A major preoccupation at the moment, though, was finding a permanent abode, since he could not stay with Mame indefinitely. Inevitably, his thoughts turned to Greenwich Village, where a spacious floor-through flat could be had for $25 to $30 a month. And he needed a large place because Kirah—under parental orders to come home if she could not find an acting job—was to join him, at least for a time.

The Village was now entering its Golden Age. Recalled the poet Orrick Johns, "The winter of 1913–1914 was the fine flowering of the village, a period of sincere, hard-working and productive social freedom." This was the Village of John Reed, Max Eastman, Harry Kemp, Floyd Dell, Art Young, John Sloan, George Bellows, Louis Untermeyer, and *The Masses;* of Polly Holladay's restaurant, the Liberal Club, and the Boni Brothers' bookshop next door.

In July Dreiser took a flat at 165 West Tenth Street, a nondescript brick tenement. His place consisted of two large rooms with broad, splintery floorboards that had cracks between them so wide a pencil would fall through. The back chamber he used as a bedroom, and the larger front room served as his living room and study. A small kitchen and a bathroom completed the amenities. He had to boil water on the stove when he wanted a bath. The only other source of heat was a small coal-burning grate. At times the place was so cold that he would go to Polly's to write.

The most prominent piece of furniture was a large rosewood desk fashioned from a piano that had belonged to his songwriting brother, Paul Dresser. This would be his worktable for the rest of his life; it was large enough to hold piles of books and the various manuscripts he was always engaged on simultaneously.

By fall Kirah had joined him. Their happiness was not spoiled by the proximity of Jug, who had moved in with her sister Ida on nearby Waverly Place. Kirah remembered seeing Jug, who did not recognize her, in the neighborhood shops. She felt no remorse, for Dreiser had told her what a narrow conventionalist his wife was, how he had married her when he had been too green to know better, and how she refused to give him a divorce. Still, the younger woman must have perceived the wife as a kind of hostile presence, for she later claimed that Jug would stand for hours beneath the streetlight, watching the apartment. (Oddly, Dreiser has Kirah doing the same thing in a story about her.)

But there were more congenial neighbors, he would discover, and a stream of visitors, who were told not to call until after five, when Dreiser's working day was over. He remained aloof from the Village scene. Louis Untermeyer recalled that when Dreiser occasionally showed up at *Masses* editorial meetings, he cast a pall over the proceedings because he was considered—or was thought to consider himself—a "Great Person." Yet he could be sociable when he chose. For a time he and Kirah had regular "at homes" on Sunday evenings, though he eventually gave them up, he said, because the guests always became noisy and argumentative, giving him a severe headache.

But Dreiser blocked off a part of life for work, a compartment in which he remained solitary. He never held any illusions about the quality of the art the Village rebels were producing: "Genius? I doubt if there was ever much more than a trace of it in the entire Village." But he enjoyed the spectacle. The Villagers seemed to him a gaudy group of strolling players, performing a commedia dell'arte in a grim slum.

• • •

While waiting for *The Genius* to be typed, Dreiser had composed three one-act plays, with the idea of Lane's advancing him money for a collection to be called *Plays of the Natural and the Supernatural*. The new efforts fell into the latter category. In one, *The Blue Sphere,* a monster child is lured to its death by a benevolent spirit holding an azure globe. In the second, *In the Dark,* a poor Italian immigrant who murdered his brother is hunted down by police while spirits hover above crying murder most foul. That play may have had its origin in a nightmare; Dreiser had recurrent ones of being pursued by some menacing foe. The origin of the third play, *Laughing Gas,* was another kind of dream: his hallucinations under nitrous oxide while his carbuncles were being removed. A brilliant scientist—a useful tool in the evolutionary scheme, like Cowperwood—lies on the operating table while his unconscious self speeds through uncharted dimensions of time and space and discovers the meaning of the universe: humans are "mere machines being used by others." We have lived before, and "Society has done the things it has done over and over." The scientist must by an effort of will create himself, or else he will die.

These dramas were "reading plays," not intended to be staged, Dreiser explained to Mencken with a hint of salesmanship, adding defensively, "I am not turning esoteric, metaphysical or spiritualistic. These are merely an effort at drama outside the ordinary limits of dramatic interpretation." They show a revival of Dreiser's preoccupation with the spirit world, where the dead are alive. The pieces meld expressionism and realism; there are spirits as well as human characters, and fluid scene changes that dissolve the frame of the realistic stage (making them virtually unstageable) and the psychic wall between past and present, the visible and the invisible worlds.

This esoteric subject matter left Mencken undaunted. By all means send them, he said; he had a "particular reason" for wanting to see them. This soon emerged: he and George Jean Nathan had taken over the editorship of the *Smart Set* and wanted to "blaze out with some Dreiser stuff."

Dreiser was glad to give Mencken the plays and, in an entirely unrelated gesture, offered him the manuscript to any of his books. Accusing Dreiser of having taken to "heroin, Pilsner, formaldehyde," Mencken said he would esteem the manuscript of *Sister Carrie* "more than the gift of a young virgin."

He saluted the German invasion of France with a "God's benison upon the Kaiser." His loyalties lay with the land of his ancestors, and he blazed out with pro-German sentiments in his "Free Lance" column in the Baltimore *Sun.* He closed each column with "In Paris by Thanksgiving" which inevitably gave way to "In Paris by Christmas!" In October he wrote Ellery Sedgwick that he was being "bombarded daily" by letters from angry readers and that "public sentiment seems to be rapidly turning in favor of England."

●   ●   ●

Dreiser emitted some modest cheers for the Kaiser in his letters to Mencken but devoted his writing time to the completion of his autobiography. In early August he reported that he expected to be done by September, and then—on to *The Bulwark*! Although he didn't come close to meeting that schedule, he accomplished an amazing amount. One day he disgorged a torrential eight thousand words—and spent the next day in bed, recovering.

Then, as would happen so many times, his momentum ran out, and he turned to shorter projects in the hope of raising some quick cash. He concocted an exotic *Arabian Nights*–style tale, "The Princess and the Thief," which he hoped to sell to Pathé Frères, a movie company; but he sent a copy to Mencken for possible use in the new *Smart Set,* along with a short story, "The Lost Phoebe," which his new agent, Gabrielle Welch, had futilely been trying to sell. According to her tally, it had been rejected by sixteen magazines. Mencken thought "Phoebe" was "fine stuff—a story in your best style," and wondered if they might come to terms on it. But after the plays, what they really needed was something representative of the Dreiser with whom the public was most familiar, the Dreiser of *Jennie Gerhardt* and *The Titan. The Genius* promised to be that Dreiser, so perhaps they should run an excerpt from it next.

Dreiser, however, still hoped to serialize *The Genius* in a better-paying magazine. He had told Mencken that he needed at least $1500 to carry him through the writing of *The Bulwark*. Mencken suggested that they publish a short excerpt from *The Genius* different from the material selected for serialization. On October 13 he confessed with chagrin that "Nathan is so full of the notion that this 'Lost Phoebe' lies far off the Dreiser that we want to play up that I begin to agree with him." What they really wanted was something from *The Genius*.

Dreiser darkly interpreted this turnabout as a slap from Nathan, of whom he had formed a vague mistrust. He complained that in order to help them out he had recalled "The Lost Phoebe" from *Red Book*, which had offered $125 for it. That was not quite the truth. Ray Long, the editor, had expressed lukewarm interest but said the price was too high, and Dreiser refused to lower it.

Unaware of all this, Mencken assumed the entire blame for the confusion about the story. Dreiser forgave him but requested the return of "The Lost Phoebe," for which he probably still hoped he could get a higher price elsewhere. He said the editors could postpone the plays and run an episode from the novel. Visibly relieved, Mencken replied, "We are in your hands, and damned glad to be." In early November Dreiser forwarded the first half of the *The Genius* manuscript, apologizing that it was an unedited version.

Despite their differences over money, Dreiser and Mencken were finding a new bond between them: the war. Many other German-Americans felt as they did. After the lurid propaganda about atrocities in Belgium, popular opinion turned against Germany and then German-Americans. America's linguistic, historical, cultural, and legal ties to Britain were too strong; and the German propaganda efforts were clumsy and exuded arrogance.

Anglophobia tinged Dreiser's pro-German views. That prejudice derived from his quarrel with Grant Richards. He considered Richards to be representative of all British intellectuals and lumped him with the fox-hunting nobs who oppressed the poor. And so Dreiser's attitude toward the war was different from that of most American intellectuals, who opposed the war out of pacifism or because they thought the munitions profiteers were pushing America into it or because of the disastrous effects of war fever on constitutional liberties.

$$\bullet \quad \bullet \quad \bullet$$

Mencken had plowed through *The Genius* with mounting distress. He delivered his verdict in person while visiting New York in January 1915. There was a "friendly row," which became so noisy that Kirah Markham fled the house. Mencken's chief complaints were verbosity and repetitiousness. He also was bothered by the novel's sexual frankness, not because of personal objections but for fear of Comstock. In later years, he recalled suggesting that a scene in which the hero touches a female character's knee be eliminated. Dreiser refused, saying, "But that's what happened." *The Genius* was the most autobiographical of his novels, and he was adamantly opposed to cutting the script. The immediate result of their meeting was that no excerpt appeared in the *Smart Set*. As it turned out, no other magazine was interested, and the serialization income Dreiser was counting on did not materialize.

And so *The Genius* was the first of his novels since *Carrie* to go to press untouched by his favorite critic's hand. Dreiser had, however, heeded the objection of Eleanora O'Neill, a Boston book critic and old friend, that Eugene's interest in Christian Science seemed mere New York intellectuals' faddishness, not worthy of a truly pagan novelist. He altered the chapters about Eugene's visits to a practitioner so that they do not represent conversion but rather a form of emotional therapy. And, realizing that the description of his hero in the title was open to challenge, he hung quotation marks around "Genius," explaining to Mencken that he wanted to inject a note of doubt; also, another book with the same title had recently appeared.

The most important change was his own idea. He jettisoned his original ending, in which Eugene and Suzanne are wed, and substituted a new one that was truer to life. In his revised version they see each other only once, at a distance, and Eugene snubs her. In the end he has returned to painting and lives alone with the child Angela conceived to hold him, only to die of complications of a Caesarean section.

Jones, at least, found the manuscript publishable, and he turned it over to Chapman for editing. Chapman cut fifty thousand words, but in the proof stage Dell was hired, at Dreiser's suggestion, to slash even more. Dell succeeded in lightening the novel by another twenty thousand words, but Dreiser restored much of what he had taken out.

Much of what was cut was fat, but some problematic allusions to the sex drive were purged, as well as animadversions on Angela Blue's possessiveness and conventional mind. The specter of Comstock probably explained the former cuts; as for the latter, Dreiser had reasons at this time not to offend Jug, on whom Angela is based in more ways than the play on her maiden name (White). Yet, for all her jealous rages, Angela Blue is one of the most sympathetic characters in the novel. Dreiser later explained that he never regarded Angela as a repellent person; she was merely a limited one who was unfitted to be Eugene's wife, "the kind of woman who regards a man as property."

By "property" Dreiser meant that Jug clung to him for financial support. When he could no longer afford his hundred-dollar-per-month payments, she hired a lawyer, and Dreiser was forced to sign a separation contract under which she agreed to an eighteen-month reprieve of his obligations. In consideration for this concession, he gave her all his property. The "consideration" part may have been legalese, since she had their furniture and he had conveyed to her some property he owned in New York and Washington states two years previously.

Kirah was understanding. She wrote him bravely from Chicago, where she had been spending time with her family and rehearsing a play, not to worry about "the madame." She said it didn't matter to her whether they got married or not.

There was probably as much prudence as emancipated thought in her attitude. She must have realized by now that any marriage to Dreiser would be an unconventional one. His varietism was already showing, for she remarks in another letter that he seems to be seeing a lot of people she hasn't met, including Mrs. Roberts (undoubtedly Mary Fanton Roberts, an old friend; his interest in her was almost certainly professional—which cannot be said of the other women, including Lillian Rosenthal, whom he met clandestinely). Kirah charged that when she was away he found others to console him, and when they were together he treated her like a jailer. Such a primitive emotion as jealousy was passé for a New Woman, and she begged him either to assure her that she was first in his affections or to drop her.

For all his strayings while they were apart, Dreiser would always regard Kirah as one of his great loves. She was undoubtedly drawn to him as an older, stronger man, a father figure. Explaining his attraction for her, she told biographer W. A. Swanberg that Dreiser was an "emotional steamroller" possessed of "animal magnetism" rather than charm. He also had a strong will and an "utter sense of loneliness" that brought out her maternal instincts. What she remembered most was their walks through the mean streets of the Lower East Side. "Few realize how the man suffered over Life," she said. "Many nights we walked the streets, Theo holding my hand in the pocket of his overcoat while the tears poured down his face."

●　●　●

Meanwhile, his closest masculine friendship, that with Mencken, had during the spring of 1915 undergone another shakeup, an aftershock of the quarrel over *The "Genius."* There followed a four-month hiatus in their correspondence. In the meantime Dreiser had found another critical champion, who, it happened, lived in the Village—John Cowper Powys, who was about the same age as Dreiser. A displaced Englishman, Powys made his living lecturing on literature to American audiences in the hinterlands. He had been drawn to Dreiser since the time he had picked up a newspaper on the train and read an interview in which Dreiser said, "I have no hope, yet I do not despair, life drifts." Astounded to hear such stoical sentiments from the lips of an American writer, he eagerly hunted down *Carrie* and *Jennie* and became a convert. In Philadelphia, in December 1914, he paid tribute to the living American novelist he admired most, before a full house of 1500 avid matrons at the Broad Street Theater, including an admirer of Dreiser who sent a detailed report of Powys's "epileptic enthusiasms"—a reference to the Englishman's flamboyant platform style.

The acquaintanceship with Jack Powys began in gratitude and progressed to respect for a fellow artist and philosopher. They were both strong individualists and mystics. Powys's religiosity ran to animism; he was also something of a latter-day druid and prayed to his Welsh ancestors. But he was open to all phases of the supernatural and thus in sympathy with the occult side of Dreiser's temperament.

•   •   •

J. Jefferson Jones was beginning to worry about Dreiser's next book, which was nowhere in sight. The autobiography, *Dawn,* was on the shelf and *The Bulwark,* inspired by Anna Tatum's story about her family, still mulching in his unconscious. He told Mencken he was planning a short novel or story about a man condemned to die in the electric chair. This was apparently his first try at the novel about a murderer that he had told friends he wanted to write as long ago as 1907.

He had, through Elias Rosenthal, obtained the record of the murder trial of Roland Molineux, who had fatally poisoned a rival for the hand of a wealthy woman, using a slow-acting substance that mimicked the symptoms of diphtheria. Dreiser made a start on the novel, which he called *The Rake*, borrowing the title of the aborted novel he had begun after *Sister Carrie.*

The hero, Ausley Bellinger, resembles young Theodore Dreiser more than he does the calculating socialite Roland Molineux—or any type of that class. Bellinger has an artistic temperament, love of beauty, and a "keen passion for sex." Through his father's connections he obtains a job in a factory, where he ogles the female workers, who exemplify natural sexuality. Dreiser had done the same thing at the Chicago laundry where he worked as a boy. Ausley meets a wealthy young woman, and another man enters the scene. Perhaps Dreiser intended the two men to compete for the heiress's hand, leading to Ausley's murder of his rival. But he lost confidence in the story well before the key incident.

According to his later reckoning, this effort was his first step on the road leading to *An American Tragedy*.

56 / *Desire as Hero*

> Don't despair. The philistines will never run us out as long as
> life do last. Given health & strength we can shake the Amer-
> ican Jericho to its fourth sub-story.
> —Dreiser to Mencken (1914)

In early August Masters came to town. At the age of forty-six, he could be
said to have awakened to find himself famous. The publication of *Spoon River
Anthology* in April had caused a sensation, and the book had become that rarity,
a best-selling work of poetry.

Dreiser and Kirah invited a congenial group to honor him at one of their
regular Sunday evening receptions. A reporter was on hand to describe the
festivities for uptown readers. The guests included "parlor socialists, artists,
bobbed-haired models, temperamental pianists, girls in smocks and sandals
and a corporation lawyer in a soft boiled shirt." People seated themselves on
the floor, and Miss Kirah Markham, "Mr. Dreiser's secretary," presided over
the punch bowl. Among the guests were Franklin Booth, the artist; Bobbie
Edwards, a poet who wrote songs about Village life; Floyd Dell; Charles Fort;
Berkeley Tobey, of *The Masses*; Ben Huebsch, the publisher; Virginia Forrest,
an actress; and Willy Pogany, a Hungarian artist.

Dreiser was a rollicking host. As Masters described him, "His teeth stuck
out, his face was red from health and excitement. His eye turned up with added
bubbling of spirits, as he folded his handkerchief and poured forth thunder-
lizard words. Altogether he was the most waggish, quizzical serio-comical,
grotesque, whimsical character I had ever seen." The highlight of the party
was a reading from the *Anthology* by Masters.

In the course of the revelry, Franklin Booth casually asked, "How would
you like to go out to Indiana in my car?" Booth, in his early forties, was a
prosperous illustrator and maintained a studio in his hometown of Carmel,
Indiana, in addition to his New York atelier. Since beginning *Dawn*, Dreiser
had thought about returning to his home state, visiting the towns where he

had lived as a boy—Terre Haute, Vincennes, Sullivan, Warsaw, Bloomington. And so he proposed that he write a book about the trip and Booth illustrate it. The latter agreed, and all that remained was for Dreiser to raise his expense money. On August 6 he called on Jones, who agreed to advance him $200 for *Plays of the Natural and the Supernatural.*

On August 11 they set out in Booth's large open touring car, a gleaming sixty-horsepower Pathfinder, driven by a chauffeur nicknamed "Speed." As they tooled through New Jersey, Dreiser noted in his diary, "40 miles an hour!" Motoring was a new experience for Dreiser, and venturing into the interior on unpaved roads was akin to an African safari.

When they arrived in Warsaw, Indiana, the first stop on their itinerary, Dreiser was overcome by nostalgia, a keen pang of change and loss. The sites he had known were altered or gone; the house belonging to the richest family in town was now a Knights of Pythias home, and the slough where red-winged blackbirds used to flock in the spring to eat wild rice had been drained and planted in corn. Wraiths of girls he had once yearned for materialized in the corner of his eye.

As he walked in the yard around the old brick house where he had once lived, mentally restoring vanished things, he felt that "somewhere down in myself, far below my surface emotions and my frothy reasoning faculties, something was hurting. It was not I, exactly. It was like something else that had once been me and was still in me, somewhere, another person or soul that was grieving, but was now overlayed or shut away like a ghost in a sealed room."

Terre Haute was the next stop. They drove about aimlessly, looking for the house where he had been born, but, lacking the correct address, they could not find it. He did locate the large house where the family had lived the longest, on a grimy, treeless street. And then the last stop: a dreary slum. The houses all looked alike to him: any of them would serve to mark the nadir of the Dreiser family fortunes, when there was nothing to eat but fried mush and the children picked up coal along the railroad tracks.

Next they drove to Sullivan, traveling past fields of rich black soil baking under "a blazing hot Egyptian noon." The house where Sarah Dreiser and the three youngest children—Theodore, Ed, and Claire—had lived was still there, considerably run down. A new chauffeur, named Bert, drove them to Evansville, where more than thirty years ago Paul Dresser had magically transported them to a clean new house. Dreiser visited the German Catholic school he had unwillingly attended years ago, where he was terrorized by the nuns in their batlike robes and flaring headdresses and the priests who whipped wrongdoers.

On August 26, the eve of his forty-fourth birthday, they arrived in Bloomington. It had grown considerably from the dusty little country town he had seen in 1888 when he came to attend Indiana University as a special student.

"New life. New age. A rich town, instead of a poor one," he records. Though they went on to Indianapolis and Carmel, he had reached the end of his pilgrimage into the country of memory. He had returned as a somewhat famous native son, an author in a state that had produced an unusual number of them. But no one had heard of him; when folks thought of a writer, they thought of Gene Stratton Porter, author of *A Girl of the Limberlost* and other sentimental best sellers.

His journey carried him to his Midland roots. He deplored the conventional rural minds in the small towns along the way, the narrow provincialism, the illusions about religion and morality, but he was half-charmed by their friendliness, the easy democratic ways, in contrast to "smug and sophisticated" New York. "America is so great, the people so brisk. Everywhere they are fiddling with machinery & production & having a good time of it."

This was the rural America he evoked in *Newspaper Days,* the countryside that produced a Lincoln, a Jackson, a Bryan; Elwood Haynes, making the first automobile in Kokomo; General Lew Wallace, writing *Ben-Hur* under a beech tree in Crawfordsville. An idyllic land, where the judge lent a copy of Shakespeare to the poor boy, who dreamed of the big world beyond. A dream of equality and opportunity that was only a dream, now that the trusts and monopolies had gained control. But a good dream.

But he also remembered the places where he grew up, a lonely outsider. He had gone home to where he never had a home.

•   •   •

The rush of memories stirred him, and back in New York he immediately set to work on a book about the trip, which he called *A Hoosier Holiday,* tapping a reservoir of memories, observations, contrasts with the past. As was becoming his practice, he had *The Bulwark* on the go—started sometime in 1915. Because of the money Dreiser owed on *The "Genius,"* Jones was in no mood to advance him any more for *A Hoosier Holiday.* The same held for *The Bulwark,* in its embryonic state. *The "Genius"* was now out, however, and Jones—and Dreiser—had reason to hope that it would be a strong seller. In October the reviews began pouring in, and they were the most vehemently pro and con of any of his books. Literary opinion in the United States was sharply split, and the battle line was drawn along a growing fissure in American culture.

On the liberal side were, first, the familiar Dreiser partisans, Reedy, J. C. Powys, and Edgar Lee Masters, all of whom held forth at considerable length and eloquence on the virtues of the novel. Floyd Dell temporarily defected to the anti-Dreiser camp, with whose values he had little in common; however, his review was full of compensatory praise. Mencken had sworn to Dreiser that he would reread the novel with an open mind, but he was not converted. His notice was a grand clash of negative and positive judgments, all cymbals and kettledrums, like the final movement of Beethoven's Seventh Symphony, and really a tribute of a kind. But Dreiser was wounded by the lash of Mencken's incomparable invective, in passages such as this one: " 'The "Genius" ' is as shapeless as a Philadelphia pie-woman. It billows and rolls and bulges out like a cloud of smoke, and its internal organization is as vague. . . . The thing rambles, staggers, fumbles, trips, wobbles, straggles, strays, heaves, pitches, reels, staggers, wavers."

Rallying behind him, though, was a new set of boosters, the younger generation of poets and novelists who saw him as a leader in their rebellion against literary conservatism. A critic for Margaret Anderson's *Little Review* who called himself "Scavenger" hailed Dreiser as "the greatest novelist in the country . . . the only real, uncontaminated genius of these States."

A review by Randolph Bourne, the spokesman for the literary radicals, titled "Desire as Hero," singled out the "subterranean current of life . . . that desire within us that pounds in manifold guise against the iron walls of experience," against "the organized machinery of existence." Dreiser writes about the erotic "with an almost religious solemnity." Eugene Witla is lashed and tossed by passions he does not understand. "One feels," Bourne writes, "that this chaos is not only in the Genius's soul, but also in the author's soul, and in America's soul."

Bourne pointed out that Dreiser's conception of desire stemmed from Herbert Spencer's philosophy: "What Mr. Dreiser has discovered is that 'libido' which was nothing more than the scientific capturing of this nineteenth-century desire." The post-Victorian novelists, of whom Dreiser was the pioneering voice, glimpsed the Freudian tragedy of civilization and its discontents, the beating of the wings of desire against the cage of convention. Yet Bourne and the other voices of the American Renaissance with youthful optimism believed that an upwelling of repressed forces of desire or vitalism would shatter the crust of outworn morality, law, and convention, creating a freer, more just society. As Dreiser said, they were out to shake the American Jericho to its foundations.

• • •

All this ferment among the literary radicals sparked a counterreaction from the conservatives, who invoked a kind of clubman's code to blackball Dreiser. According to the code, there were only two types of male characters suitable for fiction—gentlemen and muckers. As a corollary to this, a gentleman did not write sympathetically about a mucker. But in *The "Genius"* Dreiser had taken a mucker for his hero. The Kansas City *Star* scored the novel as "a procession of sordid philandering." The New York *Times* charged that Dreiser had chosen "an abnormal character and written an abnormally long novel about him." Eugene Witla was denounced as a "contemptible cur," a "drummer in a frock coat, a Don Juan of the streets"—certainly no gentleman, asserted H. W. Boynton in *The Nation*.

And, driven by the wave of anti-German sentiment that swept America after the sinking of the *Lusitania* in May, a new note of prejudice appeared in several of the reviews, exemplified by the flag-waving of Elia W. Peattie in the Chicago *Tribune*: "I have not yet lost my patriotism, and I will never admit such a thing until I am ready to see the American flag trailing in the dust dark with stains of my sons, and the Germans completing their world rule by placing their governer general in the White House in Washington."

Ironically, Dreiser himself had described the disasters that Eugene's wayward desires had brought down upon him. He had not written a tract for sexual freedom. Witla agrees that "the licentious were worn threadbare and disgraced by their ridiculous and psychological diseased propensities." But Dreiser did not judge him by Christian morality; his values were closer to those of the success code, which called for hard work and sublimation.

Dreiser did not really believe in sublimation, at least now; his impulse was for expression, in art and in life—expression of sexuality. His ideal was Cowperwood, not Witla. Yet the latter was a part of him too, the compulsive, guilt-ridden side of Dreiser's sexuality, which had its origins in the Victorian sexology of his boyhood. Dreiser's heroism lay in his attempting to say, more assertively than any other novelist of his day, that society must recognize subterranean urges as part of human nature, and that his "pathological" hero was more normal than official morality admitted. So-called decent people, in the privacy of their hearts, would confirm the existence of similar urges in themselves.

•   •   •

The battle over The *"Genius"* represented a wider war in American culture, one that was related to strong political passions unleashed by the real war in Europe. The forces of the Old Order reacted to the alien threat and sought to restore the primacy of Victorian or "Anglo-Saxon" culture and to purge the nation of "foreign" values clustered around naturalism, Freudianism, and socialism. It was an intellectual war, but a sociological one was well. Behind the genteel critics stood the cruder forces of the old nativism on one hand and the punitive powers of the state on the other.

Dreiser had become a larger symbol of all that those groups deplored. Most of the reviewers of the patriotic school lacked the intellectual equipment to challenge the hypotheses of modernism, so they retreated into moral criticism or patriotism. In the December 2 issue of *The Nation*, however, Professor Stuart

P. Sherman, of the English faculty at the University of Illinois, unlimbered the big intellectual guns.

Sherman's polemic, meaningfully titled "The Barbaric Naturalism of Theodore Dreiser," was in parts the most effective statement yet uttered of the conservative case against Dreiser's method. But it was fatally marred by a descent into a kind of polite nativism. Asserting that "In the case of the realist, biographical details are always relevant," Sherman notes that Dreiser was born of German-American parents. Turning to Dreiser's five novels, he continues, "I am greatly impressed by them as serious representatives of a new note in American literature, coming from the 'ethnic' element of our mixed population which, so we are assured by competent authorities, is to redeem us from Puritanism and insure our artistic salvation"—a reference to Bourne's call for a "trans-Atlantic" literature. (He makes no mention of such American-stock rebels as Sherwood Anderson, Edgar Lee Masters, Floyd Dell, Max Eastman, Ezra Pound, and Bourne himself.)

Like Darwin, he says, the naturalists have a theory; it is a philosophy "such as we find in the mouths of exponents of the new *Real-Politik*" (read, the German militarists). This view holds that society is a jungle, that civilization is window dressing to conceal brute instincts, which are the real determinants of human behavior. "By thus eliminating distinctively human motives and making animal instincts the supreme factors in human life," Sherman continues, Dreiser "reduces the problems of the novelist to the lowest possible terms . . . he has confined himself to a representation of animal behavior."

Sherman's attack made Mencken itch for battle. It was "a masterly exposure of what is going on within the Puritan mind," indicative "of its maniacal fear of the German." Dreiser agreed. In a letter to Harold Hersey, a poet who was working in the copyright office of the Library of Congress, Dreiser revealed how deeply Sherman's and others' personal attacks had affected him: "These moonbeam chasers are trying to make a devil of me. . . . I am now being tied up with all the evils which the Germans are supposed to represent. I am anti-christ."

●　　●　　●

Morality aside, *The "Genius"* had serious technical flaws: the inept language, the silly lovers' dialogue, the lack of clear point of view. Dreiser had been unable to detach himself from his central character. He later wrote that Eugene Witla was not autobiographical, and he does make him softer, more easygoing than himself. But he had too deep an emotional investment in his characters to discuss them with detachment.

Despite all, *The "Genius"* succeeds as a portrait of the artist's life in America. Without irony or artifice it relates the journey of an ambitious young man, driven by dreams of wealth, fame, and beauty, from his rural backwater to the city. That is the archetypal Dreiser story: the young man from the provinces, illusioned and naive, who escapes a dull Middle Western village and dreams, miraculously, of Beauty (often in the form of a young woman, the most immediate form beauty takes in a small town.) This young Eugene is appealing, as he shoots up like a green plant from the common soil. There are moving descriptions of his gropings for expression—such as the scene at the Chicago art school when he begins painting.

Although the early chapters are the best, the later ones contain individual scenes that rank among the finest that Dreiser had written: the vicious office politics at the United Magazines Corporation and Angela's death after giving birth to a child by caesarean section, for example. Depicting the ferocious battle between Eugene and Angela over Suzanne, Dreiser does achieve detachment, presenting Angela's side of the argument fully. He makes Eugene a breathing, suffering man rather than an unwitting fool; both partners are caught in a marital trap after desire has died and only hatred and pity are left.

• • •

In January 1916 Dreiser decided to seek a milder climate in which to finish *A Hoosier Holiday* and work on *The Bulwark*. He suffered from bronchitis in New York's cold winters, and this lowered his spirits. He was also enduring a siege of prostate trouble.

On January 26 he boarded a steamer bound for Savannah, Georgia. Once at sea, Dreiser felt a deep exhilaration as onshore entanglements fell away.

When he disembarked in Savannah, the rosy clouds dissipated. Conserving his funds, he rented a room in a private home for $2.50 a week and then walked around the city. Southerners, he decided, were a "thin, anemic prejudiced people." Puritanism was to blame for their character. The "respectable" whites suppressed their natural instincts and became envious, gossipy, hypocritical. Feminine purity was idealized; the women were "like saints craving subconsciously what they sniff at openly—sex." In its present culturally arid, repressive incarnation, the South had no future.

He was "Very lonely." The main cause was that he missed Kirah and had not heard from her. He managed to complete chapter 48 of *A Hoosier Holiday*, and he then sent her a telegram asking why she hadn't written. It was raining; he couldn't work. Bypassing Western Union, he transmitted a telepathic appeal. A little later a wire arrived : SWEETHEART HAVE WRITTEN EVERY DAY SINCE FRIDAY LOVE, KIRAH.

With that boost he was able to work on his book, despite the unseasonably cold weather, his painful prostate, and bad food. After finding a more pleasant room, he pounded steadily toward the finish of *A Hoosier Holiday,* completing the final chapter on February 13. The next morning he took out the draft of

John Paul Dreiser in the
1890s, wearing the full beard
he sometimes affected. (UP)

Sarah Schänäb Dreiser in
her fifties. "No one ever
wanted me *enough,* unless it
was my mother." (IU)

Theodore Dreiser, the St.
Louis reporter, aged 22. "I
have a semi-roman nose, a
high forehead and an
Austrian lip, with the
edges of my teeth always
showing." (IU)

Sister Emma Dreiser, prototype of Carrie, "vain, silly, childlike, beautiful, a nerve harp to be played upon by every wind of circumstances." (Courtesy of Vera Dreiser)

Paul Dreiser at the zenith of his Broadway celebrity. "His songs spoke a wistful, seeking, uncertain temperament, tender and illusioned. . . . He was generous to the point of self-destruction, and that is literally true." (UP)

Jug and Theo in their new
apartment, around the
time he became editor-in-
chief of *The Delineator.*
(UP)

Anna Mallon, who lured
Henry away from Dreiser
at a crucial time. Her
Infant Class typed *Sister
Carrie.* (Courtesy of Donald
T. Oakes)

Arthur Henry, who
encouraged Dreiser to
write *Carrie.* "You are to
me my other self a very
excellent Dreiser minus
some of my defects. . . . If
I could not be what I am, I
would be you." (Cornell
University)

Following in the Financier's footsteps. Dreiser, left, on the Riveria in 1912, with Grant Richards, center, and Sir Hugh Lane. (UP)

H.L. Mencken, Dreiser's early critical champion: "He was my captain in a war that will never end, and we had a swell time together." (Alfred A. Knopf)

Estelle Bloom Kubitz (aka "Gloom," "Bert," "Bo"), Dreiser's secretary during the Village years. (UP)

Helen Richardson in 1920: "Full of delightful and innocent dreams of beauty and peace under simple circumstances." (UP)

Dreiser in 1920. The inscription—"For the returned Helen"—was prophetic. She always came back. (UP)

Dreiser in Russia. Left to right: L'Etienne, a Latvian agronomist; Dr. Sophia Davidovskaya, personal physician; Dreiser; Ruth Kennell, his American-born interpreter; and a guide. (UP)

Chester Gillette on the witness stand, as depicted in the New York *World*, 1906.

Dreiser correcting a typescript in the 1920s. (UP)

Helen and Dreiser on the
veranda at Iroki, his
country place. (UP)

Helen and Dreiser in the
front yard of their home on
North Kings Road in
Hollywood in the 1940s.
(UP)

Marguerite Tjader Harris, without whose help *The Bulwark* might have never been written. (UP)

Theodore and Vera Dreiser, who knew him as his niece and as a psychologist. (Courtesy of Vera Dreiser)

The Bulwark and began revising chapter 1, having good success and breaking off at three to go to town to buy five hundred sheets of paper and check the post. On the way he spied a broken horseshoe, then a whole one. He interpreted these conflicting omens as meaning, "My spiritual guardian & enemies are fighting."

Kirah arrived for a short, inconclusive visit, and Dreiser left Savannah alone at the end of March, returning by rail via Washington.

57 / *Battle of* The "Genius"

The exact specifications are these.
Lewd:
    Pages 20-21-43-44-46-51-52-55-56-7—70-71-79-
124-125-126-127-128-129-130   131-150-151-154-155-
156-159-160-161-163-164-167-168-171-179-180   183-
245-246-340   341-342-343-344-345-348-350-351-445-
446-531-533-539-540-541-542-551-552-553-554   555-
556-557-558-567-569-585-588-595-596-597-599.
    Profane:
    192-335-356-379-389-408   409-410-421-431-469-
566-618-678-713-718-722
    Greeting.
    Visit me in my cell.
                                    —Dreiser to Mencken (1916)

Back in New York, correspondence between Dreiser and Mencken in May was consumed by inquiries from Mencken regarding Dreiser's books; he was composing a critical study and wanted to get the facts right. Mencken planned to combine it with three other essays—on Huneker, Conrad, and "Puritanism as a Literary Force"—in a book that John Lane would publish.

Sherman and Comstock surely headed the list of contemporary Puritans. Others ranged from Bible-thumpers such as Billy Sunday, moralizing lady journalists, anti-German academics, and the antivice societies, which had stepped up their attacks on alien ideas—dangerous new viruses rampant in the social body. Censorship was about *control* of the strange and thus threatening, from foreign agitators to extramarital sexual drives.

Anthony Comstock had died in 1915, but his successor, John Sumner, was emerging as an effective smut smiter. He was more public relations–conscious than his predecessor, and more legalistic. Comstock was a brute, a hard-eyed cop with gamboge whiskers who boasted about the number of filth merchants who had committed suicide as a result of his persecutions (fifteen) and who loved to invade the dens of evildoers, gun drawn (in addition to pornographers, he went after abortionists and lottery-ticket sellers).

When Sumner took over as executive secretary of the antivice society, he apparently realized that he must broaden his attack. Old Anthony had been so effective against the clandestine pornography peddlers that there were few of them left, so Sumner redirected his fire at the above-ground publishers. Whereas Comstock's main challenge had been to purveyors of well-known classics, Sumner plunged into the briar patch of contemporary literature. His pristinely literal mind saw a radical younger generation demanding free expression and access to the franker literature produced on the Continent, and concluded that the chief menace to the innocence of young women was the Village radicals who preached and practiced the doctrine of free love. One of his first raids was on *The Masses* bookshop, where he seized a sober sex manual.

Early in 1916, tipped off by a Mencken rival and surely not unaware of Mencken's columns guying the Baltimore antivice league, Sumner had turned on the *Smart Set*—or rather *Parisienne*, a subsidiary publication. But he miscalculated. Mencken and Nathan had cynically chosen the title to capitalize on pro-French sentiment generated by the war (privately they called it "the parasite"). Although the name also connoted naughtiness—at least to the average cigar store patron—they expunged the slightest hint of it from the stories, many of which had first been published in *Smart Set* and transplanted to a French setting. Sure enough, Sumner's complaint was dismissed by the judges.

•   •   •

The "Genius" continued to draw the conservatives' fire. In a discussion of recent books in the May *Atlantic*, the anonymous author defending literary romances against the realistic school chose *The "Genius"* to exemplify the faults of the latter, and added a sly reference to Dreiser's "quite Teutonic" thoroughness. Mencken pounced on that tactic as "typically and beautifully Anglo-Saxon" and said he wanted to mention the review in his book. For he was constructing a defense of Dreiser, neutralizing the nativist attacks by demonstrating that "He shows even less of German influence than of English influence"—which happened to be true.

As Mencken was polishing his argument, Dreiser asked him to edit the manuscript of *A Hoosier Holiday*. Not only that, could he dash off one hundred and fifty words of jacket copy? And not to stint on requests, he also wondered if Mencken might find an editorial job for Anna Tatum, "one of the best and sanest brains I know anything about." As usual, Mencken was amenable, asking for the typescript as soon as it was ready and meeting with Tatum. He had no openings on the *Smart Set* staff, but he did promise Dreiser that he would give her some literary work to do.

Mencken was probably relieved to find that he liked his friend's latest effort. "The book is full of splendid stuff—some of the very best you have ever done," he wrote Dreiser. He was, however, "outraged . . . by banalities," and his hands itched to clean them up. Also, the book was too long—two hundred thousand words, he reckoned. No, only about one hundred twenty-five thousand, Dreiser countered. Fine, Mencken retorted, he could suggest cuts to bring it down to a more seemly one hundred thousand. Subsequently, he did slash repetitions, mostly philosophical passages, and some of the descriptions of Dreiser's clumsy attempts at seduction at Indiana University, which Mencken thought "very unwise." Dreiser chuckled at the thought of Mencken's removing all "lewd, obscene and lascivious references."

•   •   •

Three weeks later a more drastic censor struck. One of the jewels in Anthony Comstock's empire—almost the peer of Boston's almighty Watch and Ward Society—was the Western Society for the Suppression of Vice, based in Cincinnati. Its secretary, F. L. Rowe, was a tireless soldier of the Lord. But it was one of his vigilant supporters who started it all. The Reverend John Herger, a Baptist divine, received a telephone call from an anonymous informant complaining about The "Genius," which he purchased in a local bookshop. Reverend Herger passed on the trip to Rowe, who acquired a copy and found it riddled with "obscenity and blasphemy." He promptly demanded that stores remove it from their shelves and filed a complaint with the U.S. Postal Department to have it banned from the mails. The department dismissed the complaint as improperly drawn.

Rowe reported his actions to New York, but Sumner already had been alerted. He had received in the mail pages torn from the novel, containing allegedly obscene matter. Rather than swear out a warrant for the publisher's arrest, however, he went directly to the offices of John Lane and requested that Jones either consent to delete the obscene passages or withdraw the book and stop advertising it. This move was in keeping with Sumner's new, low-profile strategy. As the New York Tribune explained: "The essential feature of the new method is to get rid of objectionable publications without giving authors and publishers the benefit of free advertising, such as followed Comstock's attack on the picture 'September Morn' and the novel Hagar Revelly."

On July 27 Dreiser sent a laconic bulletin to Mencken: "In passing—the censor has descended on The 'Genius' and ordered Jones to withdraw it from the market. . . . Jones is apparently anxious to compromise and I do not intend that he should unless I have to but I have promised silence until the specific objections are laid down." In fact, Jones had capitulated, halting shipments and requesting stores to return their copies of The "Genius." Sumner also notified the local postal authorities, and two inspectors duly collected copies of the novel to determine if it should be barred from the mails.

On July 28 the Cincinatti and New York societies jointly issued a list of the pages containing lewd, profane, and blasphemous matter — nearly ninety in all. Thanks to this scholarly industry, depraved persons could easily locate the ripe stuff, starting with page 20, where they were confronted with the following "lewd" passage (Eugene is skating with a girlfriend): "She stood before him and he fell to his knees, undoing the twisted strap. When he had the skate off and ready for her foot he looked up, and she looked down on him, smiling. He dropped the skate and flung his arms around her hips. 'You're a bad boy,' she said." On the next page, Eugene plants "a long, sensuous kiss" on her lips.

With such a lecherous hero, the book becomes steamier. By page 44 Eugene is involved in a physical relationship (not described) with another feminine acquaintance, and Dreiser notes, "his sex appetite became powerful" (no further details). On page 51 he is seduced by Bourguereau's nudes — "great, full-blown women whose voluptuous contour of neck and arms and torso and hip and thigh was enough to set the blood of youth at fever heat." After that his downhill slide is rapid; on page 55 he is painting a "naked model."

• • •

After receiving Dreiser's letter of July 27, Mencken went on full alert, sending advice and encouragement. However, the upshot of his thinking was that a compromise might be best. It could be that only a few sentences would have to be removed; better that than the suppression of the book. To resist would be folly, advised Mencken the realist. "After all, we are living in a country governed by Puritans and it is useless to attempt to beat them by a frontal attack — at least, at present." Besides, Sumner was a boob; he could be gulled into restoring most of the questioned matter.

Dreiser, however, wanted action. He briefly considered mailing a copy to see if the federal authorities would arrest him. He would gladly go to jail, he told Mencken; it would save him living expenses. Worried by his friend's seeming lust for martyrdom, Mencken tried unsuccessfully to telephone him when he was next in New York, and then wrote him to do nothing until Mencken had perused the society's complaint.

In his next letter Mencken asserts that Sumner had overplayed his hand by enumerating so many allegedly obscene passages. He was all bluff, and if Jones stood up to him, he would "compromise on a few unimportant changes." Of course, if Sumner demanded the excision of "essential things," Dreiser should fight — but he must give up the idea of going to jail. There was "very heavy work" before the war was over, and he would be needed.

Mencken was a shrewd, worldly man, but he leaned toward the side of caution in matters of sexual material. That was understandable at the *Smart Set,* which was too wobbly to risk a run-in with the comstocks. But a novel by the man he called America's greatest writer was surely a different matter. Mencken's distaste for the novel may have swayed his judgment: he thought the thing so grossly overweight that "a few thousand words might be easily cut out without damaging the whole in the slightest." Hence it was not worth fighting over a few obscene passages.

Mencken should have known better than anyone how much the novel meant to Dreiser personally, and how fiercely protective of every word of it he was. But Mencken had been badly bloodied for his pro-German opinions in "The Free Lance," and though he would never back down, he decided it was time to lie low. The real battle against the Puritans could wait until after the war, he told Dreiser.

•   •   •

Despite the Sumner shock, Dreiser continued to work on *The Bulwark,* and Jones was preparing a dummy volume, containing the first chapter, for his salesmen to circulate among the bookstores. But a minor complication had arisen: Anna Tatum was "down" on Dreiser, raising the possibility that she might bring some sort of "spite" suit.

The quarrel with Anna may have been an indirect result of his break with Kirah Markham, who was in self-styled exile in Chicago. He may have turned to Anna out of loneliness, and she had demanded a commitment that he would not make. At any rate, she returned to her home in Pennsylvania. As for Kirah, Dreiser still insisted on his freedom to cultivate friendships with other women, while she held out against all outside emotional entanglements. She didn't want to spend the rest of her life in his "intellectual harem." Some women thought so little of themselves that they would give a "big man" their "dog-like devotion," but not she.

In May he rejected her demand that he devote himself only to her: "If I could for any living woman I would for you, but I can't. You are a ranging vigorous intelligence, each day growing more individual. Our fates are slowly, but surely, diverging . . . . On the long roads that we go alone my thoughts— loving thoughts will always be with you. Goodbye and good luck. If I can serve you in any way let me know."

Possibly he didn't send that letter, since it is the only one to her that survives. She wrote him a few more times that month. In the last one extant, dated May 31, she says she is coming to New York and expresses her hope that they won't have to separate. But it was over between them. She could not live with those unknown rivals, whose letters she occasionally discovered, and he could not give them up. But even more, as she once told him, "You want me to compete with a wraith, an illusion, a phantom. Well it can't be done and I don't propose to try." She meant that ideal woman, who would forever be younger, prettier, richer, more loving, more brilliant, more sacrificing than the woman he was with. She was not the first to be defeated by this rival—or the last.

•   •   •

By the fall he had taken up with thirty-year-old Estelle Bloom Kubitz, small and pretty, with bobbed hair and dark eyes, a bright, cynical, yet vulnerable flapper. Mencken had met her sister Marion in Washington in 1914 and grown fond of her. He encouraged Marion's literary ambitions by publishing her epigrams in the *Smart Set*.

Estelle, whom Mencken had nicknamed "Gloom" because of her liking for dark Slavic novels and her moodiness, had read Dreiser's books and greatly admired them. While Kirah was away he took her for rides and deep conversation on the top deck of the Fifth Avenue bus. Eventually he enlisted her to do some typing for him in connection with the *"Genius"* case, and they entered into an informal arrangement under which she did his secretarial work. She refused to accept a regular salary, for she liked the job and wanted their relationship to be on a personal rather than an employee-employer basis. In any case, he couldn't pay her regularly. She continued to live apart from him, at his behest, and at times shared Marion's rooms.

Knowing all about Dreiser's philandering, Mencken worried that Estelle was letting herself in for trouble. The affair thrust him into a backstairs intimacy with Dreiser. He became Estelle's father confessor, and this put him in the awkward position of knowing more about Dreiser's private life than Dreiser knew he knew and, what's more, disapproving of what he heard.

Meanwhile he had charged into the thick of the *"Genius"* affair, writing friends to solicit their support and counseling Jones on strategy. His shrewdest idea was to circulate a petition supporting Dreiser among prominent writers. On August 9 he had written to Dreiser's young admirer Harold Hersey, who was now assistant to Eric Schuler, the executive secretary of the Authors League, suggesting that the organization back Dreiser. "A public protest signed by twenty-five or thirty leading American authors would have a tremendous effect," he pointed out. Although still hoping for a compromise, he realized there was safety and power in numbers. And an attack on Dreiser was an attack on all writers: "If the moralists score a victory against a man of his range and attainments, they will undoubtedly run amuck." Indeed, Sumner had let it be known that after suppressing The *"Genius"* he intended to slap bans on Dreiser's other novels.

Possibly as a result of Mencken's overture, Dreiser was invited to plead his case before the league's executive council on August 24. He delivered a grim warning: "A band of wasp-like censors has appeared and is attempting to put the quietus on our literature which is at last showing signs of breaking the bonds of Puritanism under which it has long struggled in vain." He concluded, "A literary reign of terror is being attempted. Where will it end?"

Impressed, the council members passed a resolution affirming that *The "Genius"* was not "lewd, licentious or obscene" and warning that the present "too narrow and unfair" test for obscenity might choke off the circulation of literary classics. They sent a statement to the Post Office opposing a ban from the mails, and Hersey was instructed to circulate a protest petition among the members.

Jones continued to mark time, but he told Dreiser that if the authorities did not act within two months, he would test the *de facto* ban by selling a copy of *The "Genius."* Dreiser remained steadfast in his determination "to stand pat and fight." He, Jones, and others apparently hoped that the popular protest would pressure the postal authorities and Sumner to drop the threat of prosecution.

At least it gave Dreiser and his supporters a feeling that something was being done. In addition to those Hersey sent out, statements were circulated by Mencken, Francis Hackett, Willard Huntington Wright, and John Cowper Powys, who contacted British authors. Powys struck gold when Arnold Bennett, H. G. Wells, W. J. Locke, Hugh Walpole, and others cabled their support. The press was also sympathetic, and editorials critical of the ban appeared in the New York *Tribune* and *Sun,* and the Des Moines *Register,* among others. Even the conservative *Saturday Evening Post* criticized the comstocks.

Mencken was determined that the protest signers be impeccable members of the literary establishment, meaning no red-ink boys, who, Mencken believed, wanted to hijack Dreiser's cause for their own revolutionary ends. When Dreiser relayed a request from the Liberal Club, a Greenwich Village forum, for Mencken to speak on censorship at a symposium, his Baltimore adjutant fulminated against "tinpot revolutionaries and sophomoric advanced thinkers." Mencken grumbled to Ernest Boyd that Dreiser was unable to extricate himself from the clutches of the "Washington Square mountebanks" and that he was "a fearful ass and . . . it is a very difficult thing to do anything for him."

The letter to Boyd was an expression of his growing disillusionment with Dreiser personally. In part, ideological differences were to blame: mention the Liberal Club, and Mencken saw Reds. When Dreiser mailed a flier to two hundred secondhand book dealers asking them to display *The "Genius,"* and included a preliminary list of signatories to the Authors League protest, Mencken went off like a Roman candle: "Despite our talk last week," he wrote, "you have inserted the names of four or five tenth-rate Greenwich [sic] geniuses, including two wholly unknown women and left out such men as [Winston] Churchill and [George] Ade."

Dreiser reacted angrily. He resented Mencken's "dictatorial tone" and his constant carping about ties to the Village radicals, whom he insisted that he had little to do with socially, and even if he did, it was none of Mencken's business. He added: "I still seem to sense something in this letter which is not on the surface by any means and which I resent . . . if you have any real downright grievance come across."

Mencken wrote back that he had no secret grievance. He just thought it bad politics to cite "professional revolutionists." Such people dragged Dreiser's banner into the muck of free love, birth control, and other dubious causes, giving "the moralists the very chance they are looking for."

A few of the Old Guard in the Authors League did growl about the executive council's support for Dreiser. One of the most vociferous dissidents was Hamlin Garland, who thought the petition "a shrewd advertising move" on Dreiser's part. On October 2 he warned Executive Secretary Schuler that it would promote discord.

In November Mencken launched "a general offensive against the lice who have refused to sign the protest." With the help of a stenographer he churned out letters at the rate of twenty-five a day. To the reluctant ones, he wrote personal notes, sometimes three or four of them, patiently answering the objections they had raised. The tactic worked on some, but others recused themselves, pleading that they were unfamiliar with Dreiser's writings, still others, however, knew them only too well. William Dean Howells, who had disapproved of *Sister Carrie* in 1900, wrote, "I have no doubt that half literature, prose, and poetry, could be reasonably be suppressed as Mr. Dreiser's book." Nevertheless, he supported censorship to protect immature minds.

Unsurprisingly, the younger writers better grasped the issue of freedom of expression at stake than the Old Guard. The poet William Rose Benét regarded Dreiser as "the most overrated writer in America" but signed because "the freedom of American letters" was at stake. Robert Frost was not familiar with Dreiser's novels ("beyond that they are honest"), but he joined "with all my heart" because of the principle involved. The doyenne of imagism, Amy Lowell, wrote, "Nothing would be more pernicious to the future of literature in America than to have it in the hands of bigoted and fanatical people, who judge it for reasons quite other than its artistic merit." And Ezra Pound indited an editorial in *The Egoist* condemning "the suppression of serious letters" in the United States and particularly the ban on "poor old Dreiser, who is, perhaps, the most serious and most solemn of contemporary American prosists."

Despite the variegated opinions of this highly individualistic group, the basic language of the protest held, and Mencken's yeoman work significantly lengthened the list of signers to 458 in all. Such a collective statement was unprecedented in American letters, and it temporarily united a broad swatch of the literary community, radicals and conservatives, younger and older generations, behind the principle of opposition to *unreasonable* censorship.

Sumner, however, was unfazed. In a communication with George T. Keating, a liberal editor, Sumner got to the heart of his complaint about *The "Genius"*:

> through the story there are very vivid descriptions of the activities of certain female delinquents who do not, apparently, suffer any ill consequences from their misconduct but, in the language of the day, "get away with it." It is wholly conceivable that the reading of the book by a young woman could be very harmful, and that is the standpoint from which this society views the matters which become the subjects of its activities to wit: the effect on the young and impressionable mind.

There it was in a nutshell: any book that might corrupt a young girl must not be published. For forty years American literature had labored under that sweeping, vague standard, applied informally by editors and legally by Comstock and his epigones. Now the informal editorial consensus was slowly being eroded by the new literature and the growing public demand for that literature, but the laws that formed the superstructure of the Victorian sensibility still stood.

The only way to undermine that superstructure was in the legislature and the courts. There was little hope that the former would happen, but *The "Genius"* case conceivably provided an opportunity for a sapping operation via the latter, depending on how vigorously Dreiser's lawyers pressed his cause. And he now had lawyers. The firm of John B. Stanchfield and Louis Levy had agreed to take the case for no fee. Stanchfield was a conservative, but he was a bitter foe of Sumner's; according to Mencken, he intended to fight the case through to victory and then sue Sumner for libel.

In early December Dreiser wrote Mencken with excessive optimism that the lawyers would bring suit "by Monday" and that he might be "arrested here to accommodate" Stanchfield and Levy. But the lawyers brought no action until the following year.

•   •   •

The "Genius" had been out of the stores for nearly six months now, a considerable financial loss for Dreiser. Although sales had dropped in early 1916, the novel seemed destined for a continuing life, had Sumner not quashed it. According to his most recent royalty statement, Dreiser owed his publisher $1600.

Jones did handsomely by *A Hoosier Holiday*, which was published in November in a pale green, gold-stamped binding that Kirah Markham had designed and which contained Booth's charming pencil sketches in the best smudgy *Masses* style. The book had hardly come off the press when a controversy arose. A telegram from John Lane himself arrived objecting strenuously to two anti-British passages. These were mild by Dreiser-Mencken standards but certainly would hurt sales in England. Dreiser refused to permit any changes, but Lane went ahead and made them.

John Lane's reaction aside, *A Hoosier Holiday* elicited glad cries from American reviewers, who regarded the relaxed, ruminative style as a refreshing departure for Dreiser. A majority of the reviews were favorable, though coverage was sparser than for previous books. Sales were sparse too—only about sixteen hundred copies in the first six months. Perhaps the price was too steep, the book was too thick, and, above all, it was not a novel. Or had Dreiser's name been irreparably linked with Germany and immorality?

•   •   •

A Hoosier Holiday is perhaps Dreiser's most accessible book, philosophical in parts and pessimistic in outlook, yet steeped in the sights, sounds, and talk of the Middle West and leavened by his rather ponderous humor. At the outset he compares his memories of his Indiana boyhood to a "rose window" in his life, like that at Chartres: "In symphonies of leaded glass, blue, violet, gold and rose are the sweet harmonies of memory with all the ills of youth discarded." He tests these illusions by going back, and in the end they remain, though now tinted by the darker hues of maturity. The memories themselves were not illusions—they were *of* illusions, the illusions of youth, the dreams that briefly gild the world before disillusionment sets in.

He sees Americans living by a similar set of illusions, the old dreams of the founding fathers, of equality, liberty, and justice for all. The determinist in him doubts that Americans were really free. Yet why not dream the old dreams? Someday historians would say, here was a country where "men were free, because they imagined they were free—"

58 / *Neurotic America*

> We are to have no pictures which the Puritan and the narrow,
> animated by an obsolete dogma, cannot approve of. We are
> to have no theatres, no motion pictures, no books, no public
> exhibitions of any kind, no speech even, which will in any
> way contravene his limited view of life.
> —Dreiser, "Life, Art, and America" (1916)

Jones had announced *The Bulwark* for spring 1917, extravagantly predicting that it would be "the greatest novel that has ever been written." The Lane Company also published a promotional brochure, "Theodore Dreiser: America's Foremost Novelist," containing a garland of poetic tributes by Masters and Arthur Davison Ficke and a reminiscence by Harris Merton Lyon, originally published in *Reedy's Magazine*. It was the late Harry Lyon now; Dreiser's old protégé at *Broadway Magazine* had died in the summer of 1916, and Dreiser was helping his widow find a publisher for a collection of short stories.

Jones's commercially inspired festschrift was his last hurrah for Dreiser. He had advanced him $1800 and was pressuring Dreiser to sign a contract, rightly fearing that he might take *The Bulwark* elsewhere. Dreiser complained to Mencken that the publisher had made him a "distinctly wrong" financial proposition. What was more, the Lane manager was a "bag of mush" and had "no real publishing acumen." In late November Dreiser had Schuler of the Authors League vet the proposed contract but put off signing it. By then Jones's failure to test the ban on *The "Genius"* had created further ill feeling. Under the circumstances, Dreiser did not really want Lane to have the novel and asked Mencken to help him find another house. Actually, his reluctance to give Jones *The Bulwark* may have been the main cause, at this time, of the slow progress he was making. Dreiser may have psychologically resisted working on a novel, seeking to punish Jones for his timidity.

•   •   •

Dreiser's difficulties with the novel were not due to any fear of Sumner. That is shown by a play he wrote in November called *The Hand of the Potter* (an allusion to *The Rubáiyát of Omar Khayyám*: "What! did the Hand then of the Potter shake?"). The subject was sexual perversion, and the central figure was Isadore Berchansky, a child molester. Dreiser had drawn this sordid theme from a real-life case. The sensationalistic press treatment of it—and what this revealed about American prurience—was a motif in the *Potter*.

Another was sexuality itself; Dreiser's own drives, his womanizing, had earned him the censure of Jug and Mai Dreiser and his sister Claire. There was some feeling in the family that he was abnormal, even talk that he should be sterilized. He had attempted to write about his strong sexual drive in *The "Genius,"* an effort that drew moral condemnation from literary conservatives. And gossip about his private life was fanned by his literary reputation as a writer of a banned book. Exaggerated accounts of his amours were circulating in New York literary circles.

Dreiser still bore the childhood scars of social censure in Terre Haute and Warsaw, when his sisters' affairs had brought obloquy on the family. His projected autobiography was a kind of apologia for their own lives. He intended to show with scientific detachment how an individual could not control his or her chemical makeup; it was shaped by the hand of the Potter, by Nature, and thus individuals could not be held to the illusory standards of traditional ethics: "Life and the individual should be judged on their chemical and physical merits and not on some preconceived metaphysical, religious notion or dogma," he had written.

He sought to tie together American sexual attitudes and censorship in an essay called "Neurotic America and the Sex Impulse." In it he accuses Americans of being both puritanical and "sex struck," citing the example of a Southern city he had recently visited—obviously Savannah—where books and movies are vetted by censors and the old-fashioned morality is dominant. And yet the young people flock to roof gardens, where they cling together in "suggestive dances," after which they go off to lovers' lanes in Model T Fords to consummate their aroused desires. Their behavior, however, is normal, he insists; what is neurotic is the official denial of the instinct driving them and the artificial conventions set up to regulate it. Sex is "an all but dominant force of life," superior to man-made laws. It underlies both love and lust; it is protean, surfacing in many guises, often displaced or sublimated, but always the mainspring of human effort. The conflict between the "amazing super-impulses of sex" and the rules of those who fear it has continued throughout history, generating all that is poetic and tragic in life.

• • •

Dreiser finished the first draft of *The Hand of the Potter* in early December working uncharacteristically at night, six to eight hours at a stretch, stimulating himself with cups of strong black coffee à la Balzac. He was aware of the touchiness of the theme and did discuss it with Edgar Lee Masters and Hutchins Hapgood, a journalist and prominent Villager, before writing the play. They approved, but with such a topic, execution was all. Deeply immersed in the drama as he was, he thought he had handled it with discretion; and so when he sent it to Mencken for an advance reading, he mentioned that "the one thing I am concerned about" was the accuracy with which he had rendered a character's German dialect, and he asked Mencken to "look after" it.

He must have been taken aback by the vehemence of Mencken's reaction—the most outraged critique in all their friendship. The first letter was comparatively mild. The play was hopeless, he said "not only because the subject is impossible on the stage, but also and more especially because the treatment is lacking in every sort of dramatic effectiveness. . . . Nor does it seem to me that you illuminate the central matter in the slightest. . . . The whole thing is loose, elephantine and devoid of sting." The very mention of certain subjects, Mencken insisted, "is banned by that convention on which the whole of civilized order depends. In no country of the world is such a thing as sexual perversion dealt with in the theatre." What was even more appalling was the timing. Dreiser's worst enemy could not have conceived of a more tactically stupid move. The comstocks would fall on this play with knives drawn.

Dreiser lashed back. He had told the story of a family that had concealed a "weak pervert" in its bosom "for social reasons." The man commits a crime—not shown—bringing disaster on the entire house. If the play was a total botch, the critics would duly condemn it. But when Mencken told him what could and could not be shown on the stage, he was revealing his own prudishness. As for Dreiser's alleged mishandling of the social problem he had dramatized, "I wonder really what you assume *the central matter* of this play to be. You write as if you thought I were entering on a defense of perversion . . . if you would look at the title page you would see it is labeled *a tragedy*. What has a tragedy ever illuminated—unless it is the inscrutability of life and its forces and its actions."

Dreiser urged Mencken not to reveal his opinions to anyone or publish a review in advance of the other critics, lest he doom the play before it had a chance. (Mencken seems to have heeded the first part of that request, but, he told Dreiser: "As for the review, my chaplain advises me to promise nothing. For such a disease as you show the most violent remedies are indicated.") With the dismissal of *The "Genius"* and now the bitter attack on *The Hand of the Potter,* Dreiser was beginning to feel that his champion was turning his back on him. Then too, he resented the way that Mencken was taking the upper hand in their relationship, signified by the hectoring tone he sometimes used.

On his side, Mencken felt that Dreiser was writing "cheap pornography," as he later told B. W. Huebsch. Mencken had staked his reputation on Dreiser's books, so he felt a proprietary interest in his career. But he didn't want to be known as Dreiser's house critic and was beginning to fear that he had become too closely identified with him.

Taken aback by Mencken's hostility, Dreiser kept asking, why so angry, why so violent? He had now tried the script on Powys, Stanchfield, and Levy, who thought it "great"; ditto Rella Abell Armstrong and Estelle Kubitz. But Mencken had admonished: "Take the advice of men with hair on their chests—not of women." That dig, out of the blue, let slip Mencken's private view of Dreiser as a sultan surrounded by an adoring harem that fanned his brow and cheered his every venture into pornography. Such gibes in turn fed Dreiser's suspicion that Mencken's distaste for his recent writings reflected a bourgeois judgment on his lifestyle rather than a criticism of the works themselves. In this theory he was not entirely wrong. Mencken could not stomach the promiscuous way his friend conducted his romances. Significantly, Mencken's animadversions on Dreiser's sex life in letters to friends began after Dreiser took up with Estelle Kubitz and, to Mencken's mind, treated her rottenly.

As they had in the past, both men eventually backed down. Mencken fired a final blast, then emphasized his respect: "You are the one man in America who can write novels fit for a civilized man to read and here you waste yourself upon enterprises not worth ten minutes of your time."

On Christmas Day, Dreiser returned to the salutation "Fairest Mencken," which he used when he had a favor to ask or gratitude or affection to convey, and invoked their common ethnic ties: "In the face of so much pro-British subterfuge how can you turn on a fellow Menschener [man] in this cruel fashion." He closed with an uncharacteristic "Merry, Merry Christmas."

• • •

In February 1917 the *"Genius"* case at last began its snail-like journey through the legal system. Stanchfield persuaded the parties to agree to a plan whereby Dreiser would launch a friendly suit against the John Lane Company for breach of contract. To start the wheels turning, Dreiser wrote his publisher a letter asserting that the novel was not obscene and therefore its withdrawal from the market constituted a violation of their agreement. Jones replied that he would allow the courts to decide whether or not it was obscene. To whet the judges' interest, Dreiser claimed to have suffered $50,000 in damages, though he admitted that the exact amount was difficult to ascertain. In March the controversy was submitted to the Appellate Division of the New York Supreme Court.

Dreiser did what he could to keep the censorship issue before the public in an article entitled "Life, Art and America," published in a new literary magazine called *Seven Arts*. It is one of Dreiser's most durable, certainly most impassioned essays, an extended critique of American culture, which Dreiser considers to be dominated by capitalism and the Anglo-Saxon–Puritan ethic, with little space for independent thought or artistic beauty. By virtue of his talent for selling paint or coal or stoves, the businessman "has strayed into a position of counsellor, or even dictator, not in regard to the things about which he might readily be supposed to know, but about the many things about which he would be much more likely not to know: art, science, philosophy, morals, public policy in general." As a result, the nation has produced few poets, painters, and writers comparable to those of Europe.

Dreiser's essay previews some of the themes of the intellectual revolt of the 1920s: the artistic poverty of a business civilization, the provincialism of the average American, the unchecked power of Big Business, the overriding materialism. The generation of Frank, Bourne, Van Wyck Brooks, and the others to come would push further in the coming years, and abandon or take for granted the battles fought by Dreiser's generation. But in 1917, young and old rafted together the rapids of change.

As an artist, Dreiser had claimed the privilege of remaining aloof and superior. Now he saw that he was not above the battle.

59 / *Surrounded by Women*

> Dreiser is going on with women like a crazy college boy; his
> place is full of them all day and all night. Result: he has
> stopped the Bulwark and is doing nothing.
> —Mencken to Ernest Boyd (1918)

To launch an anticensorship campaign, Dreiser, Frank Harris, Harold Hersey, and Theodore Schroeder, head of the Free Speech League and an expert on obscenity and the law, convened at Harris's home at 3 Washington Square for the purpose of founding an "author's aid society," which would extend financial assistance to talented writers (chosen by a panel of critics) whose work was too advanced for conventional publishers. Legal assistance to authors under attack by the censors would also be provided.

Although the critical-society idea would sporadically occupy Dreiser for the next two years, it never got beyond the stage of a proposed dinner to which wealthy patrons of the arts would be invited, along with artists, intellectuals, writers, and editors.

On April 6, 1917, Congress declared war on the Central Powers, and Sumner exchanged his vice crusader's mufti for the khaki of a YMCA officer. He was posted to France. While Sumner was trying to shield American manhood from the temptations of Paris, the Vice Society struggled on, but its work was eclipsed by the government agencies set up to mobilize public opinion behind President Wilson's crusade to make the world safe for democracy.

Once war was declared, Mencken saw his worst caricatures of democracy as mob rule come true as local governments and vigilantes mobilized to purge the country of Teutonic influences. To avoid the slightest note of controversy, he and Nathan kept the war out of the *Smart Set*. Publisher Eltinge Warner kept an eye on them lest they preach sedition or run a spy ring from the office. In his letters to Dreiser, Mencken confined himself to mock pledges to serve his country. Upon hearing that suffragists were enlisting, he proposed that he and Dreiser volunteer as midwives.

•   •   •

In May Stanchfield and Levy filed their brief in the *"Genius"* case. A member
of the firm, Joseph S. Auerbach, had prepared it, and his basic strategy was
to prove that the novel was actually a moral work demonstrating how Witla's
libidinous excesses led "to artistic futility and business disaster"—a not inaccurate description. Since the novel did not "exult in debauchery" or glorify vice,
it could not tend to "deprave or corrupt those whose minds are open to such
immoral influences." The brief also argued that *The "Genius"* was no worse than
other works challenged by the society that the courts had refused to ban, such
as *Arabian Nights, Tom Jones,* and *Madame Bovary.*

It would be a year before the case was argued, however, and Dreiser again
found himself financially pressed, subsisting at times on ten dollars a week.
He sold the publishing rights to *Sister Carrie* to Frank Shay, who had purchased
the Washington Square Bookstore from the Boni brothers and who planned an
edition of one thousand copies. Previously, Dreiser had been selling by mail
the copies he had on hand. He mailed out a flyer saying that his books "have
been continuously attacked by Puritans solely because America is not used to a
vigorous portrayal of itself." The recipient could obtain *Sister Carrie* by writing
to "George C. Baker," who happened to live at 165 West Tenth Street. The
cutoff of royalties from *The "Genius"* bothered him, especially when the book,
which was listed at three dollars, was being sold under the counter for five or
ten dollars. Later he and Mencken tried to obtain fifty copies of the novel to
sell at the black-market rate, but Jones's board of directors, fearing that the
comstocks would get wind of the scheme, refused to approve it. His books
with Harper's had at last earned back their advances—*Jennie* and *The Titan* had
sold some twenty-four thousand copies, *Carrie* only four thousand—but sales
were down to a trickle now.

His relationship with Estelle Kubitz was now complicated by sexual possessiveness. The first entry in a diary he began keeping in May 1917 reads:
"Little Bill cold to me. We have argument in bed as to how many women I have
watched suffer under my indifference." "Little Bill" was one of his nicknames
for her, along with "Bo" and "Bert" ("Gloom" was really Mencken's appella-
tion). Their quarrel was the usual one over his desire for "freedom" and fear
of a woman dominating him. The eternal issue was, as he wrote in his diary,
"Tension of opposition—who is to control?"

So it went, quarrels and reconciliations accompanied by bouts of strenuous
lovemaking. Sometimes she was "a gay, laughing girl," at others sulky, tearful,
and depressed, consumed by jealousy after discovering the remnants of the tea
he had served a recent visitor. Her favorite song was "Poor Butterfly." She was
the prototypical flapper, at once cynical and idealistic, one of a train of literary-
minded young women drawn to Dreiser by a need to give meaning to their lives

by serving a great artist. As she told Marion, she knew she was a doormat, but life was an "empty dance card" anyway, and the only solution was "to live in somebody else."

She obsessively recorded his flaws and betrayals and inconsistencies while complaining of being left to do work while he went out and played with others. She called him "Old Moloch" because of his stinginess. Mencken urged her to leave him and offered to lend her the money to go to Washington and find a job. "Why in hell a woman of your talents should be a slave of a man is beyond my comprehension," he admonished her.

Dreiser marched with Estelle in a suffragist parade, buying her flowers beforehand (and guiltily noting that it was the first time he had ever done so), but he compulsively lived by the double standard. He seemed to fancy—and sometimes seriously advocate—polygamy. Once he was talking to an attractive woman who had come to his studio. When she said that the independence of women led to unhappiness, he agreed. He describes in his diary what happened next: "I advocate Mormonism and prove that she already accepts it in fact while denying it in theory. As we talk I pull her over to me and feel her breasts. She kisses me, and in a few minutes I persuade her to undress . . . ." So much for theoretical discussions.

He was fonder of Estelle than she seemed to think, but his feelings were, at best, tenderness and pity, never love, which requires a loyalty and reciprocation he could—or would—not give. One of the other women he was still romancing was Lillian Rosenthal, now a singer in vaudeville, who would visit him at odd times for passionate liaisons. And that same turbulent spring he formed still another feminine friendship. She was Louise Campbell, young, pretty, spirited, cynical—a "hoyden" he called her—from Philadelphia. She had sent him a fan letter after reading *A Hoosier Holiday,* describing her vague ambition to be a writer and adding, coquettishly, "I seem to have more success in being decorative than intellectual. My friends all seem to think I make a much better fashion model than a writer." A month later, when she was in the city, she called him and he invited her to drop by. She was impressed by the Bohemian ambience of his studio, through frightened by the pet mouse he kept on his desk in a wire cage. He had caught it in a trap and couldn't bear to kill it. (Some might find the caged mouse a symbolic expression of his possessive attitude toward women.) He asked her to read a short story he was working on and, after listening patiently to her criticisms of his style, took her to lunch at the Brevoort. Like many women, she was impressed by his sympathetic attention, his way of listening closely and asking questions that got to the heart of the matter.

In May he arranged a tryst with her at a hotel in Trenton. Telling Estelle he had an appointment, he spent a rainy afternoon with Louise at a "fierce" (shabby) hotel, returning that night to pick up a cross Bert at her apartment. He comforts her, and "we fall to screwing. Work at this almost an hour. During afternoon I come four times, Louise seven or eight. We finally come down to studio and go to bed . . . and after an hour of tossing about get excited and have one more long fierce round. Then am able to sleep."

Such accounts of his sexual adventures are sprinkled throughout Dreiser's diary. They were confirmations of his potency, which he had, irrationally, worried about since adolescence. He felt the same documentary urge to record that a day ended with lovemaking that he did to describe the weather, or the name of a caller, or the price of a purchase at the store. Once he noted, "No sex." Sexuality had become as much a part of his relationship with a woman as a meal or a conversation.

At times, his promiscuity resembled addiction. He worried about his health, writing, "I must give up so much screwing or I will break down." He did not drink to excess, except on occasion, or take drugs. Women were the most delightful drug of all.

•   •   •

Despite these affairs, he never got over the old loves—or they him. Thelma Cudlipp, now a successful magazine artist for *Vanity Fair* and other magazines, saw him in a restaurant accompanied by a drab-looking woman and thought he looked "oh, so down-at-heels." Kirah Markham turned up in New York after spending a year in California working with a little theater group and trying to get into the movies. On the rebound from Dreiser, she had married Frank Lloyd Wright, Jr., son of the architect. Lengel told Dreiser that when he saw her last she had burst into tears at the mention of his name. When she came to Dreiser's apartment he cleared out the mementos of their life together; another time he imagined she was willing to make love, but he made no move; he did not want another affair to start. She separated from Wright but returned to him, speaking for many New Women when she told Dreiser, "What's the good of a freedom I don't want and can't use?"

Nor was the oldest love of all, Jug, ever completely out of his mind—or his life. Walking by their old place on 123rd Street would trigger a rush of memories of those "sad, beautiful days." Lengel's untalented wife's trying to sing reminded him of Jug's irritating desire to "be someone"; and when Lengel described his own sexual restlessness, Dreiser was reminded of the frustrations in his marriage.

In November 1917 Jug wrote him that she'd lost her job at *The Delineator* and demanded that he provide financial help. Still under an obligation to her, he had been thinking seriously of a divorce. He had sent her little if any money, pleading poverty because of the ban on *The "Genius."*

"It is so hard for me to completely rid myself of old loves," he wrote after seeing Kirah. But he could also write: "I believe it would almost kill me—be absolutely impossible for me to be faithful to one woman." Yet he had not forgotten the times as a young man when he thought himself homely, unattractive to women, and unable to interest any. As he wrote in the diary: "I have so many girls now compared with my one-time luck." He adds in the next sentence, "Will I ever have money, I wonder, to contrast with my poverty?"

Hutchins Hapgood, who regularly dropped by for a chat, concluded that, despite his amorous reputation, Dreiser placed work first. He was no one until the end of the day. His talk was almost always about literature or the moral restraints on it.

Hapgood was apparently unaware of Dreiser's many amorous visitors, but even they were pressed into service as readers, typists, or copy editors. When Louise came, he would give her a manuscript to critique "between rounds." And he used events in their lives as raw material. Campbell's account of her marriage provided him with the theme for a short story called "Love" (later called "Chains"). The sight of places associated with Jug generated two stories, "The Victim" (which he apparently never finished) and "The Old Neighborhood," which he conceived while walking through the Bronx neighborhood where they once lived. When he bought Estelle some new lingerie and watched her trying it on, he thought of a play called *The Nobody*, "the story of a poor drab of a woman who never gets anything." He never wrote the play, but the incident tells volumes about his relationship with her.

For all the competition, Bert remained at the center of his life, and they spent many hours of quiet domesticity, reading together in bed, going to restaurants or the theater. He stayed with her not only because she had a "perfect body" and was (when not in one of her moods) bright, companionable, gay, and loyal, but also because she helped him make his way through the tangle of projects in which he was embroiled. He needed her to type and edit the manuscripts he wrote with such prolific haste, cutting excess words and improving grammar as she typed.

• • •

The two of them spent a working vacation in June and July at her brother-in-law's farm. Dreiser alternated *The Bulwark* with a new project, the second volume of *A History of Myself*, which he called *Newspaper Days*. He wrote his old Warsaw schoolteacher, May Calvert Baker, that he had finished twenty-eight chapters of the Quaker novel.

When Mencken drove up to the farm, he found himself in the middle of a spat between Dreiser and Estelle. She accused him of planning an assignation with Louise Campbell, which was very likely the case. When Dreiser asked Mencken to drive him, he refused and watched with growing displeasure as Estelle meekly withdrew her objections. Later he attacked her for giving in to to Dreiser: "If you fall for that bunk again I'll have you arrested. When you went back last time, I wrote to Marion that you were ripe to be read out of the human race."

While at her brother-in-law's, Bert did some writing too—a play with two characters: Old SOB and Miss Damn Phool. Lying in a hammock with Miss DP sitting at his feet, Old SOB announces that he must go to New York on business. She tells him that if he leaves she will walk out for good: "I've worked and played with you for a year now and done ten times as much of your work as you have, and yet this business I'm to know nothing about. . . . I'm just raw enough to want some return for what I do for you and am for you."

It really wasn't a very funny skit. The author was too close to her subject matter.

60 / Over Here

> As for Dreiser, he is full of some obscure complaint against
> me, which I can't understand, and so I don't see him. In brief,
> I suddenly find myself very lonely in New York.
> —Mencken to Boyd (1918)

Dreiser and Estelle patched up their differences, but Marion refused to speak to him, in protest of his treatment of Estelle. As a result, he declined an invitation to dine with her and Mencken but relented after she sent him a conciliatory letter. They capped the evening with a session at the Ouija board at Dreiser's studio—to Mencken's disgust. Mencken took his revenge by pushing the Ouija. Dreiser sought cosmic, rather than mundane, answers from the spirits: at a previous session an anonymous shade informed him that there was no evil, no God, and perforce no reason to lead a moral life.

Ten days later, August 13, Mencken again intervened in Dreiser's destiny. Merton S. Yewdale, the Lane editor, told him that Mencken, in his *Book of Prefaces,* which Alfred A. Knopf was about to publish, had dismissed The *"Genius"* as "a mass of piffle" and said that Dreiser's early work was his best while the recent stuff represented a deterioration. This news hit Dreiser hard, and Estelle did not help his self-esteem when she remarked that Mencken's evaluation would influence posterity's verdict on Dreiser's entire oeuvre. Later, when Lill called and asked how he felt, he told her he was "horribly blue and sad, feeling eventual failure staring me in the face."

The article was far from an attack—quite the opposite. It was the fullest, most sympathetic account of Dreiser's artistic struggles and achievements yet written, save perhaps for Randolph Bourne's essay in the June *Dial.* But after reading it Dreiser felt that his Baltimore scourge was taking an unholy glee in enumerating his faults. One passage in particular drew blood. Mencken says that one half of Dreiser's mind is usually intelligent and thoughtful,

> but there come moments when a dead hand falls upon him, and he is once more
> the Indiana peasant, snuffling absurdly over imbecile sentimentalities, giving a

grave ear to quackeries, snorting and eye-rolling with the best of them. . . . The truth about Dreiser is that he is still in the transition stage between Christian Endeavour and civilization, between Warsaw, Indiana, and the Socratic grove.

Dreiser later said he objected to Mencken's "slapstick familiarity and condescension in regard to myself personally, which at times becomes a little too familiar to be agreeable." He decided Mencken had fallen behind the times, preferring earlier works like *Sister Carrie* and *Jennie Gerhardt,* which "represent really old-line conventional sentiment."

As a result, their friendship went into a deep freeze. When they met by chance in a New York restaurant, and Dreiser came over to shake hands, Mencken would have none of it.

•   •   •

Although Dreiser made scant progress on *The Bulwark* during the winter of 1917–1918, he became engrossed in volume II of his autobiography, *Newspaper Days,* completing nearly forty chapters. He also rescued the manuscript of *Dawn,* the first volume of *A History of Myself,* from J. Jefferson Jones's safe and sent it to Louise Campbell, who had volunteered to type and edit it. And he accumulated enough short stories for a book. He was also reworking some of his early stories and sketches, hoping a publisher would issue a collection. In most cases his revisionary pen deepened and improved them.

He took another look at *The Hand of the Potter.* Dissatisfied with the authenticity of his Jewish characters, early in 1918 he asked David Karsner, an editor at the socialist *Call,* to suggest someone who could introduce him to a typical family on the Lower East Side. Karsner chose a young member of the *Call* staff named Irwin Granich—who in the 1920s would take the nom de plume of Mike Gold and write a classic Lower East Side memoir, *Jews Without Money,* which appeared in the 1930s.

Honored to help Dreiser, who was a hero to him, Granich invited him to Friday night sabbath dinner at his mother's East Side tenement. The visit enabled Dreiser to add some touches of Jewish life to the play, but apparently it was all for naught. Hopkins demanded more substantial changes than Dreiser was willing to make, and in April the producer bowed out, saying, "It is the best American play that has been submitted to me, and I would eagerly have produced it had not Dreiser imposed on me so many bulls, caveats, and salvos."

•   •   •

Not long after the falling out with Hopkins, he found a publisher, if not a producer. His name was Horace Liveright.

Their meeting came about in the summer of 1917 when Dreiser discovered that *Sister Carrie* had been issued by the house of Boni & Liveright, which had purchased the rights from Shay, who was about to be drafted. The firm had been formed the previous year by Liveright and Albert Boni, who had hatched the idea for the Modern Library of contemporary classics—cheap editions bound in limp lamb's-leather covers and retailing for sixty cents each.

Liveright had done a stint as a bond salesman on Wall Street and then married the daughter of a wealthy paper manufacturer. He was the dynamo of the firm, a salesman with flair. Dreiser, he decided, would be the figurehead on the prow of the Boni & Liveright ship. He was interested in publishing new American writers, preferably undiscovered Village geniuses, and Dreiser's name on his list would give the house prestige and attract the young talent.

Liveright called on Dreiser and wove his spell, promising to put twice as many copies of *Sister Carrie* in the stores as Shay would have and, what is more, to advertise them. As for the future, he proposed that B & L acquire the rights to all of Dreiser's books, including *The "Genius,"* and publish them in a uniform set—something Dreiser had been longing for. And of course they would bring out all his new works and would support him with generous advances. Liveright coveted that much-rumored novel, *The Bulwark,* which he had heard was a devastatingly ironic swipe at religion. Liveright was already years ahead of the Genteel Age.

Dreiser had recently been talking to Harper's. The older house seemed a safer home than a new outfit like Boni & Liveright. The fact that both partners were Jewish may also have given pause, but it was probably not a major issue. He had well-off Jewish friends such as Elias Rosenthal and his daughter Lill, and when he later met Abraham Cahan, novelist and editor of *The Daily Forward,* he deeply admired him, telling Nathan, "I don't believe in saints, but there's one man on this earth who strikes me as being one, and he's Abraham Cahan."

A Jewish-run publishing house was a novelty in New York in 1917. There were two others besides Boni & Liveright: Alfred A. Knopf and B. W. Huebsch. Barred by anti-semitism from joining the established houses, Jewish publishers became the innovators on the scene, the ones who were most open to foreign writers and new, "daring" American ones. Partly this was a matter of sophisticated tastes and partly it was because they could not compete with the establishment houses for the best-seller writers or literary gentlemen and had to look elsewhere. Huebsch published not only James Joyce's *A Portrait of the Artist as a Young Man* but also Sherwood Anderson's *Winesburg, Ohio.* Knopf had Mencken, of course, and a growing list of distinguished foreign authors.

Liveright, the ex-stockbroker, analyzed Dreiser's portfolio—his books— and found it underperforming. In September he reported to Dreiser that the total sales of his eight titles in print for the year ending June 30, 1917, came to only about two thousand copies, bringing in $700 in royalties. That was "ridiculously small"; B & L could easily double it. He wondered if there were any additional titles that could be included in the package. Might he obtain *The Bulwark* without having to pay anything to Lane?

Dreiser pointed out that there was the matter of the advances Jones claimed he owed the company; perhaps Liveright could be induced to make good on those as part of the price for his transferring to B & L. But money wasn't the only thing. Did Liveright sympathize with what he was trying to do artistically? Could Dreiser depend on him not to succumb to a faint-heart attack as Jones and Harper's had done on occasion?

Liveright outlined what he would guarantee: he would publish everything Dreiser submitted, promote the books to the hilt, fight any legal challenges raised by the comstocks, and pay advances of $500 to $1000 on each title, more for a novel. Those were astonishing concessions. But Dreiser still wasn't sure and so responded with a test. He offered Liveright *The Hand of the Potter* and also a collection of his short stories. When Liveright balked at the play, Dreiser told him the deal was off. The publisher came down to his studio and tearfully agreed to do the play.

The Hand of the Potter was scheduled to go to press in February 1918, but Dreiser began making extensive revisions to reflect his recent researches. When he felt doubts about something he was working on, he would gather more background material (hence the visit with Granich) and seek scientific confirmation on problems of character.

There was another delay. A wealthy couple dabbling in the theater wanted to produce *Potter* and paid Dreiser $1000 for the option. Liveright postponed publication until after the play was staged, to take advantage of the publicity. But after scoring a Broadway success with another, more conventional drama, the backers had second thoughts and backed out. The book was not issued until 1919.

The short story collection, *Free and Other Stories,* also ran into delays because of Dreiser's insistence on revising it "on the stone." In June, shortly after the *Potter* debacle, Liveright was complaining that "you have practically rewritten the whole book." It too would have to be postponed. But when Dreiser accused his publisher of caring only about the costs (rather than his desire to improve the book), Liveright swallowed his anger and apologized. It was becoming a habit.

•　　•　　•

Meanwhile Dreiser plugged on with *Newspaper Days.* He was in truth blocked on *The Bulwark*, later explaining to Mencken that he did not think a novel about a Quaker was appropriate in the prevailing martial atmosphere. At a time when the top sellers were stirring accounts of life at the front, it would have had a poor sale, and the antireligious passages in a book by him would bring out the comstocks in force. Also, he needed money to carry him through the writing of the novel, and he was having trouble selling short stories.

Although on Christmas Day 1917 he received a timely $750 check from *The Saturday Evening Post* for his story "Free," the New Year ushered in hard times. W. A. Swanberg added up Dreiser's rejections in 1918 and came up with the figure seventy-six. As Swanberg suggests, some of the pieces were rejected because they were pessimistic, radical philosophical essays such as "Hey, Rub-a-Dub-Dub!" "Equation Inevitable," "The American Financier," and "Neurotic America and the Sex Impulse." As Douglas Doty, now at *Cosmopolitan,* told Dreiser: "Once again you have written over the heads of our audience."

The short stories were another matter. Some, including "Free," "Love," and "The Old Neighborhood," were among Dreiser's best work in the form. Most of them were eventually published in magazines—but not in 1918. His score for that year was four stories and articles sold, bringing in a total of $1650.

Dreiser was out of step with the national mood and the taboos of commercial magazines. "Butcher Rogaum's Door" was rejected by *Red Book* because the characters were Germans. At *The Saturday Evening Post,* "Free" drew a tide of angry letters objecting to its implicit endorsement of divorce. As a result of the protests, the *Post* shelved another story by Dreiser that it had purchased in the interim. In April 1919 he sold three stories, including "Love," to Burton Kline at the New York *Tribune* magazine section for only $150 each. Kline had rejected a fourth, "Sanctuary," about a prostitute, telling Dreiser that "it might get me scalped if I put it in this polite family journal." He proved a poor judge of his employers' threshold of tolerance. "Love," an account of a faithless wife and an older husband who cannot break with her, cost him his job.

The message was not lost on Dreiser. In the summer of 1918 he attempted a patriotic article called "Rural America in Wartime." It describes home-front activities in and around a farming community in Maryland. His own contributions to the war effort were few, however. In July 1917 Dreiser received a request from E. L. Harvey, publicity director of the superpatriotic National Security League, calling him to the colors "as a member of the Vigilantes" to write an editorial of two hundred words on "What the Victory and Defeat of Germany Means to Every American." Seven months later, Harvey asked where his statement was. In 1919 Harvey was back to tell him that, the war having been won, the League was concentrating on "the menace of Bolshevism to America."

Again no response. Dreiser's attitude toward communism was, in fact, favorable. In November 1917, when Lenin's forces overthrew the parliamentary

Government of Alexander Kerensky, he wrote "Good" in his diary. And when Senator Hiram Johnson later made a speech criticizing U.S. participation in the Allied intervention against the Bolsheviks, Dreiser requested a copy of the speech from the senator's office.

In a March interview with David Karsner, associate editor of the socialist *New York Call,* he unburdened himself of some near-seditious thoughts: "The United States is intolerant because she is grossly ignorant, and knows nothing, cares for nothing and boasts of it, but money, money, money. We worship the man on top of the human pile and kick the man underneath who holds up the man on top."

The omnipresent smog of wartime patriotism nauseated him. In his diary he grouses, "The present political and war situation makes me sick. The canting fol de rol of American politicians!" While dining at Lüchow's he was disgusted by the spectacle of "Germans singing *America!*" But he no longer cheered on the German army. Hearing news of a recent German victory, he comments, "I hope they get a draw out of the war anyhow. It would never do to let England win."

Mencken's estrangement from Dreiser deepened at a time when both men felt acutely isolated. He told Boyd that Dreiser was "full of some obscure complaint against me, which I can't understand so I don't see him." Mencken would never, never apologize for his essay, dismissing Dreiser's grievances as "idiotic petulance." His letters were peppered with jabs at Dreiser's amorous proclivities. "He is doing little writing but devotes himself largely to the stud." "He still keeps his manly powers and is first cock in Greenwich Village."

The coolness between them had become common knowledge in literary circles, and when in March Ben Huebsch wrote them offering to mediate, Mencken replied that Dreiser had the mistaken idea that he was engaged in a critical vendetta. Far from it: "All I propose to do is to let him alone. . . . He has his own work to do, and I may be wrong. But my experience with the Dreiser Protest showed me exactly how susceptible he is to the flattery of self-seeking frauds, particularly those with cavities between their legs." To Estelle he wrote: "It goes without saying I would do anything in the world to help Dreiser as an artist, but I have a feeling I have written my last word about him."

In his reply to Huebsch, Dreiser sounded a wistful note: "I am overly fond of Mencken, literally. He is and always will be to me a warm, human, boyish soul, generous, honest and superior—so far above the average run that I cannot even think of him in connection with it." But he thought nothing could be done to repair the breach.

Although the exchanges with Huebsch had no immediate result, they served to draw off some of the venom. In May Dreiser apologetically sent Mencken a play, *Phantasmagoria,* and the essay "Hey, Rub-a-Dub-Dub!" which outlined his skepticism of all ethical credos. Mencken replied politely but foisted on Nathan the job of rejecting the play. He declined the essay on the ground that the *Smart Set* was in precarious financial health, and "a serious article would appear in it like a flash of common decency in a Methodist." But to Boyd he described the play as "awful stuff" and the essay as "ghastly," adding, "The latest news is that he is at work on a 'philosophical book.' You may well guess that fornication will be defended in it." A truce was in effect, he said: "I still avoid the old boy, though we do not quarrel."

In November Mencken revived the humorous note that had been missing from their letters. He reported that while in New York recently he had "succumbed to alcohol" with a friend and while in their cups they discussed Dreiser's sterling virtues and decided to pay him a call. Finding no one home, they deposited their "cards" — joke presents such as religious tracts; Black Hand threats; menus of Armenian restaurants; frankfurters tied with red, white, and blue ribbons; and inscribed photographs of the Czar.

At Christmastime, Dreiser sent Mencken an inscribed copy of a novel by Bertha M. Clay, a writer of sentimental romances, conveying "all my best wishes for your dearest happiness throughout the coming year May heaven protect and prosper you, Henry dear." To "Bertha Clay," Mencken wrote gratefully on Christmas Day: "What angel whispered to you to send me your lovely book? Last night, anticipating a heavy strain upon the liver and lights today, I took a dose of castor oil. Unluckily, my mind was upon other things, and so I swallowed a whole seidel of the damned stuff. Today I have been a prisoner within white-tiled walls, but my long vigil has been made happy by your incomparable tale of true love."

And so their anger cooled.

•   •   •

Mencken later said that in one way the war had been a boon to him. It had freed him from daily journalism, giving him the leisure to write five books, recharging him with new ideas and new material. Dreiser, however, drifted into a backwater. True, he wrote a handful of good short stories (the reviews of *Free and Other Stories* were mostly unsympathetic, however), but much of his work was dedicated to keeping himself afloat.

•   •   •

In July the Appellate Court at last handed down its decision in the *"Genius"* case. In essence, the justices ducked the issue; they held that since no prosecution had been brought, the question of obscenity was not before them. It was a narrow, legalistic ruling, and the upshot was that Sumner had banned

Dreiser's novel without a court's determining that it was obscene. *The "Genius"* was now adrift in a legal limbo.

So, it seemed, was *The Bulwark*. Dreiser's contract on *The "Genius"* gave Lane an option on his next novel, and Jones had advanced him $1800 and had made up salesmen's dummies. Dreiser contended that the sums advanced him had come from a general drawing account and were not for a specific title. He could point to letters from Jones suggesting that the publisher thought so too. He also argued that Jones's failure to issue *The "Genius"* in effect voided the present contract. Jones countered that Dreiser's contract contained a standard clause warranting that the book "contains nothing of a scandalous, immoral or libelous nature." Since the high court had refused to say the book was not obscene, Sumner's informal finding of immorality held.

•   •   •

Early in 1919 Mencken wrote Dreiser, "Why in hell don't you move out of New York, settle down in some small town, and finish *The Bulwark?* In brief, get away from visible America." Dreiser suspected he was playing mother hen: "I have the feeling that you are under the impression that I am idling in the extended arms of a harem dreaming sweet dreams and killing time. It is your Dreiser complex I fear." He defended his recent production: he had completed volumes I and II of his autobiography, known as *A History of Myself*, which was not quite true. A part of volume I, *Dawn*, had been retyped by Louise, but he had abandoned it, fearing family censorship; volume II, *Newspaper Days*, was still not done, but he had it well in hand. He had also written thirty-one essays; assembled sketches about turn-of-the-century New York, many of them written years ago for the collection called *Idylls of the Poor*; and composed some two hundred poems. And he planned to write another play: "I like tragedy and am looking for a great picture to be done briefly."

Dreiser was optimistic and hoped that the play and short stories would provide money to see him through *The Bulwark*, but he closed: "Personally, at this age, I have concluded that literature is a beggars game."

61 / *The Tragedy of Desire*

> Cries and moans all night. Claims she has no friends now and
> cannot leave me. I try to cheer her up, but no use. She lies
> beside me all curled up and weeping. Of such is the tragedy
> of desire.
> —Dreiser, Diary (1917)

Following the *"Genius"* decision, Dreiser tried again to form a group that would
help authors muzzled by the comstocks. In early 1919 he engaged in two
projects toward this end: (1) an organization with the clumsy name of the Society
for Certification and Endorsement, an attempt at setting up a mechanism to subsidize the publication or exhibition of worthy but uncommercial manuscripts
or art works; and (2) a radical literary magazine similar to *Seven Arts.*

A small sum of money was raised for the society and Harold Hersey hired
at a minuscule salary to invite prominent figures in the arts to join. He sent
out 275 letters in all and received only 50 favorable responses. In March he
reported to Dreiser that artists were an antisocial lot; he had spent $200 to
raise $140. The critical society quietly died of inanition.

As for the magazine, Liveright had volunteered to back it, and Merton
Yewdale agreed to serve as unpaid managing editor, supervised by Dreiser, who
would personally select the material. The journal would be a quarterly, sold in
bookstores. Mencken, who had been thinking about starting a magazine of his
own, suggested the name: *The American Quarterly.* Among potential contributors Dreiser listed the names of several radicals, including Eugene Debs, Emma
Goldman, John Reed, and "Big Bill" Haywood. Yewdale protested, pointing
out that Reds in the magazine's pages would bring the postal authorities down
on their neck. Wartime sedition statutes were still in effect. Indeed, Mencken
offered Dreiser the satirical "Declaration of Independence in American," then
withdrew it for fear of trouble with the law.

When Yewdale resigned to take an editorial post with Harper's, Dreiser abandoned the project. He was undoubtedly sincere in his efforts to advance the twin causes of serious literature and free expression in the United States. Reedy, a member of the editorial board, was skeptical, though, pointing to the high rate of failure of such ventures, which "have more freedom than they have art and the number of people who can really appreciate either freedom or art is very thinly dissipated through the mass of the population."

•   •   •

Dreiser's relations with his old critical champion had been rather distant during the war, for Reedy was strongly anti-German and privately thought Mencken's Nietzschean ideas were a bad influence on Dreiser. After Harris Merton Lyon, the young genius both men had encouraged at different times, died in 1916, Dreiser asked Reedy to write a foreword to a book of Lyon's stories (which was never published). But Reedy admitted he no longer cared for Lyon's work. To Dreiser, Lyon represented a martyred American genius, killed by America's indifference to artists. And so he grew cool toward Reedy and avoided him when he was in New York. On his part, Reedy was disturbed by Dreiser's portrayal of Lyon's mother in a sketch called "De Maupassant, Jr." He had shown it to Mrs. Lyon, who complained of its inaccuracy.

•   •   •

That sketch had appeared in Dreiser's new book, *Twelve Men*, published in April 1919. It was not the big novel his publisher was hoping for, but it was vintage Dreiser, and Mencken hailed it as "a capital piece of work." Dreiser accepted the kudos in silence; the book was, after all, a return to his earlier style and to turn-of-the-century America—as though he had at last heeded Mencken's criticisms of his avant garde stuff. And perhaps he had.

Some of the sketches in *Twelve Men* had been written as long ago as 1902 and 1903. But Dreiser reworked them considerably. They exemplify Dreiser's idea that goodness comes in unconventional guises. Most of the twelve men are the opposite of churchgoing do-gooders; their virtue is natural, uncontaminated by dogma.

This theory of unconventional goodness was embodied most fully in the portrait of Paul Dresser, the Broadway rounder and womanizer, who is tender-hearted and "generous to the point of self-destruction." There are contradictory aspects of Paul's character he doesn't touch on, but the essence of that corpulent figure was packed into the sketch's thirty-four pages.

Reviews of *Twelve Men* were generally good, but they did not win him a wider audience. Sales through June 30 totaled 1600 copies, and only 125 more were disposed of in the rest of the year. Still, it would be one of Dreiser's most enduring books. His vision of life is expressed movingly in the last sketch, the tribute to the artist W. L. Sonntag, Jr., who died young: "We toil so much, we dream so richly, we hasten so fast and lo! the green door is opened. We are through it, and its grassy surface has sealed us forever from all which we apparently so much crave—even as, breathlessly, we are still running."

Dreiser told Mencken that "for years" he had been planning a counterpart to *Twelve Men* called *A Gallery of Women*. "God what a work! if I could do it truly—The ghosts of Puritans would rise and gibber in the streets." Actually, an editor had suggested he do a series of articles on emancipated women in December 1917. But that would require new material and more research; besides, some of the subjects he had in mind were still in his life. During the past decade he had followed the program he conceived in the early 1900s—*Jennie,* the Cowperwood trilogy, and *The "Genius."* He had virtually abandoned the third volume of the Cowperwood saga, leaving only *The Bulwark* and that elusive novel about a murderer. After the aborted effort with Molineux, he persisted. He continued to research murder trials, seeking the "right" one. In July 1916, for example, he had read the morgue clippings on the William Orpet case, which involved a young man who had murdered his former sweetheart after taking up with a new girlfriend. He clipped some stories on the 1906 trial of Chester Gillette for the murder of his pregnant sweetheart, Grace Brown. And he very probably discussed these and other cases with Edward Smith, who was planning a book on criminology that would elucidate a glandular theory of criminal behavior.

Vying, so to speak, for Dreiser's attention was *The Bulwark*. As he now envisioned it, that novel would be ironic in tone and expose the illusory nature of religion and idealism. As he wrote in the *Call:* "All truth is inherently un-Christian, for Christianity—its theory—is a delusion." But the novel was a product of his Cowperwood period; indeed, the hero, Solon Barnes, is a pallid, pious antithesis of the philandering financier: "Solon was an idealist and as such it was his disposition to turn away from the hard cruel facts of life." He does not appear to like Solon very much; the man is a stick—almost a caricature. In later chapters he toys with making Solon a bluenose reformer. Reflecting Dreiser's own troubles with the censors, the novel seems to have evolved into an attack on the comstocks.

Dreiser's great strength as a writer was his ability to present sympathetically a wide range of characters, to become them and think as they did. If the vital energy of sympathy did not flow, the character lay dead on the page, and that is what happened to Solon Barnes.

•   •   •

His intellectual drift in these years had been away from a character like Solon, who represented the problem of goodness (in the conventional, religious sense). Now he was drawn to the problem of evil in the social sense—that is, crime, murder. In Savannah he had read Dostoevsky's *Crime and Punishment,* with its portrait of the murderer as a sinner outside the human community. But Raskolnikov had no ambitions; he was contemptuous of society's rewards. Dreiser's heroes and heroines struggled in the social web (save Cowperwood, a spider who preyed on the flies).

Not incidentally, he had around this time met Aleister Crowley, the self-proclaimed witch and devil worshiper, who fascinated him. Dreiser later told Burton Roscoe that Crowley represented the principle of misrule, of anarchy and disorganization. For all his unconventional ways, Dreiser viewed society, at least in the abstract, as requiring organization and stability. This need for order, deriving from his rootless childhood, represented one side of his temperament, the other being his hatred of convention and his need for spontaneity and creative and erotic freedom.

In *The "Genius"* Eugene Witla, reflecting on his amorous drives, believes he is possessed by the devil. Freud was opening the door to another closed room of Dreiser's life: sexuality. In 1918 Edith De Long Jarmuth had introduced him to Freud's basic essay "Three Contributions to the Theory of Sex." Dreiser later described the effect of his first reading of Freud: "At that time and even now quite every paragraph came as a revelation to me—a strong, revealing light thrown on some of the darkest problems that haunted and troubled me and my work." He likened psychiatry to a key that unlocked the mental prisons where guilty secrets were entombed.

Dreiser had personally experienced the tangled motives of sex, jealousy, and violence in his relationship with Estelle Kubitz. In November 1917, while they were dining at the Café New York (the prewar Kaiserhof), they quarreled over her possessiveness and his philandering, and he delivered an ultimatum: henceforth he would come and go as he chose, sleep with her or not as he liked. She burst into tears and fled to the ladies' room. When she returned, she announced that she was going to walk out on him. Dreiser told her, "If you do I'll run a knife through you. . . . If you go and leave me here before all these people I'll kill you. They've all seen you crying." "Yes," she sobbed, "every restaurant in New York has seen that, thanks to you." Afterward they went to a movie and then returned home. Dreiser resolved that he must break with her, but they made up.

•   •   •

Following his introduction to Freud, Dreiser sought to describe the role of the unconscious in an unpublished article he wrote some time in 1918, titled "It." *It,* inspired by Freud's id, is a primal animating force "compelling the body to act, and act vigorously, often violently." *It* is a dynamo humming silently in the basement of the mind, "ever at work, apparently, wishing, dreaming, ceaselessly planning. And of a sudden, growing weary of wishing or Its method of procedure finally thought out, It presents you, the general organization (the body), with Its idea. . . . The ego which lifts the poison to Its own lips (the machinery by which It eats), that whips from Its pocket the knife or the revolver, that defies laws, scoffs at governments, taboos, philosophies—what does It know or sense that we do not?"

He was too wedded to the physical and chemical explanation of human conduct to embrace Freud completely. In particular, he was troubled by the lack of laboratory verification of the Viennese doctor's theories. As he wrote A.A. Brill, the American translator of Freud, in December 1918, "Just below Freudianism lie the outer clouds of pure mysticism." But Freudianism provided an "X" factor that was missing from the behaviorist equation—that locked room of psychosexual compulsions that Dreiser recognized in himself. Estelle exemplified "the tragedy of desire," of love that is not returned.

•   •   •

On May 11, as Dreiser was crossing the street at Columbus Circle, he was struck by a car and suffered lacerations on his right hand and scalp. After receiving first aid, he was released, in considerable pain. Estelle insisted on nursing him, and he stayed with her for a time. Among his visitors were Kirah and her new friend, a husky blond engineer named Howard Scott, who was known in Village coffee shops as an eccentric advocate of a new economic doctrine called Technocracy. Scott had picked up some medical knowledge and performed chiropractic manipulations that relieved Dreiser's pain.

On June 15, his pain nearly gone but his writing hand *hors de combat,* Dreiser boarded a Pullman for Indiana. His first stop was Huntington, for a reunion with his old "mother-teacher" from Warsaw, May Calvert Baker, now nearly sixty, who lived there with her sister. Interviewed by a reporter from the Huntington *Press,* Dreiser blasted the Horatio Alger myth. An ambitious lad, he said, had no more chance of becoming another Rockefeller here than he did anywhere else in the world. And he scored the Red Scare sweeping the country, charging that anyone who criticized the "monied class" was clapped into jail as a Bolshevik.

While in Indiana he thought about a crime story he was writing, called "Her Boy." It was not based on an actual case, though Dreiser may have been recalling his brother Paul's boyhood friend in Sullivan, "Red" Bulger, who was executed at Sing Sing for a robbery-murder. The protagonist in the story had a brutal father, like Bulger's, but he grew up not in Sullivan but in the Philadelphia slums. He was no ordinary hoodlum; he had "an errant mind, subject to dreams, vanities, illusions, which had nothing to do with practical affairs"—a description that would have served for Clyde Griffiths.

•   •   •

For Dreiser 1919 was a time of uncertainty and ambiguity in both love and work. He had long wanted a liberal publisher and now had him in Liveright. But his frustrations with The "Genius" and The Bulwark remained. He needed money; his landlord was raising his rent. Also, he was tiring of the place, now so full of Estelle's presence.

They were sinking into a kind of Bohemian domesticity. They went to restaurants and plays together, had dinners at Marion's, spent weekends at the shore, and he found this routine dangerously close to monogamy. But when she announced a new plan "to stay away nights," he immediately suspected that she had a lover, noting, "She has so little interest in sex now." Jealousy was followed by reconciliation. "Feel very sad to think affection is always jealous and painful, in myself and everyone," he writes after a quarrel. Like the couple in "Chains," they were locked together by bonds of need and sexual desire. He had written of such a love in a poem: "And love that need is, and would love its need—"

A month later he told Estelle that he was through. Again she threatened to walk out, but he called her bluff and she backed down. He sums up his attitude toward her: "I feel sorry for her, truly, but what can you do in this world, which is so unbalanced, all running after the few successful, all ignoring the hopelessly poor or unsuccessful or defective. Life is made for the strong. There is no mercy in it for the weak—none."

In August 1919, "worried about my work & income," he summoned his "psychic control"—the genius or oversoul he believed watched over him—and asked it to send him a sign. That night he had a dream: "I was possessed of a key by the aid of which I was able to fly—much to my delight." He flew over cities and vast territories, to the admiration of all. Then he landed on a high rock, and was unable to go farther because his magical key's powers had run out. Interpreting the dream, he wondered if it meant that his "mental & literary soaring days were over."

If he had consulted Freud's book on dreams, he would have read: "The close connection of flying with the idea of birds explains how it is that in men flying dreams usually have a grossly sensual meaning, and we shall not be surprised when we hear that some dreamer or other is very proud of his powers of flight."

The dream obviously derived from his fears that he was losing his potency and, concomitantly, the literary power that enabled him to soar above admiring crowds in cities. In the dream appeared "one with a key like mine who imitated me"—a generic younger rival, sexual and literary.

A month later he wrote in his diary: "This day I met Helen."

Part Ten

• • •

HOLLYWOOD

62 / *The Golden Girl*

We whisper & dream of New Orleans & Los Angeles & what
the west will bring us. Such dreams. Helen wants a bungalow
& a car & flowers and a pet lion & what not. It is a fairy tale
come true.

—Dreiser (Diary)

On Saturday, September 13, Dreiser was writing at his desk when the doorbell
rang. He slipped on the Chinese robe he wore about the house—in his haste
putting it on inside out, an omen of impending change. Standing shyly on the
stoop was a young woman he judged to be nineteen or twenty. She told him she
was a distant cousin from the western branch of the family—her grandmother,
Ester Schänäb Parks, was Dreiser's aunt, whom he had never met. She asked
for Ed Dreiser's address, and he gave it to her, then requested hers. His left
eye—the good one—was, he felt, sending him a message, meaning he was
extraordinarily attracted to her. He gave her a copy of *The Hand of the Potter*,
autographed "To my little Oregon cousin."

That was the first meeting of Dreiser and Helen Patges Richardson. She was
not nineteen but twenty-five, beautiful with a kind of "lympathic sensuality"
that acted on him, he said, like an aphrodisiac. Her golden-brown hair hung
down to her shoulders, her figure was full and shapely, and her eyes glowed
with a mischievous gaiety.

He tossed most of the night thinking about her, and the next morning
called her and asked her to meet him at the Pennsylvania Roof. She agreed
to come in the afternoon, and over a late breakfast they talked for hours. She
showed her sympathy to his work by praising *The Hand of the Potter* and promised
to read all his novels. He asked her to dinner with him on Tuesday, but she
said she couldn't. He was desolate; maybe she didn't like him after all. They
walked to the subway station, where he parted from her plunged in gloom.
She promised to come again on Wednesday, but he didn't believe her. He was
sure he had lost her forever.

All day Wednesday he waited for her call. He was trying to revise his book of philosophy but could not concentrate. A letter from Lill arrived, boasting of her triumph in a new show, but that merely bored him. He visited Estelle, "but my interest in her is so dead that I merely wonder how I can get away— once & for all." He was amazedly in love and recording as evidence his lack of attraction for others.

At 6:30 Helen appeared at his door. He took her in his arms and kissed her; she responded passionately, but she refused to stay with him that night. He told her there must be a physical relationship between them; he could not just be friends. Finally, she agreed to come Friday.

After their first night together, he wrote in his diary: "a new chapter in my life is opening which [may] lead anywhere. . . . My life seems torn up by the roots. Feel that I am in for a long period with her, maybe years."

•   •   •

The dreams and omens were right. Change had come. In the space of less than a month, he and Helen decided to go to Los Angeles, where she would try to break into the movies; he accepted an offer from Jesse Lasky, head of the Famous Players–Lasky studio and a friend of Liveright, to write screenplays; he signed a contract with Liveright for *The Bulwark* under which he would receive an advance of $4000, to be paid in twelve monthly installments of $333.33; and he sublet his apartment to his old friend Eleanora O'Neill, now married to William McQuaid.

Lasky had bought out Mirror Films, for which Dreiser had written a few scripts. Lasky apparently hoped a writer of his stature would produce some usable scenarios, while Dreiser hoped to reap bushels of Hollywood dollars by tossing off screenplays and selling his novels to Famous Players or some other studio. A Hollywood agent had offered to represent him.

Possibly, Dreiser's arrangement with Lasky precipitated the signing of *The Bulwark* contract in August. Liveright wanted the novel badly, and his lawyer had advised him that although Lane could be expected to sue, he had no con-tractual claim on the book that would stand up in court. For a gambler like Liveright it was worth a flutter.

And so with a stroke Dreiser cut through his publishing entanglements, and Helen, through her powerful sexual magnetism, provided the solution to his romantic ones. He couldn't have gone off with any woman, but she seemed to be All-Woman.

•   •   •

Born in Oregon, she was the daughter of the former Ida Parks and George Patges, a Danish immigrant who one day walked out for good, leaving his wife with two daughters to raise. When Ida's mother, Esther, sold her farm and bought a hotel in Portland, Ida and her children tagged after her; Helen was around five at the time. The hotel was frequented by vaudevillians who performed at the theater next door. There was also a local repetory theater nearby. The little girl was fascinated by the actors and longed to accompany them on their travels. She had the run of the theater, sometimes taking children's parts in the rep company's productions. By age fourteen she was performing in amateur theatricals. She had also worked in an art supply store since she was ten. A beautiful child, she caught the eye of older men and learned to exploit them for money and presents. One old man gave her a dollar if she would let him fondle her. By the time she was a teenager, she was prematurely wise to the ways of sex and strung along a wealthy old man, who gave her presents.

When she was sixteen, she met nineteen-year-old Frank Richardson, a slender, handsome visitor from Charleston, South Carolina, who was as stagestruck as she was. They fell in love and were married, and Frank formed an act with three young men, singing in saloons around town. With that experience he worked up a ballroom dance routine for himself and Helen. They had a modest success, making up to ninety dollars a week playing cities in the Northwest. After bouncing around the circuit for three or four years, they decided to try San Francisco. But there the act reached the end of its run. Richardson decided to return to his family in Charleston, while Helen tried to go it alone.

After a year of struggling, Helen became discouraged and joined him. Fed up with the theater, Frank had embarked on a business career. But the marriage was on its last legs; she found southern ways too confining for her Bohemian spirit and hankered for New York. In 1918 William E. Woodward, a friend of the Richardson family and vice president in charge of public relations at the Industrial Finance Corporation, owner of the Morris Plan loan societies, visited Charleston, and Helen told him of her ambition to go to New York someday. He was attracted to her and offered to help her if she ever did make the move. In 1918 she did, leaving Frank for good. Woodward hired her as his secretary after she took a refresher course in typing and shorthand, and they had an affair.

Woodward confided in her that he was bored with business and planned to quit his job when he was fifty and write a novel. He admired Dreiser and gave Helen a copy of *Twelve Men* to read. When she told him Dreiser was her second cousin, he urged her to call on him. She naively extolled her new lover's prowess to her boss, who was not at all pleased to hear about it, and she realized it was time for her to leave.

She had saved some money toward her goal of becoming a film actress. When she revealed her dreams to Dreiser, he immediately fell in with them because of his own movie ambitions. Both of them were drawn by the golden dream of an abundant life and an Edenic climate that was luring thousands of Americans from the Middle West.

• • •

On October 8 Dreiser and Helen boarded the liner *Momus* (God of Ridicule and Censure, he noted in his diary) bound for New Orleans. Sequestered in their cabin, they told each other fairy tales of a land of perpetual sunshine, rose-trellised bungalows, fruit trees, and shiny automobiles. "We were like two children, hand in hand, united in a common bond—the love of beauty," Helen later wrote.

In New Orleans they holed up in a romantic old hotel on a picturesque square. It was there that she gained her first insight into him. There was a picture in the room showing a farm scene, and he remarked it was like one his mother had. Watching him gaze fondly at the picture, Helen realized how strong was the cord of memory that bound him to Sarah Dreiser; later she would learn how much the loss of her had instilled in him "a fear of losing anything he loved very much."

The four-day train trip to Los Angeles was an erotic fantasy come to life. "Her beauty just knocks me. It is unbelieveable. . . . She looks like an angel or a classic figure & yet is sensuality to the core." The allure of her naked body was "simply maddening," her white skin was blue-veined like marble. He couldn't believe "she is as insane over me as she seems. It seems as though some one must have hypnotized her & told her that she was in love with me." He was in the perilous role of adorer and worried about it: "The constant distrust of Helens beauty & how it may make me suffer tortures me."

After continuing their idyll in Los Angeles, they rented the lower floor of a two-story house in the small town of Highland Park, set amid rolling golden hills. The area was swarming with cults. Their landlord would greet them each morning with a stentorian "PRAISE THE LORD!" Dreiser sent a jaundiced report to Mencken: "The place is full of healers, chiropracters, chiropodists, Christian Scientists, New Thoughters, Methodists, Baptists, Ana-Baptists and movie actors. . . . This climate is 90 percent over advertised. There's not one decent restaurant & the drinking water has alkali in it. I have lost 10 pounds in weight."

His disenchantment may have been caused in part by the obstacles he was encountering. The first time he dropped in at the Lasky studio in Hollywood, he was turned away at the gate. The same day he received a telegram from Liveright saying that Jones was threatening to sue over *The Bulwark*. Liveright tactfully inquired about his progress on the novel, which had been promised for delivery on August 1.

He had put in a day or so on the manuscript, then set it aside for two months to work on photoplays. He at last gained admission into Lansky's sanctum on December 30, only to learn that all his screenplays had been rejected. It was a depressing finale for the year of 1919.

Dreiser and Helen explored the hills near their rented home and made excursions to Catalina Island and San Diego. After a month of this, Dreiser wrote in his diary, "More idling with H——which worries me—however delightful." The weather was bad, prices were too high, and they were discovering irritating qualities in each other. Helen had petulant streaks; she was like a child who becomes angry when real life doesn't live up to her dreams. She would throw tantrums in shops when they didn't have what she wanted.

He was liable to fits of jealous fury when he imagined she was flirting with some man or when she received letters from former male friends. She thought he was pompous and overly critical of her. Once, when she forgot to take his silk shirts to the laundry, he blew up and called her "the most infernally lazy creature I ever knew." Such outbursts would make her freeze with anger, then burst into tears, and Dreiser would console her and feel guilty afterward.

For all the minor frictions, he was crazy about her. He called her his "Golden Girl." She had an intuitive love of beauty, combined with a crass materialism; she admired a sunset and a dress in the store with equal rapture. He liked her earthy humor and recorded her mannerisms in his diary under the heading "Babes Cute Ways." He liked her wisecracks, the way she said "Next" when coming out of the bathroom and her baby talk. She was vain, bawdy, and refined. She wore high heels wherever they went, applied makeup before going to bed, and favored beribboned shortie nightgowns called teddy bears. She was the most wanton and sensual woman he had ever known; in her transports she recited "the most coaxing and grossly enervating words . . ." But her seductive presence distracted him from his work: "From 10 to twelve I work on mss. Two to 4:30 play with Helen. We copulate 3 times. At 5 return to work & at 7 get dinner. 9 P.M. to bed."

•   •   •

As their stay in California lengthened into months, Dreiser began observing the curious folkways of Hollywood. The movie industry was rapidly taking over the conservative little agricultural town. Land formerly planted in orchards was overrun by actors and camera crews; sets were erected under the skies and covered by canvas when an indoor lighting effect was desired. The whole town was a set, and its citizens watched as cars full of Keystone Kops careered along the streets. By 1920 large, walled studio complexes were rising up, with massive gates before which hordes of hopefuls gathered each morning for casting calls.

Ever more grandiose sets were being erected, sparked by the success of D. W. Griffith's *Intolerance*.

Dreiser's first impression was that he had landed in a unique colony of anti-Puritans. In a letter to Margaret Johnson, an actress he had known in New York, he writes approvingly of Hollywood's amorality: "When I watch these men & beauties in the seething movie world where success and pleasure hold their proper place as goals, I see what a brilliant interesting thing a pagan world is. Moralistic cant & religious theory kill life."

Once, he and Helen strolled by the Beverly Hills Hotel and Douglas Fairbanks and Mary Pickford's mansion. As Helen spoke fervently of her movie career and her bungalow dreams, Dreiser cursed his financial state: "*She is too beautiful not to have a car & I resent our poverty.*" A few days later, in a kind of symbolic protest, she pawned her ring and went on a shopping binge, buying two hats, a dress, a pair of shoes, and some stockings. It was, Dreiser thought, an act of "wild desperation over not having all the money she wants." He grew more depressed about the paucity of money coming in and the impending cut-off of the Liveright subsidy for *The Bulwark*. Helen, who had been devoting her time to typing his screenplays, decided to launch her long-planned assault on the studios. They moved to 588 North Larchmont Street, within walking distance of Hollywood and Vine.

In early May she landed her first job as an extra. When she came home, she tactfully presented him her first paycheck — for $7.50 — then regaled him with stories of how the director and the producer had flirted with her. Although she swore she rejected their overtures, it was for Dreiser an unsettling introduction to the pressure on pretty young women to be friendly with their male bosses if they wanted a job.

One day, "horribly" lonely, he conceived a story called "Bleeding Hearts," about a drab clerk who grows jealous of his beautiful wife's success in the cinema and murders her.

At times he felt himself a has-been, and this crept into another story, called "Fulfillment." To the extent that the story is autobiographical, it shows Dreiser purging his sense of failure, symbolized by having the hero's paintings command higher prices after his death than they did in life.

Helen's next job (ironically, at Famous Players–Lasky) required her to work nights. "Helen gets in at 7 A.M. — delivered by auto. She has made a big impression," he records. She gossiped about the intrigues on the set and fending off passes and the resentment of the rival actresses and about the star, Bebe Daniels. Helen was filmed undressing behind a screen and in a teddy bear nightgown; in another scene she danced on a table. "This sex struck country," Dreiser sniffs in his diary. The houri of his private fantasies would display her beauty on the screen before millions of strangers.

She scaled the Hollywood ladder rapidly—a week's work at $10 a day, directors asking for her by name, an increase to $12.50. In contrast, he was alone all day, futilely trying to write serious stories and screen "hoakum." His confidence ebbing, he was losing his way. He felt depressed because he could not offer her a life as exciting as she was leading on the set. He seriously wondered if she might leave him for her more exciting friends in the movie world—even as she was accusing him of growing bored with her! They were a symbiotic pair, need feeding on need.

But he grew fascinated with her career, vicariously participating in it by helping her choose a new wardrobe, suggesting the materials for three new gowns, supervising the taking of a set of glamour photographs. He admired her "youth & beauty & force & ambition" and hoarded her gossip about the movie business, amassing enough material for several articles. She held herself superior to the actress who submitted to the directors' demands. It was all right, she told him, for a "low" type of woman to rise via the casting couch, but not a "refined" woman.

Then some money came in from the sale of two short stories to *Live Stories* for $400, and an optimistic letter arrived from Lengel about a possible sale of the abridged version of *The "Genius"* to the same magazine for $3000. His gloom lifted temporarily.

• • •

At the center of his literary troubles was *The Bulwark*. He returned to it at the end of February, but after a few days' desultory work, he and Helen made a trip to Santa Barbara. When they came back, he was in no better frame of mind about the novel. On April 4 he writes in his diary "I am depressed about Bulwark" and five days later he announces that he has finished reworking chapter 13, but it was "terrible hard work. No gayety of soul here." On April 22 he wrote Liveright that he was drudging on the book "with little joy and with small expectations." The small expectations part was a dig at his publisher for the poor sales of *Twelve Men*, although those had reached a fairly respectable 4000 by this time and were continuing. Liveright reminded him that it was unfair to compare a collection of short stories with a novel—speaking of which, where was *The Bulwark*?

But Dreiser was fatally blocked. In July he mentioned to Lengel that he might start another novel. A month later he wrote Mencken that "*The Bulwark* lags but should be along by Christmas or if not that—then a novel of equal force." He said nothing further about this mysterious other novel, but the evidence suggests that he began writing it in August. The first allusion to it in his diary does not occur until September 6: "In the morning Helen & I walk over the hills above Echo Park Ave. into Alessandro Street. The woman on the hill who looked like Mrs. Dreiser. . . . I work on 'An American Tragedy' till 4 P.M."

•   •   •

Helen wrote in *My Life with Dreiser* that the fundamentalist religious atmosphere in Highland Park "supplied the necessary climate" for starting *An American Tragedy,* which at this point he sometimes called "Mirage." The generative climate was also the Hollywood air, electric with sex, success, and money, charging Dreiser's and Helen's yearnings. Murder was, surprisingly, also in the air for one whose mind was attuned to suggestions of it. At a restaurant Dreiser frequented, the Welcome Inn, the owner was an Englishman who quarreled viciously with his wife. After seeing one of those rows, Dreiser wrote in his diary in July, "I suspect he plans to kill her."

A sensational murder that dominated the front pages when he arrived may have revived his interest in the novel about a murderer. Harry New, the illegitimate son of Senator New, now postmaster general of the United States, had killed his lover. Harry's sweetheart had become pregnant, and he demanded that she marry him. When she refused, he murdered her and immediately confessed. New pleaded guilty to second-degree murder and was considered mentally unbalanced.

More strongly influencing Dreiser's choice of a protagonist was the book he had just completed, *Newspaper Days,* in which he recalls standing on Euclid Avenue in Cleveland, gazing at the mansions and "envying the rich and wishing that I was famous or a member of a wealthy family, and that I might meet with some one of the beautiful girls I imagined I saw there and have her fall in love with me."

The reacquaintanceship, as it were, with the struggles of his youth predisposed Dreiser to choose a protagonist with a similar background, making the crime a tragedy of youthful ambition and desire. He had abandoned the novel about Molineux because he could not work up empathy with a character from an upper-class background. He had tried, in "Her Boy," to tell of a slum-born criminal, but Eddie Meagher's criminal career is a product of environment—the slums—which Dreiser did not know.

The most recent false scent was the Richesen case. In 1914 the Reverend Clarence Richesen had killed Avis Linnell, his pregnant lower-class sweetheart, after being called to the pastorship of a fashionable church in Boston, where he met a beautiful young woman from a good family who fell in love with him. Dreiser later said, "I planned to write this as *the* American tragedy, and I did write six chapters of it before I decided to change Clyde Griffiths." The character of a minister who was educated and from a good family was not what he had in mind.

After eliminating the Richesen murder, Dreiser turned to the one that he had been looking for all along: the 1906 murder of Grace (Billy) Brown by Chester Gillette. On August 13 he wrote to W. Earl Ward, district attorney of Herkimer County, New York, who had prosecuted Gillette, requesting the records of Gillette's appeal, which would include transcripts of the court proceedings. Ward was unable to furnish it, but suggested he try Gillette's lawyer, Charles D. Thomas. Dreiser did not get hold of the transcripts, since they comprised three huge volumes. The only other source would be newspaper accounts, and he relied on the New York *World*'s coverage of the trial in writing his novel.

In Chester Gillette Dreiser must have seen a poor, ordinary, seeking young man with whom he instinctively indentified. Another link was the fact that Gillette's parents had been Salvation Army officers. He had once told Mencken that he intended to write a story about a "street preacher," and it was no great step to imagine his protagonist's parents running a small mission. Perhaps the precipitating factor was a cinematic image that became the opening scene of the first draft and remained in the book when it was published more than five years later:

> Dusk—of a summer night.
>   And the tall walls of the commercial heart of an American city of perhaps 400,000 inhabitants—such walls as in time may linger as a mere fable. And up the broad street now comparatively hushed, a little band of six—a man of about fifty, short, stout, with bushy hair protruding from under a round black felt hat, a most unimportant-looking person, who carried a small portable organ such as is customarily used by street preachers and singers. . . .

And then the description of a twelve-year-old boy named Clyde Griffiths, unwillingly trudging behind his family of street evangelists, as though ashamed of them and of the work they did and their willful poverty and illusory faith that "God will provide," when He obviously hadn't, feeling the first stirrings of a desire to escape the drab piety of their lives.

Now this Clyde Griffiths bore little relation to Chester Gillette other than having the same initials. Dreiser had only a sketchy background to work with, but the precise details weren't important. What struck him was Chester's strict religious background, his seemingly ineffectual father and stronger mother, his poverty, his early wanderings, his chance meeting with his rich uncle, who offers Chester a job in his factory—like a scene from a Horatio Alger novel, his ambiguous social position as a poor relation, his affair with Grace Brown, his involvement with a girl from a wealthy family, his murder of his pregnant factory-girl sweetheart.

In fact, there was no love triangle in the Gillette case. A young woman named Harriet Benedict, daughter of a wealthy lawyer, was called to the stand because letters to her were found in Gillette's effects. But she testified that she had only one date with Chester, and that he went out with several girls from well-off Cortland families whom he met at various parties and church socials, while carrying on with Grace. The yellow press, taking its cue from the prosecution, blew up Harriet's role in Chester's life to that of the "other woman." From that fiction, Dreiser took his plot: poor, ambitious young man falls in love with a rich girl and kills his pregnant lower-class sweetheart.

Another element in the case that intrigued Dreiser was the manner in which Gillette murdered Brown. According to the prosecution, and the jury concurred, he took her out in a boat on Big Moose Lake in the Adirondacks, struck her with a tennis racket, and pushed her overboard. This more dramatic crime had a private resonance for Dreiser, relating to his subconscious fear of drowning that traced back to his childhood experience in a boat on the Wabash River with his black-sheep brother, Rome.

Although the facts of the Gillette case provided the framework for *An American Tragedy,* the true source lay deep within himself.

63 / *The Tangled Web*

> I am and have been conducting an individual struggle to live
> and write and I will continue so to do as my best wits help
> me.
>
> —Dreiser to Mencken (1920)

While Dreiser made a tentative start on the *Tragedy,* Helen's career gained momentum. In September she won a small role in Metro's production of *The Four Horsemen of the Apocalypse,* starring Rudolph Valentino. She scored "a great hit" on the set. Her modest rise, fueled by extravagant hopes, made success seem almost in hand. Now she was torn between Dreiser and her career—and feeling guilty about neglecting him.

He was making some progress on *An American Tragedy.* One day he took time off to visit a storefront mission, for background on Clyde's parents. He worked a bit on another project at this time, an article on Edgar Allan Poe. Even this was not completely alien to the novel. Poe's phantasmagorical stories reflected the nightmarish aspect of modern life, a dimension, Dreiser believed, that traditional realism neglected.

In a 1921 interview he said that much contemporary realistic fiction lacked "the power of imagination." Alluding to the current celebration of the seven-hundredth anniversary of Dante's death, he said that if the Italian master were alive today, "he would have gone beyond mere realistic description and shown us the half-monstrous proportions of our city like a giant sphinx with wings. The power of such imagination would lift a modern book into glorious fantasy. . . . [Contemporary novelists] are content to examine the inside of a boarding house or chronicle the mere number of windows in the colossal stone and steel shells of our buildings. They stick close to the curbstone. They rarely climb any such heights as Dante climbed to look out over the tremendous wastes of lives."

A related influence, surely, was the cinema. He had seen *The Cabinet of Dr. Caligari* and was much taken by its expressionistic style, which suggested, in surreal backdrops and cinematography, the subconscious—or soul, as the Germans would have it—and which evoked the subjective world of madness. The

film graphically dramatized the power of delusions; dream and reality inter-
mingle, and nothing is what it seems. (And in the movie there was a somnam-
bulistic murderer—a killer without volition.)

But there was also an element of identification with Poe. Probably drawing on Mencken's essay on puritanism, Dreiser had concluded that Poe was a
martyr to the Puritans, who had "a horror of reality" and who drove him to
drink and despair. Dreiser sometimes felt that he too had been hounded by the
Puritans into obscurity. Poe's temperament, being artistic, was too sensitive
and vulnerable, Dreiser believed. Few respectable people had any conception
of the mental torments these "physically denuded spirits" suffered. Drink provided Poe an escape into illusion; religion served that function for others. As
he wrote to Edward Smith, who accused him of embracing Christian Science
in The "Genuis," "Religion is a bandage for sore brains. Morality ditto. It is the
same as a shell to a snail. The blistering glare of indefinable forces would destroy most, were it not for the protecting umbrella of illusion." And he added,
"My next novel, which will soon be ready, will clear the air once and for all."
At this point he could have meant either The Bulwark or An American Tragedy,
also known as "Mirage."

•   •   •

The psychological motifs of those letters would find their way into the first
draft of An American Tragedy. He writes that Clyde Griffiths was teased by other
children and as a result developed "a concealed somberness or morbidity which
grew directly out of the wounds inflicted upon a sensitive and decidedly respon-
sive psyche." And a fight with another youth causes a "deep psychic wound . . .
which was destined to fester and ramify in strange ways later on." Dreiser concludes with a pseudo-Freudian interpretation. The wound "by some psychic
process of inversion . . . gave him a greater awe of wealth and comfort—or at
least a keener perception of the protective qualities of a high social position in
life."

Inevitably, the narrative became bogged down in Dreiser's own history.
The plot, after some twenty chapters, had not moved Clyde out of adolescence.
Dreiser seemed to have had no conception of where he was going. He needed
more information on the crime and the trial, and the execution too, so that
he could extricate the narrative from the bog of his own life and move it to a
fictional plane. Dreiser needed reality on which to ground his fiction.

•   •   •

In June, having received nothing from his author beyond fifteen chapters of The
Bulwark, Liveright took the offensive: "Everyone is waiting for a Dreiser novel.
When I tell some of the most important people in the trade that I have already

received the first third of the book, they laugh and say, 'Oh, that was written several years ago.'" And he twisted the knife a little by mentioning that Francis Hackett, in his unfavorable review of *Hey, Rub-a-Dub-Dub!*, a collection of his philosophical essays, which had been published in January, called Dreiser "our leading novelist," implying that Dreiser should stick to his last.

If Liveright meant to shame his author, which he surely did, he was going about it the wrong way. *Hey, Rub-a-Dub-Dub!* was close to Dreiser's heart, and the reviews of it had been by no means all bad. Dreiser's philosophical effusions, while subjective, unconventional, even eccentric, expressed the temperament (in all its contradictions) behind the books. Mencken roasted the book in *Smart Set*, as he had warned Dreiser he would do. He explained to Dreiser, "I could have done that book much better myself, whereas I couldn't have done a single chapter of *Twelve Men* or *Sister Carrie*."

Liveright continued his hectoring. "You are keeping your public waiting entirely too long," he said. "Everyone is clamoring for a novel from you and what they get instead is short stories, essays, plays or whatnot." Dreiser countered by accusing Liveright of not promoting his books, and he informed Mencken, "Quietly and under cover I am negotiating a return to Harper and Brothers."

Unaware of Dreiser's maneuvers, Liveright appealed to Dreiser's vanity: "We simply must not let Sinclair Lewis, Floyd Dell, Sherwood Anderson, etc. do all the writing of the 'great American novel.' "

This tactic succeeded in drawing from Dreiser a confession that he was unable to finish *The Bulwark* and had begun another novel, about which he would have nothing further to say until it was completed. As for those writers who were threatening his preeminence: "The truth is, as you ought to know by now, that my love is for the work itself and after that I would like to see it sold so that I might get a little something out of it. Beyond that little interests me, not even the arrival of a thousand geniuses. They do not help me to write my books and they do not stop me. As I say I do the very best I can."

•   •   •

Then Liveright heard that Dreiser was dickering with other publishers over *Newspaper Days*—or, rather, *A Novel About Myself*, as Dreiser was now calling the book. He dispatched a telegram: PLEASE ASK LENGEL OR MENCKEN TO SEND ME IMMEDIATELY MANUSCRIPT NOVEL ABOUT MYSELF FOR SPRING PUBLICATION. WIRE ANSWER.

Dreiser drafted a tortuous reply to Liveright's telegram. Because of Liveright's harping on *The Bulwark*, Dreiser said, he had assumed he was not interested in *Newspaper Days*. He said that Harper's had offered him $2000 for *Newspaper Days*, but he had no objection to Liveright as a publisher: "Where you are really interested you seem to do a great deal. The only thing for an author to do though is to get your real interest or move. For more reasons than one I always feel that I am entitled to considerable interest and aid, because . . . my public connection with a house is of great value to it."

As ever, Liveright backed down. He wired Dreiser an offer of $1000 for *Newspaper Days*. It might not be as good as the Harper's tender, he explained, but "after all you know that an advance is really more or less in the nature of an evidence of good faith." The ideal plan would be to publish *Newspaper Days* in the spring and the new novel in the fall. Naturally, he would not regard the latter as a substitute for *The Bulwark* but would advance an amount commensurate with what it was worth.

The bid of $2000 that Dreiser mentioned was a fantasy. Harper's had simply asked to see the manuscript. On January 4, 1921, William H. Briggs, editor-in-chief of the firm, wrote Dreiser that he thought *Newspaper Days* a "splendid work"; however, Dreiser's proposal that Harper's issue all four volumes of his projected autobiography was out of the question. "The present is not the time to announce and to begin the publication of a three or four volume autobiographical work. It is the time for a fine big piece of creative imaginative fiction by Theodore Dreiser." Now, if he would only send them a novel, one that was not contracted to another house and preferably "one with some commercial possibilities," then Harper's would be willing to talk about publishing the four volumes of the autobiography.

What Dreiser needed was a publisher whom he could trust, who would fight the censors, and who was willing to wait five years for a Dreiser novel. Actually, in Liveright, he had such a paragon, though neither of them knew it.

He could be pardoned for being disheartened by the poor commercial prospects of a serious writer in America. He told Edward Smith, who was preparing a profile of him for *The Bookman*, "I can safely [say] *all* who have attempted liberal and artistic writing in the best sense in America have failed, not of artistic achievement in the main but of public recognition and support." To write a book that criticized the American businessman, or father or mother or family, ensured unpopularity: "the writer of a serious interpretation of America is more or less a scoundrel, a low fellow. I hope I have the honor to be one."

•   •   •

After nearly a year's correspondence, Liveright and Dreiser were no further along than when they started; nor had Dreiser found another publisher. Nor had he progressed on his novel. Nor had his screenwriting career advanced a fraction of an inch. Lasky and others had rejected all the scenarios he wrote, causing him to mutter darkly to Estelle Kubitz of a "plot" against him at the studio.

He took his revenge on Hollywood by writing a gossipy, three-part series called "Hollywood: Its Morals and Manners," which ran in late 1921 in a film magazine called *Shadowland*. Apparently, movie executives were shocked by the series, which appeared not long after the Fatty Arbuckle scandal hit the front pages. Dreiser had excised from the piece some gossip about the case, in which the rotund comedian had been charged with raping and fatally injuring a starlet during an orgy in a San Francisco hotel. Three juries failed to indict Arbuckle, but he was barred from the movies for life, and Will Hays, a Republican politician, was brought in as "czar" to clean up the movies. The effect on Dreiser of all this was to make novels like *Sister Carrie,* with its heroine who goes unpunished for her sins, and *The Financier,* with its immoralist hero, unfilmable.

Up to that point Dreiser had envied the movies their sexual frankness, and a producer had even been interested in filming *The Hand of the Potter,* though that project fell through. But in November came the news that the avant garde Provincetown Players wanted to stage the tragedy. George Cram Cook, the director, dickered with Dreiser over the guarantee, with the latter demanding $500 and Cook pointing out that in the small theater the maximum weekly gross was only $1400. They compromised on a lower figure, and the play quickly went into rehearsal.

Opening night was December 5. In their notices the next day the critics from the major dailies were divided on which was worse, the production or the play. The headline over the *Herald*'s review read: PROVINCETOWN PLAYERS IN REPULSIVE PLAY. The *World*'s tag was "A Misuse of the Theatre," and its critic's verdict was that the play was "conspicuously offensive." Most of the major papers did not send their top reviewers, and the notices that appeared were brief and dismissive.

And so *The Hand of the Potter* faded into theatrical history, one of the most controversial plays to appear in the decade. Clumsy as it was, Dreiser's tragedy had stretched the moral boundaries of the theater in a healthy way.

• • •

In January Dreiser wrote in his diary: "Am wishing for money & success in my work." He sat in a dark room and meditated, "trying *to repeat Experiment of 1909.*" He meant 1919, when he had asked his control—the genius or guiding spirit that he speaks of only in his diaries—to send him a sign, and dreamed of flying. This time the message was, "Help will come." But it didn't.

He missed the energy and intellectual stimulus of New York. "There is no art in Los Angeles and Hollywood," he complained to an interviewer. "And never will be."

Even the financial insecurity that chronically plagued him was absent, despite his unproductiveness. Helen's movie earnings enabled them to achieve their original dream of buying a little bungalow. Both had tired of the gypsy life they were leading; they had lived in six different places since they had arrived. Driving through Glendale one evening, they spotted a white cottage with green shutters on a small plot of land with a vacant lot next door. They decided to buy it. The price was $4500, and they paid $1000 down and $50 a month on a mortgage, which was cheaper than their rent at their previous residence, a tiny brown stucco house in Hollywood.

For a while Helen's sister Myrtle and her boyfriend, Grell, were their constant companions. Grell conveyed the four of them around in his automobile on weekends. The young couple livened up Dreiser's cloistered existence, and he unconsciously absorbed their slangy banter, their fascination with cars and clothes, and their tastes in popular songs. No longer did he play gloomy Slavic symphonies on the Victrola; now it was "Whispering," "Avalon," and "Cherie" (which Lill had written).

Helen came down with severe stomach pains while visiting friends in San Francisco, and on the strength of testimonals by poet George Sterling (to whom Mencken had introduced him in New York) and Llewelyn Powys (Jack's younger brother), she and Dreiser consulted Dr. Albert Abrams, a well-known quack. The piercing-eyed, bearded physician was brisk and authoritative; after analyzing their blood he informed Helen that she had a sarcoma and Dreiser that he harbored tuberculosis. Helen says she didn't believe the diagnosis, though she continued to experience what Dreiser calls "cancer pains" in his diary. Her pains were probably chronic gastritis related to stress.

Helen's indisposition deeply worried him, but rather than urging her to go to a doctor, he encouraged her to take the Abrams treatment from a Los Angeles disciple, apparently hoping for a miracle cure. When the pains persisted, he ordered the man to administer longer doses of electricity from Dr. Abrams' patented "oscilloclast" and wrote in his diary: "Get a little frightened of what I would do in case she died."

With her it was the same. On the eve of her birthday, when they were lying in bed together, she cried, "Hold me, Teddie. We have such a little time on earth and we will never have each other any more in any other world forever."

•   •   •

Meanwhile, back East, further complications reared up that made Dreiser regret his isolation from the publishing center. Edward H. Dodd, head of Dodd, Mead, which had recently purchased John Lane's American branch, told Dreiser's lawyer, Arthur Carter Hume, a friend, that he was interested in clearing up Dreiser's debts and becoming his next publisher. In March Hume and Mencken conferred with Dodd, and Mencken dispatched a favorable report of the session. Dodd, he said, stood ready to publish The "Genius" with a few cuts to make it acceptable to Sumner.

Dreiser recalled Ben Dodge's characterization of Dodd, Mead as "pious Presbys" and told Mencken, "The Dodd people . . . approach me about as a Baptist snouts a pervert. . . . They do not want *The 'Genius'* unless it is properly pruned around the vitals."

Mencken assured him that the Puritans were on the run. If Dreiser weren't so obsessed with preserving every precious word of *The "Genius,"* Mencken could get it past Sumner with a few, hardly noticeable deletions. He volunteered to negotiate with the antivice crusader—on the condition that Dreiser approve and not back out later. Dreiser told him to go ahead, but insisted he make only the minimum number of cuts necessary to placate Sumner. Mencken promised that if Sumner's demands were too extreme, he would instantly adjourn the meeting.

Liveright too had designs on *The "Genius"* and had independently spoken to Sumner and secured from him a list of the cuts demanded, which Dreiser forwarded to Mencken, asking him if the number could be reduced. Mencken made an appointment with the antivice lord for May 31 and persuaded Sumner to abandon perhaps four-fifths of his original demands and to acquiesce in "reasonable" cuts, a list of which he appended. Dreiser was willing to accept many of the trims, but some he found impossible to stomach—with reason. For example, Sumner had insisted that all of page 534 be lopped off—actually a few paragraphs ending a chapter. The compromise Mencken wrested from him called for cutting the part implying that Suzanne experienced physical desire. The language is elliptical, to say the least: "Were there ever thoughts and feelings like these in so young a body?" The other compromises were along those lines: where Sumner had wanted to excise an entire page, Mencken succeeded in limiting the damage to a specific passage.

Dreiser swallowed his qualms, thanked Mencken profusely, and admitted that any chance *The "Genius"* had of selling "was done for long ago." And so there the matter rested. But Dreiser did not give Dodd his approval of the expurgated version; indeed, the publisher heard not a word from him.

• • •

Meanwhile, Liveright had at last received the manuscript of the elusive *A Novel About Myself*—a title, he informed Dreiser, no one at the house liked. Dreiser really preferred *Newspaper Days,* but Liveright and his editors decided on *A Book About Myself,* which was the worst of the lot.

With the tensions over *The Bulwark* dissipated (Liveright had finally agreed to accept the autobiography in its stead), Dreiser and Liveright worked smoothly on this book. The publisher edited it himself and was "tickled to death" that Dreiser approved of his surgery (with some exceptions). There were no expensive changes in the page proofs, and the book appeared in December on schedule.

Dreiser's original handwritten manuscript, which he and Estelle Kubitz cut down, was full of scenes and language that would have brought Sumner and his minions swarming to the doors of Boni & Liveright; for example, a description of one of his landlady's "passionate transports" and "brief blazing orgasms."

What remained was a compelling narrative. The critic H. W. Boynton, one of the Greenwich Village literary radicals, was correct in saying that the book, like Hamlin Garland's *Son of the Middle Border*, "ought to be read as a novel. . . . " Dreiser created the figure of an untrained young man drunk on the exhortations of Horatio Alger and Samuel Smiles, going east to make his fortune as a journalist. In city rooms along the way he learns that life is a stinking, cutthroat game. He sees the jarring contrasts of wealth and poverty of a country in the "furnace stage" of industrialization where the "big brains" exploit the workers. The book ends with Theodore in New York, without a job after quitting the New York *World,* worrying about his future.

● ● ●

"Before we realized it the summer of 1922 had almost passed," Helen recalls in her autobiography. "Teddy was becoming noticeably restless. . . . " Actually, he had begun to grow restless long ago, and his various chaotic negotiations had emphasized to him the extent to which he had become a literary exile.

With his writing career in the doldrums, seemingly stalled on *An American Tragedy,* and unable to finish other projects, he spent much of the year in search of a quick financial return. He even considered going back to article writing, and forwarded some ideas to Lengel at *Hearst's International.*

Then in September a letter arrived from Ray Long at Hearst, rejecting four of his "Gallery of Women" sketches. It was a painful blow, since Long had contracted for six of them for *Cosmopolitan.* The entry in Dreiser's diary that day reads: "At the moment see no very clear way out of money troubles or that I am making any real artistic headway with work. The relentless push against the individual on and away into dissolution hangs heavy on me."

It was time to return to New York and reality. He could not work in California; life was too easy. Around this time he told a Los Angeles reporter, "I want to be back where there is strugle. . . . I like to wander around the quarters of New York where the toilers are. . . . I don't care about idlers or tourists, or the humdrum, or artistic pretenders that flock out here. . . . "

More practically, he knew he must do further research on the Gillette-Brown murder—pore over detailed reports of the trial and visit the scenes of the crime and the trial. But he would need an advance to live on, and so it was time to huddle with Liveright; possibly show him the twenty-one chapters he had completed; talk about other books, including *The "Genius"* and the woman sketches (which he had described as a book that would "rub Sumner the wrong way"); and untangle his publishing affairs.

Helen was reluctant to go. Dreiser later said she gave up a promising movie career, but it is doubtful that she would have gone much further than bit parts. Then too, she feared that Teddie would find someone else in the East. On his part, he had given her three years of fidelity—a long time for him. Although he still regarded her as the most beautiful woman he had ever known, he missed the romantic tensions of his former life in New York.

Helen says she did not hesitate about choosing to go with Dreiser: "I longed to develop spiritually, mentally and artistically. Where, I thought, could I do this better than at the side of so great a man as Dreiser?"

Part Eleven

. . .

TRAGEDY AND TRIUMPH

64 / Scenes of the Crime

And what did you do after coming back to South Bay?
We went up toward the east end of the bay again to get some
lilies. We rowed around for a short time and we talked . . .
about what we were going to do. We talked about how we
were going to meet the condition which confronted us. . . .
We were talking this way when she sprang up suddenly on
the side of the boat and it tipped over. . . . As she went into
the water I grabbed for her, but I was not quick enough.
—Chester Gillette on the witness stand (1906)

Helen and Theodore arrived in New York in late October. After two weeks'
search they found an apartment in Greenwich Village at 16 Luke's Place.

After living so long in California, New York struck Dreiser as "immense,
congested, smoky . . . smeared over by millions of insignificant people. I never
saw such a change in a city." The frantic commercial pace, the building
boom that was throwing up new skyscrapers that fragmented the skyline,
the febrile flush of prosperity on Wall Street—all seemed a change for the
worse. The "old vivid searching idealism has gone," he told Margaret Johnson. He blamed the decline on "Too many unidealistic Jews." He confided to
Mencken, who had just returned from a trip abroad, that he might head for
Chicago.

Mencken's spies in New York had reported that an unexpurgated issue of
The "Genius" was in the works, and he politely asked Dreiser, Was it true? If
so, he must notify Sumner, who "acted very decently and I don't want him to
think that I was stringing him."

It was true. Liveright was more eager than ever to challenge Sumner and
publish *The "Genius"* without the cuts Mencken had so laboriously negotiated. The main obstacle was Dodd, Mead, which claimed the sanitized version
by right of succession to John Lane's American branch. Dreiser confessed that an

uncensored edition was indeed a distinct possibility, but said if that fell through he would let Dodd, Mead issue the pruned version.

But Edward Dodd wanted none of second best. He wrote Arthur Carter Hume, who had been acting as intermediary in the negotiations, "He must not get the idea that . . . he is free to go on with *The 'Genius'* with another publisher." He had offered Dreiser a contract for it and *The Bulwark* or another novel, but Dreiser had not replied while in California, probably waiting to see what kind of deal he could make with Liveright, who for all his faults was a liberal publisher.

Once in New York, Dreiser sent Dodd an intemperate letter on Boni & Liveright stationery demanding that he publish an unexpurgated edition or nothing; he had forty-eight hours to answer. As it was probably intended to do, the ultimatum angered Dodd, who decided to rid himself of the vacillating Dreiser in return for suitable compensation.

The bargaining with Liveright went smoothly, probably because the publisher gave Dreiser just about everything he wanted: a drawing account of $4000 a year, paid in monthly installments, through 1927; Liveright to secure the copyrights and plates of all his books formerly owned by Lane and those now owned by Harper's; in January 1927, B & L to publish a collected set of all of Dreiser's titles in a limited edition of one thousand copies, guaranteeing the author a minimum of $10,000 in royalties; the house to take a five-year lease on Dreiser's books and pay him a 20 percent royalty on all save *The "Genius"* on which he would receive 50 cents a copy.

Thus Liveright had *The "Genius"* and Dreiser's backlist as security for money he would advance on future books. There was, of course, no guarantee that the old books would sell, but Liveright was willing to take a chance.

In return, Dreiser promised to deliver two new books a year, through the spring of 1926. Those included titles already finished or nearly so: *A Gallery of Women,* volumes I and III of *The History of Myself* (volume II, *A Book About Myself,* aka *Newspaper Days,* having already been published), *The Color of a Great City,* a volume of poems called *Moods,* and a collection of short stories. But he also pledged two new novels — the prizes, Liveright really thought; he had small commercial hopes for the other books.

The contract was signed on February 7, and Dreiser's fortunes were changing. In January Lengel sold the serialized version of *The "Genius"* to *Metropolitan Magazine.* That, of course, was not the Mencken-expurgated version; it was a condensation, of about one hundred thousand words, to run in three installments. Dreiser netted $2700 from this transaction, and suddenly he was relatively prosperous. Later he sold two of the woman sketches — "Reina," a portrait of Helen's sister Myrtle (who would also appear in *An American Tragedy* as the mercenary Hortense), and "Ida Hauchowout" — to the *Century,* and he resold, as it were, "St. Columba and the River," the story on which *The Saturday Evening*

Post had reneged, to *Pictorial Review* for $800. And Helen had sold two lots she owned in Montrose at a $1000 profit.

• • •

By then they were quarreling. They had hardly settled in when Helen began overhearing telephone conversations between Dreiser and people she did not know, who belonged to a world of which she was not a part. Like Kirah and Estelle, she resented being segregated from his friends. The engagements were mostly with male acquaintances, but there was a Mrs. Howey with whom he said he was discussing the Russian theater. The painful exclusion drove home to Helen the precariousness of her position. Insecure and fiercely jealous, she realized that she was losing the hold over him she had in California, when they were cut off from his world back East.

At last she rebelled, announcing that she would find a place of her own. This thrust hit Dreiser in his weak point: his fear of abandonment. The "mother-boy" inside him cried out. "Helen packing. We discuss this move. I do not want her to go. The pathos of it." The next day: "Helen begins to pack & then I realize that actually she is leaving. The sinking sensation in the pit of my stomach. The sense of loss. I can hardly believe that she is going. . . . " He went out for a luncheon engagement but could think only of her. "What will the future be like now. So they slip away from me, one by one, & periods close . . . forever."

But she could not stay away for long; his pleas and promises brought her back. After an intensely passionate reunion, Helen returned to 16 St. Luke's, at least part-time, and took singing lessons as a substitute for her abandoned career. They attended the theater and made excursions to Newark and Asbury Park on the New Jersey shore, where Dreiser was seized by nostalgia for his earlier great loves — Jug, Kirah, Estelle. Each affair had ended, closing an epoch of his life never to be reopened, reminding him of the inexorable passage of time. He simply could not write finis to Helen, whom he still loved, but neither could he give up all those other women, past, present, and future.

• • •

While passing through this turmoil with Helen, Dreiser found more public distractions. Early in the spring of 1923 the antivice crusaders were astir. Sumner had formed an alliance with New York Supreme Court Justice John Ford to lobby for passage of the Clean Books Bill in the state legislature. The measure was designed to negate every defense or legal argument raised by defendants in obscenity cases in the past decade.

Dreiser jumped into the fray. In an interview published in the New York *Evening Telegram* he called censorship "bunk and hokum" and proceeded to deplore the arid state of American culture, which put philistinism in the saddle. Businessmen, he said, talked like nine-year-olds, while university graduates could converse only about Babe Ruth. "America," he summed up, "is a hopeless country for intellectuals and thinking people. . . . The majority of its people have the mentality of a European or Asian peasant."

He got into a public row with the Authors League, which had been slow to take a stand against the bill (which was ultimately defeated) and, when the chips were down, confined itself to a telegram and a letter of opposition. What triggered Dreiser's outburst was a form letter from Rex Beach, the adventure novelist, inviting him to attend a conference "to advance the artistic and cultural standards of motion pictures. . . . " Dreiser wrote Beach that the league should be mobilizing against the depredations of the comstocks instead of conferring with movie magnates. His letter received wide publicity, and league vice president Gelett Burgess, complaining that Dreiser hadn't attended the hearings, boasted of the league's effective behind-the-scenes lobbying, concluding that if Dreiser devoted "as much time furthering the cause of literature as he does to seeking personal publicity, he wouldn't need to ask an association he doesn't belong to to help protect his dubious sex fiction."

Dreiser pounced. Drawing on inside information provided by Liveright, he demolished Burgess's claim that the league had helped defeat the bill. As for his debt to the league for its help in the *"Genius"* case, beyond a statement of support he had "received no further aid of any kind from the Authors' League, and I fought the *"Genius"* issue single handed for five years. And I am still fighting—single handed."

Mencken sullied Dreiser's triumph slightly by reminding him that "a critic in Baltimore" had "laid out $300 in cash" to round up authors to sign a petition. Said Baltimore critic had another, unrelated gripe: a Boni & Liveright advertisement had quoted him as saying, "In 'The Bulwark' especially the big power of Dreiser's massive impetus is evident." Mencken had, of course, written no such moonshine (unless while in his cups), and he hadn't even read the manuscript of *The Bulwark*.

The culprit was Liveright, whose vaunted promotional skills had been unleashed. The offending passage was part of a series of advertisements treating Dreiser "as an institution," as Liveright put it. The version that had aroused Mencken was apparently an early one, for in August, to coincide with the publication of *The "Genius,"* Liveright poured $2000 into a revised, more dignified campaign, conducted primarily in the pages of *The New York Times Book Review* and announcing "with pleasure and pardonable pride" that B & L had acquired the rights to Dreiser's books.

Liveright's claim that he was the best promoter of Dreiser's work was no idle boast, but Dreiser was impatient for results, and even the prominent bust of him in the ornate "Italian Renaissance"–style reception room at B & L's new offices did not pacify him. When Liveright informed him that *A Book About Myself* had sold only "a lousy 3,000 copies," he did not hang his head in shame. He all but accused his publisher of cheating him — and of not advertising enough.

Liveright usually replied to such complaints with soothing words: "In spite of your letter, which it is possible I have misinterpreted, my admiration and affection for you remains the same"; he was for Dreiser's work "heart and soul." In another communication he outlines his advertising plan, offers to go over it with Dreiser, and promised "real results" with *The "Genius"* even though "it's only a *republication.*"

Liveright shone the publicity spotlight on the new edition of *The "Genius."* The novel was relentlessly promoted and took off, selling more than twelve thousand copies by the end of the year; sales would reach fifty thousand copies before the decade was out.

• • •

Now Dreiser was ready to resume the novel on which Liveright would gamble some $25,000, the book he described to Helen as "our dream." He spoke confidently of finishing by fall 1924.

But first he shored up the foundation of reality on which he must erect his book; he carefully amassed facts, not for their own sake but as a kind of backdrop, a real world bolstering the imagined one in which his characters moved and lived. He needed to form a scientific confirmation of his vision of the workings of that world, so he met with psychiatrist A. A. Brill, his informal technical adviser on matters criminological, and listened to his tales of murderers he had analyzed.

Brill's *Psychoanalysis,* which Dreiser perused in 1919, interprets fairy tales as expressions of forbidden wishes. It contains a passage about children who took fairy tales literally and became "phantastic dreamers entirely unfit to cope with the stern realities of modern life." When these individuals grew up, Brill asserted, they subconsciously clung to the childish desire for omnipotence. They were "constantly wishing for the unattainable that could only be gotten through some of the charms of fairy land, such as magic books, invisible caps, Aladdin's Lamp. . . ."

The Aladdin tale would become a central motif in the *Tragedy.* It tells of a poor young man who acquires magic powers and wins the Sultan's beautiful daughter. It appealed to Dreiser as a metaphor for every poor youth's desires for power and wealth (he had in *Sister Carrie* used Aladdin's cave as a simile for opulence and luxury) and the hand of the princess.

In an unscientific (but artistically necessary) way he linked these ideas with the seemingly contradictory findings of the early behaviorist Jacques Loeb, particularly his theory of tropisms. In January Dreiser called on Loeb at the Rockefeller Institute. He found the scientist "quite old" and deeply pessimistic about the future of the human race, perhaps a lingering aftershock of the Great War. In his notes on the meeting Dreiser writes that the old man was "very positive that all is accidental—no thought, no plan—no intelligence and great danger of dark ages returning. Thinks intelligentsia ought to hold together in a kind of brotherhood." The words "all is accidental" confirmed Dreiser's predisposition to tell the story of a crime not as an act of free will, but as the product of a chain of circumstances, "physico-chemical" (shortened by Dreiser to "chemic") compulsions, and the workings of the subconscious. The sexual chemism hypothesized by Freud was the link between psychiatry and behaviorism.

• • •

The next step was research on the ground. He and Helen left on July 1 for upstate New York to inspect the places associated with the Gillette-Brown murder. They were in a holiday mood, and on the way to the Hoboken ferry they stopped at Mame's place to pick up three bottles of gin. She and her husband, Austin, were now managing the Rhinelander apartments, a row of ornately balconied buildings on West Eleventh Street.

At Big Moose Lake, surrounded by vast forests, in the heart of the rugged Adirondack country, they took a room at the Glenmore Hotel, where Chester and Grace had registered on the morning of July 11, 1906, the young man using a false name. According to Dreiser's diary, he and Helen went for a row on the lake, then had dinner, and afterward listened to the music and watched the dancers at the hotel. In her autobiography Helen describes the lake as "an isolated spot, very beautiful. One felt the weight of the surrounding woods stretching for miles in every direction." Dreiser matter-of-factly records the price of the rooms and the fact that it rained from 3:00 A.M. until dawn, suggesting he spent a restless night.

By Helen's account, the next morning they hired a rowboat at the hotel dock. Dreiser merely notes that the attendant remembered seeing Grace and Chester on the fatal day, and he repeated the gist of his testimony at the trial that Chester had taken his suitcase with a tennis racquet strapped to its side in the boat. The prosecution later theorized that the racquet was the murder weapon, and the presence of the suitcase showed that Chester intended to flee after killing Grace.

In Helen's account they rowed to the inlet called South Bay, where Chester and "Billy" Brown had drifted around during the blazing hot afternoon and she had picked the pond lilies that grew in profusion near the shore.

Even today, South Bay can seem—at least to one mindful of the tragedy that took place there—a forsaken place. The water is almost black, except near the shore, where Grace's body was found, and the weedy bottom can be faintly discerned. Along most of the shoreline a tangle of pine and hardwood trees crowds close to a narrow beach, and the cottages are barely visible. The horizon is dominated by the green-furred humps of the Adirondacks. A smaller inlet, known as Punkey's Bay, where searchers dredged up Grace's body with a boathook, her bloodshot eyes open and staring, was probably uninhabited when Dreiser was there. Beyond the shore is a marsh matted with tangled grass and weeds. Elsewhere the trees press claustrophobically against the water's edge, some growing grotesquely atop huge glacial rocks, their roots clutching them like tentacles. One can imagine—as Dreiser must have—Grace and Chester drifting purposelessly about on a blazing July afternoon, not in a lovers' intimate seclusion but rather lost in a profound solitude, remote from human eyes, mutual desperation and recrimination seething below the surface. The fat, round, yellow-and-white blooms of the pond lilies protrude on thick stems above the surface like pods of some primitive plant—or, to a fanciful eye, clenched fists stabbing up from the dark depths.

Certainly, Helen's imagination worked overtime. As they both sat transfixed by the "quiet, deathlike stillness" of the spot, she thought: "Maybe Teddie will become completely hypnotized by this idea and even repeat it, here and now."

While Helen reflexively identified with the victim, Dreiser slipped into the skin of the boy, contemplating murder. There was no likelihood of his committing some violent act, of course. Envisioning the scene for his novel, he understood why he (Clyde) would not, could not, do such a thing. Beyond moral compunctions, enough of him was in Clyde that the fictional projection would have shared Dreiser's inclination, when trapped in a dilemma, to procrastinate; his tendency (as when he let Grant Richards take charge of his life) to drift, to let fate decide. Drifting in a boat on the opaque glassy surface was the dominant image of that July day in 1906, as he would imagine it. No, he (Clyde) could not do it.

The thoughts that actually ran through Dreiser's mind he didn't record in his diary; but surely his photographic memory registered the atmosphere of this forsaken place, where Nature seemed hostile, a sinister landscape out of Poe, under a pitiless sun.

•   •   •

Dreiser's research consisted of speaking to at most two or three people with direct knowledge of some aspect of the murder of Grace Brown. A historian later discovered that he did at some point visit Mrs. Ward, widow of the Herkimer County district attorney, who showed him her husband's scrapbook of clippings on the case. He may have taken some notes on the contents, but he depended

mainly on morgue clippings from the New York *World,* which he could as easily
have obtained in New York City. He evidently did not visit the shirt factory in
Cortland that had replaced the Gillette Skirt Company, where Chester worked.
But in the novel he puts Clyde in a collar factory, and he subsequently did tour
such a factory.

There were still many people in Herkimer with knowledge of the trial,
including the defense lawyer, the presiding judge, and the undersheriff who
arrested Chester and saw him daily in jail. But Dreiser had no particular desire
to interrogate them. None of them could have provided the key to his story,
the essence of the case: why Chester Gillette murdered Grace Brown (if he did)
and what went through his mind that day on Big Moose Lake. Even if they
could have, Dreiser might not have been interested. He would formulate his
own theory of what happened to Clyde and Roberta Alden on the lake.

Later that month, seeking privacy and relief from the city heat, they rented
a secluded cabin they had noticed on the way to Cortland, near Monticello in
the Catskills.

News from New York invaded his rural hideaway in the form of a momentous communication from Mencken: "Confidentially I am at work on plans for
a new review—something far above anything hitherto seen in the Republic."
That "review" would become *The American Mercury.* He and Nathan had wearied
of editing the *Smart Set,* and they persuaded their publisher, Alfred A. Knopf,
to back a new journal. Mencken wanted a magazine that was more serious than
the dandyish *Smart Set,* with iconoclastic articles on history, science, and politics, and fiction of uncompromising realism. To Dreiser he proclaimed a New
Freedom: "You may attack the Methodists by name, and call the Baptists the
Sewer Rats of God if you please."

As Mencken planned the magazine that would make him the most influential social critic of the 1920s, Dreiser was making a painful beginning on
the book that would win him his greatest fame. That summer he worked at
an improvised desk under a tree, fair game for ambient mosquitoes, worms,
and spiders. He was racked by doubts. He mentions his trepidations in letters
to Sally Kusell, a pretty young blonde woman from Illinois with literary ambitions whom he had hired as a literary assistant. She had previously worked
for her brother, a theatrical producer, and gained some experience at "play construction," as he put it, leading Dreiser to think she had the editorial skills
that Helen lacked.

Kusell's first task was to edit and type the "studies," as Dreiser called
them, for *A Gallery of Women.* By the time he left for the country, he was calling her "my little Yankee Zulu" and "my bobbed-haired pirate." In early August
he wrote that they had much to do together and he wished she were there;
however, he realized that working with her would be fatal: "The trouble with

you is that you have a gripping sex appeal for me. I doubt—apart from *that*—if much would be done because I'd fag myself daily and then lie about. . . . "

While Helen was packing she noticed a bundle of Sally's letters on top of his bag. "Ordinarily I would not have touched them," she writes ingenuously, "but at that moment I could not overcome the feeling that they concerned me in some way and I should read them. After reading two or three, I replaced the rest, for I had seen enough to know that this was a more serious triangle than I had supposed." Confronting Dreiser with the evidence, she told him she was through. They drove back to New York in a sulfurous silence, and she let him off at St. Luke's Place with the advice that he need never try to see her again. Nevertheless, she was back at the studio the next morning, and he looked tired and distraught. "I walked the streets all night long," he told her. "Where were you?"

She softened but could not take him back. They decided they would live apart but continue to see each other. Helen suspected that he was still seeing Sally, but there was little she could do, other than reproach him when he stayed away for days at a time. After one such flare-up at Christmastime, he took her to Atlantic City. She cried most of the way, but eventually he soothed her and they had a relaxed holiday. They returned home on December 27, and the next day Dreiser writes that he was "glad to be back & working." By then he had finished thirty-two chapters of the *Tragedy*.

•　　•　　•

A hint of his thinking about the novel—and The Novel—emerged in an interview published in *The New York Times Book Review*'s Christmas issue. "Realism is not literature; it is life," he told Rose Feld. He attacked the brittle novels of cynicism and disillusionment that were in vogue. The younger generation of writers "choose one dark dank, ugly corner of life . . . forgetting that life consists of many corners, many open spaces. . . . The realistic novel of America is not the torpid, sick neurasthenic novel. Life in America is not like that." Here there was opportunity, said the immigrant's son. He quoted a "foreign writer" who had told him, "There is always a push upward . . . the life, or the soul if you will, of an individual needn't stay poor."

Contemporary novelists, he complained, were overly preoccupied with form and technique—"Gertrude Stein stuff"—at the expense of substance. As for the inevitable topic of sex, Dreiser took a moralistic swipe at the current wave of flaming-youth novels, saying he was "sick of the exaggeration of sex in our novels today. But the person who ignores sex is as much a fool as the person who over-emphasizes it. You can't write a novel of realism and let sex out of the picture, even as you can't write a novel full of sex and call it realism."

The allusive realism of Stein's lost generation could not have produced a *Madame Bovary* or *Crime and Punishment*. The Russians and the Victorians needed "breadth and length. They took the trouble to make their picture complete. The little canvases of today will never displace the larger ones of yesterday." Writers had abandoned the social novel and were retreating into subjectivity, he declared. As he would observe of another novelist, now forgotten, he "is thinking more of himself than he is of life."

Caught between the Victorian and modern ages, Dreiser in his *Tragedy* was writing a large-canvas novel documenting American society and its false values. Though he was sensitive to the changes in those values, Dreiser, unlike the writers who emerged in the 1920s, could not believe that the old idols were shattered. His entire career had been one of struggle against the reticence of the genteel tradition and official censors and popular taste; he had defined himself by opposition. As he wrote David Karsner in December 1923, "Like a kite I have risen against the wind—not with it." He needed the wind to keep aloft.

The young people in Dreiser's work in progress faced a dilemma that urban sophisticates would regard as quaintly antique, something more typical of 1906 than 1923. (In his first draft he set the novel in Chester Gillette's day—remarking on the rarity of automobiles, for example. But in subsequent versions, the story is vaguely located in the late teens and early twenties, as evidenced by scattered references to clothes, songs, and movies of the time.)

Although the situation of a pregnant girl who fears disgrace and ostracism might seem anachronistic in Manhattan, it would not in Cortland or Herkimer, New York. As the sociologists Robert S. and Helen M. Lynd would write in *Middletown*, their 1925 study of Muncie, Indiana, "A heavy taboo, supported by law and by both religious and popular sanctions, rests upon sexual relationships between persons who are not married." Moreover (as the Lynds discreetly point out), it was the young people of the upper middle class who were sexually sophisticated, who knew about contraceptives and doctors who, for a price, got girls out of trouble. Dreiser was well aware of this class barrier of ignorance, so to speak; it was one link in the chain of circumstances connecting Clyde Griffiths to his doom.

65 / An "Unholy Task"

But by this time a change had come over the affections of
Chester Gillette. He had discovered that the name of Gillette
was a social one in Cortland. He had found out that it would
open the doors of Cortland's exclusive circles. He had found
out that the name would bring him in contact with girls of
a different class, girls of education, and whose families had
position; girls who moved far from the sphere of the class of
factory and farmer girls to which Grace Brown belonged.

—District Attorney Ward's opening statement (1906)

Toward the end of March Helen decided to go west. They were still living
apart, but the strain of typing his manuscripts all day and going out with him
at night was too much for her, she explained. But jealousy was at the heart of
it; she resented not only Dreiser's affair with Sally but also the fact that she was
playing a more important role in the writing of the book than Helen was. And
so, in what would become a pattern, she fled to her mother's in Portland.

He assumed the separation would be short-lived. He would finish the novel
by August 1 at the latest, he told her. When he was free they would take a trip
and then "settle in a little dream place with a garden," preferably in San Francisco. The day after she left, he received "troublesome" telepathic waves from
her and thought he heard her crying (she cried all the way to Chicago). He
continued to believe that they were in mental communication (as did she).
Sometimes he received hostile thought-waves, sometimes loving ones. He repeatedly reassured her that he was interested in no one in particular. "I know
you think I have a girl hanging on my arm every night," he wrote in April. Not
so. He told her about a couple of his engagements, one an invitation to a soirée
at the actress Clair Burke's, which he had accepted only because Mencken would
be there. He promised, "If this seeing people without you is going to torture
you I am content never to see anyone save with you." He had, he reminded
her, done that for three years in California.

He was attuned to her moods, "so like my own," and sent her copies of
poems. The first one would bring him an unwanted fame. It was called "The
Beautiful," and he had not written it at all. He had borrowed the words from

Sherwood Anderson's story "Tandy," added a few sentences, and rearranged the lines on the page. It is a tribute to a long-suffering woman, who says, "They think that it is easy to be a woman—/to love and be loved,/ But I know better." But Dreiser adds some lines describing the kind of love he needs: "Complete and ceaseless/ And insatiable and yet generous." Such was his demand of Helen.

• • •

Helen remained in Portland for several weeks, trying to put the pieces of her life back together. By April she felt better and went to Hollywood, where she had once been happy, and rented a room in a private home belonging to a family with three daughters. For a time she occupied herself with buying and selling real estate and discovered that the properties she still owned could yield profits greater than 100 percent. After making a fair sum and speculating in other tracts they owned, using additional money Dreiser sent her, she decided to resume her voice lessons. But she missed Dreiser, and he began begging her to come back, swearing that he loved her more than anything in the world, promising to do better. But she had set a more drastic condition: marriage.

He forwarded periodic reports of his progress on the *Tragedy*. At first he is full of doubts, and he tells her that he had finished a chapter, but "I boast not. I only hope for the best and that I may not destroy [the manuscript] in a crazy dark mood." His room, he said, had become a kind of prison where he was "fixed & struggling all the time." The novel was an "unholy task." "I might as well be chipping it out of solid rock," he told her. "But I am chipping." At times he feared the task was beyond his strength. His attitude toward the story was at times almost religious. "When the book is finally done maybe I'll get credit for the contest & maybe I won't," he told Helen. "But just the same & failure or no failure I feel it an honor to be permitted to even attempt to tell such a tale & on that basis I am working on."

By April he felt more confident, telling Helen that he was "surer now than I have been in a long time that I will bring it to a successful conclusion." He had pushed the story "to the point where . . . I know now that it will come through & I am not suffering mentally like I was before." When he has finished part 2, which ends with the death of Roberta (the Grace Brown figure) on the lake, he will know that "the top of the range is crossed & I'm descending the other side. . . . For the approach of this story is longer than the conclusion." That is, he must establish the causes of the murder, and then the rest—the trial and execution of Clyde Griffiths—would inexorably follow.

He was unable to write this novel as rapidly as previous ones: "It is too intricate in its thoughts & somehow my method if not my style has changed. I work with more care and hence difficulty. My style is not as fluid. Whether it's worse I can't say—yet." This was in part because of the more painstaking care with which he handled the progression of the story, the placement of scenes, the sequences of events.

For example, after Clyde has seduced Roberta Alden, his co-worker in the collar factory, he meets the dazzling Sondra Finchley: "I'm to where the factory girl & the rich girl in Clyde's life are entangling & by degrees destroying her. Hard! . . . It seems simple. I know the story. The right procession & selection of incident should be as nothing but it just chances to be everything and so I write and rewrite."

He couldn't, for example, decide when to show Roberta's awareness of the developing triangle. In the first draft he has her reproaching Clyde for breaking a date with her to attend a dance, in early December. But in later versions the dance takes place at Christmastime. Dreiser felt that it would be more revealing to show Roberta waiting for Clyde, alone in her room, with the simple presents she has bought.

• • •

In June he complained to Helen that he felt wretched and "spiritually alone." The July heat wilted him: "My body appears to be made of heavy, wet leather & my nerves & joints of rusty wires & iron." He had so much to do and didn't have the right person to help him.

She asked who was typing for him (read: Was Sally Kusell still around?). He replied that he was using no one at the moment and that he had a backlog of six chapters and an article. Liveright had offered one of his secretaries to help out, but he had refused. He did not want his publisher to read the book now: "He might begin with annoying suggestions & I'd have to pull out." He was working under conditions of virtual secrecy.

Liveright reveals his state of ignorance in a letter written on April 2: "The new book, as I understand it, is to be called An American Comedy . . . ." Apprised of the true title, he suggested it be changed to "Griffith, An American Tragedy." Dreiser stuck to the one he had used from the beginning: "I call it *An American Tragedy* because it could not happen in any other country in the world."

Liveright was now "yelling for the book," Dreiser reported to Louise Campbell, whom he had recently enlisted as an editor-typist. Louise's recollection was that he was about one-third finished when she began. She had arrived in the city in early April to audition for the chorus of the Ziegfeld Follies. But she took part of the manuscript with her to the theater, began reading it while waiting her turn onstage, and decided then and there that she would rather work for him. Louise was a faster typist than Sally, and he gradually came to value her editorial suggestions. She lived in Philadelphia, removing any sexual complications; and, in any case, their affair was probably over.

•   •   •

He was working late into the night, marking the hours by the ghostly face of the Jefferson Market Place clock. But he was not always cloistered in his room as he led Helen to believe. While continuing the relationship with Sally, he had casual affairs with Mrs. Howey; Maude Guitteau, a former showgirl whose quick seduction made him think, "Without the fame of my books I personally could not achieve this relationship at all"; and Magdalen Davis, who aspired to be a writer but worked for the Standard Oil Company and had some connection with the Greenwich Village Theatre.

These transient amours provided companionship and sexual release: "Magdalene [sic] & I meet here at 10:30 P.M. for pleasure." "When I invite [Mrs. Howey] in & close the door she immediately begins to undress—which makes me laugh. I hadn't assumed that copulation naturally followed. However—always willing to oblige."

Sally provided companionship. They went to the theater frequently. He roared at W. C. Fields in *Poppy*, and at Jimmy Savo and Fred Allen in *Vogues*. He took Magdalen to hear Sumner debate on censorship at the Civic Club. He attended a soirée at the drama critic Alexander Woollcott's rooms. He went to a writers' dinner and had four drinks, he wrote Helen, but no feminine companionship. He spent a weekend in April at the actress Laurette Taylor's place, accompanied by T. R. Smith, the Liveright editor. In May he stayed at the rented Larchmont mansion of W. C. Fields and was bored by the smart Broadway chatter.

•   •   •

So the summer passed. His eldest sister, Mame, kept a worried eye on him. The book, that "unholy thing," was taking a toll on his nerves. To soothe them he started smoking cigarettes, something he had rarely done in the past because of his bronchitis, and he was increasingly resorting to gin as a creative stimulus. Once, in a fit of drunken despair, he told Mame that he would never finish the book and began weeping.

In July he confessed to Liveright that he was stuck and could not possibly meet the deadline for fall publication. By September his morale hit bottom. Sometimes he was troubled by nightmares in which Helen figured. The dreams reflected guilt feelings about his treatment of her, and he asked for forgiveness, or rather understanding: "I may have seemed cruel and to you have been cruel but I have tortured myself more in so doing because within me you have always been—safe and centered in my very heart—and when I have hurt you I have felt so sad afterwards—ah—so very sad."

Like a child petitioning his mother, he pleads, "If I promise to be very, very good from now on . . . do you suppose you could be happy with just me." Perhaps he was worried about the "handsome" movie star friend she was now dating. It is difficult to believe that a woman of Helen's strongly sensual nature was celibate.

He assured her that compared with the other women in his life she was "on a pedestal and quite alone." Once her beauty had struck fears of inadequacy in him; now, from a distance, he was idealizing her. She played hard to get, peremptorily dismissing his offer to divorce Jug or hiding behind her refinement, coyly suggesting, "Perhaps you like a coarser type." Recalling their private orgies in California, he responded, "since when have you become delicatessen in that field?" He did indeed need a "coarser type," in the sense of an illicit relationship. The mistress became the wife, who inevitably became the controlling mother, making him *mind*. And then the Golden Girl was gone.

Now he was in the uncomfortable position of petitioner, like Clyde with Sondra, like Roberta with Clyde. Helen felt her power over him and used it to negotiate a renewal of their relationship on her terms. He stepped to her tune, making every possible promise to lure her back, every plaintive appeal to her sympathy.

The transcontinental debate continued through November. He wrote her that he had had a dream that they were seated at a table in their own place, and all sorts of people were with them. On the walls were drawings by a woman he had known, but somehow Helen wasn't jealous. As they were going out, they came to a pile of discarded woman's clothes. He feared that Helen would see them and throw a jealous fit, but she merely kicked them into a corner.

The pictures were, of course, Thelma's. And the pile of clothes symbolized all the old loves whom Helen briskly kicked out of his life.

• • •

He was waiting for her when her train arrived at Pennsylvania Station in mid-December. "Well," he kept saying foolishly, "it's Babu, all right." She thought he had "a hollow look about him, a seeming lack of vitality," which worried her.

Her presence had a rejuvenating effect on him, and they spent a few days in Washington while he researched in the Library of Congress. But when they returned, as they were getting out of a taxicab, a woman rushed up and said something "sharp and accusing" to him. Calmly, he told Helen to go inside, and while she waited she could hear them talking, his voice low and firm, the woman's shrill and insistent. To Helen it must have seemed a new variation on an old triangle. But she had come this far, and there was no going back.

66 / Death by Water

HE SWAM AWAY
AND LET GIRL DIE.
PRISONER NEAR COLLAPSE AS DEFENSE RESTS CASE.
Lies Outright and Is Trapped
Repeatedly in Gruelling
Cross-Examination.
                    —Headline, New York *World*, December 1, 1906

Overwhelmed by the distractions of Manhattan, Dreiser suggested that Helen find a place in Brooklyn. In March, at the suggestion of J. G. Robin, a
lawyer friend, he took an office in the Guardian Life Building at 50 Union
Square. Robin was associated with Arthur Carter Hume, who had an office in
the building, and the two of them advised Dreiser on legal points in the story.

Brooklyn and Union Square would be the poles of his life for nearly nine
months, as he completed book 3 of the *Tragedy*. He worked at both places but
used the office also as a staging area for nocturnal forays and, presumably, for
assignations.

Helen later offered the theory that he needed a romantic triangle to stimulate his creativity. "He tried to place himself between opposing forces in order to
gather reactions of a stimulating quality and character, and at the same time to
safeguard himself against being weakened or destroyed by the indispensability
of any one person."

Although the second part of that proposition was probably true, the first
seems a rationalization or defense mechanism for preserving her self-esteem.
Dreiser craved the ego boost and stimulation, sexual or mental, of other women.
One triangle necessarily bred another, so that he could feel that no single woman
dominated him.

•   •   •

The pages of manuscript proliferated. Louise Campbell said that at times he
seemed knee-deep in paper, for there were always several versions of each chapter

in circulation. Esherick called on him and found the living-room floor and every other available surface covered with pages.

A kind of editorial assembly line had been set up. A note he wrote on the final typescript shows how many hands it had passed through: "Finally revised and cut copy—with cuts by myself, Sally Kussell, Louise Campbell and T. R. Smith." Sally and Louise took the manuscript in turn, editing and typing successive drafts. They both cut and condensed chapters with Dreiser's approval.

Having refused to have any dealings with Liveright on editorial matters, he worked with T. R. Smith, an erudite, cherubic man who wore a pince-nez. Smith often invited Dreiser to the legendary parties Liveright gave at the four-story brownstone at 61 West Forty-eighth Street, which had become the firm's offices in 1923.

The alcoholic excesses and hedonism of the time foamed over into novels, from Fitzgerald's *The Great Gatsby* to Van Vechten's *Firecrackers*, in which a writer intones a Dreiserian credo: "that life is largely without excuse, that if there is a God he conducts the show aimlessly, if not, indeed, maliciously, that men and women run around automatically seeking escapes from their troubles and outlets for their lusts." In *Gatsby* Fitzgerald caught the callousness, the success-at-any-price materialism, the cynical egoism, the indifference to communal ties of the decade. Everyone came to Gatsby's parties, but no one went to his funeral.

Everyone came to Liveright's parties that year. . . .

• • •

Dreiser was not impervious to his times, and the novel he was writing in the 1920s would be different in its setting and the relationships among the characters from those he wrote before the 1920s. He had absorbed, almost unconsciously, the social and intellectual influences that went into the making of the decade's literature. But his cynicism was more weathered, his hedonism more tired, his alienation more profound than that of most of the younger writers. His despair was philosophical, almost detached, sometimes almost cheerful; life had on the whole used him fairly well, he liked to say on his better days. He had the weary air of one who has peered into the black deeps of space and found nothingness.

In writing he paid back the universe for its implacable indifference, siding with humanity against it, pityingly tracing the careers of characters in his novel, plotting their fates as he believed the Unknowable often cruelly plotted his and all men's. There was Roberta, experiencing "the first flashing, blinding, bleeding stab of love" for Clyde, and then, just after discovering she is pregnant, sitting alone in her room because he has fallen in love with Sondra. Love, to

Dreiser, was pain. Clyde feels the "stinging sense of what it was to want and not to have." When Clyde's attempts to arrange an abortion for Roberta come to naught (for these scenes Dreiser drew inspiration from Mame's search for a doctor reputed to perform the operations in Indiana when he was a boy in Sullivan), the trap closes and the mirage of love vanishes, leaving barren hostility.

•   •   •

Dreiser had reached the point where Clyde formulates his plot to kill Roberta. Here he summons up a figure in the *Arabian Nights*—the mysterious efrit, who whispers to the boy the answer to his problem. The efrit is a kind of perverse genii—genius, control. The efrit is *It* (which is perhaps why Dreiser chose the archaic word for genii):

> . . . the very substance of some leering and diabolic wish or wisdom concealed in his own nature and that now abhorrent and yet compelling, leering and yet intriguing, friendly and yet cruel, offered him a choice between an evil which threatened to destroy him (and against his deepest opposition) and a second evil which, however it might disgust or sear or terrify, still provided for freedom and success and love.

This was no textbook or theological representation of evil, but a force Dreiser had read into Freud and sensed in himself. Helen recalled, "His was a dual nature, and there were times when I felt the opposing force struggling for control within him so powerfully that I felt he might be torn apart by it."

The efrit, or genii, personifies Clyde's "darker self," Dreiser often said, leaving it at that. It could be called a projection of a forbidden wish which the conscious mind cannot countenance and so imagines in the form of an external spirit. Once Clyde opens the subterranean prison where the efrit dwells, he is in its power. Like the fisherman in the *Arabian Nights*, he cannot put it back in the bottle.

The efrit speaks in calm, reasonable tones, overwhelming the objections of Clyde's conscience, his fears of punishment, his repugnance toward such a deed. The efrit makes murder seem a sensible course—the rational way out of his dilemma.

But in the end, on South Bay of Big Bittern Lake, Clyde loses his nerve and "confides his dilemma to circumstances." Dreiser sets the boat adrift in a moral void—"in endless space where was no end of anything—no plots—no plans—no practical problems to be solved—nothing." The lake is like "a huge, black pearl cast by some mighty hand." As they drift on the opaque cobalt water, Roberta sings a banal little song, "I'll Be There Sunday If You Will," evoking her long wait for him to come for her. The relentless sun in the blank sky is focused, as if through a magnifying glass, on the boat, so that it becomes a single burning nodal point. Clyde nerves himself to act; the conflict within him is reflected in his face, "distorted and fulgurous." He is torn between a "chemic revulsion against death" (deeper than conscience) and a subconscious desire to kill (personified by the voice of the efrit); behaviorism and psychiatry, Loeb and Freud, clash at the "cataclysmic moment"—and nullify each other. All volition is gone; he suffers a "palsy of the will." It is as though a giant invisible hand is now writing the script. In his prose Dreiser shifts to the passive voice to describe somnambulant beings—mechanisms controlled by a higher Author:

> And yet fearing to act in any way—being unwilling to—being willing only to say that never, never would he marry her. . . . But angry and confused and floundering. And then, as she drew near him, seeking to take his hand in hers and the camera from him in order to put it in the boat, he flinging out at her, but not even then with any intention to do other than free himself of her—her touch—her pleading—consoling sympathy—her presence forever—God!
>
> Yet (the camera still unconsciously held tight) pushing at her with so much vehemence as not only to strike her lips and nose and chin with it, but to throw her back sidewise toward the left wale which caused the boat to career to the very water's edge. And then he, stirred by her sharp scream . . . rising and reaching half to assist or recapture her and half to apologize for the unintended blow—yet in so doing completely capsizing the boat—himself and Roberta being as instantly thrown into the water. And the left wale of the boat as it turned, striking Roberta on the head as she sank and then rose for the first time, her frantic, contorted face turned to Clyde, who by now had righted himself. For she was stunned, horror-struck, unintelligible with pain and fear—her lifelong fear of water and drowning and the blow he had so accidentally and all but unconsciously administered.

In the end Clyde's lethal act is a reflex triggered by a subconscious rejection of Roberta's entwining, mothering arms. Then, out of the depths of the lake rises the efrit to persuasively whisper the forbidden wish: how convenient simply to let her drown. Clyde swims to shore, thinking of "that last frantic, white, appealing look in her eyes. . . . "

His bottled-up rage had lashed out against the pregnant wife, the Mother, who is his only love but who betrayed him; the Mother who kept him in her thrall, denying him forever (God!) sexual happiness. He is free to go to the all-giving Mistress-Mother, Sondra the Golden Girl.

Dreiser lived deeply in his characters. In the tragedy on Big Bittern Lake, he had expressed his own tangled forbidden wish, not Clyde's.

• • •

On January 9, 1925, Dreiser wrote a cheerful letter to Louise Campbell, announcing he had finished book 2. Then, in an aside, he opened a window into his mind: "This book will be a terrible thing."

67 / Her Boy

When I was leaving mother,
Standing at last in solemn pause,
We looked at one another,
And I—I saw in mother's eyes,
The love she cannot tell me . . .
—Chester Gillette's last poem (1906)

Book 2 passed through further revisions before it reached T. R. Smith's desk. On June 3 the editor told Dreiser that he had read "the last five or six chapters . . . with real agony. The slow, fatal working-up to the death of Roberta is one of the grimmest and most gripping tragedies that I have read in years. The whole idea was so powerful that I had difficulty in re-editing it for you." But with barely concealed anxiety he asked, Where was book 3? They had received no copy whatsoever.

In July Smith sent books 1 and 2 to the printer. Planning on October publication, he urged Dreiser to finish the final section as speedily as possible. Liveright was aiming for the novel to be out in time for the Christmas season and had already begun beating the drums, stimulating advance interest among booksellers and reviewers.

On August 17 Smith begged Dreiser to forward all of the manuscript that had been typed. But Dreiser would not be rushed, and he continued to revise. He was still wading through the proofs of books 1 and 2, working night and day to keep up, and Louise came up from Philadelphia to read and cut on the spot.

• • •

Despite his immersion in the novel, he might have been sardonically amused to hear of an episode that summer at the Fire Island cottage of Gene Fowler, the flamboyant journalist from Denver. On a weekend in August, while Dreiser was sweating over proofs, Fowler entertained Jug. Among her male friends was an editor of the New York *Times*, and that connection probably explains her acquaintanceship with the raffish Fowler. The latter was struck by her obsession with Dreiser more than a decade after their marriage had ended. After reciting a litany of the sacrifices she had made for his career, she said, "Theo hasn't written anything worth while since our separation—and he never will."

Jug appeared in the *Tragedy*, as to a lesser extent did all the women who had tried to bind Dreiser with the chains of marriage or guilt. (Clyde's nickname for Roberta is "Bert"—the same name as Dreiser's for Estelle Kubitz.) Significantly, Dreiser made Roberta two years older than Clyde, the same discrepancy as between his and Jug's ages (Grace Brown was twenty when she died and Chester nearly twenty-three), strengthening the subconscious triangle of wife-mother versus giving mistress.

● ● ●

Having completed the first two parts of the *Tragedy*, Dreiser had crossed the mountain range. For Clyde's trial he drew on the *World's* account, quoting snatches of testimony and counsels' remarks, but significantly rearranging the order of events. His most notable borrowing was several passages from Grace Brown's love letters, the reading of which had stunned the spectators at the Gillette trial. The headline from the *World* the following morning conveys some of the impact:

COURT IN TEARS
AS LOVE LETTERS
BARE GIRL'S SOUL.
MISSIVES EPIC IN THEIR
WOMANLY SWEETNESS.

The letters had been found among Gillette's possessions. Indeed, he had accommodatingly told the DA where they were located, almost pronouncing his own death sentence, for no upstate New York jury in 1906 would have let him off after hearing the plaintive voice of Grace Brown reincarnated in court. To show the letters' effect at the trial, Dreiser quotes passages from Grace's, compressing them and changing the wording slightly—muddying their simple pathos in the process.

He altered the facts in the 1906 trial in more important ways. To emphasize the political ambitions of the district attorney, who is a candidate for county judge, he sets the trial before the election. In real life there was partisan rivalry between prosecutor Ward and defense counsel Mills, a former state senator, but Ward had been elected before the trial. The fictional DA, Mason, is also given a more extensive background in local politics than Ward had.

The most significant departure was Dreiser's staging of the courtroom drama. In the first place, he altered the sequence of the trial. For obvious dramatic reasons he has the DA read Roberta's letters last. Ward introduced them before the crucial testimony of the five doctors who signed the autopsy report. (In Dreiser's first draft he follows the sequence of the trial more slavishly.) Clyde's attorneys do not make an issue of the bungled autopsy, as did Chester's—who had good reason to do so.

He also transformed the tactics of the lawyers, particularly Ward's. Mason in the novel is a much more aggressive and adroit cross-examiner than was the real-life DA. The latter jumped around in time and place in an attempt to confuse Gillette, which succeeded. But to follow that course would have confused the reader of the novel as well. Rather than tediously exposing each of the inconsistencies of Clyde's alibis, Dreiser stages a dramatic confrontation: Mason hauls in the very boat in which Roberta and Clyde rowed on the lake and has Clyde reenact what happened. Ward had Chester describe the overturning of the boat in the witness chair.

And while Ward contemptuously dismissed Chester's story that after looking around for Grace and seeing nothing, he swam ashore, Mason dwells far more on the fact that Clyde let the girl drown, since that is an element of his moral guilt. Ward, of course, was espousing the blow-on-the-head theory, so Clyde's omission was not as important to his case, although he stressed that Chester was a good swimmer and boatman.

In contrast to Gillette's defense team, Clyde's attorneys press the theory that Clyde was bewitched by love. "A case of the Arabian Nights," observes the philosophical lawyer Jephson, "of the ensorcelled and the ensorcellor." "I don't know what you mean," Clyde says. Jephson replies: "A case of being bewitched, my poor boy—by beauty, love, wealth, by things that we sometimes think we want very, very much and cannot ever have. . . . "

Far from slavishly cribbing from the transcript, Dreiser staged the trial in masterly fashion and wrote dialogue that stated afresh the themes of his novel.

•   •   •

After the verdict and the sentence, Dreiser follows closely real-life events: Clyde's transfer to the death house at Auburn prison, his appeal, the clemency hearing before the governor (although the cast in the novel is different), the execution. Little was known about how Gillette endured his last months. As his appeals dragged on to their fruitless conclusion and his hopes that he would ultimately be freed were dashed, he saw virtually no one but his mother, his sister, and the Reverend Henry MacIlravy, an evangelist who had met Chester's mother during her unsuccessful lecture campaign to raise a defense fund for her son. With Louisa Gillette's approval, MacIlravy set out to convert Chester and succeeded. The minister is the inspiration for one of Dreiser's strongest characterizations, the Reverend Duncan McMillan.

The nature of the spiritual transactions between Gillette and MacIlravy is unknown, but in a state of intense isolation and after all hope of a reversal on appeal had vanished, Chester confessed his sins and accepted Jesus Christ as his Redeemer. The scenes when the minister is exhorting Clyde parallel Ward's cross-examination in court; each inquisitor cracks the young man's defenses, but he retains intact a core of belief in his innocence of murder and of unbelief in a Hereafter. Just as Clyde was also preserving a false innocence in court—his lawyer's concocted version of how Roberta met her death—so he at first withholds the true story from McMillan because he does not want to undermine his legal appeal. But when the appeal fails, and then the governor turns down his pleas for clemency, he confesses to McMillan, revealing the ambiguity in his own mind about whether he was guilty, legally or morally, of murder.

Weary, alone, and afraid, Clyde composes a statement, with McMillan's help, addressed to the young men of America, calling on them to accept Christ and live clean lives. Here Dreiser quotes verbatim the statement that Gillette issued on the eve of his execution. He confessed to MacIlravy and the prison chaplain that he had killed Grace; the details of the confession were never made public. Just before the execution, Governor Charles Evans Hughes, who had conducted exhaustive inquiries into some alleged new evidence, finding it neither credible nor relevant, called the prison and was told of the confession. The news eased his conscience, Hughes wrote in his memoirs, and he slept soundly for the first time in many weeks.

In Dreiser's version, only the minister and Elvira Griffiths plead with the governor. And it is the man of God who betrays him. Asked point-blank by the governor if he knows any reason why Clyde should not be executed, McMillan retreats into theology: Clyde sinned in his heart. The one man who might have saved Clyde forsakes him—does not even mention his sincere contrition, or the extenuating circumstances, which seemed so compelling when related to him by Clyde and which, Dreiser implies, might have moved the governor to grant clemency. Instead he adheres to the letter but not the spirit of the Word.

●　　●　　●

As Clyde is awaiting word on his appeal, a letter arrives—typed, unsigned, mailed from a large city, but unmistakably from Sondra. She can never understand his deed, but she "is not without sorrow and sympathy" and wishes him "freedom and happiness." No words of love to confirm that the dream for which he had risked all had not been a mirage: "His last hope—the last trace of his dream vanished. Forever! It was at that moment, as when night at last falls upon the faintest remaining gleam of dusk in the west. A dim, weakening tinge of pink—and then the dark."

Once upon a time Dreiser and Helen had shared a dream of the West. She was the Golden Girl, so beautiful that he feared she might suddenly vanish. California for a time held the promise of a life of sensuous ease and fulfillment, of money and luxury and beauty. But the mirage had dissipated, and he reluctantly returned to the reality of New York. Of course, Sondra was not literally modeled on Helen, but what she represented was. She did, however, share Helen's penchant for baby talk. With touches like this, and the initials C. G. for Gillette/Griffiths, the nickname Bert, the disparity between Clyde's and Roberta's ages, Dreiser dropped clues to his plagiarism from life—and his own subconscious.

•   •   •

Reverend McMillan accompanies Clyde on his last walk, and after it is over he is sick, thinking only of Clyde's eyes. Those eyes are his most prominent feature throughout the novel. Marguerite Tjader Harris, who was Dreiser's literary companion in later years, wrote that "eye magnetism fascinated Dreiser. His right eye impaired from birth and virtually useless to him, he believed he himself had become mystically endowed with eye magnetism at the moment of his mother's death." To Dreiser, the eyes were potent, flashing power and ambition, and instruments of artistic voyeurism, gatherers of "material," registering coldly and clinically. McMillan recalls Clyde in the chair: "his eyes fixed nervously and . . . appealingly and dazedly upon him. . . ."

•   •   •

As he approached the end of book 3, Dreiser became uneasy about the death-house scenes. On November 14, more than two weeks after the chapter had been set in type, he asked Mencken to intervene with friends at the *World* and wangle him a pass to the death row at Sing Sing prison—though "not the Execution room," he added. He had no desire to witness what went on behind that metal door. Mencken wrote James M. Cain, then an editorial writer on the paper. Cain replied that the visit could be arranged.

But when a judge granted the necessary order, Dreiser was surprised to learn that it authorized him to interview a convicted murderer named Anthony Pantano and that, moreover, the *World* expected him to write a story about it. The day after the visit Mencken received a telegram from the newspaper saying that Dreiser had demanded $500. Mencken wired his displeasure to Dreiser: "THIS PUTS ME IN A NICE HOLE INDEED." Furious, Dreiser hit back: "THE WORLD LIES YOUR TELEGRAM IS AN INSULT." Caught in the middle, Mencken called down a pox on both sides. Dreiser wrote him a spluttering letter belaboring the *World* and the American press in general, and insisting that he had never been told that he was supposed to write about Pantano for nothing.

The paper had probably induced the judge to approve the visit by saying that Dreiser was on assignment to check out a rumor that Pantano was about to make a confession. But after granting the request, the judge heard about Dreiser's novel and suspected that the assignment was not bona fide. The *World*, fearing that he would deny them access to convicts in the future, pressed Dreiser to write the article to prove the commission was legitimate. Dreiser, oblivious to these maneuvers, busy packing and closing up the Brooklyn apartment, and assuming that the visit was arranged through Mencken's connections, demanded a fee. The *World*, which had expected him to do it out of gratitude, refused. The affair was settled amicably: Dreiser related his impressions to reporter Dudley Nichols, and it was published on page 1 under the banner: "Dreiser Interviews Pantano in Death House: Doomed Man Avows Faith in a Hereafter."

In the interview Dreiser described the layout of death row, the "heavy silence" that hung in the cellblock, the guards in their black uniforms and felt-soled shoes, who reminded him of an apparition in *The Cabinet of Dr. Caligari*, "a strangely stretched-out being, with thin, twining arms that twist above his head. . . ." — an odd association, but evidently to Dreiser the place had a surreal quality like the movie. The inmates lay silently on their bunks. "One opened an unwinking eye and regarded me stilly, as if he were in another medium beyond communication, like a fish in an aquarium."

Dreiser told Mencken that the visit added little to his description of death row in the novel: "my imagination was better — (more true to the fact) — than what I saw." He did add a few details on the galleys — describing how the men played checkers with numbered boards; changing "No newspapers" to "No privacy," because the prisoners were allowed newspapers; changing a "solid Irish trusty" to a "tall cadaverous guard," like the one he had seen. Otherwise, the layout of his death house and the one at Sing Sing were completely different, and he may have made up his out of whole cloth. Clearly, he wrote his descriptions before he visited Sing Sing, and that description, save for a few touches, remains. The visit served to confirm his point that the death house was a psychological torture chamber.

The contretemps with Mencken soured their relations after five years of relative harmony. Mencken chose to ignore Dreiser's squawk, but privately he was exasperated, as was Dreiser with him for initially taking the *World*'s side in the dispute. On December 5 he sent Dreiser a copy of Isaac Goldberg's recently published biography, *The Man Mencken*, inscribed, "For Theodore Dreiser, Enemy for 18 years!" — a joke, of course.

•   •   •

Dreiser completed the novel on November 25, Helen writes. He made some small changes on the proofs, mostly corrections in the death-house scenes. He had done more extensive rewriting on earlier galleys, particularly in book 2 (book 1 was little changed). Many of these changes consisted of adding scenes, rearranging events, clarifying motivation, or altering or expanding Clyde's perceptions. For example, Dreiser inserts some language to intensify Mason's hatred of the rich, emphasizing the force of class behind his early determination to "get" Clyde, who he assumes is a wealthy young idler. There are some minor changes in the trial, including interpolations of legal maneuvers by another hand—probably J. G. Robin's—to make the lawyers' tactics more authentic.

•   •   •

Now the book was too late for the Christmas season. What is more, the manuscript was already long—some four hundred thousand words—and it would be necessary to charge five dollars for each two-volume set. Smith, and Manuel Komroff, production manager at B & L, had already sought to lighten it by some fifty thousand words. When they told Dreiser the news, he supposedly said, "What the hell is 50,000 words between friends?"—and then restored more than half of them.

But he had at last delivered the book begun six years before, and meditated even longer. Liveright set December 10 as the publication date, although finished books weren't available until the fourteenth. The publisher also planned to issue a luxury edition at $12.50 a set, signed by the author. He had advance orders for ten thousand copies of the trade edition, and excitement was building. By that time Dreiser was too exhausted to care and was desperate to get out of town, partly for a rest and partly to escape the reviews, which he expected to be hostile.

Helen was worried about him. He had been "battered" by the book (and by the love triangle in which he had been embroiled). From the novel, however much he tried, he could never escape; the writing machine kept pumping relentlessly, never giving him surcease for long, until the job was finished. At times depression radiated from him like a malign aura. Louise Campbell recalled: "You'd almost feel the air was black around him as he sat there for long stretches and said nothing." Sally Kusell thought him megalomaniacal, totally self-absorbed.

Helen was spiritually battered too. She later summed up that last year: " 'The dark days of Brooklyn,' he once wrote. And so they were. Dark days for all of us."

Walking with Clyde that last mile had taken him to a private philosophical dead end: for if the individual could be swept into dissolution without help or fellow-feeling, meaning, or hope of hereafter, life was a bleak business. Dreiser had faced the implications of his mechanistic philosophy before, but never so emotionally as in writing about the death of Clyde, alone and afraid, without hope of eternal life or any consolation of religion or philosophy, without even understanding why he must die. The door of hope clanged shut.

68 / "The Great American Novel"

> Your writer, your scientist, your chief official, all have lost
> the power to revive the early illusion concerning fame and
> high place. Their beauty and delight is like the mirage in the
> heavens only plain to the eye outside. Within is nothing. . . .
> —Dreiser, "The Bubble of Success" (ca. 1898)

After vacating the Brooklyn apartment, Helen and Dreiser moved to temporary
quarters. He was considering a walking trip, his favorite therapy for bad nerves,
but the weather was too cold, and they decided to drive to Florida. Helen had
to rush about obtaining a new license plate. Dreiser let few people know of his
plans. Just the previous Saturday he had told Sally Kusell what he had earlier
written Mencken—that he was going hiking in the mountains of Virginia—
alone.

That was propaganda. Sally had retreated to Larchmont and thus did not
work on the final ten chapters of the *Tragedy.* But she and Dreiser managed to
sneak a "glorious Saturday together." Dreiser did not tell her that Helen was
driving him to Florida.

They got away on December 8. Dreiser climbed into the Maxwell beside
Helen, and they were off. Helen had a terrible cold, and he had caught it.
When they reached Philadelphia, both were miserable.

After consulting with Louise about editing *The Financier* for a new, trim-
mer edition, he joined Helen at the Wharton Eshericks', near Philadelphia.
Then they drove to Baltimore, and Dreiser called on Mencken unannounced,
leaving Helen in the car. After almost an hour, Mencken suddenly realized that
Helen must be with him and rushed outside to invite her in. He had just that
day taken his gravely ill mother to the hospital for an operation, and was too
distraught to talk about much but his fears that she would not survive an operation. Dreiser, however, appeared to be more interested in obtaining a bottle of
scotch from Mencken's private cellar. After some desultory conversation, Dreiser

left without saying anything about Anna Mencken. Helen uttered some plati-
tudes at the door, but it was too late. Mencken was deeply offended by Dreiser's
apparent insensitivity.

•   •   •

In Florida the great land bubble was just then passing its zenith. Dreiser wrote
Mencken: "The state is all ready completely sub-divided in lots 50 × 80—and
being sold off at from 150.00 to 50,000 per lot. . . . All the awnings, water
piles & lanterns—domes and lattices of Venice, Sorrento, Capri—and Spain
& Italy are being copied in plaster & papier-maché, and sold to crackers as
romance, gaiety."

Mencken's reply, written six days later, carried a subtle reproach: "My poor
mother died the day after you were in Baltimore. I suppose that you noticed
I was rather disturbed when we met." Unfortunately, he didn't know Dreiser's
address and so sent the letter c/o Liveright, so Dreiser didn't receive it until his
return to New York, in early February. Only then did he pen some consolatory
words: "These things are in the chemistry and the physics of this immense thing
and *'wisdom'* avails not at all. Yet fortitude is exacted of us all whether we will
or not. I offer—understanding."

•   •   •

Donald McCord, brother of the artist Peter, was one of the first to congratulate
him on the *Tragedy*. Dreiser replied, "Letters such as yours—(not the general
run of criticism by any means) have satisfied me that the work is sound. I hear
the usual drivel concerning style." He was putting up a bold front, for he had
received no word about the reviews. On publication day, Liveright wired that
he had ordered paper for another large printing, but the critics were still to be
heard from.

At first the news was not very encouraging—a letter from T. R. Smith
saying that Sinclair Lewis had declined to compose a prepublication blurb after
reading the galleys. A more flattering letter arrived from the poet Arthur Ficke.
Dreiser displayed his usual phlegmatism, saying he had fled New York "to avoid
a deluge of knocks." But whatever the critics said, the book was done: "And
that's that. I hope it soothes some. It entertained me for many a day."

Then came a telegram from Sally Kusell reporting that Stuart P. Sherman
had written a favorable review in the *New York Herald Tribune Books* on January
3. Sherman's prominent notice was only the beginning. On January 9, Smith
wired: THE REVIEWS ARE AMAZING ENTHUSIASTIC AND DIGNIFIED YOUR POSITION IS
RECOGNIZED THE SALES ARE EXCELLENT.

This was followed by another telegram from Kusell on January 12 informing him that 17,000 copies had been sold. According to Liveright's figures, 13,378 copies were sold in December alone, netting Dreiser $11,872.02 in royalties. In one month he made more money from the *Tragedy* than he had from any of his previous books. Dreiser wrote Lengel: "It seems to have gone over the top. And none more surprised than myself."

It was ironic that the bellwether review had been written by his old foe. Sherman even alluded to his earlier crusade against Dreiser, but he explained that, in the years since The *"Genius,"* Dreiser had grown to understand American society, a polite way of saying he had become assimilated. As a result, his books had gained a greater artistic "detachment," "objectivity," and "impartiality." Dreiser's analysis of the psychological forces that drove Clyde to his doom, he said, was "complete and convincing"; more significant, his understanding of the predicament of poor Roberta showed that Dreiser had become a "good moralist." One need only compare Dreiser's "romantic glozing" of Jennie Gerhardt with his "exhaustive and astoundingly intelligent study of the shame and misery and torment of Roberta Alden in being pregnant, penniless, without a husband" to grasp how much he had matured since he published "that earlier sentimental tale."

The real comparison was between the Jennie who "got away with it" and the factory girl who pays for her transgression; the portrait of Roberta is true, Sherman says, because it illustrated the wages of sin. Sherman was an accurate barometer of middlebrow taste. Only a decade earlier, reviewers could praise Dreiser's realism but warn of his immorality. Now Sherman certified Dreiser's realism morally pure.

•   •   •

Late in January, Dreiser told Helen, "Well, it looks as if I've hit the mark this time. I think I'll go back home and collect some of the spoils." On January 25, 1926, they sailed from Miami on the *Kroonland,* the ship on which Dreiser had returned from Europe in 1913.

A pile of reviews—the finest of his career—awaited him in New York. The writers heaped on the superlatives:

> . . . the biggest, most important American of our times. (Sherwood Anderson, *Saturday Review of Literature*)
>
> The appearance of "An American Tragedy" is an event of first-class importance in the history of American letters. . . . (Abraham Cahan, *Jewish Daily Forward*)
>
> "An American Tragedy" is, in fine, the greatest of its author's works, and that can hardly mean less than that it is the greatest American novel of our generation. (Joseph Wood Krutch, *The Nation*)

. . . the Mount Everest of American fiction, and . . . one of the high hills in all the fiction of the world. (Heywood Broun, New York *World*)

. . . the best novel yet written by the greatest of American novelists. (Gretchen Mount, Detroit *Free Press*)

[*An*] *American Tragedy* is . . . one of the very greatest novels of this century. (H. G. Wells)

The *Tragedy* was praised for the soundness of its construction ("as solid as a bank building"); its exhaustive documentation ("He has fortified his charges with informing detail of every sort, biological, erotic, anatomical, contraceptual" [sic]); the tragic power of the narrative, especially the final scenes ("Oh, it is a painful story, a harrowing story, relentless and awful in its inevitability"); the catholicity of understanding shown the characters ("the author, with large sympathy and admirable impartiality brings out all that is strong and touching in the narrow and deluded religionist [Elvira Griffiths]"); the probing critique of American culture ("a tacit record of a parching absence of beauty in the common life").

Being Dreiser, he could not escape "the usual drivel concerning style." One critic insisted that the style was the man. Dreiser could not write as he does, "mixing slang with poetic archaisms, reveling in the cheap, trite and florid, if he were not, in himself, something correspondingly muddled, banal and tawdry." But in a letter to the editor of *The New Republic,* a poor young novelist named Henry Miller took issue with this attack, contending, "He uses language, consciously or not, in the manner which modern writers, notably Joyce, use deliberately: that is, he identifies his language with the consciousness of his characters."

Moralistic reviewers read the *Tragedy* as an exposé of Errant Youth. It was true that as an inveterate observer of the conflict between generations, Dreiser had unintentionally probed in a profounder way than the flaming-youth novels the youth culture that flowered in the 1920s, when young people of the white middle class were drawn away from the parental authority by mass cultural forces—magazines, movies, styles, music, dances—and had become independently mobile in their own Fords as well as socially mobile in their separate peer worlds centered in high school and college, a subculture with its own mores, initiation rites, secret societies, dress codes, slang, and manners and morals.

In the 1920s, mass culture (which Dreiser had amply observed in Hollywood films) set the styles. Clyde's initial break from his family is via a working-class peer group—his fellow bellhops, who teach him to drink, patronize prostitutes, and speed to roadhouse dances. He acquires the hedonistic values that clash with his parents' religious ones. Later, in Lycurgus, when he infiltrates Sondra's set, he is exposed to broader vistas of youthful pleasure—summers at the lake, tennis, dinner dances.

It is in Lycurgus that the barriers of class rear up in Clyde's path. Dreiser's inspiration is to delineate the tenuousness of his position as a poor relation of one of the town's wealthiest families. To his fellow employees at the shirt factory, to the clerks in the stores he patronizes, and above all to Roberta, Clyde is a Griffiths, part of the Lycurgus elite of power and money, and he begins playing this role to the hilt. Roberta sees rich and poor in Lycurgus "divided by a high wall."

Clyde's vain, snobbish cousin Gilbert is invidiously contrasted with his father to make another observation about American society: the change from a manufacturing to a consumer economy. The honorable, commanding Samuel Griffiths exemplifies the old producer class, living by an inner-directed credo, the Protestant ethic of hard work and postponement of gratification. Gilbert embraces this ethic as an ideology of control over the employees, but he expects material and social rewards as a matter of right, not as the result of hard work. Clyde, the arriviste, is drawn to the conspicuous-consumption lifestyle of the "fast set" and tries to slip into their ranks by imitating their dress and manners and by love, just as Carrie Meeber rose by attracting men of higher social position and then by practicing her allure on audiences in the theater.

Just as Dreiser made Carrie's career upend the values of the shopgirl novels of the 1890s, so he uses the Alger myth (hoary but still honored by the business society of the 1920s) to ironic effect in the *Tragedy*. Dreiser subverts the Alger story not because he thought it pernicious (the idea of a poor, worthy lad rising in the world had inspired him as a boy) but because he believes that American culture has betrayed it by making the end, success, more important than the means and by condoning a money-oriented, inegalitarian society. Even Samuel Griffiths belies the myth, for he started his business with $15,000 he had inherited (the luckless Asa Griffiths was cut out of the will).

With the scalpel of irony Dreiser probes the dreams—and nightmares—of American culture, its ordinary terrors and tawdry illusions. Therein lies his lasting claim as one of America's most acute social analysts—not of mere manners (like Sinclair Lewis) but of the psychological, economic, and social structures that undergird class and manners. Not that Dreiser wrote a Marxist analysis or a sociological study. He molded his massive indictment of American society out of the pain of exclusion and hunger for material success. The prosaic dream of wealth and romance is heightened into a craving for beauty—and so it would be seen by one who has known the dirt and humiliation of being poor. Yet it is all a mirage.

At the core of the novel is not the American dream but the American nightmare, a vertiginous fear of falling, of social extinction, of being a nobody. (Dreiser had once considered titling the novel *Icarus*.) This dread is carried to the ultimate nightmare—of being a criminal hounded by society for a horrible crime one both did not and did commit. After the terror of flight from the Furies, Clyde is tried and found guilty. He is taken to death row, dressed in drab prison garb, and placed in the company of pariahs like himself. He has been stripped of all the symbols of his former status. And then the great machine of the state impersonally, indifferently exterminates him.

Dreiser's power not only emanates from his patient accretion of facts; it also comes from the psychological resonances behind the facts. He drags the reader beneath the social surface into black depths of terror and desire, death and dreams.

Dreiser sensed that he must avoid the philosophizing that marred his earlier books; perhaps he had learned something from the younger novelists about understatement and from the visual power of film. He later told an interviewer, "I never once intruded upon this book my own point of view or interpretation or philosophy, nor even indulged myself in the relief of painting a word picture here and there. . . . " When he was finished, "the result seemed so foreign to me that I simply couldn't adjust myself to it at all. . . . It struck me as being . . . a monumental failure."

69 / *"Opulent, Opulent"*

> Now we waited about the large bare table, while the lady set
> the cake before her and sat down. "A chocolate cake!" Dreiser
> licked his lips. The lady cut a slice. Dreiser grew nervous. The
> lady cut a slice. Dreiser's eyes bulged, his hands thrummed.
> She cut a slice. Dreiser tipped his chair, sprawled forward.
> . . . Swiftly, as if working against a possible crisis, the good
> lady put a piece of cake on a plate and handed it to Dreiser.
> He fell to, happy, rolling his eyes.
>
> —Waldo Frank (1926)

No one, least of all Dreiser, would have predicted that his novel would strike
the lucrative vein it did. The first intimation of wealth came not long after
his return, when Liveright suggested dramatizing *An American Tragedy*. He
needed a Broadway hit, and it looked promising—an acclaimed novel that his
showman's instinct told him could have a sensational impact in the theater. To
do the adaptation, Liveright chose an unknown, Patrick Kearney, a young actor
with one produced play to his credit called *A Man's Man*, which had caused a
minor stir in a little theater production.

The publisher told Dreiser in his March 8 letter that the question of movie
rights was academic. Given the present moralistic climate in Hollywood, "it's
extremely doubtful that *An American Tragedy* can even be done on the screen.
Tremendous pressure would have to be brought on Hays to let him pass it, and
then the theme is such that it's rather unlikely that any company who would
make a good picture out of it would care to go on it."

Liveright was repeating what Jesse L. Lasky (whose readers had rejected the
Tragedy in galleys) told him. But after the studio head saw Quinn Martin's movie
column in the New York *World* on March 7, he changed his mind. Martin wrote
that *An American Tragedy* "if courageously treated would make the greatest film
yet produced."

The upshot was that the movie mogul vowed he must have the book;
price was no object. Also, he was on good terms with Will Hays, whom he

had helped install as president of the Motion Picture Producers and Distributors of America after the Fatty Arbuckle scandal, and may have thought that given the novel's reputation as a serious work of art, the arbiter of movie morals could be persuaded to approve it.

On March 17 Dreiser wrote Louise Campbell that he had decided to stay in New York for a while rather than take Helen on a long-promised junket to Paris, because "they're making a play of the *Tragedy* & there's something else in the wind." Two days later, when he appeared at Liveright's office to sign the play contract, the publisher announced that he was having lunch with Lasky and his special assistant, Walter Wanger, to discuss terms for a movie sale. This surprising intelligence planted in Dreiser's suspicious brain the idea that Liveright had been lying to him about Lasky's lack of interest and had some kind of sub rosa arrangement with him. Hadn't Liveright told him ten days ago that it was doubtful a movie could be made of the book, and that Lasky would pay $35,000 at most and only if the play were produced? The publisher's friendship with Lasky (Liveright later said he gave "absolute loyalty" to the movie company) exuded the smell of collusion.

Dreiser didn't know that Lasky had suddenly blown hot and had been trying to reach him for several days. Once he had decided to buy the novel immediately, he didn't need Liveright's play—or Liveright. In his autobiography Lasky says that the publisher had engaged in "delaying tactics" by concealing Dreiser's whereabouts.

Thus began a chain reaction of misunderstandings. Presumably, all Liveright knew was that the movie sale hinged on the play. For taking the risk of producing the dramatic version of *An American Tragedy*, he felt he was entitled to a portion of the Hollywood gold. Horace was suffering from chronic cash-flow shortage. He planned two new productions (*The Best of Us* and *Black Boy*, a play about a Negro prizefighter, starring Paul Robeson), and producing the *Tragedy* as well would be costly.

Liveright asked Dreiser what he wanted for the film rights. When he said $100,000, the highest amount ever paid for a novel, Liveright opined that $60,000 was more realistic, but told Dreiser to stick to his guns and invited him to come to lunch with the film people and state his demand in person. Then he asked if Dreiser would "take care" of him: anything above $60,000 should be his. To that Dreiser merely smiled sardonically—amused, he later said, at how Liveright had so quickly changed his tune. The publisher, however, took the smile as a sign of assent. The two of them had a few drinks and strolled to the Ritz. En route, Liveright again asked Dreiser if he would take care of him, and Dreiser said he would.

And so they joined the two movie men in the soigné dining room. Over coffee Liveright, in one last try at steering the negotiations, announced that he and Dreiser had agreed on a price: $100,000, of which he would receive $30,000 and Dreiser $70,000. The two men's recollections of what happened next diverge. Liveright said Dreiser seemed to assent to that formulation. Dreiser insisted that he had promptly told Lasky and Wanger that such a split was news to him. Liveright then excused himself from the table.

In the ensuing discussion Dreiser bluntly asked Lasky why he was buying the film. The other replied: "The way it is, the movies are under criticism today and we want to do something; as a matter of fact, we want to make a gesture and we can do it through this book." Dreiser then asked Lasky if he would make "a great feature picture" out of the book. The other promised he would. Then, Dreiser said, my price shouldn't stop you. He also claimed he requested an additional fifteen or twenty thousand for Liveright as part of the deal.

When Liveright returned to the table, he inquired about the 30 percent share. Dreiser protested that he was obligated to give him only 10 percent. (This was true. Quite apart from their agreement on *An American Tragedy*, an earlier contract awarded Liveright 10 percent of any movie sale he made.) The publisher protested that they had agreed on the higher figure. Dreiser retorted, "That's a damn lie." The publisher's smiling mask vanished. "You're a liar!" he shouted. The other diners looked on in shocked silence as a furious and red-faced author rose to his full 6 feet ½ inch, shouted an oath, and told his publisher to stand up and fight. When the 130-pound Liveright prudently remained seated, Dreiser picked up a cup of warm coffee and dashed the contents in his face. A waiter mopped up the drenched victim as Dreiser stalked out.

The following week Lasky and Dreiser agreed on a total price of $90,000, of which Liveright would receive $10,000. Liveright was hurt by what he saw as Dreiser's ingratitude and stunned by the sudden turn his fortunes had taken at that lunch. In private he remained embittered, telling friends that his efforts alone had made the sale possible. As for Dreiser, he firmly believed that Liveright had tried to pull a fast one by concealing Lasky's interest. Yet the entire quarrel had come about because Lasky, after telling Liveright about the difficulties of filming the novel, had changed his mind upon reading Martin's column and talking to his associates. Liveright acted on the basis of what Lasky told him before the column. Moreover, Dreiser might well ask, how could Liveright claim a 30-percent slice before the play was produced, contrary to their agreement? In the light of what Lasky told him at lunch, about trying to reach him, Liveright's conduct seemed suspicious indeed. Dreiser already mistrusted the man; this was the proof.

Still seething, Dreiser dispatched a harsh letter to Liveright demanding a written apology. As usual, the publisher turned the other cheek. He really could not afford to lose his now-profitable author. In his first reply, he swore that the Ritz meeting was not a "set-up" to bilk Dreiser. His main desire all along was to see that Dreiser "got everything possible out of this book."

Six days later, Donald Friede, who had lunched with Dreiser in the interim, reported to him that Dreiser had been hurt by the charge that he had lied. Liveright formally apologized and tried to put the fracas behind them. He dangled the promise of a new promotional campaign for the *Tragedy*, which he would personally supervise and which would exploit the movie sale.

That campaign was duly launched with a statement by Lasky to the press that the movie of *An American Tragedy* "will be the most ambitious effort made by our company." Every studio in Hollywood had wanted the book, he said, and Famous Players won the contest only "after the payment of a record sum, and also after we had given a guaranty to Mr. Dreiser that the book would be filmed exactly as it is written." Dreiser would later have reason to question those words.

• • •

Another imbroglio marred Dreiser's return to New York. H. L. Mencken's review did not appear until *The American Mercury* hit the stalls in late February, but he had written it in January. On January 28 he had warned Dreiser, almost apologetically, "I have taken a dreadful hack at the book in the Merkur for March, but there is also some very sweet stuff in the notice. I am sending a proof to Schmidt [Smith]."

It was devastating. Mencken calls *An American Tragedy* a "shapeless and forbidding monster—a heaping cartload of raw materials for a novel, with rubbish of all sorts intermixed—a vast, sloppy, chaotic thing of 385,000 words—at least 250,000 of them unnecessary!" Whole chapters could be spared; it is full of "banal moralizing and trite, meaningless words." "Is Freudism stale, even in Greenwich Village? Ahoy, then, let us heave in a couple of bargeloads of complexes. . . . " And, quoting an awkward sentence: "What is one to say of such dreadful bilge? What is one to say of a novelist who, after a quarter of a century at his trade, still writes it?"

He relents a little in his summing up, writing, "'An American Tragedy,' as a work of art, is a colossal botch, but as a human document it is searching and full of solemn dignity, and at times it rises to the level of genuine tragedy. . . . Hire your pastor to read the first volume for you. But don't miss the second!" But the damage had been done.

Mencken had come of age as a critic when the chief literary battles were against the Puritans. Now Dreiser not only was acceptable in the better literary circles; he was popular with Puritans such as Stuart P. Sherman. The broadside in the *Mercury* had little effect on the sales of the *Tragedy* or the canonization of Dreiser, but it would destroy a friendship. A few years later, writing in his diary, Mencken blamed the *World* quarrel for the rupture, along with Dreiser's insensitivity about his mother's death. He wrote that Dreiser did not offer any condolences, forgetting that he had written a sympathetic letter upon his return from Florida. Mencken says nothing about his hostile review of the *Tragedy*, and he had often urged Dreiser not to take critical opinions personally. But Dreiser did; to him the review was a betrayal.

In a letter to Mencken written February 8, Dreiser starts out normally enough, reporting that he and Helen are staying at the Empire Hotel and inviting Mencken to dine with them sometime. But then his anger boils up in a postscript; "As for your critical predilictions [sic], animosities, inhibitions, — et cet. Tush. who reads you? Bums and loafers. No goods. We were friends before ever you were a critic of mine, if I recall. And, — if an humble leman may speak up—may remain so—despite various—well—choose your insults."

Mencken disdained to reply; the feud was on. Encountering Mencken's assistant, Charles Angoff, a few months later, Dreiser remonstrated, "That boss of yours ought to stay in Baltimore on the *Sun* and keep out of writing about books. [Eugene] O'Neill is luckier than the rest of us. He has George Nathan to write about him. Now, Nathan knows playwriting. I can feel it inside me. But Mencken—oh well. What does it matter, anyway?"

Mencken acted throughout as though he couldn't understand why Dreiser was angry, and he professed indifference to the sudden chill in their relations. But Dreiser had expected Mencken to hail it, and instead he had hurled the same kind of wounding invective that he'd used in his review of *The "Genius."*

•   •   •

Around the time Dreiser lashed out at Mencken he shed another friend, Sally Kusell. The provocation seems trivial. Apparently, she had asked him to give her a personally autographed copy of the *Tragedy*, recognizing her contribution to it, and he resented the request, having begun to feel she was crowding him too close, calling him "Master" and all that. It may have been ingratitude on his part, or else she demanded more credit for the success of the book than he was willing to give her. Like Dreiser's other lovers, she made the mistake of finding her identity in his greatness. She admitted she was jealous of Helen but assured him that she didn't aim to intrude on his life with her, as she had done when they were in Florida. To put a stop to that, Dreiser had refused to give her his New York address. A week later he hit her with a formal indictment, as it were:

> The trouble between us springs . . . from the firm conviction that your interest in me is somehow based more on a desire for mental and artistic recognition through me than it is on any innate personal and ineffective as well as effective qualities which may characterize me. . . . The matter of inscribing the book was one of those chance flashes which reveal so much. There must be some form of written recognition consoling to an ego that sees—or did see in me as a writer—not as a man, —some form of personal achievement & stimulation for you.

Sally sent him a stream of beseeching letters. Finally, in March, she departed for California. Helen, whose resentment against Sally had erupted in Florida, could claim a victory. Indeed, she had the satisfaction of personally receiving her rival's surrender. Just before Sally left for California, she called Dreiser to tell him that her train was scheduled to depart Penn Station at such and such a time. Helen, who had answered the telephone, politely agreed to relay the message. Then Sally told her, "You are the only one I was ever afraid of. . . . You have him *always*, he comes *home* to you." Helen agreed that he did, though that had not made life any easier for her. Sally commiserated with her sufferings, then confessed she knew she had lost after Helen's return from California, when she noticed "a definite change in him, a psychic strength I felt I could not beat." Sally conceded first place to Helen. "I felt as though I wanted to put my arms around her," Helen writes.

• • •

Scarred by many disappointments over a twenty-year career as a full-time novelist, Dreiser found himself at the age of fifty-four in the promised land of wealth and ease that Clyde Griffiths had died trying to attain. Innately frugal and suspicious of wealth (he had seen it destroy his brother Paul), his instinct was to hoard what he got. Financial security and freedom to write what he pleased were his primary aims; money would give him more independence in his dealings with publishers.

But he was not an ascetic. As his bank account was enriched, his wardrobe blossomed. Waldo Frank, in a *New Yorker* "Profile," offers this snapshot: "If you see him nowadays, his ruddy face shining above the dapper clothes and his spatted boots pounding along beside the pumps of a flapper, you have a grotesque sense of an old college boy on a vacation. . . . "

Around this time Dreiser strode into John Cowper Powys's shabby Patchin Place flat and announced, "I am opulent, opulent! What can I give you?" Powys asked for a particular rare edition he had long coveted, and Dreiser bought it for him. Powys, a novelist never fully appreciated in his lifetime, once wrote that success "is an invariable sign, not of superiority, but of vitality . . . more brute force than imagination, and more *luck* than anything else!" Dreiser, however, was a "special case . . . one of those formidable Men of Destiny . . . . For once in human history the exploiters of genius have met their match in Dreiser. He can give as good as he takes, and a little more."

• • •

Dreiser's reputation, fanned by Liveright's publicity mills, grew apace. His public correspondence became so voluminous that he was forced to hire a secretary to handle it. The letters fell into four general categories: fan notes, appeals for money, pleas for advice from young writers, and requests for autographs, public statements, lectures. In the first category were heartfelt thanks for writing *An American Tragedy*, which was "comparable to no story I know of in its sympathy for the ignorance and weakness of young men. . . . " People wanted advice or understanding. An actress hoped that he was not in the "mist [sic] of a story, for my heart wants to pour out its life story all the secrets and heart aches the world must never know are mine."

One of Dreiser's correspondents was a voice from the past. On March 31 Jug sent him congratulations on his "wonderful good fortune," meaning the movie sale. She followed that with a second letter in which she asked if he might provide for her so that she could go back to Missouri and adopt her late sister Rose's daughter, Rosemary (now an orphan), thus fulfilling at last the dream of motherhood that Dreiser had thwarted. Dreiser replied, Wasn't it wonderful that, after all these years without a comment from her about any of the twelve books he had published, she should suddenly take an interest in his literary career? Did the fact that he had come into a considerable sum of money have something to do with it?

Unfair, Jug protested. Her admiration for his writing had been just as great before *Carrie* was even published. As for the other books, well, she had leafed through a few of them but had no time for reading. She reminded him that she had supported herself and had not bothered him about money over the years (though that was not for want of trying) because he had told her his income was erratic. Now, she assumed, he could afford to help her. At the age of fifty-seven and in frail health, she was in danger of losing her job in a dress store. In May, having heard nothing from Dreiser, she advised him to get in touch with her attorney.

Dreiser's old bitterness resurfaced. He told his lawyer, Dudley Field Malone, that when they were living together Jug had never been sympathetic with his work "and did everything to discourage me from proceeding with it." Her idea of success "was along very different lines." He had done his best writing while living apart from her. As for the alleged shower of wealth, he estimated that he would earn $20,000 from sales of *An American Tragedy* that year (too low by half, it turned out) and that he had "tentatively" sold the movie rights to the novel, receiving $35,000 as a "binder" (no mention of the additional $45,000 he had coming). He intended to invest as much of those funds as he could, "in order that the income . . . may keep me independent of publishers — permit me to work in my own way — guarantee me against a rainy day in the future, and possibly permit me to do at least a few of the things I have always wanted to do."

Having vented his old grudge, he agreed to pay her $200 a month for the rest of her life. In return she absolved him of liability for any debts she might incur and relinquished any claims on his estate after his death. There seems to have been some promise that she would agree to a divorce—or so Helen always insisted. But it is not at all clear that Jug would permit one. And Dreiser may not have pushed her for fear that a divorce settlement would have cost him even more. Also, there were advantages in preserving the status quo: The tie to Jug gave him a convenient out when other women started importuning him about marriage, as they usually did.

• • •

He was contemplating a separation of another sort. His contract with Liveright ran out in January 1927, and he entertained feelers from Harper's and Double-day. The spat with Liveright had inflamed his distrust of the man, though they were still speaking on business matters. He assiduously cultivated Arthur Pell, treasurer of the firm, and took up Liveright's offer to inspect the sales ledgers, though Bennett Cerf considered the procedure something of a joke.

Harper's was the more serious suitor, and Dreiser retained a nostalgia for the prolific years of his association with the firm, when he wrote *Jennie, The Financier*, and *The Titan*. In May the company offered to publish a uniform edition of his books. Such a proposition was not as risky as it had been a few years earlier; thanks to the success of the *Tragedy* and Liveright's institutional advertising campaign, sales of Dreiser's other novels had picked up. *Carrie* sold 3412 copies in 1926 (twice as many as the previous year), *Jennie* nearly 1400, and *The "Genius"* more than 8000. Harper's thus stood ready to harvest the fruits of Liveright's investment. In return, the house promised to throw the full weight of its publicity apparatus behind the collected edition and spend $10,000 annually for an advertising campaign hailing Dreiser as "America's greatest author." Half of the money for this "fund" would be siphoned from Dreiser's royalties, however.

Liveright rose to the challenge and performed his usual financial leg-erdemain, weaving a spell of future wealth that lured Dreiser despite his misgivings. He counseled Dreiser to stay with B & L, whom he knew, whom he could trust [sic]—especially if it was a matter of a ten-year contract, which was one of Dreiser's demands, along with "a sense of absolute security" and greater participation in the business affairs of the company. His offer, which after further discussion was embodied in a memorandum of agreement running for five years, amended the 1923 contract in the following particulars: 20 percent royalties on all of Dreiser's books; a $500-a-month drawing account; in the fall of 1927, B & L to launch the "great Dreiser set," the long-promised collected works of Theodore Dreiser in a limited edition; in the spring of 1929, the publisher to print a "popular library edition" from the limited-edition plates; $10,000 to be expended on advertising the *Tragedy* during the remainder of the year; commensurate sums to be laid out on future books; and a weekly advertisement of Dreiser as institution or of one of his books to run in *The New York Times Book Supplement* throughout 1927. Dreiser could hardly refuse such an alluring package, which came as close as any agreement could to fulfilling his dream of artistic independence and absolute financial security.

But what had he really won? He had bound himself tighter to the fortunes of a man whom he distrusted, who embodied the spirit of ballyhoo he found undignified yet approved when it was his books that were being touted, and whose profligate spending and plunges into the stock market and the theater should have sounded alarm bells. In return he was put on a dole of lavish advances that must be earned back by royalties from future books. He was betting on two long shots: his ability to produce more best sellers and Liveright's continued solvency. Swollen by the success of the *Tragedy*, he seems to have forgotten that he was an artist and could not crank out books to order. Of course, he had the uncompleted manuscript of *The Bulwark* and an outline of *The Stoic*, the third volume of the Cowperwood trilogy, in his trunk; they should do well, based on his current fame—*if* he could finish them in reasonable time, which was by no means certain. As he himself had said, his books never came in an orderly progression.

• • •

His business affairs presumably in order, and his desk cleared of literary projects (which that year consisted chiefly of an article on the Florida boom and the preparation for press of a limited edition of his poems, *Moods Cadenced and Declaimed*), Dreiser decided it was time to enjoy the fruits of his success. Helen would at last have her trip to Europe.

They sailed on June 22 and spent four months abroad, meeting prospective publishers in Scandinavia, cruising Norwegian fjords and trekking through still pine forests, visiting the graves of Ibsen and Björnson. Then on to Germany, where Helen "felt a strange harmony come over Teddie" as he communed with his ancestry. Yet he did not call on relatives in his father's birthplace, Mayen, and, echoing his father, criticized the Prussians as "too drastic. . . . They think too much about abstruse and esoteric problems—life, death, the destiny of man—too little of their immediate surroundings." He saw this heredity in himself but was helpless to change.

In Vienna he missed Freud, to whom he had a letter of introduction, and in Prague stayed with Tomas Masaryk, the nation's first president and an admirer of his books. In Paris he met his translator, Victor Llona, who took him to visit Balzac's home. Deeply moved, he gazed on Balzac's memorabilia. Dreiser stayed a long while, saying little, perhaps thinking of his own amazing and unsettling prosperity and envying this monastic cell where Balzac hid out from creditors and completed his Human Comedy.

After ten days in London, where he researched Yerkes' career for the third volume of his long-postponed trilogy, bantered with George Bernard Shaw, and formed a fast friendship with Otto Kyllmann of his British publisher, Constable, they boarded the *Columbus* on October 15 and docked in New York on the twenty-second.

In September Franklin P. Adams had reprinted side by side in his column an excerpt from Sherwood Anderson's story "Tandy" and a poem of Dreiser's called "The Beautiful," which had appeared in *Vanity Fair*. That poem was the one Dreiser had written—or rather "adapted"—in 1923 and sent to Helen as a plea for forgiveness. Anderson defended Dreiser when reporters called him and later wrote a friend: "My own private notion is that the man—perhaps as an exercise—tried to put some of my prose into verse form. He might have left it lying about, forgetting in the end the source. . . . It does not matter except that it must make him feel very foolish and uncomfortable when it comes to his notice. . . . I admire him greatly."

Dreiser maintained a public silence on the controversy, but it was an object lesson in the pitfalls of celebrity. A poem he had sent to Helen three years before and forgotten had branded him a plagiarist. Critics had already retailed the erroneous idea that he had copied his novel from the court records of the Gillette trial.

He now had a "position" to maintain and must be more careful. Helen begged him to let her look for more appropriate quarters. Liveright was also urging him to establish himself in a suitable place where he could play host to Manhattan's literary world as befitted a great American novelist. More practically, the publisher needed to know how to find him. Only Arthur Pell was entrusted with his address, and this arrangement had become inconvenient since a new collection of his short stories, *Chains*, was in the works, and Dreiser was needed to read proofs.

Dreiser gave Helen an equivocal go-ahead, but she had already seen just the place: a large duplex in the Rodin Studios at 200 West Fifty-seventh Street, across from Carnegie Hall. The lower floor had an enormous living room with large windows admitting the north light, a wall of glass-fronted bookcases, and an adjoining dining room and kitchen. A stair led to the upper level, which was divided into two bedrooms.

Dreiser, however, bridled at the rent: $3500 per year. At the time he was negotiating some lucrative deal that Helen does not identify. But how could she keep them straight? He was deluged by offers—$5000 from Hearst for a newspaper serialization of the *Tragedy*, $1000 from Abraham Caham for a story to appear in the thirtieth anniversary issue of the *Jewish Daily Forward*. The magazines were crying for his stories, and he sold "Fine Furniture," a slick tale that had been rejected nine times in 1923, to *Household* magazine and "Typhoon" (based on one of the murders he had considered for the *Tragedy*) to *Cosmopolitan* for hefty fees.

In addition, the dramatized version of *An American Tragedy* was grossing $30,000 a week, of which Dreiser's share was more than $2000. And the novel continued to sell steadily. Liveright partner Donald Friede wrote Dreiser in Europe in July that it was receiving almost daily mention in the press: "if it's not the book it's the play; if it's not the play it's the movie." By year's end more than fifty thousand sets had been disposed of, earning Dreiser some $47,000 in royalties. His total income that year was $91,225.65, according to his tax return.

At last Helen got her way, after persuading the landlord to lower the rent by $500, and by mid-December they were able to move into what she calls "my dream home."

• • •

In October Friede took Dreiser to see the Broadway version of the *Tragedy*. Dreiser was totally caught up in the spectacle of the characters he had lived with so long in his mind materializing onstage. He would not even leave for intermission, and when Clyde was led away through the steel door and the curtain fell, Dreiser had tears in his eyes. "The poor boy!" he said to Friede. "The poor bastard! What a shame!" In a way, he was weeping for himself and the unsated desires of youth.

Part Twelve

• • •

RUSSIA

70 / Thursdays at Home

> I was beginning to realize that genius was like the sun. One could be warmed, nourished, sustained and strengthened by it or horribly burned. . . .
>
> —Helen Dreiser, *My Life with Dreiser* (1951)

After Dreiser and Helen had settled in their new apartment, they began entertaining at regular Thursday-night "at homes," an attempt to create a kind of salon for a mix of personalities from publishing, Broadway, Wall Street, and the Village.

The venue for these affairs was the large drawing room, which rose the full two stories. Dreiser was often to be found seated in a high-backed ducal chair, listening, absorbing.

Claude Bowers, an Indiana politician turned editorial writer for the *World*, attended the Thursday-night levees from the start and observed Dreiser's attire evolve from a soiled blue artist's smock to a dinner jacket, sartorially recapitulating, presumably, his rise from a cold-water flat in the Village to an uptown duplex. Initially, Dreiser was pink-cheeked and as enthusiastic as a boy at his own birthday party. But he began to worry that the affairs were becoming dominated by the speakeasy crowd, who were more interested in sampling his excellent whiskey than in conversing about art. He confided his anxiety to Bowers.

The following week, Bowers noted, the cultural level of the guests had edged a few notches higher: first-nighters in evening dress, fresh from the premiere of *The King's Henchman*, an opera by Deems Taylor with a libretto by Edna St. Vincent Millay. Max Reinhardt, the director, was there, looking like a stockbroker, as was the short, seigneurial financier Otto Kahn.

Although the conversation did not markedly improve and Dreiser continued to fret about the lack of culture, the affairs became a popular stop on the Manhattan circuit. As many as a hundred people would show up. The mix included literati such as the novelist Ford Madox Ford; the beautiful Elinor

Wylie, who posed "like a peacock spreading its tail" to invite admiration; the inevitable "Carlo" Van Vechten; big, rumpled Sherwood Anderson; Fannie Hurst; tiny Anita Loos; dapper George Jean Nathan; erudite Ernest Boyd; the Van Doren brothers; Joseph Wood Krutch; Broadway luminaries including actress Lillian Gish and torch singer Libby Holman; artists such as George Luks, Jerome Blum, and Willy Pogany; and business and professional people such as Liveright, Dr. Brill, the Reverend Percy Stickney Grant (who had defended *The "Genius"* from his pulpit), and Liveright's lawyer Arthur Garfield Hays.

Dreiser was working hard, but his energies were dissipated among various projects, including hasty, superficial feature stories for the lucrative syndication market that his new agent, George Bye, diligently cultivated. For the Metropolitan Newspaper Service, he undertook a series of three articles, at $400 each, on American manners and morals. One, on the theme of "American Restlessness," was an expression of his own itch for change, variety: "Moving from place to place, and more because of a desire for change than for economic betterment," he wrote, "appears to be an innate part of the American spirit." Another, "Fools for Love," subliminally advertised his success-guilt. He extols a woman (Louise?) "endowed with ample equipment for success in novel or play writing," who chose to take care of her mother and help other relatives. Some would say her life was a failure: "What nonsense! What rot! To me she is really a great and appealing success." He concludes that he prefers to cast his lot with "those who feel and respond emotionally, and poetically, in simple and inconspicuous ways—not with those who thunder and battle and, at the last, find their hands and hearts empty and their strong boxes stuffed with gilt-edged and meaningless 'securities.'"

He, of course, had a strongbox at the Central Hanover Bank and Trust Company stuffed with bonds. The market was heating up, and Pell sent him tips: Financial and Industrial was now up to 82. . . . Too bad he hadn't purchased Manufacturers Trust at 600; it was now 785. . . . He should keep some cash on hand so he could act quickly when a hot issue came along.

• • •

Wealth had not made his life with Helen any more idyllic. He had taken an office in the Manufacturers Trust Building on Columbus Circle, which he used for romance as well as for work. As a result, his companion was experiencing the pangs of neglect. Out of need, and in retaliation, she developed a passion for a handsome young Hungarian-born pianist-composer named Ervin Nyiregyhazi.

"I felt myself physically drawn to him," she confesses in her autobiography. Dreiser left her alone night after night until the early-morning hours "in that tomb of a studio," she once told Ralph Fabri, the Hungarian artist who became the confidant of both of them; yet with "his terrible ego he thought I was not human and could go on and on and on with *no one.*" In her autobiography Helen writes that she held back, but to Fabri she spoke of a "short (so terribly short) intimacy."

Late in March, overcome by restlessness and nerves, Dreiser departed on a walking trip through Pennsylvania. He may have been having love problems of his own; he was involved with three or four women at this time. Helen decided to join him and caught up with him at a hotel where he was spending the night. There she asked if it would be all right if she formed "a constructive emotional attachment to help me live through the time you leave me so much alone." He exploded: "Do as you please. But when you do, I'm out!" He demanded the name of her lover. Much distressed, she told him. Helen mulled over her problem and finally concluded that if she must choose between the Hungarian and Dreiser, she would choose the latter.

Helen telephoned Nyiregyhazi that the affair was off. Later the Hungarian wrote Dreiser a letter describing the affair with Helen in the "most evil & shocking way." Dreiser was so furious that he sat down at the typewriter and copied it. When Helen happened by and asked what he was doing (he rarely used the typewriter), he showed her the letter and shouted, "This finishes you, I can tell you that!" The pianist was a "cad" for writing such a letter, and Dreiser never wanted to see him again.

Dreiser wasn't letting Helen off easily, however. After the incident of the incriminating letter, her life became more lonely. "An impregnable door was closed against me," as she puts it. Dreiser still came home to her—most nights—but that was no consolation. She would lie awake for hours waiting for the sound of his key, crying herself to sleep.

Desperate for peace of mind, she began reading books on yoga and talking with the swamis from the Vedanta Society. She took up breathing exercises and achieved "the distinct sensation of an expanding consciousness, as though my mind was opening to a deeper understanding and wider perception of life."

The arrival of Helen's mother for a visit bolstered her morale, and since Dreiser liked Mrs. Patges, an earthy woman who did not hesitate to tell him that his neglect was to blame for Helen's affair, peace of a kind returned.

• • •

In 1927, partly to breathe new life into the novel, Liveright decided to protest the ban of *An American Tragedy* in Boston. Actually, it was not officially banned, but it was rumored that the police might act. Liveright's motive was not entirely publicity-seeking. Censorship was heating up in Boston, and nine books had been suppressed in 1927, two of them published by B & L. And on April 12,

Sinclair Lewis's *Elmer Gantry* was barred, and the police had said that the *Tragedy* was one of several books under scrutiny.

To challenge the ban, Donald Friede sold a copy of the novel. He was arrested and tried by one of the pro-censorship judges, who found him guilty and fined him $100. His lawyer appealed, but it would be two years before the courts would get to it, and meanwhile the *Tragedy* was unavailable in Boston.

Dreiser attended Friede's trial and on the train to Boston met Clarence Darrow, who had delivered a highly favorable verdict on *An American Tragedy* in a review for the New York *Evening Post*. The two men were inveterate determinists and shared the belief that murderers were driven to their acts by uncontrollable forces. Indeed, the novel echoed in spirit Darrow's summation in the Leopold-Loeb trial, which saved the two thrill-killers from the electric chair.

• • •

In May he made a substantial investment that would bring him much joy and pain. This was the purchase of thirty-seven scenic acres overlooking one of the lakes in the Croton reservoir system in Westchester County, about four miles from the town of Mount Kisco.

When Dreiser bought the land, the only structure on it was a hunting lodge constructed of white birch logs. To reach it from the main road, one had to drive along a narrow, winding dirt track through high grass. The lodge was perched on a rocky hill, with a view of the surrounding meadows, woods, and the rolling green Berkshires. Below the house was a small spring-fed pond, which Dreiser would deepen for a swimming pool. He also enlarged the house and the porch and commissioned Wharton Esherick to design two gates painted Prussian blue and emblazoned with the word "Iroki," a Japanese word meaning "the spirit of beauty."

For all his restlessness, he had long hankered after a country seat where he could write undisturbed and sink some roots. He found a modicum of tranquillity as he gazed from his veranda at the rolling hills. "The peace of that place," he wrote in his diary that fall. "The silence of the stars."

• • •

In early October came another distraction: an invitation from the Soviet government to attend the November 3–10 celebration of the tenth anniversary of the Bolshevik revolution. Dreiser was intrigued but wary. He grilled the man who conveyed the summons, F. G. Biedenkapp, executive secretary of International Workers Relief, a Communist party auxiliary: how could he learn much about the country in a week? He did not want merely to ornament the Moscow celebration. He could stay as long as he wished, Biedenkapp told him—a month, six weeks. "Go where you will, accompanied or unaccompanied by Russian officials, and judge for yourself what has been done and what is happening." Finally, Dreiser agreed to go, provided he receive official letters confirming that he would be reimbursed for all his expenses, including travel and his "time," and guaranteeing freedom of movement. He told Biedenkapp that he wanted to visit "the real, unofficial Russia—the famine district on the Volga, say— some of the small towns and farms in Siberia and the Ukraine, some of the mines and fisheries." The Russian said the letters would be produced but that he must be prepared to leave within nine days if he was to arrive in time for the celebration.

Dreiser's interest in the Soviet experiment went back to the Village years, but he had no deep commitment to radical programs or causes. He did not, for example, join the intellectuals who protested the verdict in the Sacco-Vanzetti case, which radicalized many American writers in the 1920s. He was sympathetic to communism as an experiment in making life better for the masses, but he still believed that the strongest individuals would dominate the weak, that the big brains would—and should—rule, though he opposed the excessive power of Big Business. Yet he was inwardly restless, an individualist wondering if there weren't something more than self. Could a system dedicated to eliminating greed and inequality work?

After Biedenkapp departed, he discussed the Russian's proposal with Helen. She begged him to take her with him, but he told her that he would want to travel under rough conditions, and she would not like that. She teased him about becoming involved with Russian women. "Who me," he replied. "Russian girls? Those wild Bolsheviks? Aren't these American girls bad enough?"

71 / A Contrarian Abroad

> This enormous giant is at last rousing itself from the sleep
> of centuries—equipping itself—entering . . . upon a strange
> new day and mission.
> —Dreiser's Russian Diary (1927)

Dreiser was booked on the *Mauretania*, sailing October 19 for Cherbourg,
whence he would proceed via Paris and Berlin to Moscow. He was but one
of fifteen hundred Americans invited to the decennial festivities, but the only
one to rate a private tour with all expenses paid. The official notification he had
requested soon arrived in the form of cables from Maxim Litvinov, assistant foreign minister, and Mme Olga Kameneva, Leon Trotsky's sister and director of
VOKS (Society for Cultural Relations from Abroad), the government agency
that was in charge of his tour. From Joe Freeman, a young American Communist who had worked in Moscow, he received letters of introduction to various
artists and officials.

Aboard the *Mauretania* were several congenial passengers, including publisher Ben Huebsch, the lawyer Morris Ernst and his wife, and Diego Rivera,
the Mexican muralist, a Communist, with whom Dreiser got on famously, even
though the artist spoke little English and the writer knew no Spanish.

After a placid crossing, Dreiser lingered briefly in Paris and sat for an interview by a reporter from the Paris edition of the New York *Herald*. After Paris
the way of the pilgrim led through Berlin. Dreiser traveled with Huebsch, and
en route they had a long talk about communism. Dreiser resolved to look hard
at "its theory & actual practice" and "its consonance or conflict with human
nature as we find it."

Arriving in the German capital, he checked into the luxurious Adlon Hotel, where he was met by some Soviet officials. In a letter to his old friends
Franklin and Beatrice Booth, he vowed that "once out of the hands of these
government agents I will prove more simple—even to the extent of riding

third class" with the mujiks and "sleeping on a mat." He complained about the strain of travel, and two days later his bronchitis was "worse than ever." Nevertheless, he met various delegations and a representative of the Hearst papers, who offered him $3600 for two articles on Russia. He wrote Louise Campbell that he was ill, "but I'll be better tomorrow I hope. The doctor just left."

The doctor had prescribed some medicines and a Turkish bath to decongest him. The steam relieved his symptoms temporarily, and he sat up that evening with Huebsch and Sinclair Lewis, who had pursued the foreign correspondent Dorothy Thompson to Berlin in the course of a whirlwind European courtship. Dreiser's distaste for Lewis had not abated and was compounded in part by jealousy over Lewis's great success with *Main Street*, a book in the realist mode, in which Dreiser felt he had staked the original claim and for which he had fought a lonely battle against the comstocks. Lewis seemed eager to be friends.

The next day Dreiser felt worse and consulted two other doctors, who advised him to have an X ray. This disclosed that his health was "very bad," the doctors said. There was an enlargement of the aorta, which was pressing against his left lung, producing bronchitis. The physicians advised him to cancel the trip to Russia and enter a German sanitarium immediately. "I am not going into any sanitarium," Dreiser told them. "I am going into Russia. My condition may be bad but I do not happen to be afraid of death."

He talked over his situation with Lewis, who was worried. Then, alone in his room, he was overwhelmed by depression and cabled Helen, explaining later in a letter to her that he had experienced "a case of real homesickness, almost to the point of vomiting. . . . " In his diary he wrote that he felt "like a cast away in a small boat. Here I am—nearly 4000 miles from N.Y. . . . Supposing I were seriously ill—to die. And Helen so far away. And I have been so bad to her."

• • •

On November 2, with a group of American delegates, Dreiser boarded the Moscow train. Once he had crossed the border into Russia, the people all reminded him of characters in Tolstoy, Gogol, and Dostoevsky—"the heavy and yet shrewd peasants; the self-concerned and even now, under communism, rather authoritarian petty officials." On the afternoon of November 4 he arrived in Moscow.

His hotel, the Grand, was "rococo and shabby grand." Later Sergei Dinamov, from the American section of Gosizdat, the state publishing house, arrived to welcome him, accompanied by a tall, attractive American-born woman named Ruth Kennell. Dreiser gave Dinamov a list of people he wanted to see and dashed off a report to Esther McCoy, a young woman friend who had moved to New York: Russia was "an armed dictatorship. Workers and peasants are drilled like soldiers to fight and can be called to fight at any time." And to Helen: "The only difference between the Russian government & ours that I can see is that it is poorer—as yet. And that no one is allowed to pile up large fortunes—or not to work at something." The people voted just like in America, and he predicted that in ten years Russia would be "as gay & wonderful & happy a place as any on earth. I hope so. There is no lack of liberty. . . . I think really there is much less liberty in America than there is here. For one thing there is no Negro or Catholic question—the church is down here. A child cannot receive religious instruction & education is the watchword everywhere." So much for first impressions.

He was now in open rebellion against his officious hosts from VOKS. When a guide from the agency arrived the next day, he sent him packing. The American radical Scott Nearing called and found Dreiser sulking in his room, morosely drinking vodka and complaining that VOKS was trying to push him into a package tour, with a "Russian lackey as a guide."

He felt trapped, harried by manipulative strangers. He needed someone whom he could trust to translate and to take notes during interviews, and to handle the logistics of travel in this huge, baffling country.

Nearing suggested Ruth Kennell; she was American, spoke Russian, and knew the country. Dreiser liked the idea, "since we are already so close." He interviewed her, learning that her political sympathies had drawn her and her husband to Russia in 1922 as technical workers. Her husband eventually returned to the States, but she had insisted on staying. Now Dreiser offered her a job as his secretary, and she accepted.

On November 7, the anniversary of the Bolsheviks' seizure of power, Dreiser was awakened by the sound of bands and the tramp of soldiers' boots in Red Square. Later he went to a grandstand to watch union and nationality delegations stream past bearing red banners with slogans such as "Workers of the World Unite" and effigies of obese capitalists and swinish kulaks and speculators. From 11:00 until 7:00 that night the human river flowed past the reviewing stand atop Lenin's mausoleum. The marchers waved to the Party leaders smiling down at them. Deeply moved, Dreiser wrote in his diary, "I think—if only human nature can rise to the opportunity—here is one for the genuine betterment of man. But mayhap the program is too beautiful to succeed;—an idea of existence to which frail & selfish humanity can never rise. Yet I earnestly hope that this is not true—that this is truly the beginning of a better or brighter day for all."

That evening he and Ruth were joined for dinner by Dorothy Thompson, who was writing a series of articles on Russia. Dreiser and the Junoesque

Dorothy discussed the relative advantages of communism and capitalism. She thought the Russian system a "drab affair—more a matter of mental or idealistic enthusiasm on the part of its members than of actual material improvement." Later, with Nearing, they went out to a dance recital. On the way home Dreiser received an impression that Thompson was "making overtures" to him. At the hotel, Dreiser notes, "D T—& I continue our flirtation. After a supper with the American delegation she comes to my room with me to discuss communism & we find we agree on many of its present lacks as well as its hopeful possibilities. I ask her to stay but she will not—tonight."

He was surely exaggerating the lady's attraction to him. She was radiantly in love with Lewis and later wrote him that she was bored "with being face-tiously nudged by old Dreiser, who has turned quite a gay dog in Moscow, con-stantly making rather lumbering jokes." Yet she found him "sympathetic be-cause he has a sort of healing common sense about life. And, curiously enough, he has a genuine—if rather elephantine—sense of humor. Last night . . . both he and I were almost in hysterics with the accumulated laughter of the day, and irritated our earnest friends highly thereby." Evidently her conspiratorial laugh-ter encouraged Dreiser (who usually needed little encouragement) to think she was available.

•　•　•

One evening he and Ruth were invited to Dinamov's apartment, and Dreiser got his first view of crowded living conditions in the capital. He questioned the thin, dedicated editor-critic, who, with his thick glasses and ascetic face, looked like a student in a Dostoevsky novel, about living conditions. His host had foresightedly invited three workers who lived in his building to join them, and Dreiser interrogated each of them in turn. He was most attentive to the textile worker, who said he had no ambitions for his daughter to become a respectable married woman. She could live with a man and divorce him for another if she liked. "The important thing is that she should be an independent person, able to support herself." Thinking of his own marital state, Dreiser whispered to Ruth, "Get this all down."

He called on the filmmaker Sergei Eisenstein, *auteur* of the revolutionary classic *Potemkin*, who plumped for realistic dramas illustrating historic princi-ples and explained his theory of movies without a plot or professional actors, in which daily life was the drama. Eisenstein admitted the cinema was under strict government controls but argued that in America the churches exercised similar censorship. Dreiser accused him of being an "uplifter," a propagan-dist, and defended the drama of the individual, saying that "only through the individual could the mass and its dreams be sensed and interpreted." Eisenstein was not persuaded, but he greatly esteemed Dreiser's work. He was somewhat disillusioned, however, to find the author rather slow of speech and, by the Russian's lights, provincial in outlook.

During an audience with Constantin Stanislavsky, cofounder of the Moscow Art Theater, Dreiser was lectured about the political role of theater, though when he asked if communism had generated any great plays, Stanislavsky said no, dutifully adding that such plays as had been written were "good as chronicles of the revolution."

Dreiser would become personally acquainted with the mysterious ways of the censor when he submitted the dramatic version of *An American Tragedy* to Stanislavsky, who seemed enthusiastic about doing it. Several weeks passed, and then the director told him that, regrettably, the play had been disapproved. When Dreiser asked why, Stanislavsky explained that the censors had objected to the religious scenes in the death house between Clyde and the Reverend McMillan and also "the relationship between employer and worker" — presumably not sufficiently evocative of the class struggle. The incident gave a double edge to Stanislavsky's statement that "The line of art is eternal and passing conditions do not change it."

Yet this was the time of the flowering of "NEP culture," after Lenin's New Economic Policy, which permitted a measure of economic and political freedom, and Dreiser witnessed experimental productions of American plays at the Jewish theater and attended opera and ballet at the Bolshoi Opera House. A spectacular dance drama based on Victor Hugo's *The Hunchback of Notre Dame* caused Dreiser to note approvingly that the novel's anticlerical message was highlighted. Over a late supper at a gypsy restaurant, William Reswick, correspondent for the Associated Press, urged Dreiser to speak to Otto Kahn about bringing the Russian Ballet to America.

He learned more about the Party schism over collectivization versus extension of the NEP when he received a surprise visitor at his hotel — Karl Radek, a veteran Communist who would be purged along with Trotsky. Dreiser had tried several times to telephone him at the Kremlin but was always told he was out. Now Radek proceeded to elucidate Kremlin politics: he was being watched because the anti-Trotskyists feared that he and other members of the left opposition were plotting against them. He gave his version of the doctrinal dispute between Trotsky and Stalin and reminisced about Lenin.

Radek was the only high official Dreiser had seen thus far, and he was beginning to feel like a capitalist orphan adrift in a Communist sea. Finally, at a glittering banquet of the Presidium of the Moscow Soviet, he had a tantrum. Spotting an American who worked in the New York office of VOKS, he berated her until she trembled. "I have been treated vilely," he thundered. "Madame Kameneva and the Soviet government can go to hell." He demanded reimbursement for all his expenditures, including his steamship fare and Kennell's pay, and then he would go home. Mumbling that she was sorry, the woman scurried off, and soon Kameneva herself appeared, an interpreter in tow. There had been a mistake; tomorrow her secretary would help arrange a trip—anywhere he wanted to go; any interview he wanted would be arranged. Dreiser looked at her "meaningfully" and said he would let it pass—for now.

After this outburst several officials granted him interviews. His social life picked up as well. He was invited to a cocktail party, where he met the English-born Madame Litvinova, wife of the assistant foreign minister. She extolled the "restfulness" of life in Russia compared to her homeland. There was no competition for wealth, no social climbing. The onus of economic failure was not placed on the individual; everyone was guaranteed a minimal living, housing, health care, old-age assistance, and fifteen rubles a month if he or she couldn't find work.

Although this side of the Soviet system drew his warm approval, he would obsessively return to the theme of individualism—free enterprise, in economic terms—versus socialism and collectivism. He told Commissar of Trade Anastas I. Mikoyan that Russian consumers would soon crave more luxuries. Mikoyan replied sternly, "Russia will never be a luxury-consuming country. Luxury can only lead to the destruction of communism." Dreiser was silent but later said, "I wonder."

• • •

The "big brain versus little brain" controversy came to a head in an interview with Nikolai Bukharin, leader of the "right socialists," heir apparent to Lenin and the Party's top theoretician. Now co-ruler with Stalin in an uneasy duumvirate, he was a tough, doctrinaire Communist, but unlike the suspicious, conspiratorial Stalin, he was charming and popular. After Lenin's death in 1924, Bukharin had become the architect of the New Economic Policy and advocated a more humane and open form of socialism than Stalin, who supported rapid and massive industrialization from the top down.

Bukharin, a handsome, boyish-looking man, greeted the American delegate heartily and sat back for what he probably thought would be an exchange of polite generalities. But Dreiser had come to debate. He declared that communism led to "intellectual despotism." He accused the Russian state of being as doctrinaire and authoritarian as the Catholic Church or the czarist government or "any form of tyranny or propaganda of which you can think. You take the ignorant and make them believe your way because you are sure your way is best. But is it? Do you know yet?"

Bukharin said communism was "the fairest form of human government yet devised. Our dream is to make all happy." Dreiser responded, "Personally I think good often needs as much tyranny to establish and maintain it as evil. A benevolent tyranny—at least until all men have brains sufficient to appreciate good. Why not adopt that as a defense?"

Bukharin said he did not believe it. "Left alone humanity moves in the general direction of its best ideals."

Dreiser pressed on to the heart of the matter: "Should the big mind rule the little one?" Bukharin contended that the proletariat could produce great minds and that under capitalism workers were denied equal education. Gesturing toward the window, Dreiser asked if the man sweeping the street was Bukharin's class equal. Bukharin said he was, that all Russians had the same opportunities and rights. Dreiser countered, "I think big minds will always sit in high places and have comfortable rooms [like Bukharin's office] and lead the little minds in the street."

Bukharin riposted that under communism personal ambition would disappear, replaced by a universal ambition to serve the general good. Given proper education, the socialist ethic would ultimately become ingrained.

"So you're going to have a perfect world, against human nature," Dreiser said. "And you think God will accept it? That's the bunk. Contrasts will remain forever; that's what makes life interesting. That's the way the universe is run, in spite of your Marxian theories."

"My God, take him away!" Bukharin muttered to the VOKS interpreter. "I can't stand any more." Outside the Kremlin walls Dreiser watched a ragged street sweeper cross himself before the Chapel of the Siberian Virgin. "I suppose next year he'll have Bukharin's place," he said, having the last word.

•   •   •

Turning to literary business, Dreiser met with representatives of Gosizdat to discuss a contract for the Russian rights to his past and future works. He complained about pirated editions and the state publishing house's recent abridged versions of *Color of a Great City* and *Twelve Men*. Ossip Beskin, head of the Department of Foreign Literature, offered Dreiser 750 rubles ($375) for the rights to those two titles. Dreiser acted insulted and said Gosizdat could have them as a gift. At length, he settled for $1000. After further haggling, it was agreed that he would receive advances of between $600 and $1000 for each new title and semiannual royalty statements. They shook hands, and the staff was summoned to welcome the new author on the Gosizdat list. Afterward he attended a banquet for foreign writers given by the state publishing house, where the poet Mayakovsky perceptively toasted him as the first visiting American to admit he had formed no definite impressions or conclusions.

•   •   •

Meanwhile, there seemed to have been no progress on arrangements for his trip to the hinterland. Now he had a financial incentive to see "what these Russians are up to," as he liked to say: a contract with North American News Alliance (NANA) for five 1200-word articles on his trip, at a total fee of $6000. Irritated by the foot-dragging, Dreiser decided to go to Leningrad. He was put up at the Hotel Europa, a truly *luxe* establishment, and was surrounded by obsequious VOKS employees wherever he went. "It would be easy for a fool to get a false impression of his importance," he wrote in his diary. He was homesick for West Fifty-seventh Street and Mt. Kisco.

• • •

At last Dreiser was summoned to Madame Kameneva's office, but when he arrived she was just leaving. She told him airily that there were only 2000 rubles left in the budget for his expenses. He said he would take that and go back to New York. She told him nothing had been said about paying his expenses to and from Russia. Later, VOKS relented; Dreiser got his tour.

On December 12, with $1000 in expense money his agent, George Bye, had cabled him, Dreiser and party boarded the night train for Kiev. It departed three hours late, setting the pattern of rail journeys to come. In Stalino, bundled up in furs against the brisk, sleety wind, they were driven in an open car to a large state farm—ten thousand acres in all. Then on to a coal mine, followed by a good dinner of beer and schnitzel at a cooperative restaurant. A violinist rendered "Yankee Doodle" in honor of the American delegate.

For all his lambasting of the Russian system, a part of him was absorbing the socialist message, and he wrote in his diary: "In America our task is to catch and harness for the good of all that escaped, world-making, world-running thing industrial & financial enterprise & bring it back to the service of the general good." Whether communism was achieving this was an open question. Still, "One sees really a country with no abandoned—if as yet wretched poor; no foolish and meaningless rich."

Yet he still played capitalist's advocate during interviews with local officials, and he and Ruth had almost daily arguments. The cold, damp climate had revived his bronchitis, and he was coughing alarmingly into his handkerchief. As they reached the last leg of their journey, Dreiser and Ruth continued to rag and wrangle. For all their disputation, however, they had formed a close camaraderie. When they weren't arguing, their talk was full of shared jokes; both had a fine sense of the ridiculous, which could dissipate any lingering rancor from their doctrinal disputes. She treated him as a kind of lovable if eccentric rich uncle, and he regarded her as his companion "Ruthie"—and the only person in all of Russia he could trust.

So the little group made its way along the Caspian Sea to Tiflis, where they spent a quiet New Year's Eve. The following night they caught a train to Batum, and there boarded a ship that would take them to Odessa. At this point Dreiser's spirits were at their lowest ebb. As he huddled next to a stove, Ruth looked at him pityingly: "His smart light-gray topcoat was grimy, his scarf bedraggled, his suit untidy, his bow tie missing, and he himself was unwashed. There was something touching in the spectacle of America's foremost novelist at the age of 56 braving the Russian winter to examine the workings of a new social system which was at variance with his own theories."

They arrived at their final destination, Odessa, at 8:00 A.M. on January 8, a dank, cold day. Dreiser was told he would not be allowed to take his notes and manuscripts out of the country without a special permit. And, oh yes, he could not take out more than 300 rubles. These official intrusions into personal papers and personal funds represented to him the final blows of Soviet petty tyranny. And so, when a reporter from the *Odessa News* came to interview him, he gave the country a piece of his mind: "I made him a long speech about what I thought of conditions, that it was an interesting experiment, but—they had a long way to go before they could try to put the system in other countries. I had no objection to their trying it out here, but they should not try to change other countries until they had proved the system here."

The next day permission to take out his papers and money came through, as Ruth had predicted it would. Back at the hotel he dictated another statement, summing up his impressions. He confessed a bias: "Personally, I am an individualist and shall die one. In all this communistic welter, I have seen nothing that dissuades me in the least from my earliest perceptions of the necessities of man. One of these is the individual dream of self-advancement, and I cannot feel that even here communism has altered that in the least." He said that "more individualism and less communism would be of great advantage to this mighty country." And: "There is too much effort to make the laborer socially comfortable, and too little to make him thoroughly efficient. Really, there should be no talk of the seven-hour day until the workers are earning enough to pay for the latest type of machinery which would make such a day possible."

His statement was never published in Russia, but he sent a copy to an American correspondent, Junius Wood, and it appeared in the United States. In one of the two papers Wood represented, the Oakland *Tribune*, the headline read: SOVIET PLAN TO FAIL, DREISER SAYS ON RETURN. The Chicago *Daily News* was more accurate: THEODORE DREISER FINDS BOTH HOPE AND FAILURE IN RUSSIAN SOVIET DRAMA.

72 / A Contrarian at Home

> Russia has a dream. Human nature is malleable. Government
> can exert pressure on the individual and make him a collec-
> tivist. I don't care about that. Ideals are what I want.
> —Dreiser in an interview (1927)

The next Ruth heard from him was a letter from the Hôtel Grand Terminus in
Paris. His relief at escaping from Russia was palpable, and he exhorted her to
do the same: "Come out into the sunlight. Only Russians can solve that mess
if they ever do." Paris was "warm and bright. . . . And not a smell anywhere
since leaving."

Obviously, Dreiser was happy to be back in the land of sanitation, clean
sheets, and palatable food, but he was, Helen says, haunted by memories of
the poverty he had seen, talking about it as he luxuriated in the fleshpots of
Paris and the Riveria. He had come to believe that, whatever its demerits, the
Communist system was seeking to help the wretched of Russia.

Ever the contrarian, he began defending Russia to the West just as he had
stood up for the United States in Russia. In London he interviewed Winston
Churchill for a syndicated article and was incensed by the Tory politician's prediction that the Communist government would collapse within seven years.
Dreiser praised the growing military and economic power of the New Russia
and challenged Churchill to explain why England didn't improve the living
conditions of its millworkers.

He was of two minds—at least—about the Soviet experiment. Arriving in
New York on the S.S. *Hamburg* on February 21, he faced a battery of shipping
reporters eager to learn about his views on the Soviet Union. "I wasn't a Communist when I went abroad and I don't return as one," he assured them. Still,
although Russia was no utopia, there were programs there that the United
States might emulate. When one of the reporters asked him to comment on
the breadlines on the Lower East Side, Dreiser said, according to the *Evening*

Post, "Nowhere in Russia, whether the nation is prospering or not, will you find men without overcoats standing in breadlines." The *Post* also quoted him as saying, "Contrasting the free and uncontrolled grafting we face here with the regulated accumulation centered in the Soviet government, I much prefer the Russian system." His quotes made him seem to favor communism over the American way of life. No matter that he also criticized artistic censorship in Russia and quoted the conservative Winston Churchill as favoring more social spending in Britain to forestall a Communist revolution.

Dreiser had been trying not to let the personal discomforts he experienced on the trip color his public statements. He later explained his shipboard remarks to Ruth Kennell:

> I decided that, however little I might, I should not seriously try to injure an idealistic effort. Besides, learning that there were bread lines here—the first since 1910—I became furious because there is too much wealth wasted here to endure it. Hence, while I am going to stick to what I saw favorable and unfavorable, I am going to contrast it with the waste and extravagance and social indifference here. I may find myself in another storm. If so, well and good. . . .

His first interview did not result in a storm, but there were gale-force winds. An American Legion official charged that Dreiser had been on a "cooked" tour. A week later Simon Strunsky, writing in *The New York Times Book Review,* made the same point more elegantly. How could Dreiser say that there were no unemployment lines in Russia, when Stalin himself had declared that "unemployment is Russia's No. 1 problem"? It was a well-known fact that there were long queues at food stores and "conditions suggesting famine."

In a letter to the editor of the *Times,* Dreiser pointed out that he had not said there was no unemployment in Russia. As he had told the New York *Herald Tribune,* "Russia will not let anyone starve. If people can't pay their rent, the Government pays it. The Government feeds the hungry." His claim that there was no famine in Russia was generally correct. There were food shortages, the result of peasants withholding grain from the market because of low prices, and queues at the shops, but no famine.

•　•　•

In the ensuing weeks he wrestled with his conflicting impressions as he wrote the series of syndicated articles for NANA. The result was hasty but not unbalanced journalism.

He begins by describing the virtues of the Communist system: "pursuit of this ideal of work for everybody, unearned idleness for none and the elimination of the individualist who wishes everything for himself and as little as possible for any other. . . . " He provides more specific examples of Communist concern for the people's welfare: improved education ("which seeks to eliminate from the human brain or chemism all personal self-interest"—an echo of Bukharin's argument, which he pooh-poohed at the time), "the legal and political emancipation of women," the ease of divorce, and the absence of the "clatter . . . covering immoral plays, books, vice societies and their crusades, public censors, police raids, elopements, shooting, rape, sadistic murders, due to sex repressions and the like."

But Dreiser's critical faculties were overrun by his prejudices and predilections. He continues, "There are sex murders in Russia to be sure, and rapes also," but then announces, a few sentences later, "If there is no rape and no murder there is no real crime." And after seemingly praising the absence of sexual censorship, he complains in a later article, "plays that glorify religion or dwell too heavily on love or sex are mostly taboo."

Those confusions aside, he could be bluntly critical, deploring "the endless outpour and downpour of propaganda," the omnipresence of spies and secret police, the censorship of the stage and the cinema and overemphasis on didactically optimistic plays, the repression and intolerance of dissent by the ruling single-party state. He chides the press for its uncritical praise of the government and suppression of any news "which does not tend to glorify the principles of Marx and Lenin. . . . " He describes and quotes some of the various dissenters he encountered, and he tells of complaints by farmers that they could not afford to buy boots or coats. He also bemoans the lack of sanitation, the uncleanliness of the people, the overcrowded apartments, the shortage of bathing facilities (later implying that such conditions were the result of a communal philosophy imposed by the government). He is disturbed by the indoctrination of schoolchildren, the pervasive garrison psychology, and the "spyhunting" mania with its "rumors of secret trials and executions."

He wonders if the workers' state caters too much to the industrial workers at the expense of the peasants, and if "the elimination of the old-time creative or constructive businessman" is engendering a society "from which the urge and tang of competition had been extracted." He questions Marx's dictum "From each according to his ability, to each according to his need." Who is to determine need and hence reward? "Is Edison to receive the same as a swineherd? Rockefeller no more than a steelpuddler?" And what of the lack of private incentives under communism: "can man be made to work as enthusiastically for others as for himself?" He decides that communism is a "semi-religious, semi-moral theory," no more scientific than Christianity or Islam, yet by the same token no less compelling.

Perhaps the Communists are right, he sums up, and men and women's selfish instincts can be trained out of them. Stalin and his colleagues would testify to the affirmative, but "Mr. Darwin, Mr. Haeckel, Mr. Spencer, and Mr.

Voltaire will tell you no—that these Russians are fools, dreamers and that some day that great people will wake up." In the end, he throws up his hands, writing that the final word has not been written on "that fascinating, stimulating, crazy topsy-turvy land."

Emotionally, however, he had committed himself to the socialist ideal. In a single aside, he gets to the personal heart of the matter:

> [Under communism], this collective or paternalistic care of everybody for everybody else, it is possible to remove that dreadful sense of social misery in one direction and another which has so afflicted me in my life in America ever since I have been old enough to know what social misery is. . . .
>
> For if [communism] has lessened the glitter and the show it has at any rate taken the heartache and the material tragedy from millions and millions of lives.

NANA was anxious to publish a paperback edition of the articles, but Liveright objected, asserting his contractual rights to Dreiser's writing. He proposed that B & L publish a hardcover book of Dreiser's reflections on Russia. Dreiser was not averse to the money or the chance to propound his views on a country that was badly misunderstood in America. The problem was that he would have to pad the articles to have enough material for a respectable-sized hardcover book.

He enlisted Louise Campbell to help him cobble together his material. He sent her a rough draft of a manuscript that built on the newspaper articles, which he had reworked or sliced up and sandwiched between new material. Working with his notebook and newspaper clippings, including a set of Dorothy Thompson's articles, which had run in February, Louise edited and expanded the manuscript and organized it into chapters.

He might have been better advised to bring in Ruth Kennell as a collaborator. At least in hindsight, she had a better conception of the book than he did. She thought he should have written a more personal, chronological account, drawing upon the diary she had helped compile. The result might have been a more relaxed, less self-important travel book in the rambling style of *A Traveler at Forty* and *A Hoosier Holiday,* but doing it that way would have meant writing a new book rather than building on the newspaper series. Instead he reorganized the material under subject headings such as "Russia's Post-Revolutionary Political and General Achievements," "The Russian Versus the American Temperament," "The Current Soviet Economic Plan," and "Communism—Theory and Practice."

•   •   •

In July he and Helen drove their new Chrysler Imperial convertible to Woods Hole on Cape Cod, where they had rented a cottage and where he intended to finish his various writing projects. Construction was under way on the Iroki house, so it was impossible to work there. But also, through the Russian-born scientist Boris Sokoloff, he had been invited to spend a month at the Marine Biological Laboratory as a sort of writer in residence.

He interrogated the scientists in his deceptively naive way. A writer for the *Collecting Net*, the weekly newspaper published by the laboratory, described him in action: "He has that rare talent developed in his earlier experiences as a Chicago newspaper reporter, of asking questions which require hours of enthusiastic monologue to answer. Silent scientists have burst into profuse verbiage at his questions, to explain themselves. . . . Mr. Dreiser sits, profoundly interested, and listens."

But two nonscientific questions kept recurring: Is there a God? Is there life after death? He reported to Franklin and Beatrice Booth that the scientists were "all mechanists & in so far as life is concerned hopeless. It is a good show—sometimes—but ends for man here." But the longer he peered into the microscope, the more he thought he saw clues to God's existence. For there must be some creative intelligence behind the intricately beautiful forms of even the lowliest creatures. He lived, John Cowper Powys said, in a universe of chaos, but, peering into the microcosm, he glimpsed form and design.

• • •

The manuscript of *Dreiser Looks at Russia* was rushed to the printer, and by mid-August he had received galleys. At this juncture he consulted Ruth, now in Palo Alto visiting her mother. He asked her to check the text for accuracy of names and facts and to make any other changes she thought necessary. He explained that "Some of the bits are material verified by others and offered me for use."

She found the book in its present state "a hodgepodge, a carelessly thrown together conglomeration of impressions, facts and evaluations," but she wrote him an encouraging letter, praising the "delightful and true pictures." There was not much she could do beyond rearranging the order of chapters, correcting errors, and quarreling with some of his interpretations as well as his bad grammar. She objected to some anecdotes that reflected unfavorably on the Revolution, such as a description of pigs living in peasants' huts. He accepted many of her factual emendations but declined to cut the story about the pigs because Tolstoy's daughter Olga had told it to him.

• • •

As he was revising proofs of his next book, *A Gallery of Women*, another woman from his past surfaced in his life. He had already written about her in *The "Genius"*—his old love from the Butterick days, Thelma Cudlipp. After *An American Tragedy* appeared, she had read *The "Genius"* and been touched by the account of his sufferings for her sake, although she also felt he had been unfair to her mother. She wrote Dreiser a social note and later invited him and Helen to dinner.

Thelma had married Edmund Grosvenor, a rich, socially prominent attorney, in 1918 and now, at thirty-six, with two children, was living the life of a Park Avenue matron. For Dreiser the reunion was fraught with emotion. When they had a moment alone, she told him, "I have read your *'Genius.'*" "You have been a long time coming to it," he said. When she told him that her mother had committed suicide, he said, simply, "I am glad." He made a movement as though to embrace her, but let his hands drop, saying, "It is too late." Or so she describes the scene in her unpublished autobiographical novel, "October's Child." The dinner went well, but like many other women before and after her, Thelma noticed that he ignored Helen the entire evening. Helen didn't seem to mind, Thelma thought. Later she and the children visited Iroki, and she and Dreiser maintained an occasional correspondence until he died.

•   •   •

That fall he and Helen resumed the Thursday "at homes." Now, friends noticed, he could talk of nothing but his Russian journey. Claude Bowers and W. E. Woodward, Helen's one-time boss and now a debunking historian, both remembered his passionate defense of the Soviet government. He also praised Russian culture and spoke about bringing over the Russian Ballet. At one of his soirées he presented the Russian soprano Nine Koshetz, who had been a favorite in Czarist days. When she finished her recital, he announced to Bowers, "The best is yet to come." And then a group of leaping, sweating, near-naked African dancers hurtled into the room, shouting and menacing the guests. Dreiser thought the dancers wonderfully primitive. That evening was considered the highpoint of his Thursday salons.

•   •   •

The appearance of *Dreiser Looks at Russia* in November injected further turmoil into his life. On November 13, two days after publication, Franklin P. Adams once again found it his droll duty to point out in "The Conning Tower" some curious correspondences between a Dreiser book and one by another author. This time it was Dorothy Thompson, whose *The New Russia* had been published on September 7. The next day Percy Winner, in the *Evening Post,* which had run Thompson's articles, provided a detailed list of the "amazing similarities" between passages in both books. Dreiser's initial reaction when he first saw Winner's article was: "I never read her Goddamn book."

Dreiser denied that he lifted words from Thompson and countercharged that he had given *her* material while they were in Moscow, which he later used in his book, thus explaining the similarities. Thompson hotly challenged this theory: "I wonder when he gave me that material. As I recall it, we met only two or three times and then had merely casual conversations." But Dreiser wrote Ruth Kennell, "She took three separate pieces of stuff I gathered . . . all of which I talked over with her & when I didn't know she was rushing off daily letters to New York or contemplating a book. . . ."

Then he offered another explanation: they had obtained material from the same source, the weekly bulletin of the Soviet Foreign Ministry. Thompson retorted that she had drawn on official handouts only to verify some transcriptions of speeches. Furthermore, the plagiary involved descriptions of Moscow scenes, not the kind of stuff that would be found in government releases.

She had a good case. For example, Dreiser wrote: "There are the N.E.P. men. . . . They sit moodily in the restaurant of the Grand Hotel, drink Russian wines, watch the dancing and think themselves lucky if a ballerina from the opera dances with them." Thompson's account reads: "The businessmen sit moodily in the restaurant of the Grand Hotel watching the dancing and thinking themselves lucky if they have a ballerina from the opera to dance with." There were several other parallels. Thompson later wrote a friend, "The old beast simply lifted paragraph after paragraph from my articles; I'm not speaking of material—we all got that where we could—but purely literary expressions. And, of course, ideas as well, because it never occurred to anyone else, for instance, to write about the social life of Moscow."

The irony of the entire affair was that he didn't need to borrow any material from Thompson. He had spent three months in the country, whereas she had spent a month in Moscow and then hurried off to join Lewis. Take the preceding account of the scene with the NEP men. In his diary Dreiser describes a similar group he had encountered in Leningrad's Hotel Europa. He could well have used that description but perhaps felt that he must provide some Moscow color.

Rushed and needing filler material, he took a shortcut. The Thompson passages appear in the original manuscript. They are written in Dreiser's own hand. He had always regarded newspaper stories as grist for his novels, and it could be that he lumped Thompson's articles with their conversations in Moscow. This was the material he told Ruth Kennell had been "offered to me for my use."

• • •

A scandalous trial was brewing, with lawyers on both sides primed to impugn the character and integrity of the opposing parties. Dreiser seemed eager for battle, writing Kennell in December, "I have good lawyers & she & Lewis will know something more about plagiarism than they do now before it's all over." His attorneys planned to introduce a fourteen-page concordance between Thompson's book and New York *Times* columnist Anne O'Hare McCormick's previously published Russian memoir, *The Hammer and the Scythe*.

Amid all the fuss, the reviews of *Dreiser Looks at Russia* were somewhat anticlimactic. Many critics alluded to the Dorothy Thompson imbroglio, but most were bemused rather than indignant. Lewis Gannett in the New York *Herald Tribune* put it best: " . . . the impression is abroad that Dreiser's book is like Dorothy Thompson's. Except in a few details it isn't. It is as different as Theodore Dreiser is from Dorothy Thompson. . . . Dreiser is not sure of anything about Russia. And who else has ever written a book about Russia without being abundantly sure?"

73 / *This Madness*

> But in the interim ... there came a form of satiation most
> characteristic of my disposition — and perhaps of all nature in
> one form or another. ... The changefulness of my moods! The
> cruelty of them!
>
> —Dreiser, *This Madness* (1929)

Dreiser Looks at Russia found no strong response among readers; U.S. sales eventually totaled only four thousand copies. As usual, Dreiser blamed his publisher's inadequate advertising for the poor showing. In February Thompson withdrew her suit, which might have publicized the book. Probably she had no heart for a bruising court battle.

Dreiser's complaints about the book's sales were just another shot in his running battle with Liveright. A larger grievance was the failure of Horace Liveright Inc. (as the company was now known) to bring out the limited edition of his complete works, which under the contract was to have been launched in 1927. Once again Dreiser was entertaining suitors, including his old but apparently constant love, Harper's, which had offered to take over all his books for ten years and invest $75,000 in advertising; Dreiser would receive a flat 10 percent of sales. Another bidder was Simon & Schuster, the publishing house that the crossword-puzzle craze built. It would guarantee him $16,000 a year for ten years, regardless of sales, and spend $50,000 on promotion over the first five years of the contract.

Liveright once again baked a savory financial pie to tempt him into staying. He had hopes for another Great American Novel — *The Stoic* or *The Bulwark*. In the meantime there was *A Gallery of Women*, for which a presumably large public was waiting. Dreiser on women — well, his reputation was getting around. At any rate, Liveright dangled a guarantee of $15,000 a year for ten years, plus one hundred shares of stock in the company, currently selling at $275 a share.

Dreiser was surely aware that Liveright Inc. was falling on hard times. The glory days of 1927 and 1928, when its titles regularly rode the best-seller

447

list—six of them simultaneously, at one point—were behind it. The year 1929 would be the worst in the company's history; its only best seller would be Francis Hackett's *Henry VIII*. And without the Modern Library, which he had sold to Bennett Cerf to raise some quick cash, or any other backlist, Liveright needed multiple best sellers just to stay afloat.

On April 29, 1929, Dreiser signed the new contract with Liveright Inc., calling on him to deliver a new book every other year.

•   •   •

Dreiser's Russian trip embroiled him in another project at this time, one close to his Slavic soul: bringing the Russian Ballet to America. The idea had been suggested to him by William Reswick, the AP man in Moscow, who proposed that Otto Kahn be the chief angel. At least $250,000 would be needed. The logistical problems were formidable, and the impoverished company needed new sets and costumes.

Kahn (now president of the Metropolitan Opera, he had sponsored Nijinsky's American tour with the Ballet Russe) was receptive. He pledged $25,000 seed money and promised to underwrite half of the $250,000. As business manager Dreiser engaged Hy Kraft, the producer whom he had authorized to mount *Sister Carrie* for the stage (the project was abandoned when Dreiser refused to approve John Howard Lawson's script and the writer left for Hollywood).

With the prestige of Otto Kahn behind the enterprise, a few society people pledged money. But then some snags reared up. According to Kraft, communication with the Moscow authorities, with whom he was dealing through Reswick, broke down.

In early April Kraft set a deadline for a decision by Moscow, and when none came, Dreiser decided to cancel the tour. On April 14 he wrote Kraft that the "deal is off. Sorry. Financial responsibilities will be quickly determined and I will see about meeting them. . . . I'm off for Boston."

•   •   •

"Boston" meant the long-awaited obscenity trial of Donald Friede for selling a copy of *An American Tragedy*. Liveright and his attorneys, Arthur Garfield Hays and Clarence Darrow, were optimistic about winning the case. Dreiser was ready to testify in behalf of his book, and there was support among Hub intellectuals. But the city's Puritans—Protestant and Catholic—were all-powerful.

In his presentation, the district attorney needed only to cite the twenty-four questionable pages in the novel. The level of argument was epitomized by his comment on the scene in which Clyde visits a prostitute: "Well, perhaps where the gentleman published this book, it is considered not obscene for a woman to start disrobing before a man, but it happens to be out in Roxbury where I come from." In his charge to the jury, the judge backed the district attorney, telling the panel they need only consider whether the passages were obscene and tending toward the corruption of the young. Artistic intention or quality was irrelevant.

Hays knew the game was up, and he telegraphed Liveright that the jury would "vote Catholic." It did on April 18, leaving Friede the choice of paying the $300 fine or appealing. After a discussion among the principals, Liveright agreed to finance an appeal to the Massachusetts Supreme Court (which, a year later, upheld the lower court's verdict).

At the trial, Dreiser audibly chuckled at the district attorney's concern for the moral sensibilities of the good folk of Roxbury, but the Boston banning was a fire bell in the night, activating his anticensorship juices. He laid the blame on the altar of the Church. When Claude Bowers sent him an editorial he had written for the *World* condemning the banning of the *Tragedy* and the confiscation by a Boston customs official of thirteen copies of Voltaire's *Candide,* Dreiser replied in fury: "I have stated over and over that the chief menace to the world today is the Catholic Church because it is a world wide organization and because chiefly it attacks intelligence . . . since for its own prosperity's sake it believes in mass stupidity."

He suspected that religious groups were also behind the delay in the filming of *An American Tragedy* in Hollywood. Three years had passed since the stormy luncheon at the Ritz, and not a line of the script had been written. Dreiser had received reports that Will Hays was holding the picture hostage on moral grounds. Paramount-Publix (as Famous Players–Lasky was now called) was probably complicit. When Lasky announced with great fanfare the purchase of the screen rights to the novel, the studio had received a deluge of protest mail, and the recent verdict in Boston was a sign that, in some quarters at least, *An American Tragedy* was an immoral book.

●　●　●

Dreiser then found himself encountering another kind of censorship with a serial, *This Madness,* which he had sold to *Cosmopolitan.* The stories were semi-autobiographical, describing the love affairs of a famous novelist who goes by the nicknames "Dodar" and "T" and whose books include *The Financier* and *The Titan.* The editors played up the autobiographical angle, and Dreiser gave the series his imprimatur: "You people may not realize it, but in 'This Madness' you are publishing the most intimate and important work so far achieved by me." To which the editors chorused, "We do realize it, Mr. Dreiser. We realize that no man, certainly no American, has written so honestly, so frankly, about the part love plays in the life of a great artist."

Whatever its confessional value, *This Madness* was second-drawer. The stories lack irony, tension, detachment; the language is at times turgid, weighing down the slight subject matter, and at times lushly romantic.

After the first two episodes appeared, Ruth Kennell chastised him for writing "pseudobiography with the unreality and romanticism of a schoolboy, and the social snobbery of Robert W. Chambers." The stories encouraged the "false conception engendered by capitalism . . . that woman is a commodity for the use of men, which loses its value when youth or beauty decline." She was right. The women in *This Madness* are figments of desire.

Dreiser at least deserved credit for not completely succumbing to the formula of slick magazine fiction; there are no happy endings. But he did have to conform to the standards of woman's-magazine morality. The material was cut by almost a third, he told Grant C. Knight, a University of Kentucky English professor, in order to make it "suitable to the censorship in various states and possible prejudices of some of their readers. . . . " Dreiser's final typescript suggests that the trims were not as large as he said, but cuts there were. The phrase "I let my hand wander to her breasts outlined beneath the filmy material of her dress" was deemed unsuitable. The outcome of a romantic rendezvous between the author and a scantily clad woman one moonlit night in the country was not left to the imagination in the manuscript. Nor would the editors permit Dreiser to allude to the character becoming pregnant and visiting an abortionist. The "uncompromising realist" shown in the author's photograph had made some compromises.

Dreiser told Knight that he intended to publish the complete stories, along with four others, accompanied by "an introduction and a philosophic commentary at the close, which will throw some light on the book as a whole." He was not coy about their source: "In regard to the material—it is autobiographical."

•   •   •

Now that he had money, he was able to subsidize a group of researchers, some of whom were mistresses. He was secretive about his affairs, so that, like the members of a Communist cell, each woman rarely knew the identities of the others. One of his later women friends says he did this to avoid hurting anyone's feelings; avoiding jealous confrontations may have been another motive.

Among those who did literary work for him at this time was Marguerite Tjader Harris. She recalled their first meeting, at one of his Thursday nights: "He turned to look down at me as if I were a glass and he wanted to see what sort of liquid was in it." She was living the life of a society matron, and he teased her about being a "parasite" and offered to put her to work. She was interested and began performing various research tasks, commuting from Connecticut during the week to a rented room in Manhattan. He visited her infrequently, never notifying her ahead of time, as though he were trying to conceal his movements. But the uncertainty also gave a romantic piquancy to his affairs, Harris thought; he preferred to respond to "the urgency of the moment" rather than adhere to a fixed routine. She was struck by his "utter simplicity" and his strongly emotional nature. "Dreiser simply *was* his own emotions, his own instincts, or intuitions, attempting to communicate them directly, often in terms contradictory to each other."

A tall, intelligent woman with a determined chin and wide brow, Harris came from a wealthy family. Dreiser liked to take her to fashionable restaurants, the opera, or the theater. He would don a tuxedo and she, evening finery. She provided a glamorous outlet for his secret craving for admission to society, Harris thought.

All this extracurricular life generated constant tensions with Helen. By June their relationship was approaching a crisis. Ralph Fabri, the Hungarian painter, became Helen's confidante. Dreiser had admired Fabri's portrait of Helen's singing teacher, Maria Samson (who complained to the artist that Dreiser made advances to her), and asked Fabri to do one of Helen. She posed with her wolfhound, Nick, at Fabri's studio on Washington Square, often walking all the way from Fifty-seventh Street. During the sittings she poured out her troubles with Dreiser. He recorded in his diary that she told him they hadn't had sexual relations for two years, but that there was a durable spiritual affection between them.

Helen was particularly wounded by his taste for younger women, and she also feared he was endangering his health. He boasted that sex was the most important business of his life and once told Helen he had slept with three women in the same day. His run of amorous luck made him more libidinous but also more lonely. As he had written in *This Madness,* he could never be sure a woman cared for him or his fame. And clearly some of them were drawn to him by a combination of hero-worship and literary ambition, which he always encouraged to the point of commending their work to his agent of the moment. And in most cases his praise was sincere.

But women only satisfied a need; they did not provide the answers he was seeking or soothe his restless spirit (indeed, on balance, they brought him more unrest). It was in a philosophically questing mood that he returned to the Woods Hole Marine Laboratory in August. Accompanied by Calvin Bridges, the Nobel Prize–winning geneticist from the California Institute of Technology, he spent the weekend on Nantucket with Marguerite Harris and her husband. He had developed a friendship with Bridges, a towheaded, boyish man with an easy grin, who was as dedicated an admirer of femininity as Dreiser. They picnicked on the beach and talked well into the night about the philosophical questions that obsessed him. Bridges argued that philosophers had no hope of learning the "why" of existence, but he believed that eventually science would fill in all the "hows." His theory was that human lives are determined by higher laws of cause and effect, and the best we can do is to live to the fullest, enjoying the spectacle of the harmony of nature or the form of a beautiful woman. Dreiser liked this idea, Harris noted, but thought Bridges's scientific approach excluded "those veiled mysterious forces of darkness that [Dreiser] had believed in almost more than forces of Light. . . . " He envisioned the universe in mechanistic terms as the setting of a Manichean drama in which light and darkness clashed in an eternal struggle.

●   ●   ●

The struggle with Helen continued after his return to New York in September. One day in October she announced, "I just had a fight with Teddy. We're breaking this time. He's going to a lawyer." Later she reported, "He must be fixing up a place for himself. He probably wants to leave me in the street." But the next day, when Fabri went to 200 West Fifty-seventh to return a book, he found Dreiser at home, worrying about the stock market crash. It was October 29 — Black Tuesday.

On the whole, he weathered the storm relatively well, and he did not noticeably curtail his lifestyle. His income from bonds continued, and he had the regular monthly stipend of $1250 from Liveright plus a steady stream of article and permissions fees. He also had hopes for a good sale of A Gallery of Women, which appeared in late November in a two-volume $5 edition. He had argued for a $3 edition, but Liveright talked him out of it, saying that his prestige would be hurt by the lower price. And why take a 40 percent cut in royalties?

The advertising campaign for Gallery was the prince of literary ballyhoo's last hurrah. It was inaugurated with a full-page Dreiser-as-institution advertisement in the New York Times describing him as "the rock on which the future of American letters must be raised." This was followed by daily ads in several papers for a solid month. Posters covered the sides of trucks and buses, depicting beautiful women who were purportedly the characters in the book. No matter that one of the studies was about an Irish scrubwoman, another about a drab farmwife, and a third about the eccentric fortune-teller Jessie Spafford. Liveright huffed and puffed but could dispose of only twelve thousand copies — "a terrible flop," Donald Friede later described it. The $5 cover price and economic uncertainties surely diminished sales. And there was no titillation in the book to live up to Liveright's advertising.

If Gallery was a commercial disappointment, the critics weren't writing Dreiser's epitaph. A majority of them were favorable if unenthusiastic. Most of the stories were praised as honest, unadorned examples of realism, devoid of stylistic tricks and imitating life in all its inconclusiveness and ambiguity. There was criticism of Dreiser's "monotonous" preoccupation with sex, but his perception that most women are troubled by sexual problems happened to be one of his acutest insights. As Harry Hansen observed, most of the women in the book are undone by love: "Success does not attend them. Whether they restrain their passions, or become 'varietists' . . . happiness is not for them."

A Gallery of Women stirred up some objections among those who knew the real-life models. "Ernestine," for example, was based on Florence Deshon, a beautiful young actress Dreiser had met in Hollywood, who had been the mistress of Max Eastman and Charlie Chaplin before she committed suicide. Eastman wrote, "His portrait corresponds only in two small remarks to my knowledge of her life and character: She was 'sensuously and disturbingly beautiful and magnetic' and she was 'almost abnormally ambitious.' " Eastman appears in the story as Varn Kinsey, a radical poet with a talent for fund-raising for political causes, who keeps some of the money for himself as a salary. All this material was based on Dreiser's conversation with Florence Deshon in Hollywood.

Ruth Kennell would be another aggrieved party. The sketch "Ernita" describes in some detail her personal troubles. After at first leaving to Dreiser the decision on whether to print the story, her domestic situation altered, and she asked him not to do it. Her shock when she read it in the book was considerable. Dreiser had offered her $500 for the story, but she refused to take it. Sergei Dinamov, to whom she confided her troubles, agreed with her that Dreiser had not adequately disguised her identity but shrugged, "a writer is always a writer."

Hutchins Hapgood was another disgruntled victim. He is portrayed as J.J., the wealthy, cold-blooded lover of Esther Norn, who is based on Mary Pyne, as Dreiser recalls her from his Village days on West Tenth Street, when she would come to his studio from the unheated flat she shared with Harry Kemp and warm herself before his fire like a cat. Kemp is shown as a mountebank, egoist, and self-promoter who treated Mary rottenly, having affairs while she was ill. Hapgood felt that Dreiser had taken an unpardonable liberty with his life by saying he and Mary were lovers; he insisted their relationship was platonic.

In "Rona Murtha," the tale of Anna Mallon and Arthur Henry, Dreiser pays back his friend of *Sister Carrie* days for the depiction of himself as a fussy neurotic in Henry's book *An Island Cabin* more than twenty-five years before. But there is sympathy, too, for Henry's futile dreams and for the woman he casually tosses aside when she no longer serves him.

Dreiser was drawing his material from life, as he had always done. No one sued, but there were psychological repercussions. Hy Kraft received a call from him one Saturday, and when he arrived at the Rodin, Dreiser announced,

"Kraft, I'm going to die." He had no particular complaint or physical symptoms, just a premonition of doom. He had not gone out for two days because he was afraid he might collapse in the street. Kraft, who had recently undergone psychoanalysis, attributed Dreiser's depression to the publication of *Gallery*. He was ashamed of it, thought it "pretty cheap stuff, and [was] overwhelmed with a sense of guilt."

That explanation seems superficial. One guesses Dreiser felt more guilty about the slick and lucrative *This Madness* than *Gallery*, on which he had worked for nearly ten years and which could not be considered cheap exploitation. What he felt may have been an anxiety attack, triggered by fear of some nameless retribution for his exposés. All but three or four of the women were dead, but he had taken liberties with their lives, broken the sheer membrane between fact and fiction, and he now regretted it.

Depression over the book was just one of the clouds hanging over him. There were his stormy relations with Helen, various woman troubles, the Crash, and the failure to bring over the Russian Ballet, which had embarrassed him socially. As it was for many people, 1929 had been a bad year for Dreiser. He had heard the beating wings of the Furies.

Part Thirteen

. . .

EQUITY

74 / Going Left

> I say this country is facing Communism. Is it to be met like a political doctrine—soberly—in a civilized way—or tyrannically?
>
> —Dreiser (1930)

Dreiser's personal demons seemed distinctively those of a rich man, the anxieties of surfeit—juggling the financing of a country home and a luxury studio in Manhattan, conserving his capital against the gyrations of the stock market, extracting his rightful share from an increasingly shaky publisher, parceling himself among various mistresses. Many of his fellow Americans were not so fortunate in their neuroses. As the country slid into the worst depression in its history, their anxieties focused on starker problems. Speaking for the 1920s intellectuals, John Dos Passos pronounced the end of an era: "Anyway, the Jazz Age is dead." Gone was rebellious hedonism and private angst; in came politics, social conscience, the writer *engagé*.

Dreiser was still groping toward an economic philosophy that would explain the weird malaise stalking America. He considered communism in some form to be the sovereign remedy, but he had doubts that it would work in the United States. In his last public utterance on the subject, he had affirmed to readers of *Jewish Day* that he was still an individualist and praised America as "the ideal country for the individualist who is capable of getting ahead" (Jews, who were "natural-born traders," being a prime example). He had the "greatest interest" in the Communist experiment in Russia and predicted that even if it didn't bring heaven on earth in fifty years, it would "eventually alter the relationship of the people to their governments." But communism was the antithesis of individualism: "It's the cutting off of every kind of independence! You've got to obey every law and rule of the community; you've got to swear you'll do it."

•   •   •

Meanwhile, early rumors emanating from the Swedish Academy in Stockholm indicated that Dreiser had an excellent chance of winning the Nobel Prize for Literature. He had an adoring German admirer who boosted him in Europe, and he also paid his secretary-mistress Esther Van Dresser's way to the Continent. Her dual mission was to talk him up for the prize and to collect past-due royalties from his foreign publishers. A man who met her on the ship said she had claimed she was really Dreiser's daughter and described "the horrible life she was leading under his mistreatment." In Prague Esther was successful in collecting money from Dreiser's Czechoslovakian publisher. In the course of her business dealings she fell in love with the son of the American consul, and they were later married.

To replace Esther, Dreiser hired Kathryn Sayre, a brilliant Columbia graduate student in philosophy. Then, in March, plagued by bronchitis; unable to work on his next book, the autobiographical *Dawn,* because of distractions, particularly a love affair he was trying to break off; and curious about the state of the country under the lengthening shadow of the Depression, he boarded a train for Tucson, stopping off at the Grand Canyon on the way.

He rented a car, but was a blundering driver. In cities he maneuvered the vehicle as he used to drive his laundry wagon in Chicago, weaving in and out of traffic and ignoring stoplights. On country roads he was liable to fall into a reverie and veer into a ditch. After a week or so he realized he was a hazard to himself and others, and he summoned Kay Sayre to chauffeur him around and help him with *Dawn,* which he was trying to work on en route.

In transit he wrote his new Hollywood agent, I. M. Sackin, assigning him the task of selling his novels for the screen. His minimum price was $75,000 for each title, he told Sackin — more for *The "Genius"* and the *Tragedy,* which was still stalled at Paramount. He was also willing to write scripts if the price was right. He explained to his artist friend Willy Pogany, who had steered him to Sackin, that stiff demands were necessary to command respect from the studios.

En route, he shed his cloak of anonymity and began sounding off in interviews. In Albuquerque he inveighed against reformers and YMCA secretaries who censored books. He gave the horse laugh to the Hays Code and moral movies, and dismissed the Ten Commandments as "a bunch of bugaboos." Prohibition was "bunk," he told the press, and he couldn't wait to reach El Paso, where he could cross the border and get a decent drink. Capitalism also drew his ire: "Money is the hallmark of all that is best in America," he proclaimed. "Because he has money, Henry Ford is an authority."

In Dallas, less than a week later, he told the *Morning News* that a communist revolution was possible in America and that democracy was a "farce." He loosed another blast at American materialism, offering himself as a leading sinner. For thirty years, he said, he had dreamed of owning a place in the country, but now that he had one, he had spent $50,000 fixing it up—and he didn't like living there.

Dreiser's tone in these interviews, as conveyed in newsprint, sounds unvaryingly irascible. Gone was his wariness of the press. Politics brought angry emotions seething to the surface. His views were fired by passion rather than analysis. He was getting sore (as he might have said) about the way the country was being run. Also, as he once confessed, he liked to shock reporters with outrageous statements.

• • •

Next Dreiser set forth to tangle with Hollywood. Warner Brothers, it seemed, was vaguely interested in filming his books. Helen was now along. She joined him in Dallas with their nine-passenger Chrysler. Warner Brothers' interest turned out to be ephemeral, so they pushed on up the coast to San Francisco for a visit with one of Dreiser's causes, Tom Mooney, at San Quentin. They found America's most famous political prisoner, a labor leader who had been convicted by perjured testimony of bombing a patriotic parade in 1916, desperately longing for freedom. Dreiser tried to comfort him by reminding him of the worldwide renown he had gained while in jail; once out he would be a nobody. But that was small consolation to Mooney, who was weary of martyrdom and began weeping. Dreiser, deeply moved, promised that he would do all he could to win his release and traveled to Sacramento to speak with Governor C. C. Young, who was weighing a pardon. Young told him he couldn't act until a decision was handed down on the appeal of Mooney's codefendant in the San Francisco bombing. Concluding that publicity was Mooney's best hope, Dreiser tried to interest publisher William Randolph Hearst in the case, and he and Helen had lunch at San Simeon. Hearst was sympathetic but noncommittal.

Stopping at Los Angeles en route to Portland, Dreiser conferred with a director from Universal Pictures, who intimated that his boss, Carl Laemmle, Jr., was interested in filming the *Tragedy*. Fine, Dreiser told him, but he was leaving in two days. No summons came, but a telegram from the studio asking him if he would return arrived in Oregon. All right, Dreiser said, but send $500 for expenses. This was done, and Dreiser met with Laemmle, who was trying to move the studio away from its customary low-budget output to more ambitious films. But nothing further was heard from Universal.

So, empty-handed as far as Hollywood was concerned, Dreiser and Helen drove homeward, pausing at Rochester, Minnesota, where he was scheduled for a checkup at the Mayo Clinic. The examination revealed signs of youthful fibroid pulmonary tuberculosis. His left lung was "so densely scarred that multiple small cavities are present." This condition was equivalent to a chronic bronchitis, producing persistent coughing, repeated respiratory infections, and quantities of sputum, often foul-smelling and sometimes containing blood. Dreiser also had an enlarged prostate, which was of no medical concern. And so, as Dreiser had always believed, as a boy in Chicago he had contracted TB while working in the hardware warehouse (perhaps the scar was the "tumor" the doctor in Berlin saw on the X ray).

The next stop was Chicago, where they picked up his long-missing brother Rome. Dreiser had suspected that the money he had been sending to his brother's hotel was being diverted into other pockets. His suspicions turned out to be correct. They decided to take Rome, who was physically debilitated, to New York, where the recently widowed Mame would look after him.

When they arrived in New York in June, more reporters were demanding his views on the state of the nation. He held forth in the *World-Telegram* under the headline DREISER NOW REDISCOVERS AMERICA. The corporations were running the country, he charged, so why not draft prominent tycoons into the cabinet? Make John D. Rockefeller secretary of oil and gas, for example. He let fly at wealthy business leaders with their "gold swimming pools at their country houses. They can buy thousand-acre tracts to keep off neighbors and indulge in all that swill, but they can't arrange things so a man can have a job."

Perceiving like everyone else that the national economy was coughing along on one cylinder, he lashed out at an old Populist demon—monopoly capitalists extorting money from the masses to pay for their gold-plated swimming pools. But the problem was much more complicated than swimming pools, whether gold-plated or spring-fed, like his own at Iroki.

• • •

By this time, Liveright's own financial situation had deteriorated badly. He had used his shares in the company as collateral to borrow from his treasurer, Arthur Pell. In July Pell called in his loan, forced Liveright out, and began slashing costs. Liveright told friends and the press that he was going to Hollywood to take a vaguely defined job with Paramount (which Otto Kahn had arranged for him), but he hoped to return to the business he loved.

Dreiser owed his publisher *Dawn* by the end of 1930, so he retired to Iroki and brought Campbell up from Philadelphia to assist him. He would not complete the task until January. The original manuscript was graphic about Mame's and Sylvia's illegitimate babies and other sexual matters, including Dreiser's youthful masturbation. Although some of this was cut, he got in much of it in condensed form. And he had Kay Sayre go through the manuscript and camouflage his sisters' identities by giving them fictitious names and eliminating telltale descriptions such as a reference to Sylvia's belief in Christian Science. As a disciple of Rousseau, he was determined to include at least partial glimpses of his and his family's sexual history.

• • •

Politically, he continued his leftward march. When International Labor Defense, the Communist party's legal arm, asked him to speak at a rally, he declined but authorized it to use his name, thus inaugurating a practice that would become habitual. He agreed to become chairman of the Emergency Committee for Southern Political Prisoners, an adjunct of ILD and the John Reed Club. The real power in this organization was Joe Pass, a young Communist party member. The group had been formed to draw attention to the harassment (and worse) of Communist labor organizers, who had become active in the South. Dreiser's only pronouncement in its behalf was indited at Pass's request—a condemnation of the arrest in Atlanta of several Communists who had been distributing literature demanding jobs and higher wages. The charge, under a hoary statute, was inciting to insurrection, which carried the death penalty. The two blacks in the group, Herbert Newton and Henry Story, were to be tried first.

The issue, Dreiser asserted in his hastily written statement, was not communism, the desirability of which was not for him to say, but whether Communists could get a fair trial in this country. The tactic of trying the Negroes first looked like "a frame-up to convict the whole lot," since in the South blacks were considered guilty as soon as they were arrested, and some were simply lynched without even that formality. It was better to respect the Communists' rights and permit them to advocate peaceful change. This was hardly a radical position, even though the John Reed Club, a Communist party auxiliary, was behind it. The club had in May persuaded 135 intellectuals to sign a statement protesting arrests of labor organizers and workers. Among the signatories was H. L. Mencken, a vehement anti-Communist.

Dreiser was more lucid in an article on the Mooney case for the Scripps-Howard newspapers, which had decided to campaign editorially for the imprisoned man's release. Working people, he said, should stop being indifferent to the growing concentration of power in the hands of "a financial autocracy already too anxious to enslave them."

• • •

Just before Liveright left for the Coast, he wrote Dreiser that Lasky needed to be sold on the idea that a talkie of *An American Tragedy* would succeed at the box office; otherwise Paramount might vend the rights to another company.

Dreiser contended that the silent-film rights he sold to Famous Players–Lasky (Paramount's predecessor) in 1926 had lapsed because of the company's failure to film it. If Paramount wanted to make a talkie, it must negotiate a new contract with him; otherwise he could vend the rights elsewhere. He had been advised by the Dramatists Guild that Paramount held only the silent rights.

At his end, Liveright was still trying to claim the 30 percent of the motion-picture rights. He asserted that Dreiser must pay him $5000 if he sold the talkie rights. He said that he had "stirred up great interest" in a movie version directed by Sergei Eisenstein, whom he and Lasky had met in Paris and signed to a six-month contract. Perhaps at Liveright's suggestion, Eisenstein was offered the *Tragedy,* which several directors, including D. W. Griffith, had already turned down. Liveright was appointed supervisor of the project and tried to involve himself in the writing, but Eisenstein disliked him. In a diary he wrote at the end of his life, he says he can remember nothing about Liveright other than his reputation as a publisher of "daring" books.

Eisenstein had his own perspective on the novel. The real tragedy of this book, he decided, was the "tragic course pursued by Clyde, whom the social structure drives to murder." Clyde lost his nerve at the crucial moment and thus was innocent of the crime. To underscore this point, Eisenstein alters Dreiser's story by having Clyde try to rescue Roberta after the boat overturns. "But the machinery of crime has been set in motion and continues to its end, even against Clyde's will. Roberta cries out weakly, tries to retreat from him in her horror, and, not being able to swim, drowns." That version eliminated the last semblance of Clyde's guilt in a legal or moral sense. Eisenstein was primarily interested in showing the implacable operations of fate. An innocent man is subjected to a sham trial that is actually a political contest between the district attorney and his opponents before a prejudiced jury.

Eisenstein made another major alteration in the book: he eliminated the character of the Reverend McMillan and has Clyde confess to his mother in the death house that he had originally planned to kill Roberta but changed his mind. At the pardon hearing it is she who seals Clyde's doom. Unable to free herself from her religious belief that "the thought of sin is equivalent to its execution," as Eisenstein puts it, she cannot affirm his innocence to the governor.

Thus, rather than recognize the moral claims of Christianity, in the powerful presence of McMillan, as Dreiser did, Eisenstein makes the mother's "purblind fanaticism" the villain. Outside the governor's chambers, she regrets her silence and cries out, "My son is innocent!" But it is too late. The scenario coldly contemplates her guilt: "The mother's fatal moment of silence cannot even be washed away by her tears." Perhaps Eisenstein was expressing a subconscious hostility toward his own mother, who had temporarily deserted him when he was a child. Elvira Griffiths in the movie is no longer the *Pietà* figure of the book who pleads for mercy before the governor.

The script was warily received by the film company. Eisenstein recalled that studio head B. P. Schulberg asked, "Is Clyde Griffiths guilty or not guilty — in your treatment?" When Eisenstein replied not guilty, Schulberg said, "But then your script is a monstrous challenge to American society." The screenplay followed the book in showing how Clyde's early life made his crime inevitable.

Also, as Eisenstein wrote his mother while traveling to New York for talks with Lasky and Dreiser, "there are many questions in connection with the 'propaganda' theme" in the light of Representative Hamilton Fish's investigation of communism in Hollywood.

While Eisenstein and Montagu were in New York, talking to Dreiser and preparing to scout locations upstate, telegrams were presumably flying back and forth between the coasts. Then, on October 23, Lasky announced that the contract between Paramount and Eisenstein had been "terminated by mutual consent." What had swung him against the picture, he later said, was the pile of mail from patriotic Americans objecting to a film by the Red Dog Eisenstein. Lasky called Eisenstein and his collaborator, Ivor Montagu, into his office, showed them the letters, and said, "Gentlemen, it is over. Our agreement is at an end."

· · ·

In November Sinclair Lewis was awarded the Nobel Prize for Literature, the first American author to win it. Earlier, the Associated Press had reported that Dreiser was favored and that he had "several champions" in the Swedish Academy. Closer to the announcement day, however, a Swedish paper had reported on excellent authority that the choice was between Lewis and Dreiser. When the three-man committee from the Swedish Academy met, Dreiser had only one champion. The other two members reportedly preferred Lewis's satire to Dreiser's more ponderous, solemn style.

Some consolation for his loss came with the news that the sale of the talking rights to *An American Tragedy* had finally gone through. After Eisenstein's abrupt departure, Paramount boss Adolph Zukor begged Josef von Sternberg, the director of *The Blue Angel*, who had brought its star, Marlene Dietrich, to Hollywood, to make a low-budget talkie and salvage the studio's already large investment in the property. Dreiser got his $55,000. The contract was signed on January 2, 1931, and Dreiser approved von Sternberg as director and Samuel Hoffenstein, whom he knew socially, as scriptwriter.

Liveright got nothing at all. It was still another blow for the former publisher, who badly needed the money. An affair with an actress had broken up, and he was drinking heavily. In Hollywood, the splendor and flair of Horace Liveright died, leaving the ashes of a man.

75 / *Droit Moral*

> I have a literary character to maintain and I contend that I
> have a mental equity in my product and in the character of my
> product. Even though [the movie companies] buy the right
> of reproduction they don't buy the right to change it into any-
> thing they please.
>
> —Dreiser (1931)

By early 1931 Dreiser was more than ankle-deep in politics. He was now being asked for statements on this or that issue by leftist groups and publications. Anxious to say the right thing, he wrote somewhat self-importantly to Ann North, editor of *Solidarity*, "Although I know the Marxian theory thoroughly, and satisfied myself, by going there, of the experiment in Russia, I do not know the details of the larger issues which confront the Communists here in America." He proposed that she or Mr. Pass or the John Reed Club or *The New Masses* suggest pertinent topics and provide data "which could be either selected from or recast by me so that I would not be outside the facts most interesting to the Party and would be able to speak with the knowledge which is so necessary." He would consider any subjects they proposed and perhaps write an article, which publications like hers or *The New Masses* would be welcome to publish.

In May he took that offer a step further. When the *Daily Worker* required a contribution for the May Day issue on the press and political prisoners, he told them to write it themselves—"to assure you have just the statement you want"—and he would edit and sign it. "Make it strong," he told the editor.

• • •

Before he could proceed any further down the Communist road, he became embroiled in another time-consuming dispute with the capitalists in Holly-wood. Hoffenstein had in five weeks completed his screenplay of the *Tragedy*, a straightforward job of work that lobotomized the novel of all social meaning

464

and found Clyde guilty as charged. This was in keeping with von Sternberg's ideas about the picture. As the director explained, "I eliminated the sociological elements, which, in my opinion, were far from being responsible for the [murder] with which Dreiser had concerned himself."

Fearing some such jiggering, Dreiser had insisted on a clause in the contract stating that Paramount must send him the script and consider his "comments, advice, suggestions or criticisms." The company promised to "use its best endeavors" to accept them, but it was not legally bound to do so. There followed a series of errors, evasions, and missed meetings, with Hoffenstein trying to fulfill, pro forma, Paramount's part of the contract by showing the script to Dreiser so the filming could begin and the latter rejecting the screenplay and carrying his objections to Lasky.

For all the words expended on this issue, Dreiser was claiming what the French call *droit moral*, the artist's right to preserve his or her work unaltered by subsequent purchasers—which was fine with a statue but harder to do in a collaborative, commercial medium like the movies. After much back-and-forthing, Paramount flew Dreiser and Hy Kraft, who was working at the company's Long Island studio, to Hollywood, where they proposed a number of small, feasible changes that would suggest the hardships of Clyde's early life and reinject a tithe of Dreiser's social message. These were eventually added, but von Sternberg's movie, in the end, followed Hollywood morality. Where Eisenstein showed Clyde having a change of heart, von Sternberg shows him confessing his guilt to his mother in his cell; she gazes Heavenward and says, "I know that somehow, somewhere, you'll be given the right start."

Before the film was released, Dreiser's lawyers sought an injunction to stop its showing. They warned their client that he had little chance of winning, and that if he did sue, Paramount might demand a sizable bond to indemnify it against loss. But Dreiser wanted to place his side of the dispute before the public. The case went to trial in July in White Plains, New York. Paramount's lawyer attacked the novel as a "cold-blooded plagiarism" of the trial record of the Gillette case and accused the author of being anti-Christian and a publicity-seeker. To that Dreiser shouted, "It's a lie!" and was cautioned by the judge. His counsel, Arthur Garfield Hays, was more effective: if the novel was mere plagiarism, he wondered, why hadn't Paramount based its script on the court records in the Gillette case? But Judge Graham Witschief ruled that Paramount had a perfect right to change the novel any way it liked, for it must answer to a higher court: "In the preparation of the picture the producer must give consideration to the fact that the great majority of people composing the audience before which the picture will be presented will be more interested that justice prevail over wrongdoing than that the inevitability of Clyde's end clearly appear."

Dreiser had to content himself with a moral victory. As he said when he left Hollywood, "I feel, in a way, that I am acting for the thousands of authors who haven't had a square deal, in having their works belittled for screen exploitation." And he had succeeded in forcing Paramount to make at least some of the changes he and Kraft devised.

•   •   •

Midway in the movie war, Dreiser agreed, at Joe Pass's behest, to invite a group of intellectuals to his apartment to discuss forming a successor to the Southern Emergency Committee, to be know as the National Committee for the Defense of Political Prisoners. This body was envisioned by Pass as a sort of intellectuals' auxiliary of International Labor Defense. Dreiser's new secretary, Evelyn Light, a tall, efficient woman and former assistant editor of the leftist weekly *Plain Talk,* sent out fifty-three invitations. The subject of the meeting was declared to be "the matter of political persecution so rabid in the US today."

There was a good turnout at Dreiser's apartment on April 16. Malcolm Cowley, literary editor of *The New Republic,* thought only a writer of Dreiser's stature could have drawn such a crowd—editors, writers, reporters—"almost everyone in the literary world." Standing behind a table, white-maned, tall, and massive, Dreiser rapped for attention, mumbled something unintelligible and then, folding and unfolding his handkerchief, read a prepared statement. He described the absymal state the country was in. Millions were unemployed; no one knew how many, for the government published no figures. Hoover and his cabinet had no idea of how bad things were. People were out of work, starving, hiding in holes. Striking miners in western Pennsylvania and Harlan County, Kentucky, were being shot by deputies and gun thugs hired by the mineowners. After this sorrowing litany, he looked up and said quietly, "The time is ripe for American intellectuals to render some service to the American worker." He proposed to his guests that they all join the NCDPP, which opposed politically motivated persecutions or deportations of union organizers, lynchings, and violence against workers. Mumbling a few more phrases, he then opened the floor for discussion.

For a while no one said anything. As Louis Adamic wrote, "Dreiser's own great honesty and bewilderment had engulfed everybody." Eventually, the old muckraker Lincoln Steffens rose to speak, recounting examples of how workers were crushed in labor struggles and how the press suppressed the truth. When the meeting ended, most of those who had come had no idea of what they were expected to do, but they wanted to do something. The answer arrived later, when they were contacted by Pass and enrolled in the NCDPP. An impressive steering committee was recruited for the letterhead, including

Burton Rascoe, Edmund Wilson, John Dos Passos, William Rose Benét, Franz Boas, Clifton Fadiman, Granville Hicks, and Elmer Rice. Dreiser was made honorary chairman and Steffens treasurer, but Pass was "the real, practical head of the committee," according to Evelyn Light, and served as liaison with the Party.

The committee's first project was raising money for the defense of the Scottsboro Boys, nine black youths in Alabama who were accused of raping two white women in a freight car. The boys were probably not guilty. The NCDPP's role in the case consisted mainly of sending out fund-raising appeals and an open letter to the governor of Alabama. All contributions were channeled to International Labor Defense; the NCDPP was merely a conduit, a front if you will (which is not to deprecate the able defense the ILD conducted for its nine clients).

Dreiser kept a low profile, declining to address an NCDPP rally for the Scottsboro boys at New York's Town Hall later that month. Instead, he prepared or signed an eleven-hundred word statement that traced the history of racism in the South. The death penalty for rape was "definitely aimed at the Negro male," he noted, rather than the white equivalent, "who miscegenates without serious opposition. But mixing the blood of a white man with that of a Negro woman is certainly the same as mixing the blood of a black man with that of a white woman." He closed by urging a "general broadening and humanizing of the universal treatment and condition of the Negroes, especially in the South."

● ● ●

The Party was a demanding mistress; issuing open letters and inviting intellectuals to his apartment wasn't enough. It was as though Dreiser were being put through a series of courtly tests to prove his devotion. In June the Party decided he was needed in Pittsburgh. A brushfire of protests and strikes was racing through eastern Ohio and western Pennsylvania, touched off by the Communist-led National Miners Union, which was seeking to supplant the enfeebled United Mine Workers. When tensions were at their zenith, Pass and Foster urged Dreiser to go to Pittsburgh. He agreed, though he specified, despite Pass's urgings, that he would not go as a representative of the CP or the NMU.

Arriving in Pittsburgh on June 24, Dreiser told reporters that he was gathering material for a book. At his hotel he questioned twenty-five miners and wives about living conditions. The following day he visited a mine at Horning, where an NMU organizer named Philips had been arrested. Confronting constable Deal Snyder, he demanded to know on what charge Philips had been incarcerated and was told "disorderly conduct." "Watch out or I'll take you in too," the officer warned.

Unintimidated, Dreiser visited mines and talked to strikers. He interviewed Sheriff Robert V. Cain, who denied that his deputies had interfered with the strike in any way. When Dreiser asked him about the case of a deputy shooting a miner that had been reported in the press, Cain replied that the reporters had lied. Later Dreiser witnessed state policemen driving pickets off the highway, even though they had a legal right to march there.

The next day he released a statement to the United Press describing the miners' tribulations:

> . . . from each person I interviewed I extracted a corroborated story of pay that insures a living only a little above the starvation line. . . . I learned the rent paid for company houses . . . ranges from seven to twelve dollars a month. . . . The houses were unbelievably bad, colorless, unrepaired, and sometimes enclosed and forbidden to strangers. The villages were slums.
>
> The workers were so poor they were unable to obtain decent clothing and decent food or enjoy entertainment of any kind, not even so much as a moving picture show, a radio or a phonograph.

Moved by what he heard, Dreiser abandoned his stance of impartiality by coming out in favor of the NMU as the miner's only hope. The statement blasted the AFL for collaborating with corporations and utilities and the United Mine Workers for abandoning its members.

•   •   •

Embroiling himself in the political struggle provided an escape from the personal problems that were dogging him, particularly those involving women, what Helen described as "The latest phase of what Dreiser once frankly wrote about as *This Madness*. . . ." It had, she said, "brought about a new pattern of behavior that I found difficult to accept." As was her habit when the pressure became too much, she ran away, this time to Iroki. In effect, they agreed that she would live there and Dreiser would remain in the city, visiting her on weekends as he chose. Her mother and sister would join her from Portland, and Mame and Rome were now living in one of the guest cabins.

The swank studio on West Fifty-seventh Street would soon be no more. They had decided not to renew the lease, which ran out in the fall. In addition to their need to live apart, economizing was a consideration; expenses of remodeling Iroki were mounting. Not that he was hard up; that year he had a gross income of at least $40,000. But for his struggling publishers, *Dawn*, which appeared in May, was another disappointment; the book would sell some six thousand copies.

With its intimate family revelations, the book had infuriated his sisters, particularly Mame. The next time Dreiser came to Iroki, Mame began berating him as soon as she spied him from the window. When a Terre Haute historian later asked her some questions about family history, she sniffed, "How *Dawn* could have been written is beyond human conception."

Reviewers marveled at the candor of the autobiography, and only a small minority were put off by its sexual revelations. The New York *Evening Post* critic called *Dawn* "one of the most ferociously frank and sensitively candid biographies I have ever read."

• • •

In August he wrote Louise Campbell, "I've had a hell of a summer. Hot. Work. Mental worries. Law suits. Just a day to day drive. Add to that moving." What with the Paramount suit, a suit against Liveright over stock-company rights to *An American Tragedy,* as well as his political activities, his writing, and a hectic love life, Dreiser was pushing himself to the edge.

When he came out to Mount Kisco for weekends, Dreiser seemed restless and tense, as though under a great strain, Helen thought. He took only fitful pleasure in the newly completed house, which she had filled with furniture from their apartment.

He may have been thinking about the cost of the place. The house and outbuildings represented four years of expensive labor. The main structure was a squat two-story stone and wood structure, with a steeply slanted roof covered with irregularly arranged log shingles, the bark left on, in imitation of a farmhouse he had seen in Norway. Louise Campbell thought it "looked as if a demented child had playfully tossed rough-hewn logs" on the roof.

Dreiser's Folly became a *cause célèbre* in Mount Kisco. Neighbors would drive by just to gape at the totem pole on the front lawn, near the four squat stone mushrooms from Russia. That summer he put up a large tent, decorated with colorful Indian designs. On hot nights, wearing a monk's habit and carrying an old-fashioned lantern, he would sleep in it. He thought of turning Iroki into a kind of monastic retreat for writers, and he inquired of the Catholic diocese in New Mexico if he could purchase wood beams from abandoned monasteries there.

To Helen the place was "her child" — literally a substitute for the infant she and Dreiser never had. To Dreiser it was a substitute for the novel he couldn't write; but it was also a nightmare of bills and quarrels. That August he turned sixty and was in a somewhat dyspeptic frame of mind when a reporter cornered him for the obligatory birthday wisdom. The talk turned to his wealth, and Dreiser insisted it had not made him happy. "When you get money you get encumbrances. . . . You find things to worry about that never entered your mind before."

76 / "Which Side Are You On?"

> The minin' town I live in
> is a sad and a lonely place
> For pity and starvation
> is pictured on every face.
> —"Aunt Molly Jackson's Ragged Hungry Blues"

In its September issue *The New Masses* published a special birthday salute to Dreiser. The editors said he had moved from critic and observer of America to a higher stage of social activism. The International Association of Revolutionary Authors cabled: "We are very glad to be able to call you comrade." In its editorial, "The Titan," *New Masses* proclaimed that although Dreiser was not a Marxist, he had the courage "to take sides openly with the world revolutionary movement of the working class."

Izvestia joined the happy-birthday chorus. The newspaper traced Dreiser's conversion to communism to his trip to Russia. To be sure, his book *Dreiser Looks at Russia* contained many "mistakes," but the trip changed Dreiser's thinking, and he began "attacking capitalism and America's pseudo-democracy." And so he had joined Romain Rolland and George Bernard Shaw on the literary barricades. Apparently, *Izvestia* was too anxious to proclaim its latest convert to engage in haggling about the depth of his ideological commitment. There was a fear in Soviet political-literary circles that the bourgeois press would ignore Dreiser's baptism, so Moscow made sure it was broadcast to the world.

• • •

In New York the object of these tributes busied himself with moving out of his luxurious studio on Fifty-seventh Street. He found new quarters in the Ansonia Hotel, a sixteen-story rococo edifice on upper Broadway that attracted a colorful clientele of musicians, playwrights, editors, prizefighters, baseball players, and showfolk. Dreiser's two-room suite had three French windows opening on a balcony with a spectacular view of the city and the Hudson River, and cost him $110 a month; he took a room on another floor as an office for Evelyn Light. The suite was sparsely furnished—the inevitable rocking chair, the rosewood-piano desk, some paintings, and a few other nondescript pieces—and he lived simply, eating his meals at the hotel restaurant or a nearby Horn & Hardart Automat.

With the help of Kay Sayre, Light, and various researchers, he was making good progress on a new nonfiction book about the economic crisis. Dreiser had Party leaders Earl Browder and William Z. Foster read an early draft of the book and asked for their advice on certain economic matters that were vexing him. The Party's researchers probably supplied considerable data for the book. Using this and other material he had collected, Kay Sayre worked up a first draft, which Dreiser later revised and expanded.

In October the Party summoned Dreiser for his most important mission yet: a trip to Harlan County, better known in the press as "Bloody Harlan." A brushfire war was raging there between the operators and the miners, most of whom were backwoods people who had been lured by the high wages during World War I. The demand for coal fell steadily throughout the 1920s and plummeted in the Depression, causing drastic retrenchments. Thousands of laid-off miners were stuck in squalid mining camps that dotted the rugged hills. They had grown too used to wage work and town life to go home (assuming they could find jobs) and had long since lost the plots of land they once farmed. Mining had destroyed a way of life, as well as scarred the hills.

Most men worked in virtual peonage, and their families lived at the subsistence level. So the companies' latest pay cut pushed the miners into open rebellion. As one said, "We starve while we work; we might as well strike while we starve." They turned to the National Miners Union for aid, and the operators responded by blacklisting those who attended union rallies and evicting them from their houses. As organizing efforts continued, Sheriff John Henry Blair's deputies, led by imported thugs such as Jim Daniels (who boasted he had killed four men) and Marion ("Two Gun") Allen, launched a reign of terror.

A news blackout had descended on the county. Two reporters were shot, one while fleeing after he had been taken to the county line by Allen and other gun thugs and told he had five minutes to live. Two writers from *Scribner's* magazine were searched and intimidated; only the Knoxville, Tennessee, *News-Sentinel* provided objective coverage. Reporters from the Associated Press, which took care not to offend the powers that be, were tolerated, but much of the press service's information originated with its stringer, Herndon Evans, editor of the Pineville *Sun* in Bell County, who was in the owners' pocket.

•　　•　　•

That, more or less, was the gist of the ILD report that Dreiser read. The ILD wanted the NCDPP to conduct an investigation that would publicize the wholesale trampling on civil rights in Harlan. Dreiser was dubious, however, contending that a lay committee would face brutality or else no one would talk to it. He proposed instead forming a blue-ribbon panel of distinguished citizens. That idea was accepted, and Dreiser sent telegrams to a list that included Senators Robert La Follette and George Norris, newspaper publisher Roy Howard, William Allen White, and journalists, ministers, and educators from the region. (He had wanted to invite Arthur Garfield Hays, but Browder advised against this; Hays had helped the NAACP in the Scottsboro boys case and was considered a class enemy by the ILD.) All the invitees tendered their regrets, save for Bruce Crawford, the publisher of a weekly in Norton, Virginia, who had written stories critical of the owners and officials. His comments had aroused such anger that he was shot in the leg by a sniper while crossing a bridge near Pineville.

Abandoning that plan, Dreiser was forced to call for volunteers from the NCDPP membership. Lester Cohen and Samuel Ornitz, both novelists who had published with Liveright, immediately offered their services and met with Dreiser at the Ansonia. With a toothy smile, he told them he had hoped to have a committee of "representative Americans" but, having failed, "we are now reduced to writers."

Dreiser sent out some twenty invitations in all, but only seven accepted on such short notice: John Dos Passos; Charles Rumford Walker and his wife, Adelaide; Melvin P. Levy; and Crawford, Cohen, and Ornitz.

Aware of the danger he and his committee faced, Dreiser dispatched telegrams to Governor Sampson and Sheriff Blair demanding full protection and holding them "personally responsible for the lives" of the group. He said the committee's findings would be turned over to Senator Norris, a farm-belt liberal who planned to hold hearings on the Harlan war. The governor responded that he would send a detachment of state militia to Harlan; he also appointed a committee of his own to look into the charges that miners were going hungry. Sheriff Blair apparently did not deign to answer. County Judge David Crockett Jones inveighed against the "snake doctors from New York."

Having turned a protective spotlight on themselves before they left, the members of Dreiser's committee departed on November 4 for Pineville. The others were surprised when a young and attractive woman boarded the train in Cincinnati and sat with their chairman for the remainder of the journey. Dos Passos thought her most elegant in her manners, and "her neatly tailored gray suit gave off that special Chicago chic I so appreciated." He thought it odd of Dreiser to bring a lady friend along, but later wrote it off as a flouting of convention, a "fetish" of Dreiser's generation. Esther McCoy, who knew Dreiser better, said he was just "doing what came naturally." Dreiser made no introductions, but his companion was later identified as Marie Pergain, probably a pseudonym.

In Pineville the committee checked in at the Continental Hotel, where Dreiser was interviewed by reporters from the wire services and the Louisville *Courier Journal* and chatted with the mayor, who promised to assist the committee without taking sides.

The next day, November 6, a fine fall morning, the committee traveled to the town of Harlan, commandeered a public room at the Lewallen Hotel, set up a long table on a platform, and began what resembled a congressional hearing. This staging was an on-the-spot improvisation, but it was effective. Word of the inquiry had got out, and a stream of gaunt men and women in clean, patched-up clothes arrived to vent their grievances, ignored by townspeople, who were more interested in the high school football game with Pineville. They had "faces out of American history," Dos Passos thought, their speech "the lilt of Elizabethan lyrics." Dreiser, wearing a blue suit and a bow tie, with his shock of white hair and probing blue-gray eyes, looked like a judge or a senator. Dos Passos thought "there was a sort of massive humaneness about him, a self-dedicated disregard of consequences, a sly sort of dignity that earned him the respect of friend and foe alike." Dreiser led the questioning of each witness, briskly pinning down the facts like an old newspaperman.

The burden of the testimony confirmed what they had already heard: miners blacklisted for joining the NMU, homes searched without warrants, men arrested for possessing copies of the *Daily Worker,* soup kitchens blown up by deputies, unionists jailed without formal charges and set free if they promised to leave the county. As a miner's wife put it: "The gun thugs are the law in this county now and not the judge and juries."

What made the national press, however, was an exchange between Dreiser and Herndon Evans. After undergoing some rather hostile questioning by the chairman on his income and a lecture on the need for "equity" in America, the Pineville editor asked if he might put some questions to his inquisitor. Certainly, said Dreiser. How much had he received in royalties from *An American Tragedy,* Evans wanted to know. "Two hundred thousand dollars approximately. Probably more," was the response. And how much did he make in a year? Why, he earned around $35,000 last year, Dreiser estimated. Did he contribute anything to charity? No, he did not. That is all, said Evans. Dreiser begged leave to expand his answer, saying he supported several relatives, paid four secretaries to gather data on economic conditions, and kept up the property he owned. Triumphantly, Evans pointed out that he gave more to charity than Dreiser did. What kind of equity was that? Dreiser launched into a garbled summary of his writing career, pointing out that for many years he had made probably $150 a month at most, but the damage was done.

The wire service reports on the Harlan hearing focused on that single exchange, and the thrust of their stories was "Country Editor Turns Tables on Famous Novelist." Lost were Dreiser's long-held views that charity was inadequate to meet the problems of mass unemployment and that the government should assume the welfare responsibilities. Lester Cohen noticed that the miners in the audience listened to his admissions "with a sort of reverence and awe." Not because he had made all that money, but because they shared his attitude toward handouts. A mountaineer said, "I don't keer for charity myself. I only want what's coming to me." The audience also knew editor Evans as head of the local Red Cross, which denied aid to those who supported the union.

On the following Sunday, the committee split up. Dreiser's group went to Wallins Creek, where the novelist ate beans and bulldog gravy in an NMU soup kitchen and talked with miners and children at the school. They visited a dying man in a shack with rotting floorboards and a flimsy wall that collapsed when Dos Passos pushed against it to steady himself. That night, at a "free speech speakin' " at the Glendon Baptist church, they heard Mistress "Sudy" Gates praise the NMU for bringing the womenfolk into the fight. Aunt Molly Jackson sang her "Hungry Miners' Wife's Blues," and Jim Garland said the operators called the miners Red because their low wages had made them so thin and poor "that if you stood one of them up against the sun you'd see red right through him." George Maurer of the ILD told the audience that one day in America they would have courts like those in Russia, "where the workers are the judges . . . and where workers decide who is guilty and who is not guilty."

Watching Dreiser as he listened to the speeches, Cohen was struck by his deep attentiveness. He seemed somehow kindly and giving—qualities Cohen knew well enough were not usual with him; he had been profoundly moved.

•   •   •

On Monday, November 9, carrying a bulky transcript of the hearings, Dreiser boarded a train for New York. Marie Pergain was still with him; she had attended the hearings, saying nothing, and the other committee members still did not know what her role was. Before the day was out, however, they would have an answer of sorts.

The previous Friday night, two moral vigilantes, perhaps tipped off by clerks at the Continental Hotel in Pineville, learned that Pergain had entered Dreiser's room at a late hour. The "highly reputable citizens," as Judge Jones later described them, tiptoed to the room and placed some toothpicks against the door in such a way that they would fall if it was opened. The next morning the toothpicks were intact, proof that Dreiser had spent the night with a woman who was not his wife. On Monday, when the grand jury met, Judge Jones called on it to indict the culprits for adultery. And while they were at it, the veniremen should ponder an indictment of members of Dreiser's committee for criminal syndicalism. The purpose of the committee's visit, he maintained, was to "capitalize on the poor miners" and to "dupe them into joining some communistic organization."

The jury dutifully returned an indictment on the adultery charge, a misdemeanor carrying a maximum fifty-dollar fine and not an extraditable offense. Was the citizen-detectives' zeal prompted merely by small-town prurience, or were the authorities out to get something on Dreiser in order to run him out of the county? After all, he was too prominent for the usual night-rider treatment—or to shoot in the back, as some hotheads were talking about doing. Better to trump up some legal pretext for expelling him and tarnishing his inquiry.

Learning of the charge while on the train, Dreiser was inspired to claim that he could not possibly have committed adultery because he was "impotent." Typical of Dreiser's literary career, the AP refused to publish the statement until the eight-letter word had been censored. Its story reported merely that he was *incapable* of adultery.

• • •

Safely in New York, he renewed the offensive against Harlan and Bell county officialdom. On November 12 he held a press conference at the Ansonia, with Dos Passos at his side. Choking with anger, he said, "Something will have to be done about the state of things down there, and damned quickly, and put that in your papers if you dare." When the *Evening Post* interrupted him to ask what should be done, he snapped, "I'll tell you what they have to do, darling, they have to give them a living wage and damn quick." Dos Passos, who was terribly shy and hated speaking, exhibited miners' pay slips to illustrate how a man could end up earning nothing after the operators deducted rent, supplies purchased at the company store, and other charges.

Four days later the grand jury of the Bell County Circuit Court indicted the entire Dreiser committee. The bill charged that its members had banded together unlawfully "to commit criminal syndicalism and to promulgate a reign of terror" in the coalfields. The NCDPP's attorney asked New York Governor Franklin D. Roosevelt to meet with committee members before considering any extradition request the State of Kentucky might make.

In the end, the criminal syndicalism charges were quietly forgotten. Prosecuting attorney William E. Brock's talk of bringing Dreiser and friends back for trial was partly a publicity gesture intended to counter the negative image Pineville had acquired. On the publicity front, Dreiser, his committee, and, most important, the miners and their union were the clear winners. Dreiser's indiscretion in bringing a young woman along and taking her into his hotel room provoked some criticism, even on the left, but the press generally treated the adultery indictment as a joke or a red herring. Leftists tended toward the latter view—with the exception of Max Eastman, who was delighted by Dreiser's improbable claim of impotency: "It is both funny and sublime—an event in the cultural history of man."

The new journal of Henry Luceian capitalism, *Fortune,* confirmed Dreiser's achievement when it wrote: "For the past year (as everyone knows since Theodore Dreiser and his committee went down to investigate and tell the world) Harlan County has been the scene of a bloody and bitter struggle between the soft-coal operators and their miners." If the public had learned just that, it was something.

Predictably, neither Congress nor the Hoover administration did anything to help the miners. Senator Norris met with Dreiser and reviewed the testimony the NCDPP had taken. He promised to introduce a resolution calling for an investigation, but doubted that Congress had jurisdiction.

Faced by overwhelming force, the Communist party again admitted defeat. The miners, whose hopes the NMU had raised so high, were left to fight alone. In 1933 the United Mine Workers returned to the state in force, armed with the National Industrial Recovery Act, which endorsed unionism and barred yellow-dog contracts. John L. Lewis negotiated a comprehensive bargaining agreement in which, as a writer for *The New Yorker* put it, "the defeated mine-owners agreed to all the things that deputy sheriffs usually shoot people for demanding." Meanwhile the Comintern heaped ignominy on the beaten NMU, criticizing its tactics and the "dual union" strategy. Thus was the courage of many Party "agitators" tossed in the ash can of history.

● ● ●

The Harlan trip was the high point of Dreiser's romance with communism. Sometime before he went to Kentucky, probably in the early fall, he had applied for Party membership, but, he told Lester Cohen, "they wouldn't take me." And he explained to Alva Johnson of the New York *Herald Tribune,* "I have been told over and over that I am much too much of an individualist and that I do not subscribe to the exact formulas [of] the Communist program, and therefore I would never be admissable."

When Browder turned him down, he was "surprised and hurt." Browder explained to Dreiser that he was more valuable to the Communists outside the Party: "If he surrendered his right to be publicly wrong on very important issues he would no longer be Dreiser—but the Party could not afford to have a prominent member conspicuously wrong on anything in its then existing stage of development." This was a nice way of saying that the Party distrusted Dreiser. In Browder's estimation he was really an old-fashioned Populist. Then, too, he was more useful speaking out as an independent rather than as one under Party discipline, Browder may have thought. Not that Dreiser could ever be a dutiful soldier in the ranks, as Browder knew from personal experience; quite the opposite—he might use the Party to publicize his own ideas.

Dreiser would remain a Communist, but a highly unorthodox one. In the Marxist lodge he never moved beyond the degree of bourgeois liberal. He was motivated by a burning sense of injustice and unfairness and a deep sympathy for the poor. His radicalism had its origins in boyhood poverty and early ambitions mingled with youthful envy of those who had undeservedly made it to the top by dint of family wealth and connections.

But if Dreiser vented in pamphleteering and political action his sympathy for the lonely individual at the mercy of inscrutable forces, which had motivated his best work, from *Carrie* to the *Tragedy,* would there be any energizing anger and pity left for a novel? He had not published one in five years. It was one of the ironies of Dreiser's career that, in his most radical period, the next book on his agenda was *The Stoic,* the third act in the life of Frank Cowperwood, arch-Robber Baron and individualist *par excellence,* whose motto is "I satisfy myself."

77 / *The Stoic*

> As for my Communism, it is a very liberal thing. I am not an
> exact Marxian by any means. . . . My quarrel is not so much
> with doctrines as conditions. Just now, conditions are ex-
> tremely badly balanced, and I would like to see them more
> evenly levelled.
>
> —Dreiser to Evelyn Scott (1932)

As though to exorcise the old Cowperwood before taking up *The Stoic*, Dreiser
wrote an essay attacking individualism that appeared in several leftist publications and in the foreword to *Harlan Miners Speak*. Untrammeled individualism,
he said, leads to a state of nature in which every creature "is for itself, prowls
to sustain itself, and deals death to the weakest at every turn." But society "is
not and cannot be a jungle." Societies evolve like organisms; they progress by
creating "more and more rules to limit, yet not frustrate, the individual in his
relation with his fellows." The objective of organized society should be to make
it possible for "the individual to live with his fellow in reasonable equity, in
order that he may enjoy equity himself."

He saw no new Soviet Man on the horizon, only the same Old Adam. Communism, he told the Russian novelist Boris Pilnyak, endured because "Stalin
uses the same ruthless procedures as dictators in other countries to maintain
his power. With the difference that Stalin is really exceptionally gifted and a
splendid character." Stalin was the apex of the Soviet state, which represented
the congealed force of the masses, enforcing equity and curbing the excesses of
individualism, according to the Marxian Golden Rule: "From each according
to his ability; to each according to his needs."

He could not have envisioned the democratic use of government under
Roosevelt's New Deal to tame the free enterprise jungle—despite the unwittingly prophetic working title for his recently completed book, *A New Deal
for America*. But Stuart Chase's *A New Deal* had appeared earlier that year (it

probably was the inspiration for Franklin D. Roosevelt's use of the phrase when he accepted the Democratic nomination for president), so the title was changed to *Tragic America* to capitalize on *An American Tragedy*.

Browder had read the manuscript in October and made some suggestions. But he wrote Dreiser, "It is entirely understood by us that you are taking only those opinions which can express your own profound convictions, and that our contribution is merely in the nature of assistance to help get the sharpest formulation of them."

●   ●   ●

From a literary standpoint, *Tragic America* is indisputably Dreiser's worst-written book. It is an eruption of rage; a venting of the molten core of felt injustice in *An American Tragedy*; a vision of America, just as the *Tragedy* is a vision of America. His "characters" are trusts and monopolies and plutocrats, which as Edmund Wilson notes, he presents "as blind and uncouth organisms with a kind of life of their own which expand and contract, galvanize and kill, and fight each other on international arenas."

As economic analysis or a statement of policy, as reportage or history, *Tragic America* is not worth much; but as a jeremiad, it was appropriate to the times and expounded a coherent vision of a real economic tragedy. It ends with Dreiser imagining a New Communist Utopia—an egalitarian society patterned after Russian communism (and Edward Bellamy's nineteenth-century utopian novel *Looking Backward*, a book Dreiser was advising his literary assistants to read) but tailored to the American character. His central message is *"for the masses to build themselves new institutions."* This would entail scrapping the present Constitution and adopting one that would "guarantee official domination by the masses, rather than private interests. . . . "

●   ●   ●

Although *Tragic America* was a "communistic" book, Dreiser had been edging away from the Party even before it was published. In the spring he had discussed with friends the formation of an American League for Equity. As he explained to Charles Yost, a small-town newspaper editor from Ohio, it was a matter of semantics: "Communism as technically stated by the Russians will not be accepted [by Americans]. Communism as practiced by the Russians, or at least most of it, can certainly be made palatable to the average American if it is properly explained to him and the title Communism is removed." He proposed that he and Yost, Bruce Crawford, Morris Ernst, and others get together to discuss his proposed league. He would take the leadership if enough followers could be attracted. The following year, when a reader suggested he organize

Dreiser study clubs, along the lines of the John Reed Clubs, using *Tragic America* as their basic text, he was flattered enough to ask Esther McCoy, now living in Los Angeles, if she would be interested in starting such a club.

As a manifesto, however, *Tragic America* was a bust. It sold only 4600 copies the first year, but the author received scores of letters from strangers, troubled citizens looking for answers. Some reported incidents of censorship (one correspondent said that his Carnegie library had refused to put the book on its shelves because of its ideas; Los Angeles bookstores were telling people they couldn't obtain any more copies), and Dreiser began to suspect that the Catholic Church had blacklisted the book.

While in California for a "free Tom Mooney" rally, Dreiser made a quick change from radical advocate to capitalist writer, selling *Jennie Gerhardt* to B.P. Schulberg at Paramount. The terms were $25,000 to Dreiser for the rights plus 7 percent of Schulberg's one-third share of the profits as producer. Conspicuously absent from the contract was a clause giving Dreiser any say on the script. But Dreiser received oral assurances from director Marion Gering that the picture would be true to his book.

•   •   •

He had taken up *The Stoic* in earnest and acquired a new assistant to help him write it. Her name was Clara Clark; she was twenty-two, a dropout from Wheaton College and daughter of a distinguished Philadelphia Quaker family. Their collaboration started true to what was now a pattern: she wrote him an admiring letter after reading *An American Tragedy* and *Dawn*, and received an intimate reply: "Clara, Clara—Intense, aesthetic, poetic, your letter speaks to me . . . from Philadelphia, where, once, for a time I dwelt . . . would you come to see me here in New York, and we can talk?"

To Clara—bored, restless, unsure of what to do with her life, vaguely aspiring to be a novelist (she had two unpublished manuscripts in her drawer)—his summons seemed "an open door, the only door on the horizon, a door leading to life." She decided to go to New York. He told her to stay at the Hotel Ansonia, and after she checked in he came to her room, and they talked for a while. At first he was suspicious. Was she after publicity? So many were. She explained that she had recognized herself in *Dawn*, a misfit like him. He softened and told her to be thankful she was that way, rather than a dull conformist, and took her to his favorite French restaurant for dinner. When they returned to her room, he followed her in, shutting the door behind him. She realized that he had no intention of leaving.

He gave her a chapter of *The Stoic* to edit as a kind of test. She passed, and he offered her the job—six months' work at $25 a week. They settled into a routine. She would go to his suite in the morning, and he would sit in his rocking chair, an outline and research notes on Yerkes' career before him, and dictate the story to her. She decided that "for a famous novelist he was extremely humble about this writing. . . . "

He was trying hard to finish the book. As he wrote Louise, "If I can get it done I can do a lot with it because it completes a trilogy." He planned to "do some trading when the book is done." Not only would he have a new novel on the market, but after it had run its course his publisher could sell the trilogy as a set.

He was worried about money because in July, in an economy move (and also because *The Stoic* was overdue), the Liveright company had cut off his monthly stipend, "which means ⅞ of my annual income," he told Campbell. "That means Horn & Hardart, I guess. But with time I'll get down to bed rock—say $50 a week maybe. The good old days. . . . You don't need a janitor, do you?" He was thinking of moving to his old love, Harper's—soon, he hoped.

His other sources of income had dwindled. The mass magazines weren't paying as well as in the 1920s, and they weren't interested in the polemics he was writing. His name sold two controversial articles to *Liberty* for $1000 apiece, however. One, "The Seventh Commandment," was an attack on the laws against adultery and white slavery, and the editors added a disclaimer saying they disagreed with some of Dreiser's facts. (An excerpt from the article was clipped by an unidentified informant and sent to the Bureau of Investigation, U.S. Department of Justice. It is the earliest item in the security file that the FBI kept on Dreiser until his death. The extract referred to the federal authorities' reluctance to prosecute Mann Act violations except in actual prostitution cases.)

As a gesture of atonement to Helen, he instructed Arthur Carter Hume to draw up a new will leaving her two-thirds of all his property, including control of the Authors Holding Company (a corporation he had formed for tax purposes), the copyrights to his books, Iroki, and the property they still owned in California. The will confirmed her status as the permanent woman in his life, however he might stray. He told Louise Campbell that in these chaotic times he admired Helen as much as anyone. "She keeps up a strong front & looks toward a simple form of existence under a new government. She likes flowers & dogs & the country & so I think she may come out OK. As for me!!?"

He must economize; no more sables for Helen. It was the simple life now. He let go some servants and reduced the payments to his sisters, who sent up a loud outcry. He decided to go to the Southwest for a month or so, where he could work undistracted and live more cheaply than in New York. He needed also to escape the myriad demands on him by this or that cause or organization. As he wrote Campbell, "I am sick of running a bureau & of being a clearing house for nothing. . . . Me for a simple hut in the west where I can write & save expenses. Everything seems to be going under."

And so in May 1932, Dreiser headed south, via ship to Galveston, taking Clara Clark along to do the driving and to help him work on *The Stoic*. From San Antonio, he wrote Helen that he was relieved to be out of New York. Now he wanted to get on with "writing or just living—and if it were not for my present women troubles I think it would be just living—certainly for a time anyhow—or vegetating." He wished he could talk to her without the usual "trouble waves of emotion & resentment . . . that lies between us. . . . I wish so much that we might be together in freedom & peace. But whether that can be I wonder. We are so individual and both of us were born free."

•   •   •

By June Dreiser had finished thirty-two chapters of *The Stoic*. In a letter to Esther McCoy from San Antonio he said he was working hard every day and believed that he could finish the book "in a month or so." But the fires of inspiration of 1912–1914, when he launched the trilogy, no longer burned as hot.

There was also the matter of his new political commitment. Dorothy Dudley had asked him about his "turn away from interest in the financier to interest in the laborer." In a delayed reply he told her that "conditions as they are now are certain to be addled and to make ridiculous literary achievements. . . . " Nevertheless, he would complete the last volume of the Cowperwood trilogy, "which, I am sure, most of my critics will pounce on as decidedly unsocial and even ridiculous as coming from a man who wants social equity. Nevertheless, I am writing it just that way."

This *défi* to the Marxist critics was not entirely candid. For he did infuse his new views into *The Stoic,* though not in any obvious or didactic way. His main method was to soften Cowperwood so that he becomes less blatantly antisocial. The financier's motto is still "I satisfy myself," but Dreiser added a rationalizing gloss to those words in the early 1930s: "Intelligently or unintelligently [Cowperwood tells his mistress, Berenice Fleming], I try to follow the line of self-interest, because, as I see it, there is no other guide. Maybe I am wrong, but I think most of us do that. It may be that there are other interests that come before those of the individual, but in favoring himself, he appears, as a rule, to favor others."

He began casting about for opinions and sent the manuscript to his old sounding board, Will Lengel, who liked it but wondered what sort of ending Dreiser had in mind. As the novel now stood, there was no foreshadowing of Cowperwood's ultimate fate: "Things come about almost too easily for him." It was a fair comment; the narrative lacked conflict and passion. Cowperwood is too bland; he sails smoothly through one squall after another, encountering few real storms save those of a domestic nature with his wife, Aileen. He meets some opposition to his plan for monopolizing the London transport system but easily overcomes it by wooing away its most powerful figures and upsetting the remaining rival. So it goes, punctuated by happy interludes with Berenice.

After completing a draft of chapter 54 (which corresponds to chapter 48 in the published book), Dreiser broke off. He would work on the novel sporadically in the coming months, but to no avail. Possibly he had lost interest in the story. The last phase of Yerkes' career lacked the raw, dramatic conflicts that Dreiser had exploited so effectively in *The Financier* and *The Titan,* the revelations of the corrupt relationship between business and government that had stirred the cynical reporter years before. And he hadn't the visceral familiarity with London that he had with Philadelphia and Chicago, where the previous volumes had been set. Then, too, his English publisher, Otto Kyllmann, had warned of libel suits; some of Yerkes' rivals were still living. Cowperwood's financial maneuverings in Britain were just as audacious as his earlier schemes, but they didn't engage Dreiser, for the writing is flat. That left Frank's half-hearted social ambitions as a possible spark for irony, but Dreiser was not a novelist of manners.

Also inhibiting him were his problematic relations with the Liveright company. The publishers were breathing down his neck, and he always reacted hostilely to pressure. Canceling his monthly advance may have goaded him to retaliate by holding back the novel. Moreover, he did not believe his publisher could sell the novel. He later told Claude Bowers that the book business was so poor he had decided to keep *The Stoic* out of the market until better times.

• • •

A more immediate pretext to postpone the book was a new and interesting project that had come up in August. That was a literary magazine; Clara Clark had heard him discussing it with George Jean Nathan in a speakeasy the previous spring. Now Nathan had found a publisher and had invited Dreiser, Eugene O'Neill, James Branch Cabell, and Sinclair Lewis to serve on the editorial board. Ernest Boyd would be managing editor.

The magazine, to be called *The American Spectator,* intrigued Dreiser, and after various conditions were met — the most important was that he would have a say in the editorial decisions — he signed on with an eagerness that suggests he was glad to get back into editorial harness. From Iroki and the Ansonia, and later from the *Spectator*'s offices, where Evelyn Light was given a desk, he loosed a swarm of letters to potential contributors.

In January 1933, however, signs of editorial disharmony began to appear at the *Spectator.* In a letter to Nathan, Dreiser complains that the others aren't pulling their weight. "I do not think it is fair that . . . I should do all the pushing." And for the first time a piece he commissioned had been vetoed by his confreres. He told the contributor, a University of Wisconsin professor, "I cannot get the other editors to agree to any mention of Christ in connection with the economic and social dilemma in which we now find ourselves." More ominous was his complaint to Boyd and Nathan about an article by Thomas Beer that they had accepted and that Dreiser thought lightweight. His objections were overruled, and the piece ran.

•　　•　　•

Meanwhile, he had become involved in a film project, a movie called *Revolt*. It was based on a historical event, the rebellion of impoverished tobacco farmers in 1907 against the Duke tobacco trust. Hy Kraft was collaborating with him, and Dreiser sent him a three-page treatment: "It could be enormous—a sensational thing. I have not suggested here even a tithe of the powerful scenes, the sociologically and economically illuminating conversation that can and will be introduced." The picture would illustrate "the enormous profits that go to the top and the insignificant grains of reward that sift down to the man on the bottom. I think that now such things as that will not only be enormously illuminating but grimly and truthfully irritating, as well as sad."

This was to be Dreiser's contribution to the genre of revolutionary art. He even planned to direct the work, although he knew nothing about the technical aspects of filmmaking. He envisioned a powerful, even epic story à la Eisenstein, seething with social conflict and rebellious workers and heroes and villains. No love interest, though, he says in the brief treatment: "High drama in this instance will not require it. Tensity [sic] of economic emotion will replace love." The strike would result in a temporary victory for the farmers, but the great octopus of the trust will reach out to new sources of supply all over the world. "In the end . . . for all his struggles and pains, the worker will be where he was in the beginning—not much better and not much worse." No Hollywood *or* Marxist happy ending for Dreiser.

In February Kraft lined up a New York distributor and theater owner named Emanual J. Rosenthal to back the film, along with some others, including General Motors executive Joseph Fischler, who was serving as Dreiser's business adviser. In late January the principals decided to inspect locations for the film on the site of the actual tobacco wars in North Carolina and Kentucky, where the Night Riders, a group of tobacco growers, had burned out planters who would not join them in their fight against the Duke tobacco trust. In Hopkinsville, Kentucky, a firefight had erupted between armed growers led by an idealistic doctor named David A. Amass and a local militia defending the Duke interests. Amass became the model for Dreiser's hero.

The party, comprising Rosenberg, Kraft, Rothman (the director), and Dreiser, set off on January 29 in Rothman's car. By February 2 they were deep into tobacco country, in Durham, North Carolina. They inspected warehouses where auctioneers chanted their incantations and where ragged farmers, accompanied by their hollow-eyed children, brought their small crops to be sold for amounts that could provide only a bare subsistence.

By early March they were back at Iroki, and Dreiser, Kraft, and Rothman brainstormed a script while Clara Clark took notes. As she recalled, "I was set up in a corner of the studio to take dictation, which went on for several days, with a colossal amount of discussion and argument. We didn't get very far because suddenly they all disappeared."

Dreiser forwarded a draft of his own to Kraft in May. At this point the collaborators began to veer apart. In May he received a letter from Kraft, who reported, "I am still in the throes of preparing and adapting 'Revolt.' I am quite sure that this will be done before the end of the week. You know that I have worked diligently so that our joint efforts in this connection will meet with much hoped for success." Dreiser immediately suspected that Kraft was attempting to steal his script and wired him: YOU ARE NOT 'PREPARING' OR 'ADAPTING' 'REVOLT' FOR ME. YOU SHOULD BE ARRANGING A TECHNICAL SCREEN SHOOTING SCRIPT OF MY ORIGINAL MANUSCRIPT OF SAME AND NO MORE.

Dreiser soon linked Kraft with Rosenthal in a plot to steal his film and turn it into Hollywood moneymaker, complete with love interest. All of his partners happened to be Jewish, including Kraft and Fischler, and quarrels with them stirred up Dreiser's prejudices. All but Fischler had some connections with the movie business, and Dreiser was feuding with B. P. Schulberg over whether he, Dreiser, approved of the movie adaption of *Jennie Gerhardt*—a pointless quarrel spurred by Dreiser's chronic suspicion of Hollywood. It all came to nothing, and when Dreiser saw the picture in June, he wired Schulberg and Gering that he wholeheartedly approved of it. Schulberg replied that the movie had "previewed beautifully" and that "audience interest held throughout and steady tears from Vesta's death to end." Gering had made a four-handkerchief picture, which touched a sentimental nerve in Dreiser.

But the fracas with Schulberg may have soured Dreiser's relations with the producers of *Revolt*. He accused them of misleading him about the financing of the picture. The denouement came after Dreiser began referring to the financial arrangements as "kikey." Kraft was personally offended, and in Dreiser's suite at the Ansonia they had a violent argument and nearly came to blows. (In his autobiography Kraft improbably compares Dreiser to the Nazi Hermann Goering.)

It was a sad breakup for both men. Dreiser had relished the company of Kraft, who had an irreverent New York wit and acted as a kind of court jester and confidant—a younger Mencken, perhaps. For five years they had been very close. Dreiser would come to Kraft's room and talk to him for hours. Kraft would entertain him and sometimes tease him. For the younger man, who shared Dreiser's leftist politics, the breakup meant the toppling of an idol, a novelist whose sympathy for the oppressed he deeply admired.

In the aftermath, Dreiser and Kraft copyrighted their respective scripts so that if one tried to make the movie, the other could sue. In Dreiser's more literary version, *Revolt* is a documentary about the tobacco industry, full of his brooding pessimism. In the end the doctor is fatally wounded in the skirmish following the torching of the tobacco warehouses; just before he dies, he learns that President Teddy Roosevelt has ordered the government to bring an antitrust suit against Duke's American Tobacco Company. The final scene is an unmistakeably Dreiserian touch: a shot of a neglected grave in a rural cemetery. The tombstone reads: "Amos Haines—A Country Doctor."

Dreiser continued to try to interest a producer and changed the title to *Tobacco,* perhaps to make the picture seem less militant. When Fischler showed the script to an independent film company, the president suggested that the two leads—the doctor and the son of Duke—be rivals for a woman. Dreiser commented: "Just as I feared, what is on his mind is a picture narrowed down to the usual love story with some tobacco smoking in the background."

•   •   •

May 1933 was not a merry month for Dreiser. The break with Kraft was followed closely by the bankruptcy of Horace Liveright Inc. The latter news could not have come as a surprise, since the company had been in an increasingly feeble state. An estimated $115,000 was out in unearned advances to authors, including some $17,000 to Dreiser, who had not produced since *Tragic America.*

Dreiser was probably not completely aware of the disaster facing him, for the contract he had renewed in January 1932 carried a provision that in case of bankruptcy the agreement was nullified. Eugene O'Neill had negotiated a similar provision and transferred from Liveright to Random House with no problems. But Liveright had owed him back royalties, while Dreiser was in arrears. If Dreiser had handed over a completed *Stoic,* there would have been no further trouble. But Dreiser had no intention of staying. He disliked Pell and had no confidence in him as a publisher. Now he wanted to use the unfinished novel as a bargaining counter in negotiations with his next publisher.

Dreiser's next step was to exercise his rights under the bankruptcy clause in his contract. According to this provision, he was entitled to purchase plates, sheets, and bound volumes on hand at the manufacturing cost. If the parties couldn't agree on the price, the dispute would go to arbitration. Pell demanded a large sum, and Dreiser offered a fraction of it. Pell eventually reduced his price and counterclaimed for some $14,577 in unearned advances (mainly the total of the monthly $1250 paid to Dreiser between April 1929 and July 1932) and $2400 for copies of the luxury edition of a poem, *Epitaph,* he claimed had been sold to Dreiser. After further to-and-froing between the lawyers, Dreiser's side refused to go to arbitration, and the various claims and counterclaims were tossed in the lap of the judge. He ruled that the value of the plates and books must be submitted to arbitration per the contract but that the question of unearned advances must be settled in court.

All this came as a shock to Dreiser, who still thought that the new company had no right to print or sell his backlist titles because of the bankruptcy clause in his contract. Furthermore, he told his lawyer, Arthur Carter Hume, that Pell had assured him in the past that his name had been worth $15,000 to the firm, and if the company went out of business, he would write off that sum against Dreiser's debts. Now, however, Pell was suing him as a common deadbeat. Dreiser's backlist books were like contraband; some had creditors' liens on them, and others were concealed in a warehouse somewhere. He feared, with some reason, that Pell was surreptitiously dumping them on the market. And the plates were in danger of being sold at a creditors' auction.

Dreiser wrote Hume that he was "dreadfully worried" about the entire business; further delay would do him "great harm," hampering him in finding another publisher and preventing the sale of his old books, notably *Jennie,* for which the movie might have created a demand.

In a sad footnote to these unpleasant proceedings, Horace Liveright died on September 4, alone in a shabby hotel room in New York City, of pneumonia. He was only forty-six. At the time of his death he was supposed to have been readying a play called *Hotel Alimony* for Broadway production and writing his autobiography, *The Turbulent Years,* but those projects were only the last of Horace's ballyhoo. Dreiser attended the funeral along with a handful of others. If all the authors and editors whom Liveright had given a starting push had shown up, it would have been the literary event of 1933, if not the decade—O'Neill, Hemingway, Faulkner, Anderson, Katherine Anne Porter, E. A. Robinson, and S. J. Perelman, among others.

> What I cannot understand is why there are so many groups
> and why they waste so much time critically belaboring each
> other and ridiculing each other for their interpretation of
> Marx, when the world situation and particularly the Amer-
> ican situation requires a united front against a very obvious
> problem.
>
> —Dreiser to Max Eastman (1933)

Another incident in May 1933 had delayed consequences for Dreiser. This was the notorious "Editorial Conference (with Wine)," which appeared in *The American Spectator*. In May, Nathan, Boyd, Dreiser, Cabell, and O'Neill met for a sometimes facetious discussion of Jews, with a stenographer taking it down. The backdrop, if not the occasion, was the rising incidence of attacks on Jews in Germany and Hitler's accession as chancellor.

For Dreiser, the symposium, published in the *The Spectator*'s September issue, had lasting reverberations. He uttered some anti-Semitic statements that took him almost the rest of his life to live down. For example, Jews were "altogether too successful in the professions, as well as in science, philosophy, education, trade, finance, religious theory, musicianmanship . . . painting, poetry, and the other arts." His "real quarrel with the Jew" was "that he is really too clever and too dynamic in his personal and racial attacks on all other types of persons and races." In certain professions "where shrewdness rather than creative labor is the issue" Jews unfairly excelled. They should be made to accept a handicap: "Thus 100,000 Jewish lawyers might be reduced to ten and the remainder made to do farming."

For weeks afterward, Dreiser was full of his great plan to solve the "Jewish problem." Eleanor Anderson, Sherwood's wife, made the following entry in her diary following a luncheon with Dreiser not long after the symposium appeared: "Teddy is really an evangelist raving about how you can get anything over. . . . He's now all hipped on a big exposure of Catholicism."

Dreiser's ideas were a bizarre amalgam of Zionism and anti-Semitism, the former picked up from Ludwig Lewisohn, an early American Zionist, and the latter a ragbag of stereotypes and subrational resentments, common to his times and indigenous to his provincial, Catholic boyhood. A precipitating cause was his rancorous business dealings with Liveright, Lasky, Rosenthal, and Pell, though none of them had treated him unfairly.

He sincerely believed that Jews should have a national homeland; unfortunately, he expressed this half-digested idea in sweeping language that echoed the rhetoric of the brutal anti-Semites in Europe. At other times he seemed to advocate assimilation as an alternative to emigration: Jews should drop their insistence on a Jewish identity, Jewish customs, and more outrageously, Jewish "sharp practices" and become "Americans," as all the other immigrant groups had done.

An interested reader of the "Editorial Conference" was Hutchins Hapgood, unwitting model for the character J.J. in "Esther Norn." Hapgood conducted a lengthly correspondence with Dreiser, he playing the righteous prosecutor. Hapgood was of old WASP stock, but he had written a book, *The Spirit of the Ghetto,* in the early 1900s that portrayed immigrant life sympathetically, and he had a more sophisticated, liberal attitude toward discrimination than Dreiser (though he, too, favored assimilation).

Dreiser was still convinced that a Jewish state was the best solution for anti-Semitism and that "the Zionist movement being what it is," Jews would choose that option. But if no homeland were available, then there should be "a program of race or nation blending here in America. . . ."

Although Dreiser had begun to retreat from his extreme proposals, he still regarded Jews as an indigestible remnant and blamed them for provoking anti-Semitism. He ignored the historical, medieval Christian roots of anti-Semitism. And he assumed Jews were a monolithic "race," which they weren't—certainly not in America.

• • •

Meanwhile, more trouble had befallen him in September. The three arbitrators had at last rendered their decision in his dispute with Pell, and it was an expensive one for the author. The panel set a price of $6500 for the plates—more than three times what Dreiser had offered and $2500 more than the receiver had paid for them at the bankruptcy auction.

At least he had by then found a new publisher. On September 28 he signed a contract with Simon & Schuster. He received an advance of $5000 for three books—*The Stoic,* a collection of short stories, and volume III of his autobiography—and an additional $2000 toward purchasing the plates of published books from Liveright. Simon & Schuster would acquire the stock of his old books from his former publisher; this outlay was also considered an advance against royalties, making a total of $10,000.

Messrs. Simon and Schuster had a prickly genius on their hands, and they were determined to humor him. The first test came when Dreiser submitted a manuscript. It was not, as they had hoped and expected, *The Stoic*, but a revised and expanded edition of *Moods*. M. Lincoln Schuster rose to the challenge. He read the manuscript over the weekend and sent an enthusiastic report to the author: "It is an outpouring of selfhood — in your own words, 'The demon of a secret poet.' What a sweep of phantasms, exaltations, dirges, and defiances." Dreiser replied that he was, at long last, happy to have " a publisher who speaks my own language."

•   •   •

After joining Simon & Schuster, Dreiser filed for a divorce from *The American Spectator* in January 1934, citing irreconcilable differences. He had the previous fall threatened to resign, and Nathan made placatory gestures. But the problems he complained of were not remedied. In his bill of particulars Dreiser charged that Boyd and Nathan rejected articles of merit without consulting him. The two had blackballed a piece he commissioned, calling it "junk," and so, "I now find certain definite mental processes of mine being commented on as junk." Also, although he did not say it, Dreiser favored publishing more political material in the magazine. Not "direct social arguments" or ideology, he explained to John Dos Passos, but "presentations of specific instances of extreme social injustice as it relates to the individual."

Nathan and his ally Boyd would not relinquish editorial control of the magazine, so there was little Dreiser could do but resign. Asked if the editors had bickered, he told the *World Telegram*, "Of course there were quarrels. . . . That's why it was so good. There were enough fights to wreck a building."

Not long after the rift with Nathan, Dreiser reconciled with his oldest living enemy — H. L. Mencken. The reunion came about when Dreiser corrected an erroneous statement made by Burton Rascoe in a history of the *Smart Set*. Breaking the nine-year silence, he wrote to Mencken, explaining what he had done. His old comrade thanked him and added, "I am seriously thinking of doing my literary and pathological reminiscences, probably in ten volumes folio. This is my solemn promise to depict you as a swell dresser, a tender father, and one of the heroes of the Argonne."

Dreiser's answer began with a one-word paragraph that seemed a sigh of relief: "Thanks." He proposed they meet on neutral ground in New York, "white flags in hand," and invited Mencken and his wife, the former Sara Haardt, a young writer whom he had married in 1930, to visit him at Iroki. "Helen and I still hold together," Dreiser said, speaking one couple to another. Mencken responded that he would be delighted to have a session with Dreiser, and he forwarded a "recent portrait so that you might recognize me"—a fat, balding old man with a walrus mustache.

When Dreiser's Harlan investigation made headlines, Mencken was unimpressed, telling a friend that the Communists were "making a dreadful fool of him, and taking him off his work. . . . I have no animosity to him, but he has become too tragic to be borne. Seeing him would be like visiting an old friend who has gone insane, or had both legs cut off."

Their first rendezvous took place on December 4 at the Ansonia. Mencken found Dreiser a bit grayer, a bit thinner, and possessed of two legs. Both men were at first uneasy, and Dreiser had taken care to have a third party present— Arnold Gingrich, editor of *Esquire*, who was awed by the two giants. But after downing two bottles of vodka, they began disputing as raucously as ever. They steered away from politics, though, and their fiercest argument was over which German restaurant they should dine at.

Hardly had they reconvened when Dreiser asked Mencken's advice on whether to accept an invitation from Henry Seidel Canby to join the National Institute of Arts and Letters. Mencken replied as if it were still 1915: "Canby's letter offers you a great honor, and if you were a man properly appreciative you'd burst into tears." He pointed out that membership would elevate Dreiser to the august company of fogies such as Struthers Bart, Owen Davis, Hermann Hagedorn, and Edna Ferber—not to mention the venerable Hamlin Garland, who had refused to sign the *"Genius"* petition. Dreiser turned Canby down.

In a phrase Dreiser often used, it had been a long time between drinks.

•   •   •

Dreiser's relations with the Communist party reached their nadir in 1935. Hapgood published his correspondence with Dreiser, who had given his permission, in *The Nation*. The Party, which had a large Jewish membership in New York City and which was also anti-Zionist, felt it had to come down on its most prominent literary icon. It dispatched a delegation to Iroki to pray with the sinner, but the meeting produced only a partial recantation. In a statement published in *The New Masses*, Dreiser insisted that he made a distinction "between the Jewish worker and the Jewish exploiter. Everybody knows that I am an anti-capitalist. . . . I have no hatred for the Jew and nothing to do with Hitler or fascism. . . . " He admitted for the first time that perhaps his contentious business dealings with Jews had influenced him, but he resented the Party delegation's dictating to him what to think and reacted with predictable truculence, especially after some members insultingly hinted that perhaps he was getting old—in other words, a little soft in the head. He told them, "I am an individual, I have a right to say what I please."

The Nation exchange (headed "Is Dreiser Anti-Semitic?") sullied his reputation—if not among the general public, then certainly among leftist intellectuals. Friends such as Ruth Kennell stood by him, but she told him she was constantly having to defend him and asked him to explain himself; he evaded her. Gradually, though, he backed off his extreme ideas. To a later correspondent, he pointed out that his books contained not a scintilla of anti-Semitism, citing *The Hand of the Potter*. He also cited the banning of his books in Germany as proof that he was *not* anti-Semitic. Dreiser believed that his blacklisting was the result of a mistaken idea that he was Jewish. Actually, the Nazis banned him because they considered him a Communist.

As the Hitler regime's outrages against German Jews became more brazen, Dreiser reconsidered his view that the mistreatment was the victims' fault. In 1934 he called for Jews to defy the world and "take whatever steps necessary to overcome" the persecution to which they had been subjected for centuries. If they did not act, they might face increasingly cruel measures. At last he had begun to recognize the abyss to which anti-Semitism led.

•   •   •

The sensational 1936–1938 Moscow trials of alleged traitors to the state puzzled Dreiser, as it did many Communist sympathizers. He had even met some of the accused: the charming Bukharin, the disenchanted Radek, and fellow novelist Pilnyak, who had earlier denounced one of his own books as heretical. In March 1937, participating in a symposium on the tribunal in *The Modern Monthly,* Dreiser confessed that he found the affair "very confusing." The parade of abject confessions, for example, he saw as "a real triumph of the spirit of self-abnegation. . . . " The psychology was puzzling, but, unless they had been tortured, these men seemed to be nobly sacrificing their lives to preserve the system. It was all a Dostoevsky novel, full of murder and revenge, sin and repentance. The Russians stood revealed as "more capable than any other nationality of proceeding by devious, subtle, fanatical methods, incomprehensible and unjustified for the western mind."

Stalin's wholesale purges began to hit home. In the summer of 1937, Calvin Bridges came to Iroki with a list of Soviet physicists whom Stalin had purged. Bridges had been sympathetic to the Russian experiment but denounced this rape of intellectual freedom. Shocked, Dreiser strongly agreed. And in 1938 Sergei Dinamov, his staunch Russian admirer, was arrested. Dreiser could not understand what had happened, since Dinamov was a loyal Communist, and attempted to learn his whereabouts, but to no avail. He wrote Ruth Kennell, "What has become of Sergei? Not a word in 7 months! . . . Are they going to try him? And he's so truly sweet and good." (It was not until 1943 that Kennell learned his fate: imprisoned for embezzlement and later killed in the war.)

Dreiser's doubts about the Soviet experiment emerged in a shaggy colloquy with John Dos Passos, which was published in Marguerite Tjader Harris's little magazine, *Direction*, in January 1938. He admits, "Well I was strong for Russia and for Stalin and the whole program, but in the last year, I have begun to think that maybe it won't be any better than anything else." When Dos Passos confessed that he didn't understand what was going on in Russia, Dreiser said damned if he did either. Dreiser thought that although the Communists' economic and social program had succeeded, severe ideological constraints remained in force. Those perhaps represented "a temporary condition . . . an attempt to achieve cohesion and unity." He predicted that eventually "Russia will be liberalized" as a result of the people demanding religious freedom and "less standardization in life."

What he wanted for America, he later said, was "What Russia has plus mental freedom." Yet he gave the Soviet state the benefit of the doubt. As he had said to Bukharin in Moscow, a " benevolent tyranny" was needed "until all men have brains sufficient to appreciate good." But Dreiser's communism was a dream of justice and equity rather than an ideological creed. And he savored the joke about the Communist speaker in Union Square who promises, "Comes the Revolution you'll all eat strawberries and cream." A heckler cries, "But I don't like strawberries and cream." The speaker replies, "Comes the Revolution you'll *have* to like strawberries and cream." Dreiser realized the jest was on him: he wanted strawberries and cream for all—but he didn't want anyone telling him to eat them.

79 / *The Formula Called Man*

> The mystery of life—its inexplicability, beauty, cruelty, tenderness, folly, etc., etc.—has occupied the greater part of my waking thoughts; and in reverence or rage or irony, as the moment or situation might dictate, I have pondered and even demanded of cosmic energy to know *Why*.
>
> —Dreiser, "What I Believe" (1929)

Disillusioned with politics, though not with the cause of equity, Dreiser was also stymied artistically. "I've written novels," he once said to Marguerite Tjader Harris, "now I want to do something else."

Messrs. Simon and Schuster would not have appreciated that news. They were expecting *The Stoic,* the big book they believed would revive Dreiser's reputation and sales of his backlist titles; it was due by the end of 1935. But all they got was *Moods,* the volume of poetry, regarding which Richard Simon said, frankly, it would help sales if the book were shorter; it now ran to 570 pages. Dreiser complained that Simon's suggestions left him "very dubious as to the attitude of the house in regard to the book and to me." This book was different from an earlier edition that Liveright published. Dreiser had added many new poems and revised others in line with his scientific speculations. The new *Moods* was not a volume of lyrical poetry; it was an attempt "to express an individual philosophy lyrically, that is, cadenced and declaimed. . . ."

Moods appeared in 1935, trailing the unwieldy subtitle *Philosophical and Emotional (Cadenced and Declaimed)*—Dreiser's best effort to come up with a new name. Neither author nor publisher was happy with the result. It was sparsely reviewed, the critics apparently assuming that it was not a new work. It yielded the author about $400 in royalties.

Simon and Schuster continued to press for a delivery date on *The Stoic.* On January 21, 1936, Dreiser wrote Simon that he could not give them the novel, and he added, "Will it make much difference if I give you a really important

494

book and follow it later with *The Stoic?*" Schuster replied that the firm was "deeply disappointed"; could they talk with him? Dreiser remained evasive, and the publishers did not track him down until the summer.

Another event had complicated relations between author and publisher. In June 1936 *The Nation* ran an article by the labor writer Ben Stolberg called "The Jew and the World." In a lengthy letter, agreeing with most of Stolberg's points, Dreiser's tone was sadder and wiser. He admitted that his attitude toward Jews was emotional, even prejudiced, resulting from unpleasant experiences with them in business matters. He confesses, "No doubt, today I look for what I dislike in Jews, and dislike what I would normally pass over in another. *Mea culpa!*" Such an attitude "in a time like this of social unrest, nationalism, jingoism, etc. . . . might in some groups lead to a pogrom. Yet this is decidedly what I do not want. Rather I have been always seeking a solution, for in a day of violence the obvious causes might not be the real ones. We in America might have as false justifications as there have been in Germany. We would have, of course, economic jealousy as a base. But still, there is always the much more powerful factor of the intangible fanaticism against the scapegoat through which we must always rationalize our unfulfilled desires and disappointments. *Mea culpa!*"

After the letter to *The Nation* was published, Dreiser worried about the effect on his publishers, and he wrote them that he had heard they were "surprised" about his views on the Jewish question. He assured them, "My personal friendship for you has nothing to do with the problems that Stolberg discusses." Simon and Schuster seemed not to have taken offense, but Dreiser got the idea they had, and this belief would have delayed consequences.

●　　●　　●

The "really important book" he offered them was the work of scientific philosophy that would obsess him for the next five years. In 1934 he had begun writing essays for it. As he explained to Sherwood Anderson: "What I am really doing is seeking to interpret this business of life to myself. My thought is, if I ever get it reasonably straight for myself I will feel more comfortable." He was at bottom seeking scientific confirmation of God, or a creator; but he was also seeking some consolation for the ultimate tragedy—death. The hope of a form of afterlife was the answer he wanted.

An insight into his inner turmoil was a series of rambling conversations he had with Dr. Abraham A. Brill two years before, intended for publication in the *Spectator* under the title "Chaos." At one of these sessions, which were held at the psychiatrist's apartment on West Seventieth Street, Dreiser asked Brill: "Does life have any objective which means anything? Or is there nothing to hope for, nothing to live for, nothing to be honorable for, nothing to be honest for?" Brill responded, "Blessed are those who expect nothing, for they shall not be disappointed." Dreiser said: "I ask about rewards because I'm trying to establish from you that the whole process is practically chaos. Why don't you say so?" Brill countered: "You have never detached yourself from your early Christian training—you expect rewards." Dreiser yearned for a just God in Heaven; otherwise all was meaningless.

Once he told a woman whom he accused of being unfaithful, "God, how is one to live without faith? Hell is that lack of faith that breeds lack of hope." Hell, Dostoevsky said, is the inability to love. Love presumes a capacity for trust; in a universe of chaos there can be no trust.

Somewhere in the shadows of Dreiser's early boyhood, in the poverty and secret sorrows, his ability to trust had been severely crippled. This impediment left an aching void of loneliness inside him. Only his mother had given him the unconditional love he needed, and she had abandoned him. "I am the loneliest man in the world," he often said. Kirah Markham had long ago noted his "utter sense of loneliness." Hy Kraft had seen it in the 1920s: "He was . . . suffering a loneliness that must have been beyond his own powers of description," Kraft told Marguerite Harris.

Dreiser imagined, on the one hand, "some great elemental spirit holding for order of sorts. . . . " and on the other, the Prince of Misrule—chaos—"vast schemes of chicane grinding the faces of the poor, and wars brutally involving the death of millions whose lives are precious to them because of the love of power on the part of someone or many. . . . Brute strength sits empurpled and laughs a throaty laugh." Life fed on life. There were blinding flashes of beauty in creation, moments of pleasure and tenderness, but how to reconcile them with the principle of blind cruelty that seemed the driving engine of a mechanistic cosmos?

• • •

In February 1935 Dreiser was laid low by bronchitis, accompanied by an unusually severe and bizarre attack of depression. This psychic storm undoubtedly had physical causes, but its resemblance to a spiritual crisis, according to the criteria of William James, has been noted by Robert Elias. Dreiser wrote of this experience to George Douglas, the San Francisco journalist he met while living in Hollywood, in whom he perceived a similar mystical bent. He had already discussed with Douglas their collaborating on the work of philosophy that he had titled "The Formula Called Man." He had sent the journalist two essays to critique. Douglas's response, Dreiser told him, was the only one that was "*completely* understanding."

At the heart of Dreiser's thinking was the idea of man as a tool or mechanism of the creator, an idea he had entertained since at least 1914 (and injected into *The "Genius"*), after his vision, under nitrous oxide, of the universe as "the same thing over and over." In the play *Laughing Gas,* about that vision, the central character discovers that human beings are "mere machines being used by others." In a recent essay, "You the Phantom," Dreiser said much the same thing. Man is "a mechanism for the mind and the intention of some exterior and larger mental process which has constructed [him] . . . for some purpose of its own."

He told Douglas that he was prepared to devote "a considerable period of time" to writing the book. He did not want to hurry his thinking, and he worked very slowly, doing "an enormous amount of revising. But that is the only way I can work—thinking out illustrations from my experience, jotting them down, enlarging upon them, finding the proper subject head under which they belong and eventually combining them in some form as essays on the different topics I have in mind." He also took illustrations from magazine articles and scientific journals and pasted extracts or clippings on sheets of paper, then covered the page with his preliminary thoughts. These were filed under the several headings and later expanded into a short essay or quoted in a longer one.

He assigned researchers to write précis of scientific and philosophical works. He questioned eminent scientists, seeking information that would confirm some preconceived notion. For example, he asked Simon Flexner of the Rockefeller Institute if a paper the latter had written did not establish that the line "between matter and energy is lost or not to be determined. This seems to unite the two worlds, and on the plane of immensely creative intelligence."

He wanted confirmation that energy and matter were one, or rather, "two phases of the same thing," as he already believed. The two are united "on the plane of creative intelligence"; in other words, all is Mind. He had long believed in a nonmaterial or spiritual dimension of life, as stated in the Hindu Upanishads and in the doctrines of Christian Science, and now he sought scientific "proof" that the mind-matter dualism was false.

•   •   •

In January 1935 Dreiser proposed that Douglas come east and help him with the book. A gentle, erudite man who could quote poetry by the stanza, Douglas was deeply unhappy turning out editorials for Hearst's Los Angeles *Examiner.* But he had a daughter in college and was reluctant to throw up his job. So Dreiser decided to go to California. Douglas insisted that he stay with him; his family would be away. Dreiser left at the end of April. The next five months were for both men one of the happiest times of their lives and a period of emotional and intellectual communion. During the day, while Douglas was at his job, Dreiser would read scientific books or write at a table littered with notes and the abstracts of articles and books he and his researchers had compiled. When inspiration flagged, he would wander into the garden and lounge by the pond, watching the goldfish and the birds.

In the evening the two of them would sit under the stars "saying over and over and over that life is what it is," as Dreiser later recalled, and then going inside and "opening Swinburne or Shakespeare or Shelley or [George] Sterling." A cook/housekeeper looked after them, and a Frenchwoman named Brenetta Yerg, whom Helen and Dreiser had befriended, did secretarial work. Later, Helen came out, living in a rented room so as not to distract the men. She did some typing, handled correspondence, and occasionally joined the two men for dinner. Dreiser visited Calvin Bridges at the California Institute of Technology to talk over problems. He also looked up Peter McCord's brother Donald, a retired Army officer.

With Douglas, Bridges, and others providing stimulus and support, Dreiser felt he was making good progress on the *Formula*. He and Helen enjoyed life in California so much that they extended their stay into October, living in a house they owned in the Montrose section of Glendale. When it came time for them to go back, Douglas was miserable. He had been starved for intellectual companionship, and Dreiser's visit had been a revivifying experience. Now it was over. The night before they parted, he said, "There is a taste of death in every parting."

In a letter to Douglas at the end of the year, Dreiser was sanguine, if vague, about his progress on the *Formula*. "I am slowly but surely lining up the answers to a series of propositions," he said. "The result should be presently visible." He had found a secretary to type and file his effusions, organize his research, and, of course, look after his correspondence. She was Harriet Bissell, a young woman recently graduated from Smith College. Dreiser's intuition told him that she was brilliant, a genius. When Harriet learned this much later, she was appalled. She thought herself unqualified for such a role, having had one course in philosophy and two in physics at Smith. She had assumed that her duties would be strictly secretarial and had taken a two-week cram course in Gregg shorthand before going to work.

For Dreiser and Harriet the day started at nine. She worked at her typewriter, set up on a card table, while he wrote at the larger table Wharton Esherick had made for him. She noticed that, after two or three hours of work, his concentration would flag and he would break off and talk to her. He was a wonderful storyteller, with a sense of humor. Sometimes they would trade puns. "Perhaps we spent too much time doing this when we were supposed to be working," she later recalled.

He seemed incapable of putting in eight or ten hours of sustained writing anymore. And he took less interest than formerly in the details of his business affairs — the twenty or so contracts with foreign publishers, the royalty statements, tax matters, and bills. He could hardly balance a checkbook, Harriet said. The upshot was that business matters devolved upon the slender shoulders of a twenty-one-year old woman just out of Smith.

That February his book received a serious setback when George Douglas died of a heart attack. Dreiser immediately wired Donald McCord in Pasadena: GEORGE'S DEATH HURTS BEYOND BELIEF. WILL YOU PERSONALLY SELECT FOUR DOZEN ROSES. SEND WITH CARD SAYING FROM DREISER TO GEORGE.

Dreiser had lost a friend he loved and a sympathetic ear to his speculations. It was a devastating blow at a time when he was beginning to comprehend the magnitude of the task he had set for himself. The notes and paragraphs continued to pile up, but what he had was to a finished philosophy as the pieces of a jigsaw puzzle are to the picture on the front of the box.

All cosmic laws, he had decided, are "manifestations of some gigantic mind." But what was the nature of that Mind? What was it thinking, feeling? And why? Was it intelligent? Loving? Cruel? And if all individuals were ultimately reducible to matter — energy, atoms, and electrons, as science showed they assuredly were — and were mere extensions of the greater being, as science assuredly did not show, wasn't life itself a nullity? It was as though he had at last stepped behind the screen and discovered the ultimate mechanism in its laboratory, stamping out endless life forms, and within the machine — Mind. Such a perception yielded neither faith nor serenity.

• • •

In the spring Helen and Dreiser had a cataclysmic row over another romance of his. In mid-May she decided to flee to Portland and stay with her mother and then go to Los Angeles. Dreiser accompanied her. He had a lecture engagement at Purdue University and also wanted to discuss the *Formula* with George Crile, author of *The Phenomena of Life,* a book that deeply influenced Dreiser, in Cleveland. Esther McCoy, who was moving to California after a futile job-hunting stint in New York, also hitched a ride. Dreiser and Helen were amicable on the trip, but she seemed nervous and tired. They dropped Dreiser off at West Lafayette, Indiana, and Helen and Esther continued westward. They stopped in a small city for the night, and Helen immediately went shopping, as though, Esther thought, she was feeling a sense of heady freedom and expressed it by buying shoes, although she could have had a far better selection in New York. After leaving Esther in her hometown in Kansas for a visit with her parents, Helen pushed on to Oregon. After a few weeks in Portland, she settled in Los Angeles.

Esther had dispatched Dreiser an anxious bulletin on Helen's health. He replied, "I care for her truly although often enough we don't get along. . . . So often I wish I wish I could make her wholly happy and when she leaves me I am sorrowful and grieve for her and myself. . . . I will always look after her to the best of my ability, as she knows. . . . I want her to get well. I want to pull myself together and then maybe we can make a go of it out there."

They had decided to put Iroki up for sale. The house was in Helen's name, but she used it as a hold over him, a way of financing their move to California, where, she thought, he would be healthier and happier—not to mention three thousand miles from his women friends in New York. He agreed to the move in principle but lingered on in the East.

That summer he rented the main house to a Manhattan doctor and moved into the cabins on the lower end of the property. Harriet did his secretarial work and sometimes prepared meals or kept him company when he went out to dinner.

Harris visited him, and one night while they were cooking supper in the cabin over a huge fire, Dreiser told her of seeing a large snake near the house—a puff adder. He shot it, only later to learn it wasn't dangerous. A few days later he saw another one and decided it must be the first snake's mate. He spoke to it, telling it he thought it was beautiful and was sorry that he had killed its mate.

"It stopped," he went on, "and I took a few steps toward it, telling it not to be afraid; that I was not going to harm it. Then slowly it turned and came toward me, passing right across the toe of my shoe—and disappeared into the grass on the other side." Was there more to Nature than the survival of the fittest?

•   •   •

In August Helen wrote from Los Angeles that she wanted to return. He told her to come home. "I feel unhappy about this whole business because if there were any chance or hope of my living with you affectionately and peacefully I'd like to do that." He said they must adopt a much simpler lifestyle. His first priority was to sell Iroki. Then he would cash in all his stocks and bonds, hide the money somewhere, "and tell Mrs. D. to go to —"

His resentment at those monthly $200 payments to Jug had been mounting for some time. What particularly annoyed him was her continuing use of his name. Now he received letters from total strangers saying they had met his delightful wife.

Helen returned from California in November. That winter was so severe that they moved into the Park Plaza Hotel, adjacent to the Museum of Natural History. The Liveright suit over his unearned royalties came to trial in February, and it was an expensive defeat. The judge ruled that the author had plainly failed to deliver *The Stoic* and thus was liable for 75 percent of the money advanced him by the publisher between 1929 and 1932. The total came to $12,789, plus $3000 for copies of *Epitaph* and other books that Dreiser had ordered.

He quarreled with the woman who had come between him and Helen, and she left New York. Helen thought she had won again and urged him to move to California. But Dreiser could not leave his work—or break with the woman, to whom he wrote letters full of sexual longing. In the spring of 1937 the affair resumed, and Helen again fled to Portland. She later said the winter in New York had been "a terrible one for me . . . terrible or useless." But she felt she had to be there, to make one more attempt to reclaim him. He treated her absence as a trial separation that might become permanent.

Iroki was rented, so he stayed at the Park Plaza for much of the summer, retreating into his work. In late August Calvin Bridges invited him to spend a month at the biological research laboratory at Cold Spring Harbor on Long Island. While there Dreiser had another epiphany. After an afternoon of peering at minuscule creatures under the microscope, he was walking along a path and noticed some small yellow flowers. He stooped down to study them and was struck by the beauty of the *design* of nature. There must be an aesthetic mind behind all creation, manifesting itself in the sublime correspondences among the microcosmos under the microscope, a flower, the star-seeded deeps of space.

That fall he moved to the Rhinelander apartments on Eleventh Street, where Mame had lived and he had written part of *An American Tragedy* in 1923. His quarters were comfortable, with French doors opening on a New Orleans–style wrought-iron balcony; a small bedroom; a large living room; and a kitchen with a stove, refrigerator, and counter, which he used mostly as a bar.

Dreiser had been told to cut down on his drinking after tests showed signs of diabetes. Knowing he wouldn't, his physician suggested he switch from bourbon to sweet vermouth. So he filled a medicine bottle with sweet vermouth and took occasional swigs from it during the day, with no visible effects. He was subject to morning depressions, when his energy level was low. In addition, he gulped vitamins and other pills and kept an array of medicine bottles on his desk.

Robert Elias, a graduate student in English at Columbia who had written his master's thesis on Dreiser because he thought him a forgotten pioneer, called on him. They gossiped about Ernest Hemingway's fight with Max Eastman in Maxwell Perkins' office (Dreiser took Eastman's side) and discussed philosophy, free will, and man as a mechanism. If it were true that people were bundles of electrons powered by a central dynamo-mind, Elias wondered, why ask, Why? Dreiser didn't really answer the question.

Elias's final impression of that first meeting was, "When you see him close up, hot, in his shirt, standing above you pouring whisky, you realize he's not young. In a sense, I felt sorry for him. There seemed to be something so lonely."

•   •   •

During the winter of 1937–1938, Dreiser began writing quickie articles on such topics as "Lessons I Learned from an Old Man" and "Is College Worthwhile? No!" Hearing that Dreiser had abandoned fiction for philosophy, Sherwood Anderson begged him to return to storytelling. He said that the "notion of the writer being also thinker, philosopher etc." was wrong. He and Dreiser should "always be trying to tell the simple story of lives." Science wasn't the answer. "There is this terrible loneliness of the people in America. . . . This goddam science and mechanical development you talk of doesn't help all this while the other part of your work . . . the telling of the story always does."

There was really nothing Anderson could say that would persuade Dreiser to return to storytelling. Dreiser confessed to Mencken that he read "very few novels—mostly science and current sociology & economics." He thought the novel was dying "not only because of multiplicity but because of the movies, the radio and what is sure to be, television." After reading Pietro di Donato's violent *Christ in Concrete* in 1939, he wrote, "Literature cannot grow much more realistic, of that I am sure. I have a feeling that the tide is likely to turn (give way out of sheer weariness and news of horrors) to something less dramatic. Maybe." He admired John Steinbeck, considering *The Grapes of Wrath* one of the best novels of the decade, and Clifford Odets, and he praised a book by William Saroyan. In a letter to Saroyan he teased the younger man about being a "first rate pessimist" who thought that "life is a lousy mess, sex being the only thing that offers any letup and even that isn't what it is cracked up to be."

He still regarded the movies as a potentially great art form, but his only dealings with Hollywood in the late thirties were entirely mercenary. Lengel, who had left the magazine business to work as a story editor for Columbia Pictures and then became an agent, spearheaded a 1937 campaign to sell *Sister Carrie*. Warner Brothers gave the project a definite maybe, but Jack Warner was worried about the moral acceptability of the book and asked Joseph Breen at the Hays Office for an advisory opinion. Breen replied that the story's "kept woman" theme violated the production code. "At no time throughout the story," he wrote, "does she pay the penalty for her sins, and at the end is shown to be a highly successful actress." It was the same thing, over and over. For the story to win approval, Breen said, there must be "no suggestion of illicit sex anywhere." Also, Hurstwood's suicide violated a specific prohibition in the Production Code. "With this in mind could you find some other way to dispose of Hurstwood?" Warner backed out because of the censorship difficulties and economic conditions.

● ● ●

In December 1937 Dreiser wrote Helen, "I am in the midst of so many financial ills that I scarcely see how I can go on." As a result of not writing any books, Dreiser had fallen in debt to two publishers for some $22,000. He paid Liveright, but the advances from Simon & Schuster were becoming a millstone around his neck, and he resented their pressuring him, however politely, for a new book.

He tried to interest a new publisher in advancing him all or part of the money he owed Simon & Schuster, in return for rights to his entire oeuvre, past and future. In January 1938 he offered such a package to Charles Scribner, telling him, "I have the new book under way and I do not plan to be hurried into finishing it, or to have any kind of publishing pressure put on me about it." Scribner declined, as did others. The Liveright suit had probably hurt him in their eyes; unaware of all the facts, they regarded him as an author who welshed on a contract and then countersued his publisher for $52,000 in unpaid advances.

80 / Oh Change!

> I went on down to Spain (Barcelona) to see if I couldn't be
> killed I guess.
>
> —Dreiser to Donald McCord (1938)

The spring of '38 passed quietly, save for the Great Fire at Iroki. The Mount
Kisco fire department saved the house, but there was considerable water damage
inside, and Dreiser asked Ralph Fabri to submit a bill for the decorating work
he had done, leaving the amount blank "to be filled in by me" for insurance
purposes.

He had rented the property for the summer, and so in June he moved to
Pratt's Island near Noroton, Connecticut, and set up housekeeping in a beach
cottage rented by Marguerite Harris, who was otherwise engaged with her magazine, *Direction*. On weekends guests arrived, and there were picnics on the
beach. Edgar Lee Masters came with his friend Alice Davis a couple of times,
planting himself in a porch rocker like a courthouse loafer.

In early July a telegram arrived from the League of American Writers, asking Dreiser to attend, all expenses paid, the International Convention for International Peace to be held in Paris, July 23–24. Dreiser agreed; it was his first
mission for a Party auxiliary since Harlan. But he was quite casual about it: "Last
Sunday wires from the League of American Writers and the American League
for Peace & Democracy began to arrive asking me to attend—all costs paid. . . .
All I had to do was to go and say I represented them and that I believe in peace.
That seemed easy, so, since I needed a lot of peace just then, I decided to do it."

Franklin Folsom, then executive secretary of the League of American Writers, recalled journeying to Pratt's Island to try to persuade a reluctant Dreiser
to attend. It took much cajoling, and Dreiser was apparently unwilling to become associated with the league because of its Party ties. He insisted that the
money for his expenses not come "from Russia" and said he didn't want it to
look as if he were "bought and paid for" by the Soviet Union. Folsom assured
him the writers group was paying his way.

Then, on the eve of his departure, Dreiser consternated his sponsors by refusing to join the league; he apparently wanted to go as an independent citizen, representing no group. Also, his sponsors expected him to speak out on the Spanish Civil War. He had sided with the Loyalists from the start, liking their anticlericalism, writing Ruth Kennell that he was working hard for the cause and "I think we'll pay for our indifference if Spain goes fascist." But that spring John Dos Passos, who had just returned from Spain much disillusioned because of the way the Soviet Union was acting, had visited Iroki. No doubt Dos told Dreiser about the purges and assassinations of anarchists and socialists being carried out by Soviet agents and sympathizers. So Dreiser was cautious and wanted no involvement with any group.

Aboard the elegant *Normandie,* he fretted because he had forgotten his dress suit, and lots of people were wearing black tie in the dining salon. Then he turned around and inveighed against the status-seeking chatter of the first-class passengers. The only person he liked was "a small, intense Jew driven out of Germany who is a natural thinker and of course shrewd."

His name was Samuel Groskopf, and he was a Parisian merchant. Groskopf loaned Dreiser an English-language abridgment of the Talmud. He wrote Harriet Bissell of his reaction:

> And now I see if it were fully condensed & expressed it would . . . make clear that Christ must be a myth since all that he said is quite clearly there and thousands of years before. No wonder they [Jews] could never be converted. Even [Christ's] "love one another" is put in a more practical & possible way. Their strange dietary laws are now clear to me. And much of their shrewdness seems to [be] ordered by this book. Thus & so must they do—or fail & be unworthy of their Lord! Well, I stand illuminated as to that at last!

This basic text gave him a new understanding of Judaism, at a time when his philosophical studies had made him more open to religion.

He was scheduled to speak at a session on "The Bombing of Open Cities." Despite the recent pulverizing of Guernica and Madrid by Italian and German planes, mention of the war was forbidden. Dreiser learned that his remarks, originally scheduled for the beginning of the session, had been put off until the end, following some boring committee reports. This maneuver made him more determined to be heard, and so when his time came he called to the delegates who were beginning to walk out. "Don't go! Don't go! I have something of importance to say!" He told them that public sentiment against war and the bombing of civilians was "very strong in America" and he called for an international conference "such as this one would like to be" to bring about a plan "to avoid the old cutthroat competition" among nations. It was his familiar call for equity extended to the international arena. Wars, he believed, were started by nations controlled by corporate and aristocratic interests seeking economic gain. Equitable societies (e.g., Russia), it followed, did not start wars. His address was enthusiastically received, and the Paris *Herald Tribune* gave it a prominent play.

Despite the minor triumph of his speech, he was feeling dreadfully lonely, slept poorly, and experienced "stupendous" morning depressions—"My blue devils," he wrote Bissell. "I am wholly too miserable to think of anything except dying or finding some soothing drug. All this business of living begins to pall on me. . . . Richard the III it was who screamed a horse! A horse! My kingdom for a horse. I would make it a drug. If I could only find one that would pull me through." He added that he expected soon to be in Spain.

He left toward the end of the month with an escort and car provided by the Spanish Republic's delegation in Paris. He later wrote: "I felt war immediately as we crossed the border. . . . A sense of impending catastrophe difficult to define at first."

In besieged Barcelona the effects of war were more visible. It was a "dangerous atmosphere," he wrote Harriet. "They are expecting a big push from Franco & more intense bombings every hour. Strange—sitting in a hotel room & being ready any moment to hear sirens all over the city & to have to grab your bag & make for an underground shelter."

He had come to Barcelona at the invitation of Republican Foreign Minister Alvarez del Vayo and Premier Juan Negrin, who had a mission for him: to persuade President Roosevelt to authorize the U.S. government to send humanitarian aid—food, medicines—to both sides. Dreiser agreed to try.

After a brief, restful visit with John Cowper Powys at his ancestral village of Corwen in Wales, Dreiser sailed home on the *Lucania*. Folsom met him aboard ship, and when Dreiser saw him he said, "Folsom, we've got to do something about getting milk for the Spanish children."

The journey had imbued him with a deep sympathy for the Spanish people. He wrote Bissell: "Their courage. They have so little to go on—their desire for their own type of Govt. . . . The pride. They won't beg! And their looks— how handsome the men & women even in poor clothes." His political batteries recharged, he gave interviews, wrote articles, and made speeches to raise relief funds. He wrote President Roosevelt to request a meeting at which he could relay the Loyalist leaders' message. On September 7 he spent the afternoon with FDR on his yacht on the Hudson. Roosevelt listened attentively but said the U.S. government must remain neutral. Since the Neutrality Law permitted private donations of food and medicine, he advised Dreiser to organize a committee for Spanish relief with a board of distinguished professional, business, and religious leaders.

Dreiser immediately set about this task, pleading with people of whom he disapproved, such as Father John A. Ryan, president of the Catholic University, and Nelson A. Rockefeller. He talked to Joseph Medill Patterson, the newspaper magnate (who, although he styled himself a socialist, was not enthusiastic), and Rufus Jones, chairman of the American Friends Service Committee, which had been engaged in relief operations in Spain for a year. Jones was the only one who was supportive, and Dreiser was impressed by the big, homely Quaker philosopher, with whom he had a two-hour talk at Haverford College. Shortly thereafter he formed the idea of using Jones as a model for Solon Barnes, the father in *The Bulwark*.

His efforts on behalf of the Spanish people were a failure. The dignitaries he approached declined to lend their names for fear they would be accused of endorsing either the Communist or Fascist side. Possibly they did not regard Dreiser, a well-known radical, as the man to organize a neutral committee. President Roosevelt later arranged for shipments of flour to Spain through the Red Cross.

• • •

That fall, Iroki being let to a doctor who was interested in buying it, Dreiser moved his cache of notes and books into a room at the George Washington Hotel in Manhattan and worked on the introduction to *The Living Thoughts of Thoreau*. This book was part of a series of selections from great writers published by Longmans, Green, which had offered him $500 for the job. While he was away, Harriet Bissell had plowed through fourteen volumes of Thoreau's journals at the rate of one a day in the summer heat, culling key passages. Dreiser had read *Walden* and other Thoreau works as a young man, and they had influenced one of his first published stories, "McEwen of the Shining Slave Makers," almost a half century ago.

Dreiser did not find his Walden at the George Washington Hotel. There were cocktail hours with old friends, including Richard Duffy, the sympathetic editor who published him in the dark days at the turn of the century. But there were also quarrels with a woman friend, whom we shall call the Dark Lady, not because she was evil or sinister—quite the contrary—but because their love had a dark-of-the-moon side, causing much torment for them both.

Although he had promised to join Helen in California, he now felt a stronger pull to the younger woman. He told Helen bluntly that he was bored; although she had "a certain untutored and uncontaminated emotional response to beauty which is very moving," she was not interested in the scientific problems that were engaging him. And so he had "gone abroad for intellectual and emotional reactions which I felt necessary for me at the time." He was "in the midst of so many financial ills that I scarcely see how I can go on." In another letter he evoked the past: "it was lovely—unforgettable. . . . But today—the way things are—I don't seem to care whether life keeps or not. So I don't cry much. I think generally I am too sad."

As for Helen, she wanted him in California, away from temptresses. She was lonely, and also practical. She told Fabri, "he should be using his personality in a way so as to be able to make a little money for himself so that he won't have to sit day and night writing articles. He is much too old for that slavery and I know that he would not have to do it" if he came to Hollywood. She was confident that she could make some movie sales of his books that would enable them to live comfortably. But she was in a kind of limbo: "I have hung on and hung on and stayed away because I thought it best. But soon I have to make a move. Can you tell me anything." She found consolation in a quote from Voltaire: "The friendship of a great man is a gift of the gods."

•   •   •

In November Dreiser announced to Mencken, "I am moving out to the Coast for an extended period." Mencken wondered, How long would he be gone? Would he be back before the end of winter? "I am not planning an early return, maybe no return," Dreiser replied. He had decided, at last, to make the move.

He explained to Mencken that in 1935 he had found he could work well in California. "George Douglas and I ran a great household together—a fascinating group assembled about three times a week." This time, he said, he might tie up with Bridges or McCord. As for Helen, he was vague. "Helen will be with me a part of the time anyhow. She spends a good deal of her time with her mother in Portland." The doctor had made a good offer for Iroki.

•   •   •

From Germany that November came news of the anti-Semitic atrocities of *Kristallnacht*. The following month Dreiser issued a statement to a symposium published by the League of American Writers. He reiterated that he did not believe in the "social torture" of any race or sect "for reasons of difference in appearance or custom." Prejudice, though, had ancient roots, and its victims were many:

> You do not eat as I do; pronounce my native tongue as I do; dress, walk, talk or respond as fast or in the same way to this or that, as I do. Hence you are accursed. You should not live in the same world—or at least the same land or city with me. Out! I cannot induce you and I cannot wait for you to change. . . . Just now it is the Jews in Germany; the Negroes in America, the democratic-minded loyalists in Spain, the backward in China, the swart fellaheen in Egypt, the Moor in Africa, the Czechs in Czechoslovakia, who are being seized upon and exploited, restrained, oppressed or murdered—each according to some theory as to their unfitness in the past of some other nation or group—as often as not—really more often than not—for economic purposes; the desire and hope of profit on the part of the exploiters.

Dreiser had conducted a long and damaging education in public, admitting his prejudices with a candor few would dare, save the native anti-Semites and Fascists (with whom he never had any truck). He had come a long way toward understanding that the "Jewish problem" lay within himself.

Just before Thanksgiving Anderson and Eleanor, Masters and Alice, and Harriet and Dreiser gathered for a farewell dinner at Lüchow's. Bissell recalled that Dreiser mentioned Helen's need for an operation and his desire to be with her as the primary reason for his departure.

He left New York in a blizzard, and joined Helen in Portland. In her diary for November 30 there appears this entry: "8 A.M. T.D." They had been separated for more than fifteen months. As for the future. . . .

Part Fourteen

• • •

EQUATION
INEVITABLE

81 / *Exiles*

All who come here come to lie down & take the count—die
& go to heaven (this being heaven).

—Dreiser to Masters (1939)

Dreiser returned to Helen dispirited and in shaky health. Helen believed he didn't eat well or rest when she was away; he may also have been feeling the effects of his stormy love affair. He wrote the Dark Lady, "Living with you is a kind of fever coupled with strain. It plays on my vitality." As for returning to Helen, it was a trial reunion—she was on trial and "I am the judge." They would "come to some working agreement that will give [Helen] plenty to do and leave me wholly free. . . ." But Dreiser was not sure where he stood with the Dark Lady. He had left her because of the conflicts between them but hoped they would "come to a clarifying and reforming sense of what is needed to make the relationship permanent."

Money was now a pressing problem. He had cashed in all his securities, and his hope was to sell *Carrie* or another novel to the movies before the nest egg ran out. Some of his California friends thought he was on his uppers. Part of the impression was conveyed by the place he and Helen took in Glendale in early December: a small "court" apartment.

Edgar Lee Masters was worse off. He wrote, in January 1939, "I am hanging by tired fingers to the edge of the cliff." Dreiser tried to help. He talked up a movie based on *Spoon River Anthology* and suggested to Longmans, Green that it sign up Masters to do an edition of *The Living Thoughts of Emerson.* That commission was extended and worked out well, for the scholarly Masters knew his Emerson.

Helen and Dreiser had some old friends in the area: Lillian Rosenthal, now married to Mark Goodman; Donald McCord; the artist Willy Pogany, whom Dreiser had known since he lived in the Village; Clare Kummer, Arthur Henry's widow, who went back to the *Delineator* days, as did Upton Sinclair and his wife, who lived in Pasadena. The actor Edward G. Robinson, one of the many Hollywood "progressives" at the time, invited them to dinner; John Howard Lawson, who had adapted *Sister Carrie* for the stage and was now a rising screenwriter and active in Communist party affairs, dropped by for literary and political talks. He later remembered the social world of Glendale as an intellectual atmosphere in which "wild ideas and concepts were always floating around."

Dreiser was living with a woman he didn't love and had nothing to say to, while the one he did (sometimes) love (but could not live with) was three thousand miles away. And then he received a letter from her informing him that she was getting married. It had come about suddenly, she later explained— "on the rebound," a chance meeting. She still felt a great affection for him, but she was adamant. She wanted no more triangles; it ran against her conscience and pride to come running after him, only to play second fiddle to Helen. She had recognized, like others before her, Helen's tenacious hold on him, which he described variously as pity, a sense of obligation, guilt, or memories. The bond between them was like a cable composed of all these strands, individually weak but together severable only by death.

Now he experienced the pain of unreturned love. "Lord, lord but this life is cruel," he wrote her. "Life is hateful to me. I seem often a fly entangled in a net by an invisible spider. Ills. Ills. Ills." The next day he sent her a telegram: "ALL THAT IS LEFT IS WORK. THE ONLY REFUGE." She held the high hand—the strength and freedom of youth.

On New Year's Day 1939 Helen wrote her resolutions in her diary:

> *Let no destructive thoughts in*
> *Hold to course*
> *Steadfast*

"He won't let anyone go really," she fretted to Fabri, who was acting as her eyes and ears in New York. In February he reported that the marriage had taken place. Helen was exultant.

•   •   •

Not only romantically but also professionally, Dreiser was caught between two stools. He should be working on *The Bulwark* but felt the pull of the *Formula*, which he regarded as practically finished, a matter of assembling his examples under the appropriate headings. That was wildly overoptimistic. He had a jumble of notes and typescript packed in cardboard boxes; some of his files were still stored at Iroki. Privately, Harriet Bissell had become convinced that he would never finish it. He was no philosopher, had no talent for metaphysics or logic; nor was he a scientist.

His inability to reach a final conclusion about the nature of God and the universe lay at the heart of his inability to write *The Bulwark*. All along, his skepticism had inhibited him from sympathizing with his central character. Now he had Rufus Jones as a model for his hero, Solon Barnes. To Harriet he had given Jones's autobiographical volumes a lukewarm review: "He strikes me as sincere, if nothing more." But that was not entirely candid: he had heavily annotated his copies. Beside a passage describing the influence on Jones of John Woolman's *Journal*, he wrote "Solon." The writings of the eighteenth-century antislavery Quaker mystic had also touched Dreiser. In January he ordered from a Friends bookstore in Philadelphia copies of George Fox's *Journals* and of the 1871 edition of Woolman's *Journal* that Jones had read.

He traveled to Whittier College to look up Quaker sources in the library, and while there he spoke with some professors. They were so charmed by the transparent sincerity of his interest in Quaker thought that they invited him to speak to the students. He told them, "Up until I was forty years of age I believed fully that the world belonged to the Devil." In a letter to the Dark Lady, written in December, while in a state of depression, he conjured up a chilling vision of the Supreme Being he now (sometimes) believed in:

> I look at all I see now—all life really—as the product of either a blasé or disordered super-genius that can find no comfortable, workable illusion into which to enter and rest. And death & despair for all save the chemically fresh and immature— those brief and so futile extensions of his own restless, irritable, irrational crav- ings for an escape that is, after all, no real escape—but only a savage, chattering, creaking and screeching process called life that will not come through to any real smoothness of functioning & so peace for the creative energy that produces it. It seems to me to have been seeking to make a protoplasmic bed—in or on which to lie and dream. And yet only to have achieved a hairy or wiry board on which is no rest but veritable phantasms of aches and stings . . . . I write all this because I am so truly sad—disappointed with myself & all else.

He knew that his vision originated in his own sense of despair over the way his life was going, and the dwindling of the life-renewing energy of youth. As he wrote Masters, "Edgar, all that is needed to beat this sustenance and pleasure problem in this world is *youth*—ignorant, energetic desirous youth. . . . Age is an old man on your back and much too much to carry."

• • •

But in July he wrote Harriet a letter in a decidedly different tone: "I hang over the markings & colorings and formation of a flower or an insect—or a worm or snail and at such times, and only so, seem to *see* and *know* something of the instincts, and intents as well as powers of the sublime creative force that permits and maintains us all. Then the only other question is *why?*" But, even if one could not answer that, in the sheer comtemplation of design one found "a kind of peace and rest. For—be life what it will—this aesthetic skill . . . seems so not only respectable but awesome. I *admire* until I border on affection— maybe love." Now he understood how Thoreau had "sensed and was comforted by the presence of not an *invisible* but a visible personality. One so wholly and so magnificently mental. And so wholly beyond all good or evil as man senses those things."

•   •   •

Rumors of the imminent sale of *Sister Carrie* rose and fell with the fickle Hollywood tides. In September Lengel began negotiating with RKO. The agent assured the studio that Dreiser had "agreed to permit changes" that would take care of Breen's objections. Later that fall Breen approved an outline, but, as Dreiser tried to explain to Masters, in Hollywood "even selling does not mean production because political and financial and religious whispers and interpretations stalk like ghosts all over the place." And, even more darkly, he confided to another friend, the writer Dayton Stoddart, "This is a selfish, self-concentrated, mean, loafing town. The business and political world is hard boiled & cruel. The movies are solidly Jewish. They've dug in, employ only Jews with American names and buy only what they cannot abstract and disguise. And the dollar sign is the guide—mentally & physically. That America should be led—the mass—by their direction is beyond all believing. In addition they are arrogant, insolent and contemptuous."

The poison of anti-Semitism had not been entirely cleansed from his system. He concealed it from all but Stoddart, who was once called "the American Céline." His animus contained a seed of paranoia; more, he may have fantasied Jewish revenge for his past anti-Semitic statements. A tired, lonely old man desperate for money, he was scapegoating those remote, powerful executives who held his survival in their hands and who seemed as arbitrary and capricious as the inimical Creator he sometimes believed in.

He now owed Jug $4000 to $5000 in support payments and wrote her lawyer, Leo Rossett, who was threatening to sue, that he was in a low period financially and in poor health. To whom was his obligation—a woman who had been out of his life for thirty years and in it for only ten? "I have had the help of another woman for twenty years through my creative life and that woman has asked nothing. She makes no demands. But she helps. To whom is my moral duty, I ask you." He would pay when he sold something; as for now, "you can't get blood from a turnip."

The object of his moral duty was watching *her* rival's moves. Receiving a report from Fabri that the marriage was breaking up and the Dark Lady might come to California, Helen said, Let her come; *she* had a hold on Dreiser that was deeper than youth or sexual attraction: "There is a blood tie between T. and me, and that stays." She meant their distant cousinhood, but something more. Not only was "he . . . in a *position*, which I have helped him achieve more than anyone else in the world, but . . . he is the same as a Father to me. . . . Our relationship is exactly the same as father and daughter with a little added." Dreiser was the parent who abandoned her long ago.

She hoped to "give him some comfort in himself," spiritually. His health also gave her cause for worry—a painful blockage of the urinary tract and related bladder and kidney complications. His symptoms had their origin in his chronic prostate troubles. One doctor advised removal of the enlarged gland— devastating news, he wrote the Dark Lady. That meant impotence. "What woman could endure me—save as a companion?" He put off the operation, took medicine, and visited a top urologist, who was, he told Lengel, "famous for his success with mental and nervous cases." The treatment cleared up the blockage, making unnecessary the operation he feared.

The $10,000 in unearned advances from Simon & Schuster preyed on him. He complained to Lengel that the publisher had dumped his backlist books at low remainder prices to avoid paying him royalties. He had telephoned Leon Shimkin, an S&S executive, about it, and Shimkin, in Dreiser's recollection, told him that it was all a "mistake." Dreiser complained to Alfred Mendel, editor at Longmans, Green, that S&S could have liquidated his debt long ago if they had kept his titles in print, but because of "their determination to extract the next novel from me" they preferred "to hold this debt over me as a club."

But to his friends he offered another reason: his publishers were punishing him for his allegedly anti-Semitic opinions and were bent on "taking me off the market entirely." He found it very significant that Arthur Pell's former secretary was now working for Simon & Schuster. He failed to realize that there was no plot by his publishers to suppress him. The reading public had forgotten him.

In December Shimkin wrote him regarding the publisher's share of a reprint fee, of which Dreiser wanted to keep the entire amount. "It is our feeling," Shimkin said, "that if we are to be your publisher and can look forward to the privilege of publishing your books, as was called for by our contract, we would be entirely happy to overlook the contractual details and accept your suggestion to send the entire fee."

Dreiser replied that "since Horace Liveright died I have never had a publisher." He accused S&S of failing to live up to its obligation to promote his back titles. "It is my personality and reputation alone that is keeping this and my other books alive and selling—through old book stores—and will so keep them alive and selling, but not because of anything that Simon and Schuster has done in connection with them. For it so happens I am not a dead author." With those words, he severed his ties to Simon & Schuster.

As he wrote to the Dark Lady regarding *their* relationship, which, finally, was over, "If a thing is truly dead it is dead and it will not come to life, that I know. . . . I still care for you and always will, I think."

Helen might have taken some satisfaction in Dreiser's being the rejected one, but she was no longer worrying about her rival in the East. She had one in California: Elizabeth Coakley, the actor Patrick Kearney's sister, who had become Dreiser's unofficial driver. One can see the suspicion forming in her diary, in odd items such as "T. came home late" and "Teddie out with the car." That September she noted that she had planned to attend a speech he was giving, "but interference prevented. In other words Miss Kearney and car racket. She has moved up since May 2 — my birthday when she called for a job in Glendale."

After an evening at the Goodmans', during which Dreiser insulted her, Helen complained, "I wonder where equity starts for him. Surely not at home. Equity he talks and lectures & writes so much but does not practice. Mormanism [sic] is rank capitalism — a certain form of slavery. Profitable too. Like any other form of slavery linked with the capitalist side of life." He always said he believed in fifty-fifty, but where was her fifty?

On September 1 she wrote: "War declared by Germany on Poland."

•   •   •

Dreiser didn't know what to make of the situation in Europe. He did not trust Hitler after Spain, but he despised the leaders of Britain and France. He concluded: "If Russia is not to sweep Europe soon, I would prefer to see a strong German state to the rotten financial dictatorship now holding in France and England and Hungary and the Balkans and elsewhere."

In his mind, France, England, Belgium, and the Netherlands were all corrupt capitalist states exploiting the masses, and he welcomed the deposal of their governments, if not by the masses then presumably by Hitler.

He began speaking out against social injustice in the United States. California was controlled by the corporations, he wrote Kennell; labor didn't stand a chance. The jobless were sleeping in movie houses. "I talk all the time — violently — and write. But one voice! One person!"

In June 1939 an agent of the Federal Bureau of Investigation called at Dreiser's house in Hollywood. At the conclusion, according to the agent's report: "Mr. DREISER stated that he is not a Communist and has never engaged in any Communistic activities and has never been a member of any group which was engaged in radical activities, but he stated that it is well known that he has always been a liberal in all his thoughts and actions."

On New Year's Day 1940, like thousands of other Californians, Dreiser and Helen watched the Pasadena Rose Parade. Dreiser's vitality was at a low ebb, and a few weeks later, after a siege of flu and neuritis, he had what the doctors termed a minor heart attack, confining him to bed for nearly six weeks. To friends Helen downplayed the seriousness of the attack, lest a prospective publisher find him a bad risk.

Undoubtedly, worry and depression contributed to his general debility. Fortunately, the medicine he needed arrived in time. The *Sister Carrie* deal was closed on February 12 by his new agent, A. Dorion Otvos, and Dreiser's health immediately began to improve. The price was $40,000, and RKO paid a binder of $3000. A sizable chunk of the movie money was committed to paying off debts, including $5000 to Jug. (According to Helen, Jug offered Dreiser a divorce if he would give her $10,000, but he refused.) With this financial breathing space, his spirits improved; by April he was back at his desk.

In June came a summons to battle. "Do you feel keenly enough to keep the country out of war to write a book of 70–100,000 words?" Lengel asked him. Dreiser was interested but pointed out that the war might be over before a book came out. Paris had fallen, and France was about to surrender; British troops had their backs to the Channel at Dunkirk. Dreiser predicted that "by August 15 Germany will have shot up England sufficiently to make her see the light regardless of what aid we can bring to bear." The publisher believed the book could be rushed out in time if copy was in by September 1. Lengel suggested that Dreiser hire editorial help. The terms were: $1000 on signing, $2000 on delivery of the manuscript, and $2000 on publication.

The publisher was Veritas Press, a small house specializing in scientific and philosophical books, which was run by Oskar Piest, a German émigré. Piest proposed as a working title "Keep Out, America" or "Let's be Pro-American." The thesis of the book should be that America not sacrifice its freedom and constitutional ideals by becoming embroiled in a European war.

While discussions on the purpose and tenor of the book continued, Dreiser pushed ahead on the research and blocked out some chapters. As editorial assistant he hired Cedric Belfrage, a young English novelist who was trying to survive in Hollywood by writing for movie magazines. Belfrage had read and admired Dreiser's novels but was unaware that he was living in Hollywood. His first impression was of a lonely old man, a forgotten writer living in a small apartment surrounded by people who had no inkling of who he was. He also discovered that Dreiser had some odd ideas, which Belfrage wasn't sure were on the right or the left.

Belfrage soon discovered that Dreiser was good for about two hours of work in the morning. Then they would walk to Schwab's Drugstore, where the older man would buy a half-pint of whiskey. The alcohol would affect him almost immediately, and soon he couldn't talk intelligibly. "It was pitiful to see how he crumpled up. He couldn't hold it."

Belfrage later said, "He couldn't have possibly written the book by himself, so in fact I wrote the book." A few of the chapters have a distinct Dreiser flavor, but most of the writing is not in his style and lacks his familiar phraseology and sentence structure. There are occasional Anglicisms he would never have used (e.g., "up a gum tree" and "like a Girl Guides' Field Day"). Still, the book surely reflected what Dreiser wanted to say, his outline, his data, except in places where Belfrage steered him away from his more extreme obsessions, as Belfrage saw them. Either Dreiser or Belfrage coined a key term, "the International of Privilege," to convey the idea of an interlocking directorate of financial and business leaders, including Germans, conspiring against the common people to profit from the war.

On September 9 Dreiser sent the final chapter to Piest. Lengel's reaction arrived ten days later: "Considering the fact that the book was designed to show the futility of America getting into the war and to show that our interests lie in developing our own national identity, you have wandered pretty much afield at times and the book indicates that you believe our salvation rests in communism rather than in the development of democracy within the frame-work of the Constitution."

Dreiser explained his position: the Constitution should guarantee economic as well as political rights. America has "wandered so far from the ideals of the Constitution that we can't be said to have real democracy — rather the rule of a financial Oligarchy." These were the points he wanted to make in the book, and he believed they accorded with Piest's outline.

Piest had a personal problem: he had applied for citizenship and evidently feared that he would be accused of Communist sympathies. Dreiser made some revisions in line with Piest's criticisms and assured the publisher that he had kept the Constitution and the Declaration of Independence on his desk. Piest seemed satisfied and sent the book to press. But on October 24, while Dreiser was reading galleys, the publisher wired that rumors were being spread by a competitor that he was part of the covert Nazi propaganda effort in America. The charge was untrue, of course, but he feared the gossip would stigmatize Dreiser, and he thought it best that someone else publish the book, which in fact was both anti–Hitler and anti–British imperialism.

Piest and Lengel quickly arranged for Modern Age Books, a radical house, to take over. David Zablodowsky, of Modern Age, asked for some cuts, primarily material critical of the Red Cross. Dreiser stubbornly reinserted the material in the galleys. Still, Modern Age was enthusiastic, and Lengel predicted that it might take over his other books.

America Is Worth Saving was published in January. *Time* brushed it off as "a spiteful, wretchedly written tract by great, aging Theodore Dreiser … who lives in Hollywood, lectures to California's women's clubs." (Dreiser had spoken to the Beverly Hills Junior League.) Less ideological critics found that Dreiser's book made some good points, however intemperate his style and inaccurate some of his facts. (He is at times oddly prescient — predicting the decline of the British Empire and the importance of the splitting of the atom.) But they were put off by his anti-British rhetoric, such as calling England "this black widow of the nations" and characterizing the war as between "Hitlerdum and Hitlerdee." Even recent CP apostates such as Granville Hicks, caught in a seismic ideological shift, could not swallow Dreiser's contention that British imperialism was as bad as Hitlerian fascism.

But history, the most merciless critic of all, would give his book its worst review.

• • •

In December, while driving on North Kings Road in Hollywood, Dreiser and Helen spied an attractive white stucco Spanish colonial house with a red-tiled roof and a "For Sale" sign in front. It was situated on a quiet street lined with oak trees and had a large yard with a pond in back. They bought it immediately.

Reinvigorated, Dreiser took to the stump in January. He spoke at an American Peace Mobilization rally in Los Angeles, looking "flushed" and "leonine," according to *People's World*, and had the audience of three thousand roaring with laughter at jokes about FDR (whom he was "down on" for Lend-Lease aid to Britain) picnicking with the King and Queen at Hyde park: "Damned if I don't think the man has lost his mind. He's delighted when a queen comes over and eats a hot dog with him. I think we're worth more than that—they can't buy us off with a hot dog." At the end of February he flew to New York City for a speech to the American Council of Soviet Relations. Marguerite Tjader Harris found him "full of tumult, argument, very much on the offensive about his book, his opinions." She had never seen him "more violent in speech and action and flaunting opposition with almost diabolic glee." He was full of himself, and once more bubbling over with save-the-world schemes, which may have explained his good health.

But his speech at the banquet was a fiasco. He had no prepared text and grew morose as he listened to a parade of speakers who droned on about Soviet-American friendship. Out of nervousness he did not touch his food, and he drank one highball after another. After three hours, in a tipsy state, he heaved himself up to the lectern and began talking about how the press lied about communism. Then his emotions welled up and he segued into an emotional dirge about the poor and wretched of the earth, recalling mining towns in Wales and London slums, breaking into sobs at times. Finally, the Reverend John A. Kingsbury, chairman of the council, collared him during a burst of applause and led him off the platform.

The next day he spoke soberly to the League of American Writers. The novelist Richard Wright, who had been inspired by *An American Tragedy* in writing his own novel *Native Son*, was moved by Dreiser's plea to young writers to fight for social justice. Then, at a mass meeting in Newark, he told the audience, "After all is said, it is the People who run the world. . . . Or should. Henry Ford, and all our big corporations are nothing without the people." He warned them that the big corporations were trying to steal their liberties: "Realize what they are trying to do and remember that when you want to YOU CAN DO IT!" And then he waved briefly and lumbered off, to thunderous applause.

While in the city he consulted with Stanley M. Moffat, the attorney handling negotiations to wind up his contract with Simon & Schuster. The sticking point was the amount of his debt to the house, which the publisher estimated at over $10,000, and Dreiser at $8000. He also lunched with Earle Balch, editor-in-chief of G. P. Putnam's Sons, who was definitely interested in taking over his books but would make no commitment until Dreiser had extricated himself from his present publishers.

A piece of good news arrived from Hollywood: the musical version of "My Brother Paul," to be titled *My Gal Sal*, had been sold to Twentieth Century–Fox. The price was in the neighborhood of $35,000, which included the rights to Paul's songs, the money to be split among the brothers and sisters. Only Theodore, Ed, Mame, and Sylvia remained of the ten children born to Sarah and John Paul Dreiser in Indiana.

•   •   •

Early in the morning of June 22, three hundred German divisions crossed the Russo-Polish frontier in Hitler's long-awaited Operation Barbarossa. Dreiser, who had supported the Nazi-Soviet Nonaggression Pact, was furious at this perfidy. His first public comment on the invasion, for *The New Masses*, was almost incoherent, as though spat out in blind fury. It was, he said, planned from the very beginning by the "Money International" and its servants in England, Germany, France, and the United States.

On July 14, in a calmer mood, he dispatched a statement to the Union of Soviet Writers. "Nothing in the history of mankind . . . not even the senseless, barbaric devastation and massacre" by the great scourges of the past, such as Genghis Khan, Tamerlane, Attila, Napoleon, Alexander, could compare with the evil of Hitler's invasion. While he could not forget "Hitler's primary and quite respectable struggle to restore the German people, once they had been struck down by their capitalistic trade rivals of 1914–1918," the dictator's successes had gone to his head, and he was pursuing "a dream of Empire for Empire's sake." But Dreiser could not resist adding, "I mistrust England as much as I mistrust Hitler . . . ." He predicted that if Russia defeated Hitler, England would resume its old game of seeking to undermine Russia. Those opinions were stricken from the statement when it appeared in the Soviet Union.

His Anglophobia was no worse than that of many Irish-Americans or isolationists or the Chicago *Tribune* editorial page. And his opposition to fighting a war to save the British Empire was shared in theory by most liberals, including Norman Thomas and FDR privately. After Hitler attacked Russia, Dreiser refused to allow the isolationist America First Committee to distribute off prints of an anti-British chapter from *America Is Worth Saving*. He told the committee he was pro-Russian and not pro-Hitler, and did not wish to be associated with it in any way.

• • •

At home, he found few forums to address. When a group in Indianapolis asked him to speak, he accepted on the conditions that he could criticize England for not doing enough to help the Soviet Union and that the proceeds of the meeting go to Soviet relief. The sponsors acceded to his terms, and he departed in mid-November, after a row with Helen, probably related to Elizabeth Coakley.

From Indianapolis he traveled to New York to meet with Balch. Putnam offered him a contract, which he characterized to Helen as "not very good but maybe the best I can get." The good news was that Moffat had liberated him from Simon & Schuster, at a price of $8500. He returned to Helen in Portland in a conciliatory mood. "I can't stand ruling by others," he wrote her, "and so we clash often so uselessly it seems to me since nothing is gained by it. We go on as before." He was trying to do better. In September she had undergone a hysterectomy to correct a chronic gynecological problem. She had complained to Fabri of poor health for about a year. Her nerves were bad; she was "too sensitive a variety of person for the force that played on me." She had tried to find "*some sort* of relief. But T. never really realized it. He can't. He is too powerful—too ambitious—too self-centered. But that is genius. And my fate." And his too.

She came through the operation in good shape, returning home after about two weeks. Dreiser and Pearl, the maid, were there to greet her, and she cooed in her diary, "I *love* my home with Teddie *so* much and I love *him* so much." But a fortnight later she wrote: "T. out at 4 with Coakley to dinner etc. etc."

• • •

On December 7, 1941, the Japanese attack on Pearl Harbor wrote finis to the Great Debate on keeping America out of the war. In the immediate aftermath, rumors of enemy bombers in home skies and invasion fleets offshore flickered up and down the West Coast. The Japanese attack had the effect of drawing Dreiser closer to his country. He told the *Daily Worker* that Americans "ought to be willing . . . to serve the officials of this government to produce a united front . . . we have a country that is democratic in spirit, and once its dream of real democracy is made effective, it may actually democratize the whole world."

When Louise Campbell wrote him of her worries about being killed by a bomb and her depressed state of mind, he comforted her. America was in for "storm & stress, but it certainly has had a long run of ease, peace and plenty—so much so that it has grown cocky, indolent, self-pleasuring and inequitably indifferent to the needs of its own underprivileged." He closed on a patriotic note: " . . . we're all in this together & instead of spending time brooding on who's going to get killed first we'd better be figuring out how to kill some of our enemies first."

82 / The Avocado Tree

> I am not an "isolationist" in the sense that people define this slogan any more than I am a 'communist' in the sense that the *word* is interpreted by the American people as meaning something dark and mysterious and antiAmerican and this and that.
>
> —Dreiser to Hortense N. Dillon (1942)

Dreiser had joked to Louise that he had some "defense work" on his desk—probably *The Bulwark*. In a schedule he furnished Lengel, he had placed the novel second on his agenda. But Lengel and Balch insisted he begin with it. Dreiser acquiesced, adding, "It is far enough along to finish it in the time that I said," that is, by fall 1942.

In reality, *The Bulwark* was an even more problematical novel for him now than when he had abandoned it to work on *An American Tragedy*. He must reconcile the four different versions of the novel that he had on hand, all written prior to 1920. And his conception of the central character, the father Solon Barnes, had changed. But one scene at least remained the same. He had written it before he even started the novel to test whether he could do justice to the tragedy inherent in the material. That is the scene in which Solon steals downstairs late at night to view the body of his son Stewart, who has been charged with murder and, rather than face his parents, commits suicide in jail. In that confrontation was buried the autobiographical seed of the novel—Dreiser's long-repressed need for his father's approval. The suicide of Stewart was his own symbolic suicide, a cry for love and a reproach, and a turning upon himself of his hostility toward John Paul Dreiser.

Although in April he reported to Mencken that he was "doing quite well" with the book, he saw now that much writing lay ahead. He confessed to Lengel that the novel would not be ready for some time. "It is a very intimate and touchy problem in connection with religious family life—and, like The [sic]

American Tragedy I find it difficult." He offered to repay the advance if it would ease Balch's mind.

Putnam had announced *The Bulwark* in its catalogue and set a deadline of September 1. This unnerved Dreiser. "You understand it is a long book and not an easy one to write," he told Balch, "something on the order of *The Financier* or *The 'Genius.'*" Still, he assured Balch that he was working every day.

•   •   •

Typically, he confided hints of his state of mind to a woman friend, Sylvia Bradshaw (a fictitious name), an American living in Toronto and working in a war plant. Bradshaw had been drawn to Dreiser's novels several years before and, on a whim, decided to send him a Christmas card in 1941. He immediately launched one of his epistolary flirtations, which received a sympathetic response. They had unhappy marriages in common, and her grandmother was a Quaker, so Dreiser queried her about ordinary life among the Friends sixty or seventy years ago, when the novel, as it now stood, was set. He was specifically interested in "arresting incidents of one kind or another connected with the average human attempt to live up to a religious or moral ideal," the "amusing results of spiritual striving" when one fails in the attempt.

After more letters, he arranged a rendezvous with Miss Bradshaw. Abandoning plans for a romantic interlude at Niagara Falls, they agreed that she should travel to Los Angeles in July, and he sent her train fare. They spent eleven days together, which he later called "the sweetest, lovingest days of my life." Sylvia was no young thing; she was forty—intelligent, pleasant, attractive, though no beauty. But she instinctively gave him the mothering, adoration, and sensual warmth he hungered for. He compared her to the heroine of "The Darling," his favorite Chekhov story. The heroine personified his ideal woman, sacrificially loving one man after another, a maternal figure.

Almost fifty years later she remembered sitting in the car with him at the beach; hulking, sausage-shaped barrage balloons loomed in the sky, and barbed wire and machine-gun emplacements lined the shore. "He liked to talk on and on . . . and I loved to listen." Sometimes he would watch her swim. Exercise was out for him; he was physically incapable of walking even short distances.

•   •   •

The idyll with Sylvia would have an untoward effect. In August he received an invitation from the Toronto Forum to speak on the necessity of an Allied invasion of Europe to relieve the German pressure on Russia. Like most on the left, Dreiser strongly advocated such a second front. He was still sore at

England, he wrote Louise Campbell. "Its sole aim is to save the British Empire with its sacred *clauses*. . . . So I'm out to go to jail before I'm through."

He had no qualms about carrying an anti-British message into a British dominion, and in a letter to Sylvia he jocularly wondered why he had been asked, "for I plan to roast the English beef as I always do. If they want to take me to the border afterwards and throw me out into the night, that's their business."

When Dreiser arrived in Toronto early on Sunday, September 20, there were no signs of potential trouble. Realizing that their visitor was "box-office in Toronto," as the *Telegram* had written, Forum officials postponed the speech until September 22 so that a bigger crowd might be assembled. According to Dreiser, the Forum asked him to participate in a press conference on the morning of the twenty-first to stir up additional publicity. He agreed and met with a motley collection of reporters, including two from the gossip sheets *Flash* and *Hush*, a radio interviewer, and Margaret Aiken of the *Evening Telegram*. Bradshaw and Sir Charles G. D. Roberts, a Canadian novelist whom Dreiser had known in his Village days, were also present.

The reporters were well aware of his distaste for England, particularly Aiken, a niece of press magnate Lord Beaverbrook and a fervent Anglophile. Her paper was Tory in politics and had recently published some dismissive editorials about a second-front rally in the city sponsored by two leftist trade unions. Her hostile questions stunned Dreiser, who later said, "She seemed like a nice girl." He no doubt noticed that she was also an attractive one, which caused him to lower his guard. As he remembered it, he began outlining the ideas in his speech, only to be interrupted by sharp questions about his past statements on England and the second front. Under fire, he became defensive and lost his temper.

Her story generated front-page headlines in the afternoon edition: "ABUSE FOR BRITAIN DREISER'S CONTRIBUTION TO ANGLO-U.S. UNITY." She quoted him as saying, "Should Russia go down to defeat I hope the Germans invade England. I would rather see Germans in England than those damn, aristocratic, horse-riding snobs there now." He scored the "unbelievable gall and brass of the English," who had received lavish aid from the United States but had done nothing to help the Russians. He accused Churchill of not opening a second front because he was "afraid the communists will rule the world."

Dreiser's remarks were extremely impolitic, and Aiken did everything possible to make him look like a Nazi sympathizer, stressing his German background, his stern German father, his supposed admiration for Charles Lindbergh and the isolationist cause, and portraying him as a Red. Even when Dreiser insisted that he was anti-Hitler, she sniffed, "He also claims to hate Hitler—and most of his 'hymn of hate' was directed against Hitler's most formidable enemy, Britain."

After Aiken's version hit the streets, the telephone lines at the offices of local and national authorities in the city were jammed with calls from angry Canadians demanding that Dreiser be arrested and either deported or interned. In urgent session the city council adopted a resolution calling on the mayor to meet with the commissioners of police and ask them "to take such action as is necessary to prohibit Mr. Theodore Dreiser from addressing any public meeting in this city. . . . " This was done, and the commissioners banned the meeting, fearing violence, they said. The federal minister of justice issued an order forbidding Dreiser to make any speech in Canada or even to issue a statement. Canada's minister for external affairs advised the American embassy in Ottawa that if a Canadian had said what Dreiser did, he would have been clapped into jail. The American consul in Toronto made a report directly to the secretary of state, assessing the potential damage to U.S.-Canadian relations.

Following the fatal press conference, Sylvia, worried about Dreiser's health (he had a severe cold), took charge. They had lunch and did some sightseeing until the afternoon papers appeared. When they saw the *Telegram*'s headline, they agreed that they must leave the city. She remembered that the Detroit train stopped briefly at a station in the western part of the city and decided to catch it there. The central station had several flights of stairs, and she did not think he could make the descent to the platform.

They returned to the hotel, hurriedly packed, and caught a taxi, arriving only a few minutes before train time. No warrant for his arrest had been issued, but the Royal Canadian Mounted Police kept track of their movements.

Before fleeing, Dreiser took telephone calls from two Canadian reporters and told them that he had been misquoted and misinterpreted. In a long-distance interview with the New York liberal paper *PM*, he said that he did not remember saying he would rather see Germans in England than the snobs now in charge, but admitted he had said, "I would be perfectly happy to see the Germans remove the 15 percent that is holding down the English people." When his other quotes were read to him, he agreed they were more or less accurate, but he denied that he was, as Aiken reported, an admirer of Lindbergh. That had been "before Pearl Harbor." Now, of course, he was no isolationist: "I want Germany defeated, in self-defense and to save the heroic Russian people."

The train ride was uneventful, and no one tried to stop them. They got off in Port Huron, Michigan. Sylvia, who had trained as a nurse, feared he might develop pneumonia — his cold had spread to his chest, and he was having difficulty breathing — so they holed up in a hotel room for three days.

But the Port Huron *Times-Herald* was tipped off about his presence by a hotel employee and when Sylvia emerged, reporters confronted her. She persuaded them to go to their adjoining room, and once they were inside, she slammed the door and turned the key they had left in the lock. While they were immobilized, she and Dreiser checked out of the hotel. She went off to purchase train tickets, telling him to meet her on a certain corner, but became lost. As he anxiously waited for her, the liberated reporter-photographer team found him and asked for a comment. Dreiser groused that he didn't give a damn about what the Canadian press said about him and asked caustically what the reporter thought of the "Canadian ideal of free speech." The photographer snapped his picture, which ran under the headline SECOND AMERICAN TRAGEDY.

A few editorial writers criticized him for jeopardizing Allied unity. The Writers War Board, a group formed to turn out propaganda for the government on a voluntary basis, issued a statement signed by its president, Rex Stout, and several others, including Pearl Buck, expressing regret that "an American writer of Mr. Dreiser's eminence should thus insult and offend our allies." And in a crueler cut, it observed: "Our enemies would pay him well for his disservice to our country's cause."

In his public reply, Dreiser charged that the board had, "without troubling to investigate the facts concerning my remarks made about England's titled class, proceeded to ally me with Hitler and against the allies." He reiterated that his remarks were directed at the British aristocracy; he did not want "to see Hitler rule the English people as a whole." America's true allies were the "great masses of India, Russia, China and the common people of England," not the titled snobs. He asked Pearl Buck how she could sign such a document after all she had written about "the brutal rule by the British Tories of the colonial peoples of the Far East."

Later Pearl Buck wrote him that the statement of the Writers War Board had been issued without her knowledge. Although she did not agree with what he had reportedly said in Toronto, "I still believe in free speech." In his statement Dreiser had asked for an apology, but she declined, telling him, "I think your stature is too great to take this matter as seriously as you are doing." Dreiser agreed, writing her on November 19, "I am sick of the entire affair." The final indignity was a letter from Norman Cowan, the Forum's program director, demanding a refund of the traveling expenses advanced him.

•   •   •

Even before Toronto, the FBI's file on Dreiser had graduated to a full dossier, a "Custodial Detention" card listing his left-wing affiliations. This had been compiled in November 1941, under a Bureau program to detain enemy aliens and "subversives" in a national emergency. Dreiser made the list as a Communist, though the Bureau usually identified him as a sympathizer or an "intellectual Communist." Following his Toronto speech, his "dangerousness classification" was upgraded to "A–1." (This index was the Bureau's creation, and the following year Attorney General Francis Biddle ordered that it be dropped because it had no legal standing and served no legitimate purpose.)

An agent from the Detroit field office was assigned to the case. He reported that Dreiser had stayed in a hotel with a woman not his wife, and Washington conceived the idea of prosecuting him for transporting a woman for immoral purposes under the White Slave Traffic Act. Detroit was ordered to look into the matter further, although a high Bureau official admitted that "Dreiser is 71 years of age and the possibility of his having had natural relations with [Sylvia Bradshaw] seems unlikely." Then the U.S. Attorney in Detroit said that if the Bureau would present him the facts he would bring a Mann Act prosecution. But the attorney general later instructed Director Hoover to drop the investigation.

Although the Mann Act prosecution died a well-deserved death, the Bureau continued to track Dreiser. One informant charged he had an immoral relationship with a woman in New York who worked for the government and was in a position to feed him classified information. In an earlier letter Hoover had pointed out to the attorney general that "allegations to the effect that Dreiser had consorted with women had been called to the Bureau's attention." It was a close question whether the FBI was more interested in his consorting with women or his "subversive" activities. By 1943 the Bureau was monitoring his communications to and from Russia, including cables, through the Office of Censorship, a wartime agency that inspected foreign mail. His correspondence with Sylvia Bradshaw in Canada was sometimes opened.

•   •   •

Other than providing grist for J. Edgar Hoover's gossip mill, the Toronto trip may have had a positive result. Dreiser vowed to cut down on his speaking and finish his book.

In fact, he was in an unsettled mood and asked Sylvia to send him a "strength wave—something that would inspire me in connection with my book. It's hard to work when your troubled in your mind about love & desire & financial complications." He urged her to move to Los Angeles, where there were plenty of high-paying jobs. She was reluctant; like others before her, she didn't want to share him with Helen. He told her what he had told them—that he owed Helen something and could not just throw her out. Once he came into some money he would pay her off.

His letters to Bradshaw expressed affection and gratitude for her pluck and her care for him in Canada. In one he describes a flaw in his nature that he had never admitted before: "I'm in the main a bad egg—selfish, self-centered, interested in large problems which concern the welfare of millions but fails [sic] to take into consideration the poor failure at [my] door-step.

And that is very bad. I can see it clearly—the Lone Wolf complex. And yet I love & respect those who, like you, do look after the individual as well as the mass."

He would also write Sylvia: "Life, apart from the love and desire and satiation in the arms of the beloved, is scarcely worth the living. And it is because of that so often I think of death as a door to rest or peace—the end of strain and disappointment."

On October 1, 1942, Sara White Dreiser had passed through the door to rest or peace. She died in Missouri of what her niece called "a complication of illnesses." The funeral was held at the Methodist Church in Mexico, Missouri. The minister read a statement Jug had requested, that she and Theodore had been separated but not divorced. It was her life's triumph to cling to his name until it could be carved in the stone that marks her grave in the little cemetary near Montgomery City, next to her father and mother. He never commented on her death. She was someone he had known long ago.

•   •   •

How goes *The Bulwark?* Mencken asked Dreiser, seeking news and trying to revive their flagging correspondence. Dreiser replied he was on chapter 34 and promised "it will come through." He was supposed to be finishing the first third of the book to submit to Balch, but he wrote Sylvia that he had been hard at work on his tax return and outlining a script for *The "Genius."* Then he inexplicably agreed to write an article for the *Writers Digest Yearbook*, though the fee was only $75. He proposed to describe "his general stand as to world politics."

The essay contained Dreiser's familiar criticisms of England and praise of the Soviet Union; he closed with a peroration: "stop the fight, stop the destruction. Send the men behind the guns back to the fields and the laboratories, and let's welcome the new day." A. M. Mathieu, the assistant editor, promptly submitted the article to the Office of Censorship, which had the power to forbid the export of magazines, movies, or books containing material that was considered harmful to the war effort. In the case of Dreiser's article, the office provided an advance ruling that the article contained "Propaganda detrimental to the war efforts of the United States or the United Nations" and material "whose dissemination might directly or indirectly bring aid and comfort to the enemy or interfere with the war effort. . . . " If the *Yearbook* were banned overseas, the publisher would lose money.

Mathieu grauitously added a second reason: Dreiser's appeal for an end to the fighting was Nazi propaganda. To publish it "would be treason. I cannot see it any other way except treason."

An outraged Helen warned the editor not to be so "glib throwing accusations of treason around." Mr. Dreiser, she said, didn't need the $75 and hadn't written for such a small amount in years. Mathieu brushed aside Helen's letter, telling her that *he* knew what Dreiser meant when he said "stop the fighting." It wasn't like Dreiser to let these aspersions pass without a murmur. But coming a few months after the experience in Toronto, the charges apparently stunned him into silence.

· · ·

Despite his optimistic words to Mencken about his progress on *The Bulwark,* he wrote Sylvia that he felt a sense of failure. His trouble was psychological. His niece Vera Dreiser thought that he was "identifying his own father with the character in his trials and tribulations. He was also suffering from self-identification, which happened with all his writing." This self-identification confused him as to who he was or should be. Solon was hard to live in, and with; Dreiser could hardly claim to emulate the Quaker's morality in his own life, yet he could no longer view him with the distancing irony of his original conception.

In response to his pleas, Bradshaw agreed to come to Los Angeles for an indefinite stay. She found a small apartment on North Hayworth, and Dreiser visited her there. She obtained a job at the Los Angeles *Times* in the classified department to support herself. The work was hard, the wartime hours long.

Sylvia's presence did not inspire him to work on the novel, however. She recalled that he quizzed her about her Quaker forebears but otherwise did not discuss it. In August Helen's mother suffered a stroke. With Helen's tacit approval, Sylvia moved in with Theodore at the Kings Road house for a few weeks; someone must take care of him while Helen went to Oregon. But Sylvia knew it was a temporary arrangement. Since Jug's death, Helen was fiercely determined to marry Dreiser. "She carried a gun of some kind," Sylvia recalled. "I didn't want to be involved in any shooting accidents. Helen wasn't fooling as to marriage."

Although he urged her to stay, Sylvia decided to return to Canada. "I had to look ahead a little," she explained, "and I knew that Theodore did not look after himself too well and no one else did. If anything happened to him, L.A. had no attraction for me." Although in a letter to her he mentions her "fiery jealousy" and her constant threats to leave, her memory was "We never quarreled. Never! Helen was the problem."

· · ·

Shortly after Sylvia withdrew from the field, Dreiser wrote Helen in Portland that he had decided to drop *The Bulwark* and take up the third volume of his autobiography instead. But surely he realized that finding a new publisher was no easy matter. And his general mood was not conducive to starting another book. In September he told Sylvia that he had developed a case of "nerves," which evoked "a sense of dread or fear in regard to myself. . . . Suddenly the ability to write . . . to go on with *The Bulwark* or in fact anything in the way of work that is before me is up the chimney."

Stanley Moffat had written Helen that the entire relationship with Putnam depended on his finishing *The Bulwark,* and he warned that the company might lose interest or even bring a breach of contract suit. She agreed that he must finish the novel. Dreiser had been making good progress on it, she said, but now his mood was not right, and he was "not a well man." It would be "cruel and wicked" to bring a suit against a man his age; he would gladly refund the $1000. Moffat met with Balch and reported that the latter was willing "to let the situation go along just as it stands in the hope that the book will ultimately be produced." The thought of a suit was "the farthest thing from Putnam's minds."

·   ·   ·

In early November Dreiser wrote Sylvia that he had come down with chills and a fever because he had been so worried about *The Bulwark* and "got tired struggling over an essay, 'My Creator.' " The essay had come to him while he was spading around an avocado tree in the garden. It was a beautiful and flourishing tree, he wrote, its roots extending down some twelve feet into the earth, its "smooth and shiny leaves—graceful as a warrior's shield is graceful," bearing in November a dark-green fruit. The tree was a symbol of all created things, "an illustration of the supreme genius of this creative force that so overawes me. . . . " The design and beauty and intelligible purpose "of this so carefully engineered and regulated universe—this amazing process called living" were the abundant tokens of an intelligent, benign mind at work. Contemplating its handiwork, he was

> moved not only to awe but to reverence for the Creator . . . concerning whom— his presence in all things from worm to star to thought—I meditate constantly even though it be, as I see it, that my import to this, my Creator, can be but as nothing, or less, if that were possible.
>
> Yet awe I have. And, at long last, profound reverence for so amazing and esthetic and wondrous a process that may truly have been, and for all that I know, may yet continue to be forever and forever. An esthetic and wondrous process of which I might pray—and do—to remain the infinitesimal part of that same that I now am.

The thought had long been in his mind, but it needed to be clothed in the foliage of words. He was a writer, not a philosopher; he needed the image, the metaphor, of belief.

·   ·   ·

In December came the news that Edgar Lee Masters had been discovered ill and penniless in his room in New York's Chelsea Hotel. A sculptor friend found him and took him to Bellevue Hospital, where, due to wartime crowding, he was given a bed in the hall. Alice Davis, his long-time companion, bowed out of his life, and his wife—the young, capable Ellen Masters, from whom he had been estranged for years and who was now a teacher—strode in and took over his care. Financial help arrived from the Authors League and the Carnegie Fund, as well as checks from Mencken and other friends. He was transferred to a hospital room and was soon recovering.

Dreiser was luckier than Masters. Out of Russia came a miracle, even as the Red Army was mopping up the remains of the Wehrmacht at Stalingrad. Having heard that some American authors were receiving royalty payments, whereas he had received little on an edition of his books published in 1940, he wrote Stalin demanding equity. Two months later his bank notified him that a sum had been transferred to his account. He read the figure as $3.46 and wondered why they bothered him with such a petty amount. But his eyesight was dimming. Helen looked at the figure: it was $34,600. A call to the bank verified that it had come from the Soviet government: payment in full for royalties due. Dreiser's face lit up.

"I refuse to worry any more," he said. "This will carry me through to the end."

83 / *Closing the Accounts*

Dreiser came to New York to accept a prize from the American
Academy of Arts and Letters. I didn't come to see him, for I
simply couldn't endure any such transaction. . . . For him to
now take a cash prize from them seems to me to be intolerable.
I think I'd rather starve first.
                                    —Mencken to James T. Farrell (1944)

In early January Dreiser received another piece of news, a letter from Walter
Damrosch, the conductor and president of the National Academy of Arts and
Letters, informing him that he had been chosen to receive the Award of Merit,
bestowed every five years and carrying with it a gold medal and a $1000 prize.
He accepted but wrote Damrosch that his health and the state of his affairs
might preclude his accepting in person.

How could Dreiser tell Mencken that he had decided to accept an honor
from their old foe, the Academy, symbol of the literary establishment? (Neither
may have known that Sinclair Lewis had led the fight by younger members to
give the award to Dreiser.) Almost sheepishly, Dreiser wrote that he planned
to be in New York in May, for reasons he would explain later. But he couldn't
evade Mencken. "I can only deplore the fact that you are having any truck with
that gang. . . . If they have actually offered you a hand-out, I hope you invite
them to stick it up their rainspouts," he said.

But he truly needed Mencken's emotional support for the ordeal and
apologetically invited him to the dinner Damrosch was giving after the cer-
emonies on May 19. He would feel "forlorn, deluded, even impostor like" if
Mencken didn't come but would consider himself "justly reproved" if Mencken
refused. The latter would not bend his principles: "Unhappily I can't join you at
the orgies. . . . Some of the chief members of that preposterous organization
made brave efforts to stab you in the back in 1916, and I am not disposed to
forget it."

Dreiser expected this rebuke, though he really could see nothing wrong with accepting $1000 and a free trip to New York; he planned to ease his conscience by padding his travel expenses. Helen had intended to accompany him and parley with a possible buyer of Iroki, whom Moffat had located after the doctor backed out. But she had to go to Portland and nurse her mother in February, leaving Dreiser alone.

Well aware of how lost he was when on his own, Helen alerted Ralph Fabri to look after him in New York, making sure he ate regular meals. Swallowing her jealousy, she also enlisted Marguerite Tjader Harris, who replied, "You know *I love him more than almost anyone* on earth. I'm always so glad that he has you, to be with him. I don't think anyone has ever understood or loved him as you have, and do . . . so you know you can depend on me to take the best care of him. . . . " Helen had no choice; her mother was seriously ill. Besides, she was about to play her trump card, which would eliminate all her rivals.

●   ●   ●

Marguerite met his train and took him to his favorite hotel, the Commodore, near Grand Central Station. He was so much thinner, almost gaunt-looking. She made a remark about God bringing him here safely, and he announced, "Well, I believe in God, now—a Creative force."

Also greeting him was Margaret Carson, a bright, attractive young woman who was handling publicity for the awards ceremony. Dreiser was entranced by her and told Marguerite, "My that was a smart girl. It's really these women who should run the world nowadays. The men ought to retire." Carson later discovered that after a few drinks he became flirtatious and tried to embrace her.

His sister Mame had written him before he left that she was ill. She was now in Kew Gardens Hospital; cancer of the bladder was suspected, and a later operation confirmed the preliminary diagnosis. The visit to the hospital was an emotional experience. He was surprised to find Ed and Mai and Vera there when he arrived. Mame cried when she saw Theodore. She fretted about the expense, and asked if she might go home to die. He kissed her, held her hand, and told her everything would be taken care of. Mame said, "You've always been so good to me. I can never repay you." She urged him to get to know Ed's daughter Vera—"there are so few of us left."

He had lunch with Earle Balch at the Century Club; Richard Duffy, who had volunteered to work up a prospectus for a collected edition, outlined his plan. But the Putnam editor said he could not spend any more money on Dreiser since he was already in too deep. A Dreiser novel would sell itself and create demand for his other works. Dreiser wearily agreed to the familiar condition.

Balch had not been enthusiastic about the new chapters of *The Bulwark* Dreiser had sent him in May 1943; they consisted largely of background on the characters and did not advance the story. After a long lunch, Dreiser returned to the hotel a bit worse for liquor.

Meeting no encouragement from other publishers he saw, Dreiser began to lose heart. He was like Willy Loman, dragging a sample case of old books from one publisher to another. They were more or less polite; they knew who he was (or had been), but with wartime paper shortages the idea of a complete set was out of the question.

Dreiser told Robert Elias that he felt like Kipling, who said that one day his genius had abandoned him. He saw his new agent, Jacques Chambrun, who advised him to stop being obsessed with the old novels: write something new—some short stories. Dreiser said he had written lots of them. Weren't they still good? Was what he had achieved nothing? Here in this noisy, confusing, changing city, old men were consigned to the ash heap unless they kept up with the literary procession.

James T. Farrell called at the Commodore and got the impression that Dreiser "was closing out the accounts of an entire past." But he seemed mentally alert and quizzed the younger man about the new writers. Were they any good? What were they writing about? He said he had recently read Charles Jackson's *The Lost Weekend*, a harrowing tale of an alcoholic's bender, and simply did not get it. "What kind of subject is that? For years I've been burying relatives who drank themselves to death."

He himself had avoided the alcoholic's fate, but as he had told Mencken about whiskey, "I love and need it so." He carried a half pint of cheap rye in his pocket and would take a nip whenever he felt bored or tired. "I don't know what's the matter with me," he would tell Marguerite. "I guess a little whiskey will fix me up." He would gulp down vitamin pills, almost absentmindedly. He could not adjust to the fact that he was nearly seventy-three and slowing down.

• • •

On May 19 he taxied to the rambling brick building that housed the National Institute of Arts and Letters on 155th Street. He had prepared an acceptance speech, on a pet idea of his, which seemed suitable for this august gathering— the creation of a cabinet-level secretary of the arts.

He submitted a short statement in advance, but someone at the Academy, the Institute's parent body, told him that the speech raised controversial issues and must be reviewed. Since there was no time for such a proceeding, he was requested not to deliver the speech. So he told Marguerite. However, Felicia

Geffen Van Veen, Damrosch's assistant, had no recollection of anyone's asking Dreiser not to give the speech. Nor did she think there was any practice of reviewing the nominees' speeches.

With Edgar Lee Masters beside him for moral support, he watched the sedate procession of academicians in black gowns to the stage. There were four honorees: Dreiser, Willa Cather, S. S. McClure, and Paul Robeson. Institute president Arthur Train made some gracious remarks.

Then it was Dreiser's turn. Whereas Train had introduced the preceding winners as old friends, Dreiser was presented by Professor Chauncey B. Tinker as a kind of literary fossil. In a speech many thought condescending, Tinker said Dreiser was chosen as a pioneer and leading exponent of the naturalistic school. But he made it clear that the views of said school, and certainly of its chief exponent, were definitely not those of the Academy, which "is neither conservative nor radical. . . . It sponsors no school and has no programme." Its sole aim was to honor ability in whatever guise it appeared.

Undampened by Tinker's remarks, the audience applauded warmly as Dreiser rose and walked to the podium. To Marguerite he looked like a caged lion. He retreated into his own dignity, turning his back on the audience to bow and accept the medal from Damrosch. His speech remained in his pocket as he mumbled a few words of thanks. He probably hadn't the heart to say more after the equivocal tribute from Professor Tinker.

• • •

He spent several evenings with Masters, who was visibly slowed but receiving devoted care from his wife, the kind of brisk, take-charge young woman Dreiser liked (needed). At Lüchow's the headwaiter recognized them and seated them at their favorite table near the orchestra, which did not strike up "Nearer My God to Thee" as Mencken once predicted. (How they must have missed him!) Hearing Dreiser mildly complain that the music was not as romantic as it used to be, the headwaiter spoke to the conductor, who played a round of Gypsy airs. Over *wurst* and beer they reminisced about their past escapades and the women they had pursued. They agreed they were paying for those excesses of the flesh, but it was too late now.

Also entertaining him was his niece Vera, now a practicing psychologist. Vera was intensely curious about her famous uncle, to whom she had hardly spoken since she was a teenager. One evening she accompanied him to see Robeson in *Othello*. After the performance they went backstage to invite the actor out for a bite, but he told them that no restaurant in the theater district would serve him because of his race, so they would have to go to the Village. Dreiser was too tired to make the journey.

The next day Vera took him for lunch and a drive in Fort Tryon Park. He asked her, "How would you like me as a patient?" She told him it would be too difficult a job. They talked of his many women, and he confessed, "I've been in love a thousand times . . . or maybe never at all. . . . most likely never at all. . . . " She asked him, "Is that why you had so much hostility toward women?" This took him aback, and he changed the subject. She asked him if he believed in God. He said, "not only do I believe in God, but I will go into any scientific laboratory and prove it to you."

The following weekend he visited Ed and Mai at their large home in Far Rockaway, Queens. The brothers spent most of the afternoon reminiscing about their childhood. Ed, still firm and fit, looked fifteen years younger than Theodore, though he was only two years his junior. When Ed sang an old German folk song about leaving the gates of the city, which their father used to sing to them, the memory of it came back in a rush to Theodore, bringing tears to his eyes. He spoke sympathetically of John Paul Dreiser.

He thought it amazing the way Mai and Ed still held hands after forty years of marriage. Sitting in that comfortable home with a brother he loved, he perceived the void in his life, Vera thought, the lack of a stable home and a family.

The next day they visited Mame, who was sinking rapidly. One by one they slipped in to say goodbye. Outside the hospital they gathered for a moment. Ed had to go to work, and as he was about to leave, Theodore kissed him on the cheek and said, "Long life, Ed." They embraced silently and Ed strode off to the subway, tears in his eyes.

Driving back to Manhattan, Dreiser suggested to Vera that she come to California and help him with the novel. He needed someone with her intelligence and energy. When she told him she had a baby daughter and a career and could not possibly leave, he shrugged and said, "If you really wanted to, you'd arrange it."

On another day he paid a farewell visit to Iroki, which Helen, working by long-distance phone, had sold for $22,000. He and Marguerite wandered about, taking a last look at the big house, now empty and desolate-looking. In a window Dreiser found a dead starling, its beak impaled in the mesh of the screen. He carefully extracted it, smoothed its iridescent feathers, and laid it on the ground, as though laying to rest a dead dream that had once fluttered about this place.

• • •

And then came a request from the Office of War Information to make two broadcasts, one to the people of America and the other to the people of Germany, to be beamed on the eve of the Allied invasion of Europe. This assignment was the best tonic of the whole trip. He sat before the microphone, speaking the words in a husky voice:

> I have just come across the country . . . this great America of ours . . . and I wish you could have been with me. You would have seen, as I did, in railway stations, or trains, in hotels, or the streets . . . an amazing display of youthful vigor, enthusiasm, youthful yet manly love of country. . . . I see millions of the finest type of fighting men, who seek nothing as much as the day and hour when they can try their young strength, their American vitality and brains, their American alertness and inventiveness, against the Nazi brutes, whom they do not fear but whom they abhor, as do all Americans.

He went back a few days later to speak to the enemy. Identifying himself as the son of a German-born father who had left his native land to escape Prussian militarism, he called on the German people to recover their past greatness, which had produced statesmen, scientists, and artists, and to help bring a new era of justice in the world. He closed, "Just as a tryout, let's have a few hundred years of the brotherhood of man."

And then a farewell cocktail party for all the New York friends who had rallied around him during his stay. Those present included Edwin Seaver, Marguerite's co-editor on *Direction;* Charles Scribner, still talking about publishing a Dreiser set; Dorothy Norman, a columnist for the New York *Post,* who later wrote, "[Dreiser] has never lost his passionate interest in all movements, all work that reaches out to enrich life"; William Gropper, the artist; Isidore Schneider, literary editor of *Soviet Russia Today,* for which he had written an article; George Seldes; Richard Wright; Elias; and various wives and children. Wright found Dreiser refreshingly humble, unlike most writers: "If you asked him a question, he would say a little something in reply; and later, a little more, and perhaps later, still more—as if any idea was enough to start some deep emotional, psychological movement in him."

As people were making motions to depart, Dreiser received a telephone call informing him that Mame had died. He lay down awhile in the darkened bedroom and then came out to say his farewells.

And then more interviews with Elias, whom he liked now. Elias, seconded by Marguerite, urged him to finish *The Bulwark.* Dreiser agreed; he always said that work was the only cure for a low mental state. Turning to Marguerite, he said, "If you come to California and help me, I think I can do it." Marguerite agreed to come—but only with Helen's permission.

And then Mame's funeral. She looked beautiful in death, the lines of suffering smoothed from her face. Dreiser was moved by the young minister's reading of the traditional funeral service. "What beautiful words," he told Marguerite. "He reminded me of Alyosha Karamazov."

•   •   •

On June 5 he boarded a train for the West. But his destination was not Los Angeles; it was the town of Stevenson, Washington, where Helen awaited him. Stevenson was noted for its spectacular scenery and its quick marriages. Dreiser had at last agreed to marry Helen, after some diplomatic interventions by Helen's sister, Myrtle (herself engaged to Chester Butcher, a rancher), and surprisingly, by Mai, who had come to accept their unconventional union and who now thought it only fitting that they seal it.

What Dreiser really thought about this step can only be guessed, since he did not discuss his plans in New York. But he seems to have done it to please Helen—a gesture of atonement, putting a legal seal on their long relationship. That bout of loneliness earlier in the spring had reminded him of his need for her care. He had seen what Ellen Masters had done for Edgar, and even joked about how he was lucky to have his "lawful wedded wife" looking after him. Bradshaw seemed no longer interested, and he wrote her later that, although his feelings toward her were the same, he could not bring himself "to break up the practical relationship here." Helen's hold over him was too strong. She provided a well-run home where he could store his books and papers; she was someone he could depend on to look after him and perform routine secretarial chores.

The ceremony was performed by a justice of the peace, with only Helen and Dreiser, Myrtle and her fiancé present. To avoid newspaper attention, Dreiser signed the register with his baptismal first name, Herman. Helen wanted no publicity, since it might remind the world of their twenty-five-year unsanctioned liaison. She had sometimes passed as Helen Dreiser, though she rarely used "Mrs. Theodore Dreiser," feeling he would resent it. Now the title was legally hers. Soon after the ceremony she proudly wrote it at the top of a letter to Fabri.

•   •   •

He was kinder to Helen now, but he looked forward to Marguerite's arrival. They had been close in New York, and she had also served as hostess, typist, companion, schedule keeper, and morale booster. He expected her to help him finish both the novel and the philosophy. The details of *The Bulwark* were clear in his mind, he wrote her, and he "could easily outline the successive chapters or structure and when that was done paint in the various scenes—their respective colors and emotional qualities."

Although he had Helen, he needed an opposing feminine magnetic pole to draw forth the erotic energy that still fitfully drove his creativity. Vera diagnosed oedipal longings in him, "the force that had drawn him to all women." He was "borrowing strength" from women "to enhance his own security."

Marguerite formally requested Helen's permission to come. Helen warned her about wartime conditions in Los Angeles — the housing shortage, the necessity of a car, gasoline rationing. Although both spoke in the most high-minded way, a hint of potential rivalry broke through. Marguerite assured Helen that she would be strictly business. "I'm sure there'll be no discord between us," Helen replied. "Surely we are beyond that." And she went on: "I know you love Teddie dearly. . . . Perhaps I love him more like you love Hilary [her son]. It's that kind of love. Once I allowed myself to worship him. But that was corrected by a realization that came through difficult years, that it was wrong. . . . It is very bad to worship any human being be it man, child or woman. . . . It is so characteristic of a woman to worship. But it's not the way." The words showed a hard-won maturity. She told Marguerite she would be welcome.

In August she and Hilary drove out in an old convertible. They arrived in time for the celebration of Dreiser's seventy-third birthday on the twenty-seventh. He hated such occasions, so Helen disguised the event as a kind of party for *The Bulwark,* complete with a cake in the shape of a book on a revolving stand that played "Happy Birthday." The guest list grew to sixty people. Along with friends from the old days, including Lillian and Mark Goodman, Clare Kummer and her daughter Marjorie, the Tobeys, and Masters's daughter Marcia and *her* daughter, there were the new recruits to his Hollywood set: Clifford Odets and spouse; the Al Manuals; the A. Dorian Otvoses; the Russian consul Ivan Boutnikoff; their neighbors the Wards (she was the actress Jane Wyatt); Dr. Chang, the Chinese consul, and family; Will and Ariel Durant; and others.

Dreiser looked fresh and dapper in a cream-colored suit, and Helen glowed with some of her old radiance in her white hostess dress. It was an odd assortment of people. Clare and Lill played songs they had composed long ago, which no one remembered. A pupil of Lill's sang Dreiser's favorite air, "Jeannie with the Light Brown Hair." The Chinese consul's daughter played Grieg's Piano Concerto. The men hunted for some hard stuff, which they knew Dreiser kept in his desk, rather than go on with Helen's famous orange punch. "It was one of our most successful parties," Helen summed up, "and the last one of any size."

•   •   •

Marguerite and Hilary settled into temporary accommodations in a motel. The housing shortage was fierce, but they eventually secured a tiny three-room house located in a cul-de-sac near Cahuenga Boulevard.

The Putnam contract had been weighing on Dreiser's mind, and he decided to refund the advance. With that obligation lifted and Marguerite to edit and type his various drafts, his mind was eased. But much remained to be done. Helen says he quoted frequently from the Bible at this time, and one line recurred while he worked on the novel: " . . . this night thy soul shall be required of thee."

84 / The Bulwark

> Nature, machine-like, works definitely and heartlessly, if in
> the main beautifully. Hence if we, as individuals, do not make
> this dream of a God or what he stands for to us, real, in our
> thoughts and deeds — then He is not real or true.
>
> —Dreiser (1934)

Dreiser had only one deadline now: the time remaining to him. Their workday began at ten, when Marguerite picked him up and drove him to the little
house on Cadet Court. He would be carrying a stack of manuscript or a bundle wrapped in twine or stuck in a decaying brown envelope — material he had
excavated from his files and decided was usable. "This is the stuff on Isobel,"
he would say. "This is about Stewart at school." Once he brought an unusually
thick sheaf of pages. "Fifty thousand words more. Now this will send you back
to Connecticut!" Piles of manuscripts littered her tiny living room until she
dragged in her steamer trunk to serve as a filing case.

They read through the four extant typescripts and decided that two were
worth salvaging. One dealt with the various family members, and the other
recounted Solon's business career. The latter was too detailed, so it was cut
drastically and merged with the family version. They cannibalized from a third
manuscript, which had been too severely cut but which carried Stewart's story
further than the other two. These three scripts were merged into a working
draft, to which more cutting and fleshing out and rewriting was done.

In this fashion — and probably Marguerite did much of the stitching
together — they built up the novel on the foundation of the thirty introductory
chapters he had written in 1942–1943 and submitted to Balch. After rereading
them in the light of his more recent work, Dreiser was appalled that he had
parted with them. Now, with Marguerite's help, he would be able to compress
them.

Marguerite worked a double shift, going over the manuscripts by day
and editing and typing the reorganized material at night. When the pages had

been spliced into a coherent narrative, they made a diagram of the story, show-ing where each character stood and what remained to be written, and from this Dreiser prepared a fourteen-page outline for submission to a publisher. Al Manuel, now with the Goldstone Agency in Hollywood, had interested Dou-bleday in the manuscript, but Dreiser did not want to sign a contract until he had completed the book.

His uncertain health slowed their progress. In October he wrote Sylvia that he was "too weak and nervously shaken to work," and that he was "doctoring and—or vitamining." He told Masters he was continually tired and "laying off of work of any kind and as much as possible." His doctor had diagnosed a thyroid condition of an unspecified nature and prescribed medication. That complaint would have contributed to his lethargy and weight loss.

During a visit in September, Vera thought he looked weary and ill. He was almost childishly dependent on Helen, who mothered him in the good-humoredly dictatorial way of a nurse long accustomed to the crotchets of her charge. Once she and Vera went out shopping and stayed away longer than planned. When they returned he was pulling at his hair and almost screamed: "Where were you? I was going to call the police in another few minutes. I was worried sick!" Helen merely laughed and walked off. She represented, Vera now realized, "the one person he could depend upon to be there when he needed her," and when she wasn't he became distraught.

Once when he and Vera were alone he pulled her to him and tried to kiss her. She broke away but later thought she had been "cruel" and that he had not been making a sexual advance but seeking affection and reassurance from her.

She diagnosed sagging self-esteem. Once when she wished to see some movie people about several songs she had written, his name gained her imme-diate entrée. When she told him this, "He could not believe that anyone was really interested. He had to be reassured constantly, by word, by deed."

In fact, he was regarded as a sort of literary monument in a town where reputations were planted in shifting sands. His parties drew many admirers, most of them displaced New York intellectuals of the liberal-left persuasion. One guest recalled, "You always felt as if they were going to collect for some-thing." Folk singers Woody Guthrie and Pete Seeger had sung ballads in his living room. Charlie Chaplin performed impromptu sketches that made Dreiser laugh until the tears streamed down his face. In 1945 Paul Robeson came to tea, and he and Dreiser talked intently about the problems of Negroes. Dreiser pro-posed an article on the subject. When Robeson had to leave for a performance, Dreiser asked him to sing one song. Robeson leaned against the living-room table and boomed out "Ol' Man River."

•　　•　　•

As he became more engrossed in the novel, his social life tapered off. On Sundays Helen took him to one of the churches in the area, in keeping with her project of helping him find spiritual peace. They attended a Christian Science church for a while, but he preferred the Mt. Hollywood Congregational Church, whose pastor, the Reverend Alan Hunter, was a liberal in politics as well as theology. The ritual at his church featured a period of individual meditation, which may have made it seem to Dreiser more Quakerly and nonsectarian. On Good Friday he insisted on attending an evening service at the Congregational Church, and when they emerged under a starry sky and palm trees, a setting Hunter had compared to the Holy Land, he said little but seemed profoundly moved.

In January he ran into a block on the novel and was laid up by a cold that led to a severe depression. "He could be so difficult at times," Marguerite recalled of her charge, "so sunk in a negative mood that death, and all sorts of disasters seemed actually lurking around him, as if he were deliberately drawing them to himself." He had reached the stage in the narrative where the rebellious Etta (loosely based on Anna Tatum), encouraged by her freethinking friend Volida, runs away to the University of Wisconsin. (Volida, who exhibits mannish traits and wants to study medicine, is a discreet shadow of her prototype, the lesbian doctor who had seduced Anna Tatum.) One night he dreamed of Solon in a hotel room in Madison; indeed, he *was* Solon. It was a breakthrough; he had achieved the needed identification with the character and could move ahead with the story.

By March he had reached a point in the narrative where Stewart, joyriding with his friends, is involved in the death of a girl, an incident inspired by a case Dreiser had read about some thirty years ago. When he dictated a description of the scene in which Stewart decides to plunge the knife into his chest rather than face his father and mother, he became the boy. At the point where the press trumpets the family's disgrace, he suddenly stopped. "That's enough," he sighed, emotionally drained. This was "the works."

Without Marguerite's energy to draw upon, the book would have been impossible for him. She roused him in the morning and gently pushed him through the day. She lavished encouragement and at times physical affection on him. His virility was waning, but age hadn't diminished his need for physical love, even if it consisted of her sitting in his lap or simply hugging him. He needed this physical touching.

And she provided the sympathetic ear he needed to overcome his inhibitions about writing a religious story, for she had recently embarked on a spiritual search of her own. But she strongly denied exercising a Svengali-like influence over him. As she wrote Robert Elias at the time, "I do know that the ideas, and all the ideas . . . expressed in the *Bulwark,* are his own, and not planted by me, or anyone. . . . we were close in what we both believed, especially about that universal element of Love, flowing from God and through all created things."

•   •   •

By March they were approaching the last chapters. On fine days he would work on the patio. He might suddenly eject a phrase or describe a scene so fluently that she would grab her pencil and copy the words down on a box lid or whatever paper was handy. Now in relatively good health and feeling the story carrying him along to the ending he had imagined thirty years ago, he was as happy as he had ever been. He loved to sit on the patio and hum to himself (a sign of serenity) or watch the antics of Hilary's guinea pigs, which ran loose in the garden.

But although Marguerite was an ideal midwife, she was no editor. Inevitably, he thought of Louise Campbell and wrote her that he would be finished within a month. Could she take over the manuscript? "For you are, as you know, —a swell editor," he cajoled, "the best I have ever known and I'll feel troubled if you find yourself unable to edit."

It took him a month longer than he had anticipated, but the final scenes contained the novel's most moving passages, written in simple, Biblical prose. He spoke the phrases to Marguerite as if they had been patiently waiting, fully formed, all these years. Solon had become a Jobian figure, battered by the world. Having resigned from the bank where he was treasurer in protest against financial chicanery, and mourning Stewart, he is haunted by a sense of failure. His children have all but abandoned Quakerism and no longer care about him.

At this point Dreiser gave Solon words hard-earned in his own quest for meaning. One day Solon walks in the garden and observes a glittering green fly feeding on an insect. In a reversal of the squid and lobster scene of *The Financier,* Dreiser uses this encounter to demonstrate Solon's vision of the unity of all creation; cruelty and strife are but transitory shifts as Nature ceaselessly seeks a balance between opposing forces in the equation inevitable. Solon studies the flowers and the grass, as Dreiser had done in "My Creator," and concludes, "Surely there must be a Creative Divinity, and so a purpose, behind all this variety and beauty and tragedy of life." Later he encounters a puff adder and, as Dreiser had done at Iroki, assures it that he means no harm. As the snake crawls across his shoe, Solon realizes that the creature understood his loving intent and was no longer afraid. Similarly, God must feel good intent—love— toward all things. All creatures are a part of the design of creation, of God.

Hearing of Stewart's suicide, blaming her own rebellion for inspiring Stewart, and regretting the lies she told her parents, Etta returns to ask her father's forgiveness and to take care of him. One morning while shaving he looks in the mirror and asks her, "Daughter, what has become of that poor old man who was dying of cancer?" What old man? she asks him. "Why . . . why . . . that poor old man whose son killed himself." Solon's words carried a faint echo of an ironic comment Dreiser made to Esther McCoy about himself being forgotten: "Is that man still alive? Why doesn't he die?"

While reading to the dying Solon from Woolman's *Journal,* Etta comes to understand her father's faith. She grows more spiritual. At Solon's funeral, her brother Orville, now a stolid, conservative businessman, asks her how she can weep when it was she who started all the family's troubles with her rebellion. She tells him, "Oh, I am not crying for myself—or for Father—I am crying *for life.*" In an outline of the novel, written nearly thirty years before, Dreiser had anticipated this scene: "Orville's request to Etta not to cry, and her answer." (And even before that, he had written in his European Diary, "I fancy my tears are for the whole world. . . .") No one is blameworthy, all life is a tragedy of desire. All traces of individual strivings are immersed in the solvent of universal tears.

• • •

All that remained was for Marguerite to type the final version. This provoked a minor clash with Helen because Dreiser had promised that she could type the chapters that made up part I—the chapters on family history and Solon's boyhood that they had worked on before Marguerite came upon the scene. When Helen saw how severely this section had been cut, she felt betrayed and blamed Marguerite. But Dreiser managed to convince her that the deletions were necessary, and she completed the job.

He sent a copy of the script to Campbell, who read it with growing dismay. She found herself out of sympathy with the talk about God and the Inner Light. She thought the novel inferior work, poorly written, and it espoused values that contradicted Dreiser's entire career. She gently conveyed her opinion to him, and it awakened his own doubts. "While I am not sure that all you say is correct," he wrote her, "I will have to go over it and see how much I agree, and what I can do." He instructed her to hold on to the manuscript because he might want her to cut it. Then he asked James T. Farrell to read it and advise him.

Marguerite suspected that Helen was behind his fear of seeming too religious. But Helen, pagan though she was, had no opposition to the religious passages, and indeed had written Marguerite, "The Bulwark . . . is a beautiful book. It is full of poetry, philosophy and a lot of truth. He is using many quotations from the bible and this truth & beauty takes hold of one. It is, to me, almost hypnotic, especially now in this crazy world. And, working on it, has the power of absorbing one so that the rest seems more or less unimportant."

Helen was more concerned about Dreiser's reputation and his well-being. Not long after he had sent Louise the manuscript, Helen urged her to look for weak spots with *"a critical eye."* She went on, "When the Tragedy was in the making, I was absolutely sure about the outcome of it. I can't say that I feel that same absolute confidence in this book. And it worries me." Better the novel not be published than for it to fail. An adverse critical reaction would be too painful for Dreiser to bear.

Dreiser was also worried. He knew that his first novel since the *Tragedy* would draw much critical attention and that, given his age, the book would be taken as a kind of summing up. He did not want to be seen as having embraced religion, like the old radical Heywood Broun, who had converted to Catholicism on his deathbed. He and Mencken often joked about Broun as though challenging each other not to weaken in the end.

Dreiser had not embraced Quakerism. It's clear that in the final chapters Solon is more a mouthpiece for Dreiser's views than those of the Society of Friends. The revelations the author granted him stemmed from his own experience. Indeed, Rufus Jones later criticized *The Bulwark* on the ground that Dreiser "never gets inside of this Quaker family or of a Quaker Meeting, and his characters remain too much like constructed frames for presenting the author's theories."

Dreiser describes not Quakerism but a nonsectarian religion in *The Bulwark.* He uses John Woolman's *Journal* as his vehicle. Speaking for the author, Etta says, "Here was no narrow morality, no religion limited by society or creed, but rather, in the words of Woolman, 'a principle placed in the human mind, which in different places and ages had different names; it is, however, pure and proceeds from God. It is deep and inward, confined to no forms of religion, nor excluded from any.' " That was Dreiser's view of "pure religion and undefiled," a direct, unmediated perception of a God, of beauty and unconditional love at the center of all things.

• • •

Despite Louise's dissent, there was good news from Doubleday: it wanted to publish the novel. But associate editor Donald B. Elder insisted that it be cut. Dreiser replied that he preferred to do his own trimming first (or rather have Louise do it, subject to his approval), but he was heartened by the news and regained some of his old energy. Soon he was outlining short stories to Marguerite, and an idea for a series of articles on why men leave their wives.

But first he wanted to tackle *The Stoic,* and so they took out that much-worked-over manuscript. Marguerite found the writing slick and mechanical. The business scenes didn't come to life. Also, she thought the scenario he had written was too rigid and schematic—a potted biography. Her impression was that he was chiefly interested in winding up the book, not reworking it. Marguerite offered to help him with the philosophy instead, but he was bent on finishing the novel, sensing that his time was growing short.

Marguerite had to return to Connecticut in June, and although she offered to extend her stay a few weeks, he did not press her. Helen probably played a role in Marguerite's banishment. She suspected a triangle forming and resented the other woman's literary influence over him. After Marguerite left, he wrote her wistfully, "So my golden girl is gone!"

He was anxiously awaiting Farrell's reactions to his novel, for he respected the younger man's judgment. In June Farrell delivered his verdict, which was positive. Sensing that Louise's objections had been partly to the old-fashioned style, he telephoned her and she confirmed this. He also discovered that she had most disliked those scenes in the final chapters describing Solon's spiritual revelations. Farrell had liked them best; he had years before recognized Dreiser's mystical streak in *Hey, Rub-a-Dub-Dub!*

•   •   •

Meanwhile, a complication was brewing. Dreiser had given Marguerite a letter to the Doubleday Company authorizing her to look over the manuscript and to inspect the galleys when they were completed. Upon her return, she called on Donald Elder, who told her he liked the novel but described Campbell's and Farrell's reactions. Marguerite now felt fiercely possessive toward the book and resented the outsiders. She asked Dreiser what was going on. To avert her wrath, he downplayed their roles. Farrell, he said, "seemed to feel that it had some minor errors or inconsistencies which he wanted to correct. . . . " Louise had called the book "a strong piece of work likely to do better than I think," but had suggested "a few corrections." He only wished Marguerite were there to help him discuss their suggestions, which were really trivial.

In fact, he had already authorized Louise to cut the manuscript within Farrell's guidelines of preserving style and religious material. She had forwarded to him the first sixty pages, and he had approved her work. He instructed her to continue her editing "in the same spirit." In another letter he warns her that if Mrs. Harris should come to see her, not to be disturbed.

Dreiser was indecisive but inclined to entrust the book to Campbell and Farrell. Anticipating that Marguerite would try to interfere, he had written Elder on August 10 that Louise was preparing "a revised version for me based on suggestions made by James T. Farrell and myself. This might result in a much improved script, in which case I prefer this be the one to use,—after I have approved it, of course."

Torn between his longing for Marguerite to return to Hollywood and his dependence on peace with Helen, he seems to have psychologically collapsed. On August 14 he wrote Marguerite that he wasn't feeling well—"decidedly lethargic"—and needed an "action program—something constructive that will stir me to labor. If I did not feel so sickish—so lethargic I could think something out." He left it to her to decide whether to return. And then, two weeks later, a shakily scrawled note arrived:

> Double, Double, Toil and Trouble
> Fire burn and cauldron bubble.
> I run and fret and worry. I had your understanding letter days ago, but as for an agreeable Solution for you and for me?—*not so easy.* Worry, jealousy. Discord. The feeling of injustice—unfairness. A sense of unjustified scheming and plotting. And eventually *for some one*—retribution. And because of all this the difficulty of creative labor.

The "some one" was surely Helen. Dreiser had observed her hiding a letter and suspected she was reading his mail. Perhaps she opened an affectionate missive from Marguerite, realized for the first time how close the collaborators had grown, and put her foot down. Whatever "unjustified scheming" she was doing involved *The Bulwark;* Marguerite suspected that Helen was trying to purge her influence.

In September Marguerite returned to California. As soon as he had a chance, Dreiser led her into the garden, where they could talk privately. He told her that Helen was helping him finish *The Stoic* and resented her being there. The upshot was that they couldn't work together until the novel was finished. Marguerite said it might be best if she went home, but he gave her such a beseeching look that she agreed to stay.

On August 31 Dreiser sent Elder the "authorized" *Bulwark* manuscript and asked him to use it as a guide in his own editing. Although Louise had very reluctantly agreed to cut it, she had done her best, working to a tight deadline. She sensed that Dreiser was under a strain—desperately trying to finish. She said later that she did a "considerable amount of rewriting of parts of *The Bulwark*," and, as was her practice, she retyped the manuscript.

And then, in another twist in the convoluted history of *The Bulwark,* Elder wrote Dreiser, "Frankly I feel that Mrs. Campbell's revision has damaged the manuscript. . . . " She had cut too much, he said, made the style too slick. He thought her work had distorted the book, and that the pace of the narrative should be slower "so that the reader can assimilate the many details which are so important to the total picture." Elder felt a strong obligation to preserve Dreiser's style.

Confused and weary, Dreiser authorized Elder to use his own judgment. The latter attacked the manuscript with considerable vigor. Actually, he accepted some of Campbell's revisions or substituted his own (better) versions, and sometimes went beyond her proposed cuts. All in all, he compressed the book considerably, excising many of the tedious introductory clauses that Dreiser so favored, simplifying his prolixity, speeding up the narrative. Most of the changes were improvements, resulting in a simpler, plainer style. To be sure, many of Dreiser's old-fashioned locutions still stand, so it cannot be said that Elder (or Campbell) modernized the book in the way Farrell advised against.

While much of the editing was helpful—indeed, improved the book's style and readability—religious and philosophical passages were jettisoned. Esther McCoy felt that the stylistic improvements removed Dreiser's personality: "Dreiser was reduced to good clear English in *The Bulwark* and it lost much of its relation to him." Marguerite was incensed by the streamlining of those convoluted sentences she had heard him dictate with such deep emotion, in his tired but musical voice. And she suspected censorship of the religious passages by Helen.

Of course, she did not see what they had done until much later. Her last chance to look at the book was when the proofs arrived in September. She telephoned Dreiser and asked if she might help him read them, but Helen wanted no more of her involvement. Receiving an ambiguous reply from him, Harris jumped in her car and drove to North Kings Road. There followed a wrenching scene. Marguerite insisted that she and Dreiser read the proofs at her place. Helen refused, and, as Marguerite told Elias, she "was almost driven out, while he stood looking, strangely helpless. . . . " Helen's version of the confrontation in *My Life with Dreiser* has him siding with *her*, though one suspects she was rewriting history to claim a final victory.

The fight was more than a clash between two jealous women. Each was doing what she thought was best for *him*, and for the book. Helen may have been jealous of Dreiser's involvement with Marguerite, but she believed, with considerable justice, that he trusted Louise and Farrell more than he did Marguerite to edit the script. Marguerite may have been in love with Dreiser, but she was also jealous of the version in which she had invested so much of herself. And indeed, with the strength and energy of her own body and spirit, she had literally pulled him back to life as he was sinking into the fatal torpor and lassitude that settles on old people when they have given up.

Dreiser was so torn between the two women that he was rendered helpless. As Marguerite left, driven out by Helen's implacable hostility, he could only mumble to her at the door that he would call her after looking over the galleys. All the women, all the triangles he had known! And now the final one, forming over a book.

The galleys were returned with scarcely a mark on them. Dreiser apparently did not notice the cuts that had been made—or was too tired to care. In his accompanying letter to Elder, he praised the editor for an excellent job, adding, "I am glad to see that you did incorporate some of Mrs. Campbell's ideas . . . but I do not know why she cut so much. It isn't quite like her, as I remember her work."

85 / *Equation Inevitable*

> Any why, since you know what is here to be the merest wisp
> or rumor . . . of that totality, do you cling so fearfully, desper-
> ately to it when outside of this little stage play, rounded by
> a sleep, is all reality—the ultimate essence or base of it all?
> —Dreiser, *Notes on Life* (1974)

In the last months he seemed to friends more at peace. Robert Elias saw him in
September and found him "obviously tired and in the home stretch." Sometimes
his mind was sharp, but at other times it would drift into a fog. His memory
of recent events was capricious.

Helen arranged a small party on his seventy-fourth birthday, a quiet affair
under a pall cast by the recent death of his agent A. Dorian Otvos. Dreiser had
grown fond of the playful Otvos, one of those precious people who made him
laugh, and spoke movingly at the funeral.

In September his favorite sister, Sylvia, died. Now only Ed and Theodore
were left—and possibly Al, of whom he had lost track. With a heightened
consciousness of his dwindling time, his actions took the form of valedictories.
The most notable was his decision to join the Communist party in July. John
Howard Lawson said that Dreiser was worried about the postwar world and
feared continuing conflict. He had written of this to Louise: "the world seems
so topsy-turvy that I mentally feel distrait most of the time. . . . I wonder how
this world mess is to end for us. We are so mixed in everything . . . that I fear
sometimes that we'll be warring for years with this country & that."

In an essay called "Interdependence," written in September, a month after
the end of the terrible war, he said that only cooperation among the masses could
prevent the destruction of civilization (he had in mind, presumably, the atomic
bombs that were dropped on Hiroshima and Nagasaki in August 1945). But he
took care to explain that by "mass" he meant the individuals composing it. "As
soon as one begins to think of the other side as a mass or a crowd, the human
link seems to go." He believed now that small actions by myriad individuals
could cumulatively make a difference.

Joining the Party was consistent with those sentiments. And the CP was now hospitable to his application. It had been rocked by an ideological upheaval resulting in the ouster of Earl Browder by a faction, led by William Z. Foster, opposing Browder's "Teheran Doctrine" of postwar cooperation with the capitalists. No doubt the Party was eager to exploit the publicity of Dreiser's affiliation at this turning point in its history. But there is no reason to question John Howard Lawson's opinion that the decision was Dreiser's alone. As Lawson recalled, "He felt that the Socialist solution was the ultimate solution and he wanted to go on record about this." Dreiser was, in his own way, trying to put himself "right" with the world. And there was a quasi-religious element in his approval of communism. He considered the Russian leaders to be spiritual men—austere, selflessly dedicated to serving the people.

Dreser saw no conflict between religion and the ideals of communism, just as he saw none between undogmatic religion and science. He regarded communism as a practical social program, but like the Populists of his youth, he invoked Christ's Sermon on the Mount to express its ideals. He was an enthusiastic reader of the books of Dean Hewlett Johnson, the Archbishop of Canterbury, who professed to find a kinship between communism and Christianity.

He was also saying, though less clearly, that communism *should* have a spiritual basis, without which it is mechanical and inhuman. The principles of communism, he believed, were ultimately those of Christ, and thus the leaders of the world's only Communist country were "spiritual" because they were Communists—which, as bloody history attests, did not follow at all.

Finally, it should be said that Dreiser didn't join the Party in more than a formal sense. One could say he lent it his name as he had sometimes done in the 1930s. The announcement, which was probably written by Lawson or some other Party members, reads like a CP press release rather than a personal statement by Dreiser of his convictions.

Few of his friends were surprised by the gesture. Mencken wrote him, "I have been thinking of you as a comrade since the beginning of the second holy war against sin." He meant that he had considered Dreiser a Communist since Germany invaded Russia. They had "had it out" regarding Dreiser's political views in 1943, when Mencken asked him, "What, precisely, are your ideas about the current crusade to save humanity?" Dreiser replied, probably to Mencken's discomfiture, "Personally, I do not know what can save humanity, unless it is the amazing Creative force which has brought 'humanity,' along with its entire environment into being." He digressed to his contemplation of suicide in 1903, his experiences as Butterick editor-in-chief, his disillusionment with the rich, his affection for the "common man." And then he gets to the heart of the matter:

> You see, Mencken, unlike yourself, I am biased. I was born poor. For a time, in November and December, once, I went without shoes. I saw my beloved mother

suffer from want—even worry and wring her hands in misery. And for that reason, perhaps—let it be what it will—I, regardless of whom or what, am for a social system that can and will do better than that for its members—those who try, however, humbly,—and more, *wish to learn how* to help themselves, but are none-the-less defeated by the trickeries of a set of vain-glorious dunces, who actually believe that money—*however come by*—the privilege of buying this and that—distinguishes them above all others of the very social system which has permitted them to be and to trick these others out of the money that makes them so great. . . .

As for the Communist System—as I saw it in Russia in 1927 and '28—I am for it—hide and hoof.

There was much more in the letter, including praise and love for Mencken and gratitude for his battles on Dreiser's behalf. And from Mencken, vociferous dissent as to the loveliness of the Communist system and the rectitude of Comrade Stalin, and a reminder that he had not exactly been born rich; he had supported himself since the age of sixteen. Paradoxically, over the ideological gulf between them flowed the warmest sentiments in several years, as a result of Dreiser's expressions of love.

Resigned to Dreiser's radicalism, Mencken was more worried about a deathbed conversion and issued a humorous warning: "In case you are now approached by a Jesuit or Trappist, perhaps disguised as a Jewish rabbi or a Wall Street customers' man, be on your guard. Remember Heywood Broun. If you are fetched I win $2."

Dreiser's answer was a joke—a Catholic indulgence card on which he wrote, "Here's another device for reducing your stay down below. It's going to be hot down there and those hundreds of days off will be welcome I'm sure." It was a signal he had not succumbed.

Mencken's private opinion, later voiced to James T. Farrell, was that "Dreiser was led into the Marxist corral" by Helen. But he goes on to lay the blame on a familiar complaint—Dreiser's gullibility toward quacks and religious nostrums. "I always predicted that if he lived long enough he'd leap back upon the bosom of the holy church."

There is no evidence that Helen played a part in Dreiser's conversion, though she might have encouraged it as a way of helping him to achieve serenity. In Marguerite Harris's opinion, however, Helen wanted him in the Party to counteract Harris's religious influence on him while they were working together on *The Bulwark*.

• • •

Marguerite's idea that Helen influenced *The Stoic* is more plausible. When Dreiser took up the novel in June, it was two-thirds done. Seated in his rocking chair, he dictated to Helen at the typewriter. They would work until one or so and have a light lunch. Then they might go out for a drive, often taking dinner at a restaurant. Evenings were spent quietly at home, Helen typing up the day's work and Dreiser reading and editing the already typed manuscript. "It was incredible the way he persisted in his job," she writes of this period; "in fact it was all he wanted to do with the exception of an occasional diversion."

They drew closer during this time, and she writes, almost too glowingly for credibility, "If a woman ever experienced a complete renewal of her love life combined with a new depth of spirit, I had that joy." And she on her part hovered over him. A friend said she "kept putting an invisible shawl about his shoulders."

But there were episodes Helen doesn't talk about: a bender that ended up in a fancy Hollywood brothel, episodes of senile dementia. At 3:00 A.M. one morning she found him prowling about the house in a distraught state. He told her he was looking for Helen. When she assured him she was Helen, he replied, "Everyone thinks she's Helen." The delusion sometimes lasted for days. Once Marguerite discovered him lying on a couch, his eyes gleaming, his hands hot and feverish. "I don't know where Helen is," he told her. "There was a strange person here this morning. Maybe you can find out for me." Marguerite assured him that Helen, who was out, would return. That pacified him, and when she did come back he recognized her. Marguerite consulted a psychiatrist, who told her that at Dreiser's age there was little to be done, and it was best not to upset him by challenging his hallucinations or whatever they were. Rest and quiet were what he needed.

His visions strikingly symbolized his essentially ambivalent relationship with Helen. He feared that she had abandoned him but also denied her presence, as though he were wishing her away (indeed, Marguerite thought he feared Helen). And so it had been for a long time: she was always there, even when he was away with another woman, and when he was with her he dreamed of another woman. Now only Helen was left, and she was all women.

•   •   •

In late October Dreiser wrote Farrell that he had finished *The Stoic;* as soon as it was typed he would send it to him. He did not do so until early December. The last two chapters had caused him some difficulties. He had no trouble describing Cowperwood's death; his fortune fought over by lawyers, business rivals, and tax collectors; and all the planned memorials to his name—the hospital, the art museum—never built.

But the problem of what happens to Berenice remained. Here, too, reality had suggested a possible outcome: she takes a trip to India, like her prototype, Emilie Grigsby, to study Eastern philosophy. After four years, Berenice's spiritual education is complete, and she returns to America and founds a charity hospital with some of the money Cowperwood left her. She trains as a nurse and then takes charge of the children's ward. Her special fondness for some blind children was probably inspired by Dreiser's own visits to a Hollywood orphanage for such children. She comes to a deeper understanding of Cowperwood, realizing "that his worship and constant search for beauty in every form and especially in the form of a woman was nothing more than a search for the Divine design behind all forms — the face of the Brahman shining through." Thus did Dreiser rationalize his own lifelong pursuit of the feminine as a quest for beauty. The manuscript ended with an almost perfunctory essay on the relativity of good and evil, intended as a coda to the trilogy.

Seeking confirmation of the authenticity of his treatment of yoga, he and Helen visited Swami Prabhavananda, head of the Vedanta center in Los Angeles. The holy man described the visit to Alan Hunter: "It was she who did the talking. She wanted to know if they were right in their expression of the Vedanta teachings. I told them I could not tell this, unless I saw the manuscript myself. This they did not have with them. Mr. Dreiser said nothing at all."

Inaccuracy is not the problem with the chapters on Berenice's conversion. The ideas are not integrated into the narrative; they are not dramatized in terms of character. It might have indeed made an interesting conclusion to relate the spiritual quest of this once frivolous and calculating woman, but Dreiser does not tell that story. Instead, he provides a copybook of wise sayings, their self-evident truth assumed to be sufficient to explain Berenice's acceptance of them.

That Dreiser had doubts about the ending is shown by a letter to Farrell, written on December 14: "Would you prefer, personally, to see the chapters on yoga come out of the book? If so, what would be your idea of a logical ending?" Farrell suggested that the passages about yoga be recast to show Berenice's feelings and reactions and "the ironic inadequacy of her efforts." He was also unhappy with the essay about good and evil, regarding it as too sketchy to serve as the finale of this great trilogy. Dreiser replied equably, "You are dead right about the last chapter in regard to Berenice," and said he intended to rewrite it. "As to the essay on Good and Evil," he went on, "well that is something that can be discussed at length, and there is plenty of time for that."

But there was no longer plenty of time.

• • •

In December he and Helen attended a wedding. A photograph taken for the occasion — the last one of him — shows a very ill and tired man. On Christmas Eve he visited Elizabeth Coakley, spending most of the day watching her children decorate their Christmas tree and listening to Elizabeth play the harp. She drove him home in a freezing rain. When they arrived at his door, he said, "Oh how I dread to leave you. I am the loneliest man in the world." He spoke of "paying off" Helen—as he had to so many women in the past. Had he ever really meant it?

On December 27 he worked on the next-to-last chapter of *The Stoic*. The earlier yoga chapters he let stand; the job of revising them in line with Farrell's criticisms was beyond his powers. He continued until five o'clock, and then they drove to the beach and watched a brilliant Technicolor California sunset, all flame and crimson and gold, the most beautiful Helen had ever seen. He suggested they buy hot dogs for dinner from a stand on the boardwalk. They chatted with the jovial vendor, who told them he supported his wife and five children on what he made from his business. On the way home they talked of how some people could be happy with so little.

He said he was tired and intended to turn in. Helen retyped the chapter he had dictated that day, and when she finished at around 9:00 P.M. she looked in on him. She was disturbed by his appearance; his skin had a glossy look and his face was pale. She said she would show him the script in the morning, but he insisted, "*No,* read it right now!" So she read it to him, and he seemed pleased. Later she turned on the radio so he could listen to the ten o'clock news. He complained of kidney pains, and she brought him a heat lamp. After a half hour he felt better and turned out the light.

At 2:45 A.M. she awakened to see him standing in her room in his dressing gown. "Helen," he said, "I have an *intense* pain!" The urgency in his voice made her quickly get up, but he crumpled to the floor before she could reach him. He was in agony, and the cliché of so many World War II movies occurred to Helen: "This is it." She did not want to leave him even to go to the phone. Frantically she piled up pillows and blankets under him and tried to administer a teaspoon of brandy, but his teeth were clenched. His physician, Dr. Hirshfeld, was out, but his assistant, Dr. Chier, came within ten minutes. Helen and the doctor took Dreiser's arms and helped him to his room; he collapsed on the way but they managed to get him in bed and the doctor gave him a shot of morphine. Dreiser told him, "A pain like that could kill a person."

• • •

It was a heart attack, a massive one, and Dr. Chier thought Dreiser's chances of recovery were slim. Lillian and Mark Goodman had arrived and stayed with Helen through the night. The next day Dreiser was placed in an oxygen tent and a male nurse brought in.

While driving home from her job with an architect, Esther McCoy remembered she had two books by Theodore Reik and James T. Farrell that Dreiser had asked her to report on, so she decided to drop them off. Helen answered the door and told her that Teddy had had a heart attack. Esther went into his bedroom and found him under the oxygen tent looking "very gray." She noticed how his long eyelashes made him look childishly vulnerable. She asked him how he was. "Bum," he said.

Helen hovered over him, making him comfortable, and Esther walked through his study into the living room, noticing with sudden clarity the familiar talismans on his rosewood desk: the Chinese fisherman, the American Indian, the kewpie doll. There was the high-backed ducal chair he had sat in during parties at the Rodin Studios and now wrote in. She had a feeling that he would never sit in the chair again.

Helen asked Esther to spend the night with her, so Esther went home to get her things. The day had been hot and humid when she arrived, but now a fresh wind was blowing up. A fog rolled in, blurring the Christmas lights on the houses and then blanketing the street lamps. Soon it was so thick she could barely see the road and had to follow the white center line. She recalled Dreiser's idea of death as a fog that slowly, silently blurs the contours of reality, until the world is obliterated.

Meanwhile, Dr. Hirshfeld arrived and examined Dreiser. He seemed better and might pull through. When Helen went into his room, he was lucid. Suddenly he said, "Kiss me, Helen," and she did—on the side of his lips, just as she had in a dream a few weeks before. She kissed him again, and he said, "You look beautiful."

A little later, while Helen was resting, she heard the nurse talking on the telephone in an urgent voice. Dreiser's breathing was shallower; the doctor must come at once. Helen hurried to him. He seemed to be asleep. She held his hand; it was icy. He exhaled once, and then stopped breathing. She could not believe he had gone. The spirit slipped free, and the atoms and protons that composed him began the final dissolution that would return all that had been Theodore Dreiser to the primal source, the ultimate matter-energy. The doctor arrived to pronounce him dead at 6:50 P.M.

As he had foretold, Helen was there at the end to close his eyes.

• • •

Esther and her husband, Berkeley Tobey, were first to hear the news. When they arrived, Helen seemed in control of herself. The funeral home attendants arrived. They placed the corpse on a gurney and wheeled it toward the door. At that moment Marguerite Harris burst into the room and threw herself on the body. The attendants tried to remove her, but she insisted that she go with Dreiser to the funeral home. Helen, who had been quietly watching, said, "Let her go." Esther could not help thinking that Helen, who had shared him with so many women, was now generously sharing him in death. Helen recalled her feelings as the men took him away: "The biggest and best part of my life went through the door with him. I simply crumbled."

The next day Helen was strong enough to go to Forest Lawn to select a lot, explaining that Dreiser had told her he wanted to be buried there. She purchased a site "along a ridge, open to the sky, the sun & moon," she wrote Elias. "There are stately pines, like sentinels all about. . . . It's a heavenly spot." And then she selected "a beautiful dark rich red hardwood mahogany casket lined with a beautiful shade of velvet" and commissioned the sculptor Edgardo Simone to make a death mask and a cast of his right hand.

A gravediggers' strike delayed the burial, allowing time for differences over how the funeral should be conducted to fester. There were two factions: the religious camp and the progressive camp. Marguerite, who belonged to the former, arranged, with Helen's permission, for the Reverend Hunter to preside. The progressives, led by Lawson and James, lobbied for a political statement. Helen's main wish was that Charlie Chaplin read one of Dreiser's poems at the end of the service. She was leery of the CP representatives turning the service into a political rally. On the night before the funeral she was about to discuss it with them, when Marguerite arrived and shouted angrily that no Communist officials should speak.

At this usurpation by her rival, Helen forgot that she felt the same way and began berating Marguerite. The two women seemed locked in a contest for Dreiser's soul. Helen had earlier pretended a reconciliation, but now her jealousy spewed forth. She threatened to cancel Dr. Hunter's appearance and then ordered Marguerite out of the house.

Somehow the arrangements were completed. Helen wanted a great man's funeral. He belonged to the world now—he who had never belonged to her, or to anyone. Pallbearers were selected from a cross-section of Dreiser's friends. Upton Sinclair, however, declined because, he explained, he and Dreiser were merely acquaintances, causing Helen to burst into tears. "We went several times a year, at their invitation! He and Teddie had the warmest of relations!"

●   ●   ●

On January 3, 1946, more than a week after Dreiser's death, the obsequies were held at Forest Lawn. Helen had been distraught that morning. She kept running to the window and saying that Marguerite was outside in a car "spying" on her. Vera could see no one, but Helen would not believe her. Finally Vera got her dressed and with Esther they rode in one of limousines to the Church of the Recessional. On the way Esther began crying, and Vera efficiently produced a flask of water, a little cup and a pill. It was a cold day, and Helen wore the new fur jacket that Vera had urged her to buy, rather than the borrowed coat she planned to use.

The services represented a carefully scripted compromise between the two factions, a kind of stiff tableau with politics and church receiving equal time in eulogies by John Howard Lawson and the Reverend Alan Hunter. Marguerite called it "a farce or a least a tragic dividing of, & clashing of forces. . . . " But in that sense the ceremony truthfully reflected two contending forces in Dreiser's life. All that was lacking was a veiled woman from out of the past flinging herself on the coffin. As it was, several former lovers were present, but Helen was gracious to them. There was none of the spontaneous human drama that Dreiser loved, none of the moving extemporaneous tributes such as he sometimes delivered over the bier of a friend.

Lawson's talk—or lecture—was a scholarly summation of Dreiser's literary career, relating his works to American society, emphasizing the social consciousness and the desire for equity that ran through all his books. He reminded the mourners that Dreiser's decision to become a member of the Communist party was the logical consequence of his life and work, and he warned that fascism was abroad in the land. Then Charlie Chaplin read a poem from *Moods*, "The Road I Came," which would be engraved on Dreiser's tombstone. Esther had preferred Emerson's "The Red Slayer," with its affirmation of the triumph of the spirit over death. Chaplin intoned the lines in his mellifluous voice:

Oh, what is this
That knows the road I came?

The next speaker was Dr. Hunter, looking somewhat ill at ease, as though he was there on sufferance. He quoted from *The Bulwark*, John Woolman, and George Fox. He did not claim Dreiser for any church—nor could he; he suggested only that the deceased had struggled against the "image of life as a mere machine." He quoted, as Dreiser's most "characteristic cry," the Biblical words, "Lord, I believe, help Thou my unbelief." He closed with a prayer.

Through it all, Dreiser lay in his coffin with what Helen called an "indescribable expression of peace" on his strong countenance. Possibly the tranquillity was cosmetic, a tribute to the embalmer's art, begging the more important question: Had he, before the end, found the answers? Had a truce been achieved among the warring elements within him, those eager, contending desires for love, wealth, power, equity, beauty, God? In his last years he had sought to escape the lonely torment of selfhood and immerse himself in a larger whole, to find some unified-field theory of science and religion that would redeem the pain of life. He searched for a constancy of love from outside himself that would assuage the chilling loneliness of the ego in a bleak universe.

But this faith of his last years — if indeed he had found it to his satisfaction — was grafted on earlier, deeper roots: the belief in a universe governed by chaos, life preying on life. That faith he could never have entirely renounced, because it had been formed and fed by his observations of life, the sensory data of experience, and the "laws" of science as revealed by Darwin and Spencer.

But always he retained that tantalizing conception of an Unknowable behind the veil of appearance. As a child at Communion, hearing that the Spirit was in the bread and wine, he had cried "Give me God!" It was a hunger that was never appeased; in the end, like other desires of the flesh, it wearily surrendered itself to a philosophical monogamy, a metaphysical fidelity, to a single Creator.

The sea is ever dancing or raging, he had written in the epilogue of *The Titan*. At best a temporary balance is struck between belief and unbelief; and in the end, Equation Inevitable, a final balance, the cessation of all striving. "Nirvana! Nirvana! The ultimate, still, equation."

Envoy

From Baltimore Mencken did what he could for Helen, progressing from "Dear Mrs. Dreiser" to "Dear Helen," advising her on publishing affairs, and writing an introduction for the reissue of *An American Tragedy* by the World Publishing Company, which did not, however, undertake the complete set that had been Dreiser's dream. Mencken had been one of the first she notified, ending the telegram with her special grace: "He loved you." That same day, among the mail at 1524 Hollins Street was a letter Mencken sent the previous day. He had forgotten to put a stamp on it, and to his relief it was returned. It was the usual chaff, but no longer appropriate. He had closed, "I trust you are in ruddy health and good spirits. As for me, I grind away at dull tasks and hope for a club-house ticket in Heaven."

He quickly sent Helen a more suitable message: "He was lucky to have you. . . . It is hard to think of his work ended. What a man he was." And later: "Theodore's death leaves me feeling as if my whole world had blown up . . . there was a time when he was my captain in a war that will never end, and we had a swell time together. No other man had a greater influence on my youth."

Helen pulled out of the depths of her depression and devoted herself to disposing of Dreiser's literary remains, helping prepare a collection of his short stories, and writing her memoirs, *My Life with Dreiser*. Although in her refined way she suppresses many unpleasant memories, she is surprisingly candid about the love affairs that had made life with Dreiser at times hell. She dedicated the book "To the unknown women in the life of Theodore Dreiser, who devoted themselves unselfishly to the beauty of his intellect and its artistic unfoldment."

She eventually sold the house at 1015 North Kings Road and moved in with her sister Myrtle on a ranch in Oregon. Her health was not good, and in time she had a stroke, and then another one that completely incapacitated her. She lay in a special large crib, plump and rouged like a large doll, living out her days. She died in 1957.

• • •

At his death, Dreiser's estate was valued in excess of $100,000, not counting the gold coins stuffed in a strongbox, which the government allowed Helen to redeem. *The Bulwark* sold well, earning over $40,000 in royalties.

When the novel appeared, most reviewers took the occasion to sum up Dreiser's career, and most acclaimed him as a major force in American letters. The novel itself received mixed notices, with much speculation on whether the old materialist had embraced religion at the end. *The Stoic*, published the following year, had been completed by Helen from his notes; the final chapter, however, consists of Dreiser's outline of what he intended to write. The essay on good and evil was dropped. The book was widely judged a tired performance, though some Dreiser loyalists felt in it faint tremors of the old power.

Neither novel was up to the great works that ensured that his name would endure: *Sister Carrie, Jennie Gerhardt, The Financier, An American Tragedy*. But neither was a meretricious performance, and *The Bulwark* surely belongs in the second rank.

He had an enormous influence on American literature during the first quarter of the century—and for a time he *was* American literature, the only writer worth talking about in the same breath with the European masters. Out of his passions, contradictions, and sufferings, he wrenched the art that was his salvation from the hungers and depressions that racked him. It was no wonder that he elevated the creative principle to a godhead and encouraged by word and example truthful expression in others. If there was one central, unifying theme of his contradiction-riddled life, it was that he was totally subsumed in the role of author. Like many novelists, he was a congeries of different selves, from Hurstwood and Carrie to Cowperwood and Clyde. Moreover, he saw himself and all human beings as characters in the great, shapeless novel of life manipulated by the Author/Creator behind the veil.

He was the most "American" of novelists. His hungry curiosity probed the nooks and crannies of the national life, as he sought to perform what he saw as his mission—understanding a large, youthful, dynamic country that had no deep roots in the past and that was in a perpetual state of change and becoming. He retained a deep compassion for the voiceless mass of individuals in this land; their tawdry dreams and desires had for him the beauty of prayers.

His journey ended, ironically, in Hollywood, a factory town of dreams, beneath the expensive soil of Forest Lawn. He had frequently written of the lure of illusion and how it betrays the seeker. But art and beauty and love were themselves illusions. Or were they? In the end, he discovered, perhaps, that they were part of the greater Reality.

Acknowledgments

I wish to express my gratitude to Victor Navasky, Hamilton Fish, and Arthur L. Carter, editor and publishers of *The Nation*, for allowing me time off from my editorial duties to work on this book. Thanks also to my capable replacements, Zachary Sklar, Kirkpatrick Sale, Elsa Dixler, and Richard Pollak, and to my other colleagues at the magazine who filled in for me at various times. Helping in another way were the researchers — Sheila Dillon, Dana Seligman, Amy Singer, Vania Del Borgo, and Ken Silverstein — who saved me long stints at the library by unearthing various hard-to-find articles and publications. Thanks also to Lynn Nesbit, my agent; to Phyllis Grann of G. P. Putnam's Sons; to my editor, Faith Sale, for putting up with a dilatory author; to her assistants, Ben McCormick and Gregory Rodriguez, for helping assemble the manuscript; and to Fred Sawyer for skillful copyediting. Finally, my respects to Shirley Sulat and Denise Auclair, who typed various drafts of the manuscript.

I must also express my deep gratitude to the people who related their recollections of Dreiser, shared with me their research, permitted me to quote from letters, or aided me in other ways. To list them alphabetically: Sam Abbott, Cedric Belfrage, Alfred P. Bingham, Craig Brandon, "Sylvia Bradshaw," Margaret Carson, Dr. Francis X. Claps, Beatrice Cole, Harold Dies, Vera Dreiser, Yvette Eastman, Robert H. Elias, Clifton Fadiman, Vincent Fitzpatrick, Franklin Folsom, Shari Handlin, Hilary Harris, Harriet B. Hubbard, Clara C. Jaeger, Ernest Kroll, Herman Liveright, Hazel L. Mack, Ellen C. Masters, Ken McCormick, Esther McCoy, Thomas P. Riggio, Mrs. Dwight Robinson, Felicia Van Veen, and James L. W. West III.

Gary Giddins kindly lent me copies of financial records and correspondence belonging to Arthur Pell. Michelle Galen, then of the Nation Institute, filed numerous Freedom of Information Act requests in my behalf.

I am fortunate in having the works of previous biographers as a solid foundation: Dorothy Dudley's *Dreiser and the Land of the Free* (1932), while as much cultural study and sounding board for her own ideas as biography, does provide useful interviews with the subject as well as his contemporaries, as does Robert H. Elias's *Theodore Dreiser: Apostle of Nature,* which came out in 1949. Elias published an emended version containing an invaluable survey of the state of Dreiser knowledge as of 1970. W. A. Swanberg's *Dreiser* (1965) draws copiously on interviews with contemporaries, many of whom are gone.

Certainly, there has been no shortage of full-length critical studies of Dreiser, beginning with H. L. Mencken's in one of his *Prefaces*, and Burton Rascoe's slender volume written in the 1920s, both of which effectively defended Dreiser against his critics before he had written the novel that certified his greatness, *An American Tragedy*; and on through essays and books by such effective champions as Alfred Kazin, Irving Howe, Van Wyck Brooks, Charles Shapiro, Maxwell Geismar, F. O. Matthiessen, John J. McAleer, Philip Gerber, Ellen Moers, Richard Lehan, Yoshinobu Hakutani, Donald Pizer, Robert Penn Warren, and Lawrence E. Hussman, to name some of the most prominent.

Also helpful were Robert Elias's three-volume edition of Dreiser's letters; Donald Pizer's book of heretofore uncollected or unpublished Dreiser prose, as well as his researches into the writing of various Dreiser works; Richard Lehan and the late Ellen Moers's investigations of the sources of various Dreiser texts; Richard W. Dowell's editing of *The Dreiser Newsletter*, which published a good deal of new material, and his researches in conjunction with the University of Pennsylvania edition of *An Amateur Laborer*. Mention should also be made of James L. W. West III, who has demonstrated the importance of the bibliographer's craft to biography; Thomas P. Riggio, who has contributed fresh facts and interpretations in his introductions to the indispensable Dreiser diaries and the Dreiser-Mencken letters, which he edited; Larzer Ziff, whose study *The American 1890s* is a model of literary history; T. D. Nostwich, who generously shared with me his cache of Dreiser's journalism (which has been published in *Theodore Dreiser: Journalism, Vol. 1, Newspaper Writings, 1892–1895*); Yoshinobu Hakutani, for *Selected Magazine Articles of Theodore Dreiser* (the first of a two-volume set); and Jack Salzman, whose *Theodore Dreiser: The Critical Reception* relieved me of the burden of locating the reviews of Dreiser's books in newspapers and magazines. *Dreiser Studies*, edited by Frederick E. Rusch, and *The Dreiser Society Newsletter*, edited by Nancy Warner Barrineau, continue to provide the latest in Dreiser scholarship. None of these authorities, of course, is responsible for any errors in this book.

I must also express my gratitude to Donald T. Oakes, who has let me draw upon his inquiry into the life of Arthur Henry. And to Gupton and Grace Vogt, my thanks for helping me locate information on Sara White Dreiser. Gupton Vogt also generously and properly opened up to scholars the courtship letters from Dreiser to Jug, and he introduced me to Louise Graham, who shared with me her memories of her Aunt Jug, as did Mrs. Graham's daughter Mary Lou Ahmann.

I must express my deep gratitude to Vera Dreiser, who tirelessly answered my questions about her Uncle Theodore, about whom she wrote a valuable and insightful book that brings to bear her firsthand knowledge of family history and her training as a psychologist; and to her daughter, Tedi, who with her husband, Joel Godard, has provided warm hospitality, including, on one memorable evening, an impromptu living-room concert of several Paul Dresser ballads.

Finally, my list of credits would not be complete without mention of the various librarians who eased my path through various thickets of Dreiserana. Preeminent among these is Neda M. Westlake, a familiar name in this section of books on Dreiser. Until her retirement in 1984, she served as curator of special collections at the Van Pelt Library, University of Pennsylvania, where the Dreiser Collection resides. The staffs of the libraries holding papers relevant to Dreiser were unfailingly cooperative. First and foremost, my gratitude to Daniel Traister, Kathleen Reed, and Nancy Shawcross at the Dreiser Collection, University of Pennsylvania. Thanks also to Neil Jordahl, Vincent Fitzpatrick, and Avril Kadis at Enoch Pratt Free Library, Baltimore, where the H.L. Mencken Collection resides; to Cathy Henderson at the Harry Ransom Humanities Research Center, University of Texas at Austin; and to Saundra Taylor at the Lilly Library, Indiana University. Other libraries that provided access to Dreiser materials were: Rare Book and Manuscript Library, Columbia University; the Manuscripts and Archives Division of the New York Public Library; the Robert H. Elias Collection, Cornell University Library; Theodore Dreiser Collection (# 6220), Clifton Waller Barrett Library, Manuscripts Division, Special Collections Department, University of Virginia; the University of Rochester Library; the University Library, the University of Illinois at Urbana-Champaign; and the New York Society Library. Unless otherwise noted, all papers cited in the Chapter Notes are located at the University of Pennsylvania. Libraries are cited by the following abbreviations:

ColU—Columbia University Library, New York City
CorU—Cornell University Library, Ithaca, New York
EPFL—Enoch Pratt Free Library, Baltimore
EUL—Emory University Library, Atlanta, Georgia
EvL—Evansville Public Library, Evansville, Indiana
IHS—Indiana Historical Society, Indianapolis, Indiana
IndU—Lilly Library, Indiana University, Bloomington, Indiana
MCHS—Montgomery County Historical Society, Montgomery City, Missouri
NYPL—New York Public Library, New York City
StLML—St. Louis Mercantile Library, St. Louis, Missouri
SuL—Sullivan County Library, Sullivan, Indiana
THL—Emeline Fairbanks Library, Terre Haute, Indiana
UIll—University of Illinois at Urbana-Champaign

UP—University of Pennsylvania Library, Philadelphia, Pennsylvania

URo—University of Rochester Library, Rochester, New York

UTex—Henry Ransom Humanities Research Center, The University of
     Texas at Austin

UVa—University of Virginia Library, Charlottesville, Virginia

VCHS—Vigo County Historical Society, Terre Haute, Indiana

WaL—Warsaw Public Library, Warsaw, Indiana

For permission to quote unpublished Dreiser material, I thank the Trustees
of the University of Pennsylvania and Daniel Traister, Assistant Director of Libraries for Special Collections. Permission to publish extracts from the Mencken
letters has been granted by the Enoch Pratt Free Library in accordance with the
terms of the will of H. L. Mencken.

I am indebted to the following for the photographs used in this abridgement and the first edition:

Theodore Dreiser Collection, Department of Special Collections,
Van Pelt Library, University of Pennsylvania, for the photographs of
Theodore Dreiser, circa 1893; John Paul Dreiser; brother Paul Dresser;
Theo and Jug; and Dreiser during the writing of *Sister Carrie*.

Lilly Library, Indiana University, for the photographs of Sara Schänäb
Dreiser; Dreiser in St. Louis; Sara Osborne "Jug" White; and Dreiser
in Chicago.

Vera Dreiser for the photographs, from her private collection, of
sister Emma; and Jug as a young wife.

Donald T. Oakes for the photographs, from his private collection, of
Anna Mallon; and the House of Seven Pillars.

Cornell University Library for the photographs of Arthur Henry.

Theodore Dreiser Collection, Department of Special Collections, Van
Pelt Library, University of Pennsylvania, for the following photographs:
Dreiser, Grant Richards, and Sir Hugh Lane; Estelle Bloom Kubitz;
Helen Richardson in 1920; Dreiser in 1920; Helen in black lace dress;
Dreiser correcting typescript; Dreiser in Russia; Iroki in winter; *Jennie
Gerhardt* film still; Dreiser addressing peace conference; Dreiser and
Helen in Hollywood in the 1940s; snapshot of Marguerite Tjader Har-
ris; last photograph of Dreiser.

Alfred A. Knopf for photograph of H. L. Mencken.

Los Angeles *Herald-Examiner* for photograph of Dreiser and George
Douglas.

Emory University Library and Vera Dreiser for photograph of
Theodore and Vera Dreiser.

Clara Clark Jaeger for photograph of herself.

Notes

For frequently cited works only the author's name and short title of the book are used after the first identification. All page references with communications between Dreiser and Mencken are from Thomas P. Riggio, ed., Dreiser-Mencken Letters.

Chapter 1

"I will not say" "Dawn" (holograph), ch. I. (p. 5)

an ancient provincial town Information on Mayen and German Dreisers from Dr. Renate Schmidt-von Bardelben, "Dreiser on the European Continent," *The Dreiser Newsletter*, Fall 1971. (p. 5)

"I have never met" Henry Dreiser to TD, Dec. 23, 1900. (p. 5)

Dreiser obtained a job Robert H. Elias, *Theodore Dreiser: Apostle of Nature*, 6. Information on Paul Dreiser's early career in America obtained from the following: Pamphlet, "In the Year of 1850 in the Village of Connersville," Markle file (THL); H. W. Beckwith, *History of Vigo and Parke Countys* [sic], 142; *History of Montgomery County, Ohio*, 51, 58. (p. 6)

Sarah Mary Schänäb Information on Sarah Dreiser's background: Dr. Hale T. Schenefield, "A Personal Memoir of Theodore Dreiser. With the relations of the Dreiser, Arnold and Parks Families" (WaL); Shari Dreiser Scott to Ellen Moers, Jan. 31, 1965, EM Coll, Box 8, "Mother and Religion" (ColU); "In Memory of Rev. H. A. Snepp," St. Joseph Conference Minutes,

Sept. 4–8, 1895, Plymouth, Indiana, ibid.; Undated, unsigned letter to Helen Richardson Dreiser re Esther Ann Snepp, ibid. (p. 6)

"madly in love" *Dawn*, 4. (p. 6)

moved to Terre Haute Edwin Ellis (George's son) to TD, Feb. 6, 1906: "I have known Paul [Jr.] since his birth. His father came with my father from Ohio to this city. . . . " George Ellis came to Terre Haute in 1853, as mentioned. Actually there were two Ellis mills; Terre Haute histories variously refer to the Riverside Mill, which seems to have been George's and which ran continuously until his death, and the Wabash Mill, which Edwin seems to have managed or owned. Paul Dreiser, Sr., worked in both places. (p. 6)

three children Photostat in EM Coll from "Dreiser Family Bible" says that the children, James, George and Havrey [?] died in Terre Haute in 1854 and 1855. In *Dawn*, 5, TD writes that the children were "all boys and all taken within three years." (p. 6)

In 1857 Sarah John Paul Dreiser, Jr. (Paul Dresser) was born on April 22, 1858. A. R. Markle, "Some Light on Paul Dresser; His Anniversary Is This Month," Terre Haute *Sunday Tribune*, April 14, 1941, Markle file (THL). (p. 6)

Jewetts' venture Dr. Maple's Scrapbook, 13, 15 (SuL). (p. 7)

"ruined the business" Mary Frances Brennan ("Mame," TD's sister) to A. R. Markle, Jan. 12, 1941, Markle file (THL). (p. 7)

kindly and intelligent TD, "Sarah Schanab," MS, Box 92A (UP). (p. 7)

"the large family" Rachael Harris, "Personal Recollection of the Dresser [sic] Family," Sullivan *Daily Times*, June 14, 1937. (p. 7)

"one of the best" Quoted in Thomas P. Riggio, "The Dreisers in Sullivan: A Biographical Revision," *The Dreiser Newsletter*, Fall 1979. (p. 7)

"withdrawing from the firm" Sullivan County *Democrat*, April 15, 1869. (p. 7)

"Yankee treachery" Brennan to Markle, Jan 12, 1941. (p. 7)

"wool manufacturer" Census Roll, enumerated Aug. 30, 1870 (SuL). (p. 7)

a storm Riggio, "Dreisers in Sullivan"; Richard W. Dowell, "Ask Mr. Markle?" *The Dreiser Newsletter*, Spring 1977. (p. 7)

Deed records Dowell, "Ask Mr. Markle?" (pp. 7–8)

"laborer" Markle file (THL). (p. 8)

TD's birth date Baptismal record, Church of St. Benedict, Sept. 10, 1871. Markle to Robert H. Elias (CorU). Record also in Markle file (THL). (p. 8)

Chapter 2

"All this industry" H. W. Beckwith, *History of Vigo and Parke Countys* [sic], 482. (p. 9)

"that sacred little spot" Quoted in Nick Salvatore, *Eugene V. Debs: Citizen and Socialist*, 3, 21, 22. (p. 9)

Dreiser children The names appear in family records various ways, but Dreiser gives the original German versions in the holograph MS of "Dawn." (p. 10)

"puny beyond belief" *Dawn*, 7. (p. 10)

"I was always" Ibid., 19. (p. 10)

"velvety hand" "Sarah Schanab" (UP). (p. 10)

"My Mother was" Mary Frances Brennan to A. R. Markle, Jan 13, 1941. (p. 10)

so wrought up Vera Dreiser, *My Uncle Theodore*, 33. (p. 10)

"Oh years later" *Dawn*, 17. (p. 10)

"Long after I had" "Dawn" (typescript), ch. XXVI, 236. (p. 10)

"Aren't you sorry" *Dawn*, 19. (p. 11)

"Are you going," "Work yes" "Dawn" (holograph), ch. I. (p. 11)

"the little wise-looking" Carmel O'Neill Haley, "The Dreisers," *The Commonweal*, July 7, 1933. (p. 11)

"Give me God!" Ibid. (p. 12)

Chapter 3

"At the same time" *A Hoosier Holiday*, 390, 391. (p. 13)

"laborer," "spinner," etc. "Dreiser Notes," Markle file (THL). (p. 13)

"a great business" C. C. Oakey, *Greater Terre Haute and Vigo Countys*, 368. (p. 13)

"he could still have," "by now he" "Dawn" (typescript), ch. XV, 8. (p. 13)

"long, dreary" *Dawn*, 23. (p. 14)

"to devote his" Mary Frances Brennan, "My Brother Paul," with MFB to TD, July 5, 1906. Box 190. (p. 14)

leading to the study Catherine C. Etienne, registrar, St. Meinrad Seminary to author, June 9, 1982. The school had no record of Paul's attendance between 1873 and 1878; records prior to that time were destroyed by fire. Probably he attended the school when he was around twelve, ca. 1870. (p. 14)

Paul, Jr., lasted The account of Paul's peregrinations is drawn from "Paul Dresser" by Max Ehrmann, a pamphlet in the Markle Coll (THL); the Reverend F. Joseph Mutch, letter to *The Commonweal*, Aug 18, 1933; Indianapolis *Journal*, Sept. 25, 1899, clipping in PD Scrapbook, Box 392 (UP). (p. 14)

"vainglory, indifference" Quoted in Ellen Moers, *Two Dreisers*, 220. (p. 14)

"You have the damndest" "Dawn" (typescript), 3. (p. 15)

"wornout clothes" *Dawn*, 349. (p. 15)

" 'I don't know' " Quoted in *Dawn*, 69. (p. 15)

"They fought over" "Dawn" (typescript), ch. III, 28. (p. 16)

"It was during" Ibid., Ch. V, 30. (p. 16)

"Now we are about" Quoted, Vera Dreiser, in *My Uncle Theodore*, 35. (p. 17)

Chapter 4

"Perhaps you will" *Dawn*, 75. (p. 20)

"like the sun" Ibid., 113. (p. 20)

For a time, he traveled The account of Paul's early career is drawn from clippings in the "Evansville Biography, Paul Dresser" file, Evansville Public Library; Markle file (THL); and the PD Scrapbook. (p. 20)

"You can't get" Quoted in "Proposed Memorial of Interest to Many Here," *Evansville Journal*, Oct. 15, 1922 (EvL). (p. 21)

"It looks as if" Quoted in John H. Mackey to TD, April 27, 1923. (p. 21)

"No mah deah," "MR. PAUL DRESSER" Quoted in undated clipping, Terre Haute *Daily Tribune*, PD Scrapbook. (p. 21)

"the sensational comique," New York *Dramatic Mirror*, Feb. 10, 1906, Vera Dreiser file, Box 384. (p. 21)

Chapter 5

"In 1889 Chicago" *Sister Carrie*, Pennsylvania Edition, 15. (p. 23)

"[Theodore] would do" Edward Dreiser, "My Brother Theodore," *Book Find News*, March 1946. (p. 24)

guttural "Dawn" (typescript), ch. VI, 39. (p. 24)

"Hear me, Lyman Treadwell" Quoted in Mark Sullivan, *Our Times: The Turn of the Century*, 210. (p. 25)

records show ... rented to Paul "Proposed Memorial of Interest to Many Here," Evansville *Journal*, Oct. 15, 1922 (EvL). (p. 25)

In the two decades Statistics from James DeMuth, *Small Town Chicago*, 6. (p. 26)

"It is the only" Henry B. Fuller, *With the Procession*, 203. (p. 27)

The neighborhood the Dreisers lived in Richard Sennett, *Families Against the City* (a sociological study of the Union Park section from 1872 to 1890), 44–59. (p. 27)

"were selling themselves" "Dawn" (holograph), ch. XXI; *Dawn*, 173. (p. 28)

Chapter 6

"From contemplating" *A Hoosier Holiday*, 113. (p. 29)

The population then was Description: author's visit. Historical details: George A. Nye, *Warsaw in 1885 and 1886*, unpublished MS (WaL). *Biographical and Historical Record of Kosciusko County, Indiana*. (p. 29)

Augusta Phillipson et al. "Dawn" (holograph), ch. XXXIII. (p. 30)

"some phase of" *Dawn*, 198. (p. 30)

"money, daring" Ibid., 250. (p. 31)

"as soft and pleasing" *Dawn*, 271. (p. 32)

"Shameless creatures," "You are too rough" Ibid., 229, 231. (p. 32)

"scandal hung" "Dawn" (holograph), ch. XXXVI. (p. 32)

"A WOMAN IN THE CASE" Chicago *Mail*, Feb. 17, 1886. Quoted in Donald Pizer, ed., *Sister Carrie*, Norton Critical Edition, 375 ff. (p. 33)

"I was more" "Dawn" (holograph), ch. XLI. (p. 34)

"We knew Dreiser" Quoted in Dorothy Dudley, *Dreiser and the Land of the Free*, 53. I have been unable to locate this quotation, described by Dudley as being from a review of *A Hoosier Holiday* in *Winder's Travel Magazine* (which existed). (p. 34)

"Ma, I'm going" *Dawn*, 194. (p. 35)

Chapter 7

"Ah the horror" "Dawn" (holograph), Ch. LIX. (p. 36)

"a shadowy self-effacing" Ibid., Ch. XXX. (p. 37)

"sissy sons" *Dawn*, 330. (p. 37)

"The shadows" Ibid., 332. (p. 38)

"inured to a lean," "morbidity that" "Dawn" (holograph), ch. IX. (p. 38)

"shambling man" *Dawn*, 342. (p. 38)

"My gott" Ibid., 343. (p. 38)

"Mind and mind" Ibid., 344. (p. 38)

"buzzing dreams" "Dawn" (holograph), ch. LXXXI. (p. 39)

She would pay his In a letter to Richard Duffy, Nov. 18, 1901, Dreiser says that he paid half his tuition, but one wonders how he could have saved the money. His pride was speaking. (p. 39)

Chapter 8

"I attended the state" TD to Richard Duffy, Nov. 18, 1901. (p. 40)

"charming place" Ibid. (p. 40)

He did not get off TD's record at I.U. in Joseph Katz, "Theodore Dreiser at Indiana University," *Notes and Queries*, March 1966. (p. 40)

"I never learned" *A Hoosier Holiday*, 484. (p. 40)

He joined Philomathean Katz, "Theodore Dreiser." (p. 41)

"Never in my life" *Dawn*, 398, 399. (p. 41)

"several years" TD to RD, Nov. 18. (p. 42)

"You know," "Oh, ma," "You think" *Dawn*, 509. (p. 43)

"Well, that's" Ibid., 513. (p. 43)

Chapter 9

"Well might I" "Dawn" (holograph), ch. LIX. (p. 44)

"Theodore Dreiser, through" Quoted in Joseph Katz, "Theodore Dreiser at Indiana University," *Notes and Queries*, March 1966. (p. 45)

"The palls of heavy" *Newspaper Days*, 19. (p. 46)

" 'Theodore' he said" *Dawn*, 583. (p. 47)

"I done the best" *Newspaper Days*, 31. (p. 48)

Chapter 10

"We are dealing" "Newspaper Days" (holograph), ch. III. (p. 51)

"Why did you pick" *Newspaper Days*, 39. (p. 52)

"CLEVELAND AND GRAY THE TICKET" Chicago *Globe*, June 21, 1892. (p. 53)

"Cut the gentle con" *Newspaper Days*, 59. (p. 53)

"From surrounding basements" *Globe*, July 24, 1892. (p. 54)

"Maybe you're cut out" *Newspaper Days*, 67. (p. 54)

"A cheap coffin" *Globe*, Sept. 11, 1892. (p. 54)

"whose younger years," "glory and an," "In thine own," "Achieve thine own" *Globe*, Oct. 23, 1892. Donald Pizer, ed., *Theodore Dreiser: A Selection of Uncollected Prose*, 33. (p. 55)

"Dorse, I think" "Dawn" (holograph), ch. LXXI. (p. 55)

"though I ejaculated" "Newspaper Days" (holograph), ch. IV. (p. 55)

"buzzing dreams" Ibid. (p. 56)

"You don't care" *Newspaper Days*, 86. (p. 56)

Chapter 11

"I went into" TD to Mencken, May 13, 1916. In Robert H. Elias, *Letters of Theodore Dreiser*, I, 211. (p. 57)

"ambitious" TD to Emma Rector, March 1, 1894 (IU). Richard W. Dowell, "You Will Not Like Me, I'm Sure," *American Literary Realism*, Summer 1970. (p. 57)

"intensely uxorious," "feminine ministrations" "A Book About Myself," Part II, holograph MS, ch. XXIV. (p. 58)

"flushed like a" "Newspaper Days" (holograph), ch. XII. (p. 58)

Reedy had been a See Max Putzel, *The Man in the Mirror: William Marion Reedy and His Magazine*; Clarence E. Miller, "William Marion Reedy: A Patchwork Portrait," *Bulletin of the Missouri Historical Society*, Oct. 1960. (p. 60)

Office rumor had it Miller, "William Marion Reedy." (p. 60)

"a splendid writer," "Though you sent him" Quoted in Henry Burke, *From the Day's Journey*, 167. (p. 61)

"Olney Wade" "Dreiser Clipping File," microfilm, reel I, folder 9 (UP). (p. 61)

"Worldly experience," "When you look" TD to Rector, March 1, 1894. (p. 61)

"Many forms," "Someone will," St. Louis *Globe-Democrat*, Jan. 22, 1893. (pp. 62–63)

"the skin of the victim's hand" *Globe-Democrat*, Jan. 22, 1893. (p. 63)

"BURNED TO DEATH" Ibid. And see also "SIXTEEN DEAD," January 23, 1893. (p. 63)

"You called for me" *Newspaper Days*, 167, 168. (p. 63)

Chapter 12

"I went to" TD to Sara Osborne White, June 30, 1898. (p. 65)

"a world of unreality" *Newspaper Days*, 179. (p. 65)

"Those who are" Quoted in Robert H. Elias, *Theodore Dreiser: Apostle of Nature*, 54. (p. 65)

"brings back visions" "The Black Diva's Concert," St. Louis *Globe-Democrat*, April 1, 1893. (p. 65)

"the colored lady," "fervid tribute" St. Louis *Chronicle*, April 1, 1893. This and subsequent stories located by T. D. Nostwich. (p. 65)

"The African temperament" St. Louis *Republic*, April 2, 1893. (p. 66)

"he is even better" *Globe-Democrat*, "The Theaters," May 1, 1893. (p. 66)

"dallied with the 'black bottle,' " "so carelessly" "John L. Out for a Lark," *Globe-Democrat*, Feb. 28, 1893. (p. 66)

"McCullagh is becoming" *Chronicle*, May 1, 1893. (p. 66)

"Remember Zola and Balzac" *Newspaper Days*, 211. (p. 67)

"brute," "demon," "THIS CALLS FOR HEMP" *Republic*, January 17, 1894. Quoted in T. D. Nostwich, "The Source of Dreiser's 'Nigger Jeff,' " *Resources for American Literary Study*, Fall 1978. (p. 67)

"distorted," "wailing more like," "with a swish," "Through the broken," "came to his death," "TEN-FOOT DROP" *Republic*,

Jan. 18, 1894. Quoted in Notswich, "Nigger Jeff." (pp. 67–68)

"Mr. Joy said" *Republic*, June 20, 1893. (p. 68)

"Mere humor, such as" *Newspaper Days*, 415. (p. 68)

"the best dressed" Quoted in Harry Burke, *From the Day's Journey*, 168. (p. 68)

"a genius for overdressing" Quoted in Burke, *Journey*. (p. 68)

"parvenu" "Dawn" (holograph), ch. XLVI. (p. 68)

"an intense something" *Newspaper Days*, 242. (p. 69)

Sara's hair color and other information on Sallie White: Interview with Mrs. Louise Graham (niece), St. Charles, Missouri, Nov. 1985.

"One can understand" Quoted in Guy Szuberla, "Dreiser at the World's Fair: The City Without Limits," *Modern Fiction Studies*, Autumn 1977. (p. 69)

"a massive," "in droves," "They made one" Quoted in Szuberla, "World's Fair." (p. 70)

"who sweat" Quoted in Larzer Ziff, *The American 1890s*, 104. (p. 70)

"New York's the place" TD to Rector, Dec. 13, 1893. In Richard W. Dowell, "You Will Not Like Me, I'm Sure," *American Literary Realism*, Summer 1970. (p. 71)

Chapter 13

"I was more" "Newspaper Days" (holograph), ch. L. (p. 72)

"all the surging" *Newspaper Days*, 319. (p. 72)

he personally shepherded Arthur Henry to Dorothy Dudley, quoted in *Dreiser and the Land of the Free*, 104. (p. 73)

sympathies were with the workers "The Strike To-Day," Toledo *Blade*, March 24, 1894. In Donald Pizer, ed., *Sister Carrie*, Norton Critical Edition, 416–423. (p. 73)

posed as a union man, Pizer, 423. (p. 73)

Henry's wife, Maude MWH to RHE, April 12, 1945 (CorU), Donald T. Oakes, unpublished MS, Afterword, II. See also Helen

Dreiser to RHE, Feb. 19, 1945: "Mr. Dreiser . . . does not think he wrote most of the strike articles" (CorU). (p. 73)

"If he had been" *Newspaper Days*, 373. (p. 73)

Chapter 14

"Just about then" "Now Comes Author Theodore Dreiser Who Tells of 100,000 Jennie Gerhardts," Cleveland *Leader*, Nov. 12, 1911. In Donald Pizer, ed., *Theodore Dreiser: A Selection of Uncollected Prose*, 186. (p. 74)

"They were talking" Quoted in Jeremy Brecher, *Strike!*, 73. (p. 74)

"Higher up the tenement" Quoted in Joseph Frazier Wall, *Andrew Carnegie*, 580, 581. (p. 75)

"I'd rather have" *Newspaper Days*, 406. (p. 75)

"the general unrest" "Reed Just as He Stands," Pittsburgh *Dispatch*, April 28, 1894. (p. 75)

"After working twelve hours" Quoted in Wall, *Carnegie*, 580. (p. 76)

"a suicide by" "The Last Fly of Fly Time," *Dispatch*, Oct. 3, 1894. (p. 76)

"Hospital Violet Day" *Dispatch*, May 12, 1894. (p. 76)

"stowed away with heartaches" "And It Was Mighty Blue," *Dispatch*, May 15, 1894. (pp. 76–77)

Chapter 15

"New York . . . had" *Newspaper Days*, 452. (p. 78)

"a man of some" *History of St. Charles, Montgomery and Warren Counties, Missouri*, 707. (p. 78)

"aristocrats" Interview with Billy Joe Auchly, Montgomery City, Missouri, Nov. 1985. (p. 78)

"a very successful and good" "Life and Influence of Danville and Danville Township," undated clipping, Montgomery County Historical Society, Montgomery City, Missouri. (p. 78)

He carried her to her room "Newspaper Days" (holograph), ch. LXVIII. (p. 79)

TD's walk up Broadway Taken from *Newspaper Days*, 439, 447, and Stephen Jenkins, *The Greatest Street in the World*. (p. 81)

"Sometime you ought to" *Newspaper Days*, 449. (p. 81)

"I have never lived" "Newspaper Days" (holograph), ch. LXII. (p. 82)

Chapter 16

"To understand" Herbert Spencer, *First Principles*, 19, 39, TD's Library (UP). (p. 83)

"in the furnace stage" *Newspaper Days*, 375. (p. 83)

"an ambitious young man" TD to SOW, Aug. 14, 1896. (p. 83)

"quite blew me" *Newspaper Days*, 457. (p. 84)

"his conclusions never" Quoted in William Irvine, *Apes, Angels and Victorians*, 109. (p. 84)

"I remember that" Quoted in Richard Hofstader, *Social Darwinism in American Thought*, 45. (p. 84)

"Personal ends must be" Quoted in James G. Kennedy, *Herbert Spencer*, 69. (p. 85)

"At the approach" "Reflections," *Ev'ry Month*, Feb. 1897. In Donald Pizer, ed., *Theodore Dreiser: A Selection of Uncollected Prose*, 107. (p. 85)

"the Alexander" "Literary Notes," *Ev'ry Month*, May 1896. Ibid., 59. (p. 85)

Chapter 17

"Some transition is needed" Honoré de Balzac, *Lost Illusions*, 161. (p. 87)

"the idea of Hurstwood was born" *Newspaper Days*, 464. In the MS, TD adds the qualifier "if ever." (p. 88)

"This young man" Ibid., 466. (p. 88)

"How to Improve" "Better Tenements Wanted," New York *World*, Dec. 13, 1894. (p. 88)

Dreiser seems not to See Allen Churchill, *Park Row,* 55, and Isaac Marcosson, *David Graham Phillips and His Times,* 177. (p. 88)

"Terseness" Quoted in Churchill, *Park Row,* 39. (p. 89)

"a dropsical eagle" Ibid., 227. (p. 89)

"What was the trouble?" *Newspaper Days,* 488, 489. (p. 89)

"waiting for something" "Newspaper Days" (holograph), ch. LXXXI. (p. 90)

"He had turned fifty," "suffering from the same" Ibid., ch. LXV, 62. I used photocopies of this part of holograph MS in Moers Coll, "Two Dreisers," folder 10 (ColU). (p. 90)

By another account Vera Dreiser, *My Uncle Theodore,* 96. (p. 90)

Chapter 18

"DID HE BLOW OUT" New York *World,* Feb. 16, 1895. There is no evidence that Dreiser wrote this story. (p. 92)

"Old stuff!" "Three Contacts." (p. 92)

"I'm not to be" Ibid. (p. 93)

"felt his liver" Stephen Crane, "An Experiment in Misery," New York *Press,* April 22, 1894. In R. W. Stallman and E. R. Hagemann, eds., *The New York City Sketches of Stephen Crane,* 37. (p. 93)

"the vilest part" Quoted in Ellen Moers, *Two Dreisers,* 24. Moers provides an illuminating discussion of "Bowery journalism." (p. 93)

"emblematic of a nation" Crane, in *New York City Sketches,* 43. (p. 94)

"In adversity his father" Dorothy Dudley, *Theodore Dreiser and the Land of the Free,* 135. (p. 94)

"Life was desolate" Ibid., 134, 135. (p. 94)

One bitter cold night Clara L. Jaeger, unpublished MS, 42–44; CLJ to author, Oct. 26, 1984. In the early 1930s, when Mrs. Jaeger worked for TD as a secretary, he told her of his life on the Bowery and thoughts of suicide. He also claimed that he seriously contemplated ending it all in the East River in 1903, while he was down and out in Brooklyn, only to be saved by a chance intervention. The latter story is suspect, since he gave at least two versions of it, yet did not mention it in his most complete account of that period, *An Amateur Laborer.* The story TD told Mrs. Jaeger includes some plausible details, and I am inclined to believe there is some truth in it, that he was at least considering suicide at this time. (pp. 94–95)

Chapter 19

"It becomes not only" "Reflections," *Ev'ry Month,* Sept. 1896. (p. 96)

"While the 'ginnie' " Quoted in Mark Sullivan, *Our Times: The Turn of the Century,* 254. (p. 96)

"Thee I wish you" Emma Dreiser Hopkins to TD, ca. 1896. (p. 97)

He was also Pseudonyms listed in Joseph Katz, "Theodore Dreiser's *Ev'ry Month,*" *Library Chronicle,* Winter 1972. (p. 98)

her name would be TD to SOW, Oct. 18, 1896 (IndU). He addressed her in letters sometimes as "S. Jug White," and occasionally used "Sally Joy White" as a pseudonym. In a letter to her dated Sept. 11, 1896, answering her complaint about the use of SOW, he explains, "I intend to use SOW to indicate less familiarity." (p. 99)

"All of the literary" TD to SOW, July 10, 1896 (IndU). (p. 99)

"Like Dinah's meals" Ibid. (p. 99)

dropped a total of fifty thousand dollars Fred Haviland told Edward Marks. Marks, with A. J. Liebling, *They All Sang,* 122. (p. 99)

"firmly grounded in" TD to SOW, Nov. 4, 1896 (IndU). (p. 99)

"We are born" "Reflections," *Ev'ry Month,* Aug. 1896. In Donald Pizer, ed., *Theodore Dreiser: A Selection of Uncollected Prose,* 85. (p. 99)

"This is the law" "Reflections," June 1896. Ibid., 62. (p. 99)

"the man is wrong" "Reflections," *Ev'ry Month,* Feb. 1897, Moers Coll (ColU). (p. 100) "money changers" Ibid. (p. 100)

"[Do] you think" Ibid. (p. 100)

"I am practically alone" TD to SOW, Dec. 1, 1896 (IndU). (p. 100)

"I know I am" TD to SOW, Oct. 18, 1896. (p. 100)

"nothing but my ticket" Arthur Henry, *Lodgings in Town*, 23. (p. 100)

"And you?" Ibid., 82, 83. (p. 101)

"a lover of impossible" "Rona Murtha." In *A Gallery of Women*, II, 567. (p. 101)

"got it through" Quoted in Dorothy Dudley, *Dreiser and the Land of the Free*, 142. (p. 101)

Chapter 20

"While cynics might" PD to Mary South, Nov. 5, 1897 (IndU). (p. 102)

"hereafter devote his time" Undated clipping, Dresser Manuscripts (IndU). (p. 102)

Each song sold The standard composer's royalty was 4 to 8 cents a copy. A clipping in the Paul Dresser Scrapbook, "Popular Songs and their Writers," by Caroll Fleming, reports that "The Wabash" netted Paul $20,000 on 500,000, and "Just Tell Them That You Saw Me," $16,000 on 400,000. Paul told one writer that "The Wabash" sold 750,000, and another that he made $30,000 on the song. As a partner in the firm, he may have been credited with a higher royalty than the normal songwriter. (p. 102)

In a letter TD to SOW, May 18, 1896 (IndU). (p. 102)

As D recounts it "My Brother Paul" In *Twelve Men*, 76–101. (p. 103)

"Round my Indiana home" "On the Banks of the Wabash, Far Away," words and music by Paul Dresser. *The Songs of Paul Dresser*, 72. (p. 103)

"the words of" "The Birth and Growth of a Popular Song," *Metropolitan*, Nov. 1898. (p. 103)

"Yes, dearie" TD to SOW, May 15, 1898 (IndU). To assuage Jug's apparent jealousy, TD adds that the second verse about Mary was not his idea, and that he knows no girls of that name. (p. 103)

Ed Dreiser told Vera Dreiser, *My Uncle Theodore*, 75, 78. (pp. 103–104)

remembered being summoned Isadore Witmark and Isaac Goldberg, *From Ragtime to Swingtime*, 170, 171. (p. 104)

"Oh, the moonlight's" *Songs of Paul Dresser*, 72. (p. 104)

received an ovation " 'On the Banks of the Wabash': A Musical Whodunit," *Indiana Magazine of History*, June 1970. (p. 104)

"The 'Wabash' is going" PD to MS, Sept. 6, 1897 (IndU). (p. 104)

"The 'Wabash' is still" PD to MS, Aug. 11, 1898 (IndU). (p. 104)

"loves all women" TD to SOW, March 24, 1897 (IndU). (p. 105)

This practice so disgusted Vera Dreiser, *My Uncle*, 74. (p. 105)

Chapter 21

"I had made" Unpublished MS. Quoted in Donald Pizer, *Theodore Dreiser: A Selection of Uncollected Prose*, 273, 274. (p. 106)

For a time Theodore He mentions the *Cosmopolitan* connection in his entry in the 1900–1901 *Who's Who*. Richard Duffy to TD, Jan. 30, 1899. *Ainslee's* to TD, Sept. 22, 1899. (p. 106)

"By the way" Quoted in W. A. Swanberg, *Dreiser*, 91. (p. 107)

"It is the first dollar" "A Monarch of Metal Workers," *Success*, June 3, 1899. Reprinted, unsigned, in O. S. Marden, ed., *Little Visits with Great Workers*, 51. (Many issues of *Success* are not available at NYPL, so I have drawn from *Little Visits*.) (p. 107)

"No more significant" Quoted in Robert H. Elias, *Theodore Dreiser: Apostle of Nature*, 99. (p. 107)

"a snow storm" Ibid. (p. 107)

"I wish to discover" "A Talk with America's Leading Lawyer," *Success*, Jan. 1898. In Pizer, *Uncollected Prose*, 119. (p. 108)

"money," "I never met," "This remark," "If equally" Ibid., 120, 122. (p. 108) "nature had made me" TD to SOW, Aug. 14, 1896 (IndU). (p. 108)

"The modern young man" Marden, *Little Visits*, 435. (p. 108)

"all success is not" "Fame Found in Quiet Nooks," *Success*, Sept. 1898. In Yoshinobu Hakutani, ed., *Selected Magazine Articles of Theodore Dreiser*, 50. (p. 109)

"You should make your" Quoted in Myrta Lockett Avary, "Success—and Dreiser," *The Colophon*, Autumn 1938. (p. 109)

Chapter 22

"Man's ingenuity finds" "Scenes in a Cartridge Factory," *Cosmopolitan*, July 1898. (p. 110)

"standing and ability" TD to SOW, Feb. 23, 1898 (IndU). (p. 110)

he had sent her a ring "I mailed you a memento of our promises—the ring." TD to SOW, June 12, 1896. (p. 110)

"glared upon and outraged" "The Haunts of Nathaniel Hawthorne," *Truth*, Sept. 21, 1898. (p. 110)

"by purely photographic," "the clear crowning" Quoted in Ellen Moers, *Two Dreisers*, 12, 13. (p. 111)

"had the tone" "The Camera Club of New York," *Ainslee's*, Oct. 1899. (p. 111)

"We would also like" J. C. Brill to TD, April 29, 1898. (p. 111)

"matter copied bodily" H. J. Miller to *Cosmopolitan*, Aug. 3, 1898. Quoted in W. A. Swanberg, *Dreiser*, 94. (p. 111)

"oppressed" TD to Clarence S. Howell, May 17, 1910. Copy of letter in Dreiser Manuscripts II (IU). (p. 112)

"Right with naked hands" In Sidney A. Witherbee, ed., *Spanish-American War Songs*, 276, 277. The poem was also syndicated and a copy is among the miscellaneous papers in the Dreiser Manuscripts II file (IU). (p. 112)

"so swift and decisive" "The Making of Small Arms," *Ainslee's*, July 1898. (p. 112)

"Think of all," "Oh, but," "This was" TD to SOW, Sept. 16, 1898. (p. 113)

"Lord! one whose" Clipping in Dreiser Manuscripts II (IndU). (p. 113)

Chapter 23

"I lived in my" TD to SOW, Sept. 21, 1896 (IndU). (p. 114)

"little quarter of our" TD to SOW, July 10, 1896. (p. 114)

"Your little shoes" Ibid. (p. 114)

"I hate to be" TD to SOW, Aug. 28, 1898. (p. 114)

"Nature ... has given" TD to SOW, June 25, 1896. (p. 115)

"almost fainting" TD to SOW, May 1896. (p. 115)

"What a lover" TD to SOW, May 1, 1896. (p. 115)

"You abetted me" TD to SOW, Oct. 18, 1896. (p. 115)

"I want you" TD to SOW, June 30, 1898. (p. 115)

"Everything in such soft," "You have too" TD to SOW, Aug. 19, 1896. (p. 115)

"so many times" TD to SOW, Sept. 11, 1896. (p. 116)

"awful glad," "accept introductions" TD to SOW, Oct. 10, 1896. (p. 116)

"sacred modesty," "saintlike beauty" TD to SOW, June 25, 1896. (p. 116)

"divinely formed" TD to SOW, July 3, 1898. (p. 116)

"red-halo-ed Venus" TD to SOW, Jan. 24, 1898. (p. 116)

"to despoil your saintlike" TD to SOW, June 25, 1896. (p. 116)

"the imagination becomes" TD to SOW, July 29, 1898. (p. 116)

"my own girl" Ibid. (p. 116)

"seems like," "houses already furnished" TD to SOW, Feb. 1, 1898. (p. 116)

"As the hurrying engine" TD to SOW, June 20, 1898. (p. 117)

"the next forty days" TD to SOW, Aug. 15, 1898. (p. 117)

"and more I cannot" TD to SOW, March 24, 1897. (p. 117)

"when nothing shall be" TD to SOW, July 3, 1898. (p. 117)

"sighs and light laughter," "I'll have you" TD to SOW, Aug. 15, 1898. (p. 117)

"It seems as if" TD to SOW, Aug. 31, 1898. (p. 117)

"It is true that" Quoted in Vera Dreiser, *My Uncle Theodore*, 192. (p. 118)

"not a sentimental passage" Quoted in Dorothy Dudley, *Dreiser and the Land of the Free*, 143. (p. 118)

"the first flare" *Newspaper Days*, 502. (p. 118)

"Under the influence of" *Sister Carrie*, Pennsylvania Edition, 610, 611. (p. 118)

Chapter 24

"Married! Married!" "Rella." In *A Gallery of Women*, II, 103. (p. 119)

Six-room flats Description based on the flat Carrie lived in when she first moved to New York City. *Sister Carrie*, Pennsylvania Edition, 307. (p. 119)

A Christmas reunion Described in TD to SOW, Dec. 26, 1896 (IndU). (p. 119)

Death was instantaneous Paul Dresser to Mary South, Nov. 1, 1897 (IndU). (p. 120)

"Poor Theresa" Sylvia Dreiser to TD, Nov. 7, 1897. (p. 120)

Mame "talked about us" Emma Dreiser to TD, undated. (p. 120)

Carl's suicide Interview with Vera Dreiser, Dec. 15, 1982, tape (EUL). (p. 120)

"same tale of woe—wow—" Paul Dreiser to TD, undated. (p. 120)

"slow, miserable" Claire Dreiser to TD, Jan. 24, 1898. Dreiser manuscripts II (IndU). (p. 120)

"expressed a hearty," "had the book" The clipping is in Dreiser Manuscripts II (IndU). TD also mentions the interview and his "forthcoming" book of poems in a letter to Jug, July 27, 1898. See also Ellen Moers, "New Light on Dreiser in the 1890s," *Columbia Literary Columns*, May 1966. (p. 121)

plagiarism See Edward Mercur Williams, "Edmund Clarence Stedman at Home," *The New England Quarterly*, June 1952. (p. 122)

"at this late date" "Edmund Clarence Stedman at Home," *Munsey's*, March 1899. In his otherwise definitive article, Williams does not mention this admittedly vague qualification—which did not excuse TD for the literary

misdemeanor of using the precise wording of the Anna Bowman Dodd article. (p. 122)

"characteristic and best," "above the average," "it is impossible," "lacking in dramatic" Quoted in Moers, "Light on Dreiser." (p. 122)

"A critically admired" Ibid. (p. 122)

"ceaseless drag," "And this thing" *Ainslee's*, April 1899. (pp. 122–123)

"cool, damp soil" "Resignation," clipping in Dreiser Manuscripts II (IndU). (p. 123)

"It was a hot day" "McEwen of the Shining Slave Makers." In *Free and Other Stories*, 54. (p. 123)

thought it "asinine" TD to Mencken, May 13, 1916. In Robert H. Elias, *The Letters of Theodore Dreiser*, I, 212. (p. 123)

details of the story Ellen Moers, *Two Dreisers*, 144. (p. 123)

"strange passions" "McEwen." In *Free*, 75. (p. 123)

"with its stars" "Old Rogaum and His Theresa." Ibid., 207. (p. 124)

"bar of cool moonlight" "Nigger Jeff." Ibid., 110. (p. 124)

"with the cruel," "it was not so much" Ibid., 111. (p. 124)

"I'll get it" Ibid. (p. 125)

"The planner of this" "Little Essays on Great Problems: The Bubble of Success," unpublished MS (UVa). (p. 125)

a parody of the popular historical romances See Joseph P. Griffin, " 'When the Old Century Was New': An Early Dreiser Parody," *Studies in Short Fiction*, Summer 1980. (p. 125)

"the aristocracy, gentry" "When the Old Century Was New." In *Free*, 356. (p. 125)

"the crush and stress" Ibid., 369. (p. 125)

"something particularly" *Demorest's* to TD, Aug. 4, 1899. (p. 126)

Chapter 25

"Genius struggles up" "Edward Al," *Ev'ry Month*, June 1896. In Donald Pizer, *Theodore Dreiser: A Selection of Uncollected Prose*, 73. (p. 127)

"that some time ago" Arthur Henry to TD, undated. (p. 128)

"You owe me $26.19" Henry to TD, June 19, 1900. (p. 128)

"up to a," "had share" Henry, *An Island Cabin*, 193. (p. 128)

"girlish figure," "a complex combination" Henry, *Cabin*, 193. (p. 128)

"I too wish" Henry to TD, July 9, 1900. (p. 128)

"the old hats and peaked shoulders" "Curious Shifts of the Poor," *Demorest's*, Nov. 1899. In Pizer, *Uncollected Prose*, 138. See *Sister Carrie*, Pennsylvania Edition, chs. 45–47. (p. 129)

"as dumb brutes" Pizer, *Uncollected Prose*, 137, 139. (p. 129)

"young newspaper men trying" Howells, *Literature and Life*, 154. (p. 129)

Chapter 26

"She went to the city" "She Went to the City," words and music by Paul Dresser, *The Paul Dresser Songbook*, 240. Ellen Moers notes the connection between this song and *Sister Carrie* in *Two Dreisers*, 99. Since the song was written in 1904, one wonders if Paul had his brother's novel in mind. (p. 133)

"was blank" Quoted in Dorothy Dudley, *Dreiser and the Land of the Free*, 160. (p. 133)

"I took a piece" TD to Mencken, May 13, 1916, 232. In Robert H. Elias, *Letters of Theodore Dreiser*, I, 213. (p. 133)

"story backbone, showing his," "the master" Richard Duffy, "When They Were Twenty-One," *The Bookman*, Jan. 1914. (p. 134)

"venturing to reconnoitre the" *Carrie*, Pennsylvania Edition, 4. (p. 134)

popular, cautionary books Cathy N. and Arnold E. Davidson, "Carrie's Sisters: The Popular Prototypes for Dreiser's Heroine," *Modern Fiction Studies*, Autumn 1977. (p. 134)

"The gleam of a thousand lights" *Carrie*, 4. (p. 134)

"the threads which bound" Ibid., 3. (p. 134)

"took advantage of her uncomfortable," "wholly untrained" TD to SOW, Sept. 2, 1898 (IndU). (p. 135)

Carrie Tuttle—"Cad" for short See Thomas P. Riggio, "Notes on the Origins of 'Sister Carrie,'" *The Library Chronicle*, Spring 1979. (p. 135)

"mouth had the expression" *Carrie*, 144. (p. 135)

Theodore's memories of his arrival In the holograph MS of "Dawn" (ch. XXVIII), TD writes that ch. II of *Carrie* was drawn from his first impressions of the city and expressed "a faint inkling of what I thought." (p. 135)

changed the year to 1889 John C. Berkey and Alice M. Winters, Historical Notes, *Carrie*, Pennsylvania Edition, 558. (p. 135)

"a line of girls" *Carrie*, 36. Changed by Henry for published version to eliminate repetition. Dreiser's article on the sweatshops: "The Transmigration of the Sweat Shop," *Puritan*, July 1900. (p. 136)

"rows of blank-looking girls" Quoted in Adrienne Siegel, *The Image of the American City in Popular Literature*, 77, 94. (p. 136)

"Say, Maggie, if you'll" *Carrie*, 41. See Duane J. MacMillan, "*Sister Carrie*, 'Chapter IV': Theodore Dreiser's 'Tip-of-the-Hat' to Stephen Crane," *The Dreiser Newsletter*, Spring 1979. (p. 136)

Drouet "would need to" *Carrie*, 75. (p. 136)

"not because he was" Ibid., 63. (p. 136)

"only an average little conscience" Ibid., 89. (p. 136)

"a tide rolled between them" *Carrie*, 79. (p. 136)

"She was alone" Ibid., 90. (p. 136)

Chapter 27

"The forces which regulate" *Sister Carrie*, Pennsylvania Edition, 119. (p. 137)

"It seemed to me" Quoted in Dorothy Dudley, *Dreiser and the Land of the Free*, 162. (p. 137)

Henry apparently helped with the research Telegram, Henry to TD, Aug. 28, 1899. Henry tells TD when he will return from Fall River. The unpublished MS of "Fall River" is vividly and powerfully written, as though Dreiser had been there. TD used a few paragraphs from this article in an editorial for *1910* (no. 5) entitled "The Factory." In Donald Pizer, *Theodore Dreiser: A Selection of Uncollected Prose*, 175. (p. 137)

"a picturesque account of the lives" *Cosmopolitan* to TD, Nov. 2, 1901; H. M. Alden to TD, Oct. 24, 1899; *McClure's* to TD, Oct. 11, 1899. (p. 137)

"being left to the mercy" TD to Robert Underwood Johnson, Jan. 9, 1900, Century Coll (NYPL). (p. 138)

"the 'average' reader" Ellery Sedgwick to TD, Oct. 19, 1900. (p. 138)

"ran along by force of habit" *Carrie*, Pennsylvania Edition, 87. (p. 138)

"lacked financial functions" Ibid., 179. (p. 138)

"altogether a very acceptable" Ibid., 44. (p. 139)

"black eyes," "a cold make believe" Ibid., 45. (p. 139)

"He lost sympathy for the man" Ibid., 85. (p. 139)

"those more unmentionable" Ibid., 44. (p. 139)

"Is she a blonde?" Ibid., 48. (p. 139)

"that mystic period between the glare" Ibid., 10. (p. 139)

"that shadow of manner" Ibid., 23. (p. 139)

"Her form had filled out" Ibid., 146. (p. 139)

"secret passage" Ibid., 177. (p. 140)

". . . there is something wolfish" Ibid., 184. (p. 140)

"Remember, love is all a woman" Ibid., 192. (p. 140)

"could hardly restrain," "He would marry her" Ibid., 193. (p. 140)

Chapter 28

"Nature is so grim." TD [unsigned], "The Man on the Sidewalk." In "At the Sign of the Lead Pencil," *The Bohemian*, Oct. 1909. In Donald Pizer, *Theodore Dreiser: A Selection of Uncollected Prose*, 165, 166. (p. 141)

"You didn't do me right, Cad" *Sister Carrie*, Pennsylvania Edition, 26. (p. 141)

"liberal analysis of Spencer" *Carrie*, 87. (p. 141)

"plaything" Ibid., 198. (p. 142)

Carrie as old-fashioned heroine and modern woman See Sheldon Grebstein, "Dreiser's Victorian Vamp," *Midcontinent American Studies Journal*, Spring 1963. In Pizer, ed., *Sister Carrie*, Norton Critical Edition, 541, 551. See also Larzer Ziff, *The American 1890s*, 278, 341. (p. 142)

"Its population was not" *Carrie*, Pennsylvania Edition, 16. (p. 142)

"a lone figure in a" *Carrie*, 12. (p. 142)

"which had sucked its waxen" *Carrie*, 146. (p. 142)

Chapter 29

"At times, sitting at my little" TD, untitled MS, "Autobiographical Attack on Grant Richards," ca. 1911 (UVa). (p. 143)

"I couldn't think how" TD to Mencken, May 13, 1916, 232. In Robert H. Elias, *Letters of Theodore Dreiser*, I, 211. (p. 143)

Hurstwood's guilt or innocence was ambiguous Elias, *Theodore Dreiser: Apostle of Nature*, 107, 108. (p. 143)

"our foremost American" TD to W. Arthur Woodward, Elias, *Letters*, I, 48, 49. (p. 143)

"taking up experimental psychology" Elmer Gates to TD, March 3 and May 29, 1900. (p. 143)

"is not intellection" See Ellen Moers, *Two Dreisers*, 167, 168. (p. 143)

"slowly destroy the structure," "prevents normal" Gates to TD, Nov. 11, 1901. Here Gates presumably repeats what he told Dreiser at their meeting more than a year previously. (p. 144)

"Sister Anna" attended convent See Donald Oakes, MS on Arthur Henry, Afterword, 43. (p. 144)

"the individual whose mind" *Carrie*, Pennsylvania Edition, 269. (p. 145)

"There was something fascinating" Ibid., 271. (p. 145)

"dark, friendless, exiled" Ibid., 287. (p. 145)

"but a single point" Ibid., 299. (p. 145)

"Hurstwood was nothing," "dreams unfilled" Ibid., 305. (p. 146)

"certain poisons in the blood," "eventually produce" *Carrie*, Pennsylvania Edition, 339. (p. 146)

"a deep and cancerous sense" TD to John Howard Lawson, Oct. 10, 1928. In Donald Pizer, ed., *Sister Carrie*, Norton Critical Edition, 476. (p. 146)

"Men were posted at the gates" *Carrie*, Pennsylvania Edition, 339. (p. 146)

". . . the vagaries of fortune" Ibid., 448. (p. 147)

"Well, let her have it" Ibid., 449. (p. 147)

"Every few days" Richard Duffy, "When They Were Twenty-One," *The Bookman*, Jan. 1914. (p. 147)

"He always sat in a rocking" Ibid. (p. 148)

"Eat. Eat" *Carrie*, Pennsylvania Edition, 493. (p. 148)

"How sheepish men look" Ibid., 495. (p. 148)

"hidden wholly in that kindness" Ibid. (p. 148)

"A man is still" "Reflections," *Ev'ry Month*, June 1896. In Donald Pizer, *Theodore Dreiser: A Selection of Uncollected Prose*, 65. (p. 149)

Chapter 30

"After it was done" TD to Mencken, May 13, 1916, 232. In Robert H. Elias, *Letters of Theodore Dreiser*, I, 214. (p. 153)

"Dear Mr. Author" James L. W. West, III, John C. Berkey, and Alice M. Winters, Historical Commentary, *Sister Carrie*, Pennsylvania Edition, n. 15, 537. (p. 153)

Rather than write "bitch" James L. W. West, III, *A Sister Carrie Portfolio*, Historical Commentary, 509. (p. 154)

"her feet, though small" *Carrie*, Pennsylvania Edition, 4. (p. 154)

"When I finished it," "Two hours passed" New York *Herald*, July 7, 1907. In *Sister Carrie*, Norton Critical Edition, 432. (p. 155)

"Dream boats and swan songs," "Ames is not a matrimonial" "Carrie," holograph (NYPL). (p. 156)

"If I were you" *Carrie*, Norton Critical Edition, 356. (p. 156)

"wide awake to her beauty," "the light is but now," "O blind strivings" *Carrie*, Pennsylvania Edition, 487. (p. 156)

"poor unsophisticated," "drag to follow," "the admired way," "Not evil" *Carrie*, Norton Critical Edition, 367, 368. (p. 156)

substituted something slicker *Carrie*, Pennsylvania Edition, 513, 514. (p. 157)

Alden gave the manuscript a quick reading . . . he forwarded Vrest Orton, *Dreiserana: A Book About His Books*, 14. (p. 157)

"superior piece of reportorial realism," "below-the-surface life," "neither firm enough" Quoted in *Carrie*, Pennsylvania Edition, 519. (p. 157)

[Henry] went through the entire typescript . . . Dreiser followed West et al., Historical Commentary, *Carrie*, Pennsylvania Edition, 522. (p. 157)

The majority of the trims Ibid. (p. 157)

Chapter 31

"I had the definite and yet" "Down Hill and Up" (unpublished MS), 4 (UP). (p. 159)

"the first real American book" TD to Mencken, May 13, 1916. In Robert H. Elias, *Letters of Theodore Dreiser*, I, 211. For the record TD adds, "and I had read quite a number by W. D. Howells and others." (p. 159)

"I have found a masterpiece" Quoted in Dorothy Dudley, *Dreiser and the Land of the Free*, 168. (p. 159)

"My Dear Mr. Dreiser" Norris to TD, May 28, 1900. In Donald Pizer, ed., *Sister Carrie*, Norton Critical Edition, 434. (p. 159)

"so good a piece of work" Page to TD, June 9, 1900. In *Carrie*, Norton Critical Edition, 435. (p. 160)

"People are not of equal," "a natural" Quoted in Dudley, *Land of the Free*, 169. (p. 160) "scaled the outworks of the walls" Duffy to TD, July 3, [1900]. (p. 160)

"to join the one a year group" TD to Fremont Older, Nov. 27, 1923. In Elias, *Letters,* II, 418. (p. 160)

set to work on . . . The Rake See Thomas P. Riggio, Introduction, *Theodore Dreiser: The American Diaries,* n. 5, 8. (p. 160)

"warm argument," "straining after," "pretentious" Henry to TD, July 14, 1900. In *Carrie,* Norton Critical Edition, 435, 436. (p. 160)

"that there was something," "deep gloom," "physical derangement," "There is a tenth sense" TD to Henry, July 23, 1900. In Elias, *Letters,* I, 53. (pp. 160–161)

"Dear Teddie" Henry to TD, July 19, 1900. In *Carrie,* Norton Critical Edition, 437, 438. (p. 161)

" 'Doubleday,' he said, 'thinks the story immoral' " Ibid. (p. 161)

"Page—and all of us—" Norris to Henry, July 18, [1900]. In *Carrie,* Norton Critical Edition, 437. (p. 161)

"[Doubleday] would make no effort to sell it" Henry to TD, July 19, 1900. (p. 161)

"to be released from my agreement" Page to TD, July 19, 1900. In Elias, *Letters,* I, 55. (p. 161)

"he must have ample reasons" TD to Henry, July 23, 1900. (p. 162)

"sincere," "mistaken" Henry to TD, July 19, 1900. (p. 162)

"It was Frank who made the trouble" Quoted in Dudley, *Land of the Free,* 180. (p. 162)

"matter has been adjudicated," "Not that, after all," "are needed by society" TD to Henry, July 23, 1900. In Elias, *Letters,* I, 52, 53, 54. (p. 162)

"material injury," "The public feeds" TD to Page, July 23, 1900. Ibid., 57, 58. (p. 162)

"We arrived at exactly the same conclusion" Henry to TD, July 31, 1900. In *Carrie,* Norton Critical Edition, 446, 447. (p. 162)

"I do not have much faith in" TD to Page, Aug. 6, 1900. In Elias, *Letters,* I, 61. (p. 163)

"crushed and tragically pathetic" Quoted in Dudley, *Land of the Free,* 182. (p. 163)

The junior members met with Doubleday; McKee advised TD to Older. In Elias, *Letters,* II, n. II, 420. (p. 163)

"to take the book under my arm" Ibid., 419. (p. 163)

Chapter 32

"You would never dream" Seattle *Post Intelligencer,* Jan. 20, 1901. In Jack Salzman, ed., *Theodore Dreiser: The Critical Reception,* II. (p. 164)

a book called The Flesh and the Spirit The contract is in Letters to TD file at UP. (p. 164)

spliced one of the scenes into the MS of Newspaper Days See Robert H. Elias, "Bibliography and the Biographer," *The Library Chronicle,* Spring 1971. (p. 164)

"Dear Sir," "profanity" Doubleday to TD, Sept. 4, 1900. In Elias, *Letters of Theodore Dreiser,* I, 54, 63, 64. (p. 164)

"Since when has the expression 'Lord Lord' " TD to Doubleday, undated. Ibid., 64, 65. (p. 165)

appeared in the final book, while others were altered Donald Pizer, ed., *Sister Carrie,* Norton Critical Edition, n. I, 453. (p. 165)

"dingy lavoratory," "dingy hall," "those more unmentionable" *Carrie,* Pennsylvania Edition, 527, 528. See also James L. W. West, III, *A Sister Carrie Portfolio,* 62, 67. (p. 165)

"an evil . . . which," "clear, sound," "charming idyll," "delicate romance," "striking contrast" *Catalogue of Books Published by Messrs. Doubleday Page and Company, 34 Union Square, New York, 1900–1901* (NYPL). (p. 165)

"Such girls, however, as imagine" Quoted in Salzman, *Critical Reception,* 2. (p. 166)

"after having yielded up that" Ibid., 17. (p. 166)

"a presentation," "Not once," "has been waited for" Ibid., 15. (p. 166)

"Out in the highways," "other side" Ibid., I. (p. 166)

"Civilization is at bottom" Ibid., 4. (p. 167)

"Its veritism out-Howells Mr. Howells," "an art about it," "there lurks behind," "seems to be" Salzman, *Critical Reception* 7, 8. (p. 167)

"commonest kind of common people" Salzman, *Critical Reception*, 8. (p. 167)

"has been neither extensively advertised" Ibid., 6. (p. 168)

"It is a 'dead one' " John H. Raftery, "By Bread Alone," *Reedy's Mirror*, Dec. 5, 1901 (StLML). (p. 168)

"the mighty lift that thrills" Quoted in Larzer Ziff, *The American 1890s*, 220. (p. 168)

"You know, I didn't like Sister Carrie" Quoted in Dorothy Dudley, *Dreiser and the Land of the Free*, 197. This is Dreiser's account and may be apocryphal. I have included it because it expresses at least symbolic truth. If Howells had not disliked *Carrie* he would have reviewed it. (p. 168)

"I get a little tired of saying" Quoted in R. W. Stallman, *Stephen Crane*, 499. (p. 169)

Chapter 33

"Similarly, any form of social distress" *Dawn*, 107. (p. 173)

"I'm quite sure I didn't" TD, unpublished MS, "Autobiographical Attack on Grant Richards," ca. 1911, 17 (UVa). (p. 173)

John Paul Dreiser was living with Mame Vera Dreiser, *My Uncle Theodore*, 120. (p. 173)

"I am very sorry to hear" Duffy to TD, Dec. 30, 1900. (p. 174)

He wrote with considerable speed TD dated each chapter. See holograph MS of "Jennie Gerhardt" (UP). See also Thomas P. Riggio, Introduction to *Theodore Dreiser: The American Diaries*, n. 5, 8, and Richard Lehan, *Theodore Dreiser: His World and His Novels*, 83. See also *Jennie Gerhardt*, ed. by James L. W. West III, 423. (p. 174)

"had a most depressing effect on me" "Down Hill and Up" (unpublished MS), Part I, unpaged (UP). (p. 174)

"an error in character analysis" TD to Brett, April 16, 1901, Macmillan Coll (NYPL). Quoted in Preface, Richard W. Dowell, ed., *An Amateur Laborer*, xiii. (p. 175)

"New royalty arrangement might be made" Doubleday, Page to TD, card written in pen, Feb. 27, 1901. (p. 175)

Heinemann edition of Carrie See Historical Commentary, *Carrie*, Pennsylvania Edition, 529, 530. Also John C. Berkey and Alice M. Winters, "The Heinemann Edition of *Sister Carrie*," *The Library Chronicle*, Spring 1979. (p. 175)

Chapter 34

"In all the world, there" Arthur Henry, *An Island Cabin*, 213. (p. 177)

"wise, generous and tender," "harmony, beauty and order" Ibid., 172. (p. 177)

"Men rob and murder" Ibid., 171, 172. (p. 177)

"it might be a crab" Ibid., 173. (p. 178)

"Any conception of life" Ibid., 174. (p. 178)

"How the revelations of science" Quoted in Howard Mumford Jones, *The Age of Energy*, 313. (p. 178)

"pulled her from the trunk" Henry, *Cabin*, 193. (p. 178)

"I found a lot of your trash" Ibid., 206. (p. 178)

"It was inevitable" Maude Henry to Elias, April 2, 1945 (Cor U). (p. 179)

Chapter 35

"It is quite true that to the victor" "Reflections," *Ev'ry Month*, June 1896. In Donald Pizer, *Theodore Dreiser: A Selection of Uncollected Prose*, 64. (p. 180)

"distinct commentary on the social" Quoted in Robert H. Elias, *The Letters of Theodore Dreiser*, I, 122. (p. 180) "make it over into what we want" Steffens to TD, Oct. 23, 1901. (p. 180)

"either a definite account" Steffens to TD, Oct. 29, 1901. (p. 180)

"It is plain that" Steffens to TD, Nov. 13, 1901. (p. 180)

story that was "less drastic" "Down Hill and Up" (unpublished MS), Part I, unpaged. (p. 181)

a loss ... of between $150 and $200 Thompson to TD, Sept. 23, 1901. (p. 181)

"I believe in you and in your work" Quoted in Richard W. Dowell, ed., *An Amateur Laborer*, xv. (p. 181)

"either for the coming winter" Enclosure, Jewett to TD, Sept. 20, 1901. (p. 181)

Doubleday, Page had sprinkled Taylor to TD, Aug. 14, 1924. Taylor was, of course, recollecting his motives twenty-three years earlier. (p. 181)

"really powerful," "thoroughly good" Quoted in Jack Salzman, *Theodore Dreiser: The Critical Reception*, 20. (p. 182)

"At last a really strong novel" Ibid., 18. (p. 182)

have "done me proud" TD to Ripley Hitchcock, Feb. 27, 1903. (p. 182)

ended up selling only one thousand copies *Sister Carrie*, Historical Commentary, Pennsylvania Edition, 530. (p. 182)

Chapter 36

"The deep blue blacks of the dome" TD to Mary Annabel Fanton Roberts, Nov. 14, 1901. In Robert H. Elias, *The Letters of Theodore Dreiser*, I, 66. (p. 183)

"home like, southern and high and dry" TD to Taylor, Nov. 25, 1901. Ibid., 68. (p. 183)

"great towering lonely figures," "desire to work" TD to Roberts. Ibid., 66, 67. (p. 183)

"To the majority of readers" Jewett to TD, Nov. 13, 1901. (p. 183)

"win a much warmer," "thoroughly womanly way," "it is exactly," "simply the damnable," "Carrie would not marry" Jewett to TD, Nov. 22, 1901. (p. 184)

"I try to steer" TD to Taylor. In Elias, *Letters*, I, 68. (p. 184)

"because of the mistakes of her past" Jewett to TD, Dec. 30, 1901. (p. 184)

"our experience has taught us," "made a success" Taylor to TD, Dec. 4, 1901. (p. 184)

"I do not wonder after your," "to issue the book" Jewett to TD, Dec. 30, 1901. (p. 185)

"large sympathy" Bowler to TD, Oct. 26, 1902. (p. 185)

sent Duffy a description Duffy to TD, Jan. 9, 1902. (p. 185)

"Butcher Rogaum's Door" *Reedy's Mirror*, Dec. 12, 1901. The title was changed to "Old Rogaum and His Theresa" in *Free and Other Stories*. (p. 185)

"is supposed to be," "Hen has," "proceeding slowly," "rousingly beautiful," "Time will" TD to Duffy, Feb. 2, 1902. In William White, "Dreiser on Hardy, Henley, and Whitman: An Unpublished Letter," *English Language Notes*, Dec. 1968. (pp. 185–186)

Chapter 37

"I wandered here & there" "Down Hill and Up" (unpublished MS), Part I, unpaged. (p. 187)

"The last time I saw you" Jewett to TD, March 17, 1902. (p. 187)

Jug sent him a postcard Sara Dreiser to TD, March 26, 1902. "Forwarded to Charlottesville, Va. (Lynchburg) General Delivery, March 28, 1902." (p. 187)

"in more attractive form," "whose path crosses" Quoted in James L. W. West, III, "*Nicholas Blood* and *Sister Carrie*," *The Library Chronicle*, Spring 1979. (p. 187)

"Cooper of the," "very keen to strike" Jewett to TD, March 21, 1902. (p. 187)

he might call the book "Jane Gebhardt" Jewett to TD, April 9, 1902. (p. 188)

"You have a mind" Jewett to TD, April 16, 1902. (p. 188)

ten chapters he forwarded ... were those The typescript of "Jennie Gerhardt" is stamped "Anna C. Mallon & Co." It bears penciled editing and comment by Jewett, mentioned in his letter to TD of May 27, 1902. (p. 188)

"saw only a family, in the Gerhardts" "Jennie Gerhardt" (holograph), ch. IX. (p. 188)

"Such a wife! Such a home!" Ibid., ch. XII. (p. 188)

"The lesson Brander's action had taught her" "Jennie Gerhardt" (typescript), ch. XX, 10. (p. 189)

"Will he marry you?" "the lie falling" "Jennie Gerhardt" (holograph), ch. XXVIII. (p. 189)

"The Macheavellean [sic] manner in which Lester" Ibid. (pp. 189–190)

"an aching desire to be forever on the move" Isaac Goldberg, "A Visit With Theodore Dreiser," *Haldemann Julius Monthly*. (p. 190)

"when impartial chance decimates the rank" TD to William Dean Howells, May 14, 1902. In Ellen Moers, *Two Dreisers*, 175. (Original letter is at Houghton Library, Harvard University.) (p. 190)

"There is something so mellow, kindly," "If the common ground" Ibid., 176. (pp. 190–191)

"If the book cannot mature" Jewett to TD, June 10, 1902. (p. 191)

"Am sorry I did not have the first chapters" Gordinnier to TD, June 12, 1902. (p. 191)

"Unless Jennie reaps the proverbial" Gordinnier to TD, July 5, 1902. (p. 191)

Chapter 38

"I was hard up" Quoted in Dorothy Dudley, *Dreiser and the Land of the Free*, 201. (p. 192)

the town's "yellow sheet" McCord to TD, July 7, 1900; Aug. 9, 1901. (p. 192)

He now owed the publisher ... $700 Richard W. Dowell, ed., *An Amateur Laborer*, xv. (p. 192)

"It is not the kind of material" Alden to TD, Aug. 1, 1902. (p. 192)

"We do not want too much 'misery'" Penfield to TD, June 24, 1902. (p. 192)

mainly in the market for light amusing material Duffy to TD, July 31 and Aug. 12, 1902. (p. 192)

"morally bankrupt" Quoted in Dudley, *Land of the Free*, 201. (p. 192)

"You elaborate certain parts," "the reader becomes confused" Jewett to TD, Aug. 20, 1902. (p. 193)

"an earnest, child-heart longing" *The Color of a Great City*, 282. (p. 193)

"indissoluble link which binds" Ibid., 282, 283. (p. 193)

he complained of chest pains Dowell, *Laborer*, 6. (p. 193)

"nervous exhaustion," "amusing and companionable" Ibid. (pp. 193–194)

nearly all the textbook symptoms See, for example, Nathan S. Kline, MD, *From Sad to Glad*, from which the list was compiled. (p. 194)

"confusing physical opposition," "I am in a much" Riggio, *American Diaries*, 66, 67. (p. 194)

"purely mental exhaustion" Ibid., 67. (p. 194)

"my tendency to overindulge" Ibid., 62. (p. 194)

"Wednesday Nov. 19th" Ibid., 65. (p. 194)

were written in Jug's hand Ibid., n. 14, 65. (p. 194)

"whoever is to be really free" Sigmund Freud, "Contributions to the Psychology of Love." In *Sexuality and the Psychology of Love*, 65. (p. 194)

"the ache of modernism" Thomas Hardy, *Tess of the D'Urbervilles*, Bantam Edition, 123. (p. 195)

"mental wildness," "brain ache," "disturbing sense of error" Riggio, *American Diaries*, 62. (p. 195)

"Open the door and sweep" Jewett to TD, Nov. 5, 1902. (p. 195)

he had burned the manuscript J. W. Taylor to TD, Aug. 14, 1924. Taylor recalls TD's saying he destroyed the MS back in 1902, though there is no mention of this in the Medical Diary. (p. 195)

"Brace up, stop worrying" Jewett to TD, Dec. 19, 1902. (p. 195) he explained that he had lost interest Quoted in Montrose J. Moses, "Theodore Dreiser," *The New York Times Review of Books*, June 23, 1912. In Donald Pizer, ed., *Theodore Dreiser: A Selection of Uncollected Prose*, 194. (p. 195)

"short, pungent, vigorous," "anything which," "pay cash" Riggio, *American Diaries*, 63, 83, n. 29. (p. 195)

"Tell the truth," "honestly and without," "the discussion of" "True Art Speaks Plainly," *Booklovers Magazine*, Feb. 1903. (p. 195)

"Immoral! Immoral!" Ibid. (p. 195)

"Ah me—Ah me" Riggio, *American Diaries*, 104. (p. 195)

scopolamine, chloral hydrate, small amounts of arsenic, strychnine and quinine Prescriptions are shown in the Medical Diary. Substances prescribed were verified by Donald B. Hayes, registered pharmacist, Crawfordsville, Indiana. All dosages were in "the normal parameters." (p. 196)

"Bromide has no rational place" Louis S. Goodman and Alfred Gilman, *The Pharmacological Basis of Therapeutics*, 163. Information on the actions of these drugs from this book and also from Donald B. Hayes, letter to author. (p. 196)

Chapter 39

"[Hurstwood] buried himself in his papers" *Sister Carrie*, Pennsylvania Edition, 354. (p. 197)

"I understand now better than ever" Duffy to TD, Nov. 16, 1902. (p. 197)

"Find that I suffer from a peculiar illusion" Riggio, *American Diaries*, 61. (p. 197)

he paid back part Riggio, *American Diaries*, 76. (p. 197)

"doomed to rot," "I might as well use" Riggio, *American Diaries*, 92, 93. (p. 198)

"All the horror of being alone," "I must get something" Ibid., 94. (p. 198)

"literary and socialistic work" Ibid., 96. (p. 198)

"very poverty-stricken neighborhood" Ibid., 99. (p. 198)

"writing articles and finishing my story" Ibid., 99. (p. 199)

"Love was to come back" Ibid., 106. (p. 199)

"Not now. Not now." Ibid., 109. (p. 199)

"thinking how I would write" Ibid., 108. (p. 199)

"tottering in ugliness," "Life of the world" Envelope in Dreiser Manuscripts II (IU). (p. 199)

"To thrill with the touch of cool water" Dreiser Manuscripts II (IU). (pp. 199–200)

"We will hear more of you yet" Riggio, *American Diaries*, 102. (p. 200)

"Though one has neither," "I wish those who" Ibid., 112. (p. 200)

Chapter 40

"A word or given order" Richard W. Dowell, ed., *An Amateur Laborer*, 3. (p. 201)

"In the chill glow of a dying February" Dowell, *Laborer*, 7. (p. 201)

He found a small four-story Ibid., 7–9. (p. 201)

"bespeak an opportunity of seeing" Hitchcock to TD, Feb. 14, 1902. (p. 202)

"a long illness," "no immediate," "down in the dumps," "I seem to be" TD to Hitchcock, Feb. 27, 1903. (p. 202)

"radical changes," "certain things relating" TD to Hitchcock, March 2, 1903. (p. 202)

Barnes . . . came up Jewett to TD, May 1 and May 8, 1903. (p. 202)

"I rose to a futile effort" Dowell, *Laborer*, 11. (p. 202)

"all life—animal and vegetable" Dowell, *Laborer*, 12. (p. 203)

astrology Jeremiah MacDonald to TD, Dec. 14, 1901. (p. 203)

"It seemed as if my mind" Dowell, *Laborer*, 122. (p. 203)

because of the mental stress he was undergoing, he began seeing A theory of the reason for TD's perceptual distortions provided by Dr. Byron S. Lingeman, Massachusetts Eye and Ear Infirmary, Boston. See J. Pearlman, *Psychiatric Problems in Ophthalmology*. (p. 204) "a tall, thin, greedy individual," "taking an indifferent" Dowell, *Laborer*, 25. (p. 204)

"He was very wise and sane" Ibid., 27. (p. 204)

Chapter 41

"I long to see them" *The Songs of Paul Dresser*, 12. (p. 205)

When Mame opened the door, she was shocked Dowell, *Laborer*, 31–34. (p. 205)

"the vastness, the indifference" Ibid., 36. (p. 206)

He stood at the rail . . . He had been born with Dowell, *Laborer*, 44. (p. 206)

"Hello, Paul," "Look old man," "I know you're" Ibid., 53, 54. (p. 208)

"Enough to be clean and decent" Ibid., 59. (p. 209)

Chapter 42

"After a long battle" Quoted in Richard W. Dowell, ed., *An Amateur Laborer*. 3. (p. 213)

"wresting a man's mental control from him" "Scared Back to Nature," *Harper's Weekly*, May 16, 1903. (p. 213)

the Hardenbrooks' daughter Dowell, *Laborer*, 107, 108, 138–141. (p. 214)

"I saw that I was as unfitted to be" Dowell, *Laborer*, 160. (p. 214)

"Good for you." Jewett to TD, June 19, 1903. (p. 214)

"That none should suffer" Quoted in Dowell, *Laborer*, xxx. (p. 214)

Davis "will do something for you" Paul Dresser to TD, Oct. 18, 1903. (p. 215)

a fifty-dollar check from Paul Dowell, *Laborer*, xvii. (p. 215)

he told of seriously contemplating ending it all "Down Hill and Up," Part I, 14, 15. TD to Mencken, March 27, 1943, 688–689. In Robert H. Elias, *Letters of Theodore Dreiser*, III, 980, 981. (p. 215)

"To be maimed as an insect" Dowell, *Laborer*, 124. (p. 216)

"debarred . . . from broad and pleasant" Ibid. (p. 216)

"Fortune need not forever feel" TD to Arthur Henry, July 23, 1900. (p. 216)

Chapter 43

"But still I think of him" *Twelve Men*, 108. (p. 217)

"Where are the friends" Words and music by Paul Dresser (1903). In *The Paul Dresser Songbook*, 222. (p. 217)

"the strongest, best biggest novel" Kenton to TD, May [?] 1905. In Robert H. Elias, *Letters of Theodore Dreiser*, I, 72. (p. 218)

Dreiser told her Carrie was still, "Maybe—the gods providing" TD to Kenton, May 6, 1905. Elias, *Letters*, I, 73. (p. 218)

"Surely a courageous publisher" Kenton to TD, June 30, 1905. (p. 218)

"Young people were tired of" Dorothy Dudley, *Dreiser and the Land of the Free*, 215. (pp. 218–219)

"needlessly offensive custom" Quoted in Van Wyck Brooks, *The Confident Years*, n. 2, 296. (p. 219)

"cutting them in two" Dudley, *Land of the Free*, 206. (p. 219)

"You are purchasing one of the best" Jewett to MacLean, Jan. 19, 1905. (p. 220)

A year later Taylor to TD, July 7, 1905; April 19, 1906. (p. 220)

"tamper with the higher," "some assistance" "The Publisher's World," *Smith's*, April 1905. (p. 220)

"Great—fine, exstatic [sic]" Paul to TD, June 1905. (p. 220)

"made lots of money but none" Mabel Haviland to Vera Dreiser, Dec. 10, 1959, Vera Dreiser file, Box 384A. (p. 220)

"genuine songs of feeling," "the rich" "Writes Home and Mother Songs," "But He Is No Sentimentalist Paul Dresser Says—Facts That Contradict Him." New York *Sun*, May 29, 1904, Paul Dresser Scrapbook. (p. 221)

"The People, the People" Unpublished. The lyic is among the papers in the PD Scrapbook. (p. 221)

It was said that he had Charles K. Harris in *After the Ball* writes that Paul had a memorandum book listing all his debtors, but could not collect from one of them. (p. 221)

set up his portable organ "My Brother Paul," by Mary Dreiser Brennam [sic], typescript with letter to TD, July 5, 1906. See Mai Skelly Dreiser to Helen Dreiser, Jan. 11, 1947. She recalled: "Poor Paul when he was at Emma's he told them there would be enough for everyone when he passed on. The truth was he didn't have a quarter to buy a meal. He ate his meals at my Aunt Kate's." (p. 221)

pernicious anemia, rheumatism, dropsy, bad heart Paul mentioned some of these complaints in letters. In its obituary notice, the New York *Telegraph* mentions "dropsical complaint" and heart trouble. As for Paul's dieting, an undated clipping in the Scrapbook, "Paul Dresser Quite Ill," reports that he had been on a thirty-five-day fast, taking nothing but orange juice and water. When he began the fast he weighed 326 pounds and was gaining a pound a day. After losing sixty-six pounds, he began "making up for the meals he missed and his stomach would not stand the strain." (p. 221)

"emanated a kind of fear" *Twelve Men*, 105. (p. 221)

"PAUL IS DYING" Telegram, Ed Dreiser to TD, Jan. 29, 1906. (p. 222)

"his soft hands folded over" *Twelve Men*, 108. (p. 222)

"He made two or three fortunes" New York *Telegraph*, Jan. 31, 1906. (p. 222)

in his homily Father Van Rennselaer Mary Frances Brennan, in "My Brother Paul." (p. 222)

"And then came an angel" Typescript in PD Scrapbook. (p. 222)

Chapter 44

"she was in the walled city" *Sister Carrie*, Pennsylvania Edition, 449. (p. 223)

"My Gal Sal" royalties Herbert E. Marks to TD, July 9, 1932. Box 259. (p. 223)

"prove you can face" Henry to TD, undated. (Letter owned by Mr. and Mrs. Gupton Vogt.) (p. 223)

"Here is the way" TD to Henry, Jan. 12, 1903. (Letter owned by Mr. and Mrs. Gupton Vogt.) (p. 224)

"to see if it is not possible" Henry to TD, Feb. 8, 1904. (p. 224)

"Tom as I have depicted him" Henry to TD, Feb. 17, 1904. (p. 224)

"It is very clear to me," "should have" Ibid. (p. 224)

"Poor dear All [sic]" Mary Frances Brennan to TD, March 22, 1906. (p. 224)

"Success is what counts" TD [?] "A Word to the Public," *Smith's*, June 1905. (p. 224)

"the right use" *Smith's*, July 1905. (p. 225)

"reflect American" *Smith's*, Aug. 1906. (p. 225)

"What weakling, seeing" "A Lesson from the Aquarium," *Tom Watson's Magazine*, Jan. 1906. In Donald Pizer, ed., *Theodore Dreiser: A Selection of Uncollected Prose*, 161, 162. (p. 225)

"The Materials," "The tale is too intricate" Quoted in Philip L. Gerber, "Dreiser's *Financier*: A Genesis," *Journal of Modern Literature*, March 1971. (p. 226)

"I was always difficult" Quoted in Dorothy Dudley, *Dreiser and the Land of the Free*, 206. (p. 226)

"a careful supervision," "any personality," "the new," "illustrated" TD to Caleb L. Litchfield, April 10, 1906. In Robert H. Elias, *Letters of Theodore Dreiser*, I, 76–79. (p. 227)

"The minute I set eyes on him" Quoted in Dudley, *Land of the Free*, 109. See also Roy L. McCardell, "Benjamin B. Hampton— Publisher, Publicist and Picture Producer," New York *Morning Telegraph*, April 24, 1921. (p. 227)

"God, how I hate to go to bed" *Twelve Men*, 217. (p. 228)

"the prettiest piece of transformation" *The Standard & Vanity Fair*, Jan. 3, 1908. (p. 228)

"Christ in Hell" Quoted in Dudley, *Land of the Free*, 211. (p. 228)

"If you would call at this office" Wilder to TD, June 6, 1907. (p. 229)

Chapter 45

"From now on" *The Delineator*, Jan. 1908. (p. 230)

"a fashion sheet" Hoffman to Robert H. Elias, Jan. 10, 1945 (CorU). (p. 230)

"west of the" Frances Perkins, Oral History Coll (ColU). (p. 230)

"strange lantern of a face," "regarding me without seeing" Fannie Hurst, *Anatomy of Me*, 156, 157. (p. 231)

"the most nervous" Nina Carter Marbourg, "Some of the Editors I Have Met," *Newspaperdom*, Oct. 24, 1907. (p. 231)

"queer" Perkins, Oral History. (p. 231)

"dominating personality" Charles Hanson Towne, *Adventures in Editing*, 122, 123. (p. 232)

"curious eyes" William C. Lengel, "The 'Genius' Himself," *Esquire*, Sept. 1938. (p. 232)

"You can stay," "There won't" Quoted in W. A. Swanberg, *Dreiser*, 147. (p. 232)

"He was exceedingly" Lengel, "Genius." (p. 232)

"the one big" Quoted in Dorothy Dudley, *Dreiser and the Land of the Free*, 126. (p. 232)

"In Philadelphia" Homer Croy, *Country Cured*, 142. I have added Lorimer's and Bok's first names to the quote. (p. 232)

"a pirate selling ribbons" Quoted in Jack Salzman, ed., *Theodore Dreiser: The Critical Reception*, 71. (p. 232)

"One must live" Lengel, "Genius." (p. 233)

Chapter 46

"Mr. Dreiser" Quoted by Dorothy Dudley in *Dreiser and the Land of the Free*, 234. (p. 234)

Holly was . . . familiar with the book's history In Flora Mai Holly to James T. Farrell, July 4, 1943. (p. 234)

they had agreed on a contract Enclosure, Charles H. Doscher to Neda M. Westlake, Aug. 12, 1954. Doscher was Dodge's junior partner. (p. 234)

"This book was accepted" Quoted in

Neda M. Westlake, "The *Sister Carrie* Scrapbook," *The Library Chronicle*, Spring 1979. (p. 235)

"The Curtain Raised" Quoted in Elias, *Theodore Dreiser: Apostle of Nature*, 137. (p. 235)

sales got off to a brisk start See James L. W. West, III, "Dreiser and the B. W. Dodge *Sister Carrie*," *Studies in Bibliography*, University of Virginia, 1982. (p. 236)

"one of the most important," "literature of high class," "somber," "strongest piece of realism" Quoted in Jack Salzman, *Theodore Dreiser: The Critical Reception*, 47, 29, 38, 44. (p. 236)

"Such books are to be shunned" Quoted in Dudley, *Land of the Free*, 216. (p. 236)

"The book is not," "a matter for regret" Salzman, *Critical Reception*, 42, 32. (p. 236)

"with the dignity of psychological" Ibid., 33. (p. 236)

"one more," "No wonder England" Ibid., 38. (p. 236)

"The mere living of your daily life" Otis Norman, *The New York Times Saturday Review of Books*, June 15, 1907. In Donald Pizer, *Theodore Dreiser: A Selection of Uncollected Prose*, 163. (p. 237)

"Every human life is intensely" Ibid., 163, 164. (p. 237)

Chapter 47

"Are you writing" Quoted in Donald Pizer, ed., *Theodore Dreiser: A Selection of Uncollected Prose*, 164. (p. 243)

"partly finished" Quoted in Pizer, *Uncollected Prose*, 164, 163. (p. 243)

"I don't want" Grant Richards to TD, Dec. 6, 1905 (UIll). (p. 243)

"keen pleasure" GR to TD, March 6, 1908 (UIll). (p. 243)

"better drop" TD to GR, March 14, 1908 (UIll). (p. 243)

"All I can say" GR to TD, March 31, 1908 (UIll). (p. 243)

"The label gives" Quoted in William C. Lengel, "The 'Genius' Himself," *Esquire*, Sept. 1938. (p. 244)

Ludwig Lewisohn "An American Memory," Alfred Kazin and Charles Shapiro, eds., *The Stature of Theodore Dreiser*, 17. (p. 244)

"have some fun" TD to HLM, July 11, 1909, Thomas P. Riggio, ed., *Dreiser-Mencken Letters*, 26. (p. 244)

"in with both feet" HLM to TD, [after July 11, 1909], 26. (p. 244)

"tainted fiction," "a big catholic" TD to HLM, Aug. 8, 1909, 29. (p. 244)

Mencken's first HLM to TD, [before Aug. 9, 1909], 29; TD to HLM, Aug. 9, 1909, 31. (p. 244)

"I am getting along" HLM to TD, March 7, 1909, 22. (p. 244)

"with the confidence" Quoted in Isaac Goldberg, *The Man Mencken*, 379. (p. 244)

"Schopenhauer" TD to HLM, Dec. 16, 1909, 42. (p. 245)

"In memory of" Quoted in Robert H. Elias, ed., *Letters of Theodore Dreiser*, I, 97. (p. 245)

"Theo wants" Thelma Cudlipp Whitman, "October's Child" (unpublished MS), with W. A. Swanberg Papers. (p. 245)

"Do you like," "Then he kissed" Ibid. (p. 245)

"dwarfed his capacity" Vera Dreiser, *My Uncle Theodore*, 103. (p. 246)

"In case a man" "Concerning Us All," *Delineator*, Oct. 1907. (p. 246)

"Mrs. Dreiser was quite" TD to HLM, July 28, 1910, 50. (p. 247)

"I NEED you" TD to TC, Oct. 7, 1910. Elias, *Letters*, I, 108. (p. 247)

Chapter 48

"Here was all" *"Genius,"* 666–67. (p. 248)

"Though the young" Hoffman to Elias, Jan. 19, 1945 (CorU). (p. 248)

"Butterick ... was" Ibid. (p. 248)

"Are the Dead" See *Delineator*, Oct. 1908. (p. 248)

"have raised a storm" "Still We Think We Are Justified." *Delineator*, Dec. 1908. (p. 248)

"Our editor" Wilder to Charles W. Taylor Jr., Boston *Globe*, Nov. 13, 1908, Dreiser Manuscripts, II (IndU). (p. 248)

"the spirit" "You and the Editor," *Delineator*, Dec. 1908. (p. 248)

"might delight," "to modify" TD to Duffield, Aug. 7, 1910 (UIll). (p. 248)

"I do not consider" TD to Rider, Oct. 11, 1910. (p. 250)

"I have just" Undated memo. (p. 250)

"Nothing's up" TD to HLM, Oct. 11, 1910, 52. (p. 250)

endlessly folding William C. Lengel, "The 'Genius' Himself," *Esquire*, Sept. 1938. (p. 250)

dickering for an interest Edwin Wildman to TD, Oct. 24, 1910. (p. 250)

"not at all anxious," "You are worth" TD to Cudlipp, Oct. 3, 1910, Robert H. Elias, *Letters of Theodore Dreiser*, I, 105–106. (p. 250)

"Oh, Honeypot" Ibid., 108–9. (p. 250)

"I'm sorry" Quoted in Dorothy Dudley, *Dreiser and the Land of the Free*, 231. (p. 251)

"It was pathetic" Quoted in F. O. Matthiessen, *Theodore Dreiser*, 107–8. (p. 251)

Chapter 49

"I have just" TD to HLM, Feb. 24, 1911, 63. (p. 252)

"Little by little" McKee to Elias, March 23, 1949 (CorU). (p. 252)

"fortunate enough" Hitchcock to TD, Nov. 11, 1910. (p. 253)

"establishes a standard" Rosenthal to TD, Jan. 25, 1911. (p. 254)

"I am convinced" TD to Rider, Robert H. Elias, *Letters of Theodore Dreiser*, I, 110. (p. 254)

"There are some" TD to Holly, March 9, 1911. (p. 255)

"I sometimes think" TD to HLM, March 10, 1911, 65. (p. 255)

"I had better" TD to Richards, June 26, 1911(UIll). (p. 255)

"the 3d book" TD to HLM, April 17, 1911, 67 (p. 256)

"They may not" TD to GR, June 16, 1911 (UIll). (p. 256)

"I have just finished" HLM to TD, April 23, 1911, 68. (p. 256)

"as grim" TD to HLM, April 28, 1911, 72. (p. 256)

"the best fiction" Huneker to TD, May 16, 1911. (p. 256)

"I understand" *Jennie Gerhardt* TS (UVa) James L. W. West to author, Sept. 8, 1987. (p. 256)

"I couldn't" *Jennie*, 164–65. (p. 257)

Trites Quoted in Richards to TD, April 15, 1912. (p. 257)

"If anyone" HLM to TD, April 23, 1911, 69. (p. 257)

"Why you should" Hitchcock to TD, May 5, 1911. (p. 257)

"put back pages" Hitchcock to TD, July 14, 1911. (p. 257)

"irritated me" HLM to TD, Nov. 9, 1911, 81. (p. 257)

". . . the Harpers cut" HLM to Wilson, Oct. 25, 1911. In Guy Forgue, ed., *Letters of H. L. Mencken*, 18. (p. 258)

"We can congratulate" Hitchcock to Holly, Sept. 5, 1911. (p. 258)

"practically gathered" TD to HLM, Aug. 8, 1911, 73. (p. 258)

"marked for cutting" TD to HLM, Sept. 4, 1911, 76. (p. 258)

"the best American" In Jack Salzman, ed., *Theodore Dreiser: The Critical Reception*, 62. (p. 258)

"but don't let" TD to Mrs. Dell, Oct. 17, 1911. (p. 258)

"must be due to" Salzman, *Critical Reception*, 65, 67. (p. 259)

"with power," "Is a woman" Ibid., 58, 59. (p. 259)

"is a long" Ibid., 92. (p. 259)

"rather unpleasant" Carbon, Duneka to Mabie, Oct. 6, 1911 (Morgan Lib.). (p. 259)

"reverential," "very winning" Mabie to Duneka, Oct. 11, 1911 (Morgan Lib.). (p. 259)

Dreiser was furious TD to Duneka, Oct. 17, 1911 (Morgan Lib.). (p. 260)

"It looks to me" TD to HLM [ca. Nov. 1, 1911], 80. (p. 260)

"Dreiser simply" HLM to Ernest Boyd, Aug. 20, 1925. Forgue, *Letters of H. L. Mencken*, 281. (p. 260)

Chapter 50

"Sunday Nov. 5th" "Autobiographical Attack on Grant Richards" [ca. 1911] (UVa). (p. 263)

he let Jug fix up Rembrandt Realty Co. to TD, June 5, 1911; "Autobiographical Attack." (p. 263)

"He's gone around" Quoted in W.A. Swanberg, *Dreiser*, 151. WAS sets this incident earlier, but I assume TD was visiting Lillian Rosenthal. (p. 263)

"I think I know" European Diary, Dec. 31, 1911. (p. 263)

"If only some" *Jennie*, 396. (p. 263)

"great power to make" Jug to TD, April 19, 1926. (p. 264)

"was not helpful" Leigh to TD, Nov. 8, 1911. (p. 264)

"I have a" TD to HLM, Nov. 11, 1911, 82. (p. 265)

He was broke "Autobiographical Attack" (uva). (p. 265)

"risky," "difficult fellow" Richards, *Author Hunting, by an Old Literary Sportsman*, 179. (p. 265)

"other propositions" Quoted in Duneka to TD, Nov. 14, 1911. (p. 266)

"bluff" "A Traveler at Forty," TS, ch. III. (p. 266)

"Strictly between" TD to HLM, Nov. 11, 1911, 82. (p. 266)

"the fact that" Duneka to TD, Nov. 14, 1911. (p. 266)

"that stretch" Quoted in Donald Pizer, ed., *Theodore Dreiser: A Selection of Uncollected Prose*, 188–89. (p. 267)

"love its" "Autobiographical Attack." (p. 267)

"the American" Baldwin Macy, "New York Letter," New York *Evening Post*, Nov. 24, 1911. (p. 267)

"Greek Arcadian" European Diary, Dec. 30, 1911. (p. 267)

"We made last" Richards to TD, Dec. 6, 1911 (UIll). (p. 267)

"The prostitute" TD to HLM, Nov. 8, 1912, 105. (p. 268)

"luck with Thelma" Ibid. Dec. 30, 1911. (p. 268)

"If I were" *European Diary.* Jan. 5, 1912. (p. 268)

"With one foot" Richards, *Caviare,* 49. (p. 269)

Mme de Villiers Diary, Jan. 17. (p. 269)
news from Duneka Duneka to TD, Jan. 16, 1912. (p. 269)

"If I were you" TD to Richards, Jan. 16, 1912. (p. 269)

"Tush" Richards to TD, Jan. 28, 1912. (p. 270)

"39," "Rentier" Card with diary. (p. 270)
"eighth-rate city" TD to Richards, Feb. 12. (p. 270)

"race of" Quoted in Pizer, *Uncollected Prose,* 197. (p. 270)

affairs in America TD to Duneka, March 9, Feb. 20, 1912. (p. 270)

"I may go back" TD to Richards, Feb. 25, 1912. (p. 270)

"disloyal . . . ," "I've been" Richards to TD, March 19, 1912. (pp. 270–271)

"Such things" Richards to TD, March 14, 1912. (p. 271)

"trembling," "Not that" Duneka to TD, Feb. 19, 1912. (p. 271)

"THEODOR," "dear old" Diary March 12. (p. 271)

Mme Culp Ibid., March 15. (p. 272)
"the great fact" Ibid., March 20. (p. 272)
"I fancy my" Ibid., March 22. (p. 272)
"a true advocate" Ibid., April 4. (p. 272)
"find myself" Ibid., April 12. (p. 273)
"Youth is gone" Ibid., April 20. (p. 273)
"America today" Markham clipping with diary, Ibid., April 24. (p. 273)

Chapter 51

"Like a wolf" *Financier,* 495. (p. 274)
"I cannot grant" Jug to TD, March 14, 1912. (p. 274)

breaks between volumes TD to Richards, May 26, 1912. (p. 274)

"are civil" Ibid. (p. 274)

"I have preferred" Ibid. (p. 275)

"I am profoundly" TD to Richards, May 4, 1912. (p. 275)

"One day you" Richards to TD, June 7, 1912. (p. 275)

"For heaven" TD to HLM, May [June] 7, 1912, 95. (p. 275)

Dreiser's research See Philip Gerber, "Dreiser's Financier: A Genesis," *Journal of Modern Literature,* March 1971. (p. 275)

"your young couple" Coates to TD, April 19, July 10, July 18, 1912. (p. 275)

"He was not worse" Quoted in Philip Gerber, "The Financier Himself: Dreiser and C. T. Yerkes," *Proceedings of the Modern Language Association,* Jan. 1973. My account of Dreiser and Yerkes is drawn largely from Gerber's articles. See also Gerber, "The Alabaster Protégé," *American Literature,* May 1971. (p. 276)

"Whatever I do" Quoted in Donald Pizer, *The Novels of Theodore Dreiser: A Critical Study,* 326, n.27. (p. 276)

Jay Cooke Philip Gerber, "Dreiser's Debt to *Jay Cooke,*" *Library Chronicle,* Winter 1972. (p. 276)

"How was life" *Financier,* 5. (p. 276)
"A real man" *Financier,* 44. (p. 277)
"The strong man" Quoted in Gerber, "Financier Himself." (p. 277)

"Morality and ethics" European Diary, March 13, 1912. (p. 277)

"Wealth does not buy" Quoted in Gerber, "Financier Himself." (p. 277)

"were like wondrous" Quoted in Pizer, *Novels of TD,* 172. (p. 277)

"I want to" Hitchcock to TD, June 13, 1912. (p. 278)

Hitchcock had another worry Hitchcock to TD, July 2 and 3, 1912. (p. 278)

"the rumor" Hitchcock to TD, June 6, 1912. (p. 278)

"It looks to be" TD to HLM, Aug. 28, 1912, 97. (p. 278)

"Let me have" HLM to TD, Aug. 30, 1912, 97. (p. 278)

"No better picture" HLM to TD, Oct. 6, 1912, 99. (p. 279)

"got drunk on" HLM to Wilson, Dec. 10, 1912. Guy Forgue, ed., *Letters of H. L. Mencken,* 28. (p. 279)

"the girl's initiation" HLM to TD, Oct. 6. (p. 279)

"You always see" TD to HLM, [after Oct. 6, 1912], 102. (p. 279)

"Do you really" TD to Richards, July 7, 1912. (p. 279)

"did not care" TD to Richards, July 24, 1912 (UTex). (p. 279)

"My poor friend" Richards to TD, Aug. 8, 1912. (p. 279)

"There's something" Quoted in Grant Richards, *Author Hunting by an Old Literary Sportsman*, 205. (p. 280)

"I would give anything" Quoted in Dorothy Dudley, *Dreiser and the Land of the Free*, 284. (p. 280)

"a go between" Richards to Doty, Dec. 12, 1912 (UTex). (p. 280)

"You are gaining" HLM to TD, Aug. 1, 1913, 122. (p. 280)

"the more important" Quoted in Jack Salzman, ed., *Theodore Dreiser: The Critical Reception*, 102. (p. 280)

"Dreiser is a real" HLM to Wright, Nov. 12, 1913. Forgue, *Letters of H. L. Mencken*, 34. (p. 281)

"We live in" *Financier* (1912 edition), 250. (p. 281)

"I didn't know" William C. Lengel, "The 'Genius' Himself," *Esquire*, Sept. 1938. (p. 281)

lived together Thomas P. Riggio, ed., *Theodore Dreiser: The American Diaries 1902– 1926*, 207–8. (p. 281)

Chapter 52

"Chicago is my love" Quoted in Donald Pizer, ed., *Theodore Dreiser: A Selection of Uncollected Prose*, 193. (p. 283)

"The poetry" Quoted in Dale Kramer, *Chicago Renaissance*, 148. (p. 283)

"He needs me" Dell told Swanberg, May 19, 1963. (p. 284)

"gave herself" Thomas A. Riggio, ed., *Theodore Dreiser: The American Diaries 1902– 1926*, 207. (p. 284)

"going to place" TD to HLM, Feb. 17, 1913, 115. (p. 285)

"certain delicate conditions" Hitchcock to Holly, Oct. 17, 1912. (p. 285)

"badly written" Dell to TD, [April] 1913. (p. 285)

"would do more" Lengel to TD, March 31, 1913 (ColU). (p. 285)

"could not possibly" Quoted in W. A. Swanberg, *Dreiser*, 167. (p. 285)

fifty-two chapters Hyman to TD, May 20, 1913. (p. 286)

"relatively concise" Hitchcock to TD, March 6, 1913. (p. 286)

"the forbearance" Sutphen to TD, May 29, 1914. (p. 286)

"The country is" Quoted in Dudley, *Dreiser and the Land of the Free*, 292. (p. 286)

"because it is" Tatum, unpublished article on TD. (p. 286)

yearning letters Markham to TD, Feb. 18, 1913. (p. 286)

"I suppose when" Dell told Swanberg, May 19, 1963. (p. 287)

"Miss Kirah Markham" Quoted in Swanberg, *Dreiser*, 169. (p. 287)

"bureaucratic &" TD to Cosgrave, before July 18, 1913, Robert H. Elias, ed., *Letters of Theodore Dreiser*, I, 154. (p. 287)

"will give me" TD to HLM, 124. (p. 288)

Chapter 53

"After I am" TD to HLM, Nov. 18, 1913, 127. (p. 289)

"I think true" *Traveler at Forty* TS, LXIV. (p. 289)

"objected" TD to HLM, Nov. 18, 1913, 126. (p. 289)

"illicit relations" Quoted in Lars Ahnebrink, "Garland and Dreiser: An Abortive Friendship," *Midwest Journal*, Winter 1955–56. (p. 289)

"Back to Alexander" European Diary, March 26, 1912. (p. 290)

"Occasionally I" Ibid. (p. 290)

"It is so" Ibid. (p. 290)

"it would be" Doty to Richards, July 21, 1913 (UTex). (p. 290)

"much liked" Ellsworth to Richards, July 3, 1913 (UTex). (p. 290)

"Mr. Dreiser thinks" Ellsworth to Richards, Aug. 5, 1913 (UTex). (p. 290)

"The damn book" Doty to Richards, July 21, 1913 (UTex). (p. 291)

"dragging in tempo," "an effect" HLM to TD, Nov. 16, 1913, 125. (p. 291)

"the last half" TD to HLM, Nov. 18, 1912, 126. (p. 291)

"For heaven" [after Nov. 16, 1913], 127. (p. 291)

"He is an agnostic" HLM to TD, Nov. 16, 1912, 125. (p. 291)

"For myself" *Traveler*, 4. (p. 291)

"We can have" Quoted in Jack Salzman, ed., *Theodore Dreiser: The Critical Reception*, 163. (p. 292)

"Look, this" Quoted in Swanberg, *Dreiser*, 192. (p. 292)

"one last look" Quoted in Salzman, *Critical Reception*, 192. (p. 292)

"in marriage" *Traveler*, 498. (p. 293)

"intellectual," "will guarantee" Ibid., 500. (p. 293)

"I am an" Philadelphia *Press*, April 26, 1913. (p. 293)

"went no further" Quoted in Matthew J. Bruccoli, *The Fortunes of Mitchell Kennerley*, 74. (p. 294)

"Certainly you'll" HLM to TD, Jan. 11, 1914, 130. (p. 294)

Chapter 54

"An eternal pox" HLM to TD, March 18, 1914, 134. (p. 295)

"young, smug" *Titan*, 206. (p. 295)

"Fighting Yerkes," "Imagine them" Quoted in Philip Gerber, "The Financier Himself: Dreiser and C. T. Yerkes," *Proceedings of the Modern Language Association*, Jan. 1973. (p. 296)

"We do not" Ibid. (p. 296)

"the realism is" TD to HLM, March 6, 1914, 132. (p. 296)

"hard, cold" TD to Alfred A. Knopf, March 13, 1914. (p. 296)

"The Harpers" HLM to TD, March 6, 1914, 132. (p. 297)

"He is a" Tatum to TD, March 11, 1914. (p. 297)

"Oh, Dodo" Ibid. (p. 297)

"a far more" Ibid. (p. 297)

"commercial possibility" TD to Knopf, March 13, 1914. (p. 297)

staggering Ben Hecht, *A Child of the Century*, 205. (p. 297)

"A big city" Quoted in W. A. Swanberg, *Dreiser*, 172. (p. 298)

"a terrible thing" Ibid. (p. 298)

"I've got it" Ibid. (p. 298)

"a new philosophic" TD to HLM, March 16, 1914, 133. (p. 298)

"proud" Quoted in Thomas P. Riggio, ed., *Dreiser-Mencken Letters*, I, 137, fn.2. (p. 298)

"Too much truth" Tatum to TD, March 18, 1914. (p. 298)

"If you will" TD to HLM, March 31, 1914, 138–39. (p. 299)

"The book of" TD to Knopf, March 3, 1914. (p. 299)

"The story is" Quoted in Jack Salzman, ed., *Theodore Dreiser: The Critical Reception*, 189. (p. 299)

"a satyr," "no more" Ibid., 188, 189, 176. (p. 299)

"The book tells" Ibid., 202. (p. 300)

overworked words solecisms Ibid., 187, 177. (p. 300)

Chapter 55

"Only youth and enthusiasm" Unpublished MS, "Greenwich Village." (p. 303)

"Don't give" TD to HLM, April 5, 1914, 140. (p. 303)

He called it Thomas P. Riggio, ed., *Theodore Dreiser: The American Diaries 1902–1926*, 448. (p. 303)

"an absolutely" New York *Sun*, Sept. 28, 1912. (p. 303)

"try to edit" TD to HLM, June 22, 1914, 144. (p. 304)

"I have many" Ibid. (p. 304)

One of Dreiser's schemes TD, "Myself and the Movies," *Esquire*, July 1943. (p. 304)

Broadway waters Welch to TD, April 8, 1914. (p. 304)

"The winter of" Orrick Johns, *Time of Our Lives*, 217. (p. 304)

TD's studio Estelle Kubitz told Swanberg, Dec. 12, 1962; Ralph Fabri to Swanberg, Dec. 23, 1962. (p. 305)

Jug would stand Markham told Swanberg, Dec. 12, 1962. TD used this in the "Aglaia" episode in his serial *This Madness*. (p. 305)

Louis Untermeyer LU told Swanberg, Nov. 11, 1962. (p. 305)

"Genius?" "Greenwich Village." Unpublished MS. (p. 305)

"I am not turning" TD to HLM, July 29, 1914, 147. (p. 306)

"blaze out" HLM to TD, Aug. 11, 1914, 149. (p. 306)

"heroin, Pilsner" Ibid. (p. 306)

"In Paris" Quoted in William Manchester, *H. L. Mencken: Disturber of the Peace*, III. (p. 306)

"bombarded daily" HLM to Sedgwick, Oct. 10, 1914, in Guy Forgue, ed., *Letters of H. L. Mencken*, 52. (p. 306)

"The Lost Phoebe" Welch to TD, Aug. 21, 1914. (p. 307)

"fine stuff" HLM to TD, Aug. 29, 1914, 153. (p. 307)

"Nathan is so full" HLM to TD, Oct. 13, 1914, 160. (p. 307)

Ray Long TD to HLM, Oct. 13, 1914, 160; Welch to TD, Sept. 1, 1914. (p. 307)

"We are in" HLM to TD, Oct. 17, 1914, 163. (p. 307)

"friendly row" HLM to TD, Sept. 5, 1925, 536. (p. 308)

"But that's what" HLM told Robert H. Elias, Nov. 2, 1944. HLM in New York *World-Telegram & Sun*, March 25, 1946. (p. 308)

Dell's cuts Floyd Dell, *Homecoming*, 269. Dell told Swanberg, May 19, 1963. (p. 308)

"the kind of woman" TD to John Golden, June 17, 1938. Robert H. Elias, ed., *Letters of Theodore Dreiser*, III, 796. (p. 309)

separation contract Undated copy at UP. (p. 309)

"the madame" Markham to TD, Feb. 16, 1915. (p. 309)

"emotional steamroller" W. A. Swanberg, *Dreiser*, 181–82. (p. 309)

"I have no hope" Quoted in Dorothy Dudley, *Dreiser and the Land of the Free*, 334. (p. 310)

"epileptic enthusiasms" Albert Mordell to TD, Dec. 2, 1914. (p. 310)

through Elias Rosenthal Rosenthal to TD, Sept. 5, 1914. (p. 310)

"keen passion" "The Rake," unpublished MS. (p. 310)

Chapter 56

"Don't despair" TD to HLM, March 25, 1914, 137. (p. 312)

"parlor socialists" Undated clipping, "The First Anthology Night of the Season." (p. 312)

"His teeth stuck" Edgar Lee Masters, *Across Spoon River*, 367. (p. 312)

"How would you" "A Hoosier Holiday" Diary. (p. 312)

"40 miles" Ibid., Aug. 11. (p. 313)

"somewhere down" *A Hoosier Holiday*, 304. (p. 313)

"a blazing hot" "A Hoosier Holiday" Diary, Aug. 23. (p. 313)

"New life" Ibid., Aug. 26. (p. 314)

"smug and" Ibid., Aug. 17. (p. 314)

"America is so" Ibid., Aug. 14. (p. 314)

"The 'Genius' " is as Quoted in Jack Salzman, ed., *Theodore Dreiser: The Critical Reception*, 242–43. (p. 315)

"the greatest" Ibid., 212. (p. 315)

"subterranean current" Ibid., 234–35. (p. 315)

"What Mr. Dreiser" Ibid., 234. (p. 315)

"a procession," "an abnormal," "contemptible cur," "drummer" Ibid., 249, 252, 226, 243, 224. (pp. 315–316)

"I have not" Ibid., 243. (p. 316)

"In the case of" *Nation*, Dec. 2, 1915. Reprinted in Alfred Kazin and Charles Shapiro, eds., *The Stature of Theodore Dreiser*, 70–80. (p. 317)

"a masterly" HLM to TD, Dec. 8, 1915, 211. (p. 317)

"These moonbeam" TD to Hersey, Dec. 19, 1915. Robert H. Elias, ed., *Letters of Theodore Dreiser*, I, 205. (p. 317) "thin, anemic" Thomas P. Riggio, ed., *Theodore Dreiser: The American Diaries 1902–1906*. 128. (p. 318)

"Very lonely" Ibid., 132. (p. 318)

"SWEETHEART" Ibid., 133. (p. 318)

"My spiritual" Ibid., 144. (p. 319)

Chapter 57

"The exact" TD to HLM, July 29, 1916, 247. (p. 320)

"quite Teutonic" Quoted in Thomas P. Riggio, ed., *Dreiser-Mencken Letters*, 236, fn. 1. (p. 321)

"typically and" HLM to TD, June 6, 1916, 235. (p. 321)

"He shows" Riggio, *American Diaries*, 780. (p. 321)

"one of the" TD to HLM, [before June 19, 1916], 236. (p. 321)

"The book is" HLM to TD, June 26, 1916, 240. (p. 321)

"very unwise" Ibid., June 28, 1916, 241. (p. 322)

"lewd, obscene" TD to HLM, July 7, 1916, 242. (p. 322)

"The essential" Quoted in Dorothy Dudley, *Dreiser and the Land of the Free*, 358. (p. 322)

"In passing" TD to HLM, July 27, 1916, 244. (p. 322)

"She stood," "his sex," "great," "naked model" *"Genius,"* 20, 44, 51, 55. (p. 323)

"After all" HLM to TD, July 28, 1916, 245. (p. 323)

go to jail TD to HLM, July 29, 1916, 246. (p. 323)

to telephone him HLM to TD, Aug. 3, 1916, 248. (p. 323)

"compromise on" Ibid., Aug. 5, 1916, 251. (p. 323)

"a few thousand" HLM to TD, Aug. 5, 1916, 252. (p. 324)

"down" TD to HLM, Aug. 10, 1916, 254. (p. 324)

"intellectual harem" Markham to TD, March 29, 1916. (p. 324)

"If I could" TD to Markham, May 10, 1916. (p. 324)

"You want me" *Newspaper Days*, holograph MS, ch. XXV. (p. 324)

Estelle Kubitz Autobiographical MS (NYPL). (p. 325)

"A public protest" HLM to Hersey, Aug. 9, 1916. Quoted in Robert H. Elias, *Theodore Dreiser: Apostle of Nature*, 199. (p. 325)

"A band of" Hersey's notes, box 89. (p. 325)

"lewd, licentious" Quoted in Robert H. Elias, ed., *Letters of Theodore Dreiser*, I, 226, fn. 26. (p. 326)

"to stand" TD to HLM, Aug. 8, 1916, 252. (p. 326)

He, Jones TD to Ficke, Sept. 21, 1916. (p. 326)

"tinpot revolutionaries" HLM to TD, Sept. 5, 1916, 264. (p. 326)

"a fearful ass" HLM to Boyd, Sept. 6, 1916. Quoted in Guy Forgue, ed., *Letters of H. L. Mencken*, 90. (p. 326)

"Despite our" HLM to TD, Oct. 6, 1916, 266. (p. 326)

"dictatorial tone" TD to HLM, Oct. 9, 1916, 268. (p. 326)

"professional" HLM to TD, Oct. 10, 1916, 268–69. (p. 327)

"a shrewd" Garland to Schuler, Oct. 2, 1916. Quoted in Lars Ahnebrink, "Garland and Dreiser: An Abortive Friendship," *Midwest Journal*, Winter 1955–56. (p. 327)

"a general offensive" HLM to TD, Nov. 14, 1916, 274. (p. 327)

"I have no" Quoted in Dudley, *Land of the Free*, 358. (p. 327)

"the most overrated" Benét to HLM, Nov. 22, 1916. (p. 327)

"beyond that" Frost to HLM, Dec. 16, 1916. Quoted in Dudley, 367. (p. 327)

"Nothing would" Lowell to HLM, Sept. 18, 1916. (p. 327)

"poor old" Quoted in Louis Oldani, "Two Unpublished Pound Letters: Pound's Aid to Dreiser," *Library Chronicle*, Spring 1977. (p. 327)

"through the story" Sumner to Keating, Nov. 22, 1916. (p. 328)

"by Monday," "arrested" TD to HLM, Dec. 13, 1916, 280. (p. 328)

owed his publisher Royalty statement, Oct. 16, 1916. (p. 328)

"In symphonies" *AHH*, 18. (p. 329)

"men were free" Ibid., 513. In MS the book concludes: "Of dreams and the memory of them is life compounded. But now it is no more." (p. 329)

Chapter 58

"We are to have" "Life, Art in America" *Hey, Rub-a-Dub-Dub!*, 281. (p. 330)

"the greatest" Quoted in Vrest Orton, *Dreiserana: A Book about His Books*, 42. (p. 330)

"distinctly wrong" TD to HLM, Nov. 4, 1916, 273. (p. 330)

sterilized Paul Gormley to Vera Dreiser, Dec. 12, 1965. (p. 331)

"Life and the" Quoted in Robert H. Elias, *Theodore Dreiser: Apostle of Nature*, 181. (p. 331)

"an all but" *Hey, Rub*, 141. (p. 331)

"the one thing" TD to HLM, Dec. 13, 1916, 280. (p. 332)

"not only because" HLM to TD, [Dec. 16, 1916], 281. (p. 332)

"weak pervert" TD to HLM, Dec. 18, 1916, 283. (p. 332)

"I wonder" Ibid., 284. (p. 332)

"As for the" HLM to TD, Dec. 20, 1916, 285. (p. 332)

"cheap pornography" HLM to Huebsch, March 16, 1918. In Carl Bode, ed., *The New Mencken Letters*, 83. (p. 333)

"great" TD to HLM, Dec. 21, 1916, 286. (p. 333)

"'Take the advice" HLM to TD, [Dec. 20, 1916], 285. (p. 333)

"You are the" HLM to TD, Dec. 23, 1916, 290. (p. 333)

"In the face" TD to HLM, Dec. 25, 1916, 291. (p. 333)

"has strayed into" *Hey, Rub*, 275. (p. 334)

Chapter 59

"Dreiser is" HLM to Boyd, [1918] (NYPL). (p. 335)

volunteer as midwives HLM to TD, [April 1917], 298. (p. 335)

"to artistic" Auerbach brief, *TD v. John Lane Company*. Reprinted as "Authorship and Liberty," *North American Review*, June 1918. (p. 336)

"deprave or corrupt" Ibid. (p. 336)

"have been continuously" Card at UP. Quoted in Walker Gilmer, *Horace Liveright*, 14. (p. 336)

Jones's board TD to HLM, Oct. 25, 1917, 310; Jones to TD, Nov. 19, 1917. (p. 336)

"Little Bill" Riggio, *American Diaries*, 149. (p. 336)

"Tension of" Ibid. (p. 336)

"live in somebody" Kubitz to Marion Bloom, [Sept. 12] (NYPL). (p. 337)

"Why in hell" HLM to Kubitz, April 17, 1917 (NYPL). (p. 337)

"I advocate" Riggio, *American Diaries*, 190. (p. 337)

"I seem to have" in Campbell to TD, Feb. 26, 1917. (p. 337)

"we fall to" Riggio, *American Diaries*, 158. (p. 337)

"I must give up" Ibid., 176. (p. 338)

"oh, so down" Quoted in W. A. Swanberg, *Dreiser*, 211. (p. 338)

"What's the good" Riggio, *American Diaries*, 185. (p. 338)

"sad, beautiful" Ibid., 214. (p. 338)

"I have so" Ibid., 176. (p. 339)

Dreiser placed work Hutchins Hapgood, *A Victorian in the Modern World*, 266. (p. 339)

"between rounds" Riggio, *American Diaries*, 193. (p. 339)

"the story" Ibid., 232. (p. 339)

"If you fall" HLM to Kubitz, July 20, 1917 (NYPL). (p. 340)

"I've worked and" Unpublished MS, July 10, 1917 (NYPL). (p. 340)

Chapter 60

"As for Dreiser" HLM to Boyd, [1918]. In Guy Forgue, ed., *Letters of H. L. Mencken*, 113. (p. 341) "a mass of" Thomas P. Riggio, ed., *Theodore Dreiser: The American Diaries 1902–1906.* 181. (p. 341)

"but there" Riggio, *Dreiser-Mencken Letters.* 786. (p. 341)

"slapstick," "represent really" TD to Huebsch, March 10, 1918. Robert H. Elias, ed., *Letters of Theodore Dreiser,* I, 250–251. (p. 342)

Irwin Granich Karsner to TD, Jan. 15, Jan. 16, 1918. (p. 342)

Lower East Side Mike Gold, *Mike Gold Reader.* 161–62. (p. 342)

"It is the best" Quoted in Dorothy Dudley, *Dreiser and the Land of the Free.* 395. (p. 342)

"I don't believe" Quoted in George Jean Nathan, *Intimate Notebooks of George Jean Nathan.* 52. (p. 343)

"ridiculously small" Horace Liveright to TD, Sept. 7, 1917. (p. 344)

"you have" Liveright to TD, June 24, 1918. (p. 344)

Swanberg added Swanberg, 226. (p. 345)

"Once again" Doty to TD, Sept. 6, 1918. (p. 345)

"it might get," **cost him his job** Kline to TD, [April 9, 1919]. (p. 345)

"as a member" Harvey to TD, Aug. 24, 1917. (p. 345)

"the menace" Harvey to TD, Apr. 19, 1919. (p. 345)

"Good" Riggio, *American Diaries,* 202. (p. 346)

"The United" Karsner, "Theodore Dreiser," New York *Call.* March 2, 1918. (p. 346)

"The present" Riggio, *American Diaries,* 184. (p. 346)

"Germans singing" Ibid., 183. (p. 346)

"I hope" Ibid., 196. (p. 346)

"full of some" HLM to Boyd, [1917] (NYPL). (p. 346)

"idiotic petulance" HLM to Boyd, [Fall 1917], Forgue, *Letters of Mencken,* III. (p. 346)

"He is doing" Ibid., April 20, 1918. Forgue, *Letters of Mencken,* 120. (p. 346)

"He still" HLM to George Sterling, March 10, 1918. In Carl Bode, ed., *The New Mencken Letters,* 85. (p. 346)

"All I propose" HLM to B. W. Huebsch, Aug. 16, 1918. Bode, *New Mencken Letters,* 84–85. (p. 346)

"It goes" HLM to Kubitz, March 14, 1918 (NYPL). (p. 346)

"I am overly" TD to Huebsch, March 10, 1918. Elias, *Letters,* I, 250. (p. 346)

"a serious" HLM to TD, June 20, 1918, 312. (p. 347)

"awful stuff" HLM to Boyd, May 27, 1918 (NYPL). (p. 347)

"I still avoid" Ibid., June 29, 1918 (NYPL). (p. 347)

"succumbed to" HLM to TD, Nov. 25 [1918], 318. (p. 347)

"What angel" HLM to [TD], Dec. 25, 1918, 320. (p. 347)

He could point See Jones to TD, Feb. 16, 1917. (p. 348)

Jones countered Ibid., Sept. 20, 1918 (p. 348).

"Why in hell" HLM to TD, Feb. 1, 1919, 335. (p. 348)

"I have the," "Personally" TD to HLM, Feb. 3, 1919, 335–36. (p. 348)

Chapter 61

"Cries and" Thomas P. Riggio, ed., *Theodore Dreiser: The American Diaries 1902–1926,* 209. (p. 349)

Society for See TD to Gaylord Yost, July 5, 1918. (p. 349)

Hersey Hersey to TD, March 15, 1919. (p. 349)

Mencken suggested name HLM to TD, March 29, 1919, 341. (p. 349)

Yewdale protested Yewdale to TD, March 29, 1919. (p. 349)

Mencken's Declaration HLM to TD, May 7, 1919, 340. (p. 349)

Orpet case Gillette See Ellen Moers, *Two Dreisers,* 190–99. (p. 351)

"All truth" "The Right to Kill," in Donald Pizer, ed., *Theodore Dreiser: A Selection of Uncollected Prose,* 226. (p. 351)

Aleister Crowley Burton Rascoe, "Burn This," New York *Daily News* [n.d.]. (p. 352)

"At that time" Pizer, *Uncollected Prose,* 263. (p. 352)

"If you do" Riggio, *American Diaries,* 105. (p. 352)

"compelling the body" In Pizer, *Uncollected Prose,* 221. (p. 352) "ever at work" Ibid., 223. (p. 352)

"Just below" TD to A. A. Brill, Dec. 20, 1918. (p. 353)

"monied class" Huntington *Press*, June 18, 1919. (p. 353)

"an errant mind" Quoted in Donald Pizer, *The Novels of Theodore Dreiser*, 206. (p. 353)

"to stay away," "She has" Riggio, *American Diaries*, 217. (p. 354)

"Feel very" Ibid., 216. (p. 354)

"And love" "To a Wood Dove," *Moods: Cadenced and Declaimed*, 41. (p. 354)

"I feel sorry" Riggio, *American Diaries*, 256. (p. 354)

"worried about," "I was possessed," "mental" Ibid., 277–278. (p. 354)

"The close" Freud, *Interpretation of Dreams*, 429. (p. 354)

"one with" Riggio, *American Diaries*, 277. (p. 354)

"This day" Ibid., 278. (p. 354)

Chapter 62

"We whisper" Thomas P. Riggio, ed., *Theodore Dreiser: The American Diaries 1902–1926*, 284. (p. 357)

"lymphatic sensuality" Ibid., 278. (p. 357)

"but my interest" Ibid., 281. (p. 358)

"a new chapter" Ibid., 282. (p. 358)

Helen's life Ibid., 318–19, 339, 353; Helen Dreiser, *My Life with Dreiser*, 315–26. (p. 358)

"We were like" Helen, *Life*, 31. (p. 360)

"a fear of" Ibid., 28. (p. 360)

"Her beauty" Riggio, *American Diaries*, 291. (p. 360)

"she is as insane" Ibid., 284. (p. 360)

"The constant" Ibid., 285. (p. 360)

"The place is" TD to HLM, 369. (p. 360)

"More idling" Riggio, *American Diaries*, 294. (p. 361)

"the most infernally" Ibid., 313. (p. 361)

"Babes Cute" Ibid., 295. (p. 361)

"the most coaxing" Ibid., 291. (p. 361)

"From 10 to" Ibid., 304. (p. 361)

"When I watch" TD to Johnson, July 29, 1920. (p. 362)

"She is too" Riggio, *American Diaries*, 312. (p. 362)

"wild desperation" Ibid., 313. (p. 362)

"Helen gets," "This sex" Ibid., 327. (p. 362)

"youth & beauty" Ibid. (p. 363)

"I am depressed" Ibid., 309. (p. 363)

"terrible hard" Ibid., 310. (p. 363)

"The Bulwark" TD to HLM, Aug. 13, 1920, 382. (p. 363)

"In the morning" Riggio, *American Diaries*, 336–37. (p. 363)

"supplied the" Helen, *Life*, 37. (p. 364)

"envying the rich" *Newspaper Days*, 376. (p. 364)

Richesen case See Ellen Moers, *Two Dreisers*, 198–199, 164. See Kathryn M. Plank, "Dreiser's Real American Tragedy" *Papers On Language & Literature*, Spring, 1991, 279–281. (p. 364)

"I planned" MS, "American Tragedies." (p. 364)

wrote to W. Earl Ward Ward to TD, Sept. 7, 1920, which refers to TD to Ward, Aug. 13, 1920. (p. 365)

"Dusk—of a summer" Holograph MS, *An American Tragedy*. (p. 365)

no "Miss Rich" See New York *World*, Nov. 29, 1906. For a full account of Gillette's life see Craig Brandon, *Murder in the Adirondacks*, to which I am deeply indebted. (p. 365)

Chapter 63

"I am and have" TD to HLM, Sept. 20, 1920. (p. 367)

"a great hit" Thomas P. Riggio, ed., *Theodore Dreiser: The American Diaries 1902–1926*, 338. (p. 367)

"the power of," "he would" Quoted in Dorothy Dudley, *Dreiser and the Land of the Free*, 406. (p. 367)

"Religion is a," "My next" TD to Smith, Jan. 10, 1921. Robert H. Elias, ed., *Letters of Theodore Dreiser*, I, 337–38. (p. 368)

"deep psychic wound" Holograph MS of *An American Tragedy*. Reprinted in *Esquire*, Oct. 1958. (p. 368)

"by some psychic" Ibid. (p. 368)

"Everyone is waiting" Liveright to TD, June 28, 1920. (p. 368)

"our leading" Ibid., July 8, 1920. (p. 369)

"I could have done" HLM to TD, Dec. 11, 1920, 416. (p. 369)

"Quietly and" TD to HLM, Aug. 27, 1920, 384. (p. 369)

"We simply must" Liveright to TD, Nov. 22, 1920. (p. 369)

"The truth is" TD to Liveright, Dec. 3, 1920. Elias, *Letters*, I, 310. (p. 369)

"PLEASE ASK LENGEL" Liveright to TD (telegram), Dec. 21, 1920. (p. 369)

"Where you are" TD to Liveright, Dec. 21, 1920. (p. 369)

"after all you" Liveright to TD, Jan. 6, 1921. (p. 370)

"splendid work," "The present," "one with some" Briggs to TD, Jan. 4, 1921. (p. 370)

"I can safely" TD to Smith, Dec. 26, 1920. Elias, *Letters*, I, 326. (p. 370)

demanding $500 Cook to TD (telegram), Oct. 12, 1921. (p. 371)

"Am wishing for" Riggio, *American Diaries*, 388. (p. 371)

"Whispering" Ibid., 378. (p. 372)

"Get a little" Ibid., 369. (p. 372)

"Hold me" Ibid., 387. (p. 372)

Mencken dispatched HLM to TD, March 16, 1922, 464–65. (p. 372)

"The Dodd people" TD to HLM, March 22, 1922, 466. (p. 373)

Mencken assured him HLM to TD, April 22, 1922, 468. (p. 373)

Dreiser forwarded TD to HLM, May 22, 1922, 473. (p. 373)

Mencken made an appointment HLM to TD, June 1, 1922, 473. (p. 373)

Dreiser was willing TD to HLM, June 8, 1922, 474–75. (p. 373)

"was done for" TD to HLM, June 24, 1922. (p. 373)

"tickled to death" Liveright to TD, July 22, 1922. (p. 373)

"ought to be read" Quoted in Jack Salzman, ed., *Theodore Dreiser: The Critical Reception*, 409. (p. 374)

"Before we realized" Helen Dreiser, *My Life with Dreiser*, 63. (p. 374)

At the moment Riggio, *American Diaries*, 394. (p. 374)

"I want to be" Quoted in Dudley, *Land of the Free*, 442. (p. 374)

"rub Sumner" See Liveright to TD, Sept. 1, 1922. (p. 375)

"I longed" Helen, *Life*, 63–64. (p. 375)

Chapter 64

"And what did you" New York *World*, Nov. 29, 1906. (p. 379)

"immense, congested" TD to Johnson, Jan. 8, 1923. (p. 379)

"acted very decently" HLM to TD, Oct. 28, 1922, 479. (p. 379)

"He must not" Dodd to Hume, Dec. 13, 1922. (p. 380)

intemperate letter See Hume to TD, Dec. 20, 1922. (p. 380)

bargaining with Liveright "Memorandum of Agreement," Jan. 19, 1923. (p. 380)

"Helen packing," "Helen begins," "What will" Thomas P. Riggio, ed., *Theodore Dreiser: The American Diaries 1902–1926*, 396. (p. 381)

"to advance" Quoted in Robert H. Elias, ed., *Letters of Theodore Dreiser*, II, 408. (p. 382)

Dreiser wrote Beach TD to Beach, May 5, 1923, Ibid. (p. 382)

"as much time" Quoted in Elias, *Letters*, II, 410. (p. 382)

"received no further" TD to Burgess, [between May 19 and June 2, 1923]. Ibid., 415, 416. (p. 382)

"a critic in" HLM to TD, May 31, 1923, 493. (p. 382)

"In 'The Bulwark' " HLM to TD, March 20, 1923, 488. (p. 382)

"as an institution" Liveright to TD, Aug. 2, 1923. (p. 382)

"a lousy 3,000" Ibid., Aug. 7, 1923. (p. 383)

"In spite of your" Ibid., March 27, 1923. (p. 383)

"real results" Ibid., Aug. 2, 1923. (p. 383)

"our dream" Helen Dreiser, *My Life with Dreiser*, 66. (p. 383) "phantastic dreamers" Quoted in Ellen Moers, *Two Dreisers*, 269. (p. 383)

"quite old," "very positive" Riggio, *American Diaries*, 396–97. (p. 384)

"an isolated spot" Helen, *Life*, 84. (p. 384)

Dreiser matter-of-factly records Riggio, *American Diaries*, 401. (p. 384)

"Maybe Teddie will" Helen, *Life*, 85. (p. 385)

Mrs. Ward, widow See Craig Brandon, *Murder in the Adirondacks*, 341. (p. 385)

"Confidentially, I am" HLM to TD, July 28, 1923, 407. (p. 386)

"You may attack" HLM to TD, Aug. 2, 1923, 498. (p. 386)

"my little Yankee" TD to Kusell, July 29, Aug. 4, 1923. (p. 386)

"The trouble with" TD to Kusell, Aug. 4, 1923. (p. 386)

"Ordinarily, I" Helen, *Life*, 88. (p. 387)

"I walked the streets" Ibid, 89. (p. 387)

"glad to be back" Riggio, *American Diaries*, 406. (p. 387)

"Realism is not" Rose C. Feld, "Mr. Dreiser Passes Judgment on American Literature," *Book Review*, Dec. 23, 1923. (p. 387)

"is thinking more" TD to HLM, May 12, 1924, 516. The writer referred to was Thomas Craven, author of *Paint*. (p. 388)

"Like a kite" TD to Karsner, Feb. 12, 1923. (p. 388)

vaguely located in the 1920s See Donald Pizer, *The Novels of Theodore Dreiser*, 217. (p. 388)

"A heavy taboo" Robert S. and Helen Merrell Lynd, *Middletown*, 112. (p. 388)

Chapter 65

"But by this time" New York *World*, Nov. 18, 1906. (p. 389)

"settle in a" TD to Helen, Feb. 23, 1924. (p. 389)

"troublesome" waves TD to Helen, March 24. (p. 389)

"I know you think" TD to Helen, April 21. (p. 389)

"If this seeing people" TD to Helen, April 23. (p. 389)

"They think that it is" TD to Helen, March 24. (p. 390)

"I boast not" TD to Helen, March 26. (p. 390)

"fixed & struggling" TD to Helen, June 26. (p. 390)

"unholy task," "I might as well" Ibid. (p. 390)

"When the book" TD to Helen, June 18. (p. 390)

"surer now than I" TD to Helen, April 16. (p. 390)

"the top of the range" TD to Helen, May 3. (p. 390)

"It is too intricate" TD to Helen, April 16. (p. 390)

"I'm to where the factory" TD to Helen, June 18. (p. 391)

"spiritually alone" TD to Helen, June 26. (p. 391)

"My body appears" TD to Helen, July 16. (p. 391)

"He might begin" TD to Helen, April 12. (p. 391)

"The new book" Liveright to TD, April 2. (p. 391)

"Griffith, An American" Liveright to TD, April 23. (p. 391)

"I call it" Quoted in Claude Bowers, *My Life*, 156. (p. 391)

Louise Campbell See Campbell, *Letters to Louise*, 14–22. (p. 391)

"Without my fame" Riggio, *American Diaries*, 410. (p. 392)

"Magdalene [sic]," "When I invite" Ibid., 410, 408. (p. 392)

"I may have" TD to Helen, Aug. 4. Quoted in Helen Dreiser, *My Life with Dreiser*, 99. (p. 392)

"If I promise" Ibid., Sept. 26. (p. 392)

"on a pedestal," "Perhaps," "since when" TD to Helen, June 17, 1924. (p. 393)

"Well," he kept, "sharp and accusing" Helen, *Life*, 106. (p. 393)

Chapter 66

"HE SWAM AWAY" New York *World*, Dec. 1, 1906. (p. 394)

"He tried to place" Helen Dreiser, *My Life with Dreiser,* 126. (p. 394)

"Finally revised and cut" Quoted in Donald Pizer, *The Novels of Theodore Dreiser,* 230. (p. 395)

"that life is largely" Quoted in Bruce Kellner, *Carl Van Vechten and the Irreverent Decades,* 167. (p. 395)

"the first flashing" *An American Tragedy,* I, 300. (p. 395)

"the very substance" Ibid., II, 48–49. (p. 396)

"His was a dual" Helen Dreiser, *My Life with Dreiser,* 216. (p. 396)

"confides his dilemma" Philip Emerson Wood, "An Interview with Theodore Dreiser in which He Discusses Errant Youth," Philadelphia *Public Ledger,* undated clipping. (p. 396)

"in endless space," "a huge" *AAT,* II, 74. (p. 396)

"distorted and fulgurous" Ibid., 76. (p. 397)

"chemic revulsion" Ibid., 77. (p. 397)

a "palsy" Ibid., 76. (p. 397)

passive voice See Shelley Fisher Fishkin, *From Fact to Fiction,* 130–33. (p. 397)

"And yet fearing" *AAT,* II, 77. (p. 397)

"that last frantic" Ibid., 79. (p. 397)

Dreiser's forbidden wish For comments on TD's oedipal conflicts see Robert Forrey, "Theodore Dreiser: Oedipus Redivivus," *Modern Fiction Studies,* Autumn 1977; and Richard B. Hovey and Ruth S. Ralph, "Dreiser's *The 'Genius':* Structure and Motivation," *Hartford Studies in Literature,* Number 2, 1970. In the latter the authors write, "Witla cannot resolve his wife's dual role: she is both lover and mother, playmate-sinner and jailer-punisher." (p. 397)

"This book will be" TD to Campbell, Jan. 9, 1925. In Robert H. Elias, ed., *Letters of Theodore Dreiser,* II, 433. (p. 397)

Chapter 67

"When I was leaving" Quoted in Craig Brandon, *Murder in the Adirondacks,* 290. (p. 398)

"the last five or six" Smith to TD, June 3, 1925. (p. 398)

Smith begged Smith to TD, Aug. 17, 1925. (p. 398)

"Theo hasn't written" Quoted in Gene Fowler, *Bean James,* 37. (p. 399)

"COURT IN TEARS" *New York World,* Nov. 20, 1906. (p. 399)

"A case of the" Ibid., 274. (p. 400)

"not without sorrow," "His last" Ibid., 383. (p. 401)

"eye magnetism" *Notes on Life,* Marguerite Tjader and John J. McAleer, eds., 336. (p. 402)

"his eyes fixed nervously" *AAT,* II, 406. (p. 402)

"not the Execution room" TD to HLM, Nov. 14, 1925, 544. A year earlier Dreiser obtained permission to witness an execution, but the condemned men were reprieved. See Edward Smith to TD, Sept. 15, 17, 1924. (p. 402)

Cain replied See HLM to TD, Nov. 21, 1925, 545. (p. 402)

"THIS PUTS ME" HLM to TD, Nov. 28, 1925 (telegram), 546. (p. 402)

"THE WORLD LIES" TD to HLM, Nov. 28, 1925 (telegram), 547. (p. 402)

"Dreiser Interviews," "a strangely," "One opened" *New York World,* Nov. 30, 1925. (p. 403)

"my imagination" TD to HLM, Dec. 3, 1925, 547. (p. 403)

He did add Galley 244, *AAT,* ch. XXIX. (p. 403)

"For Theodore Dreiser" Quoted in Riggio, II, 549, n. 2. (p. 403)

inserts some language Galley 164, *AAT.* (p. 404)

"What the hell" Quoted in Walker Gilmer, *Horace Liveright,* 135. (p. 404)

"You'd almost feel" Campbell told Swanberg, June 21, 1962. (p. 404)

" 'The dark days' " Helen Dreiser, *My Life with Dreiser,* 113. (p. 404)

Chapter 68

"Your writer," "The Bubble of Success," unpublished MS (UVa). (p. 406) "glorious Saturday" Kusell to TD, Dec. 9, 1925. (p. 406)

"The state is" TD to HLM, Jan. 14, 1926, 550. (p. 407)

"My poor mother" HLM to TD, Jan. 20, 1926, 551. (p. 407)

"These things are" TD to HLM, Feb. 2, 1926, 552. (p. 407)

"Letters such as" TD to McCord, Feb. 2, 1926. (p. 407)

"To avoid a deluge" TD to Ficke, Jan. 14, 1926. (p. 407)

"THE REVIEWS" Smith to TD (telegram), Jan. 9, 1926. (p. 407)

"It seems to have" TD to Lengel, Feb. 15, 1926. (p. 408)

"detachment," "complete and," "romantic glozing," "that earlier" Quoted in Jack Salzman, ed., *Theodore Dreiser: The Critical Reception*, 444. (p. 408)

"Well, it looks" Helen Dreiser, *My Life with Dreiser*, 120. (p. 408)

"the biggest" Salzman, *Critical Reception*, 447. (p. 408)

"The appearance" Ibid., 462. (p. 408)

" 'An American' " Ibid., 471. (p. 408)

"the Mount Everest" Ibid., 473. (p. 409)

"the best novel" Ibid., 474. (p. 409)

"[An] American" Ibid. Quoted in Dorothy Dudley, *Dreiser and the Land of the Free*, 458. (p. 409)

"as solid" Quoted in Salzman, *Critical Reception*, 445. (p. 409)

"He has fortified" Ibid., 460. (p. 409)

"Oh, it is" Ibid., 437. (p. 409)

"the author" Ibid., 446. (p. 409)

"a tacit record" Ibid., 455. (p. 409)

"mixing slang" Ibid., 484. (p. 409)

"He uses language" Ibid., 486. (p. 409)

"I never once" Quoted in Philip Emerson Wood, "Interview With TD," Philadelphia *Public Ledger*, undated clipping. (p. 411)

Chapter 69

"Now we waited" "Search-Light" [Waldo Frank], *Time Exposures*, 160–61. (p. 412)

"it's extremely" Liveright to TD, March 8, 1926. (p. 412)

"if courageously treated" Quinn Martin, "The Magic Lantern: A Book that Would Make a Great Film," New York *World*, March 7, 1926. (p. 412)

movie mogul See Jesse Lasky, with Don Weldon, *I Blow My Own Horn*. See also Neil Gabler, *An Empire of Their Own*, 203. (p. 412)

"they're making" TD to Campbell, March 17, 1926. Robert H. Elias, ed., *Letters of Theodore Dreiser*, II, 443. (p. 413)

"absolute loyalty" Liveright to TD, March 26, 1926. (p. 413)

"delaying tactics" Lasky, *Horn*, 203. (p. 413)

American Tragedy negotiations See TD to Liveright, March 23, 1926. Elias, *Letters*, II, 442–46; Liveright to TD, March 26, 1926; Lasky, ibid., 222. (p. 413)

"The way it is" TD statement, June 10, 1931. (p. 414)

"got everything" Liveright to TD, March 26, 1926. (p. 414)

"will be the most" Clipping at UP. (p. 415)

"I have taken" HLM to TD, Jan. 28, 1926, 552. (p. 415)

"shapeless and forbidding," "Is Freudianism," "What is," " 'An American' " Quoted in Jack Salzman, ed., *Theodore Dreiser: The Critical Reception*, 476–78. (p. 415)

writing in his diary See Charles A. Fecher, ed., *The Diary of H. L. Mencken*, 21–22. (p. 415)

"As for your" TD to HLM, Feb. 8, 1926, 554. (p. 416)

"That boss of yours" Quoted in Charles Angoff, *H. L. Mencken: A Portrait from Memory*, 101. (p. 416)

"The trouble between" TD to Kusell, Feb. 13, 1926. (p. 416)

"You are," "a definite," "I felt" Helen Dreiser, *My Life with Dreiser*, 125–26. Helen does not name the other woman. (p. 417)

"If you see him" "Search-Light," 163. (p. 417)

"I am opulent" Quoted in J. C. Powys to Vera Dreiser, Nov. 1959. (p. 417)

"special case" J. C. Powys, *Autobiography*, 575. (p. 417)

"comparable to no" Winder to TD, Feb. 23, 1927. (p. 418)

"mist [sic] of a" Claire Windsor to TD, April 18, 1926. (p. 418)

"wonderful good fortune" Jug to TD, March 31, 1926; TD to Jug, [April] 1926. W. A. Swanberg, *Dreiser,* 309. (p. 418)

"and did everything," "tentatively," "in order" TD to Malone, carbon of memo, n.d. (p. 418)

he agreed Agreement dated June 1, 1926. (p. 418)

entertained feelers TD to Claire Windsor, after April 18, 1926. (p. 419)

"felt a strange," "too drastic" Helen, *Life,* 137. See Dr. Renate Schmidt-von Bardelben, "Dreiser on the European Continent," *Dreiser Newsletter,* Fall 1971. (p. 420)

Balzac's home Victor Llona, "Sightseeing in Paris with Theodore Dreiser," *Yale Review,* Spring 1987. (p. 420)

"My own private" Anderson to Burton Emmett, Oct. 4, 1926. In Charles E. Modlin, ed., *Sherwood Anderson: Selected Letters,* 86. (p. 421)

Only Arthur Pell Friede to TD, Dec. 8, 1926. (p. 421)

Rodin Studios Helen, *Life,* 140. (p. 421)

"if it's not the book" Friede to TD, July 20, 1926. (p. 422)

"The poor boy!" Quoted in Donald Friede, *The Mechanical Angel,* 43. (p. 422)

Chapter 70

"I was beginning" Helen Dreiser, *My Life with Dreiser,* 200. (p. 425)

"Moving" TD, "Is American Restlessness. . . . " New York *American,* April 10, 1927. (p. 426)

"endowed with ample" "Fools for Love," New York *American,* May 22, 1927. (p. 426)

He, of course, had a strongbox List of stocks in Arthur Pell papers (courtesy of Gary Giddins). (p. 426)

"I felt myself physically" Helen, *Life,* 144. (p. 426)

"tomb," "his terrible," "short" Helen to Fabri, May 22, 1939. (pp. 426)

"a constructive," "Do as you please" Helen, *Life,* 146. (p. 427)

"most evil &" Helen to Fabri, May 22, 1929. (p. 427)

"An impregnable door" Helen, *Life,* 149. (p. 427)

"the distinct sensation" Ibid., 152. (p. 427)

"The peace of that" Russia Diary, Oct. 15, 1927. (p. 428)

"the real, unofficial Russia" Helen, *Life,* 165–66. (p. 429)

Sacco-Vanzetti Liveright to TD, Aug. 24, 1927. (p. 429)

"Who me" Diary, Oct. 11, 1927. (p. 429)

Chapter 71

"This enormous giant" Russia Diary, Nov. 7, 1927. (p. 430)

"its theory" Ibid., Oct. 28. (p. 430)

"once out of the" TD to Franklin and Beatrice Booth, Oct. 26, Robert H. Elias, *Letters of Theodore Dreiser,* II, 462. (p. 430)

"but I'll be better" TD to Campbell, Oct. 28, 1927. Robert H Elias, ed., *Letters of Theodore Dreiser,* II, 463. (p. 431)

"very bad," enlargement, "I am not" Russia Diary, Oct. 29. (p. 431)

"like a cast away" Ibid. (p. 431)

"the heavy and yet" Ibid., Nov. 3. (p. 431)

"an armed dictatorship" TD to McCoy, postcard, n.d. (p. 432)

"The only difference" TD to Helen, n.d. (p. 432)

"Russian lackey as" Quoted in Ruth Epperson Kennell, *Dreiser and the Soviet Union,* 23. (p. 432)

"since we are already" Diary, Nov. 6. (p. 432)

"I think—if only" Ibid., Nov. 7. (p. 432)

"drab affair," "making overtures," "DT——" Ibid. (p. 433)

"with being facetiously," "sympathetic" Quoted in Vincent Sheean, *Dorothy and Red,* 6. (p. 433)

"The important thing" Quoted in Kennell, *Soviet Union*, 35. (p. 433)

"uplifter," "only through" Diary, Nov. 13. (p. 433)

somewhat disillusioned Marie Seton, *Sergei M. Eisenstein*, 21. (p. 434)

"good as chronicles" Quoted in Kennell, *Soviet Union*, 41. (p. 434)

"I have been treated" Diary, Nov. 15. (p. 434)

"restfulness" Ibid., Nov. 18. (p. 435)

"Russia will never be" Quoted in Kennell, *Soviet Union*, 80. (p. 435)

"any form of tyranny," Bukharin interview Quotes from Kennell, *Soviet Union*, 73–79, and Diary, Dec. 5. (p. 435)

"It would be easy" Diary, Nov. 27, 1928. (p. 437)

"In America our task" Diary, Dec. 19 (TD's hand). (p. 437)

"His smart light-gray" Kennell, *Soviet Union*, 184. (p. 438)

"I made him a long speech," Diary, Jan. 10. (p. 438)

"Personally, I am" Quoted in Kennell, *Soviet Union*, 312. (p. 438)

"There is too much" Ibid., 314–15. (p. 438)

"SOVIET PLAN TO FAIL" Oakland *Tribune*, n.d. (p. 438)

"THEODORE DREISER FINDS" Chicago *Tribune*, Feb. 6, 1928. (p. 438)

Chapter 72

"Russia has a dream" TD, interview, New York Paris *Herald*, Oct. 27, 1927. (p. 439)

"Come out into the" TD to Kennell, Jan. 17, 1928. (p. 439)

"I wasn't a Communist" "No Red Bread Line, Says Dreiser," New York *Evening Post*, Feb. 22, 1928. (p. 439)

Russia was no utopia "Dreiser Back from Russia," unidentified clip, Feb. 22, 1928. (p. 439)

"Nowhere in Russia" New York *Evening Post*, Feb. 22. 1928. (p. 440)

"I decided that" TD to Kennell, Feb. 24, 1928. (p. 440)

"unemployment is Russia's" Simon Strunsky, "About Books," *New York Times Book Review*, March 4, 1928. (p. 440)

"Russia will not let" Letter, "Mr. Dreiser Excepts," *New York Times*, March 15, 1928. (p. 440)

"pursuit of the ideal" New York *World*, March 18, 1928. (p. 440)

"which seeks to eliminate," "there are sex murders" *World*, March 19. (p. 441)

"plays that glorify" *World*, March 24. (p. 441)

"the endless outpour," "which does not" *World*, March 25. (p. 441)

"rumors of secret trials," "Is Edison," "semi-religious" *World*, March 27. (p. 441)

"Mr. Darwin," "that fascinating" *World*, March 28. (pp. 441, 442)

"[Under communism], this collective" *World*, March 22. (p. 442)

syndicate wanted to publish TD to Kennell, Sept. 5, 1928. (p. 442)

"He has that rare" *Collecting Net*, July 21, 1928. (p. 443)

"all mechanists & in" TD to Booths, July 7, 1928. Robert H. Elias, *Letters of Theodore Dreiser*, II, 469–70. (p. 443)

"Some of the bits" TD to Kennell, Aug. 18, 1928. (p. 443)

"a hodgepodge" Kennell, *Dreiser and the Soviet Union*, 220. (p. 443)

"I have read," "You have" Thelma Cudlipp, "October's Child," unpublished MS. Swanberg notes. (p. 444)

he could talk of nothing See Claude Bowers, *My Life*, 167; William E. Woodward, *The Gift of Life*, 315; W. A. Swanberg, *Dreiser*, 341. (p. 444)

"I never read" Beatrice Cole told Lingeman, Nov. 11, 1986. (p. 444)

"I wonder when he gave" New York *Evening Post*, Nov. 14, 1928. (p. 445)

"She took three" TD to Kennell, Dec. 12, 1928. (p. 445)

"There are the N.E.P." New York *Evening Post*, Feb. 22, 1928. (p. 445)

"The old beast" Quoted in Marion K. Sanders, *Dorothy Thompson*, 146. (p. 445)

"I have good lawyers" TD to Kennell, Dec. 2, 1928. (p. 445)

"The impression is abroad" Quoted in Jack Salzman, ed., *Theodore Dreiser: The Critical Reception*, 552–53. (p. 446)

Chapter 73

"But in the interim" TD "This Madness: Aglaia," *Cosmopolitan*, Feb. 1929. (p. 447)

Harper's, Simon & Schuster TD to Lengel, Oct. 19, 1928. (p. 447)

"deal is off" TD to Kraft, April 14, 1929. See also Hy Kraft, *On My Way to the Theater*, 70–73; Marguerite Tjader, *Theodore Dreiser: A New Dimension*, 14–17; Louise Campbell, *Letters to Louise*, 60–62. (p. 448)

"Well, perhaps where" Quoted in Walker Gilmer, *Horace Liveright*, 171. (p. 448)

"I have stated" TD to Bowers, May 27, 1929. Robert H. Elias, ed., *Letters of Theodore Dreiser*, II, 490. (p. 449)

"You people may not" *Cosmopolitan*, June 1929. (p. 449)

"pseudobiography," "false conception" Kennell to TD, March 10, 1929. (p. 450)

"suitable to the censorship" TD to Knight, May 13, 1929. Elias, *Letters*, II, 489. (p. 450)

"I let my hand" Cuts shown on copy of TS of "This Madness." (p. 450)

"an introduction," "In regard" TD to Knight, May 13, 1929. Elias, *Letters*, II, 489. (p. 450)

"He turned to look" Marguerite Tjader, *Dreiser: A New Dimension*, 1. (p. 450)

"the urgency of the moment," "Dreiser simply" Ibid., 10. (p. 451)

"I just had a fight" Fabri, Diary, Oct. 25, 1929 (Swanberg papers, UP). (p. 452)

"He must be fixing" Ibid., Oct. 28, 1929. (p. 452)

"a terrible flop" Friede to Swanberg, Jan. 11, 1963. (p. 452)

"Success does not attend" Quoted in Jack Salzman, ed., *Theodore Dreiser: The Critical Reception*, 568. (p. 453)

"His portrait corresponds" Max Eastman, *Love and Revolution*, 184. See also Thomas P. Riggio, ed., *Theodore Dreiser: The American Diaries 1902–1926*, 349. (p. 453)

Kennell and "Ernita" Kennell to TD, May 28, 1929. (p. 453)

"Kraft, I'm going" Kraft, *On My Way to the Theater*, 67. (p. 454)

Chapter 74

"I say this country" Statement on arrest of communists in Atlanta [Oct.? 1930]. (p. 457)

"natural-born traders" Quoted in W. A. Swanberg, *Dreiser*, 351. (p. 457)

"horrible life" Symon Gould to Elias, Dec. 19, 1949 (CorU). (p. 458)

"a bunch of bugaboos," "Money is the" Albuquerque *Journal*, April 19, 1930. (p. 458)

"farce," For thirty years Swanberg, *Dreiser*, 362. (p. 458)

"so densely scarred" Dr. Lemon to TD, June 3, 1930. (p. 459)

"DREISER NOW REDISCOVERS," "gold swimming pools" New York *World-Telegram*, July 9, 1930. (p. 460)

Kay Sayre go through the manuscript Memo, TD to Sayre. (p. 460)

"a frame-up" Undated statement. See Pass to TD, Oct. 6, 1930. (p. 461)

"stirred up great interest" Liveright to Pell (telegram), Aug. 13, 1930 (Owned by Gary Giddins). (p. 462)

Eisenstein and Liveright Eisenstein, *Immoral Memories*, 156. (p. 462)

"tragic course" Eisenstein, *Film Form and the Film Sense*, 96. (p. 462)

"But the machinery" Quoted in Marie Seton, *Sergei M. Eisenstein*, 179. (p. 462)

"the thought of sin" Scenario of *An American Tragedy*, in Ivor Montagu, *With Eisenstein in Hollywood*, 339. (p. 462)

"purblind," "My son," "The mother's" Ibid. (p. 462)

"Is Clyde Griffiths" Eisenstein, *Film Form*, 96. (p. 463)

"there are many questions" Quoted in Seton, *Eisenstein*, 184. (p. 463)

"terminated by mutual" Quoted in Seton, *Eisenstein*, 186. (p. 463)

"Gentlemen, it is" Quoted in Montagu, *With Eisenstein* 120. (p. 463)

Lewis and Nobel Prize Mark Schorer, *Sinclair Lewis*, 546–47. (p. 463)

"several champions" "Dreiser Is Favored to Win Nobel Prize," *New York Times*, Oct. 9, 1930. (p. 463)

Zukor begged Josef von Sternberg Von Sternberg, *Fun in a Chinese Laundry*, 46. (p. 463)

Chapter 75

"I have a literary" Quoted in Marguerite Harris, *Dreiser: A New Dimension*, 53. (p. 464)

"Although I know" TD to North, Jan. 17, 1931. (p. 464)

"to assure you have" Evelyn Light to *Daily Worker*, May 1930. "The American Press and Political Prisoners," *Daily Worker*, May 19, 1930. (p. 464)

"I eliminated the sociological" Josef Von Sternberg, *Fun in a Chinese Laundry*. 47. (p. 465)

"comments, advice" Contract, Jan. 2, 1931. (p. 465)

Dreiser and Kraft in Hollywood Hy Kraft, "Dreiser's War on Hollywood," *The Screen Writer*, March 1946; Kraft, *On My Way to the Theater*, 77–82. (p. 465)

Von Sternberg movie version of *AAT* Of all the new scenes Kraft and TD suggested, only seven were used. These included hints of Clyde's home life and his mother's strictness; the joyride resulting in the death of the child; Clyde's subsequent flight and shots of him riding the rails, washing dishes, getting a job as a bellhop. To show the influence of the Green-Davidson hotel in awakening Clyde's dreams of riches, a segment was added in which a wealthy young woman hands him a large tip. When her mother chastises her for giving him so much money, the girl says, "I liked his looks. . . . I wonder what a boy of his kind is doing in this kind of work." This bit of exposition served more to give credibility to Clyde's romance with Sondra than to define his shift of values. In the next scene, a maid, obviously Clyde's girlfriend, accuses him of "getting high hat." He snaps, "I'm not going to be a bellhop all my life." Enter: *Ambition*. Cut to roadhouse and clinging, tipsy couples, jazz,etc.

When Clyde flees after the little girl is killed, his mother prays for his safety and asks forgiveness: "We have always been so terribly poor. We've never been able to give him the happiness, the simple joys and pleasures that should come to every boy." The speech seems mere pious words rather than an explanation of Clyde's character. At the end of the film there is an added scene in the county jail immediately after Clyde's conviction. When his mother assures him that she believes he is innocent, he confesses, "But I'm not—not really." He tells her he swam away because he wanted Roberta to die. He wanted to tell the jury this but couldn't; he was too ashamed. His confession is intended to be taken literally, to emphasize his guilt. His mother is shocked and tells him it was not his fault: "We never gave you the right start. We brought you up among ugly, evil surroundings, and while we were trying to save the souls of others we were letting you go astray." Clyde chokes up: "Mother are they really going to——? She tells him to be brave and face his punishment like a man. Then she looks heavenward and says, "I know that somehow, somewhere, you'll be given the right start." See TD to Edwin Wilson, Oct. 22, 1931; TD to Campbell, Aug. 4, 1921. Elias, *Letters*, II, 562. (p. 465)

Paramount suit TD to Lasky, March 17, 1931. Robert H. Elias, ed., *Letters of Theodore Dreiser*, II, 522; Lasky to TD, June 3, 1931; Elias, *Letters*, II, 522, n. 12; Hays and Hume to Lasky, June 26, 1931; W. A. Swanberg, *Dreiser*, 377. (p. 465)

"In the preparation" Quoted in Elias, *Letters*, II, 562, n. 23. (p. 465)

"I feel, in a way" Quoted in Elias, *Theodore Dreiser*, 249. (p. 466)

"the matter of political" Letter dated April 9, 1931. See TD to Pass, May 5, May 12, 1921. (p. 466)

"almost everyone" Malcolm Cowley, *The Dream of the Golden Mountain*, 57. (p. 466)

"The time is ripe" Quoted in Louis Adamic, *My America*, 110. (p. 466)

"Dreiser's own great" Ibid. (p. 466)

"the real, practical head" Light to Monohan, May 20, 1931 (p. 467) "definitely aimed" Quoted in Elias, *Theodore Dreiser,* 252. (p. 467)

Foster urged Dreiser Pass to TD, June 12, 1931. (p. 467)

"Watch out" Pittsburgh *Press,* June 25, 1931. (p. 467)

"from each person" "Miners Slaves in Strike Zone Writes Dreiser," New York *World,* June 26, 1931. (p. 468)

"The latest phase" Helen Dreiser, *My Life with Dreiser,* 213–14. (p. 468)

"How *Dawn* could have" Mame to Markel, n.d. (THL). (p. 469)

"One of the most" Quoted in Jack Salzman, ed., *Theodore Dreiser: The Critical Reception,* 590. (p. 469)

"I've had a hell" TD to Campbell, Aug. 5, 1931. Elias, *Letters,* II, 561. (p. 469)

"looked as if" Campbell, *Letters to Louise,* 43. (p. 469)

"her child" Harriet B. Hubbard to Lingeman, March 20, 1989. (p. 469)

"When you get money" "Dreiser, 60, Glad He's Rich," *New York Times,* Aug. 27, 1931. (p. 469)

Chapter 76

"The minin' town" Quoted in *Harlan Miners Speak,* 201. (p. 470)

"to take sides" "The Titan," *New Masses,* Sept. 1931. (p. 470)

Kay Sayre chief ghostwriter L. V. Heilbrunn told Elias. (p. 471)

tendered their regrets Undated memo, Sayre to TD. (p. 472)

"representative Americans" Lester Cohen, "Theodore Dreiser: A Personal Memoir," *Discovery* 4, 1954. (p. 472)

"personally responsible" "Dreiser and Group Go to Harlan County," Lawenceburg [Kentucky] *News,* Nov. 4, 1931. (p. 472)

The governor responded "Troops Will Go to Harlan During Probe." Undated clipping. (p. 472)

"snake doctors" Quoted in Irving Bernstein, *The Lean Years,* 380. (p. 472)

"her neatly tailored" John Dos Passos, *The Best Times,* 228. (p. 472)

"doing what came" McCoy to Swanberg, March 4, 1963. (p. 473)

"faces out of," "the lilt of Elizabethan" Dos Passos, *Times,* 228. (p. 473)

"there was a sort" Quoted in Daniel Aaron, *Writers on the Left,* 179. (p. 473)

"The gun thugs" National Committee for the Defense of Political Prisoners, *Harlan Miners Speak,* 206. (p. 473)

"with a sort of reverence," "I don't keer" Quoted in Cohen, "Theodore Dreiser," *Discovery* 4, 114, 115. (p. 474)

"that if you stood" *Harlan Miners,* 292. (p. 474)

"where the workers are" "Dreiser Eats Beans at Miners Kitchen," *New York Times,* Nov. 7, 1931. (p. 474)

"highly reputable citizens," "capitalize," "dupe" "Dreiser Faces Arrest; Charges of Misconduct," Richmond *Times-Dispatch,* Nov. 10, 1931. (pp. 474–475)

"Something will have to," "I'll tell you" "Mr. Dreiser Speaks His Mind," New York *Evening Post,* Nov. 13, 1932. (p. 475)

"to commit criminal" "Dreiser Group Opens Attack on Extradition," New York *Herald-Tribune,* Nov. 17, 1932. (p. 475)

"It is both funny" Quoted in Eastman, *Love and Revolution,* 537. (p. 476)

"For the past year" "Harlan County Faces," *Fortune,* Feb. 1932. (p. 476)

"the defeated mine-owners" Quoted in Irving Bernstein, *Turbulent Years,* 45. (p. 476)

"they wouldn't take me" Cohen, "Theodore Dreiser," *Discovery* 4, 119. (p. 476)

"I have been told" "Theodore Dreiser Explains His Political Views," New York *Herald-Tribune,* Dec. 22, 1931. (p. 476)

"surprised and hurt" W. A. Swanberg, *Dreiser,* 393. See also Elias interview of Browder, Aug. 16, 1947, in which Browder gives somewhat different reasons for refusing Dreiser. (p. 476)

Chapter 77

"As for my Communism" TD to Evelyn Scott, Oct. 28, 1932. (p. 478) "is for itself" *Crawford's Weekly,* Jan. 2, 1932. *New Masses,* Jan. 1932. (p. 478)

"Stalin uses the same" Transcript in Joseph Brainen, "Human Nature in a Crucible," *Jewish Standard,* Sept. 30, 1932. (p. 478)

"It is entirely understood" Browder to TD, Oct. 20, 1931. (p. 479)

"as blind and uncouth" Jack Salzman, ed., *Theodore Dreiser: The Critical Reception,* 641. (p. 479)

"for the masses" Tragic America, 413 (italics in original). (p. 479)

"guarantee official" Ibid., 414. (p. 479)

"Communism as technically" TD to C. E. Yost, April 6, 1932. (p. 479)

to ask Esther McCoy TD to McCoy, March 20, 1933. (p. 480)

"Clara, Clara" Quoted in Clara Clark Jaeger, *Philadelphia Rebel,* 68. (p. 480)

"an open door" Ibid., 71. (p. 480)

"for a famous novelist" Ibid., 81 (p. 481)

"If I can get it" TD to Campbell, July 21, 1932. *Letters to Louise,* 78. (p. 481)

"do some trading" TD to Campbell, July 31, 1932. Ibid., 79. (p. 481)

"which means 7/8 of" TD to Campbell, July 8, 1932. Ibid., 78. (p. 481)

He was thinking of moving TD to Campbell, Sept. 13, 1932. Ibid., 81. (p. 481)

"The Seventh Commandment" *Liberty,* April 2, 1932. (p. 481)

sent to the Bureau TD's FBI file, received April 7, 1932. (p. 481)

instructed Hume TD to Hume, March 19, 1932. See Helen to Elias, Feb. 8, 1946 (CorU). (p. 481)

"She keeps up a strong" TD to Campbell, April 15, 1932. Robert H. Elias, ed., *Letters of Theodore Dreiser,* II, 585. (p. 481)

He must economize TD to Campbell, July 23, 1932. Ibid., 591. (p. 481)

"I am sick of" TD to Campbell, Ibid. (p. 481)

"writing or just living" TD to Helen, May 15, 1932. (p. 482)

"in a month or so" TD to McCoy, June 9, 1932. (p. 482)

"turn away from" Dudley to TD, July 14, 1931. (p. 482)

"conditions as they are" TD to Dudley, April 7, 1932. (URo). (p. 482)

"Intelligently or unintelligently" *Stoic,* 4. (p. 482)

"Things come about" Lengel to TD, Aug. 12, 1933 (ColU). (p. 482)

Kyllmann warned of libel Kyllmann to TD, Sept. 27, 1932. (p. 483)

He later told Claude Bowers *My Life,* 172. (p. 483)

"I do not think" TD to Nathan, Jan. 7, 1933. (p. 483)

"I cannot get" TD to Hammerstand, Jan. 7, 1933. (p. 484)

"It could be enormous" TD to Kraft, Sept. 29, 1932. (p. 484)

"High drama" Ibid. (p. 484)

"I was set up" Clara Clark Jaeger to Lingeman, March 26, 1989. (p. 485)

"I am still in" Copy enclosed in TD to Fischler, May 17, 1933 (IndU). (p. 485)

"YOU ARE NOT" TD to Kraft (telegram), May 18, 1933, Ibid. (p. 485)

Schulberg See New York *Daily News,* March 20, 1933. (p. 485)

"previewed beautifully" Schulberg to TD, June 2, 1933. (p. 485)

"kikey" Hy Kraft, *On My Way to the Theater,* 102. (p. 485)

"Just as I feared" TD to Fischler, July 5, 1934 (IndU). (p. 486)

Liveright bankruptcy Light to Hume, May 7, 1933; A. H. Gross memo, May 31, 1933; TD to Hume, Sept. 19, 1933; Walker Gilmer, *Horace Liveright,* 234; "Dreiser in Court Action," *New York Times,* Nov. 11, 1933. (p. 486)

"dreadfully worried" TD to Hume, July 10, 1934. (p. 487)

Chapter 78

"What I cannot" TD to Eastman, June 14, 1933. Robert H. Elias, ed., *Letters of Theodore Dreiser,* II, 633. (p. 488)

"altogether too successful" *American Spectator,* Sept. 1933. (p. 488)

"the Zionist movement" TD to Hapgood, Dec. 28, 1933. Elias, *Letters,* II, 662–63. (p. 489) rendered their decision Hume to TD Sept. 22, 1934. TD to Briggs, Sept. 21, 1934. (p. 489)

"It is an outpouring" Schuster to TD, Oct. 26, 1934. Elias, *Letters,* II, 721, n. 10. (p. 490)

"A publisher who speaks" TD to Schuster, Oct. 26, 1934. (p. 490)

"I now find certain" TD to Nathan, Oct. 7, 1933. Elias, *Letters,* II, 645. (p. 490)

"direct social arguments" TD to Dos Passos, June 14, 1933. Ibid., 631. (p. 490)

"Of course there were" "Theodore Dreiser to Quit Spectator," New York *World Telegram,* Jan. 12, 1934. (p. 490)

"I am seriously" HLM to TD, Nov. 21, 1934, 564. (p. 490)

"white flags in hand" TD to HLM, Nov. 24, 1934, 565. (p. 490)

"recent portrait" HLM to TD, Nov. 29, 1934, 566. (p. 491)

"making a dreadful fool" HLM to Garrison, Nov. 12, 1931. Forgue, ed., *Letters of H. L. Mencken,* 335–36. (p. 491)

rendezvous on December 4 Charles A. Fecher, ed., *The Diary of H. L. Mencken,* 73–74. (p. 491)

"Canby's letter offers" HLM to TD, Jan. 3, 1935, 571. (p. 491)

"between the Jewish" "Dreiser Denies He Is Anti-Semitic," *New Masses,* April 30, 1935. (p. 491)

"I am an individual" Quoted, ibid. (p. 491)

"Is Dreiser Anti-Semitic?" *Nation,* April 17, 1935. (p. 492)

not a scintilla of anti-Semitism TD to Heller, May 25, 1938. (p. 492)

"take whatever steps" Statement to H. L. Lack, March 13, 1934. (p. 492)

"very confusing" *Modern Monthly,* March 1937. (p. 492)

Calvin Bridges came Harriet B. Hubbard told Lingeman, 1988. (p. 492)

"What has become of Sergei?" Quoted in Kennell, *Dreiser and the Soviet Union,* 258. (p. 492)

"Well I was strong" Quoted in Daniel Aaron, *Writers on the Left,* 352; Theodore

Dreiser and John Dos Passos, "A Conversation," *Direction,* Jan. 1938. (p. 493)

"What Russia has plus" TD to Crawford, Sept. 13, 1939. Elias, *Letters,* III, 846. (p. 493)

Chapter 79

"The mystery of life" TD, "What I Believe," Donald Pizer, ed., *Theodore Dreiser: A Selection of Uncollected Prose,* 245. (p. 494)

"I've written novels" Quoted in *Notes on Life,* Marguerite Tjader and John J. McAleer, eds. vii. (p. 494)

"very dubious" TD to Simon, Feb. 5, 1935. Robert H. Elias, ed., *Letters of Theodore Dreiser,* II, 721. (p. 494)

"to express an individual" TD to Sulamith Ish-Kishor, Feb. 14, 1935. Elias, *Letters,* II, 728. (p. 494)

"Will it make much" TD to Simon, Jan. 21, 1936. (p. 494)

"deeply disappointed" Simon to TD, Feb. 14, 1936. (p. 495)

"No doubt, today" TS dated June 15, 1936. Other quotes are from this MS, which bears corrections in TD's hand. In the published version, Dreiser says, "I never said that as a race . . . I wholly disliked and distrusted [Jews]." He cut from the manuscript a phrase reading, " . . . as a race, I frankly dislike and distrust them." (p. 495)

"My personal friendship" TD to Simon, July 24, 1936. (p. 495)

"What I am really" TD to Anderson, Jan. 2, 1936. Elias, *Letters,* III, 761. (p. 495)

"Does life have," "Blessed," "I ask," "You have" "Chaos," TS, Sept. 23, 1932. (p. 495)

"God, how is one" TD to "the Dark Lady," Aug. 1938. (p. 496)

"I am the loneliest" Examples of this statement: Vera Dreiser, *My Uncle Theodore,* 192; also Elizabeth Coakley, quoted in W. A. Swanberg, *Dreiser,* 520; Yvette Eastman told Lingeman; Esherick told Swanberg, June 25, 1962. (p. 496) "utter sense" Quoted in Swanberg, *Dreiser,* 182. (p. 496)

"He was . . . suffering" Hy Kraft, *On My Way to the Theater,* 103. (p. 496)

"There was a sad" Eastman told Lingeman, May 21, 1982. (p. 496)

"some great elemental" "vast schemes" *Hey, Rub,* 23–24. (p. 496)

William James Robert H. Elias, *Theodore Dreiser,* 287. (p. 496)

"*completely* understanding" TD to Douglas, Jan. 11, 1935. Elias, *Letters,* II 712. (p. 496)

"a mechanism" TD, "You the Phantom," *Esquire,* Nov. 1934. Pizer, *Uncollected Prose,* 288. (p. 497)

"a considerable period" TD to Douglas, Jan. 11, 1935. Elias, *Letters,* II, 712. (p. 497)

"between matter and energy" TD to Flexner, June 1, 1935. Ibid., 745. (p. 497)

"two phases" Ibid. (p. 497)

"saying over and over" TD to Douglas, Jan. 28, 1936. Ibid., 769. See also Helen Dreiser, *My Life with Dreiser,* 249. (p. 498)

"There is a taste" Quoted in Helen, *Life,* 253. (p. 498)

"I am slowly but surely" TD to Douglas, Dec. 27, 1935 (UTex). (p. 498)

"Perhaps we spent" Harriet B. Hubbard to Lingeman, Feb. 23, 1989. (p. 498)

"GEORGE'S DEATH HURTS" TD to McCord (telegram), Feb. 11, 1936. (p. 499)

"manifestations of some" TD, *Notes on Life,* 72. (p. 499)

"I care for her" TD to McCoy, June 22, 1936. (p. 500)

"It stopped" Marguerite Tjader, *Dreiser: A New Dimension,* 73. (p. 500)

"I feel unhappy about" TD to Helen, Aug. 26, 1936. (p. 500)

Liveright suit outcome "Book Peddling and Surrealism Are Two of Issues in Dreiser Suit," New York *American,* April 19, 1937; "Dreiser Ordered to Pay Royalties," New York *World-Telegram,* June 30, 1937. (p. 500)

"a terrible one" Helen to Fabri, Oct. 27, 1937. (p. 501)

"When you see him" Quoted in Swanberg, *Dreiser,* 445. (p. 502)

"notion of the writer" Anderson to TD, Jan. 12, 1936. Elias, *Letters,* III, 768. (p. 502)

"very few novels" TD to HLM, Jan. 2, 1937, 620. (p. 502)

"not only because of" TD to HLM, Aug. 9, 1936, 608. (p. 502)

"Literature cannot grow" TD to Fischler, March 31, 1939 (IndU). (p. 502)

"first rate pessimist" TD to Saroyan, March 7, 1936. (p. 502)

"At no time throughout" Breen to Warner Bros., Oct. 11, 1937. See Lengel to TD, Oct. 30, 1937. (p. 502)

"I am in the midst" TD to Helen, Dec. 7, 1937. (p. 503)

"I have the new book" TD to Scribner, [after Jan. 10, 1938]. (p. 503)

Chapter 80

"I went on down" TD to McCord, Aug. 18, 1938. (p. 504)

"to be filled in" TD to Fabri, May 15, 1938. (p. 504)

"Last Sunday wires" TD to Yvette Szekely, July 1938. Quoted in Daniel Aaron, *Writers on the Left,* 444, n. 15. (p. 504)

Folsom recalled Folsom told Lingeman, Jan. 9, 1990. (p. 504)

"I think we'll pay" Quoted in Kennell, *Dreiser and the Soviet Union,* 257. (p. 505)

talked with Dos Passos Harriet B. Hubbard told Lingeman, 1988. (p. 505)

"a small intense Jew" TD to Bissell, July 15, 1938. Robert H. Elias, ed., *Letters of Theodore Dreiser,* III, 801. (p. 505)

"And now I see" Ibid. (p. 505)

"Don't go!" Quoted in Helen Dreiser, *My Life with Dreiser,* 260. (p. 505)

"very strong," "such as," "to avoid" "Americans Favor U.S. Action to End Bombing of Civilians, Dreiser Says," Paris *Herald-Tribune,* July 24, 1938. (p. 505)

"My blue devils" TD to Bissell, July 26, 1938. Elias, *Letters,* III, 808. (p. 506)

"I felt war immediately" TD, "Barcelona in August," *Direction,* Nov. 1938. (p. 506) "dangerous atmosphere" TD to Bissell, Aug. 2, 1938. Elias, *Letters*, II, 809. (p. 506)

"Folsom, we've got" Folsom told Lingeman, Jan. 9, 1990. (p. 506)

"Their courage" TD to Bissell, Aug. 2, 1938. Elias, *Letters*, II, 809. (p. 506)

Dreiser and Thoreau See D. B. Graham, "Dreiser and Thoreau: An Early Influence," *Dreiser Newsletter*, Spring 1976. (p. 507)

"gone abroad for" TD to Helen, Dec. 7, 1937. (p. 507)

"it was lovely" TD to Helen, Dec. 19. (p. 507)

"he should be using" Helen to Fabri, July 6, 1938. (p. 508)

"The friendship" Helen's diary, Sept. 20. (p. 508)

"I have hung on" Helen to Fabri, July 6. (p. 508)

"I am moving out" TD to HLM, Nov. 8, 1938, 629. (p. 508)

"How long" HLM to TD, Nov. 9, 1938, 629. (p. 508)

"I am not planning" TD to HLM, Nov. 10, 1938, 630. (p. 508)

"George Douglas and I" Ibid. (p. 508)

"for reasons," "You do not" TD to Folsom, Dec. 19, 1938. *We Hold These Truths . . . ,* 45–47. (p. 508)

Chapter 81

"All who come here" TD to Masters, April 12, 1939. (p. 513)

"Living with you" TD to Dark Lady, [1938]. (p. 513)

"I am the judge" Ibid. (p. 513)

"come to a clarifying" Ibid. (p. 513)

"I am hanging" Masters to TD, Jan. 1, 1939. (p. 513)

"wild ideas" Lawson told Swanberg, Oct. 16, 1963. (p. 514)

"on the rebound" Confidential source. (p. 514)

"Lord, lord" TD to Dark Lady, [1938]. (p. 514)

"Let no destructive" Helen's diary, Jan. 1, 1939. (p. 514)

"He won't let anyone" Helen to Fabri, Feb. 3, 1939. (p. 514)

"He strikes me as" TD to Bissell, Dec. 16, 1938. (p. 515)

They were charmed Marguerite Tjader, *Dreiser: A New Dimension*, 165. (p. 515)

"Up until I was" Quoted in Gerhard Friedrich, "Dreiser's Debt to Woolman's Journal," *American Quarterly*, Winter, 1955. (p. 515)

"I look at all" TD to Dark Lady, [1938]. (p. 515)

"I hang over" TD to Bissell, July 5, 1939. (p. 515)

"even selling does not" TD to Masters, Aug. 30, 1939. (p. 516)

"This is a selfish" TD to Stoddart, June 22, 1939. (p. 516)

"I have had the help" Quoted in Helen Dreiser, *My Life with Dreiser*, 267–68. (p. 516)

"There is a blood tie" Helen to Fabri, May 11, 1939. (p. 517)

His symptoms Dr. F. X. Claps told Lingeman, 1988. (p. 517)

"What woman could" TD to Dark Lady, 1939. (p. 517)

"famous for his success" TD to Lengel, Aug. 4, 1939. (p. 517)

"mistake" TD to Shimkin, Dec. 21, 1939. Robert H. Elias, ed., *Letters of Theodore Dreiser*, III, 861. (p. 517)

"their determination" TD to Mendel, Nov. 20, 1939. (p. 517)

"taking me off" TD to Lengel, Aug. 4, 1939. (p. 517)

no plot Clifton Fadiman to Lingeman, May 4, 1989. (p. 517)

"It is our feeling" Shimkin to TD, Dec. 15, 1939. (p. 517)

"since Horace Liveright" TD to Shimkin, Dec. 21, 1939. Elias, *Letters*, III, 859. (p. 517)

"It is my personality" Ibid., 860. (p. 517)

"If a thing" TD to Dark Lady, [1939]. (p. 518)

"but interference" Helen's diary, Sept. 17, 1939. (p. 518)

"I wonder where" Ibid., Sept. 22. (p. 518)

"War declared" Ibid., Sept. 1. (p. 518)

"If Russia is not" Quoted in Ruth Epperson Kennell, *Dreiser and the Soviet Union,* 273. (p. 518)

"I talk all" Quoted in Kennell, *Soviet Union,* 275. (p. 518)

"Mr. DREISER" Bureau File 100—34431, June 7, 1943. (p. 518)

Dreiser's health...began to improve. See Helen Dreiser, *My Life with Dreiser,* 275. (p. 519)

"Do you feel keenly" Lengel to TD, June 4, 1940. (p. 519)

"by August 15" TD to Lengel, [after June 19, 1940]. (p. 519)

Lengel suggested Lengel to TD, July 6, 1940. (p. 519)

"It was pitiful" Belfrage told Lingeman, July 13, 1982. (p. 519)

"Considering the fact" Lengel to TD, Sept. 19, 1940. (p. 520)

"wandered so far" TD to Lengel, Sept. 24, 1940. Elias, *Letters,* III, 901. (p. 520)

the publisher wired Piest to TD (telegram), Oct. 24, 1940. (p. 520)

asked for some cuts Zabladowsky to TD, Oct. 29, 1940. (p. 520)

"a spiteful, wretchedly" Quoted in Jack Salzman, ed., *Theodore Dreiser: The Critical Reception,* 652. (p. 520)

"Damned if I don't" Quoted in "3,000 in Biggest L.A. Peace Rally," *People's World,* Jan. 15, 1941. (p. 521)

"full of tumult" Marguerite Tjader, *Dreiser: A New Dimension,* 113–14. (p. 521)

"After all is said" Quoted, ibid., 122. (p. 522)

"Money International" TD to North (telegram), [after June 26, 1941]. (p. 522)

"Nothing in the history" TD to Fadeyev, July 14, 1941. (p. 522)

Those opinions were stricken Translation of published statement in Kennell, *Soviet Union,* 293–94. (p. 522)

"not very good," "I can't stand" TD to Helen, Dec. 2, 1941. (p. 523)

"too sensitive a variety" Helen to Fabri, Jan. 21, 1941. (p. 523)

"I *love* my home" Helen's diary, Oct. 7, 1941. (p. 523)

"T. out at 4" Ibid., Oct. 19. (p. 523)

"ought to be willing" TD to *Daily Worker,* Dec. 12, 1941. (p. 523)

"storm & stress" TD to Campbell, Dec. 31, 1941. Elias, *Letters,* III, 946–48. (p. 524)

Chapter 82

"I am not" TD to Dillon, Oct. 20, 1942. (p. 525)

"It is far enough" TD to Lengel, Nov. 13, 1942. Robert H. Elias, ed., *Letters of Theodore Dreiser,* III, 944. (p. 525)

"doing quite well" TD to HLM, April 2, 1942, 671. (p. 525)

"It is a very intimate" TD to Lengel, July 1, 1942. (p. 525)

"You understand" TD to Balch, May 1, 1942. (p. 526)

he assured Balch TD to Balch, Aug. 11, 1942. (p. 526)

"arresting incidents" TD to Bradshaw, April 2, 1942. (p. 526)

"the sweetest, lovingest" TD to Bradshaw, n.d. (p. 526)

"He liked" Bradshaw told Lingeman, 1987. (p. 526)

"Its sole aim" TD to Campbell, July 23, 1942. Elias, *Letters,* III, 963. (p. 527)

"for I plan" TD to Bradshaw, Sept. 13, 1942. (p. 527)

"box-office in Toronto" Quoted in Joseph Griffin, "Theodore Dreiser Visits Toronto," *Canadian Review of American Studies,* Spring 1983. (p. 527)

the Forum asked him TD to Norman Cowan, Programme Director, Oct. 22, 1942. (p. 527)

"She seemed like" Bradshaw told Lingeman, 1987. (p. 527)

"ABUSE FOR BRITAIN," "Should Russia" Quoted in Griffin. (p. 527)

"to take such action" Ibid. (p. 528)

The American consul Moffat to Secretary of State, Sept. 24, 1942. FBI file. (p. 528)

account of Dreiser's flight Bradshaw told Lingeman, 1987. See also Moffat to Secretary of State. (p. 528) calls from two Canadian reporters In Griffin. (p. 528)

PM interview George McIntyre, "PM Interviews Dreiser to Learn What He Said in *That* Interview," *PM*, Sept. 22, 1942. (p. 528)

TD in Port Huron Bradshaw told Lingeman, 1987. FBI memo, Nov. 11, 1942. (p. 528)

"Canadian ideal" "Novelist Dreiser Dodges Interview with Reporters," Port Huron *Times-Herald*, Sept. 24, 1942. (p. 529)

"an American writer" Quoted in Griffin. (p. 529)

"Our enemies" Writers War Board, quoted in Elias, *Letters*, III, 973, n. 20. (p. 529)

"without troubling" Quoted in Helen Dreiser, *My Life with Dreiser*, 203–4. (p. 529)

"I still believe," "I think" Buck to TD, Quoted in Griffin. (p. 529)

"I am sick" TD to Buck, Nov. 19, 1942. Quoted, ibid. (p. 529)

"Custodial Detention" FBI file. (p. 529)

"dangerousness classification" Special Agent report, Dec. 2, 1942. (p. 529)

"Dreiser is 71" Ugo Carusi to Hoover, Jan. 22, 1943. FBI files. See also Hood to director, March 24, 1943; Hoover to SAC, Los Angeles, April 30, 1943; memo for the director from Ladd, Jan. 7, 1943; agent report from Louisville, Jan. 12, 1943. (p. 530)

immoral relationship D. M. Ladd to director of FBI, Jan. 4, 1943. (p. 530)

"allegations" Hoover memo to the attorney general, Jan. 21, 1943. (p. 530)

Bureau was monitoring Hoover to SAC, Los Angeles, Jan. 14, 1943. Office of Censorship document, Aug. 7, 1943. (p. 530)

"strength wave" TD to Bradshaw, Dec. 7, 1942. (p. 530)

"I'm in the main" TD to Bradshaw, Nov. 19, 1942. (p. 530)

"a complication of illnesses" Grace Vogt to Elias, July 12, 1945. Elias Papers (CorU). (p. 531)

Jug's funeral Louise Graham (niece) told Lingeman, Nov. 1985. (p. 531)

"it will come through" TD to HLM, March 8, 1943, 685. (p. 531)

"his general stand" Helen to A. M. Mathieu, assistant editor, Jan. 27, 1943. (p. 531)

"stop the fight" Unpublished MS. (p. 531)

"Propaganda detrimental," "would be treason" Mathieu to TD, Feb. 22, 1943. (p. 531)

"glib throwing" Helen to Mathieu, Feb. 28, 1943. (p. 531)

"identifying his own" Vera Dreiser, *My Uncle Theodore*, 208. (p. 532)

Sylvia in Los Angeles Bradshaw told Lingeman, 1987. (p. 532)

"She carried a gun," "I didn't want" Bradshaw told Lingeman, 1987. (p. 532)

"nerves," "sense of" TD to Bradshaw, Sept. 2, 1943. (p. 533)

"not a well man," "cruel" Helen to Moffat, Sept. 24, 1943. See Moffat to Helen, Sept. 22, 1943. (p. 533)

"the farthest thing" Moffat to Helen, Sept. 28, 1943. (p. 533)

"got tired" TD to Bradshaw, Nov. 1943. (p. 533)

"smooth and shiny," "an illustration," "of this," "moved not only," "My Creator," unpublished MS. Donald Pizer, ed., *Theodore Dreiser: A Selection of Uncollected Prose*, 326–29. (p. 533)

Masters found ill See Hilary Masters, *Last Stands*, 166–68. Also Charles A. Fecher, ed., *The Diary of H. L. Mencken*, 297, which says, contrary to Masters' book, that Mencken did donate money to his father. (p. 534)

"I refuse to worry" Quoted in Helen, *Life*, 294. (p. 534)

Chapter 83

"Dreiser came to New York" HLM to Farrell, June 5, 1944. Guy Forgue, ed., *Letters of H.L. Mencken*, 481. (p. 535)

He accepted TD to Damrosch, Jan. 10, 1944. Robert H. Elias, *Letters of Theodore Dreiser*, III, 1001–2. (p. 535)

"I can only deplore" HLM to TD, March 27, 1944, 708. (p. 535)

"forlorn, deluded," "justly reproved" TD to HLM, May 5, 1944, 710–12. (p. 535)

"Unhappily I can't" HLM to TD, May 9, 1944, 712. (p. 535)

"You know *I love*" Harris to Helen, April 17, 1944. (p. 536)

"Well, I believe" Quoted in Marguerite Tjader, *Dreiser: A New Dimension*, 126. (p. 536)

"My that was" Ibid. Margaret Carson told Lingeman, Nov. 13, 1986. (p. 536)

"You've always been" Vera Dreiser, *My Uncle Theodore*, 178. (p. 536)

lunch with Balch TD to Helen, May 19, 1944. (p. 536)

a bit worse Tjader, *Dimension*, 128. (p. 537)

"was closing out" James T. Farrell, *Reflections at 50*, 127. (p. 537)

"What kind of subject" Ibid., 126. (p. 537)

"I don't know" Tjader, *Dimension*, 128–29. (p. 537)

Van Veen Felicia Van Veen told Lingeman, Dec. 3, 1986. (p. 538)

Academy ceremony Robert H. Elias, *Theodore Dreiser: Apostle of Nature*, 293–95; W. A. Swanberg, *Dreiser*, 499–500; Tjader, *Dimension*, 130–32. (p. 538)

"How would you like" Quoted in Vera Dreiser, *My Uncle Theodore*, 182. (p. 539)

"I've been in love" Ibid., 185. (p. 539)

"Is that why" Ibid., 184. (p. 539)

"not only do I" Ibid., 184–85. (p. 539)

"Long life, Ed" Ibid., 189. (p. 539)

"I have just come" *Direction*, Summer 1944. (p. 540)

"Just as a tryout" Quoted in Tjader, *Dimension*, 136. (p. 540)

"[Dreiser] has never lost," "If you asked him" Quoted in Tjader, *Dimension*, 138. (p. 540)

"If you will come" Quoted in Tjader, *Dimension*, 143. (p. 540)

"to break up the" TD to Bradshaw, Sept. 1, 1944. (p. 541)

"could easily outline" TD to Harris, June 15, 1944. (p. 541)

"the force that had" Vera, *Uncle*, 197. (p. 542)

"I'm sure there'll be" Helen to Harris, June 26, 1944. (p. 542)

"It was one of" Helen Dreiser, *My Life with Dreiser*, 301. See also McCoy, "Dreiser's

Last Party," *Los Angeles Times*, Aug. 21, 1977. (p. 542)

". . . this night thy soul" Helen, *Life*, 303. (p. 543)

Chapter 84

"Nature, machine-like" Enc., TD to Fabri, July 12, 1934. (p. 544)

"This is the stuff" Marguerite Tjader, *Dreiser: A New Dimension*, 156. (p. 544)

"too weak and nervously" TD to Bradshaw, Oct. 2, 1944. (p. 545)

"doctoring and—or vitamining" TD to Masters, Oct. 4, 1944. (p. 545)

"Where were you?" Quoted in Vera Dreiser, *My Uncle Theodore*, 202. (p. 545)

"the one person" Ibid., 206. (p. 545)

tried to kiss her Ibid., 204. (p. 545)

"He could not believe" Ibid., 201. (p. 545)

"You always felt" Friede to Swanberg, Jan. 11, 1963. (p. 545)

"He could be" Tjader, *Dimension*, 169. (p. 546)

Dreiser's dream Ibid., 169. (p. 546)

"That's enough" Ibid., 182. (p. 546)

"I do know" Harris to Elias [1945] (CorU). (p. 546)

"For you are" TD to Campbell, March 4, 1945. Robert H. Elias, ed., *Letters of Theodore Dreiser*, III, 1016. (p. 546)

"Surely there must be" *Bulwark*, 317. (p. 547)

"Is that man" Quoted in Esther McCoy, unpublished MS. (p. 548)

"Oh, I am not crying" *Bulwark*, 337. (p. 548)

"Orville's request" *Bulwark* notes, box 120. (p. 548)

"While I am not sure" TD to Campbell, May 21, 1945. See Campbell, *Letters to Louise*, 116ff. (p. 548)

"The Bulwark . . . is a" Helen to Harris, June 6, 1944. (p. 548)

"When the Tragedy was" Helen to Campbell, May 9, 1945. (p. 549)

"never gets inside" Quoted in Elizabeth Gray Vining, *Friend of Life*, 29. See also Carroll

T. Brown, "Dreiser's *Bulwark* and Philadelphia Quakerism," *Bulletin of Friends Historical Association,* Autumn 1946. (p. 549)

"Here was no narrow" *Bulwark,* 328. (p. 549)

"So my golden girl" TD to Harris, June 24, 1945 (UTex). (p. 550)

Farrell delivered his verdict Farrell, *Reflections at Fifty,* 136–38. For excerpts from Farrell's letter, as well as from other correspondence on the novel, see Jack Salzman, "The Curious History of Dreiser's *The Bulwark,*" *Yearbook of American Biographical and Textual Studies,* 1973. (p. 550)

had given Marguerite TD to Doubleday, June 21, 1945. (p. 550)

"seemed to feel" TD to Harris, July 28, 1945 (UTex). (p. 550)

"in the same spirit" TD to Campbell, July 27, 1945. (p. 550)

In another letter TD to Campbell, Aug. 1945. (p. 550)

"a revised version" TD to Elder, Aug. 10, 1945. Elias, *Letters,* III, 1023. (p. 550)

"decidedly lethargic" TD to Harris, Aug. 14, 1945 (UTex). (p. 551)

"Double, Double" TD to Harris, Aug. 25, 1945 (UTex). (p. 551)

Dreiser sent Elder the "authorized" TD to Elder, Aug. 31, 1945. Elias, *Letters,* III, 1027. (p. 551)

"considerable amount of rewriting" Campbell, *Letters to Louise,* 120. (p. 551)

"Frankly, I feel that" Elder to TD, Sept. 20, 1945. (p. 551)

Dreiser authorized Elder TD to Elder (telegram), Sept. 22, 1945. (p. 552)

Elder's editing of *The Bulwark* For example, Dreiser wrote "Interiorially, the old house. . . ." Louise made this "The house itself was. . . ." In Elder's final version the sentence reads, "Inside, the old house was. . . . " (Campbell MS, box 125, p. 24. *Bulwark,* p. 11.) Dreiser wrote, "Yet because of the fact that he felt himself unattractive to girls he would never at that date, or later, have ventured to think that any attractive girl was interested in him" (MS pp. 59–66). Louise left the sentence alone. Elder made it: "Yet feeling himself to be unattractive to girls, he

did not venture to think that she would be interested in him" (*Bulwark,* 32).

Marguerite Tjader Harris, in "Dreiser's Style," TS, box 384E, describes other cuts. For example, part of Solon's prayer while viewing Stewart's body in the parlor was deleted. The phrase "palely flaring candle" was changed to "a single candle in his hand, its flame wavering palely. . . . " This observation about Etta after Stewart's death was cut: "She had not learned that beauty of spirit must hang upon a cross—"

For still another account of the writing of *The Bulwark,* see Jack Salzman, "The Curious History of Dreiser's *The Bulwark.*" Salzman essentially accepts Elder's assurances, in a letter to him (Dec. 10, 1961), that he restored much of what Campbell had cut: "Working from the original version and the revised one, I produced a third, in which the book was cut, the plot simplified and a lot of subplot cut out, much earlier dialogue and some Dreiserian soliloquies restored."

My own conclusions, admittedly tentative, are that Elder did more editing than his letter indicates. I compared the published book with the MS identified by Marguerite Tjader Harris as "Original typed version—with editorial changes marked by Louise Campbell." This manuscript was checked by Dreiser in April 1945 (before it was sent to Louise), Harris says. She adds, "Any, and all other corrections were made by some one else, supposedly, Louise Campbell." However, Salzman is correct in observing that there was still another MS. This was Elder's "third" version, the setting MS. It comprises two kinds of paper, onionskin and heavier bond. A note identifies the "light paper [i.e., onionskin]" as the Campbell version and the bond paper as Elder's. Apparently, then, this setting MS is Elder's reconciliation of his version with Campbell's. The latter—the onionskin—is probably a carbon copy of the retyped MS. Apparently Campbell made her suggested editorial changes on a part of a copy of TD's TS (the one mentioned by Harris, above) and sent it to him for his approval. He looked over her changes and, in his letter of June 27, 1945, gave her his approval to proceed with the editing. As was her custom, she then retyped the MS with her changes incorporated. Elder worked with this script or a copy of it.

Regarding the galleys, Salzman writes that another hand, not TD's, made some corrections. This would be after TD had seen them but before the final version was set. According to Carroll T. Brown, in "Dreiser's *Bulwark* and Philadelphia Quakerism," the galleys were sent to Richmond Miller for verification of the Quaker references, and he made some changes. Some of the changes visible on the proofs are for style or to restore words dropped by the printer, and so are by the proofreader. But others seem to be Miller's (for example, "church" is changed to "meeting-house"). Also, the Farmers and Traders Bank, the name of an actual bank in Philadelphia, was changed in the proof stage to Traders and Builders Bank, at Dreiser's suggestion, after Elder warned him of the possibility of a libel suit (Elder to TD [telegram, n.d.]; TD to Elder [telegram], Nov. 8, 1945) (CorU). (p. 552)

"was almost driven out" Harris to Elias, Jan. 7, 1946 (CorU). (p. 552)

"I am glad to see" TD to Elder, Dec. 22, 1945. (p. 553)

Chapter 85

"And why, since you" TD, *Notes on Life,* Marguerite Tjader and John McAleer, eds., 318. (p. 554)

"obviously tired" Quoted in W. A. Swanberg, *Dreiser,* 517. (p. 554)

"the world seems" TD to Campbell, July 15, 1944. Robert H. Elias, ed., *Letters of Theodore Dreiser,* III, 1010. (p. 554)

"As soon as one" Quoted in Robert H. Elias, *Theodore Dreiser: Apostle of Nature,* 302. (p. 554)

"He felt that the" Lawson told Swanberg, Oct. 16, 1963. (p. 555)

"I have been thinking" HLM to TD, Sept. 11, 1945, 719. (p. 555)

"You see, Mencken" TD to HLM, March 27, 1943, 688–90. (p. 555–556)

"In case you are" HLM to TD, Sept. 11, 1945, 719. (p. 556)

"Here's another device" TD to HLM, [Dec. 1945], 719. (p. 556)

"Dreiser was led" HLM to Farrell, June 12, 1946. Guy Forgue, ed., *Letters of H.L. Mencken,* 498–99. (p. 556)

"It was incredible" Helen Dreiser, *My Life with Dreiser,* 307. (p. 557)

"kept putting an invisible" Friede to Swanberg, Jan. 11, 1963. (p. 557)

"Everyone thinks she's" Quoted in Swanberg, *Dreiser,* 517. (p. 557)

"I don't know where" Quoted in Marguerite Tjader, *Dreiser: A New Dimension,* 221. (p. 557)

"that his worship" *Stoic,* 327. (p. 558)

"It was she who" Quoted in Tjader, *Dimension,* 230–31. (p. 558)

"Would you prefer" TD to Farrell. Quoted in Swanberg, *Dreiser,* 580, n. 18. (p. 558)

"the ironic inadequacy" Farrell to TD, Dec. 19, 1945. See Elias, *Letters,* III, 1034. (p. 558)

"You are dead right" TD to Farrell, Dec. 24, 1945. Elias, *Letters,* III, 1035. (p. 558)

"Oh how I dread" Quoted in Richard Dowell, "Dreiser and Kathleen Mavourneen," *Dreiser Newsletter,* Fall 1977. (p. 558)

"*No,* read it" Helen to Elias, Feb. 7, 1946 (CorU). (p. 559)

"Helen, I have," "This is it," "A pain" Ibid. (p. 559)

"very gray," "Bum" Esther McCoy, "The Death of Dreiser," *Grand Street,* Winter 1988. (p. 560)

"Kiss me, Helen" Helen to Elias, Feb. 7, 1946 (CorU). (p. 560)

"Let her go" Quoted in McCoy, "Death of Dreiser." (p. 560)

"The biggest and best" Helen, *Life,* 317. (p. 561)

"along a ridge," "a beautiful" Helen to Elias, Feb. 7, 1946 (CorU). (p. 561)

Marguerite arrived and shouted Helen to Elias, Feb. 8, 1946 (CorU). (p. 561)

She threatened to cancel Harris to Elias, Jan. 7, 1946 (CorU). (p. 561)

"We went several times" Quoted in McCoy, unpublished MS. (p. 561)

"spying" on her Vera Dreiser, *My Uncle Theodore,* 238. (p. 561)

"a farce or at least" Harris to Elias, Jan. 7, 1946 (CorU). (p. 562)

"indescribable expression" Helen, *Life,* 321. (p. 562)

Envoy

"He loved you" Helen to HLM, Dec. 29, 1945. (p. 564)

"I trust you are" HLM to TD, Dec. 27, 1945, 720. (p. 564)

"He was lucky" HLM to Helen, Dec. 29, 1945. Riggio, *Dreiser-Mencken Letters,* 723. (p. 564)

"Theodore's death" HLM to Helen, Dec. 30, 1945. Riggio, II, 723–24. (p. 564)

lay in a special large crib William Targ, *Indecent Pleasures,* 73. (p. 564)

Selected Bibliography

Aaron, Daniel. *Writers on the Left.* New York: Oxford University Press, 1947.

Adamic, Louis. *My America.* New York: Harper & Row, 1938.

Angoff, Charles. *H. L. Mencken: A Portrait from Memory.* New York: Thomas Yoseloff, 1956.

Balzac, Honoré de. *Lost Illusions.* Penguin Books, 1971.

Beckwith, H. W. *History of Vigo and Parke Countys.* Chicago: H. H. Hill and N. Iddings Publishing, 1880.

Bernstein, Irving. *The Lean Years.* New York: Da Capo Press, 1960.

——. *Turbulent Years.* Boston: Houghton Mifflin, 1970.

Biographical and Historical Record of Kosciusko County, Indiana. Chicago: Lewis Publishing Company, 1887.

Bode, Carl. *Mencken.* Carbondale and Edwardsville: Southern Illinois University Press, 1969.

——, ed. *The New Mencken Letters.* New York: Dial Press, 1977.

Bourne, Randolph. *The Radical Will: Randolph Bourne, Selected Writings, 1911–1918.* Olaf Hansen, ed. New York: Urizen Books, 1977.

Bowers, Claude. *My Life.* New York: Simon & Schuster, 1962.

Bradsby, H. C. *History of Vigo County, Indiana, With Biographical Selections.* Chicago: S. B. Nelson and Company, 1891.

Brandon, Craig. *Murder in the Adirondacks.* Utica, N.Y.: North Country Books, 1986.

Brill, A. A. *Psychoanalysis, Its Theory and Practical Applications.* Philadelphia: W. B. Saunders, 1914.

Brooks, Van Wyck. *The Confident Years.* New York: E. P. Dutton, 1955.

——. *John Sloan: A Painter's Life.* New York: E. P. Dutton, 1955.

Bruccoli, Matthew J. *The Fortunes of Mitchell Kennerley, Bookman.* New York: Harcourt Brace Jovanovich, 1986.

Burke, Harry. *From the Day's Journey.* St. Louis: William Harvey Miner, 1924.

Campbell, Louise. *Letters to Louise.* Philadelphia: University of Pennsylvania Press, 1959.

Churchill, Allen. *Park Row.* New York: Rinehart and Company, 1958.

Clurman, Harold. *The Fervent Years.* New York: Alfred A. Knopf, 1945.

Cole, Arthur Harrison. *The American Wool Manufacture.* Cambridge: Harvard University Press, 1926.

Cowley, Malcolm. *The Dream of the Golden Mountain.* New York: Penguin Books, 1981.

Croy, Homer. *Country Cured.* Vol. I. New York: Harper & Brothers, 1943.

Dell, Floyd. *Homecoming.* New York: Farrar & Rinehart, 1933.

DeMuth, James. *Small Town Chicago.* Port Washington, N.Y.: Kennikat Press, 1980.

Doran, George H. *Chronicles of Barabbas.* New York: Rinehart and Company, 1952.

Dos Passos, John. *The Best Times.* New York: Signet Books, 1968.

Dreiser, Helen. *My Life With Dreiser.* Cleveland and New York: World Publishing Company, 1951.

Dreiser, Theodore. *An Amateur Laborer.* Richard W. Dowell, ed. Philadelphia: University of Pennsylvania Press, 1983.

———. *America Is Worth Saving*. New York: Modern Age Books, 1941.

———. *An American Tragedy.*, 2 volumes. New York: Boni and Liveright, 1925.

———. *The Bulwark*. Garden City, N.Y.: Doubleday & Co., 1946.

———. *Chains*. London: Constable & Co., 1928.

———. *The Color of a Great City*. New York: Boni and Liveright, 1923.

———. *Dawn*. New York: Horace Liveright, 1931.

———. *Dreiser Looks at Russia*. New York: Horace Liveright, 1928.

———. *The Financier*. New York: Harper & Brothers, 1912.

———. *The Financier*. Revised edition. New York: Thomas Y. Crowell, 1974.

———. *Free and Other Stories*. New York: The Modern Library, 1925.

———. *A Gallery of Women*, 2 volumes. New York: Horace Liveright, 1929.

———. *The "Genius"*. New York: Boni and Liveright, 1923.

———. *The Hand of the Potter*. New York: Boni and Liveright, 1918.

———. *Hey, Rub-a-Dub-Dub!* London: Constable & Co., 1931.

———. *A Hoosier Holiday*. New York: John Lane Company, 1916.

———. *Jennie Gerhardt*. Garden City, N.Y.: Garden City Publishing Company, [n.d.].

———. *Jennie Gerhardt*. James L. W. West III, ed., Philadelphia: University of Pennsylvania Press, 1992.

———. *Moods: Cadenced and Declaimed*. London: Constable & Company, 1929.

———. *Newspaper Days*. New York: Beekman Publishers, 1974.

———. *Notes on Life*. Marguerite Tjader and John J. McAleer, eds. University, Ala.: University of Alabama Press, 1974.

———. *Sister Carrie*. New York: Doubleday, Page, 1900.

———. *Sister Carrie*. New York: B. W. Dodge, 1907.

———. *Sister Carrie*. Norton Critical Edition, Donald Pizer, ed. New York: W. W. Norton, 1970.

———. *Sister Carrie*. Jack Salzman, ed. New York: Bobbs-Merrill, 1970.

———. *Sister Carrie*. Pennsylvania Edition, John C. Berkey; Alice M. Winters; James L. W. West, III; and Neda M. Westlake, eds. Philadelphia: University of Pennsylvania Press, 1981.

———. *The Stoic*. New York: New American Library, 1981.

———. *The Titan*. New York: Thomas Y. Crowell Company, 1974.

———. *A Traveler at Forty*. New York: Century Company, 1913.

———. *Twelve Men*. New York: Boni and Liveright, 1919.

Dreiser, Vera, with Howard, Brett. *My Uncle Theodore*. New York: Nash Publishing, 1976.

Dresser, Paul. *The Songs of Paul Dresser*. New York: Boni and Liveright, 1927.

Dudley, Dorothy. *Dreiser and the Land of the Free*. New York: The Beechhurst Press, 1946.

Eastman, Max. *Love and Revolution*. New York: Random House, 1964.

Eisenstein, Sergei. *Film Form and the Film Sense*. New York: Meridian Books, 1957.

———. *Immoral Memories*. Trans. by Herbert Marshall. Boston: Houghton Mifflin, 1983.

Elias, Robert H. *Letters of Theodore Dreiser*, 3 volumes. Philadelphia: University of Pennsylvania Press, 1959.

———. *Theodore Dreiser: Apostle of Nature*. Emended Edition. Ithaca: Cornell University Press, 1970.

Farrell, James T. *Reflections at Fifty*. New York: Vanguard Press, 1954.

Fecher, Charles A., ed. *The Diary of H. L. Mencken*. New York: Alfred A. Knopf, 1990.

Fishkin, Shelley Fisher. *From Fact to Fiction*. New York: Oxford University Press, 1985.

Forgue, Guy, ed. *Letters of H. L. Mencken*. Boston: Northeastern University Press, 1981.

Fowler, Gene. *Beau James*. New York: The Viking Press, 1949.

Freeman, Joseph. *An American Testament.* New York: Farrar and Rinehart, 1936.

Friede, Donald. *The Mechanical Angel.* New York: Alfred A. Knopf, 1948.

Freud, Sigmund. *The Interpretation of Dreams.* New York: Avon Books, 1965.

———. *Sexuality and the Psychology of Love.* New York: Collier Books, 1963.

Fuller, Henry B. *With the Procession.* Chicago: The University of Chicago Press, 1965.

Gabler, Neal. *An Empire of Their Own.* New York: Crown Publishers, 1988.

Geismar, Maxwell. *Rebels and Ancestors.* Boston: Houghton Mifflin, 1953.

Gilmer, Walker. *Horace Liveright.* New York: David Lewis, 1970.

Gold, Mike. *The Mike Gold Reader.* Samuel Sillen, ed. New York: International Publishers, 1954.

Goldberg, Isaac. *The Man Mencken.* New York: Simon & Schuster, 1925.

———. *The Rise of Tin Pan Alley.* New York: John Day, 1930.

Goodman, Louis S., and Alfred Gilman. *The Pharmacological Basis of Therapeutics.* New York: Macmillan, 1958.

Griffin, Joseph. *The Small Canvas.* Rutherford, N.J.: Fairleigh Dickinson University Press, 1985.

Hakutani, Yoshinobu, ed. *Selected Magazine Articles of Theodore Dreiser.* Rutherford, N.J.: Farleigh Dickinson University Press, 1985.

———. *Young Dreiser.* Rutherford, N.J.: Fairleigh Dickinson University Press, 1980.

Hapgood, Hutchins. *A Victorian in the Modern World.* New York: Harcourt, Brace and Company, 1939.

Hardy, Thomas. *Tess of the D'Urbervilles.* New York: Bantam Books, 1981.

Harris, Charles K. *After the Ball.* New York: Frank-Maurice, 1926.

Harris, Leon A. *Upton Sinclair: American Rebel.* New York: Thomas Crowell, 1975.

Hassam, Loren. *A Historical Sketch of Terre Haute, Indiana.* Terre Haute: Gazette Job Rooms, 1873.

Hecht, Ben. *A Child of the Century.* New York: Simon & Schuster, 1954.

Hendrick, Burton J., ed. *The Training of an American: The Earlier Life and Letters of Walter H. Page, 1855–1913.* Boston: Houghton Mifflin, 1928.

Henry, Arthur. *An Island Cabin.* New York: A. S. Barnes and Company, 1904.

———. *Lodgings in Town.* New York: A. S. Barnes and Company, 1905.

Hill, Thomas E. *Hill's Manual of Social and Business Forms: A Guide to Correct Writing.* Chicago: Quadrangle Books, 1971. [Reprint of the 1885 edition]

History of Greene and Sullivan Counties, State of Indiana. Chicago: Goodspeed Brothers, 1884.

History of Montgomery County, Ohio. Chicago: W. H. Beers and Company, 1882.

History of St. Charles, Montgomery and Warren Counties, Missouri. St. Louis: Paul V. Cochrane, 1969.

Hofstadter, Richard. *Social Darwinism in American Thought.* Boston: Beacon Press, 1955.

Howells, William Dean. *A Hazard of New Fortunes.* New York: New American Library, 1965.

———. *Literature and Life.* New York: Harper & Brothers, 1911.

Hurst, Fannie. *Anatomy of Me.* New York: Doubleday, 1958.

Irvine, Wiliam. *Apes, Angels and Victorians.* New York: McGraw-Hill, 1955.

Isserman, Maurice. *Which Side Were You On?* Middletown, Conn.: Wesleyan University Press, 1982.

Jaeger, Clara. *Philadelphia Rebel.* Richmond, Virginia: Grosvenor, 1988.

Jenkins, Stephen. *The Greatest Street in the World.* New York: G. P. Putnam's Sons, 1911.

Jones, Howard Mumford. *The Age of Energy.* New York: The Viking Press, 1971.

Kazin, Alfred, and Charles Shapiro, eds. *The Stature of Theodore Dreiser.* Bloomington: Indiana University Press, 1965.

Kellner, Bruce. *Carl Van Vechten and the Irreverent Decades.* Norman: University of Oklahoma Press, 1968.

Kellogg, J. H. *Neurasthenia.* Battle Creek, MI: Good Health Publishing Company, 1915.

Kennedy, James G. *Herbert Spencer.* Boston: Twayne Publishers, 1978.

Kennell, Ruth Epperson. *Dreiser and the Soviet Union.* New York: International Publishers, 1969.

Kirk, Clara Marburg. *W. D. Howells, Traveler from Altruria.* New Brunswick, N.J.: Rutgers University Press, 1962.

Klehr, Harvey. *The Heyday of American Communism.* New York: Basic Books, 1984.

Kraft, Hy. *On My Way to the Theater.* New York: Macmillan, 1971.

Kramer, Dale. *Chicago Renaissance.* New York: Appleton-Century, 1966.

Lasky, Jesse, with Weldon, Don. *I Blow My Own Horn.* Boston: Houghton Mifflin, 1963.

Lears, Jackson. *No Place of Grace.* New York: Pantheon Books, 1981.

Lehan, Richard. *Theodore Dreiser: His World and His Novels.* Carbondale and Edwardsville, Ill.: Southern Illinois University Press, 1969.

Lewisohn, Ludwig. *Up Stream.* New York: Modern Library, 1926.

Loeb, Jacques. *The Mechanistic Conception of Life.* Cambridge, Mass.: Harvard University Press, Belknap Press, 1964.

Ludington, Townsend. *John Dos Passos.* New York: E. P. Dutton, 1980.

Lynd, Robert S. and Helen Merrell. *Middletown.* New York: Harcourt, Brace & World/Harvest, 1956.

Lynn, Kenneth, S. *William Dean Howells.* New York: Harcourt Brace Jovanovich, 1971.

Lyon, Peter. *Success Story: The Life and Times of S. S. McClure.* Deland, Fla.: Everett/Edwards, 1967.

McPhaul, John J. *Deadlines and Monkeyshines.* New York: Prentice-Hall, 1962.

Manchester, William. *H. L. Mencken: Disturber of the Peace.* New York: Collier Books, 1962.

Marcosson, Isaac. *Adventures in Interviewing.* New York: John Lane, 1923.

———. *David Graham Phillips and His Times.* New York: Dodd, Mead and Company, 1932.

Marden, Orison Swett, ed. *Little Visits with Great Americans.* New York: The Success Company, 1905.

Marks, Edward, with A. J. Liebling. *They All Sang.* New York: The Viking Press, 1934.

Masters, Edgar Lee. *Across Spoon River.* New York: Farrar & Rinehart, 1936.

Masters, Hilary. *Last Stands.* Boston: David R. Godine, 1982.

Matthiessen, F. O. *Theodore Dreiser.* New York: William Sloane, 1951.

Mencken, H. L. *My Life as Author and Editor.* New York: Knopf, 1992.

Modlin, Charles, ed. *Sherwood Anderson: Selected Letters.* Knoxville: University of Tennessee Press, 1984.

Moers, Ellen. *Two Dreisers.* New York: The Viking Press, 1969.

Montagu, Ivor. *With Eisenstein in Hollywood.* New York: International Publishers, 1969.

Mott, Frank Luther. *A History of American Magazines,* 4 volumes. Cambridge: Harvard University Press, 1957.

Nathan, George Jean. *The Intimate Notebooks of George Jean Nathan.* New York: Alfred A. Knopf, 1932.

———et al., eds. *The American Spectator Yearbook.* New York: Stokes, 1934.

National Committee for the Defense of Political Prisoners. *Harlan Miners Speak.* New York: Harcourt, Brace, 1932.

Oakey, C. C. *Greater Terre Haute and Vigo Countys* [sic], 2 volumes. Chicago: Lewis Publishing Company, 1908.

Odets, Clifford. *The Time Is Ripe.* New York: Grove Press, 1988.

Orton, Vrest. *Dreiserana: A Book about His Books.* New York: Haskell House, 1973.

Pizer, Donald. *The Novels of Theodore Dreiser: A Critical Study.* Minneapolis: University of Minnesota Press, 1976.

———. ed. *Theodore Dreiser: A Selection of Uncollected Prose.* Detroit: Wayne State University Press, 1977.

Powys, John Cowper. *Autobiography.* London: Macdonald, 1967.

Powys, Llewelyn. *The Verdict of Bridlegoose.* New York: Harcourt Brace, 1926.

Putzel, Max. *The Man in the Mirror: William Marion Reedy and His Magazine.* Cambridge: Harvard University Press, 1963.

Rascoe, Burton. *Theodore Dreiser.* New York: Robert M. McBride, 1925.

Ravitz, Abe C. *David Graham Phillips.* New York: Twayne, 1966.

Reynolds, Quentin. *The Fiction Factory.* New York: Random House, 1955.

Richards, Grant. *Author Hunting by an Old Literary Sportsman.* New York: Coward-McCann, 1934.

Riggio, Thomas P., ed. *Theodore Dreiser: The American Diaries 1902–1926.* Philadelphia: University of Pennsylvania Press, 1982.

———. ed. *Dreiser-Mencken Letters,* 2 volumes. Philadelphia: University of Pennsylvania Press, 1986.

Riis, Jacob. *How the Other Half Lives.* New York: Hill and Wang, 1957.

Salvatore, Nick. *Eugene V. Debs: Citizen and Socialist.* Champaign: University of Illinois Press, 1984.

Salzman, Jack, ed. *Theodore Dreiser: The Critical Reception.* New York: David Lewis, 1972.

Sanders, Marion K. *Dorothy Thompson: A Legend in Her Time.* Boston: Houghton Mifflin, 1973.

Schorer, Mark. *Sinclair Lewis: An American Life.* New York: McGraw-Hill, 1961.

Search-Light [Waldo Frank]. *Time Exposures.* New York: Boni & Liveright, 1926.

Sennett, Richard. *Families Against the City.* New York: Vintage Books, 1970.

Seton, Marie. *Sergei M. Eisenstein.* New York: A. A. Wynn, n.d.

Sheean, Vincent. *Dorothy and Red.* Boston: Houghton Mifflin, 1963.

Siegel, Adrienne. *The Image of the American City in Popular Literature.* Port Washington, N.Y.: Kennikat Press, 1981.

Sloane, Florence Adele. *Maverick in Mauve.* Commentary by Louis Auchincloss. New York: Doubleday, 1983.

Spencer, Herbert. *First Principles.* 5th London Edition. New York: A. L. Burt, [n.d.]

Stallman R. W. *Stephen Crane.* New York: George Braziller, 1968.

——— and Hagemann, E. R., eds. *The New York City Sketches of Stephen Crane.* New York: New York University Press, 1966.

Stenerson, Douglas C. *H. L. Mencken: Iconoclast from Baltimore.* Chicago: University of Chicago Press, 1971.

Sullivan, Mark. *Our Times: The Turn of the Century.* New York: Charles Scribner's Sons, 1926.

Swanberg, W. A. *Dreiser.* New York: Scribner, 1965.

Tarbell, Ida M. *The Nationalizing of Business.* Chicago: Quadrangle Paperbacks, 1971.

Targ, William. *Indecent Pleasures.* New York: Macmillan, 1975.

Taylor, Walter F. *The Economic Novel in America.* New York: Octagon Books, 1964.

Tjader, Marguerite. *Dreiser: A New Dimension.* Norwalk, Conn.: Silvermine Publishers, 1965.

Towne, Charles Hanson. *Adventures in Editing.* New York: D. Appleton and Company, 1926.

———. *So Far So Good.* New York: Julian Messner, 1945.

Trachtenberg, Alan. *The Incorporation of America.* New York: Hill and Wang, 1982.

Vining, Elizabeth Gray. *Friend of Life.* Philadelphia: J. B. Lippincott, 1958.

Von Sternberg, Josef. *Fun in a Chinese Laundry.* New York: Macmillan, 1965.

Walker, Franklin. *Frank Norris.* New York: Doubleday, Doran, 1932.

———. ed. *The Letters of Frank Norris.* San Francisco: The Book Club of California, 1956.

Wall, Joseph Frazier. *Andrew Carnegie.* New York: Oxford University Press, 1970.

West, James L. W., III. *A Sister Carrie Portfolio.* Charlottesville: The University of Virginia Press, 1985.

Witherbee, Sidney A., ed. *Spanish-American War Songs.* Detroit: S. A. Witherbee, 1898.

Witmark, Isadore, and Isaac Goldberg. *Story of the House of Witmark: From Ragtime to Swingtime.* New York: Lee Furman, 1939.

Woodward, William E. *The Gift of Life.* New York: Dutton, 1947.

Ziff, Larzer. *The American 1890s.* London: Chatto and Windus, 1967.

Index

Dreiser, Theodore (Herman Theodore) (*continued*)
love affairs of, 47, 55–56, 58–59, 117, 214
lynching covered by, 67–68, 124
as magazine editor, 97–101, 215–216, 220, 224–226, 226–233, 237
as magazine journalist, 106–113, 121–122, 137–138, 176, 192–193, 195, 213, 215, 225
on marriage, 118, 119
marriage (to Jug), 245, 246–247, 249–250, 274
marriage feared by, 46, 56, 71, 116
marries Helen Richardson, 541
and mechanism, 496–497, 499
and Mencken, feuds with, 326, 332–333, 346, 402–403, 415–416
and Mencken, friendship begins with, 244–245
and Mencken, literary alliance forged with, 260, 307, 310
and Mencken, reconciliation with, 490
and middle age, 268
on money, 556
money as viewed by, xv, 45, 100
money earned by, 75, 88–89, 97, 106, 110, 137, 165, 182, 226, 227
and motion picture industry, 304
music enjoyed by, 102–103, 148
name of, 5, 8, 10
and Nature, 500, 501, 544
nature as viewed by, 141, 142
nervous breakdown of, 193–209, 213, 215
as newspaper journalist, 47–48, 51–77, 85, 87–91, 192, 215
nicknames of, 24, 55
nightmares of, 19, 44
and Nobel Prize for Literature, defeated for, 458, 463
as outcast, 34, 36
personality of, 249
pessimism of, 293
philosophizing of, 410–411
as plagiarist, 111, 122, 135
plays of, 305–306
as playwright, 61
as poet, 103, 105, 112, 113, 117, 121, 122–123, 175, 199, 203
political march leftward, 461, 464, 466–467, 470–472, 478–479, 555–556
on politics, 459
as Populist, 99, 100
portfolio of, 343–344
poverty of, xv, xvii, 8, 14, 16, 19, 20, 27–28, 83, 94–95, 198–209
on prejudice, 508–509
pride of, 198, 201, 203, 206
pro-German attitudes of, in World War I, 307, 345

progress as viewed by, 110, 142
as prolific writer, 111, 175
prose style of, 106, 107, 111, 124, 125, 141, 147, 154, 157, 166
prostitutes visited by, 77, 81
on prostitution, 268
pseudonyms of, 98
psychological power of, 411
public displays of affection repugnant to, 117
reading as influence on, 24, 25, 30, 34, 74, 76–77, 84–85, 186
on realism, 387
realism in fiction, 125–126, 128, 129, 142, 154, 166–167, 236
rebelliousness of, xvi, 41, 114, 226
on religion, 249
reputation of, 417–418
researchers for, 450, 497, 498
and Helen Richardson, affair begins with, 357–359
schemes of, 304
on science, 502
sentimentality of, 30
sexual promiscuity of, 246, 263, 337–338, 392, 450
and sex theme, 259
and sexuality, 316, 331, 352, 387
sexuality of, xv, 30–32, 33, 39, 41, 45, 55–56, 58–59, 77, 79, 81, 115, 116, 117, 135, 194
short stories by, 98, 123–127, 128–129, 137–138, 175, 176, 185, 192, 198, 216
shyness of, 30, 34, 41, 231
on small-town vs. city life, 29
on society, 478
solitariness of, 34, 100, 216
song lyrics by, 103–104
and Soviet experiment, 429, 444, 457, 478, 479, 492, 521, 555, 556
and Soviet Union, trip to, 431–437, 448
spiritual crises of, 47, 178, 199
and spiritualism, 264, 306, 497
and stock market crash, 452
style of, 409
suicide contemplated by, 94–95, 99, 209, 215
suicides written about by, 91, 92, 124
teachers of, 29–30, 34, 38, 39
as theater critic, 65–66, 98
train wreck covered by, 62–64
and universe, 281
vision of man, 281
Wanderjahre of, 72–83
on wealth, 469
womanizing of, 246, 263–264, 337–338, 391–392, 450–451
as writer, 351
as writer, in childhood, 34
as writer of fiction, development of, 123–127, 147

Index

About the Author

Richard Lingeman, executive editior of *The Nation*, journalist and critic, is the author of two notable works of social history, *Don't You Know There's A War On?*, about life on the American Home Front during World War II, and *Small Town America: A Narrative History 1620–the Present*, an account of the role of the small town in American society and culture. A former editor and columnist with *The New York Times Book Review*, he grew up in Crawfordsville, Indiana, graduated from Haverford College and studied at Yale Law School and Colum bia University. He has lived for many years in New York City with his wife, Anthea, and their daughter, Jenifer.